Political Economy

Political Economy

DAN USHER

Blackwell
Publishing

350 Main Street, Malden, MA 02148-5020, USA
108 Cowley Road, Oxford OX4 1JF, UK
550 Swanston Street, Carlton, Victoria 3053, Australia

First published 2003 by Blackwell Publishing Ltd

Library of Congress Cataloging-in-Publication Data

Usher, Dan 1934-
    Political economy/Dan Usher.
        p. cm.
Includes bibliographical references and index.
    ISBN 0-631-23333-4 (alk. paper) – ISBN 0-631-23334-2 (pbk.: alk. paper)
1. Economics. I. Title.

    HB 171.5 .U84 2003
    330–dc21

                                                                    2002038290

A catalogue record for this title is available from the British Library.

Set in 10/12½ Galliard
by Newgen Imaging Systems (P) Ltd, Chennai, India
Printed and bound in the United Kingdom
by TJ International, Padstow, Cornwall

For further information on
Blackwell Publishing, visit our website:
http://www.blackwellpublishing.com

CONTENTS

[People are better off today than at any time in the entire history of the world. Over the last century and a half, people in most countries have acquired a cornucopia of new types of goods, have increased income per head by more than ten fold and have doubled life expectancy. The competitive market is a necessary, though by no means sufficient, condition for our prosperity.]

[The importance of property rights is illustrated in an example where property is not secure. People may devote resources to producing goods for consumption or to taking goods produced by others. The example highlights the role of government as policeman and the danger – rarely averted until modern times – of the emergence of a predatory ruling class.]

[Once property is secure, the price mechanism can be counted on to direct resources for the production of goods and to allocate goods among people, automatically, without central direction and so efficiently that no planner, however knowledgeable, could redirect resources to make everybody better off simultaneously.]

[Demand and supply curves are the principal tools of economic analysis. Both curves connect quantity and price, the demand curve in accordance with the utility, or preferences, of

the consumer, the supply curve in accordance with the technology of the economy. Together, demand and supply curves are employed in analyzing taxes, tariffs, rules for public projects, monopoly, patents and the gain from invention. Different interpretations of the demand curve are compared.]

10 Administration   322

[Legislation is an incomplete guide to public administration. Two subsidiary criteria are that all citizens be treated equally and that the available public revenue be assigned efficiently to projects within each category of expenditure. Cost-benefit analysis acquires a political as well as an economic dimension. The executive branch of government and the civil service must be constrained in their dealings with citizens not just for efficiency in the economy, but to avoid placing citizens at the mercy of the administrators.]

11 Law   361

[The domain of political economy overlaps with the domain of law. The law's resolution of disputes sheds light on the meaning of property rights. Principles for choosing among public projects and policies can be extended to the choice among laws. The "rule of law" is a significant part of society's defense against predatory government.]

The Four Pillars   401

[Markets with private ownership of the means of production, politics based upon majority-rule voting, a rule-bound public administration and a degree of independence for the judiciary are mutually reinforcing ingredients of what most people see as a good society.]

FIGURES

TABLES

PREFACE

...by directing industry in such a manner as its produce may be of the greatest value, he intends only his own gain, and he is in this, as in many other cases led by an invisible hand to promote an end which was no part of his intention. Nor is it always worse for society that it was no part of it. By pursuing his own interest he frequently promotes that of society more effectually than when he really intends to promote it.
Adam Smith, *The Wealth of Nations,* 1776

This book is an introduction to economics for university students. As the name "political economy" suggests, the book differs from other introductory texts in emphasizing connections between the organization of the economy and the conduct of government, but, like every other introductory text, its primary focus is upon the calculus of self-interest in the everyday business of life and upon the workings of the economy itself. The book is intended to whet the student's appetite for the study of economics and to supply a foundation for more advanced courses in the subject. It is also intended to convey the lessons of economics that will prove most useful to the student – whose main interest may lie in other subjects and who may not continue the study of economics – in his role as citizen, voter and participant in the governance of society. Somewhat more difficult than other introductory texts, the book is no more difficult than introductory texts in the sciences. As the text for a full-year introductory lecture course, it should be comprehensible enough.

The book would also serve as a text for a second-year course in political economy narrowly defined, with emphasis on the economics of voting, public administration, and law. The chapters on markets and the competitive economy would then constitute a review of essential background material.

The main purpose of this book, like that of any introduction to economics, is to explain the price mechanism: how market prices emerge spontaneously and how these prices create "order without orders," allowing the world's business to be conducted without any central authority to direct the process in detail. One might suppose that nothing less than an all-powerful central authority would be required to direct millions of people producing a virtually infinite variety of goods, to align production to consumption so that the mix of goods produced is precisely the mix of goods people want to consume, and to determine each person's share of the pie. Surprising as it may seem to people unacquainted with economic ideas, that turns out not to be so. Instead, with private ownership of the means of production but without central control or conscious planning of the economy as a whole, self-interested people are guided by market-determined prices to deploy the resources of the world to produce what people want to consume. This assertion, made commonplace by repetition, is so extraordinary and so completely counter-intuitive that it cannot be strictly and unreservedly true. A central task of economics is to show when the assertion is true, when public intervention in the economy might be helpful, and when markets are best left alone because public intervention is likely to do more harm than good.

A second objective is to introduce the student to the tools of economic analysis. Demand and supply curves are derived in a simple framework and are then applied to the task of showing the consequences for the economy of monopoly, tariffs, patents, technical change and alternative forms of taxation. Demand and supply curves facilitate the analysis of the role of the government in the economy, why some countries are rich and other countries are poor, how to foster economic growth, how to reduce the gap between the incomes of the rich and the poor, when to regulate markets, when and how to reduce the level of pollution, how to identify the pros and cons of public provision of health care and education, and how to determine the appropriate public provision of the infrastructure of society – roads, bridges, the army, and basic research – that a market might not supply at all.

Third – and here is where a text on political economy differs most from other economics texts – a text on political economy emphasizes the mutual dependence of economics and politics, how the virtues of a competitive economy are conditional on other institutions in society and how economic organization may foster or corrode democratic government. Perennial questions of political economy are discussed: How can the personnel of the army and the bureaucracy – endowed with a monopoly of the means of organized violence to protect citizens from one another and from aggression abroad – be deterred from employing its authority to transform itself into a ruling class that exploits the rest of society for its own prosperity and advantage? Throughout most of history, that is exactly what happened. Why is this outcome avoided in some countries today? How can democracy with majority-rule voting be sustained when a majority of the poor can employ the power of the vote to expropriate the rich? What is to prevent a majority based upon race, language, religion, locality or any badge whatsoever from exploiting the remaining minority of the population? Until a few hundred years ago, it was generally believed that democracy had no defense against expropriation of minorities by majorities, and democracy was widely opposed on that account. Why, though some capitalist societies are not democratic, has no thoroughgoing communist society, with full public ownership of the means of production, ever been democratic, despite the intentions of its founders? A text on political economy would be expected to raise these questions, even if no definitive answers can be supplied.

Political economy is the original name for economics, abandoned a hundred years ago for the simpler term "economics" because the content of the subject had narrowed. The word "economy" is derived from a Greek word meaning "the management of the household." Political economy would be the management of the nation. In the nineteenth century, and frequently in the first half of the twentieth century as well, what we now call economics and what we now call political science would be studied under the heading of political economy in the same department of the university. Over the last fifty years or so, the unified departments split into individual departments of economics and political science, as each subject acquired a separate domain of investigation and a distinct style of analysis. The economy came to be studied entirely on its own, as a great machine that reacts to political decisions about such matters as tariffs and taxes but that runs entirely in accordance with its own laws of motion.

Just as the divorce seemed complete, there emerged on the horizon new problems that straddled the two disciplines. It became evident that voting could be usefully analyzed by methods that have more in common with economics than with political science as practiced at the time. The study of voting became the domain of scholars who may have started out as economists or as political scientists but who needed familiarity with both disciplines. It became evident that economic growth was as much a consequence of political organization as of conditions in the economy. It became evident that society's choice of laws could be explained on the same economic principles used to explain society's choice of roads, bridges, hospitals, and schools. It became evident that democratic government and civil liberties were intimately connected with the organization of the economy.

Nowadays, the term political economy may refer *either* to a sub-field of economics about overlaps with politics and law *or* to the entire field of economics broadened to include the overlaps with politics and law. Political economy may be an increment or an expansion. In this book, it is an expansion; it is economics with a political slant. The study of how markets supply goods and promote economic growth (the traditional domain of economics) is combined with the study of how markets depend on other institutions in society and of how, together, property, public administration, voting and the law uphold what most of us see as a good society.

The broadening of a field of study may or may not be desirable. In some grand sense, all knowledge is one, but we compartmentalize knowledge into fields such as physics, chemistry, biology, economics, political science, and philosophy for the same reason that different people do different jobs. The world's work is best accomplished by a division of labour in learning as well as in toil. But boundaries between fields of knowledge are not fixed forever. They change from time to time in response to new interests and new discoveries, as, for instance, when psychology split off from philosophy or when biology and chemistry gave birth to bio-chemistry. Whether it is useful to recognize something called political economy is in the end a question of how best to develop the student's understanding of society. A course in political economy may be a good beginning for the study of economics and a way to whet the student's appetite for economics more narrowly defined. Whether he begins with conventional economics or with political economy should make little difference by the end of a solid three or four year program.

It is customary to teach economics by telling little stories to illustrate the main ideas of the subject. Here, the practice (or vice, depending on how you look at it) is carried to the extreme. Predatory behavior is introduced by the story of the fishermen and the pirates. The interaction of taste and technology is illustrated by the tale of Robinson Crusoe. Prices and markets are introduced in an economy with five people, each with his own plot of land. Problems in majority-rule voting are exemplified by a choice among sandwiches, the apportionment of the national income, the construction of five roads in five regions of the country, and deals in the legislature between militarists and egalitarians. The five roads reappear in the discussion of public administration, together with a story about safety in airports and bus stations. The examples are mostly numerical rather than analytic. They rely more upon made-up numbers than upon smooth curves or functions. By comparison with other introductory expositions of economics, the style here is old-fashioned, less general and sometimes open to the suspicion that different numbers might have yielded a different story; but it allows for the presentation of ideas with much less recourse to formal mathematics. The examples are intended to convey economic ideas forcefully and memorably, supplying the student with templates or paradigms that can be applied in a variety of circumstances. After studying this book, a student of economics would proceed to solid, rigorous texts in microeconomics and macroeconomics.

The reader is expected to be familiar with high school algebra but not calculus, though some calculus ideas are developed from first principles. The student with no calculus at all will acquire a little familiarity with calculus ideas which should be of some help when he comes to study calculus later on. The student with a little calculus will follow the demonstrations more easily and will have his grasp of calculus strengthened by its surreptitious application here. The student with a strong foundation in calculus will be able to skip some demonstrations as obvious.

Chapter 1 is intended to motivate the student for the study of political economy. It calls attention to how extraordinarily fortunate we are to be living in this particular time and place, automatically raising the question of how prosperity and freedom are attained. People today – primarily, but by no means exclusively, in the capitalist democracies of Europe and North America – are enormously better off in virtually every respect than people have ever been before, with a higher standard of living, greater variety of goods, much longer lives, less pronounced inequality of income, status and rights, the elimination in most countries of torture and slavery, and greater influence of ordinary people upon the choice of leaders and the conduct of government. The common opinion that the twentieth century has been especially prone to devastation in war and civil strife is debatable; and the deficit of mortality, if any, on that account is almost certainly outweighed by the alleviation of ordinary starvation and disease. A statistical summary of these advances in prosperity, longevity, and other aspects of society leads naturally to the study of whether and to what extent the competitive economy is a necessary condition for economic, political, and social progress.

Chapter 2 is about predatory behavior. The chapter may be seen as presenting a dilemma or riddle to be solved in the rest of the course. Life in a society without strong government is "solitary, poor, nasty, brutish and short." Resources and energy may be diverted from the production of useful goods and services to the struggle over the allocation among people of the goods and services produced. Government strong enough to contain private exploitation is also strong enough to exploit the common man in the interest of a ruling class, as a shepherd exploits his sheep, allowing neither liberty nor progress. The picture of government as predator leads naturally to the study of how a competitive economy might serve to constrain and humanize the potentially corrosive powers of government.

The next five chapters are a simple, self-contained account of the mechanism, the virtues and the weaknesses of markets with private ownership of the means of production. Chapter 3 is an almost unconscionably brief description of the competitive economy. It is the story of the invisible hand referred to in the quotation from Adam Smith above. It is the story of how prices govern production and allocation of goods, determining at once how scarce resources are deployed, what is produced, and how goods are allocated among people. The principal tools of analysis are the demand curve as a reflection of taste and the supply curves as a reflection of technology. These are introduced in an economy with only one person who produces two goods on five plots of land with different productivities. Then, after a brief digression on bargaining, the five plots of land are reassigned to five different people, allowing for the emergence of a competitive market where prices guide production and trade. Simple as they are, these models are sufficient to display the virtues and vices of the competitive economy and to show how markets enable most of the world's work to be done and most of the national income to be allocated without detailed and comprehensive direction by a central authority.

Demand and supply curves are a flexible and versatile tool of analysis. In Chapter 4 they are put to work in measuring the gain from trade, the full cost of taxation, the social loss from monopoly and social gain from invention. Taste and technology are studied in more detail in chapters 5 and 6. Chapter 5 is about the diversity of types of goods and the implications for the role of government in society. Chapter 6 is about how different types of resources are combined to produce goods and about the sources of economic progress. Chapter 7 is about how people bargain and about how associations – corporations, trade unions, and political parties – supplement or circumvent markets when direct bargaining is prohibitively costly. The world's work is facilitated by a combination of price-taking and deal-making. The clean implications of price-taking in the simple economy discussed in the earlier chapters require considerable modification once bargaining is required.

The benefits of a competitive market are realized because, and only to the extent that, property is secure. Security of property is typically postulated in expositions of economic analysis. The postulate is often valid in practice, but never completely so and always because other institutions in society create an environment where markets can flourish. These institutions and their connections with the economy are the subject of the last four chapters. Chapter 8 is about criteria for economic policy. We cannot reason with one another about laws, rules or policies without some generally recognized notion – however vague or imprecise – of the common good, but there is, unfortunately, no unambiguous and universally acceptable measure. An attempt is made to be as precise as possible about the common good and its implications for economic policies or institutions. Chapter 9 is about voting. People nowadays are inclined to think of voting as unambiguously righteous, but it turns out, on close inspection, to be much more problematic than is often supposed. Voting supplies laws and leaders, but could itself become the instrument by which one group of people exploits another. The emphasis of the chapter is on how this dismal outcome is in practice averted. Diseases of voting (the reasons why government by majority-rule voting may self-destruct) and defenses of voting against disintegration are examined. Chapter 10 is about administration. Not all public decisions can be made by voting. The army, the police, the roads, the redistribution of income, and, in most societies, the hospitals, the schools, and many other aspects of life are publicly administered. Public administration requires detailed regulation that can only be supplied by a hierarchically organized bureaucracy that may turn despotic unless confined by clear principles of governance that only the legislature can provide. Cost-benefit analysis is discussed as a surrogate for the common good and as a defense against excessive discretion by the bureaucracy.

The final chapter is about how the law protects property and preserves the environment for majority-rule voting by punishing crimes, adjudicating disputes and guarding a constitutionally specified line that no administrative apparatus and no legislature may cross. Law is the guardian of rules that would otherwise be violated and misused. For product liability and for murder, it is shown how, and to what extent, laws can be designed and evaluated with references to their consequences in promoting the common good. The chapter ends with a discussion of cases pertaining in one way or another to civil rights and to the role of the courts in interpreting the constitution.

Two large interconnected themes run throughout the book. The first is the distinction between economic rights that people hold unequally and political rights that people hold equally. Economic rights are entitlement to property acquired by inheritance or by purchase. Political rights include the right to vote, to equal treatment under the law, to equal access to public education, to run for office, and so on. These rights clash at the edges. They clash over the progressivity of the income tax, or, more generally, over society's decision about how much of each person's earnings are his own to spend as he pleases and how much are to be shared with the community at large through tax-financed redistribution of income, welfare for the poor, the old age pension, unemployment insurance, public provision of health care, and so on. The clash between these rights is at the root of an ancient objection to democracy, the fear that the right to vote will be used by the poor to expropriate the rich, destroying prosperity and democracy in the process. These rights are studied together in contemporary political economy.

The other major theme is the mutual dependence of private property, voting, administration, and law. Together, these institutions constitute the foundation of what we see as the good society, defending us against anarchy on the one hand and despotism on the other. Though the competitive economy is often studied in isolation from political institutions, it cannot really stand alone because private property cannot defend itself. Property is a creature of the state. None of the virtues of a competitive economy can be realized without public administration to protect property rights, compensate for the "failures" of an unfettered competitive economy, redistribute income to some extent, and supply types of goods that markets can never supply. The law specifies the boundaries between people's property rights, resolves disputes and protects people from predatory government as well as from one another, tasks that the law cannot perform without some degree of independence for the judiciary. Voting is required as the only alternative to despotic government. But the defense is not just one-sided. Our political institutions cannot cope with the allocation among citizens of the entire national income, and can only be maintained in conjunction with an economy where most of the allocation of income to people is outside the political arena. The consensus in society to accept the will of the majority in voting, the decisions of the bureaucracy and the judgments of the courts as binding on each of us could not otherwise withstand the pressure of self-interest.

Dan Liang, now a graduate student in the Queen's School of Business, prepared the diagrams and assembled most of the data on life expectancy in chapter 1. Jill Hodgson, my secretary, miraculously preserved her cheerfulness and her sanity through revision after revision of the text. My colleague Marvin McInnis proved an inexhaustible source of information about the matters discussed in chapter 1. Charles Beach, Caroline Miller, Jim Pritchard, and Lucien Karshmar suggested sources of data. Suggestions by Barbara Goldberg have been incorporated in the chapter on law. Thank you all. For more years than I care to admit, the economics department at Queen's University has provided me with a pleasant and challenging environment for research and writing. The Social Science Research Council of Canada provided financial support.

Chapter **One**

HOW DREADFUL LIFE USED TO BE

Political Economy or Economics is a study of mankind in the ordinary business of life: it examines that part of individual and social action which is most closely connected with the attainment and the use of the material requisites of well being.

Alfred Marshall, 1890

In the ordinary business of life, mankind thrives as never before. Over the last few hundred years, first in Europe and America and then increasingly throughout the world, people have become substantially better off – materially, politically, and culturally – than they have ever been in the entire history of the world. We live longer. We eat more nutritious food. We are better clothed. We are better housed. We have access to a far greater variety of goods. We have more leisure We are healthier. We have infinitely greater access to information. We watch television, drive cars, and fly to vacations thousands of miles away from home. Ordinary folk enjoy a standard of living to which the nobility in the great empires of the past could not aspire. Our laws are more just and humane. We have greater respect for one another. We are more inclined to recognize a common humanity between rulers and ruled, and between rich and poor. We govern ourselves collectively, and are less frequently subjected to the whim of tyrants. Our present conditions of life are uniformly better than those of our ancestors.

The source of our prosperity is the organization of our economy. I claim this as a necessary rather than as a sufficient condition. But for the institution of private property and the intricate web of rules we call capitalism, none of what we now enjoy would be possible. To make such a claim is not to deny that other similar claims may be equally valid. But for the progress of science and technology, none of what we now enjoy would be possible. But for the development of political liberty and democracy, none of this would be possible. I would deny neither of these other claims. Claims on behalf of capitalism, technology, and political organization may all be true, as necessary conditions, simultaneously. This chapter does not discuss markets or explain how markets foster prosperity and economic growth. These matters will be discussed throughout this book. The main purpose of this chapter is to set the stage by reviewing the record of mankind's achievements.

A subsidiary purpose is to balance this triumphant view of contemporary capitalism as a producer of goods and services (including non-material goods such as leisure, health, and longevity) with a brief account of mankind's far less successful record in distribution. Inevitably, the apportionment among people of the benefits of material progress leaves some gap between the prosperous and the unprosperous and entails some wastage of resources, goods, effort, and lives in the struggle of each person against every other person to procure for oneself the largest possible share. Within the nation, the bread and the cheese, the cars and the bicycles, the access to medical services, and the access to higher education all have to be apportioned, so much for you, so much for him, so much for me. The nation's tasks have to be assigned. Explicitly or implicitly, society must decide who is to be the butcher, the baker, the doctor, the day laborer, the cop on the beat, the prime minister, and the beggar on the side of the road. Privileges and responsibilities have to be assigned. Society must decide who participates in the choice of laws, who obeys whom, when, and in what circumstances obedience is withdrawn. In the world at large, territories must be assigned to peoples, countries' borders must be established, citizenship must be recognized together with rights, if any, to migrate from one country to another.

The next few chapters are about how markets attend to production and distribution automatically with no central authority to determine who does what and who gets what as long as there is a prior allocation among people of the property of the nation. The distribution of property is not God-given or just in itself. It can be nothing other than the outcome of a gradual evolution through a complex interaction of skill, industry, chicanery, and theft. It is accepted (in so far as it is accepted) as the foundation of prosperity and as the only peaceful and efficient alternative to the wasteful and lethal scramble over allocation among people and among groups of people identified by race, religion, language, wealth, or territory of residence. Wars occur when the distribution of goods, property and privilege – within the nation and, especially, among nations – is not universally accepted. A sketch of the record, prosperity, equality, and conflict is presented in this chapter as preference to the analysis of these phenomena in the rest of the book.

The chapter is divided into three main sections: the material conditions of life, customs, and mass destruction. Under the general heading of the material conditions of life, I present evidence on the length of life and standard of living. Life expectancy at birth has increased from about twenty-five years in biblical times to over seventy-five years in a great many countries today. A person born today can expect three times the life-span of his biblical ancestors, of the ancient Romans or of English people at the time of William the Conqueror. The improvement in the standard of living is equally spectacular. Real national income per head – the standard measure of the availability of goods and services – has increased a full ten-fold over the last hundred and fifty years. Until very recently, a typical person came close to starvation at some time in his life, was illiterate, and rarely strayed more than a few miles from his place of birth. Today, in Europe, America, and elsewhere, starvation is a distant memory though it remains unbanished elsewhere in the world.

Under the heading of customs, I call attention to the dependence of our judgments of right and wrong upon the circumstances of the economy. What is right in a poor community may become wrong once a degree of prosperity is attained. We need no longer resort to patricide and infanticide for the survival of the community. Crimes can be punished less cruelly than at a time when imprisonment was, for the ordinary run of crimes, prohibitively expensive. Less obviously connected to the degree of prosperity, but connected nonetheless, are the institution of slavery, class privileges, heresy, and political inequality. Slavery, once prevalent throughout the world, has now been almost eliminated. Civil rights and property rights supply a degree of protection against predatory neighbors or predatory government. Political inequality is distinctly less pervasive than it once was, though economic inequality still flourishes.

Under the heading of mass destruction, I discuss the loss of life in war and the wanton extermination of large numbers of people by their own governments. Here the record of the twentieth century is much less admirable, though better comparatively speaking than is often supposed. The advance of technology has brought us prosperity but has made war more lethal and has supplied governments with new vehicles for oppression of the ordinary citizen. Death in war has been greater during the twentieth century than ever before, but not significantly so as a percentage of total population, and the depressing effect of war on life expectancy is almost negligible by comparison with the general improvement due to advances in medicine and to prosperity itself. Such matters are usually ignored in economics texts because they are not part of the ordinary business of life. Economics is above all the peaceful science with no place in its formal models for violence, terrorism, war, or extermination. These matters find their way, albeit peripherally, into a text on political economy because technical change is at once the foundation of material progress and the source of an ever-greater capacity to harm one another, creating an ever-greater challenge to hold that capacity in check.

This chapter is written with special reference to Canada, the United States, and Great Britain, in part because data for these countries are readily available but primarily because these are the countries I know best. An author with a different geographical focus could tell much the same story about other countries elsewhere. Broad trends are similar in these three countries and in many other countries as well. Most countries throughout the world have shown significant improvement in mortality rates and material well-being, but not all countries have been equally fortunate. Some worldwide trends will be examined.

THE MATERIAL CONDITIONS OF LIFE

Longevity

"Once a distracted mother came to the All-Compassionate one with her dead babe in her arms, and besought him it might be restored to life. He listened to her pleading; then sent her forth to fetch a grain of mustard seed from a house where no children had died. She sought for long and in vain, and then returned and told him of her failure.

> 'My sister, thou has found,' the Master said, 'searching for what none finds,
> That bitter balm I had to give thee.
> Thou knowest the whole wide world weeps.
> The grief which all share grows less for one.' "

The All-Compassionate one is the Buddha,[1] and this old tale of the mustard seed has for millennia been a consolation to people in grief. Today, however, the moral is not what it once was. The intended moral of the story was that every mother has seen the death of some of her children, and that no mother can expect to be exempted from this sad condition of life. That can no longer be the moral because the bowl of the grieving mother would now be full rather than empty. To be sure, children still die, but the death of a child is now a rare event, and most houses have not seen such deaths. Science, technology, and prosperity have rendered the story obsolete.

An almost unconscionably selective history of life expectancy from the cave dwellers to the present day is presented in table 1.1 with England as the "representative" country from the middle ages to the present day. The remarkable features of the story are how so little happened from the start of civilization to the beginning of the nineteenth century and how much has happened in the last two hundred years. Ten thousand years ago hunter-gatherers had a life expectancy of just over 30 years. By the year 1800, English life expectancy had crept up to 37 years. It rose steadily over the course of the nineteenth century, but, by the end of the century, was still only 50 years. Then, during the twentieth century, life expectancy increased by almost 30 to 79 years in 2000. This was the greatest increase in longevity in the entire history of humankind. In most countries throughout the world, life expectancy today is greater than ever before.

The information in table 1.1 is from three sources. For the years before the middle ages, the early data are ingenious estimates by anthropologists and archeologists from the study of ancient bones. The English data from the thirteenth century to 1841 are church records and graveyards. Thereafter, the data are from censuses of population. The experience of the twentieth century will be examined in greater detail below, but with reference to the United States rather than to England.

The main story in the table is of ups and downs with no long-term trend until the end of the middle ages, very slow growth for the next few hundred years, acceleration in the nineteenth century and rapid growth in the twentieth century. There are two sub-plots: the long-term fall in life expectancy associated with the transition from hunter-gathering to agriculture (a decline of five years from the mesolithic to the neolithic periods) and the sudden plunge in life expectancy during the Black Death in the fourteenth century. A school of anthropologists maintains that ordinary people were better off as hunter-gatherers than they were for millennia afterwards until quite recent times. People were taller than they have been at any time prior to the twentieth century. Their health was better – as measured, for example, by the number of missing teeth in their skeletons. Their diet was better, meat rather than grain. The numbers in

Table 1.1 Life expectancy at birth from ancient times to the present

	Time and place	Years
1	Palaeolithic, 500,000 BC–8,000 BC, cave men with primitive stone tools	19.9
2	Mesolithic, 8,000 BC–2,500 BC, hunter-gatherers	31.4
3	Neolithic, 6,000 BC–1,500 BC agriculture and domestication of animals	26.9
5	Bronze Age, 2,500 BC–500 BC, ancient Egypt and Mesopotamia	32.1
6	Iron Age, 1,500 BC–AD 500	27.3
7	Roman empire, first to fourth centuries	27.8
8	Hungary, tenth to twelfth centuries	28.1
9	England and Wales, generation of males born 1276–1300	31.3
10	England and Wales, generation of males born 1348–75, during the Black Death	17.3
11	England and Wales, generation of males born 1426–50	32.8
12	England and Wales, 1601	38.1
13	England and Wales, 1701	37.1
14	England and Wales, 1801	35.9
15	England and Wales, 1841	40.3
16	England and Wales, 1871	41.3
17	England and Wales, 1900	50.4
18	England and Wales, 1950	68.9
19	England and Wales, 2000	78.9

Sources: 1–6, A. C. Swedlund and G. J. Armelagos, Demographic Anthropology, *Dubuque, Iowa, W. C. Brown, 1976, table 4.6. The stages of civilization are defined by technology, attained in different places at different times. The ages are mapped in "Archelogy," an entry in Collier's Encyclopedia. 7–8, G. Ascadi and J. Nemeskeri,* History of Human Life Span and Mortality, *1970, tables 121 and 130. 9–11, J. C. Russell,* British Medieval Population, *1948, tables 8.4, 8.7 and 8.10. 12–16, E. A. Wrigley and R. S. Schofield,* The Population History of England, 1541–1871, *1981, table A3.1. 17–19, www.oheschools.org/ohech6pg4.html*

table 1.1 are consistent with this claim, but it is hard to know how much stock to put in these estimates.[2]

The Black Death was an epidemic of the plague that originated in China and swept west, destroying about a third of the population of Europe, and arriving in England in 1348. Life expectancy dropped by almost half, from 31.3 years for the generation born between 1276 and 1300 to 17.3 years for the generation born between 1348 and 1376. In 1300, the population of England and Wales was about five million. By 1377, it had fallen to about two and a half million. Additional waves of the plague drove the population down to about one and a half million by the end of the century.

The huge worldwide improvement in longevity in the twentieth century is exemplified by the experience of the United States summarized, for males and for females, in tables 1.2 and 1.3. The tables themselves are largely self-explanatory. In both tables, the right-hand columns show life expectancy. Over the century, life expectancy increased from 46.3 years to 73.9 years for men, and from 48.3 years to 79.4 years for women. By the end of the century, men lived 27.6 years longer than their great grandfathers a hundred years before. By the end of the century, women lived 31.1 years longer than their great grandmothers a hundred years before. Women not only

Table 1.2 Improvements in age-specific[a] mortality rates and life expectancy in the United States during the twentieth century (males)

[Age-specific mortality rates are deaths per 100,000 people in the designated age group].

Year	Under 1	1–4	5–14	15–24	25–34	35–44	45–54	55–64	65–74	75–84	85+	Life expectancy
1900	17,914	2,045	384	594	824	1,067	1,570	2,870	5,929	12,826	26,877	46.3
1910	14,533	1,458	310	484	693	995	1,523	2,867	5,874	12,742	25,579	48.4
1915	11,450	969	243	423	619	914	1,436	2,769	5,875	12,455	24,672	52.5
1916	11,820	1,169	261	455	660	971	1,509	2,898	6,063	12,865	25,546	49.6
1917	11,736	1,119	270	496	708	1,007	1,548	2,934	6,111	12,899	25,107	48.4
1918	12,453	1,600	415	1,215	1,902	1,528	1,671	2,870	5,850	11,812	22,756	36.6
1920	10,353	1,027	280	478	643	822	1,263	2,463	5,453	12,214	25,301	53.5
1930	7,701	602	190	350	489	746	1,360	2,661	5,582	11,912	23,671	58.1
1940	6,190	312	118	229	338	588	1,289	2,612	5,462	12,126	24,639	60.8
1950	3,728	152	71	168	217	429	1,067	2,395	4,931	10,426	21,636	65.6
1960	3,059	120	56	152	188	373	992	2,310	4,914	10,178	21,186	66.6
1970	2,410	93	51	189	215	403	959	2,283	4,874	10,010	17,822	67.1
1980	1,429	73	37	172	196	299	767	1,815	4,105	8,817	18,801	70
1990	1,082	52	29	147	204	310	610	1,553	3,492	7,889	18,057	71.8
1999	802	39	22	116	150	257	547	1,280	3,109	7,000	16,931	73.9

Sources: 1 National Vital Statistics Report, vol. 48, no. 18, February 7, 2001, table 12. Estimated life expectancy at birth in years, by race and sex: Death-registration states, 1900–28, and United States, 1928–98. National Center for Health Statistics, Health, United States, 2001. Hyattsville, Maryland, Public Health Service, 2001. 2 National Center of Health Statistics, United States, 2001. Official Website: www.cdc.gov/nchs/datawh/statab/unpubd/mortabs/hist290.htm

Table 1.3 Improvements in age-specific[a] mortality rates and life expectancy in the United States during the twentieth century (females)

[Age-specific mortality rates are deaths per 100,000 people in the designated age group.]

Year	Under 1	1–4	5–14	15–24	25–34	35–44	45–54	55–64	65–74	75–84	85+	Life expectancy
1900	14,541	1,912	388	578	815	975	1,418	2,576	5,358	11,877	25,517	48.3
1910	11,762	1,335	285	423	612	790	1,207	2,366	5,241	11,740	24,600	51.8
1915	8,995	879	216	391	544	745	1,165	2,319	5,247	11,599	23,532	56.8
1916	9,281	1,052	228	422	572	775	1,195	2,387	5,360	11,950	24,660	54.3
1917	9,147	1,012	242	442	587	785	1,202	2,399	5,336	11,921	24,206	54
1918	9,851	1,546	410	943	1,340	1,134	1,358	2,403	5,150	10,827	21,805	42.2
1920	8,067	946	247	497	713	800	1,170	2,244	5,046	11,589	24,467	54.6
1930	6,074	523	153	319	433	615	1,062	2,124	4,676	10,663	22,138	61.6
1940	4,774	267	89	181	274	452	861	1,800	4,222	10,369	22,759	65.2
1950	2,855	127	49	89	143	290	642	1,405	3,333	8,400	19,195	71.1
1960	2,321	98	37	61	107	229	527	1,196	2,872	7,633	19,008	73.1
1970	1,864	75	32	68	102	231	517	1,099	2,580	6,678	15,518	74.7
1980	1,142	55	24	58	76	159	413	934	2,144	5,440	14,747	77.4
1990	856	41	19	49	74	138	343	879	1,991	4,883	14,274	78.8
1999	658	31	16	45	67	143	313	787	1,973	4,916	14,863	79.4

Sources: *Same as table 1.2.*

live longer than men, but the improvement over the century has been greater for women than for men.

The rest of tables 1.2 and 1.3 shows age-specific mortality rates, defined here as the number of deaths per 100,000 people. For example, the figure of 17,914 in the top left-hand corner of table 1.2 means that 17,914 out of every 100,000 male children born during the year 1900 died within the first year of life. Almost 18 percent of the baby boys born in the year 1900 did not live to their first birthday. By contrast, the figure of 802 at the bottom of the column indicates that, by the year 1999, less than 1 percent were dying during the first year of life. Throughout the century, the mortality rate is high during the first year of life, is lowest for the period of life between 5 and 14 years of age and becomes steadily higher thereafter.

At every age, mortality rates are significantly lower in the year 1999 than in the year 1900, but the drop in mortality rates is most dramatic for infants and young children. With minor variations, the reduction from 1900 to 1999 in the risk of death is less pronounced as one grows older. For male children in the first year of life, the risk of death in the year 1999 had fallen to less than a twentieth (specifically, as shown in the first column of table 1.2, the ratio is 802/17,914 or 4.5 percent) of what it had been in the year 1900. The percentage fall is even more pronounced for the much safer period of life between one to four years of age. For that age group, the risk of death in the year 1999 had fallen to about one-fiftieth (39/2,045 or 1.9 percent) of what it had been in the year 1900. Thereafter the percentage gains diminish. By the end of the twentieth century, the risk of death between 5 and 14 years of age was only 6.3 percent of what it had been at the beginning. The comparable figures are 19.5 percent between 15 and 24 years of age, 34.8 percent between 45 and 54 four years of age, and 62.9 percent among people 85 years and older. The same pattern is evident for females in table 1.3.

The rows show mortality rates every tenth year with the exception of the years around the great flu epidemic of 1918. Male life expectancy which had been 48.4 years in 1917 fell abruptly in 1918 to 36.6 years, not significantly different from what it had been before the invention of agriculture 20,000 years ago. Among young men aged 25 to 34, the mortality rate rose from 708 per 100,000 in 1917 to 1,902 per 100,000 in 1918, an extra risk of death of just over 1 percent per year The figures for women are essentially the same. By contrast the rise in the death rate among men of that age group during the Second World War (not shown in table 1.2) was about 50 per 100,000 or about a twentieth of a percent. These figures must be interpreted with care. To say that life expectancy fell from 48.4 years in 1917 to 36.6 years in 1918 is not to suggest that people born in 1918 had markedly shorter lives than people born the year before. It is, rather, to say that people would have had markedly shorter lives if these temporarily higher mortality rates had persisted throughout their lives.

For young adults, male and female, the principal sources of the decline in the mortality rates are shown in table 1.4. The combined mortality rate from all causes together fell in the course of the century to about an eighth of what it had been at the beginning, from 819.8 per 100,000 people in the year 1900 down to 108.3 per 100,000 people in the year 1999, that is, from just under one person per hundred to just over one person per thousand. The greatest triumph for this age group was the elimination of tuberculosis, which killed about one person per three hundred in the year 1900. The

Table 1.4 Selected causes of mortality among young adults in the United States [Both sexes, 25–34 years, deaths per 100,000 people per year.]

Years	All causes	Tuberculosis (all forms)	Pneumonia (all forms) and influenza	Syphilis (all forms)	Aids	Cancer and other malignant tumors	Diabetes mellitus	Intracranial lesions of vascular origin (stroke)	Diseases of the heart	Diarrhea, enteritis and ulceration of the intestines	Appendicitis	Nephritis (all forms)	Complications of pregnancy and childbirth	Motor vehicle accidents	All other accidents	Suicide	Homicide
1900	819.8	294.3	76.2	—	0.0	14.0	5.0	15.4	43.4	7.5	8.9	45.2	—	*	62.6	11.2	1.8
1910	654.5	217.6	46.9	6.3	0.0	14.1	5.1	10.2	40.8	3.2	10.1	32.7	—	1.8	78.9	17.7	7.9
1920	677.5	164.9	180.6	9.6	0.0	14.7	5.6	7.5	37.5	3.0	13.7	20.4	—	7.9	46.0	11.5	18.9
1930	465.8	102.8	38.9	10.1	0.0	16.7	3.5	6.4	38.2	1.5	14.0	17.6	—	24.0	38.4	14.9	17.3
1940	305.9	56.3	17.1	7.1	0.0	17.3	2.8	5.5	29.7	1.0	7.0	11.8	—	24.8	27.4	13.5	12.2
1950	178.7	19.1	4.2	0.7	0.0	20.0	2.2	4.2	20.9	0.7	0.9	4.5	5.4	17.3	13.0	8.6	9.9
1960	146.4	2.4	4.8	0.2	0.0	19.5	2.3	4.7	15.6	0.7	0.3	2.8	2.9	24.3	18.6	10.0	9.7
1970	157.4	0.7	3.8	0.0	0.0	16.5	2.2	4.5	11.4	0.5	0.2	1.4	1.2	30.9	20.7	14.1	16.6
1980	135.5	0.1	1.5	0.0	0.0	13.7	1.5	2.6	8.3	0.4	0.1	0.7	0.4	29.1	17.2	16.0	19.6
1990	139.2	0.3	1.8	0.0	19.7	12.6	1.6	2.2	7.6	0.4	0.0	0.5	0.4	23.6	13.4	15.2	17.7
1999	108.3	*	0.9	*	7.2	10.6	1.5	1.5	8.1	*	0	0.7	0.5	17.9	13.4	13.5	11.2

* Zero or negligible – no data.

Sources: 1 Forrest D. Linder and Robert D. Grove, Vital Statistics Rates in the United States, 1900–1940. 2 Robert D. Grove and Alice M. Hetzel, Vital Statistics Rates in the United States, 1940–1960. 3 National Office of Vital Statistics, Vital Statistics of the United States, Mortality, 1932 through 1993. 4 National Center for Health Statistics, "Mortality data from the National Vital Statistics System," mortality website: www.cdc.gov/nchs/datawh/statb/unpubd/mortabs.htm www.cdc.gov/nchs/releases/0-1 facts/99mortality.htm 5 United States Bureau of the Census, Vital Statistics, Special Reports, vol. 43, "Death, rates by age, race and sex, 1900–1953."

death rate from Aids has never exceeded the death rate from tuberculosis a century ago, and was lower in the year 1999 than syphilis in the year 1930. Mortality from rheumatic fever, diabetes, stroke, influenza, appendicitis as well as complications of pregnancy has been all but eliminated. Mortality from cancer and heart disease has been reduced but not comparably to the reduction in mortality from other diseases. By contrast, the incidence of violent death remains more or less the same. Death rates from accidents, suicide, and homicide do not change much over the century, though there seems to be some considerable improvement in the last few decades.

THE INCREASE IN LIFE EXPECTANCY THROUGHOUT THE WORLD

The great increase in life expectancy in the United States is by no means unusual. Similar increases have occurred in most of the countries in Europe and America as well as in Japan and elsewhere in Asia. Most advanced countries have by now attained life expectancies of about 75 years for men and 80 for women. A sample of histories of life expectancies is presented in table 1.5. Russia is an exception. In 1965, life expectancy in Russia was about the same as in the United States. Since then, American life expectancy has risen from 66.8 to 72.0 for men, and from 73.7 to 78.8 for women. By contrast, Russian life expectancy remained about the same until 1989, falling from 64.5 to 64.2 for men but rising from 73.7 to 74.6 for women. Then Russian life expectancy plummeted to 58.9 (a fall of 5.3 years) for men, and to 71.9 (a fall of 2.7 years) for women in 1998.

For the period since the Second World War, the increase in life expectancy through-out the world is summarized in table 1.6 for three groupings of countries, more developed, less developed, and least developed. Average life expectancy has increased substantially in all three regions, and the spreads between regions are narrowing somewhat, but significant differences among regions remain.

Table 1.5   Life expectancy at birth in several countries, 1750–2000

	1750	1800	1880	1900	1930	1950	1965	2001
Sweden	37.3	36.5	48.5	54	63.3	71.3	73.9	79.7
France	27.9	33.9	42.1	47.4	56.7	66.5	71.1	78.9
Russia	—	—	27.7	32.4	42.9	64	69.1	67.3
Australia	—	—	49	55	65.3	69.6	71	80
Canada	—	35.6	49.6	56	61	68.6	72	79.6
Japan	—	—	35.1	37.7	45.9	59.1	70.3	80.1

Sources: M. Livi-Bacci, A Concise History of World Population, *Oxford, Blackwell, second edition, 1997, tables 4.3 and 4.8, supplemented by data from Angus Maddison,* Monitoring the World Economy, 1820–1992, *Paris, OECD, 1995, table A-3a; R. Bourbeau, J. Legare, and V. Emond,* New Birth Cohort Life Tables for Canada and Quebec, 1801–1991, *Statistics Canada, 91 F0015MPE; V. Shkolnikov, F. Mesle, and J. Vallin, "Health crisis in Russia,"* Population, *vol. 8, 1999, INED, appendix table 1; Canadian Historical Statistics, table, 65 and 66 (for 1966), Statistiska central-byran (www.scb.se for 1961–70); Queensland, Office of the Commonwealth Actuary (www.oesr.qld.au for 1965–7) and www.odci.gov/cia/publications/factbook/country.html*

Table 1.6   Worldwide life expectancy at birth, 1950–1999

	More developed regions	Less developed regions	Least developed regions
1950–5	66.5	40.9	35.7
1960–5	69.8	47.7	39.8
1970–5	71.2	54.6	43.6
1980–5	73.0	58.5	47.2
1990–9	75.0	64.0	61.0

Sources: **United Nations,** **World Population Prospects, The 1994 Revision,** *p. 117,*
supplemented by current data from www.prb.org/pubs/wpds99/wpds99_world.htm

Demographic catastrophe

The Black Death was by no means the only or the worst epidemic in the history of mankind. Even more dramatic was the epidemic brought by Europeans to the indigenous people of North America. Smallpox, measles, typhus, tuberculosis, influenza, and chicken pox – diseases that Europeans had coped with for millennia – were hitherto unknown in the Americas and very much more lethal. It has been estimated that contact with the Europeans diminished the indigenous population of the United States from 5 million to a low of 60,000, from which it substantially increased once people became accustomed to European-borne disease. From 1532 to 1608, the indigenous population of central Mexico fell from 16.9 to 1.1 million.[3]

From time to time over the last two millennia, China has experienced similarly rapid declines in population, but with a different cause. China has been no less subject than Europe to epidemics, but the standard explanation of the ups and downs in population is political. Variations in population are attributed to the establishment and disintegration of public order, referred to by historians as the dynastic cycle. An established ruling dynasty is said to possess the mandate of heaven. As long as the dynasty preserves the mandate of heaven, public order is maintained and the population grows. Eventually, dynasties lose the mandate of heaven. Public order is then dissolved, the land is preyed upon by armies of bandits that the government can no longer suppress, crops are stolen or destroyed, people are displaced, starvation stalks the land, and population declines until such time as a new dynasty is established, making way for fresh population growth once order is restored. The root cause of the cycle is debatable. The traditional explanation is that, with time, dynasties grow corrupt and effete. Population growth itself may be destabilizing as the standard of living is reduced, choking off the farmers' surplus production required for the provisioning of the army and the bureaucracy of the state. Disease and starvation reinforce one another in the population decline.

The story is told in table 1.7, showing the history of the population of China classified by the six principal dynasties during the last two thousand years. For each dynasty, two estimates of population are shown, one near the beginning of the dynasty and the other near the end. It is immediately evident from these data that population grew substantially within each dynasty, and then fell between dynasties, sometimes

Table 1.7   The population of imperial China, 206 BC to AD 1911

Dynasties	Population early in the dynasty (millions)	Population late in the dynasty (millions)
West Han (206 BC–AD 8)	14.0 (206 BC)	58.0 (AD 2)
East Han (AD 25–AD 208)	15.1 (AD 31)	59.8 (AD 118)
Tang (AD 618–AD 907)	17.6 (AD 624)	38.1 (AD 845)
Sung (960–1279)	24.8 (AD 959)	54.9 (1276)
Ming (1368–1644)	63.8 (1368)	99.9 (1626)
Ch'ing (1645–1911)	88.5 (1646)	405.5 (1911)

*Sources: **Cheng-chui Lai, "Man/land ratio and dynastic cycle in Imperial China: a Malthusian interpretation,"** Archives of Economic History, 1992, vol. 2, no. 1, 113–25, table 1.*

dramatically. For instance, in just 29 years from AD 2 near the end of the West Han dynasty to AD 31 near the beginning of the next dynasty, the population declined by about 75 percent from 58 million to 15.1 million. Population recovered over the next 80 years during the East Han dynasty, but then fell once again between the end of the East Han dynasty and the beginning of the Tang dynasty, five hundred years later. The last imperial dynasty was followed by the Republic of China, which lasted until 1953, when it was replaced by the Peoples' Republic of China, which rules to this day. In 1953, the first year of the Peoples' Republic of China, the population of China was 508 million. By the year AD 2000, the population of China had grown to 1 billion and 266 million people.

Today, epidemics are contained, but by no means eliminated. The world's encounter with Aids is instructive. The experience of the epidemic in the rich countries was very different from that of the experience in the poor countries. When the epidemic first struck the United States in the early 1980s, it was not recognized as a new disease, and its cause was completely unknown. In time, though no cure has yet been discovered, scientists learned the nature of the disease, its cause, and the means to contain it. Before 1980, there were in the United States no known deaths from Aids. Thereafter, the number of deaths from the infection increased steadily to a peak of 51,000 in 1995. Aggressive treatment reduced deaths to 9,000 in 2000, the latest year for which data are available. The rate of infection with the HIV virus has been reduced and expensive treatment has contained the virus so that it does not give rise to full-blown Aids. About 800,000 to 900,000 Americans out of a total population of 280 million are now thought to be infected. It is terrifying to think what might have happened if the Aids epidemic had struck a century ago when the nature of the disease could not have been discovered and when people would be unlikely to associate disease today with sexual activity as much as a dozen years before the onset of the disease.

The rate of infection with the HIV virus has been much higher in Africa. It is estimated that, by the year 2000, a full 8.5 percent of the adult population of sub-Saharan Africa was infected with Aids and that, during the year 1999, a third of a percent of the population (2.2 million people out of a total population of 596.3 million) died of the disease.[4] The cost of treatment is greater than most African countries can afford without massive foreign assistance.

Prosperity

A rough indicator of prosperity in England over the last seven centuries is supplied by the time series of average *real wages* in table 1.8. If people consumed nothing but bread, the real wage each year would be the number of loaves consumed or, equivalently, the money wage divided by the price of bread. When people consume many different goods, the real wage each year becomes the money wage *deflated* by a *price index* to reflect wage-earners' standard of living. The price index and the corresponding index of real wages are constructed with reference to an arbitrarily chosen *base year*. In the base year, real wages and money wages are, by definition, the same. In any other year, the real wage is the money wage one would require in the base year (when confronted with prices in the base year) to be as well off as one would be with the average wage in that other year. Suppose the year 2000 is the chosen base year. With respect to the year 2000 as the base year, the average real wage in the year 1950 is said to be $18,000 per year if the average worker in the year 1950 – with prices and wages as they were in 1950 – was as well off as a person who earned $18,000 in the year 2000. Actual money wages in the year 1950 may have been very much less. If prices had increased six-fold in the intervening fifty years, then the actual money wage in the year 1950 would have been only $3,000.

To deflate money wages by prices is to divide money wages each year by the value of an appropriately scaled price index. In the example in the preceding paragraph, the price index is set at 1 for the year 2000, ensuring that the average money wage and the average real wage are the same in that year. As prices are assumed to have risen six-fold from 1950 to 2000, the value of the price index must have been $\frac{1}{6}$ in the year 1950. Thus, if the money wage is $3,000 in the year 1950, the corresponding real wage must be $18,000 [3,000 ÷ (1/6)]. Alternatively, as in table 1.8, the price index might be scaled to set the real wage at 100 in some chosen base year. If the average money wage was $36,000 in the year 2000, it would be said that real wages grew by 100 percent – or 1.39 percent per year – over the entire 50-year period. The construction of a time-series of real wages is straightforward when all prices change proportionally, up or down, from year to year. The measurement of real wages becomes problematic when prices vary at different rates – some up, some down – each year, a matter to be taken up at the end of chapter 5 once the required theory of taste and demand has been developed. For the moment, think of real wages as money wages deflated by a reasonable price index without being too concerned about what "reasonable" means in this context.

Table 1.8 is a time series of real wages in England from 1340 to 1977, specifically of builders' wages corrected for changes over time in prices of commodities that builders are likely to buy. The procedure tracks standards of living satisfactorily if and in so far as percentage changes over time in the real wages of builders are not too different from percentage changes over time in average real wages for all occupations and for all regions of the country. The information is acquired from a sample of records of

Table 1.8 Real wages and population: England and Wales, 1340–1997

Date	Real wages $(1451-75=100)$	Population (millions)
1340	52	4 to 6
1377	74	2.2 to 2.8
1421	108	1.6
1552	48	3.0
1600	44	4.1
1642	48	5.1
1700	57	5.1
1750	68	5.7
1800	38	8.9
1850	84	17.9
1900	134	32.5
1950	180	43.8
1997	460	58.2

Sources: Real wages [1340 to 1950]: H. Phelps-Brown and S. Hopkins, "Seven centuries of prices of consumables compared with builders' wage-rates," Economica, 1956, *included as "Labour force, 31" in B. R. Mitchell,* British Historical Statistics, *Cambridge, Cambridge University Press, 1988. [1997]* Statistical Yearbook, 1997, United Nations, *tables 33 and 35 and B. R. Mitchell,* International Historical Statistics, Europe, 1750–1993, *London, Macmillan, 1998, tables B1 and H2. Population [1340, 1377 and 1421]: D. Coleman and J. Glass,* The British Population: Patterns Trends and Processes, *Oxford, Oxford University Press, 1992 [1552–1950], Mitchell,* British Historical Statistics, *"Population and vital statistics, 1." [1997]* Statistical Yearbook, 1997, United Nations, *table 7 for the entire United Kingdom.*

monasteries and other institutions. Sketchy and incomplete, it is the only information available for such a long stretch of time. To construct the time series of real wages, money wages were deflated by a price index scaled so that the average real wage is set at 100 over the period from 1451 to 1475. The choice of dates in the early years is determined in part by the availability of data and in part to show data before and after the Black Death. For each year in the table, population is shown as well. Figures for the early years are necessarily judgmental because there was no adequate census of population.

The history of real wages and population in England can be divided into three main episodes. The first episode was the Black Death which, as discussed above, wiped out half the population of England in the middle of the fourteenth century. From the beginning to the end of the fourteenth century, the population of England fell from about 5 million to about 2 million. The fall in population created a scarcity of labor, leading to a rise in the real wage from about 50 in the early part of the fourteenth century to a peak of over 100 in the fifteenth century, the highest level of real wages until the middle of the nineteenth century. The next episode was the gradual rise in population throughout the seventeenth and eighteenth centuries, but with no corresponding rise in real wages. Potential gains in the early years of the industrial revolution were eaten away in population growth. In the third episode from about 1800 to the present day, technical change outdistanced population growth, and real wages rose steadily from a low of 38 in 1800 to 460 in 1997, over 12 times what they were in the beginning of the nineteenth century and almost 4 times as high as they had ever been up to the twentieth century. Until about a hundred years ago, wages rose in good times and fell in bad times, with no discernible long-term trend one way or another. Only in the last hundred years or so has technical change outdistanced population growth, providing the common man with a standard of living unprecedented in the entire history of the world.

Real wages are a less than ideal measure of prosperity for a country as a whole. When available, a better measure of general prosperity is *real national income* per head where "national income" is the value of all goods and services produced by government as well as by the private sector, and for investment as well as for consumption. Time series of national income do not reach as far back as time series of real wages because national income statistics are built up from vast amounts of primary data collected by national statistical agencies that did not exist until the nineteenth century.

For Canada, from the year 1870 to the year 2000, a time series of real national income is presented in table 1.9. National income can be thought of as a family of closely related statistics, each giving rise to a somewhat different time series. The variant of national income in table 1.9 is *real gross domestic product* per head expressed in dollars for the year 2000. *Domestic product* is the dollar value of all goods and services produced in the country (including non-residents' entitlement to domestically produced goods and services, but excluding residents' entitlement to goods and services produced abroad). *Gross* means that there is no correction for depreciation of the capital stock. Conversion from money national income to real national income is essentially the same as conversion from money wages to real wages. The choice of the year 2000 as the base year of the time series is arbitrary but, nonetheless, informative, because the user of statistics of real national income wants to know how well off people used to be by his standards today, not how well off he is by theirs. He wants to know how much income grandma and grandpa would need today to be as well off as they were back in 1950, not how much income he would need in 1950 to be as well off as he is today.

Inevitably, the measurement of real national income is fuzzy because the price index is never quite what we would like it to be, because different people consume different proportions of goods, because new types of goods are introduced from time to time, and because the quality of goods changes over time. Statistics of real national income do not have the precision of, for example, distances between cities. Statistics of real national income are interesting and instructive nonetheless.

Table 1.9 is largely self-explanatory. For example, the number 2,554 in the top row of the fourth column means that people in the year 1870 were on average as well off as one would be with an annual income of $2,554 in the year 2000. Actual money income per head in the year 1870 was very much less, but prices were less too. Only for the year 2000, shown on the bottom row of the table, are money income and real income the same.

The right-hand column of table 1.9 shows the rate of growth each decade in real gross domestic product per head. The average rate of growth over the entire 130 years

Table 1.9 Canadian economic growth, 1870–2000

	Gross domestic product at prices in the year 2000 ($ billion)	Population (000)	Gross domestic product per head at prices in the year 2000 ($)	Annual growth rate of gross domestic product per head (average since the year in the preceding row: %)
1870	9.3	3,625	2,554	—
1880	11.5	4,255	2,697	0.55
1890	16.5	4,779	3,453	2.47
1900	22.6	5,301	4,265	2.11
1910	41.5	6,988	5,934	3.3
1920	49.9	8,556	5,832	−0.02
1930	76.1	10,208	7,472	2.45
1933	56.9	10,633	5,550	−11.1
1940	94.6	11,381	8,309	6.29
1950	155.4	13,712	11,343	3.11
1960	243.5	17,870	13,628	1.84
1970	402.7	21,297	18,908	3.27
1980	613.1	24,043	25,500	2.99
1990	808.5	27,791	29,092	1.32
2000	1,056	30,616	34,492	1.7

Sources: **M. C. Urquhart, Gross National Product, Canada 1870–1926, Kingston and Montreal: McGill-Queen's University Press, table 1.2, updated with data from CANSIM, Statistics
Canada. Several time series covering less than the entire period from 1870 to 2000 and with different base years are spliced together to produce one consistent time series in 2000 dollars. 1870
to 2000 and with different base years are spliced together to produce one consistent time series in
2000 dollars.**

of the time series was about 2 percent per year. Such is the power of compound interest
that this annual growth of 2 percent was sufficient to generate a more than 15-fold
increase in real income per head, from $2,254 in the year 1870 to $34,942 in the year
2000. The typical Canadian today is over 15 times as well off as Canadians used to be
130 years ago. This unprecedented prosperity is broadly consistent with the pattern
of real wages in England in table 1.8.

As the overall measure of prosperity tends to be somewhat abstract and distant
from everyday life, it may be helpful to supplement the table with information about
the specifics of the improvement in the standard of living. The increase in real gross
domestic product per head is a summing up of the changes over time in the quantities
and qualities of a thousand different goods and services. A few of these changes are
shown in table 1.10 for several years between 1935 and 1997 for which the data happen
to be readily available. This was a time of rapidly increasing prosperity in a number
of dimensions. Ownership of automobiles increased four-fold. Housing improved
markedly, as indicated by the increase in the proportion of dwellings with flush toilets
from just over half to almost 100 percent. The old term "cold water flat" has gone out
of use because virtually all apartments are now supplied with hot water. The switch
during the last quarter of the twentieth century from red meat to poultry is in part due

Table 1.10   Selected indicators of prosperity in Canada, 1935–1997

	1935	1950	1965	1974	1986	1997
Red meat, pounds per person per year	115.5	126	150	169.7	154.6	130
Poultry, pounds per person per year	10.4	11.5	27.2	43.3	55.2	67.5
Vegetables, pounds per person per year	—	—	291	321.9	380.9	409.4
Fruit, pounds per person per year	—	—	183.5	199.3	253.2	283.4
Cars per 1000 people	91	139	269	377	438	440
Flush toilets, % of households	56.3	64.2	78.7	97.2	99+	99+
Refrigerators, % of households	9.3	60	98	99+	99+	99+
Computers, % of households	0	0	—	—	10.3	39.8
Television sets, % of households	0	10.3	92.6	96.5	98.7	99+
Telephones per 1000 people	57	110	270	390	—	—
Undergraduate students per 1000 people	3	5	8.3	17	15.7	16.6
Graduate students per 1000 people	0.14	0.39	1.12	1.67	2.09	2.52

Sources: D. Usher, The Measurement of Economic Growth, Oxford: Blackwell, 1980, table 10.2, and Tanis Day, "Substituting capital for labor in the home: the diffusion of household technology," Ph.D. dissertation, Queen's University, 1987, table A. la. Supplemented with data from Statistics Canada: Road Motor Vehicles, 53–219; Education in Canada, 81–229; Household Facilities and Equipment, 64–202, Food Consumption in Canada, 32–230, Historical Statistics of Canada.

to a substantial fall in the price of poultry relative to the price of beef, and in part due a change in peoples' perception about what constitutes a healthy diet. General prosperity and improvements in food storage have resulted in large increases in consumption of fruits and vegetables. As a percentage of the population, the number of undergraduates in university increased four-fold and the number of graduate students increased twenty-fold. Equally important, though not so easily quantified, is the improvement in the quality of goods and the introduction of new goods. We have much better cars and refrigerators than we had in 1935, and we have TV sets and home computers which our grandparents in 1935 did not have at all. Progress in medical science has increased the quality as well as the length of life. New and better anaesthetics save us from pain our ancestors had no choice but to endure. We need no longer fear a tooth extraction or die in agony. Among the few goods consumed less today than in the past are potatoes and cigarettes. In 1981, 38.1 percent of Canadians smoked an average of 20.6 cigarettes per smoker. In 1996/7, 28.9 percent of Canadians smoked an average of 17.5 cigarettes per smoker.[5]

A similar story is told for the entire world in table 1.11. There is a ten-fold growth in western Europe and 'western offshoots' (meaning United States, Canada, Australia, and New Zealand) and a less spectacular but still substantial growth in the rest of the world. Asia more or less stagnated for the first hundred years, but grew faster in the last thirty years than any other region. Africa did the least well over the entire period, trebling income per head but falling relatively from 82 percent (450/661) to 24 percent (1318/5539) of the world average.

Table 1.11 Worldwide gross domestic product per head in 1990 (dollars)

	Western Europe	Western offshoots	Southern Europe	Eastern Europe	Latin America	Asia	Africa	Average
1820	1,292	1,202	806	750	715	550	450	661
1870	2,110	2,440	1,111	1,030	800	580	480	920
1900	3,092	4,022	1,575	1,263	1,134	681	500	1,305
1929	4,704	5,237	1,753	1,557	1,515	742	575	1,592
1960	7,675	10,813	2,828	3,670	3,302	1,041	933	2,931
1992	17,384	20,850	8,273	4,608	5,292	3,239	1,318	5,539

Sources: A. Madison, Monitoring the World Economy, Paris: OECD, 1995, table E-3, 210. "Western offshoots" refers to United States, Canada, Australia, and New Zealand. The comparable figures for Japan are 704 in 1820 and 19,425 in 1992. The comparable figures for the United States are 1,287 in 1820 and 22,569 in 1992. The comparable figures for Canada are 1,225 in 1820 and 18,159 in 1992.

Table 1.12 Life expectancy at birth and the number of children per woman in Canada, 1700–1999

Year	Life expectancy at birth		Number of children per woman (fertility rate)	Number of children per woman who lives to the end of child-bearing age	Population of canada (thousands)
	Males	Females			
1700	35.5	35.5	4.3	8.2	18
1831	40.2	42.4	3.9	6.5	1,124
1861	42.7	45.3	3	4.8	3,230
1891	49.3	53.5	2.5	3.6	4,883
1921	62.6	70.2	2.7	3.1	8,788
1950	72.3	79.6	1.8	1.9	14,009
1999	76.1	82.8	1.7	1.7	31,006

Sources: Demographic data from Y. Lavoie "Two centuries of demographic change," Report on the Demographic Situation in Canada, Statistics Canada, 91-209-E, 1992 and 1996. Population data from W. L. Marr and D. G. Paterson, Canada: An Economic History, Toronto: Macmillan of Canada, 1980, table 6-1 updated from Annual Demographic Statistics, 1999, Statistics Canada, 91-213- XPB, table 1.1. All data for 1999 are from www.odci.gov/cia/publications/factbook/ca.html#people

The increase in longevity and prosperity over the last two hundred years would have been impossible without a marked decline in fertility rates, defined as the number of children per woman. Consider the Canadian experience as set out in table 1.12. In the year 1700, women in Canada who lived until the end of their childbearing age would have given birth to just over eight children. With mortality rates as they were at that time, the actual number of children per woman was 4.3, equivalent to about 2.15 female children per generation. Suppose the length of a generation, from child-birth to childbirth, to be 25 years. Had that rate of increase been maintained over

Table 1.13   A fall in fertility rates and a rise in population

	Fertility rates		Population (millions)				
	1980–5	1990–9	1750	1850	1900	1950	1999
World	—	2.9	791	1,262	1,650	2,520	5,982
Africa	6.32	5.4	106	111	133	224	771
Asia	3.7	2.8	502	809	947	1,403	3,637
Europe	1.78	1.4	163	276	408	549	728
Latin America	3.84	2.9	16	38	74	166	512
Northern America	1.8	2	2	26	82	166	303
Oceania	2.6	2.4	2	2	6	13	30

Sources: **United Nations,** World Population Prospects: The 1994 Revision, *pp. 101 and 117,* *supplemented by current data from www.prb.org/pubs/wpds99/wpds99_world.htm*

the twelve generations from 1700 to 2000, the original population of 18 thousand in the year 1700 would have grown 9,756-fold (2.15^{12}), reaching 176 million by the year 2000, over five times the present population of Canada. The Canadian resource base could not support that many people at the present standard of living. Despite substantial immigration over the past three hundred years, the population of Canada is only 32 million today. Worse still, if mortality rates among women had been the same in the year 1700 as they became in the year 2000 (so that almost all women survived until the end of their childbearing years) and if the number of children "per woman who lives to the end of the childbearing age" remained as it was in the year 1700, the population would have increased over four-fold per generation. The Canadian population would have grown 22.6 million-fold (4.1^{12}). By the year 2000, the Canadian population would have reached about 407 billion people, more than sixty times the present population of the world.

Until quite recently, recognition of the consequences of this bizarre mathematics of population growth led thoughtful people to despair about the prospects for permanent prosperity or long-term economic growth. A small upper class could be kept wealthy. Forces beyond anybody's control would keep the vast majority of people permanently impoverished. Technical change may raise the standard of living for a time, but not permanently. Inevitably, prosperity lowers mortality rates, the fall in mortality rates brings population growth, population growth reduces resources per head, and the reduction in resources per head brings prosperity to an end, driving down the standard of living to whatever level is sufficient to stop population growth.

Little faith was placed in people's ability or willingness to restrict population voluntarily, though that is exactly what happened. Population has grown rapidly in the last few hundred years, but not nearly as rapidly as our mathematics would suggest, because fertility rates fell. The story is told for Canada in table 1.12 and for the entire world in table 1.13. Table 1.13 shows that fertility rates have been declining everywhere, but not sufficiently to stop population growth. Fertility rates in Africa have been especially high: enough to generate a three-fold increase in population over the last fifty years. Fertility rates in Europe and America have been much lower: enough that the population will soon decline if not shored up by immigration. In view of the enormous increase over the last few hundred years in the population of Europe and of lands occupied by Europeans, a period of voluntary decline may be no tragedy. The larger picture is that technical change has enabled national income per head to increase despite the pressure of population on land and resources. There is no assurance that past trends will continue, for current fertility rates are still well above what is required at present mortality rates to stop the growth of population. The mechanics of economic growth will be discussed in chapter 6.

Customs and Institutions

The doubling of the length of life and the ten-fold increase in gross national product per head over the last two hundred years are beneficial to humankind directly and by virtue of the customs and institutions they permit. Patricide, infanticide, brutal punishment for crime, torture, persecution of witches and heretics, a rigid class structure, and slavery have been eliminated in much of the world because people are for the first time in a position to do without them.

Patricide and Infanticide

> *For our custom up here is that all old people who can do no more, and whom death will not take, help death to take them. And this is not merely to be rid of a life that is no longer a pleasure, but also to relieve their nearest relations of the trouble they give them.*
>
> **A Netsilik Eskimo**[6]

Today, old folks retire to a life of leisure in Florida. Traditionally, the Eskimos abandoned their old folks, who were younger than most Canadians and Americans retiring today, to freeze. There is nothing unusual about such behavior. The story is told that, among the Visigoths, ancestors of much of the population of Europe and North America, old men weary of life would be expected to throw themselves off *The Rock of the Forefathers* on the understanding that a delightful abode in heaven awaited those who committed suicide and a horrible subterranean cavern awaited those who died of sickness or decrepitude. Such practices are common among poor primitive peoples, especially nomads for whom the capacity to walk long distances quickly is essential.[7] Similar considerations may lie behind the ancient Hindu custom of immolating widows on their husbands' funeral pyres.

Nor can we condemn our ancestors for these practices. A community close to subsistence may be confronted with the stark choice between the old and the young. The very survival of the group may depend on a willingness to slough off its weaker members. "The Eskimos of Baffin Island have a great respect for the aged and treat them well. But when a woman becomes so old that she is a burden, she may calmly resign herself to death, allowing herself to be walled into a snow hut and left to die. She thinks it is better; the tribe agrees."[8]

The content of our ethics depends upon the productivity of our economy. Right and wrong depend upon the level of prosperity humankind has attained. Provision for the old always draws upon resources that might be used for the benefit of the young instead. Whether that provision is warranted depends on what else those resources might procure. Today, patricide is evil because the sacrifice to the young in sending the old folks to a retirement home rather than to the ice flows is a smaller car or a shorter vacation, not life itself. Today the trade-off is between lives and goods. At other times it has been between the lives of the old and the lives of the young. We sympathize with the plight of the Eskimos in circumstances as they used to be, though we would unreservedly condemn patricide by Eskimos following the old traditions, or by anybody else, today. Patricide has become an abomination because we can afford to dispense with it.

Infanticide was equally necessary. The human female is biologically programmed to produce many more children than is consistent with the very low rates of population growth observed throughout most of history. Without modern methods of birth control, it is unlikely, bordering on impossible, that a population of hunter-gatherers could have been stabilized without recourse to infanticide.[9] Nomadic people cannot maintain more young children than can be carried for long distances. There is anthropological evidence of infanticide among the many tribal societies. Some societies did not recognize children until enough time had elapsed after birth for a decision to be made whether the child should be allowed to survive, drawing the line between birth control and murder at, for example, the tenth month after conception. Prosperity has distinct moral consequences.

The severity of the law

A similar observation can be made about the law. Prosperity and longevity cannot be sustained without a modicum of public order, and that, in turn, requires that crime be significantly deterred. The incidence of crime must be held to some tolerable limit by the prospect of punishment. Today, we can afford a police force, and we can afford to put convicted criminals in prison. In times gone by, both were prohibitively costly and other means had to be found to deter crime. As the risk of detection was low, the punishment had to be correspondingly severe.

Consider an amoral person deciding whether to steal $100. If he is sure to be caught, a fine of as little as $1 (over and above the return of the stolen $100) is sufficient deterrence because the thief is made $1 worse off by stealing than by not stealing. But if the probability of detection and punishment is only 10 percent (and if the would-be thief is risk neutral), the fine must exceed the loot by a factor of at least nine to ensure that crime does not pay. To deter a theft of $100, a fine of over $900 would be required. The general principle is that crime can only be deterred when the expected cost of punishment to the would-be criminal exceeds his expected benefit from crime. The preservation of society requires that punishment be severe enough to deter most crime, though, for reasons to be discussed later on, not all crime is deterred in practice.

To this principle, there is an important qualification. The would-be criminal must be wealthy enough to pay the fine. If not, some other form of punishment is required. The poorer the society and the less efficient the police, the less likely is this requirement to be met. Nowadays, the alternative is imprisonment which is costly to society but effective as a deterrent. Imprisonment may be insufficient in a poor society. Imprisonment may be deemed too costly or may fail to deter crime among people on the very edge of subsistence. That leaves only the infliction of pain or the death penalty, which were – and had to be – imposed almost everywhere until modern times.

English law as it was in the early seventeenth century provides a wealth of examples.[10] Treason, murder, manslaughter, larceny, abduction of an heiress with intent to marry her, forgery, malicious burning of stocks of grain, malicious injury to another man's eyes or tongue, refusal to depart on command from assembly with intent to bring down prices, and stealing of more than a shilling's worth (about two days wage of a laborer) were all capital crimes, punishable by hanging. Lying, perjury, and blasphemy were punished by piercing the tongue with a hot iron. Every village had its stocks and its whipping post for punishment of lesser crimes such as petty theft, vagrancy, wife beating, drunkenness, breaking the sabbath, or gambling. All punishment, especially execution, would be meted out in full view of the public, outside church on Sunday or in the marketplace on market day. As recently as 1833, a 14-year-old boy was hanged for stealing two pence worth of printers ink.[11]

Treason, the most serious of all crimes, was punished by hanging, drawing (disembowelling), and quartering. The great seventeenth-century English jurist, Sir Edward Coke, described the process, with approval, as follows:

> When the sentence was fully carried out – and this was not always done – the traitor was drawn backwards, with head downwards, on a hurdle from the prison to the gallows, as being "unworthy to tread any more on mother earth"... he was then hanged by the neck and, whilst still alive, cut down from the gallows and his penis and testicles cut off, since he was regarded as unprofitably begotten and unfit to leave any descendants; his bowels and entrails, which were considered to have inwardly conceived and concealed the treason, were cut out of his body and burnt by the executioner before the dying man's eyes; then his head, that imagined the crime, was cut off, his body divided into four quarters and set up in some "high and eminent place to the view and detestation of men and to become a prey for the fowls of the air."[12]

Torture – by the rack, compression, manacles, starvation, and hanging by one's thumbs – was regularly employed on witnesses and accused persons to extract information. Torture is distinct from punishment. Punishment is inflicted on someone convicted of having committed a crime; torture is inflicted to elicit information from someone who may very well be innocent of any crime. Special measures had to be taken in circumstances where conviction could not be obtained without a plea, guilty or not guilty as the case may be, by the accused and where the accused refused to plead at all. The procedure, called *pein forte et dure*, was to place one heavy stone after another on the chest of the accused until his rib cage collapsed. Knowing the consequences of silence, an accused person might still refuse to plead because a guilty verdict would mean the forfeiture of his property to the state, while a person who dies under *peine forte et dure* has not been convicted of a crime so that his heirs retain entitlement to their inheritance.[13]

These were the practices of our ancestors. English law was not unusually harsh for its time, and by the seventeenth century, the reformers were already condemning its worse excesses. Seventeenth-century England was the huge cauldron from which bubbled up a great many of our present ideas about justice and democracy. Nevertheless, a degree of savagery in the criminal justice system, like the institution of patricide among the traditional Eskimos, was once necessary to preserve society and maintain the core of order without which civilized life would have been impossible.

Witchcraft and heresy

Today, Halloween is a celebration for children. It is at the same time a collective memory of the era, four to five hundred years ago, when the church, Protestant and Catholic, treated witchcraft as a capital crime and was instrumental in its prosecution and punishment. In those days, the devil stalked the earth, capturing the souls of unfortunate people who flew off on broomsticks to their sabbats to copulate with the devil and plot mischief. As witches could hardly be expected to admit to such crimes voluntarily, confession was extracted by torture.

During the great witch craze from about 1450 to 1650, belief in the existence of witches was almost universal, in part because learned and authoritative treatises on the subject decreed that "to disbelieve in witchcraft is the greatest of heresie."[14] University students would be taught by grave and sincere professors that witches live secretly among us and must be exterminated. Throughout most of Europe, the punishment for witchcraft was to be burned alive at the stake, with the option of being strangled first if one admitted one's crimes. Estimates vary considerably, but something in the order of 100,000 witches, mostly but not entirely old women, were executed.[15]

Heresy was also punishable by burning at the stake, though lesser punishments would normally be imposed on those who confessed their crimes and accepted the authority of the true church, whatever that might be. Records of ancient tribes or musings of ancient prophets were accepted as literally and factually true, and bureaucracies of clerics were empowered with the sole custody of interpretation. Entrance to heaven became conditional on obedience to the true church, no act in defense of the true church was prohibited, and no punishment of unbelievers was too severe. The term "heresy" was usually reserved for Christians who deviated from the true church, not Jews or Muslims who had always been apart, but the definition of heresy varied from time to time and from place to place. For a layman to read the Bible in the vernacular might be heresy. Participants in religious sects outside of the established church were heretics. Converted Jews or Muslims preserving elements of their old faiths were heretics. Protestants in Catholic countries and Catholics in Protestant countries were heretics.

No one is sure how many heretics were burned at the stake in the middle ages and in early modern times. Probably tens of thousands altogether.[16] Many, many more deaths are probably attributable to the ferocity of the wars of religion in the seventeenth century when Catholics and Protestants alike could expect to be executed for their religious beliefs if their side did not come out victorious. Many innocent civilians would have been destroyed in the crossfire. Only gradually did the crime of heresy disappear. Associating freedom of belief with freedom of trade, some historians have attributed the disappearance of the crime of heresy and the emergence of the principle of toleration with the rise of capitalism.[17] Memory of the days when heresy was a capital offense lies behind the provision in the American constitution for separation between church and state.

The class structure

> For that infinite wisdom of God, which hath distinguished his angels by degrees, which hath given less light and beauty to the heavenly bodies, which hath made differences between beast and birds, created the eagle and the fly, the cedar and the shrub, and among stone given the fairest tincture to the ruby and the quickest light to the diamond, hath also ordained kings, dukes and leaders of people, magistrates, judges and other degrees among men.
>
> **Sir Walter Raleigh**[18]

How utterly foreign that sounds! So accustomed have we become to thinking of people as fundamentally equal that we have quite forgotten that our ancestors held a very different world view in which some people were innately superior to others. The pharaohs of Egypt and the emperors of China, Rome, ancient Cambodia, and many other places were not just divinely appointed, but God-like in themselves and worthy of worship. Nobility were almost biologically different from ordinary folk. It may have been self-evident to the writer of the *Declaration of Independence*, and it may be self-evident to us today, that "all men are created equal," but it was no less self-evident to our ancestors that they were not.

The cruel truth of the matter may be that, throughout most of recorded history, a sufficient degree of order in society could only be established despotically. The material conditions of life may have allowed no other options, except perhaps in small tribes where people could keep watch on one another and the community as a whole could mete out punishment where necessary. Otherwise, the choice may have been between total disorder where the life of man is, in Hobbes' famous phrase, "solitary, poor, nasty, brutish and short" and the utter subservience of the greater part of humankind to a small ruling class which comes to look upon its subjects as sheep to be cared for and protected only to the extent that the wool and meat are useful to the shepherd. And if that be the choice, the shepherd may be preferable to the wolves. Recall the passage in the Bible (1 Samuel 8) where the Israelites beg the prophet Samuel to appoint a king.

> And he [the Lord as quoted by Samuel] said, "This will be the behaviour of the king who will reign over you.... He will appoint captains over his thousands and captains over his fifties.... He will take your daughters to be perfumers, cooks and bakers. And he will take the best of your fields, your vineyards and your olive groves.... And you will be his

servants. And you will cry out in that day because of your king ... and the Lord will not hear you in that day." Nevertheless the people refused to obey the voice of Samuel; and they said, "We will have a king over us ... that our king may judge us and go out before us and fight our battles."

To be sure, the origin of kingship may have been somewhat less consensual than the story would suggest, but, had there been a choice, an absolute monarchy and the division of humankind into rigid social classes may have been the best available option.

Class structure would be reflected in the law. During the third century AD there evolved in the Roman empire a broad distinction between the *humiliores* and the *honestiores*, names which should speak for themselves. The *humiliores* could be flogged, tortured or put to death for certain crimes for which the *honestiores* could at most be exiled or deprived of property.[19] In imperial China, scholars who passed the Confucian examination and thereby established themselves as members of the ruling class were exempt from torture and corporal punishment, no small privilege when torture with wooden presses was routinely employed to exact confessions from persons accused of crimes. The legal privileges of the upper classes were enhanced by the rule that punishment, not excluding strangulation or beheading for many crimes, was commutable to fines at rates the upper classes could afford but the lower classes could not.[20] In the old Soviet Union, the privileges of the members of the Communist Party – the nomenklatura – included the right to shop in special stores that were closed to ordinary people. It has been claimed that, in practice, the nomenklatura was so favored in the application of the law that there might as well have been two distinct codes of law.[21]

In Anglo-Saxon times before the Norman Conquest, when recognition by the courts was restricted to the kindred group, the punishment for murder was the payment of compensation, called *wergild*, from the kinspeople of the murderer to the kin of his victim. The amount of compensation depended on the status of the victim: 1,200 shillings for the death of an immediate dependent of the king, though 200 shillings would do for an ordinary landowner, 20 shillings for a slave, with no penalty at all if the slave was one's own.[22] Marked class distinctions were still evident in the seventeenth century. The law allowed peers to assault, strike, and beat members of the lower classes. People who could read and write were exempted from the death penalty for certain crimes, including theft, under a curious provision of the law called "benefit of clergy."[23] The history of the law over the last two hundred years is the story of the removal of class privilege and the development of rules that are the same for all.

Slavery

The ugliest manifestation of the class system is slavery, which was once ubiquitous but has now been eliminated from most of the world. Treatment of slaves by the ancient Israelites may have been more humane than in neighboring tribes, but the authors of the Bible and the Koran saw nothing wrong in one person owning another. The list of large-scale slave-holding societies runs for pages and pages, and includes ancient

Greece and Rome, Muslim Spain, the Arab world to the present day, early medieval England, many countries of Africa before and during the period of colonialism (African slaves destined for the Americas or the middle east were mostly bought from local traders, not captured), Korea, China, Thailand, many countries in Latin America, many North American Indian tribes before the coming of the Europeans, Canada until early in the nineteenth century and the United States before slavery was abolished during the Civil War.[24]

Slavery is not a uniform institution. Slaves have no rights whatsoever in some societies and limited rights in others. Slavery merges by degrees into serfdom where peasants are tied to the land but have some protection against ill-treatment by their masters. Slavery was part of the traditional culture of Indian tribes of the Canadian west coast where slaves accounted for about 15 percent of the population and where the authority of masters over slaves was as complete as the ownership of any property today. Masters could kill their slaves with impunity. Slaves might be executed as part of the potlatch (winter festival) or on the occasion of the master's funeral. "The first whale that was killed in a season it was customary to make a sacrifice of one of their slaves the corps they laid beside a piece of the whales head adorned with eagle feathers after it has laid there a sertain time they put it in a box as usual."[25] And at the foot of those magnificent totem poles that have become symbolic of Canadian culture one might expect to find the bones of a ritually executed slave. Similar stories might be told of a thousand other cultures.

Franchise

The abolition of slavery and of the legal privileges of the upper classes is part of a larger process: the gradual emergence of a society where everybody has the same civil rights as everybody else and where people are equal politically, though they may be unequal in their incomes and in their wealth. Civil rights may be classified as rights *against* the government and as rights *over* the government. Rights against government include freedom of speech, freedom of association and the rule of law protecting people from punishment at the pleasure of the ruling class. Rights over the government empower citizens to participate in the choice of leaders and legislators. Public decisions must be binding on everybody, those who favor them and those who do not. Sometimes acquiescence is attained by force, as when a criminal is punished. Sometimes acquiescence is attained by a combination of respect for political customs and the threat of force, as when the outcome of a presidential election is accepted by the loser and when a law passed by the legislature is obeyed by those who opposed the law as well as by those who favored it. Regardless, public decision-making may be the preserve of the privileged few – as in a monarchy or under communism with an all-powerful central committee – or a right of every citizen, a right that cannot be exercised by all citizens simultaneously except by voting.

Voting is only sustainable under very special conditions which obtain now in many countries but have not always done so. As much as we admire the ancient constitution of Athens (approximately 400 BC) as the cradle of democracy, we have to recognize that its franchise was limited to about a sixth of the adult population. Franchise was limited to free male citizens. Exact numbers for residents and voters are hard to come by. One historian's considered judgment is that, at the height of Athenian civilization in the fourth century BC, the total male population of Athens was about 31,000, of whom about 12,000 were free aliens with civil rights but without the right to vote and about 10,000 were slaves, leaving 9,000 people entitled to vote out of a total population of 62,000.[26] Can we then infer from the prevalence of slavery and the limited franchise that the ancient Athenians were insufficiently imbued with the spirit of democracy as we understand the word today? There is another possibility. Restricted democracy with limited franchise may have been the only alternative to the tyranny characteristic of most countries at that time.

In the early years of the nineteenth century, the parliament of the United Kingdom was still the preserve of the grandees and the landowning classes whose dominance was upheld by property qualifications for voting, the exclusion of women, "rotten boroughs" (constituencies with almost no voters), and the open ballot (so that a bribe-giver could ascertain that the bribe-taker has voted as he promised). Gradually the franchise was extended to the entire adult population, in part through fear of rebellion by the disenfranchised, but also because economic conditions rendered universal franchise compatible with democractic government.

Over and over again, serious and well-meaning people have opposed government by voting with universal franchise in the belief that it is destined to self-destruct. The argument in a nutshell is that, with universal franchise, the poor can outvote the rich and have every incentive to employ their democratically acquired authority over the government to dispossess the rich entirely. In an age where most people are illiterate and where the poor are not permanently secure from starvation, nobody's wealth would be safe and enterprise would be rendered futile by the prospect of expropriation at the hands of a hostile majority of the electorate. In an age where heretics risk execution, supporters of a government ousted in an election might prefer civil war to acquiescence in the outcome of the vote. The argument that democracy self-destructs was probably correct until recent times. The stability of democracy today will discussed in chapter 9.

Whatever the reasons, franchise in the United Kingdom and in the United States has been gradually enlarged over the last two centuries. Property qualifications have been abolished. Women have become entitled to vote. People are no longer excluded from voting by virtue of race. Literacy tests (which could be used selectively to exclude groups of voters) are no longer employed. Focussing instead on Canada, table 1.14 is a reminder of some of the key events in that process. The table includes events elsewhere and before the establishment of Canada as an independent country because the true history of Canada is the history of the influences on its people beginning with Adam and Eve and encompassing events in many times and places.

Inequality of income

It is characteristic of modern democracies that people are equal in one respect but unequal in another. People are equal politically as voters and as citizens, but unequal economically as property holders and in their capacity to earn. Some degree of inequality of income is inevitable in any society where people's wages are a reflection of their

Table 1.14   Steps on the path to liberty and equality in Canada

1215: The Magna Carta. King John of England guarantees political and legal rights to his barons, protection from arbitrary taxation, and from punishment without trial. The Magna Carta offered nothing to the common man, but was the beginning of the extension of rights to other social classes.

1649: The beheading of Charles I. A central event in the English revolution in which the supremacy of parliament was established.

1776: The Declaration of Independence. The American revolution was the central event in the gradual dismantling of colonies and the establishment of representative government.

1832: The enfranchisement of Catholics in Canada.

1834: The Abolition of slavery in the British empire. There had been slaves in British North America and in New France.

1834–51: The *dis*enfranchisement of women in the colonies of British North America. Each province determined its own franchise. It was not the case that franchise was steadily expanded. All provinces disenfranchised women at this time.

1870: The fifteenth amendment to the constitution of the United States: "The right of citizens of the United States to vote shall not be denied or abridged by the united states or by any state on account of race, color or previous condition of servitude." (In practice, by one means or another, the right was abridged for many years to come.)

1884: Universal suffrage established, but for white males only. Prior to 1884, there had been property qualifications on voting.

1918: Women enfranchised in federal elections.

1923: Chinese immigration Act – banned the immigration of Chinese altogether. Formerly, Chinese immigration had been subject to a head tax instituted in 1884, raised to $100 to 1900 and raised again to $500 in 1903. Immigration of south Asians and blacks had been banned in 1907 and 1910.

1940: Women enfranchised for provincial elections in Quebec, the last of the provinces to enfranchise women.

1948: Chinese enfranchised and allowed to immigrate on the same terms as anybody else.

See the entries on "representative government" and "prejudice and discrimination" in The Canadian Encyclopaedia, *and John Garner,* The Franchise and Politics in British North America, 1755–1967.

talents and where property is privately owned. It is, nevertheless, of interest to measure the gap between the rich and the poor and to see whether, in what direction, and to what extent the gap between rich and poor is changing over time. The pattern in the United States from 1926 to 1998 is shown in table 1.15. Inequality might be assessed for individuals or for families. In table 1.15, inequality of family income is identified by "quintile" shares, defined as shares of each fifth of the population ordered from the poorest to the wealthiest. For example, the number 3.6 in the top right-hand

Table 1.15 The distribution of family income in the United States, 1926–1998

Quintile shares	1926	1935–6	1941	1950	1960	1970	1980	1990	1998
Lowest		4.1	4.1	4.5	4.8	5.4	5.1	4.6	3.6
Second	12.5	9.2	9.5	12	12.2	12.2	11.6	10.8	9
Third	13.8	14.1	15.3	17.4	17.8	17.6	17.5	16.6	15
Fourth	19.3	20.9	22.3	23.4	24	23.8	24.3	23.8	23.2
Highest	54.4	51.7	48.8	42.7	41.3	40.9	41.6	44.3	49.2
Share of top 5%	30	26.5	24	17.3	15.9	15.6	15.3	17.4	21.4
Disposable personal income per person in 1992 dollars									
	5,349	5,160	6,640	7,661	8,660	12,202	14,813	17,941	20,733

Sources: Historical Statistics of the United States, Colonial Times to 1970, *Series G319–336, F19 and F31, supplemented by* The Statistical Abstract of the United States, *1996 and 2000, table 692 and US Census Bureau, Series P60, Income Inequality, table 1. For 1926 only, the two lowest quintile shares are combined. The bottom row of the table is constructed by splicing series of real disposable personal income with different base years. Data for 1998 are from www.census.gov/hhes/income/histinc/inchhdet.html*

corner of the table means that, in the year 1998, the poorest 20 percent of all families in the United States acquired only 3.6 percent of the total income. If every family's income were the same, each quintile of the population would have exactly 20 percent of the income and the top 5 percent of income earners would have 5 percent of the income. The numbers in the column would be 20, 20, 20, 20, 20, 5 with average disposable income at the bottom. Deviations from this sequence reflect inequality in the distribution of income. To say that the poorest 20 percent of all families has only 3.6 percent of total income and that the richest 5 percent has 21.4 percent is to say that the poorest 20 percent acquires only a fifth and that the richest 5 percent acquires just over four times what they would acquire if total income were allocated equally. In other words, the income per family among the richest 5 percent is about twenty times the income per family among the poorest 20 percent of the population.

The trend of inequality of income in the United States is this: steadily increasing equality of income until the mid-1970s, followed by steadily increasing inequality of income thereafter, so that the gap between rich and poor was almost the same at the end of the period (1998) as it was at the beginning (1926). Consider the share of the poorest 40 percent of the population, shown in the top two rows of table 1.15. It rose steadily from 12.5 percent of total income in 1926 to 17.6 percent in 1970, and then fell again to 12.6 percent in 1998, which was almost where it began. At the same time, the share of the most prosperous 5 percent of the population fell dramatically from 30 percent of total income in 1926 to 15.3 percent in 1980, and then rose, almost equally dramatically, to 21.4 percent in 1998.

Shares must be distinguished from levels. A fall in one's share of total income need not signify that one is becoming worse off over time, only worse off relative to other people. From 1980 to 1998, the share of the lowest quintile fell from 5.1 percent to 3.6 percent, but the average income of a person in that quintile remained almost the same. Measured in constant (1992) dollars, the average income of a person in the lowest quintile is the product of (1) average disposable income in the bottom row of the table, and (2) the share of the lowest quintile as a proportion of its percentage of the population (i.e. 20 percent). In 1980, the average income of a family in the lowest quintile was \$3,777 $[14,813 \times 5.1/20]$. In 1998, the average income of a family in the lowest quintile was \$3,732 $[20,733 \times 3.6/20]$. Thus, from 1980 to 1989, the average income of a family in the lowest quintile declined ever so slightly at a rate of 0.07 percent per year. By contrast, over the same period, the average income per family of the most prosperous 5 percent of the population grew from \$45,343 $[14,318 \times 15.3/5]$ to \$89,152 $[20,733 \times 21.4/5]$, at a rate of 3.76 percent per year.

The resurgence of inequality over the last twenty-five years or so came as a surprise to many observers who had supposed that the long-term equalizing trend – shown in table 1.15 for the years from 1926 to 1970 but believed to have been maintained since the late nineteenth century – would continue indefinitely, in part because of the growing access in the American population to higher education. The numbers must be taken with a grain of salt. Average size of poor families is less than average size of rich families. In any year, observed low-income families include some whose incomes are only temporarily low. A family that earns \$500,000 one year and nothing the next is counted in the statistics as a poor family with no income every second year. The standard of living of the poor is buoyed up by charity, earnings not recorded by the tax collector and free services such as the food bank. However, to the extent that these influences persist unchanged over time, the trend of inequality in table 1.15 may be reasonably accurate. The recent increase in the number of homeless people and of beggars on city streets seems indicative of a real trend.

The significance of inequality may be changing as a consequence of general prosperity, the content of civil rights, public provision of "free" goods and services, and other aspects of modern society. General prosperity matters because relative deprivation is the far greater hardship when average income is low. Consider a society with two distinct classes, with equal numbers of people in each class, and with a ten-fold gap between the income per family of the upper class and the income per family of the lower class. A ten fold gap between the incomes of the classes may not matter very much if the income per family in the upper class is \$500,000 and the income per family in the lower class is \$50,000 because what is most important in life – an adequate diet, a decent place to live, and so on – can be had for \$50,000. The extra \$450,000 is for luxuries that would be welcome but that one can do without. A ten-fold gap between the incomes of the classes would matter a great deal if income per family in the upper class were only \$50,000 and the income per family in the lower class were \$5,000, for, depending on what society supplies free, a family with an annual income of only \$5,000 is consigned to a life of poverty at best, and perhaps to actual starvation. Prosperity moderates the sting of income inequality. Public provision of "free" goods is also significant. Obviously, poverty hurts more when medical care and access to education are purchased by each person for himself than when they are provided to each person equally by the state. Inequality hurts less when we all walk the same streets, are entitled to watch the same television programs, vote equally for legislators, send our children to the same schools and are subject to laws that do not subtly favor the rich over the poor than when these conditions do not obtain. Money matters in accordance with what money can buy, and money buys less when civil rights are strong.

With regard to longevity and prosperity, it may be asserted unambiguously that, with few exceptions, people throughout the world are better off today than people have ever been before. With regard to social customs and institutions, no such sweeping statements can be warranted. Social customs cannot be compared quantitatively. There are too many contemporary instances of horrible institutions and horrible behavior justified by ancient legends believed to be literally and completely true. The reign of hocus pocus is not yet over. What can be said is that we have rid ourselves of a great burden of superstition and misery. Infanticide, patricide, judicial torture, witchcraft, slavery, cruel and unusual punishment, and the more extreme manifestations of the class system are largely, though not entirely, gone. A great by-product of rationality in science and in markets is that such institutions are no longer necessary.

MASS DESTRUCTION

> *And Samuel said to Saul, "The Lord sent you to anoint you king over his people Israel: now therefor hearken unto the words of the Lord. Thus says the lord of hosts, 'I will punish what the Amalekites did to Israel in opposing them on the way, when they came up out of Egypt. Now go and smite the Amalekites, and utterly destroy all that they have; do not spare them, but kill both man and woman, infant and suckling, ox and sheep, camel and ass.'. ... And Saul defeated the Amalekites ... and utterly destroyed all the people with the edge of the sword."*
>
> **1 Samuel 15**

The efflorescence of science, technology, and productivity that has supplied most of mankind with unprecedentedly high standard of living has also provided us with the means to harm one another more efficiently and on a far greater scale than ever before. Societies have been exterminated in the past, but, as a vehicle for extermination, the sword and the gallows cannot compete with the machine gun, poison gas, biological weapons, and the atomic bomb. It is virtually impossible to predict whether and for how long improvements in the organization of society will restrain our usage of such weapons. We may take some consolation in the fact that the mass destruction in the twentieth may not have been significantly worse than in earlier centuries and that its impact on life expectancy has been tiny by comparison with the improvement in life expectancy brought about by the containment of disease and by prosperity itself. Table 1.16 shows the number of deaths in a selection of catastrophic events.

War

The full death toll in the Second World War is the sum of the number of deaths of soldiers in battle and the number of civilians destroyed by bombing, shelling, execution, or starvation. The total number of deaths has been estimated at 50 million, as shown in table 1.17. Estimates of the number of civilian deaths tend to be more

Table 1.16 Death toll in wars and exterminations (millions)

Number of soldiers killed in battle[a]	
Thirty Years War, 1618–48	0.6
Napoleonic Wars, 1806–15	3
US Civil War, 1860–5	0.5
First World War, 1914–18	9
Second World War, 1940–5	22
Government extermination of civilians[b]	
Collectivization of agriculture in the USSR in the 1930s	14
The Holocaust, 1942–5	12
The Great Leap Forward, 1958–60	35
Communist rule in Cambodia, 1975	1
Civil War in Rwanda	1

Sources: [a] *Urlanis, B.,* **Wars and Population,** *Progress Publishers, Moscow, 1971, 226;* [b] *discussed below.*

Table 1.17 Death toll in the Second World War (millions)

Soldiers killed in battle, died of wounds, perished in captivity	22
Civilians who perished in concentration camps	12
Civilians who perished from aerial bombings	1.5
Civilians who perished as a result of hostilities, owing to blockade, starvation and epidemics	
in European countries	7
in China	7.5

Sources: B. *Urlanis,* **Wars and Population,** *Progress Publishers, Moscow, 1971, 293.*

judgmental and less reliable than estimates of deaths of soldiers. Civil order and civilian record-keeping break down in wartime, and there is some difficulty in accounting for the fall in the birth rate. Typically, civilian deaths are estimated by comparing the actual population after a war with an estimate of what that population would be if the pre-war population had increased at the "normal" rate.[27] This method of estimation is necessarily imperfect. All of the three components of the estimation – the actual pre-war population, the actual post-war population and the rate of growth of population as it would have been if the war had been avoided – are inaccurate to some extent. Typically, this method of estimation is combined with whatever records of deaths are available and with survivors' reports. One is suspicious if different sources of information fail to correspond.

The Second World War was by far the most lethal in recent times, but it is hard to say whether it was more lethal than past wars in relation to total world population at the time. We simply do not know, for example, the full death toll, soldiers and civilians, of the conquests of Genghis Khan. Historians recorded the victories of glorious leaders, not the cost to the conquered.

Extermination of unwanted people

"As I live," says the Lord, *"What you have said in my hearing I will do to you: your dead bodies shall fall in this wilderness; and of all of your number, numbered from twenty years old and upward, who have murmured against me, not one shall come into the land where I swore I would make you dwell . . . but your little ones who you said would become a prey, I will bring in, and they shall know the land which you have despised. . . . And your children shall be shepherds in the wilderness forty years, and shall suffer for your faithlessness, until the last of your dead bodies lies in the wilderness."*

Numbers 14

As many people have been exterminated by their own governments as have died in wars. A class of people is deemed so wicked or so dangerous that nothing short of extermination is sufficient to protect moral purity or the safety of the rest. By far the best documented and the most chilling, though not the most lethal as measured in millions killed, of the non-military exterminations in the twentieth century, was the Holocaust. Of the 12 million people exterminated, about 6 million were Jews seen as polluting the Aryan race. These 6 million made up about two-thirds of the pre-war Jewish population of Europe.[28] A great many gypsies were also exterminated. Though the Holocaust occurred in wartime, the extermination of the Jews contributed neither to the security of the leaders of the Nazi party nor to the effectiveness of the German army in the war. It was a diversion of resources from the war effort to ideological aims. Victims were brought to concentration camps, worked for as long as they had the strength, gassed, and cremated.

An estimated 14.5 million people were executed or starved during the collectivization of agriculture in the Soviet Union in the 1930s. Collectivization was the transformation of agriculture from small privately owned farms into large publicly owned farms. Motives for the massacre were apparently mixed, partly to stamp out all resistance to collectivization of agriculture by farmers who had been accustomed to a degree of independence, partly to wipe out Ukrainians who were less than enthusiastic about Russian domination in a communist society, partly to transfer a larger fraction of the produce of agriculture to the cities than would otherwise have been possible.[29] The number of victims of collectivization is shown in table 1.18. The term "deKulakization" in the table refers to the elimination of the wealthy peasants, called Kulaks, an elastic term referring at first to very wealthy farmers, then, as the most wealthy farmers were eliminated, to less wealthy farmers, and so on. The killings came in two great waves. First, in the late 1920s, came the elimination of the Kulaks, many of whom were sent to die in concentration camps. Then, in 1932–3, came the mass starvation of peasants brought through the requisition of most of the harvest by the state.

Table 1.18 Death toll in the Russian collectivization of agriculture, 1930–1937 (millions)

Peasants killed or starved, 1930–7	11
Arrested to die in concentration camps	3.5
Total	14.5
Of these:	
Dead as a result of deKulakization	6.5
Dead in the Kazakh catastrophe	1
Dead in the famine of 1932–3	
in the Ukraine	5
in the north Caucasus	1
elsewhere	1

Sources: Robert Conquest, Harvest of Sorrow, Soviet Collectivization and the Terror Famine, Edmonton, Alberta, University of Alberta Press, 1986, p. 306.

The Khmer Rouge came to power in Cambodia in 1975 and remained in power until 1979 when they were displaced by a puppet government sponsored by Vietnam. The Khmer Rouge, so far as anyone can tell, were not insane in the normal sense of the term and intended in all sincerity to purify their country. According to an official broadcast by Radio Phnom Penh in 1975,

> A clean social system is flourishing throughout new Cambodia. Since 17 April, Cambodia has been totally and permanently emancipated. The sound, clean, social system formerly prevailing in the liberated zone has now been expanded to Phnom Penh, a number of provincial capitals and throughout the country. This new social system is sound, clean, free of corruption, hooliganism, graft, embezzlement, gambling, prostitution, alcoholism, or any kind of hazardous games.[30]

To achieve these aims, the Khmer Rouge emptied the cities of bourgeois and petty bourgeois elements, and collectivized agriculture at a cost of about 1.7 million lives out of a total population prior to their accession to power of about 7.9 million. The details are shown in table 1.19. About 15 percent of the native Khmer people, 50 percent of the resident Chinese and almost 100 percent of the resident Vietnamese were eliminated. Other minorities were decimated. Indigenous rural Khmers were the least affected.

The starvation of some 30 million people in China during the period known as the Great Leap Forward (1958–61) was not a natural disaster from flooding or drought, not the extermination of a hated minority, not the exploitation of one race, social class, or linguistic group for the benefit of another, and not the outcome of rivalry among would-be rulers of the country. Unbelievable as this may be, the disaster appears to have been brought about by vanity. Mao Zedong bore no animosity toward the Chinese peasants left to starve. Schooled in the Chinese classics and in Marxism, elevated to the peak of society by the Communist victory over the Kuomintang, unchallenged in his primacy, venerated in poetry and song as the great and glorious leader, his portrait displayed reverently in every house and in every public place,

Table 1.19 Death toll in democratic Kampuchea, 1975–1979

Social group	1975 population (thousands)	Number who perished (thousands)	% that perished
New people			
Urban Khmer	2000	500	25
Rural Khmer	600	150	25
Chinese (all urban)	430	215	50
Vietnamese (urban)	10	10	100
Lao (rural)	10	4	40
Total new people	3050	879	29
Base people			
rural Khmer	4500	675	15
Cham (all rural)	250	90	36
Vietnamese (rural)	10	10	100
Thai (rural)	20	8	40
upland minorities	60	9	15
Total base people	4840	792	16
Total Cambodia	7890	1671	21

Sources: **Ben Kiernan, The Pol Pot Regime, Race, Power and Genocide in Cambodia under the Khmer Rouge, 1975–59, New Haven, Yale University Press, 1996, p. 458.** *Kampuchea is the new name of Cambodia. The distinction between "new" and "base" people was drawn by the Communist Party itself. New people came under the authority of the Communist Party when it assumed control over the whole of Cambodia in 1975. Base people had been living in Communist-controlled territory before the Communist Party assumed control over the entire country.*

Mao Zedong could not imagine that he was less than infallible as an agronomist. The Great Leap Forward combined industrial and agricultural reform, including the production of steel from scrap iron in backyard furnaces, abolition of private property in land, collectivization of agriculture to the point of communal dining, and mandatory changes in farming practice. It was expected to generate huge increases in output of food and other goods. Mao could not accept the evidence that output fell drastically and that taxes levied at reasonable rates on predicted output left the peasant with virtually nothing. The cadres dared not describe what was really happening. Better 30 million people should starve than that the great helmsman should be embarrassed. So completely was the press controlled and foreign visitors restricted in their movements that twenty years were to pass before decisive evidence emerged that the famine had occurred at all.[31]

The late twentieth century witnessed a number of politically engineered episodes of mass starvation, the worst being the Ethiopian famine of 1984–5 in which an estimated 8 million people lost their lives. Typically, it is difficult to attribute famines to a single cause. A crop failure that would not lead to starvation in a rich country may do so in a poor country, or famine may be averted by well-chosen redistribution of the available food stocks. Political turmoil may or may not lead to famine depending on the productivity of the economy.[32]

The total number of deaths during the twentieth century in war and in the extermination of unwanted people has been estimated at about 175 million.[33]

A Balance

What are we to make of all this? Focussing upon peacetime prosperity – the increase in life expectancy, the increase in national income, the appearance of a host of new products, the spread of literacy, and the flourishing of democracy in more countries than ever before – observers have judged the twentieth century to have been, without question, the best time in the history of the world. Focussing upon mass destruction, death in battle, and extermination of unwanted people – observers have judged the twentieth century to have been the most terrible century in the history of mankind. Are these judgments in any way comparable. Do longevity and prosperity outweigh mass destruction, or vice versa?

Comparison of the loss of life in war and extermination with the gain of life in reduced mortality from natural causes requires a weighing of both phenomena on a common scale. That can be arranged, though only approximately, by expressing the loss of life in war and extermination in man years which can then be compared with total world population at risk over the course of the century. On the assumptions that the full toll of loss of life in war and mass extermination was 200 million people and that its victims would otherwise have lived for 50 years, the total loss of life would be 10 billion man years. As world population grew over the century from about 2 billion people to about 6 billion people, it would not be grossly inaccurate to say that the population at risk from war and mass extermination was about 10 billion as well, in which case the loss would be about 1 man year per person. But the gain in ordinary life expectancy from the decline in civilian mortality was, depending on the country, between 30 and 40 years, and the average life expectancy over the century was about 15 years higher than life expectancy in 1900. The loss of 1 expected year of life in war and mass extermination must be set against an average civilian gain of 15 or 30 years, depending on how you choose to measure it. Terrible as they were, the wars and exterminations of the twentieth century destroyed far fewer years of life than were created by the unprecedented decline in mortality from natural causes. On a life-expectancy scale, the fall in mortality from natural causes is by far the larger consideration.

Bear in mind that the comparison is between the *decrease* in mortality from natural causes and the *total* number of deaths in war and mass extermination. Strictly speaking, the comparison would only be valid if there had been no war or extermination in times gone by. If deaths in war and mass extermination had remained the same over the centuries as a proportion of the population, there would be nothing to set against the gain in life expectancy in the comparison of the twentieth century with other centuries in the past. Evidence on this matter is hard to come by. Statistics of deaths in battle are untrustworthy, and war-related deaths of civilians are not available at all. Armies were typically smaller, but decimation of innocent civilians, never far from the margin of subsistence, might have been enormous. We simply do not know the extent of the death toll of the Roman conquests, the invasions of Genghis Khan, the Islamic conquest of North Africa, or the Amalekites wiped out by

Table 1.20 The severity of war

Century	Casualties in battle per million people per year (Europe, average per century)	Deaths from all causes per million people per year (England, the middle year of the century)
Sixteenth	150	27,100
Seventeenth	370	32,100
Eighteenth	330	27,100
Nineteenth	150	23,100
Twentieth	583	11,600

Sources: For the first four centuries, the number of casualties in battle, including soldiers wounded as well as soldiers killed, is from Quincy Wright, **A Study of War,** *Chicago, University of Chicago Press, 1965, table 50*, p. 656. The corresponding number for the twentieth century is the ratio of a one-hundredth part of total deaths in battle over the course of the century to the population in the year 1950. Total deaths in battle is estimated at 35 million. The population of Europe in the year 1950 was about 600 million. English death rates from all causes are from B. R. Mitchell,* **British Historical Statistics,** *Cambridge: Cambridge University Press, 1988, tables 11 and 13.*

King Saul at God's command. Mortality rates in war and extermination may, for all we know, have been greater in biblical times than in twentieth-century Europe. An anthropological study of the Yanomamos of Brazil and Venezuela revealed that deaths in ordinary intertribal warfare once accounted for 24 percent of all male deaths.[34] History is written by the victors who may choose not to dwell on the cost of their victories and who tend not to speak well of the defeated. The story of the wanderings of the Israelites for forty years in the desert was written by those who finally arrived at the promised land, not by those whose bones lay rotting in the wilderness. Swings in the population of imperial China, as shown in table 1.7, are greater as a percentage than the swings in population in all but a very few countries in this century. It is difficult at this distance to disentangle the influences of war and epidemics, but the experience of ordinary people caught in a downturn of population must have been dreadful. In the ninth century, a breakdown of civil order in the Mayan civilization is thought to have caused a fall of 90 percent in the population of parts of Central America.[35]

For Europe only, the loss of life of soldiers in war and the normal everyday mortality from disease, malnutrition, accidents, and old age is presented for each of the last five centuries in table 1.20. The interpretation of mortality in the second column is both broader and narrower than I would have liked. It is broader because it includes wounds as well as deaths in battle. It is narrower because it excludes mass extermination of civilians together with death by starvation in the wake of war. The third column is for England only, but is probably representative of Europe as a whole. The significance of the table in the context of this chapter is that war appears to have been more lethal in the twentieth century than ever before, but, as in our stylized example, the gain from the drop in ordinary peacetime mortality has more than compensated for any increase in the severity of war.

The purpose of these comparisons is not to belittle the horror of war and of mass extermination, but to emphasize in the strongest possible way the significance of the gain in life expectancy. A premise of the comparison is that a life is a life is a life. The loss of the young man to tuberculosis is no less tragic than the loss of the life of a young man in war, and the grief of his parents is no less real, despite the absence of the flags, the speeches, and the monuments for those who die in battle. The comparison is, of course, only of lives saved or lost. The increase in national income, the proliferation of new goods and services, and the greater freedom that most people enjoy would have to be thrown into any comparison of the twentieth century with preceding centuries.

The ultimate test of whether life in times gone by really was dreadful by comparison with life today is where in time you would prefer to be located. To compare the twentieth century with, for instance, the nineteenth century, suppose you are offered the choice of living your life in either century. Your response would, of course, depend on how the question is framed. It must not be supposed that in selecting centuries you can choose to be your favorite character, an Einstein, a Queen Victoria, or an Abraham Lincoln. You must suppose that you will be a randomly chosen person with a randomly chosen life-span in a certain country or in the world as a whole, so that, for example, as a nineteenth-century American you would have a one in fifty million chance of being President and about a one in ten chance of being a slave.

As a Canadian or American – if your choice is to live in the nineteenth century or the twentieth century as a randomly chosen Canadian or American – there is, I believe no contest whatsoever. The twentieth century wins hands down. Your standard of living is significantly higher. Your life expectancy is much higher too. There is far less chance of seeing your children die of disease or of women dying in childbirth. You have greater political rights, with no chance of being a slave. Your risk of death as a soldier is significantly less, and your risk of civilian mortality in war is infinitely so: for the US Civil War was more lethal to North Americans than either the First or the Second World War. Nor is there much question about Latin America, Taiwan, South East Asia, or Japan, notwithstanding the Japanese losses in the Second World War. For the typical western European, an unprecedentedly high peacetime standard of living and life expectancy in the twentieth century must be balanced against the experience of two world wars that were very nasty but not so lethal as to outweigh the gains in life expectancy from the containment of disease. The balance is probably in favor of the twentieth century, though not for Jews or Armenians who were almost wiped out.

Elsewhere, the choice is not so clear. For Russia, the huge losses in both world wars, Stalin's wanton destruction of peasants and the experience of living in a Communist society may turn the balance toward the nineteenth century. For China, both centuries have been pretty bad, with huge losses in war and revolution, though the standard of living and life expectancy today are higher than ever before. The choice may be most problematic for Africa with low economic growth, periodic famine and civil war, and the worst ravages of the Aids epidemic.

There are dangers on the horizon. World population continues to grow, though at a slower rate than in the recent past. Population growth may eat up past gains by creating new scarcities. Scarcity of resources or the emergence of new toxic substances may eventually impede economic growth or precipitate decline. Global warming seems inevitable. Fossil energy will eventually give out, and only time will tell whether it can be adequately replaced by solar energy or other developments. Fresh water is becoming scarce. Other resources are becoming scarce too. Public order may crack, domestically or internationally. War is increasingly lethal; one well-placed bomb can wipe out as many people as died in the whole of the Second World War. The specter of nuclear annihilation that receded with the end of the Cold War is reappearing as advanced technology enables more and more countries to procure nuclear and biological weapons. Terrorism is becoming more lethal too. Democratic politics could succumb to theological madness or disintegrate into some new despotism of the great all-knowing leader. Always fragile, the web of institutions that holds democracy together may one day fail to do so.

Be that as it may, the comparison in this chapter is between present and past, not between present and future. This chapter is a description of what has happened already, not a prediction of what is yet to come. The comparison is between the way things are and the way things used to be. We live in a perpetual race between new dangers and our ability to invent our way around them. So far, we have been winning.

Beyond its role as a preface to the study of economics, this brief review of the dimensions of progress may serve as an antidote to complacency about the content of our lives. We grow accustomed to our possessions and our recently acquired freedom from misery, disease, and premature death. We tend to take our conditions of life for granted, forgetting that life was not always as it is today. This review of the dimensions of progress may preserve a sense of wonder and gratitude for our good fortune, and may provide a response to the grumps and the nostalgic among us who look back to the good old days, disparaging the present by comparison.

As an introduction to the study of economics, the purpose of this review is to raise questions about why and how. How, in what sense, and under what conditions, does the price mechanism organize the nation's resources to make people as well off as possible today and to provide appropriately for tomorrow? What is the proper role of the government in the economy? Should government be confined to the protection of private property, has it a larger role to play and, if so, what precisely is that role? How does one go about predicting the full consequences of public policy upon the economy? These questions are the meat and potatoes of any economics text, and this text is no exception. Other question are more characteristic of political economy. To what extent was the growth of the economy, year after year, and the procession of inventions that made it possible attributable to the organization of the economy? To what extent are economic progress and political developments intertwined? Are political rights and democracy the consequences of events in the political realm that are what they are independently of developments in the economy? Is economic progress independent of politics? What lessons can be learned about how we should be organizing ourselves to preserve democratic government and economic prosperity? The very term "political economy" suggests that all these questions can be usefully discussed together.

As a preface to that discussion, the next chapter is an attempt to highlight the importance of the security of property as a requirement for efficiency in the economy by constructing a world where property is insecure and the economy is distinctly inefficient. The model to be developed serves as a vehicle for raising the ancient question of whether the establishment of a degree of security is ever possible in this imperfect world except at the expense of liberty, freedom, and democracy. This chapter has been about how dreadful life used to be. The next chapter is about why perpetual dreadfulness might be expected. The rest of the book is about how, and to what extent, perpetual dreadfulness can be averted.

Chapter Two

MAKING AND TAKING

. . . it is lamentable to think how great a proportion of all the efforts and talents in the world are employed in merely neutralizing one another. It is the proper end of government to reduce this wretched waste to the smallest possible amount, by taking such measures as shall cause the energies now spent by mankind in injuring one another, or in protecting themselves against injury, to be turned to the legitimate employment of the human faculties, that of compelling the powers of nature to be more and more subservient to physical and moral good.

John Stuart Mill, 1848

. . . considering that the state of man can never be without some incommodity or other; and that the greatest, that in any form of government can possibly happen to the people in general, is scarce sensible in respect of the miseries, and horrible calamities, that accompany a civil war, or that dissolute condition of masterless men, without subjugation to laws, and coercive powers to tie their hands from rapine and revenge; nor considering that the greatest pressure of sovereign governors, proceedeth not from any delight, or profit they can expect in damage or weakening of their subjects, but in whose vigour, consisteth their own strength and glory.

Thomas Hobbes, *Leviathan*, 1651

"Do unto others," says the moralist, "as you would have them do unto you." The saying would be meaningless, unless it is supposed that you might prefer to do otherwise. To act morally is – almost by definition – to choose what is right over what is best for oneself alone. The central proposition in economics – a proposition that repetition has rendered less astonishing than it should be or than it is when encountered for the first time – is that the presumed gap between what is best for oneself and what is best for everybody is sometimes illusory.

"Do as you please" says the economist "because you serve others best when you serve yourself alone." Economics is about when and under what circumstances this is so. Economics is about how the combined effect of self-interested behavior by all of the participants in the economy is very often conducive to the common good in some sense of the term. Economics is the calculus of greed, designed in part to show when greed can be harnessed to the common good and in part to work out the less-obvious implications of self-interested behavior. We begin in this chapter with a simple example in which one's first thought about the matter turns out to be correct because everybody becomes significantly worse off doing what they please than if their activities were coordinated. This book is mostly about circumstances where the "invisible hand" of the competitive market – referred to in the quotation from Adam Smith at the beginning of the preface – works in the service of the common good. This chapter is about circumstances where that is not so. Here the invisible hand is perverse and needs to be constrained.

The Story of the Fishermen and the Pirates

Along the Canadian–American border is a region called the Thousand Islands where Lake Ontario drains into the St Lawrence River. Fishing is good in the Thousand Islands. As one might imagine, there are many fishing spots concealed by the islands from one another. This is the location of our example: not the actual Thousand Islands, but an abstract and theoretical Thousand Islands isolated from the rest of the world and populated by folk who may choose to be fishermen or to be pirates. The following assumptions describe the place completely.

(a) There are N people each free to choose between two occupations, fishing and piracy.

(b) There are L fishing locations. Every day, fishermen select locations at random, spreading themselves out so that there is never more than one fisherman at each location. There are more than enough locations to go round, even if everybody became a fisherman, i.e. $L > N$.

(c) Every fisherman catches one ton of fish per day. There is no scarcity of fish, no risk of depletion of the stock and no problem of conservation. If everybody chose to be a fisherman, the national income per day would be N tons of fish.

(d) Pirates prey on fishermen and take away their fish. Pirates do not know where the fishermen are located, and they have just time to search S locations looking for fishermen. If, on any search, a pirate discovers a fisherman he appropriates the entire catch. Otherwise the search is wasted. On a very lucky day, a pirate finds a fisherman on every search, and his income that day becomes S tons of fish. Normally, a pirate is less successful because some of the locations he visits are unoccupied by fisherman or because occupied locations are visited by other pirates as well. If more than one pirate preys on a fisherman, the pirates divide the catch equally among themselves. Think of fishermen as embarking for the fishing grounds early each morning and of pirates as venturing out later in the day after the catch is in but before the fishermen have time to return to the safety of the port. Assume for simplicity that pirates do not learn from their mistakes. Every search is at a location drawn randomly from the L available locations. Pirates never prey on one another.

(e) Everybody is equally skilled at fishing and piracy, and both occupations are equally arduous. As this is economics, there are no moral scruples in the choice of a profession. People choose to be fishermen or pirates to acquire the largest possible tonnage of fish. They sort themselves out as fishermen or as pirates until it is no longer beneficial for anybody to change from one occupation to the other. There is some uncertainty in each occupation, but people ignore risk because the largest expected income each day provides the best living in the long run.

(f) There are no police to maintain order and protect the fishermen's catch.

In these assumptions, realism is sacrificed to simplicity to focus as clearly as possible on the nature of an anarchic society. Unrealistic features and possible modifications of these assumptions will be discussed presently after the formal model and a numerical example are presented.

The moral of the story is simple but important. People choose between fishing and piracy just as they might choose between two legitimate occupations such as law and medicine. They sort themselves out as pirates or fishermen until it would be disadvantageous for anybody to change professions. If the income of fishermen exceeded the income of pirates, some pirates would become fishermen instead, lowering the income of fishermen and raising the income of pirates until the equality between their incomes is restored. Similarly, if the income of pirates exceeded the income of fishermen, some fishermen would become pirates instead, lowering the income of pirates and raising the income of fishermen until the equality between their incomes is restored. The determination of incomes is the same as in any other labor market where people are equally competent in all occupations. Yet piracy is obviously harmful not just to the fishermen on whom the pirates prey but to the pirates themselves, for everybody's income is lower than if piracy could somehow be prohibited. Self-interest drives some people to become pirates even though everybody, those who become pirates as well as those who become fishermen, would be better off if piracy could somehow be prohibited.

Three sorts of outcomes are possible, depending on the parameters of the model: There may be no piracy because fishing is the more lucrative occupation no matter how many or how few pirates there happen to be. That would be so if there were so many more locations than people that a pirate had too little chance of discovering a fisherman in the limited number of searches he is able to make. This possibility is uninteresting in the present context because it fails to illustrate the problem that this chapter is about.

There may be no fishing. For that to be so, piracy must remain more lucrative than fishing no matter how many pirates or how few fishermen there turn out to be. Were that so, everybody would become a pirate, and no fish would be caught. Society would destroy itself in an orgy of predation, or population would fall enough, and the ratio of fishing sites to people would rise enough, that it is in the interest of some people to become fishermen again.

There may be some piracy and some fishing. Piracy may be more lucrative than fishing as long as pirates constitute less than a certain fraction of the population, but less lucrative when the proportion of pirates becomes too large. We shall now show how the "equilibrium" number of pirates – the number such that no pirate would be better off switching to fishing, and no fisherman would be better off switching to piracy – can be determined from information about total population, N, the number of locations, L, and the number of searches per pirate, S.

Piracy must necessarily reduce the average income per head of fishermen and pirates together. With no pirates at all, the income per head would be one ton of fish per person. With m pirates, the average income per head must fall to $(N - m)/N$ tons of fish because a total catch of $N - m$ tons must somehow be apportioned among N people.

Denote the expected incomes of fishermen and pirates as y_f and y_p respectively. Total income must, one way or another, equal the total catch, that is,

$$(N - m)y_f + my_p = N - m \qquad (1)$$

or, equivalently,

$$[(N - m)/N]y_f + [m/N]y_p = (N - m)/N \qquad (2)$$

where $(N - m)/N$ is at once the proportion of fishermen in the population and the average income per head in both occupations, and where m/N is the proportion of pirates in the population. Equation (2) shows average income per head as a population-weighted average of income per head of fishermen and income per head of pirates.

Suppose, for example, that there are 10 people and 20 locations and that each pirate can investigate 4 locations. If everybody were a fisherman, the total catch would be ten tons of fish or one ton per head. If one person became a pirate instead, the total catch must be reduced from 10 to 9 tons and the average income of fishermen and pirates together falls to 9/10 of a ton. It is, nevertheless, in the interest of at least one person to become a pirate because, as will be demonstrated below, the income of one pirate among nine fishermen would be well above one ton of fish, and it is no concern to him that others' incomes are reduced by more than his is increased. Each person reasons that if I do not become a pirate somebody else will, and I shall be that much worse off remaining as a fisherman. A second pirate causes average income to fall to 8/10 of a ton, a third to 7/10 and so on.

To discover the number of pirates (m) for a given population (N), number of fishing locations (L) and searches per pirate (S), we first show how the incomes of fishermen and pirates (y_f and y_p) depend on the number of pirates (m), and we then deduce the number of pirates for which these incomes are equal. In other words, for given values of L, N and S, we wish to construct functions $y_f(m)$ and $y_p(m)$ which can be equated to determine the value of m that emerges when everybody is free to choose between fishing and piracy and each person chooses between occupations to make himself as well off as possible.

For any given number, m, of pirates, there must be $N - m$ fishermen who occupy a randomly chosen $N - m$ of the L available locations. The pirates search among the L locations hoping to find a fisherman. On each of his S searches, a pirate has a probability $1/L$ of arriving at any given location, so that his probability of missing that location is $(1 - 1/L)$. Recall the general principle that, when the probabilities of two events are independent, the probability of both occurring at once is the product of the probabilities of the two events. From this principle, it follows at once that a pirate's probability of missing any given location in all S of his searches is $(1 - 1/L)^S$ and that the probability of a given location being missed by all m pirates is $(1 - 1/L)^{mS}$. Since each fisherman catches one ton of fish, his net expected income – his catch reduced by the expected "tax" imposed by pirates – is exactly equal to the probability that no pirate succeeds in finding him. Thus, for any given L, S, the expected income of a fisherman as a function of the number of pirates, m, becomes

$$y_f(m) = (1 - 1/L)^{mS} \tag{3}$$

which is the probability that no pirate appears at the fisherman's location.

Suppose there are 20 locations, 3 pirates, and 4 searches per pirate. The probability that any given pirate visits any given location on any given search is 1 in 20 or 5 percent. The probability of his missing that location on that search is 95 percent. The probability of his missing that location in all four of his searches is $(0.95)^4$ or 81.45 percent The probability of 3 pirates missing that location altogether is $(0.95)^{4 \times 3}$ or 54.04 percent. With a probability of about 54 percent of retaining his catch, the fisherman's expected net income has to be about 0.54 tons per day, down from 1 ton in the absence of piracy.

To determine the expected income of a pirate, note that, when the fisherman bears a probability $(1 - 1/L)^{mS}$ of retaining his catch, the corresponding probability of losing his catch to pirates must be $(1 - 1/L)^{mS}$. Since the fisherman's probability of losing his catch must equal the pirates' share of the catch, and since there are $N - m$ fishermen, the total loot of all pirates together must be $(N - m)[(1 - 1/L)^{mS}]$, and each pirate's expected income, $y_p(m)$, must be

$$y_p(m) = [(N - m)/m][1 - (1 - 1/L)^{mS}] \tag{4}$$

A pirate's expected income is total expected loot in the economy – the average loot per fisherman multiplied by the number of fishermen – divided by the number of pirates.

How many pirates will there be? The equilibrium number of pirates, denoted by m*, is the number at which every person – fishermen and pirates alike – is content with his choice of occupation. The determination of m* depends on whether it is constrained to be an integer. To confine m* to integers is to say that both occupations must be full time. To relax that assumption is to say that m* might be a number such as 3.27, indicating that three people work full time at piracy and a fourth person devotes 27 percent of his time to piracy and the remaining 63 percent to fishing. With m* not confined to an integer, people sort themselves between occupations to equalize incomes exactly. The labor market induces a value of m* such that

$$y_f(m^*) = y_p(m^*) \tag{5}$$

and where $y_f(m)$ and $y_p(m)$ are defined in equations (3) and (4). Together, the three equations – (3), (4), and (5) – would determine the three unknowns $y_f(m^*)$, $y_p(m^*)$, and m*.

Equation (5) cannot hold exactly when, as we have assumed, each person must apply himself full time to either fishing or piracy. To generalize equation (5) for a market with a finite population, N, and where each person must choose one of the two occupations, think of people as "originally" fishermen and as switching to piracy one by one as long as it is profitable to do so. There would be no piracy at all if N were small enough that

$$y_p(1) < y_f(0) = 1 \tag{6}$$

for a fisherman could only make himself worse off by switching to piracy. With N in excess of the minimal value for which this inequality holds, the income of the first person to switch from fishing to piracy exceeds the income of the fishermen when there are no pirates. Some fisherman switches from fishing to piracy because $y_p(1) > y_f(0)$. The second switch occurs if $y_p(2) > y_f(1)$. More and more fishermen turn to piracy until the time comes when it is no longer profitable to do so. There is finally a number of pirates, m^*, for which it is no longer true that $y_p(m^* + 1) > y_f(m^*)$. Thus, the number of pirates for which everybody is content with his present occupation is m^* defined by the condition that

$$y_p(m^*) > y_f(m^* - 1) \quad \text{and} \quad y_p(m^* + 1) < y_f(m^*) \tag{7}$$

With fewer than m^* pirates, the second inequality is reversed; with more than m^* pirates, the first inequality is reversed. Think of equation (7) as the natural extension of equation (5) when m is discrete. Note that, at the equilibrium where nobody wants to change occupations, a pirate is still slightly better off than a fisherman, but not so much better off as to outweigh the fall in the income of pirates brought about by one extra person's switch to piracy. The values of $y_p(m^*)$, $y_f(m^*)$ and m^* can be computed from equations (3), (4), and (7).

The story is told by numerical example in table 2.1 for a society with 10 people, 20 fishing locations and 4 searches per pirate. The expected income of fishermen, the expected income of pirates and average expected income per person are shown for all possible numbers of pirates from 0 to 10. The first column shows m. The next shows y_f calculated from equation (3). The next shows y_p calculated from equation (4). The final column shows average expected income per head of fishermen and pirates together.

The first row of table 2.1 shows what happens when everybody is a fisherman and there are no pirates. The fisherman keeps his entire catch, and his income is one ton of fish. The second row shows what happens after one person switches from fishing to piracy. With nine rather than ten fishermen, the total catch must be reduced from 10 to 9 tons per day and the average income per person must fall from 1 ton to 0.9 tons as shown in the final column of the table. Since each pirate makes 4 searches, each of the nine remaining fishermen is now subjected to four chances of losing his catch with a probability of 5 percent, reducing his expected income to $(0.95)^4 = 0.8145$. The corresponding income of the one pirate has to be the difference between the total catch, 9, and the sum of the expected incomes of the fishermen, (9×0.8145). The pirate's income becomes 1.6696 [that is $9 - (9 \times 0.8145)$] as shown in the third column, indicating that it would be personally advantageous for one of the original ten fishermen to switch to piracy even though the average income of all ten people is reduced. All other rows are constructed accordingly. Note that the income of the fisherman in the last row cannot be the income of actual fishermen because there are

Table 2.1 How the income of fishermen, the income of pirates, and the average income per head depend on the number of pirates

[There are 10 people and 20 fishing locations. Each pirate can investigate 4 locations. The * indicates the number of people who choose to become pirates.]

Number of pirates (m)	Income of fishermen (y_f, tons per head)	Income of pirates (y_p, tons per head)	Average income per head (N − m)/N
0	1	—	1
1	0.8145	1.6695	0.9
2	0.6634	1.3464	0.8
3	0.5403	1.0725	0.7
4	0.4401	0.8399	0.6
5	0.3585	0.6415	0.5
6	0.2920	0.4720	0.4
7*	0.2378	0.3267	0.3
8	0.1937	0.2016	0.2
9	0.1578	0.0936	0.1
10	0.1285	0	0

Incomes of fishermen and pirates are computed for each value of m in accordance with equations (3) and (4). In accordance with equation (7), each person is content with his choice of occupation when there are 7 pirates and 3 fishermen, that is, $y_p(7) > y_f(6)$ but $y_p(8) < y_f(7)$.

none. It is the income of an eleventh person if there were one and if he chose to be a fisherman.

The outcome in table 2.1 is that seven out of ten people become pirates, reducing average expected income per head by two-thirds, from 1 ton of fish if piracy were somehow prohibited to 0.3 tons of fish when each person chooses in his own best interest whether to be a fisherman or a pirate. With less than seven pirates, it is in each fisherman's interest to become a pirate instead, even though his switch from fishing to piracy lowers the average income in the population as a whole. When there are only six pirates, a fisherman can increase his income from 0.2920 to 0.3267 by becoming a pirate, and he does so. Only with seven or more pirates does the switch become unprofitable. When there are seven pirates, each of the three remaining fishermen would reduce his income from 0.2378 to 0.2016 by becoming a pirate, and he chooses not to do so.

The harm is not just that pirates gain at the expense of fishermen. It is that everybody's expected income – fishermen and pirates alike – is less than it would be in a world without piracy. With no piracy, everybody would acquire 1 ton of fish. With seven pirates, every fisherman acquires 0.2378 tons and every pirate acquires 0.3267 tons, but no additional fisherman switches to piracy because the switch would reduce his income from 0.2378 tons to 0.2016 tons. However, since the pirates' income exceeds the fishermen's income, there is an advantage to the seven people who become pirates first.

The story in table 2.1 is retold in figure 2.1 with incomes on the vertical axis and number of pirates on the horizontal axis. For all values of m, the expected incomes

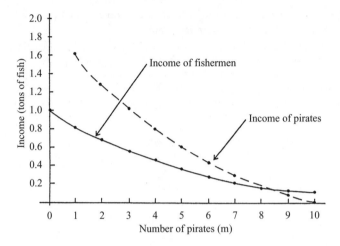

Figure 2.1   Incomes of fishermen and pirates depending on the number of pirates.

of fishermen from column 2 of table 2.1 are shown as dots connected by a solid line, and expected incomes of pirates are shown by dots connected by a broken line. Two important features of the story are brought out when the data are graphed. First, it is immediately evident that the income of the pirates starts above the income of the fishermen when m = 1, and then declines more steeply, becoming the same for some m between 0 and 10. If the income of the pirates did not start above the income of the fishermen, there would be no piracy. If the incomes of pirates did not decline more steeply than the incomes of fishermen, society would destroy itself. As mentioned above, both situations are possible. The former is uninteresting because no predation would ever be observed. The latter is unrealistic because the parameters of the problem would have to change.

Second, the joining of the dots shows incomes of fishermen and pirates as continuous functions of the number of pirates with a crossing of the curves where the incomes are equal. The smooth curve is representative of more realistic situations where m is, in actuality or for all practical purposes, a continuous variable. The number of pirates would become a continuous variable if the model were reconstructed so that people could choose how many hours in the day to devote to fishing and how many hours in the day to devote to piracy. In that case, the horizontal axis of the graph would become the proportion of total available hours devoted to piracy, and equation (7) would automatically collapse into equation (5) yielding a unique market-determined income per hour for everybody, fishermen and pirates alike. A similar outcome would emerge in a large market with a great many fishermen and a great many pirates. A small population was postulated for simplicity of exposition and to tell a story that (we hope) is intuitively appealing.

An interesting feature of the fishermen and pirates story is that population growth leads to a decline in output per head, even in circumstances where there would be no such decline in the absence of piracy. This is not the much-told tale of population growth leading to impoverishment as more and more people draw upon a given endowment of resources. That path to impoverishment will be examined in chapter 6. It is not the mechanism here because, together, assumptions (b) and (c) guarantee that each fisherman catches one ton of fish per day regardless of the population, as long as there remain more fishing locations than there are fishermen to occupy them. In the absence of piracy and as long as $L > N$, output per head would be unaffected by an increase in population.

The introduction of piracy changes the story completely. When m people out of a total population of N choose to become pirates, the output per head falls from 1 to $(N - m)/N$. If total population grew but the number of pirates remained unchanged at m, there would have to be an increase in output per head because $(N - m)/N$ is an increasing function of N. But m does not remain unchanged. On the contrary, by increasing the pirates' chance of discovering a fisherman at any given location, an increase in population creates such a large increase in the profitability of piracy that the number of people choosing to become pirates increases more than proportionally with population. The proportion of pirates increases, the proportion of fishermen falls, and the income per head falls accordingly, for the ratio $(N - m)/N$ is at once the proportion of fishermen and the output of fish per head.

To see why an increase in N leads to a fall in $(N - m)/N$, suppose first that N increases but m remains the same. Were that so, the income of fishermen, as shown in equation (3), would remain the same also, but the income of pirates, as shown in equation (4), would increase because $(N - m)/N$ would increase while $[1 - (1 - 1/L)^{mS}]$ remains unchanged. A gap would emerge between the incomes of pirates and fishermen, causing some fishermen to become pirates instead.

For average income to fall, the number of pirates at which everyone is content with his choice of occupation must increase more than proportionally with population. The ratio $(N - m)/N$ would have to be reduced. That must turn out to be so because even proportional increases in m and N would not be sufficient to maintain the equality between the incomes of fishermen and pirates in equations (3) and (4). With equal proportional increases in N and in m^{*}, the term $(N - m)/m$ in equation (4) must remain unchanged. But the increase in m must lower $(1 - 1/L)^{mS}$ in equation (3) and raise $(1 - (1 - 1/L)^{mS})$ in equation (4) accordingly, so that y_f falls and y_p rises, causing m to increase still further if the equality between y_f and y_p is to be maintained. Thus, the larger the population, the larger the proportion of pirates, and the smaller the common income per head.

This proposition is illustrated in table 2.2 for a fishermen and pirates economy where, once again, the number of fishing spots, L, equals 20 and the number of searches per pirate, S, equals 4. The first column shows total population, the second shows the number of pirates computed by trial and error from equations (3), (4), and (7), the third shows the income of fishermen, the fourth shows the income of pirates and the final column shows average income per head in the entire population. It is easy for the reader to check that the numbers in table 2.2 are what they are claimed to be. Outcomes are compared for seven populations: less than 7, 7, 8, 9, 10, 11, and 12. All populations less than 7 can be considered together because 7 turns out to be the smallest population for which there are any pirates at all. With a population of less than 7, there is no piracy, and the fisherman keeps his entire catch of fish.

Table 2.2 How the number of pirates increases by more than the increase in population, and how the average income per person declines accordingly

Population (N)	Number of pirates, (m^*)	Income of fishermen, $y_f(m^*)$	Income of pirates, $y_p(m^*)$	Average income $(N - m^*)/N$
Less than 7	0	1	—	1
7	1	0.6634	0.8415	0.8571
8	4	0.4410	0.5599	0.5000
9	5	0.3585	0.5132	0.4444
10	7	0.2378	0.3267	0.3000
11	8	0.1935	0.3024	0.2727
12	10	0.1285	0.1743	0.1667

Three important propositions are illustrated in table 2.2: First, for any given number of fishing locations, there is a minimal population below which piracy does not pay at all. Second, the increase in the number of pirates is more than proportional to the increase in total population. Third, average income per head declines substantially as the population grows. In the numerical example, the decline in income per head is from 1 ton to 1/12 tons as population increases from 6 to 12. Population growth decreases average income per head by increasing the proportion of pirates in the population for which the incomes of fishermen and pirates are equalized.

The tale of the fishermen and the pirates is about a discrepancy between private interests and the common good. This is the simplest tale one can tell of how it is in nobody's immediate interest to cooperate even though everybody would become better off with universal cooperation than when each person does what is best for himself with the means at hand. Hardly a surprising state of affairs, but one that needs emphasis at the outset of a course in economics where other, very different, tales will be told about how the combined effect of each person doing what is best for himself is in some sense the best for everybody. The essence of the fishermen and pirates example that, though everybody – fishermen and pirates alike – would be better off under a binding agreement to desist from piracy, it would be in each person's interest to break the agreement, making himself better off at the expense of the rest of the community. Public enforcement is required if such agreements are to be honored at all.

The story has been told as simply as possible. The six explicit assumptions set out above are chosen to focus upon the gap between private interest and the common good, with as little extraneous material as possible. But the assumptions are much stronger and less representative of real social conflict than one might at first suppose. Behind the explicit assumption are several implicit assumptions that should be identified to clarify the example and as pointers to considerations that might be introduced in more realistic depictions of social interaction.

(1) *There is no geography.*   The story may appear to have a geographical dimension because fishermen occupy different locations, but the geography is spurious. Locations cannot be mapped and it cannot be said within the context of the story that place A is closer to place B than to place C, or that you have to pass through place B to get from

place A to place C. There is no distance or proximity. This feature of the story should be emphasized because it characterizes most of the literature of economics, even the literature on international trade. It is perhaps remarkable how useful economics can be in spite of this restriction. There are instances where geography is explicitly introduced into economic analysis, but these are rare.

(2) *There is no time.* While it is true that the interaction between fishermen and pirates is said to take place in the course of a day, the model is *atemporal* in the sense that the economy is assumed to replicate itself over and over again forever. Nothing ever changes, not, at least, on the assumptions we have made so far. But, in this model as in many other economic models, the atemporal assumption is not fundamental. A rudimentary dynamics is introduced in the study of production in chapter 6. A thorough analysis of how societies change over time is beyond the scope of this book.

(3) *There is an exceedingly restrictive model of production.* Assumption (c) above – every fisherman catches one ton of fish, no matter how few or how many fishermen there are – implies that

$$F = n \qquad\qquad (8)$$

where F is the total catch of fish in tons and n is the number of fishermen (equal to $N - m$). The relation between input and output in the equation is the simplest imaginable example of a *production function*, the general form of which (within the fishing example) is

$$F = g(n) \qquad\qquad (9)$$

where g is any increasing function of n. The production function, g, is often assumed to be *concave*. Output, F, is assumed to increase with input, n, but at a decreasing rate, so that each additional unit of n yields a progressively smaller addition to F. Concavity would be a reasonable assumption if, for example, F stood for food grown rather than fish and n stood for the number of farmers producing that food on a given plot of land. Concave production functions will be employed in chapter 6 to explore whether and in what circumstances population growth leads to the impoverishment of mankind. Assumption (c) is that the production function for fishing is *not* concave as long as $N < L$.

(4) *There is no trade.* The model looks no further than the production of fish. Trade of one good for another and the emergence of market-determined prices are put aside until the next chapter.

(5) *The act of piracy is unrealistically, even absurdly, tame.* A pirate approaches a fisherman and says politely but convincingly, "Your fish or your life." The fisherman considers the proposal, decides he would rather lose his fish and hands over his catch to the pirate. No fish are destroyed in the struggle over possession. No part of the potential catch is lost from the diversion of the fisherman's time and effort from

fishing to the defence of his catch. No part of the potential catch is lost from the fisherman's switch from locations that are relatively more productive but more exposed to predation by pirates to locations that are relatively less productive but less exposed to predation by pirates. The only source of waste in this model of piracy is the loss of the fish that pirates would have caught if they had chosen to become fishermen instead.

The justification for this abstraction from the rough and tumble of conflict is that, though a more realistic model of conflict could be constructed, the simple model focusses more clearly on the main lesson in the example: that the national income may be lowered considerably and people may become very much worse off than they might otherwise be when resources are diverted from making things to taking things that others have made. The waste of resources occurs, notwithstanding the balance in the labor market when each person is as well off as he can be – as pirate or fisherman, as predator or prey – in response to the behavior of the rest of the actors in the economy.

(6) *Piracy is wasteful but not injurious or lethal.*   The taking of fish by pirates involves no fighting, no injury and no loss of life. This is really an aspect of assumption (5) above, but worth singling out to emphasize how much of the reality of conflict is being assumed away. From tribal skirmishes to thermonuclear war, the struggle over goods is fraught with the threat of violence which deteriorates into actual violence from time to time. The threat of violence lies at the core of the fishermen and pirates model, but actual violence is always avoided. This absence of violence is characteristic of economics in general. Fighting, injury, and death will also be abstracted away from the competitive economy in the next chapter. Instead, the world's work is undertaken peacefully as property rights convert universal selfishness into a vast web of cooperation to produce what people want to consume.

(7) *There is no rivalry or conflict of interest among fishermen.*   With enough fishing locations to go round and with all locations equally productive, there is nothing for fishermen to be rivalrous about. No fisherman gets in another's way or affects the size of another's catch. That is why a clear distinction can be drawn between fishermen as producers and pirates as predators.

Normally, the distinction is less clear-cut. At a minimum, some fishing locations would be more promising than others. Especially promising locations would have to be allocated by some competitive process or by rules specifying where each person is entitled to fish. In short, society requires a system of property rights which must be enforced against fishermen as well as against pirates. Switching from fishing to farming, the available land must somehow be allocated among farmers. Sometimes the allocation is accepted without fuss. Sometimes the allocation is the occasion for deadly rivalry.

In practice, the distinction between fishing and piracy is nothing like as precise as it appears in this chapter. People compete as voters over the privileges that government supplies. As will be explained in chapter 5, ordinary production generates "externalities" that are harmful to other people and that governments might usefully constrain. An inevitable vagueness at the edges of property rights generates rivalry among people seeking favorable interpretation. Everybody is both fisherman and pirate in varying degrees. An essential ingredient of a good society is that most of the effort of most of the people is directed toward fishing rather than piracy and that what piracy remains is wasteful but not lethal.

(8) *There is no organization.* There are no gangs of pirates, no associations of fishermen to defend against piracy, no pirate-fighters among the fishermen, and no police. Each person acts entirely alone. This assumption is to be abandoned immediately below with the introduction of an organized police force. Organized police may be quite effective against unorganized pirates, but not completely so. As we shall see, the establishment of the police force imposes a second cost of piracy. The original cost is the reduction in the total catch of fish when some people become pirates rather than fishermen. The extra cost is the additional loss of fish when would-be fishermen become policemen instead. The introduction of the police force is beneficial to the remaining fishermen if the number of would-be pirates deterred exceeds the number of police and as long as the policemen's income per head is kept in line with the income per head of the fishermen. For example, if 7 out of a total population of 10 would become pirates in the absence of a police force and if 2 policemen are sufficient to deter 3 of the 7 people who would otherwise become pirates, then the total catch must increase from 3 to 4 tons and average income increases accordingly.

Before leaving the simple world of pirates and fishermen, I should say again what the story is really about. It is obviously not about the men who fly the Jolly Roger or Sail the Ocean Blue. It is a parable, the simplest parable I could devise, about the two fundamental types of economic activity, about making and taking, about production and predation, and about the waste of resources when effort that might otherwise be devoted to the one is devoted to the other instead.

The story is about the cost of crime as the loss of potential output when some people devote their labour power to stealing or cheating, and as potential victims divert some of their labour from the production of goods and services to defence against theft. Defence against theft may be self-protection (bars on windows, burglar alarms, the hiring of guards, and so on) or the appointment of specialists in crime-thwarting (police, judges, prison guards, and so on). Less obviously, the story is about many socially undesirable but not necessarily illegal activities, as, for instance, when I pollute the air by driving my car or heating my house. In such activities, one and the same person may divide his day between fishing and piracy, between production and predation, where predation in this context is any activity that is harmful to others. That we are all to some extent pirates and that activities with a by-product of piracy may be in the common interest does not exempt me from the charge of participating in anti-social behavior when my activity is in excess of what everyone in society would agree upon if such agreements could be enforced. The story is also about lobbying, where the activity of the lobbyist is to persuade legislators to favor one industry at the expense of another or to persuade public officials to supply a valuable license to oneself rather than to one's competitor. It is also about certain kinds of speculation where the resources of the speculator are devoted to predicting prices, buying cheap now and selling dear later on, where production is unaffected by the speculator's activity and where the speculator's profit is at the expense of others who would not have sold or would have demanded a better price if the speculator's knowledge had been widely available. More remotely, the model is about monopoly where production is curtailed to raise price.

The story of the fishermen and the pirates may also be looked upon as a parable of warfare among tribes or nations. Tribes fight one another even though they would all be better off if they knew in advance what the outcome of warfare would be, could arrange for a peaceful transfer from one tribe to another of whatever would otherwise be won in battle and could divert the time and effort in fighting to the production of useful goods and services. It is in this context, however, that we see the full force of assumptions 5 and 6, which abstract from the loss of life and the destruction of product that real warfare always entails. The only cost of conflict in the fishermen and pirates example is the waste of labor power that could be used for production instead. That is sufficient for the purpose at hand, which is to demonstrate the potential wastage in predatory behavior, but one should bear in mind what a small part of the real cost of conflict is actually accounted for.

Above all, the story of the fishermen and the pirates is a counterpoint to the tales economists usually tell – and that I shall tell presently – about efficiency in a free market where the outcome is best for everybody when each person does what is best for himself. In this context, the story of the fishermen and the pirates has a double purpose: to draw attention to the many ways in which unrestricted self-interest may not serve the common good – so that the usual economists' tale turns out to be false – and, more importantly, to emphasize how extraordinary it is that there are any circumstances where the economists' tale does turn out to be true, where the combined effect of a multitude of independent agents each doing what is best for himself without a thought for the welfare of others can be anything but chaotic. The story of the fishermen and the pirates is the preface to the principal story in any work of economics. It is the preface to the story about how private greed is conscripted to the public good when property is secure and when actors in the economy recognize a market-determined set of prices for all goods and services. Familiarity with that story breeds not contempt, but a loss of a sense of wonder that the story is true in any circumstances, however restricted those circumstances may be.

FISHERMEN, PIRATES, AND POLICE

A key assumption in the fishermen and pirates model is the absence of organization. Each person acts alone, choosing to be a fisherman or a pirate to maximize his income in response to the choices of every other person in society. Of all the assumptions in the fishermen and pirates model, this is perhaps the hardest to swallow. Fortunately, it is easily replaced, though the society that emerges when it is replaced is not necessarily more attractive. The obvious replacement is to suppose that piracy can be contained, though perhaps not eliminated altogether, by a police force. To characterize the police as simply as possible, we delete assumption (f) in the fishermen and pirates model as set out above, and replace it with assumption (g) about the technology of policing combined with either assumption (h) or assumption (j), to be discussed presently, about the behavior of the police.

(g)   The police force consists of c (mnemonic for cops) people, no more and no less. No additional police would improve the effectiveness of the force, but a smaller force would have no impact on piracy at all. Ideally, the police would deter piracy completely. To do so, they would not need to detect all piracy. It would be sufficient for the police to discover a fraction of the pirates, as long as the punishment is severe enough to keep the profession of piracy less attractive than the profession of fishing. That is not what is supposed here. Instead, it is supposed that the police succeed in discovering a fraction, α, of the pirates, but never in convicting them of the crime of piracy because pirates throw their loot overboard when they see the police coming. Assume for simplicity that pirates are never actually punished, but that a fraction of the loot is destroyed by the pirates themselves to avoid detection. The police force is financed by taxation at a rate t of the residual income of fishermen after a part of the catch has been appropriated by pirates. In practice, a society would be able to choose the number of police where, the larger the police force, the greater the deterrence to crime. That flexibility is assumed away here in the interest of clarity and simplicity. Unnecessary complications are avoided by supposing that c is fixed.

Consider a society with N people and L fishing locations, where c people become policemen, the rest choose between fishing and piracy, and the police force destroys a fraction α of the pirates' loot. For such a society, the incomes in the three occupations – fishing, piracy, and policing – depend upon the number of pirates, m, and the tax rate, t, imposed by the police on the fishermen.

$$y_f(m,\ t) = (1 - t)(1 - 1/L)^{mS} \tag{10}$$

$$y_p(m) = (1 - \alpha)[1 - (1 - 1/L)^{mS}][(N - m - c)/m] \tag{11}$$

and

$$y_c(m,\ t) = t(1 - 1/L)^{mS}[(N - m - c)/c] \tag{12}$$

Equation (10) is a modification of equation (3) with the income of the fishermen reduced by taxation to finance the police force. Equation (11) is a modification of equation (4) with the income of the pirates adjusted to account for the reduction in the number of fishermen from $(N - m)$ to $(N - m - c)$ and for the destruction by pirates of a fraction, α, of the loot to evade detection by the police. The income of the pirates does not depend on the tax rate, but the tax rate affects the income of the pirates indirectly by influencing the civilians' (people other than the police) choice between fishing and piracy.

The income per policeman, $y_c(m,\ t)$ in equation (12), is total tax revenue per policeman. Total revenue is the product of the tax base and the revenue per unit of the tax base. The tax base is the number of fishermen, $N - m - c$. The revenue per unit of the tax base is the product of the tax rate, t, on fishermen and the pre-tax income per fisherman, $(1 - 1/L)^{mS}$, retained after being preyed upon by pirates.

When total population and the number of locations are large, or when m can be thought of as a continuous variable, people's opportunity to choose between fishing and piracy guarantees that the incomes of fisherman and pirates are the same. By analogy with equation (5) above,

$$y_p(m) = y_f(m, t) \tag{13}$$

Otherwise, the incomes of fishermen and pirates are connected as described in equation (7).

The total revenue of the police force is illustrated in figure 2.2 which is a development of figure 2.1 above. As in figure 2.1, the number of pirates is shown on the horizontal axis and income, in tons of fish, is shown on the vertical axis. Now, however, there are two vertical axes. The left-hand axis is carried over unchanged from figure 2.1. The right-hand axis is placed a distance $N - c$ from the left-hand axis, where $N - c$ is the civilian population of fishermen and pirates. For any m, the distance from m to the left-hand axis is the number of pirates and the distance to the right-hand axis is the number of fishermen, $N - c - m$. Three curves are shown, two for fishermen and one for pirates. The income-of-the-pirates curve labeled "y_p when a fraction α of the loot is destroyed" shows the value for each m of $y_p(m)$ in equation (11). The higher income-of-the-fishermen curve labeled "y_f before tax" shows the value of $y_f(m, t)$ as it would be if t were set equal to 0. The lower income-of-the-fishermen curve labeled "y_f after tax" shows the value of $y_f(m, t)$ as it becomes when taxation at a rate t is imposed. Equation (13) implies that, for any tax rate t, the number of pirates is determined to equate the income of the pirates and the after-tax income of the fishermen. Their common value – identified by the crossing of the income-of-the-pirates curve and the after-tax income-of-the-fishermen curve – is indicated on figure 2.2 by y. It is immediately evident from figure 2.2 that, if the tax rate, t, could be altered while the size of the police force, c, remained the same, then a decrease in the tax rate – by raising the entire after-tax income-of-the-fishermen curve – must lead to a decrease in the number of pirates, m, and an increase in the common income, y, of the fishermen and the pirates. The opposite is also true. An increase in the tax rate on fishermen decreases the common income of fishermen and pirates.

The total revenue of the police is represented by the shaded area in figure 2.2. It is a product of the tax per fisherman and the number of fisherman, where the tax per fisherman – equal to $t(1 - 1/L)^{mS}$ – is the gap between the fishermen's pre-tax and post-tax incomes. The policemen's income per head is total tax revenue divided by the number of police. At a tax rate of 0, total revenue would be 0. As the tax rate increases, so too does total revenue, but not indefinitely. Eventually, the gain in total revenue from the increase in the tax per fisherman is outweighed by the decrease in total revenue from the tax-induced increase in the number of pirates. There must, therefore, be some tax rate greater than 0 but less than 100 percent at which total revenue would be maximized.

How might the tax rate be chosen? Two possibilities will be considered: that the police are responsible to the fishermen, and that the police are predatory. A responsible police force chooses a tax rate, t, to maximize the after-tax income of the fishermen on the understanding that the income per policeman is kept equal to

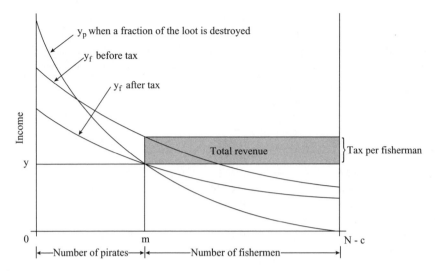

Figure 2.2 The revenue of the police.

the income per fisherman. A predatory police force chooses the tax rate to maximize tax revenue regardless of the after-tax income of the fishermen. These opposite assumptions about the behavior of the police will be examined in turn, the first as assumption (h) immediately below and the second as assumption (j) to follow.

A responsible police force

Think of the police force as established in a social "contract" among the entire population, including people destined to become pirates and police as well as people destined to become fishermen. The arrangement is that police are to tax fishermen and hunt pirates as described above, but are to levy taxes no higher than necessary to keep their incomes equal to those of fishermen and pirates.

(h)   The tax rate, t, is chosen to equalize the after-tax incomes of the fishermen and the police.

Specifically,

$$y_c(m, t) = y_f(m, t) \tag{14}$$

Combining equation (14) with equations (10) and (12), we see immediately what the tax rate must be. The tax rate, t^{**}, required to equalize incomes of fishermen and police must be

$$t^{**} = c/[N - m] \tag{15}$$

The police's share of the income of fishermen, after their encounter with pirates but before tax, must equal the police's share of the non-piratical population. Replacing

Table 2.3 How the police make everybody better off by harming pirates
[There are 10 people and 20 fishing locations. Each pirate can investigate 4 locations. One policeman is sufficient to destroy 1/3 of the pirates' loot, reducing the number of pirates from 7 to 3. The ** indicates the number of people who choose to become pirates.]

Number of pirates (m)	Income of fishermen (y_f, tons per head)	Income of pirates (y_p, tons per head)	Average income per head $(N - c - m(1 + y_p/2))/N$
0	0.9	—	0.9
1	0.7240	0.9893	0.7505
2	0.5805	0.7854	0.6215
3**	0.4631	0.6129	0.5081
4	0.3668	0.4590	0.4034
5	0.2868	0.3421	0.3145
6	0.2190	0.2360	0.2292
7	0.1585	0.1452	0.1492
8	0.0969	0.0672	0.0731
9	—	0	0

Sources: The incomes of fishermen and pirates are computed for each value of m in accordance with equations (10) and (11). From equation (7), it follows that each person is content with his occupation when there are 3 pirates and 7 remaining fishermen; $m** = 3$ because $y_p(3) > y_f(2)$ but $y_p(4) < y_f(5)$. Comparing table 2.3 with table 2.1, we see that the establishment of the police force increases each fishermen's income from 0.2378 tons per head to 0.4631 tons per head, and increases each pirate's income from 0.3267 tons per head to 0.6129 tons per head. Everybody has been made better off.

y_f and y_c in equation (13) by their values in equations (10) and (12) and using equation (15) to eliminate t, we see that

$$(1 - \alpha)[1 - (1 - 1/L)^{mS}][(N - m - c)/m] = (1 - 1/L)^{mS}[N - m - c]/[N - m] \quad (16)$$

which establishes m as a function of the parameters L, α, S and c. The new equilibrium number of pirates will be designated as m** which must be less than m*, the number of pirates as it would be if there were no police force.

The police are beneficial to fishermen and pirates alike if, and to the extent that, the equilibrium number of pirates, m, as computed in equation (16) is sufficiently less than the number of pirates in the absence of a police force to raise all incomes per head. This proposition is illustrated in table 2.3 and then in figure 2.3.

Table 2.3 is a reworking of the data in table 2.1 with the additional assumptions that 1 of the 10 people is a policeman and that the impact of policing on the economy is to destroy a third of the loot, that is, $c = 1$ and $\alpha = 1/3$, so that the income, y_p, of pirates is two-thirds of what it would otherwise be. For any given number of pirates, the expected income per head of fishermen is reduced from what it was in table 2.1 because the remainder of the catch after the fishermen's encounter with pirates must now be shared with the one policeman. The expected income per head of pirates is twice reduced, once because fewer locations are occupied by fishermen with a catch to steal, and again because the police destroy part of the loot.

Police aid fishermen by reducing the equilibrium number of pirates at which everybody is content to remain in his present occupation. With no police force, there

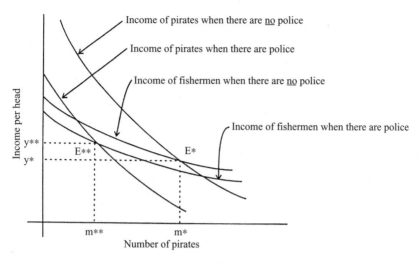

Income per head

Income of pirates when there are <u>no</u> police

Income of pirates when there are police

Income of fishermen when there are <u>no</u> police

Income of fishermen when there are police

y**

E**

E*

y*

m**   m*

Number of pirates

Figure 2.3   How a responsible police force raises the income of fishermen and pirates.

would be seven pirates, the income of fishermen would be 0.2378 tons per head and the income of pirates would be 0.3267 tons, as shown in table 2.1. With one policeman who destroys a third of the loot, the number of pirates is reduced from seven to three, the income of fishermen rises to 0.4631 tons and the income of pirates rises to 0.6292 tons. By making fishermen somewhat worse off and pirates very much worse off for any given number of pirates, the police force makes everybody better off when people are free to choose between fishing and piracy.

The contrast between an economy without police and an economy with police is illustrated in figure 2.3, an extension of figures 2.1 and 2.2. As in figure 2.1, the vertical axis of figure 2.3 shows incomes of fishermen and pirates, and the horizontal axis shows the number of pirates looked upon as a continuous variable rather than an integer. With no police force, the income-of-the-fishermen curve and the income-of-the-pirates curve intersect at E*, signifying that there are m* pirates and that the common income of fishermen and pirates is y*. The introduction of the police lowers both curves. The income-of-the-pirates curve is lowered because part of the loot is destroyed. The income-of-the-fishermen curve is lowered because fishermen are taxed to finance the police force. The new intersection is at E**, signifying that there are m** pirates and that the common income of fishermen and pirates is y**. A responsible police force lowers the income-of-the-pirates curve by significantly more than the income-of-the-fishermen curve so that the number of pirates at which people are indifferent between fishing and piracy is reduced substantially and the common income of fishermen and pirates is increased. In short, a benevolent police force works as it should when m** is sufficiently less than m* that y** is greater than y*, even though both curves are depressed.

The income-of-the-pirates curve and the income-of-the-fishermen curve in figure 2.3 are both lowered by the activity of the police, but the income-of-the-pirates curve is lowered by sufficiently more than the income-of-the-fishermen curve that everybody's net income per head is increased when each person is content with his new choice of occupation, given what everyone else is doing. This must be so, for otherwise no responsible police force would ever be established. An odd implication of this line of reasoning is that everybody, even pirates, favors severe punishment for piracy because the larger the fraction of the pirates' loot destroyed, the smaller the number of pirates in equilibrium, and the larger everybody's income will be.

A predatory police force

The life of the fisherman becomes less attractive with the abandonment of assumption (h) that the income of the police is kept equal to the income of the fishermen they serve. The assumption may seem reasonable for contemporary societies where the incomes of actual policemen are not incommensurate with the incomes of similarly skilled people in the private sector. The assumption is less self-evident when the police in our example are seen as representative of government as a whole. Throughout most of recorded history, a ruling class has ruled in its own interest primarily and has provided its members with far larger incomes than their subjects could ever hope to earn.

The story of the police has been told so far as though the police force were established in a social contract where all people combined to establish rules in their common interest, and as though, once established, the contract were respected by everybody forever. Such a contract might well have stipulated that the incomes of the policemen will not exceed the incomes of fishermen. There are, however, other less attractive and historically more realistic possibilities.

The king, ruling class or police force (whatever one wants to call it) may have emerged not by social contract, but out of conflict among pirates for control of the loot. Recall the stipulation in assumption (d) that pirates prey on fishermen but never upon one another. Why not? Would it not be more reasonable to suppose that pirates form groups which fight among themselves to acquire a monopoly of the loot, and that one group of pirates emerges victorious? Kings have sometimes been appointed by subjects, but normally kings seize power and tell nice tales afterwards to legitimize their regimes. William the Conqueror's acquisition of England is perhaps the typical case. Every dynasty in the history of China – and the present regime is no exception – began as a gang of bandits that succeeded in establishing order at a time of chaos. Eventually, successfully organized bandits acquire legitimacy but not benevolence. Society would still be ruled in the interest of rulers rather than subjects. Concern for the welfare of subjects would extend no farther than is conducive to the rulers' "own strength and glory." Within our model, society would be conducted to maximize y_c regardless of the consequences for y_f and y_p.

Even if established by social contract, a police force may turn predatory because its powers over the citizen cannot be contained. To combat piracy, the police force – representative here of the entire paraphernalia of law enforcement and government – must be organized as a hierarchy with a monopoly, or near monopoly, on the means of violence. A country can have only one army. A second army would fight with the first, destroying the order and security in society that an army is designed to protect. There can only be one head of state, one ministry of finance, one central bank, one federal bureau of investigation. This is something of an exaggeration. A country may have a federal, as opposed to unitary, government. State governments may share power with the central government. The powers of the central bank may be divided among several reserve banks in different parts of the country. There may be a sharing of powers between the Federal Bureau of Investigation and the Central Intelligence Agency. Much of this diversity is a parceling out of the different functions of government among separate branches, organizations or ministries, but there may be some genuine competition or deliberate duplication of functions. A founding principle of the government of the United States was the division of powers among executive, legislature, and judiciary, and the further division of the legislative power into the Senate and the House of Representatives, providing checks and balances as a defense against arbitrary power. Yet there remains a residue of unity of organization in government, a unity not found in the private sector of the economy where each fisherman and each pirate acts in his own interest exclusively. Regardless of how government came to be, it is precisely this unity of organization which is at once reason why a small number of police may prevail over a potentially large number of pirates and why a government may come to exploit the fishermen it protects.

Passage from responsible to predatory government can be modeled as the replacement of assumption (h) with assumption (j), or, equivalently, as the replacement of equation (14) above – specifying equality of income between the fishermen and the police – with the establishment of a higher rate of tax, t^{***}, that maximizes the income of the police, y_c.

(j)   Police tax fishermen at a rate t, chosen not to equalize incomes of fishermen and police as in assumption (h), but to maximize the income per head, y_c, of the police. Pirates cannot be taxed.

On this assumption, our description of the environment of the fishermen, pirates and police boils down to a system of five unknowns constrained by four equations. The five unknowns are y_f, y_p, y_c, m, and t. The four equations are (10), (11), (12), and (13), specifying the incomes of fishermen, pirates and police and then constraining the incomes of fishermen and pirates to be the same. In such a system the four equations can be employed to represent any four of the unknowns in terms of the fifth. As we are focussing on the police force's choice of the tax rate, it is useful to express the first four unknowns as functions of t. Thus, the incomes of the fishermen and the police – originally expressed in equations (10) and (12) as functions $y_f(m, t)$ and $y_c(m, t)$ of m and t – can be reconstructed as functions $y_f(t)$ and $y_c(t)$ of t alone.

These functions are plotted on figure 2.4 with income in the vertical axis and the tax rate on the horizontal axis. As already illustrated in figure 2.2, the income of fishermen, $y_f(t)$, declines steadily as the tax rate increases. The very best outcome for the fishermen would be for the police to provide its deterrence to piracy free of charge. The income of fishermen is as high as possible when t = 0 and it declines steadily with every increase in t. The direct effect of an increase in the tax rate on the residual income of the fisherman-taxpayer is reinforced by the indirect effect of the tax-induced increases in the number of pirates and the corresponding increase in the share of the fisherman's catch lost to piracy.

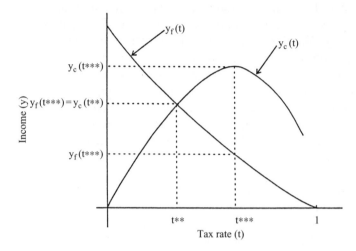

Figure 2.4 How incomes of fishermen and police are affected by the tax rate.
* (on other figures) refers to a society without police; ** refers to a responsible police force; *** refers to a
predatory police force.

By contrast, the relation between the tax rate, t, and the income of the police, $y_c(t)$, is humped. The police acquire no income at $t = 0$, and their income increases with t up to a maximum beyond which any additional increase in the tax rate reduces everybody's net income: fishermen, pirates, and even the police. The choice of the tax rate is a balancing of three considerations. The higher the tax rate, the larger is the portion acquired by the police of what is left of each fisherman's catch after the fisherman's encounter with pirates, the lower is the number of fishermen subject to tax and the larger is the pirates' share of the total catch. Recall that a responsible police force would set the tax rate at t^{**} where $y_c = y_f$. Freed from that constraint, a predatory police force chooses t^{***} to maximize $y_c(t)$ regardless of the impact on the income of the fishermen. The tax rate t^{***} must be larger than t^{**} but still less than 100 percent. (We are adopting a convention where * refers to outcomes in the absence of a police force, ** refers to outcomes when the police force is responsible and *** refers to outcomes when the police force is predatory. Necessarily, $t^{***} > t^{**} > t^* = 0$.) It is true, almost by definition, and immediately evident from figure 2.4, that fishermen are worse off when the police are predatory than when the police are responsible.

Is a predatory police force better than none?

The quotation at the beginning of this chapter leaves no doubt about Thomas Hobbes' view on the matter. Writing in the midst of the English Civil War, he saw firm government, however predatory, as preferable to the chaos around him. Our model suggests the opposite, though Hobbes' view acquires weight from a reconsideration of our assumptions.

As shown in the discussion surrounding table 2.1, the option of piracy is an unmitigated harm to fishermen in the absence of a police force. Strangely enough, the option of piracy may be converted from a harm to an advantage when the police force is predatory. Two predators may be better for the prey than just one. The private predator may neutralize the public predator to some extent. The public predator exploits his prey through taxation. The private predator constrains the public predator by allowing the tax base to shrink as the rate is increased, supplying the public predator with a motive for taxing at a rate well short of 100 percent and leaving the prey with some net, after-tax income.

The worst possible situation for the fishermen (within the context of our model) is where a predatory police force can deter piracy altogether. Without piracy or the possibility of piracy, equations (11) and (13) become irrelevant and equations (10) and (12) reduce to

$$y_f(t) = (1 - t) \tag{17}$$

and

$$y_c(t) = t[(N - c)/c] \tag{18}$$

From these equations, it is immediately evident that the income of the police is as large as possible when the tax rate, t, is set equal to 1. The police acquire an income per head of $(N - c)/c$ with nothing left over for the fishermen at all. Without piracy as a constraint, nothing within the model we have constructed stops a predatory police force from appropriating the entire catch by imposing a tax rate of 100 percent. Since fishermen retain some fish in the absence of the police force and no fish in the presence of a predatory police force, the former must necessarily be preferable. For the fishermen, under our assumptions, predatory government without the possibility of piracy is the worst of all possible worlds. Thus far, Hobbes turns out to be wrong.

However, our main question is not whether the prospect of piracy increases the income of fishermen when the police force is predatory, but whether a predatory police force increases the income of fishermen in an environment where fishermen may turn to piracy. This is the question to which Hobbes gives an unambiguously affirmative answer. Interestingly enough, Hobbes turns out to be wrong once again within the strict confines of the model we have constructed. To facilitate the exposition within the confines of the model, the matter is examined in two stages. In the first stage, the police force is assumed to be predatory but ineffectual in deterring piracy. The tax rate is set to maximize total revenue, but the value of α is set equal to 0, indicating that the police destroy none of the pirates' loot. It is hardly surprising that such a police force is no help to the fishermen. In the second stage, the value of α is set greater than 0, indicating that police do destroy a portion of the pirates' loot. This is the case for which we might suppose that even a predatory police force would be helpful, but that turns out not to be so.

The argument is developed with reference to figure 2.5 containing two variants of figure 2.2 side by side. The left-hand side shows interactions between fishermen and pirates when the police are ineffectual. The right-hand side reproduces the left-hand side together with an additional curve illustrating the response of a predatory police force to an increase in its capacity to deter piracy.[2]

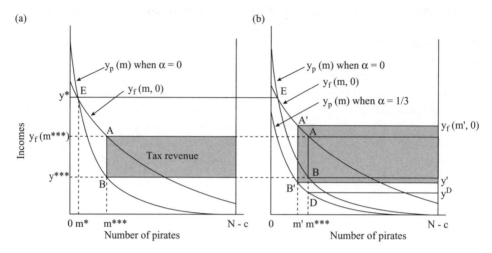

Figure 2.5 How predatory government may be worse for fishermen than no government. (a) Piracy undetected by police ($\alpha = 0$); (b) piracy detected by police ($\alpha = 1/3$).

The left-hand side shows the income-of-the-fishermen curve *as it would be* if fishermen were untaxed and the income-of-the-pirates curve *as it would be* if pirates kept all their loot. These curves can equally well be thought of as describing a society with no police at all but with a population of $N - c$ rather than N. The equilibrium number of pirates would be m* and the common income of fishermen and pirates would be y*, identified by the crossing at the point E of the income-of-the-fishermen curve and income-of-the-pirates curve. When fishermen are taxed at a rate t but pirates are left alone, a gap emerges between the before-tax income of fishermen, $y_f(m, 0)$, and the after-tax income of fishermen, $y_f(m, t)$, for every value of m. The gap is illustrated as the distance from A to B, and the new equilibrium number of pirates is that for which $y_f(m, t)$ equals $y_p(m)$ as it would be when $\alpha = 0$. The number of pirates increases from m* to m***, and the common income of fishermen (after tax) and pirates falls from y* to y***. It is immediately evident from figure 2.5 that, by levying the revenue-maximizing rate of tax, a predatory but ineffectual police force makes fishermen and pirates worse off than they would be with no police force at all.

Matters become even worse when the police deter piracy. One might expect a police force that deters piracy to be preferable to a police force that fails to do so, and, as shown in the discussion surrounding figure 2.3, this turns out to be so when the police force is responsible. It is not so when the police are predatory. On the contrary, the more effective the police in deterring piracy, the worse off do fishermen and pirates become. The reason is that, with piracy deterred, the only constraint on the police is eliminated, and the police can levy as high a tax as they please with no significant shrinkage of the tax base.

The right-hand side of figure 2.5 reproduces the left-hand side together with one extra curve, the income-of-the-pirates curve as it becomes when the police deter pirates to some extent. Specifically, this modified income-of-the-pirates curve is placed one-third below the original income-of-the-pirates curve on the assumption that $\alpha = 1/3$.

As the figure is drawn, the new, lower, income-of-the-pirates curve lies entirely below the income-of-the-fishermen curve, so that piracy would be eliminated altogether, and the fishermen's income would be as large as possible, if the police force were responsible and if the gap between the income-of-the-fishermen curve and the income-of-the-pirates curve were large enough at $m = 0$ for the police force to be adequately financed when $y_c = y_f$.

A predatory police force responds differently. The lowering of the income-of-the-pirates curve supplies the police with an opportunity to raise the tax on fishermen without decreasing the tax base. A predatory police force exploits that opportunity to expand its revenue as much as possible. The police could raise the tax per fisherman from the distance between A and B to the distance between A and D, leaving the number of pirates unchanged and lowering the common income of fishermen and pirates from y^{***} to y^D. But that is not the police's best option. Instead, the police can raise their incomes still further by lowering the tax rate slightly, reducing the number of pirates from m^{***} to m', increasing its tax base from $N - c - m^{***}$ to $N - c - m'$ and increasing the common income of fishermen and pirates from y^D to y'. Typically, as shown in the figure, y' would be still less than y^{***}, the fishermen's income as it would be if α were equal to 0. The greater the deterrence to piracy, the smaller the after-tax income of fishermen becomes.

The new, larger tax revenue of the predatory police force is the shaded area on the right-hand side of the figure. We know already that, in the limit where α increases to 1, there is nothing to stop a predatory police force from appropriating the entire catch by setting $t = 1$. As the curves are drawn, the increased effectiveness of the police against pirates raises tax revenue but leaves civilians worse off than before. Once again, Hobbes appears to be wrong. The option of piracy is advantageous to fishermen when the police are predatory. A predatory police force is harmful to fishermen with or without the option of piracy.

Another consideration may reverse this conclusion. A so far underemphasized assumption of the fishermen and pirates model (assumption c) is that each fisherman catches one ton of fish per day regardless of anything else in the model. That the catch is one ton rather than some other amount is of no importance. That the catch remains invariant is crucial because a predatory police force would acquire an incentive to moderate taxation of fishermen if a lowering of the fisherman's income reduced his capacity to work or if taxation impeded productivity in some other way. One's capacity to work may increase gradually together with one's after-tax income. A wise ruler would take that into account.

Replace the assumption that each fisherman catches 1 ton of fish with the assumption that a fisherman catches f tons, where f is a concave function of the fisherman's net (after tax) income; as the fisherman's net income increases, his productivity increases too, but at a decreasing rate. Specifically, the output per fisherman is reduced from 1 ton per day (as in assumption (b)) to f tons per day where

$$f = \text{the smaller of } \{\sqrt{y_f}, 1\} \tag{19}$$

and where y_f is the fisherman's after-tax income. The relation in equation (19) between the fisherman's net income and his productivity is illustrated in figure 2.6 with net

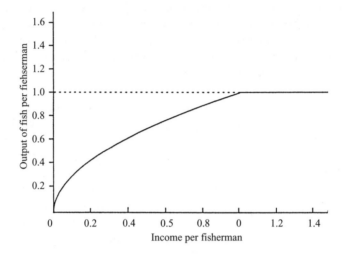

Figure 2.6   How the output of a fisherman increases with his income.

income, y_f, on the horizontal axis and productivity, f, on the vertical axis. This equation specifies that a fisherman can never produce more than 1 ton of fish, but he produces less whenever his after-tax income falls below 1 ton.

Equation (19) reduces immediately to

$$f = \sqrt{y_f} \qquad (20)$$

whenever $y_f < 1$ as it must be when fisherman are taxed. Thus, when fishermen are taxed at a rate t and when the option of piracy is eliminated altogether, the income per head of fishermen in equation (17) is transformed into

$$y_f(t) = (1 - t)f \qquad (21)$$

From equations (20) and (21), we see at once that $y_f(t) = (1 - t)\sqrt{y_f(t)}$ or

$$y_f(t) = (1 - t)^2 \qquad (22)$$

and

$$f = (1 - t) \qquad (23)$$

Also, once piracy is eliminated, the income of the police in equation (18) becomes

$$y_c(t) = tf[(N - c)/c] = t(1 - t)[(N - c)/c] \qquad (24)$$

Consider a society of 10 people where 2 people acting as policemen are sufficient to deter piracy altogether. A responsible police force sets the tax rate, t, so that $y_c = y_f$. Equating incomes of fishermen and police in equations (22) and (24), we see that $(1 - t)^2 = t(1 - t)[(N - c)/c]$, from which it follows that $(1 - t)/t = (N - c)/c = 4$, or $t = 20$ percent. Plugging that value back into equations (22), (23), and (24), we see that the productivity, f, of fishermen must be 0.8 tons of fish (rather than 1 ton) and the common income of fishermen and police together must be 0.64 tons of fish per person. By contrast, a predatory police force sets the tax rate to maximize y_c regardless of y_f. It sets a tax rate of 50 percent, reducing the productivity of the fishermen to 0.5, raising the income of the police from 0.64 to 1, and lowering the income of fishermen from 0.64 to 0.25 tons of fish per person.[1] Clearly, fishermen are better off with a benevolent police force than with a predatory police force.

Has a predatory police force become better for the fishermen than none at all? It was distinctly worse when the productivity of fishermen was assumed to be invariant. Now the opposite may be so, depending on how many pirates there would be with no police force to intercept their loot. With m pirates out of a total population of N, the common income of fishermen and pirates must be $(N - m)f/N$ tons of fish per day. From equation (20), it follows immediately that the common income reduces to $[(N - m)/N]^2$ tons of fish.

With only 1 pirate (that is, if $m = 1$), the common income of fishermen and pirates must be 0.81. Were that so, fishermen would be better off without any police, responsible or otherwise. No responsible police force would ever be established, and a predatory police force, yielding fishermen an after-tax income of 0.25, would clearly be worse than none. With 3 pirates, the common value of y_p and y_f would be 0.49, which is worse for fishermen than if there were a responsible police force, but better than with a predatory police force. With as many as 7 pirates (the equilibrium number in figure 2.1), the common value of y_p and y_f would be 0.09 which is worse for fishermen not just with a responsible police force, but with a predatory police force as well. The essence of the example is that the tax imposed by a predatory police force may be constrained by more than the threat of piracy. It may also be constrained by the impact of taxation on the productivity of the labour force, and, if so, even a predatory police force can be preferable for the fishermen to piracy.

The principal difference between piracy and a predatory police force is that a predatory police force takes account of the effects of its actions on the productivity of the fishermen. Each pirate acts in his own interest exclusively regardless of the effects of his actions not just on fishermen, but on other pirates as well. A pirate who appropriates a fisherman's catch does not consider the productivity of fishermen as a whole. Better take the fruit today even though the tree is placed in jeopardy, for, if I do not take the fruit, then somebody else will. I have every incentive to behave this way though I know full well that all pirates are worse off than they might be when every pirate acts as I do. An organized and unified police force is never confronted with this dilemma. Cognizant of the full consequences of its actions, a predatory police force allows fishermen a high enough income to work well. This entirely self-interested restraint may supply fishermen with larger incomes than they would acquire with no police force at all.

Much depends on the size of the population and the availability of resources. Within the formal model of fishing and piracy in the absence of the police, the relative advantages of the two occupations – reflected in the heights of the income-of-the-fishermen curve and the income-of-the-pirates curve – depend on total population, N, and on the number of fishing locations, L. Consider the determination of the income of the fishermen, y_f, and income of the pirates, y_p, in equations (3) and (4). With N held constant, an increase in L raises y_f and lowers y_p for any given number of pirates, m. Thus, the larger L, the smaller the equilibrium m must be, the larger is the common income of fishermen and pirates, and the less likely it becomes that any police force, responsible or predatory, can be advantageous. The same holds true when L is held constant and N is reduced. Generalizing, it is often claimed that a condition of anarchy, among people or among tribes, may be tolerable in sparsely settled regions, but becomes intolerable, and is terminated by the establishment of government, once population density is increased.

One final consideration should be mentioned briefly. Organization requires hierarchy with its own costs to society, especially to fishermen at the bottom of the economic and social scale. Until very recently, hierarchy could not be maintained without a supreme ruler at the apex and a ruling class between the emperor and the ordinary subject. As already mentioned in chapter 1, emperors were literally deified, a ruling class was raised above the ordinary run of mankind and no common humanity was recognized in the law. Members of the ruling class come to see themselves almost as a different species from their subjects and to treat them accordingly. Invested with great power over the rest of society, rulers might from time to time turn out to be foolish, evil or insane. Enormous harm can be inflicted on the innocent many at the whim of the omnipotent few.

The story of the fishermen and the pirates raises three questions that will occupy us throughout this book.

(1) *What, in practice, are fishing and piracy?*   Every society must draw a line between activities to be restricted because, in Mill's words quoted at the beginning of this chapter, "efforts and talents in the world are employed in merely neutralizing one another," and activities to be permitted or encouraged because they are "the legitimate employment of the human faculties, that of compelling the powers of nature to be more and more subservient to physical and moral good." Passing from the economy in this chapter with only one good, fish, to real economies with a virtually infinite variety of goods and industrial processes, it becomes less evident which among the multitude of privately advantageous activities are like fishing and which are like piracy. Many activities are like fishing in some respects and like piracy in others. Societies must decide which activities to permit, which to regulate and which to prohibit altogether. The great lesson of economics, alluded to in the first few paragraphs of this chapter and to be discussed in detail in the next, is that much of what goes on in the private sector of the economy is fishing and that some notion of the common good is fostered when property rights are protected and markets are otherwise left alone. As we proceed, we shall acquire lists of virtues of the market and of types of self-interested behavior with fringes of piracy calling for intervention by the state.

(2) *What is the job of the police?*   A second line must be drawn between socially advantageous activities that people undertake voluntarily because it is in their interest to do so and socially advantageous activities that have to be undertaken collectively if they are to be undertaken at all. In this chapter, the only role of government is to protect fishermen by hunting pirates. Protection of life and property is always the rock-bottom

minimal role of government, but complex societies require more. People act collectively or consign decision-making to a central authority in specifying and administering
a vast web of laws, in delineating the scope of property rights (for instance, rules about
the formation, rights and obligations of corporations), in the building and maintenance of roads and other public works and in dealings with other countries. Societies
decide collectively about the boundary between political and economic rights in the
redistribution of income and in public provision of medical care and education. Among
the considerations in drawing the line between public and private sectors is that large
governments may turn predatory. The larger the public sector, the greater the risk
of its acquiring a will of its own quite apart from the interests of the population as
a whole.

(3) *How can the police be kept responsible?*   In one variant of our story, the police were
responsible. In another, they were predatory. Nothing was said about why the police
might turn out one way or the other, or about how to design institutions to constrain
private predation without at the same time introducing public predation in its place.
"Who guards the guardians?" This fundamental question of political theory will not
be settled in an introductory textbook of economics, but it lies in the background of
the examination of voting, public administration, and law in chapters 9, 10, and 11.
There is a special connection between markets and responsible government. It will be
claimed that government cannot be responsible unless elected, that the institution of
voting self-destructs unless the domain over which we vote is constrained, and that
the market frees government from tasks it cannot perform without at the same time
ceasing to be responsible to the electorate.

Chapter **Three**

TASTE, TECHNOLOGY, AND MARKETS

A decentralized economy motivated by self-interest and guided by price signals would be compatible with a coherent disposition of economic resources....It is important to understand how surprising this claim must be to anyone not exposed to this tradition. The immediate "common sense" answer to the question "What will an economy motivated by a very large number of different agents look like?" is probably: there will be chaos.... A quite different answer has long been claimed true and has indeed permeated the economic thinking of a large number of people who are in no way economists.

Kenneth Arrow and Frank Hahn

The previous chapter ended unhappily. Unrestricted freedom of each person to act in his own interest as he thinks best led to a society where everyone, fishermen and pirates alike, was worse off than if people were constrained to act in the common interest. The required constraint could only be supplied by an organized police force, and there appeared to be no way to prevent an organization intended to suppress piracy from suppressing the rest of society as well. "Who guards the guardians?" points to a dilemma from which very few societies have escaped.

Much depends on the range of the authority of the guardians. As will be argued in detail later on, the capacity of the society to guard the guardians will depend on what exactly the guardians are called upon to do. A hierarchically organized corps of guardians called upon to direct the economy in detail would have to exert such extensive and such specific authority over the lives of ordinary citizens that, as the experience of communism in our time has abundantly shown, the guardians would evolve into a predatory ruling class and the status of the ordinary citizen would be reduced to little better than slavery. On the other hand, the great lesson of economics is that, subject to a host of qualifications which constitute a large part of the subject matter of economics, it is sufficient for the government to protect property rights. Once property rights are protected, the ordinary play of self-interest by an uncoordinated multitude of producers and consumers can be relied upon to run the economy efficiently.

This highly counter-intuitive proposition, rendered commonplace by repetition in the classroom and in public discussion, is the subject of the present chapter.

We approach the proposition in three stages. Forces governing the mix of goods produced, their prices and their allocation among people can be usefully classified under the headings of technology and taste, or, equivalently, of supply and demand. To introduce these concepts as simply and as cleanly as we can, we begin in the first part of the chapter with an isolated person who produces and consumes but does not buy or sell. His technology is represented by a *production possibility curve*. His taste is represented by *indifference curves*. These in turn are summarized for any good by a *supply curve* and a *demand curve*. The crossing of the supply curve and the demand curve indicates that the person is as well off as he can be with the technology at his disposal. Applications of demand and supply curves to the study of taxes, tariffs, patents, monopoly, and other matters will be the subject of the next chapter. The second part of the chapter is a brief introductory discussion of the indeterminacy of bargaining. This discussion may well leave the reader with the impression that the anticipation of chaos from an unregulated market, referred to in the quotation from Arrow and Hahn at the outset of this chapter, is well justified, setting the stage for the examination of market-determined order to follow. The third part is on markets and market prices. It is shown how and in precisely what sense the price mechanism conscripts self-interest in the service of the common good. The chapter ends with a list of the virtues and vices of the competitive economy.

TECHNOLOGY AND TASTE IN A ONE-PERSON ECONOMY

Technology and the supply price

Think of Robinson Crusoe alone on his island. He consumes only two goods, bread and cheese. Both goods are produced with land exclusively. Outputs of the two goods depend on the allocation of land between them. Robinson Crusoe's input of labor is fixed; he cannot increase output by working harder. Specifically, the island contains five distinct plots of land – called A, B, C, D, and E – with different fertilities depending on which crop is produced. Plots may be devoted entirely to bread, entirely to cheese or partly to both in whatever proportion Robinson Crusoe thinks best. Output is measured per unit of time. Think of the unit of time as a week. Production is assumed to remain the same week after week. Robinson Crusoe's only choice is how to allocate the available land between bread-making and cheese-making. If all the land were devoted to bread-making, he would have plenty of bread but no cheese. If the land were devoted to cheese-making, he would have plenty of cheese but no bread. As every sandwich-eater knows, a person wants some of both goods and must allocate the available land between them.

There are two aspects to production. Robinson Crusoe must decide how much of each good to produce, whether, in effect, to produce lots of cheese and a little bread, or lots of bread and a little cheese. He must also decide which plots of land to devote to each good, a simple representation of the wider problem in real economies of deciding how to deploy resources efficiently among competing uses.

Table 3.1 Outputs of bread and cheese per week on each of five plots of land

Plots	Loaves of bread when the plot is used exclusively for bread	Pounds of cheese when the plot is used exclusively for cheese	Rate of trade-off in production (loaves per pound)
A	16	4	4
B	8	4	2
C	5	10	1/2
D	6	6	1
E	12	4	3

The technology of this example is described in table 3.1. The first column of the table identifies plots. The second column shows the output of each plot if used entirely for the production of bread. The third column shows output of each plot if used entirely for the production of cheese. The last column entitled "rate of trade-off in production, (loaves per pound)" is the ratio of the two preceding columns. The meaning of the first row, for example, is that plot A can be used to produce either 16 loaves of bread per week, or 4 pounds of cheese per week, or any combination of the two (such as 8 loaves and 2 pounds, or 4 loaves and 3 pounds), and that 4 loaves must be forgone for every pound of cheese acquired by diverting production on that plot from bread to cheese.

From the information in table 3.1, we cannot say what Robinson Crusoe will do because that depends in part on his tastes, or preferences, about which we have so far said nothing. What we can say is that, whatever his tastes, Robinson Crusoe wants to produce *efficiently*. He organizes production to get as much bread and cheese as possible in the sense that no reorganization of production would enable him to obtain more of both goods. For instance, if Robinson Crusoe chooses to produce only 4 loaves of bread, he insists on producing those 4 loaves on plot A rather than plot B because, by producing bread on plot A rather than plot B, he acquires 2 extra pounds of cheese.

The key to the allocation of land to goods is the right-hand column showing the trade-off in production between bread and cheese on each plot. The lower the number in the right-hand column, the better the plot for cheese production, not absolutely, but relative to bread production. Thus, if Robinson Crusoe is a bread-lover who consumes almost no cheese, the little bit of cheese he does consume will be produced on plot C for which the loss of bread per pound of cheese is as small as possible. To produce cheese on plot C "costs" only one-half (the number in the right-hand column) of a loaf of bread, for the 10 pounds of cheese acquired when plot C is devoted to cheese is at the expense of only 5 loaves of bread which plot C could have produced instead. As long as Robinson Crusoe is content with up to 10 pounds of cheese, all cheese is produced on plot C. If Robinson Crusoe wants more cheese than can be produced on plot C, he must draw upon the next best plot, D, where a full loaf of bread must be sacrificed per pound of cheese acquired. If he wants more than 16 pounds (the output

Table 3.2   Efficient combinations of bread and cheese

Efficient ordering of plots devoted to cheese production	Pounds of cheese on the "last" plot	Loaves of bread on the "last" plot	Total pounds of cheese produced	Total loaves of bread produced	Supply price of cheese (loaves forgone per extra pound acquired on "last" plot)
None	—	—	0	47	—
First plot: C	10	5	10	42	1/2
Second plot: D	6	6	16	36	1
Third plot: B	4	8	20	28	2
Fourth plot: E	4	12	24	16	3
Fifth plot: A	4	16	28	0	4

of cheese from plots C and D combined), he must convert some of plot B from the production of bread to the production of cheese, and so on.

The information in table 3.1 is reorganized in table 3.2 to show the range of efficient combinations of bread and cheese that might be produced. The first column lists the five plots of land according to their relative efficiency in the production of cheese. The efficient ordering of plots – from most to least productive for cheese relative to bread – is C, D, B, E, and A. Plot C is first in this ordering because it yields the most cheese, 2 pounds, per loaf of bread forgone as indicated in the right-hand column of the table. No other plot supplies cheese so cheaply. The ordering of plots in the first column is a reflection of the relative productivity of the different plots of land, as shown in the final column of table 3.1 and relabeled as the *supply price* of cheese. "Supply price" means "rate of trade-off in production between bread and cheese." The latter term is the more descriptive; the former is more in accordance with common usage in economics and is better connected to ordinary market prices to be discussed later on. The supply price of cheese rises from 0.5 loaves per pound on plot C to 4 loaves per pound on plot A.

For each row, the "total pounds of cheese produced," as shown in the fourth column of the table, is the sum of the productive capacity of the plot shown in that row and all preceding plots. For example, the total output of cheese corresponding to plot B (20 pounds) is the combined output of plots C, D, and B because plots C and D would have been devoted to cheese production already before production of cheese on plot B could be efficient. Similarly, for any plot listed in the first column, the fifth column shows the total output of bread when that plot, together with all higher plots, is devoted to the production of cheese.

Three observations on the interpretation of the table: First, though the table shows combinations of bread and cheese that might be produced when each plot is used for bread or for cheese exclusively, Robinson Crusoe can produce any amount of bread up to 47 loaves, as long as the output of cheese is adjusted accordingly. To obtain 8 loaves of bread, he devotes half of plot A to bread-making, and devotes the rest of plot A and all of the other plots to cheese-making, producing 26 pounds of cheese as well. To obtain 19 loaves, he devotes all of plot A and a quarter of plot E to bread-making and the rest to cheese, producing 23 pounds of cheese as well.

Second, table 3.2 shows all *efficient* combinations of bread and cheese, where efficiency is interpreted to mean that production cannot be rearranged to yield more of both goods and where the source of efficiency in this example is the ordering of the plots devoted to bread. Any other arrangement would yield less of one good for any given amount of the other. For example, if Robinson Crusoe wanted to produce 10 pounds of cheese, he could produce them on plots D and B, but that would be inefficient because the remaining plots – A, C, and E – would yield only 33 loaves of bread rather than the 42 loaves of bread that could be produced on plots A, B, D, and E. Ordering of plots according to the supply price of cheese is efficient; every other ordering is inefficient in that there would be less of bread, cheese or both.

Third, the name "supply price of cheese" in the final column requires some explanation. When you buy cheese at the grocery store, you are quoted a price of, say, $3 dollars per pound. This means that you must give up $3 in return for a pound of cheese, $6 in return for two pounds, and so on. Price cannot be expressed that way in the Robinson Crusoe example because money is meaningless in an environment with only one person. Robinson Crusoe is, nevertheless, confronted with a sort of price, a price in terms of bread rather than dollars. Think of Robinson Crusoe as, initially, producing bread and nothing else. If he wants some cheese as well, he has to give up some bread in return. The exchange is effected through production rather than purchase, but it is an exchange nonetheless. Initially, as indicated in the first row of table 3.2, Robinson Crusoe is producing 47 loaves of bread and no cheese. Then he can acquire up to 10 pounds of cheese at a price of half a loaf per pound. If he wants more cheese, he must convert all or part of plot D from bread to cheese, raising the supply price from 0.5 to 1 loaf per pound. As more cheese is produced, the supply price rises not steadily, but in jumps, as one plot after another is diverted from bread to cheese, until, in the end, when only plot A is left, Robinson Crusoe faces a supply price of 4 loaves for each additional pound of cheese.

The supply price of cheese in table 3.2 is similar but not altogether identical to the ordinary price of cheese in the grocery store. The price of cheese at the grocery store is a *money price*, measured as dollars per unit of quantity, for instance $3 per pound. The price of cheese in table 3.2 is a *relative price*, measured as quantity per unit of quantity, the first quantity being a standard of comparison (in our example, bread) and the second quantity being of the good (in our example, cheese) that is priced. Of course, it is arbitrary, within the context of our example, which quantity is chosen as the standard of comparison. If we had chosen cheese rather than bread to be the standard of comparison, then the headings of the final columns of tables 3.1 and 3.2 would have been reversed. "Loaves per pound" would have to be changed to "pounds per loaf" and all the numbers in those columns would have to be inverted; the numbers 0.5, 1, 2, 3, and 4 would have to be changed to 2, 1, 0.5, 0.33, and 0.25.

The difference between money price and relative price is not really as sharp as may at first appear because a money price can be looked upon as a relative price where the standard of comparison (the technical term for that standard is *numeraire*) is all other goods rather than just one good as in our example. To say that the price of cheese has increased from $3 to $6 is to say that one must forgo consumption of twice as much of other goods to acquire an extra pound of cheese. (The astute reader may well ask at this point whether that is still true under inflation when all prices double. Obviously,

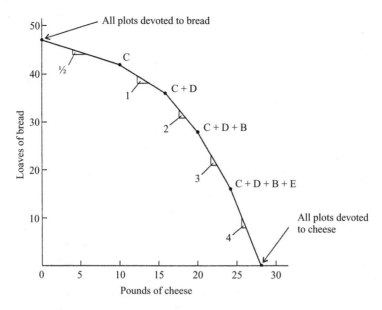

Figure 3.1   The production possibility curve. Points indicate plots devoted to cheese; slopes indicate supply prices of cheese.

it is not. To interpret a money price as a relative price with respect to "all other goods" as the numeraire is to suppose that the price of cheese rises while the price level, the average price of all other goods, remains the same.)

There is another difference between ordinary money prices and the supply price of cheese in table 3.2. The supply price of cheese is presented in table 3.2 as a list, or schedule, of the cost of cheese in terms of bread depending on how much cheese Robinson Crusoe chooses to acquire, while the money price of cheese in the grocery store is seen by the buyer of cheese as a fixed number determined by the market and independent of the amount he wants to buy. The supply price of cheese in table 3.2 could also be pinned down to a particular number if we knew how much cheese Robinson Crusoe chooses to produce, but that depends in part on Robinson Crusoe's taste for bread and cheese, which has not, as yet, been introduced in the example, but will be presently.

The economic significance of the information in table 3.2 is clarified by translation into a *production possibility curve* as shown in figure 3.1, with total loaves of bread on the vertical axis and total pounds of cheese on the horizontal axis. All pairs of numbers in the fourth and fifth columns of table 3.2 are plotted as points on figure 3.1, and adjacent points are joined by line segments. The resulting production possibility curve is the locus of all efficient combinations of bread and cheese that Robinson Crusoe might produce. He could produce at points below the curve (for instance by producing bread on plot D and cheese on all other plots), but he would never choose to do so. As an *economic man*, he would never voluntarily accept less of both goods than he might otherwise obtain. By assumption, he cannot produce outside of the production possibility curve. That would be beyond the confines of the available technology.

Robinson Crusoe must choose a combination of bread and cheese from among the combinations represented by the production possibility curve.

Notice the shape of the production possibility curve. It must, of course, be downward sloping because any increase in the output of one good must be at the expense of the other as long as the allocation of land between bread and cheese is efficient. That it is also bowed outward is a geometrical consequence of the differences among plots of land in the ratio of the potential output of cheese to the potential output of bread. The assumed productivities of the five plots of land, as shown in the second and third columns of table 3.1, could be random numbers drawn out of a hat, and still the production possibility curve would be bowed out. Different numbers would yield a different curve, but all such curves would be bowed out as shown in figure 3.1. The numbers in table 3.1 were chosen to facilitate calculation, but the main story is independent of that choice. On the other hand, the production possibility curve becomes a downward-sloping straight line when all land is equally productive for both goods. It could only be bowed inward if production of one good interfered with the production of the other as, for example, if smoke from a foundry interfered with a laundry nearby.

If Robinson Crusoe chooses a combination of bread and cheese represented by one of the six nodes on the production possibility curve, then he is using all of some plots for bread and all of other plots for cheese. If he chooses a combination of bread and cheese represented by a point on a line between nodes, then some plot (never more than one, for that would be inefficient) is being used partly for bread and partly for cheese. At each node on the diagram is an indication of which plots of land are devoted to cheese-making, on the understanding that the remaining plots are devoted to bread.

By construction, the slope of any segment of the production possibility curve is the corresponding supply price of cheese. Consider, for example, the first segment on the left. This represents Robinson Crusoe's options for the disposition of plot C, the plot with the lowest supply price of cheese, when all other plots are devoted to bread exclusively. If all of plot C were used for bread as well, the output of bread would be 47 loaves. If instead plot C were used entirely for cheese, the output of bread would fall to 42 loaves but Robinson Crusoe would acquire 10 pounds of cheese. Along that segment, one loaf would be sacrificed for every two pounds of cheese acquired, so that the relative price of cheese would be 0.5 loaves per pound as indicated on the diagram. Relative prices from the last column of table 3.2 are indicated for every segment of the figure. Supply prices at nodes are not defined.

There is yet another way of presenting this information. The production possibility curve shows the quantity of cheese together with the corresponding quantity of bread. We might instead show the quantity of cheese together with the supply price of cheese, i.e. with the rate of trade-off in production of bread for cheese. The new curve – called a *supply curve* – is shown in figure 3.2 with pounds of cheese on the horizontal axis and the supply price of cheese on the vertical axis. The supply curve may be constructed from the production possibility curve or, equivalently, from the data in the fourth column and the last column of table 3.2. The supply curve of cheese is stepped rather than smooth because the supply price of cheese remains steady as more and more cheese is produced on any given plot of land, and then jumps sharply once that plot of

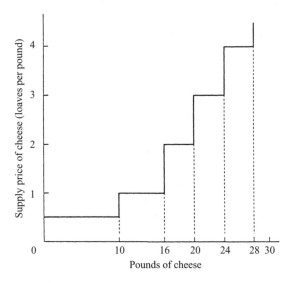

Figure 3.2 The supply curve of cheese.

land is completely devoted to cheese and any extra cheese must be produced on the next, less productive, plot. The supply curve becomes vertical at 28 pounds of cheese because no extra cheese can be produced at any price.

In choosing how much of each good to consume, Robinson Crusoe can be looked upon as picking the best point on the production possibility frontier or, equivalently, as picking the best point on the supply curve of cheese. The relation between these curves is that, for any given quantity of cheese produced, the slope of the one curve is the height of the other. That is how the curves are constructed.[1] Note, finally, that the supply curve is not just a reflection of the technology of the economy. It is a reflection of the technology of the economy when resources are used efficiently, with plots of land allocated to bread or to cheese so as to maximize the amount of cheese produced for any given output of bread or, equivalently, to maximize the amount of bread produced for any given output of cheese.

Taste and the demand price

Though it is sufficient within the terms of this example to say that Robinson Crusoe picks the best point on the production possibility curve, the generalization of the example to a more realistic economy requires that taste, or equivalently preferences, be modeled in some detail. What this means in practice is that we need a device, or picture, showing at a glance which of any two combinations of bread and cheese – or, generalizing to an economy with many different kinds of goods and services, which of any two bundles of goods consumed – is preferred. The device is a set of *indifference curves* such that (1) any two combinations of bread and cheese represented by points on the same curve are equally desired, and (2) any combination of bread and cheese represented by a point on a higher indifference curve is preferred by Robinson Crusoe

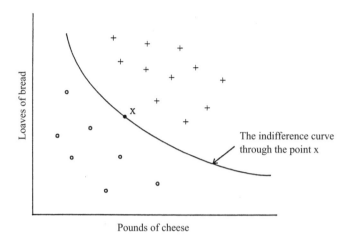

Figure 3.3 An indifference curve.

to any combination of bread and cheese represented by a point on a lower indifference curve. Since indifference curves are a reflection of Robinson Crusoe's preferences, they can only be discovered by asking him to tell us what they are. In principle, we could ask Robinson Crusoe to draw his indifference curves. Alternatively, we could elicit that information from his answers to a long series of questions of the form, "Do you prefer this to that?"

Indifference curves representing Robinson Crusoe's taste for bread and cheese can be superimposed on the production possibility curve. Start with an empty graph with loaves of bread consumed on the vertical axis and pounds of cheese consumed on the horizontal axis. Choose any point on the graph and call it "x". Then pick any other point, and ask Robinson Crusoe whether he would rather consume the combination of bread and cheese represented by the other point than to consume the combination of bread and cheese represented by the point x. If his answer is that he prefers the combination of bread and cheese represented by the other point, mark that point with a "+". If his answer is that he prefers the combination of bread and cheese represented by the point x, mark the other point with a "0". Repeat the process over and over again until the entire graph is filled up with + or 0, as illustrated in figure 3.3.

There must, however, be a boundary between the space covered by + and the space covered by 0, as illustrated by the smooth line on figure 3.3. As long as Robinson Crusoe is consistent in his responses, the point x must lie on that boundary; he must be indifferent between the point x and any other point on the boundary. Asked whether he would prefer the amounts of bread and cheese represented by the point x or amounts of bread and cheese represented by another point of the indifference curve, Robinson Crusoe would have to say he is indifferent between the two.

By choosing different values of x as the starting point for this conceptual experiment, the entire graph can be filled up with indifference curves which never cross because no combination of bread and cheese can be simultaneously indifferent to and preferred to some other combination. Three indifference curves like that in figure 3.3 are reproduced in figure 3.4. The points $\alpha_1, \alpha_2, \alpha_3, \alpha_4$ and α_5 will be explained presently.

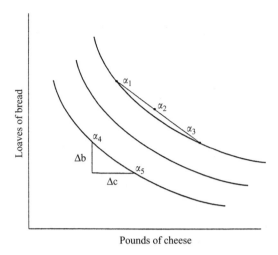

Figure 3.4   Several indifference curves.

The logic of rational choice is sufficient to account for the existence of indifference curves and for the fact that they do not cross, but something more is required to account for their shapes. As drawn in figure 3.4, the indifference curves are bowed in, as south-easterly portions of loops. This postulated shape of indifference curves is a consequence of the common assumption in economics that people avoid extremes; if I am indifferent between two slices of bread and two slices of cheese, then I would prefer one slice of bread and one slice of cheese for a proper sandwich. More generally, if Robinson Crusoe is indifferent between the combinations of bread and cheese represented by the points α_1 and α_3 in figure 3.4 (as he must be because they lie on the same indifference curve), then both of these combinations must be inferior in Robinson Crusoe's assessment to a third combination, represented by the point α_2, consisting of a fraction of the bread and cheese at α_1 *plus* one-minus-that-fraction of the bread and cheese at α_3. For instance, the combination α_3 might consist of one-quarter of the bread and cheese at α_1 plus three-quarters of the bread and cheese at α_3. By simple geometry, it may be shown that all such points must lie on a straight line from α_1 to α_3, close to α_1 if the fraction is high and close to α_3 if the fraction is low. To say that indifference curves are bowed-in is to say that any point such as α_2 lies on a higher indifference curve than the points α_1 and α_3.

The slope of an indifference curve is the rate of trade-off in use between bread and cheese. Consider the two points α_4 and α_5 on the same indifference curve, and define Δb and Δc as the changes in the amounts of bread and cheese between these two points. Consumption at the point α_5 contains Δc more cheese than consumption at the point α_4, and Δb less bread. The ratio $\Delta b/\Delta c$ is the trade-off in use between bread and cheese, the decrease in the number of loaves of bread per pound of cheese acquired leaving Robinson Crusoe neither better off nor worse off with the combination of bread and cheese at the point α_5 than he would be with the combination of bread and cheese at the point α_4. A rate of trade-off in use between bread and cheese may be identified not just between two points, but at a single point on an indifference curve.

The rate of trade-off at a point – for example, at the point α_4 – is just the slope of the indifference curve at α_4, or, equivalently, ratio $\Delta b/\Delta c$ between α_4 and α_5 when α_5 is very close to α_4.

Analogously with the supply side of this simple economy, we refer to the rate of trade-off in use between bread and cheese (at any given combination of bread and cheese) as the *demand price* of cheese. Another way to describe the characteristic shape of indifference curves is to say that the demand price becomes steadily lower from left to right along an indifference curve. The more cheese one has, the less one is willing to pay for an extra pound.

Nothing in the construction of the indifference curves supplies a numbering of the curves themselves. It seems natural to speak of indifference curves as higher and lower according to whether the person to whom the curves refer becomes better off or worse off in exchanging a combination of bread and cheese on one indifference curve for a combination of bread and cheese on the other. Of the three curves shown in figure 3.4, the lowest curve is the one closest to the origin, the middle curve is next and the highest curve is the farthest away, but there, as yet, is no basis for numbering these curves. The numberings 1, 2, and 3, or 1, 10, and 150, or $-50, -25$, and 0 would all seem to do equally well. Any three numbers would do, as long as the higher number is attached to the higher curve. Any such numbering would be consistent with the test by which indifference curves are discovered.

Representation of taste by indifference curves allows us to speak of *choosing* as *maximizing*. Once indifference curves have been identified, Robinson Crusoe's choices become logically equivalent to maximizing *utility*, where utility is any numbering of indifference curves whatsoever as long as higher numbers are assigned to higher curves. To say that Robinson Crusoe maximizes utility is just a convenient and expedient way of saying that he chooses consistently.

In general, the utility function may be written as $u(c, b)$ attaching a value of u to every combination of c and b. For purposes of exposition, it is convenient to postulate a specific functional form. A simple and useful assumption specification of the utility function is

$$u = cb \tag{1}$$

where u is mnemonic for utility. An indifference curve becomes the trace of all combinations of c and b for which u is constant. Consider two combinations of bread and cheese, $\{c_1, b_1\}$ and $\{c_2, b_2\}$. If Robinson Crusoe's tastes just happen to conform to equation (1), if $c_1 b_1 = u_1$ and if $c_2 b_2 = u_2$, then the first combination of bread and cheese is indifferent to, preferred to or dispreferred to the second according as u_1 is equal to, larger than or smaller than u_2. Bear in mind that, in postulating that tastes conform to equation (1), there is no presumption that a person's tastes should conform; it is simply supposed for purposes of exposition that they do. They might easily have conformed to some other function instead.

Though it is not possible to specify a function such as that in equation (1) without at the same time specifying a distinct value of u for any pair of values of b and c, no meaning is being attached to the magnitude of u and nothing in the derivation of the demand price depends upon it. For example, $b = 7$ and $c = 9$, then,

Table 3.3 Supply and demand curves for cheese

Plots devoted to cheese production	Pounds of cheese produced (c)	Loaves of bread produced (b)	Robinson Crusoe's welfare u = cb	Supply price of cheese (loaves forgone per extra pound acquired)	Demand price of cheese $p^D = b/c$
None	0	47	0	0.5	Infinity
C	10	42	420	1	4.2
C and D	16	36	576	2	2.25
C, D, and part of B	17	34	578	2	2
C, D, and B	20	28	560	3	1.4
C, D, B, and E	24	16	384	4	0.67
C, D, B, E, and A	28	0	0	Infinity	0

according to equation (1), u = 63, but that is of no economic significance. Robinson Crusoe's behavior is exactly the same when the utility function is u = 50cb, or u = (cb)^2 or any function of cb whatsoever, as long as the greater cb generates the greater u. Also, as will be shown presently, the utility function u = cb has the property that the corresponding indifference curves are bowed in as shown in figures 3.3 and 3.4. The reader should be warned, however, that the utility function in equation (1) has some very special properties that make it very convenient for introducing to supply and demand curves, but at the cost of suppressing some aspects of economic behavior.

The demand price of cheese corresponding to any combination of bread and cheese is defined as $p^D(c, b) = \Delta b/\Delta c$ where Δb and Δc are absolute values of small changes in b and c along the indifference curve at the point {c, b}. For the utility function u = cb, the demand price of cheese can be derived analytically. It is easy to show that.[2]

$$p^D(c, b) = b/c \qquad (2)$$

A *demand curve* for cheese, comparable to the supply curve in figure 3.2 but downward-sloping rather than upward-sloping, will be constructed presently.

Equilibrium

Now the demand and supply sides of the economy can be pulled together, first in table 3 and then in figure 3.5. Table 3.3 is a list of quantities, supply prices, demand prices and utilities. With the exception of the row entitled "C, D, and part of B," each

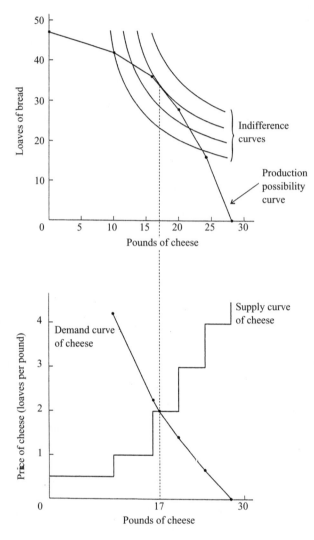

Figure 3.5 Technology and taste: supply and demand.

row in table 3.3 shows quantities and prices when plots of land are used entirely for one good or entirely for the other. Outcomes when other plots are divided between bread and cheese are not shown in table 3.3 but are easily computed. "Pounds of cheese produced," "loaves of bread produced," and "supply price" are reproduced from table 3.2. The new columns in table 3.3 show Robinson Crusoe's utility on the special assumption that Robinson Crusoe's tastes are accurately represented by the utility function in equation (1), so that the demand price of cheese becomes $p^D = b/c$. This equation is used in deriving the numbers in the final column of table 3.3.

The main story in table 3.3 is that there is a best combination of bread and cheese characterized at once by the maximization of utility and the equality between the demand price and the supply price of cheese. Start at the top row of table 3.3 where all plots of land are devoted to bread-making so that output consists of 47 loaves of bread and no cheese. Then, passing down the rows as one extra plot after another is devoted to cheese, Robinson Crusoe trades off more and more bread for cheese at an ever higher supply price (rate of trade-off in production of bread for cheese) and an ever lower demand price (rate of trade-off in use of bread for cheese). At the same time, Robinson Crusoe's utility grows steadily from a low of 0 when no cheese is produced, to 420 when plot C is converted from bread to cheese, to 576 when plot D is converted as well, to a maximum of 578 when the appropriate portion of plot B is converted to cheese and the rest of plot B remains in the production of bread. Thereafter, utility falls steadily to 560 when the rest of plot B is converted to cheese-making, to 384 when plot E is converted, and finally back to nothing when all land is devoted to cheese and no bread is produced at all.

Robinson Crusoe's best available combination of bread and cheese could be observed directly by checking the value of utility at every point on the production possibility curve, but it can also be deduced from a comparison of demand and supply prices. If the demand price of cheese exceeds the supply price, then the amount of bread Robinson Crusoe would be willing to give up to acquire an extra pound of cheese must be greater than the amount of bread he is obliged to give up in order to produce the extra cheese, and the quantity of cheese produced must be too small. Similarly, if the supply price of cheese exceeds the demand price, then the amount of bread Robinson Crusoe would be obliged to give up in order to produce the extra pound of cheese must be greater than the amount of bread he is willing to give up, and the quantity of cheese produced must be too large. In either case, a change in the mix of bread and cheese produced is warranted whenever the supply price differs from the demand price. Robinson Crusoe can only be content with the mix of goods produced when the two prices are the same. The best combination of bread and cheese can be identified by equating demand and supply prices.

The demand price of cheese is higher than the supply price – 2.25 as compared with 2 – when all of plots C and D are devoted to cheese and all of plots B, E, and A are devoted to bread. The demand price of cheese is lower than the supply price – 1.4 as compared with 3 – when the whole of plot B is shifted from bread production to cheese production. Thus, starting from a position where plots C and D are devoted to cheese, Robinson Crusoe makes himself as well off as possible by switching some but not all of plot B from bread to cheese. The appropriate share of plot B is identified by the equality between the demand price and the supply price of cheese. It turns out that demand and supply prices are equal when a quarter of plot B is devoted to cheese and the remaining three-quarters to bread.[3]

It is important to distinguish what is contingent in table 3.3 (contingent on the arbitrarily chosen productivities of land in table 3.1) from what is characteristic of all technology and taste. The exact outputs of bread and cheese and the common value of the supply price and the demand price are contingent on our choice of numbers in table 3.3 and are without general significance. What is not contingent is the equality between the demand price and the supply price, signifying that Robinson Crusoe is as well off as possible with the technology at hand.

The very same story is told twice in figure 3.5. It is told on the top half of the figure combining the production possibility curve with indifference curves. It is told again on the bottom half of the figure with the supply and demand curves. The top half of figure 3.5 contains a set of indifference curves, assumed for convenience to be in accordance with equation (1) above, superimposed on the production possibility curve from figure 3.3, representing Robinson Crusoe's options for the production of bread and cheese. In choosing among these, Robinson Crusoe seeks to make himself as well off as possible. His best option is where an indifference curve just touches the production possibility curve, for, whenever an indifference curve cuts the production possibility curve, some higher indifference curve must necessarily be attainable by moving one way or the other along the production possibility curve. For example, an indifference curve cuts the production possibility curve at the node representing 42 loaves of bread and 10 pounds of cheese, but a higher indifference curve cuts the next node to the right.

Robinson Crusoe's best option – corresponding to the highest attainable indifference curve – is characterized by the tangency of an indifference curve to the production possibility frontier. But the supply price is the slope of the production possibility curve, the demand price is the slope of the indifference curve, and the common tangency of the production possibility curve and the highest attainable indifference curve guarantees an equality between the supply price and the demand price at the best attainable combination of bread and cheese. This information is reproduced in the bottom half of the figure. The supply curve in the bottom half of the figure shows the quantity of cheese produced for each and every supply price of cheese as represented by the slope of the production possibility curve. Carried over unchanged from figure 3.2, the supply curve in figure 3.5 is upward-sloping, a reflection of the curvature of the production possibility curve.

The corresponding *demand curve* for cheese connects the demand price of cheese with the quantity of cheese consumed. At each point on the demand curve on the bottom part of figure 3.5, the demand price is consistent with equation (2). For each and every quantity of cheese, the demand curve shows the demand price of cheese representing the slope of the indifference curve cutting the production possibility curve at that quantity of cheese, together with the corresponding quantity of bread.

The crossing of the demand and supply curves on the bottom half of figure 3.5 has a double significance. First, it identifies the *equilibrium* price and quantity of cheese, the price and quantity that emerge as the outcome of the interaction between supply and demand, or, equivalently, between technology and taste. Later on, when we pass from a one-person economy to a many-person economy, the equilibrium price will evolve into the market-clearing price at which everything for sale is bought and all demands are satisfied. Second, the crossing of the supply and demand curves identifies the *optimal* quantity of cheese. It identifies the best possible pair of outputs of bread and cheese, where "best" means that Robinson Crusoe's consumption is on the highest indifference curve attainable with the technology at his disposal.

Admittedly there is not much difference between equilibrium and optimum in Robinson Crusoe's world. Equilibrium is what he chooses. Optimum is what is best for him. Why would he not choose what is best? The difference between equilibrium and optimum becomes important in more complex economies with many people where – as in the story of the fishermen and the pirates – the outcome is not necessarily for the best. There is even some question as to whether a best outcome can ever be identified.

A best outcome can be identified easily enough in the Robinson Crusoe example where there is only one person and in the fishermen and pirates example where everybody's consumption is the same. In the fishermen and pirates example, the outcome is unambiguously best when there are no pirates. What is best is less evident when people's tastes differ or when full equality of income is no longer feasible. We will return to that question later on.

A smooth production possibility curve

The supply curve in figure 3.5 is a step function because it was convenient for exposition to postulate a technology with five distinct plots of land. The supply curve can easily be made continuous. One might simply postulate a production possibility curve that is bowed-out as in figure 3.1 but that is at the same time continuous so that the derived supply curve is smoothly upward-sloping. Alternatively, one can make up a technology from which the production possibility curve is implied. Assume that Robinson Crusoe lives on a rectangular island, one kilometre from north to south and D metres from east to west. Productivity of land is assumed to be uniform on any strip from north to south, so that we need only keep track of differences in productivities from east to west, and we can speak unambiguously about production per metre, rather than per square metre, of land. Let x be the number of metres devoted to cheese and z be the number of metres devoted to bread, where

$$x + z = D \tag{3}$$

For some purposes, it is sufficient to suppose that all land is equally productive for both goods. Suppose the output of cheese is α pounds per metre and the output of bread is β loaves per metre, regardless of how the available land is allocated between the two goods. Outputs of bread and cheese are αx pounds and βz loaves. The production possibility curve becomes

$$D = x + z = (c/\alpha) + (b/\beta)$$

or, equivalently,

$$b^{max} = b + (\beta/\alpha)c \tag{4}$$

where b^{max}, defined equal to βD, is the most bread that could be produced if no cheese were produced at all. Robinson Crusoe's production possibility curve in equation (4) shows all combinations of bread and cheese he might produce. It is downward-sloping but not bowed outward. The supply of cheese, p^S, must be equal to β/α no matter how much or how little cheese is produced, and the supply curve of cheese is flat at a height p^S above the horizontal axis.

A more interesting assumption about technology is that the west side of the island is best for the production of bread, the east side is best for cheese, but there is no clear boundary between bread land and cheese land. Instead, the productivity of land for cheese increases steadily from east to west while the productivity of land for bread increases steadily from west to east. That pattern may be represented by the functions

$$c = \sqrt{(x/\delta)} \quad \text{and} \quad b = \sqrt{(z/\gamma)} \tag{5}$$

where the x metres on the west side are devoted to cheese, the z metres on the east side are devoted to bread, δ are γ parameters reflecting the productivity of land for cheese and for bread and, once again, $x + z = D$. Additional land devoted to cheese yields more cheese in total but less cheese per metre (for the output of cheese per metre is $c/x = (\sqrt{\delta x})/x = \sqrt{(\delta/x)}$ which diminishes with x). The larger δ, the more land is required to produce any given amount of cheese. The larger γ, the more land is required to produce any given amount of bread. Robertson Crusoe's only choice is the dividing line between bread and cheese production. From these assumptions, it follows immediately that the production possibility curve becomes a quarter circle if δ and γ are the same. Otherwise, the production possibility curve is squished, horizontally or vertically depending on the ratio of δ and γ.

$$D = x + y = \delta c^2 + \gamma b^2 \tag{6}$$

By an argument analogous to the derivation of the demand function in equation (2), it may be shown that the supply price – the rate of trade-off between bread and cheese along the supply curve – is

$$p^S(c, b) = \Delta b/\Delta c \text{ (along the production possibility frontier)} = (\delta/\gamma)(c/b) \tag{7}$$

where b is connected to c in accordance with equation (6).[4]

    The essential common feature of the supply curves in figure 3.5 and in equation (7) is that both curves slope upward as a reflection of the economic principle that goods are produced as cheaply as possible. The first pound of cheese is produced at the lowest possible cost in loaves of bread forgone. The next pound may be slightly more expensive because the least expensive combination of resources devoted to cheese-making has already been used up in producing the first pound. The alternative cost of cheese goes higher and higher as the total production of cheese increases. This is the fundamental principle in both examples. By contrast, the supply curve associated with equation (4) and the portions of the supply curve in figure 3.5 representing additional allocations of land to cheese within the same plot are both flat.

Income

Robinson Crusoe's problem is to maximize his utility given his options as summarized in a production possibility curve. For reasons that are not especially compelling as long as we concentrate on Robinson Crusoe alone but that become compelling later on when we turn to economies with more than one person, Robinson Crusoe's maximization can be split into two distinct components: his maximization of income given his opportunities for production, and his maximization of utility given his income.

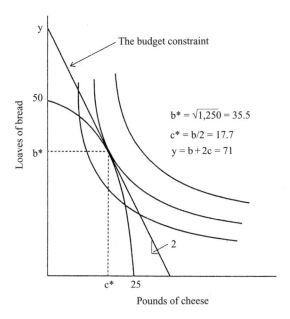

Figure 3.6   Income, the budget constraint, and the market price of cheese.

To illustrate the bifurcation of the maximization problem, replace the segmented production possibility curve of figure 3.3 with a smooth production possibility curve in equation (8) which is a special case of equation (6) where $\delta = 4, \gamma = 1$ and $D = 2,500$.

$$4c^2 + b^2 = 2,500 \qquad (8)$$

Robinson Crusoe can produce 50 loaves of bread or 25 pounds of cheese but more than half of each if he chooses to produce some of both goods. (The parameter 4 is chosen to generate an equilibrium price of cheese of 2 loaves per pound in an example to follow.) From equations (7) and (8), it follows immediately that the supply price of cheese is

$$p^S = 4c/b = 4c/\sqrt{(2500 - 4c^2)} \qquad (9)$$

Robinson Crusoe's choice of bread and cheese is illustrated in figure 3.6 which is just like the top half of figure 3.5 except that the segmented production possibility curve based on information in table 3.1 is replaced by the smooth production possibility curve in equation (8). As in figure 3.5, Robinson Crusoe's best combination of bread and cheese is identified equally well by the tangency of an indifference curve to the production possibility curve, by the equality of the demand price and the supply price and by the crossing of the demand and supply curves for cheese (not shown in figure 3.6). Equation (2) indicates that the demand price, p^D, is b/c.

Equation (9) indicates that the supply price, p^S, is $4c/b$. For these prices to be equal, their common value must be 2 loaves of bread per pound of cheese, from which it follows that $b = 2c$ when b and c are the chosen quantities of bread and cheese. Substituting this into the production possibility curve in equation (8), it follows that

$2b^2 = 2,500$, or $b^* = \sqrt{1,250} = 35.5$ and $c^* = b/2 = 17.7$ where b^* and c^* are Robinson Crusoe's chosen quantities of bread and cheese as shown in figure 3.6.

The new ingredients in figure 3.6 are *income* and the *budget constraint*. Since indifference curves are bowed in while the production possibility curve is bowed out, the common tangent of the highest attainable indifference curve and the production possibility curve touches neither curve except at the point of tangency. For reasons that will soon be obvious, the common tangent itself is called the *budget constraint*. The projection of the budget constraint onto the vertical axis is called *income* and is denoted by y. All combinations of b and c along the budget constraint are indicated by the equation

$$b + p^M c = y \qquad (10)$$

where p^M is the common value of the demand price and the supply price where the demand and supply curves cross. The letter M is mnemonic for "market" price because that is what p^M is destined to become in the multi-person society to be discussed later on in this chapter. For the present, p^M is just the common slope of the production possibility curve and the indifference curve on the point on the production possibility curve where Robinson Crusoe's utility is as large as possible. In this example, p^M is 2 loaves per person.

By construction, Robinson Crusoe's chosen quantities, b^* and c^*, of bread and cheese, conform to equation (10). Here, income is graduated in loaves of bread, but its connection with ordinary money income is straightforward. Suppose you have a money income of $20 to spend on bread and cheese when the price of cheese is $4 per pound and the price of bread is $2 per loaf. That is exactly equivalent to having a stock of 10 loaves of bread, any amount of which may be exchanged for cheese at a rate of 2 loaves per pound. Your income, y, in equation (10) is your stock of bread, your money income divided by the money price per loaf of bread. The relative price of cheese, p^M, is the ratio of the money price of cheese to the money price of bread. In short, income and price in equation (10) are converted from money income and the money price of cheese by dividing both dollar values by the price of bread.

Defined originally as Robinson Crusoe's utility-maximizing quantities of bread and cheese along the production possibility curve, b^* and c^* can be looked upon as both his best choice of bread and cheese along his budget constraint and his choice of bread and cheese to maximize his income at the going market price. In the latter choice, Robinson Crusoe's income must be thought of as a variable. Imagine a set of lines all parallel to the budget constraint in figure 3.6. Corresponding to each line is an income, defined as the height of the intersection of the line with the vertical axis. As producer, Robinson Crusoe may be thought of as choosing a point on his production possibility curve to place himself on the highest attainable line or, equivalently, as seeking the largest attainable income.

THE INDETERMINACY OF BARGAINING

Increase the population from one person to two. Robinson Crusoe splits into two people called Mary and Norman. Mary can produce cheese but no bread, while Norman can produce bread but no cheese. Mary owns a plot of land where she produces 50 pounds of cheese. Norman owns a plot of land where he produces 100 loaves of bread. Their tastes, which may but need not be the same, can be represented by indifference curves like those in figure 3.4. In short, Mary and Norman would like to consume both goods but can produce only one. For both goods, total production equals total consumption.

$$b_N + b_M = 100 \quad \text{and} \quad c_N + c_M = 50 \tag{11}$$

where b_M and c_M are Mary's consumption of bread and cheese and where b_N and c_N are Norman's consumption of bread and cheese. Any trade involves Mary giving c_N pounds of cheese to Norman in return for b_M loaves of bread, where $b_M = c_N = 0$ if they do not trade at all. The question before us is how the amounts c_N of cheese and b_M of bread might be determined. Somehow a bargain must be struck.

Mary and Norman might agree to share their produce equally, so that

$$c_M = c_N = 25 \quad \text{and} \quad b_M = b_N = 50 \tag{12}$$

If it just so happened that their utility functions corresponded to equation (1) above, an equal split of both goods would supply each party with a utility of 1,250. That seems fair enough, and, in practice, many bargains amount to a splitting of the difference between the participants. This is not the only possibility.

Suppose Norman is nasty or greedy or both. If so, he might demand a split more favorable to himself. For instance, he might insist on a 60–40 split in his favor, so that $c_N = 30$ and $b_N = 60$ while $c_M = 20$ and $b_M = 40$. This may seem unfair to poor Mary, but, if Norman is adamant or if he can somehow lock himself into a situation where he literally cannot accept less than 30 pounds of cheese and 60 loaves of bread – in effect trading 40 loaves of bread for 30 pounds of cheese – then Mary has no choice but to accept the trade, for she is better off with that disadvantageous trade than with no trade at all. If Mary accepts Norman's offer, her utility in accordance with equation (1) would fall from 1,250 to 800. If she refuses, her utility falls to 0 as long as Norman would, really and truly, reject any deal less favorable to himself.

The situation is symmetric. Mary may be the nasty one. She may be the first to bind herself so that she cannot accept any deal that is not weighted in her favor. Then Norman may be left with no option other than to accept Mary's disproportionate offer. Either party gets the better of the deal if he is adamant while the other is not. Traditionally in economics, cool reason prevails. Here, irrationality may be advantageous. If Norman is wild-eyed and secure in his belief that the God Thor entitles him to a disproportional share, while Mary is composed and rational, then Norman may get the better of the deal. Adolph Hitler is reputed to have insisted that somebody has to be reasonable in negotiation, and it is not going to be Hitler! To be sure, the parties may be nice to one another, but self-interest alone is insufficient.

Worse still, this being economics, Mary and Norman are not supposed to be nice to one another. Economics is at bottom the study of greed, of how self-interested people respond to the physical environment and to one another to make themselves as well off as possible. Recall the world of fishermen and pirates where each person chooses his occupation in his own interest exclusively, regardless of the impact of his choice on

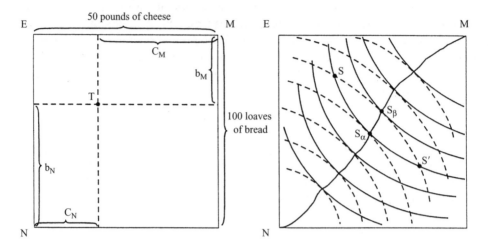

Figure 3.7 The indeterminacy of bargaining.

other people. The moral of the story was that society requires protection from pirates, enabling the fisherman to keep the whole of his catch, and making everybody as well off as the technology of production allows. But Mary's and Norman's property is secure. Norman cannot steal from Mary, nor Mary from Norman. The outcome remains not just inefficient, but indeterminate as well. Calculation of self-interest cannot predict what deal Mary and Norman will strike, or even whether they will strike a deal at all.

By analogy with Robinson Crusoe, one might suppose a unique efficient outcome could be identified. One might hope to discover a bargain that does for Mary and Norman together what the crossing of the demand and supply curve does for Robinson Crusoe. That turns out not to be so. Efficient bargains can be identified, but efficiency is no longer unique.

To see why, consider the *box diagram* in figure 3.7. The box is reproduced twice, side by side, with different information in each reproduction. Look first at the left-hand version of the box. The width of the box is Mary's production of cheese, which we assumed to be 50. The height of the box is Norman's production of bread, which we assumed to be 100. The south-west corner of the box, marked N, is Norman's "origin" in the sense that Norman's production of bread, his consumption of bread, and his consumption of cheese are to be measured as distances from that origin. The north-east corner of the box is Mary's origin. The north-east corner of the box, marked E, represents endowments, Norman's production of bread as a distance above his origin, and Mary's production of cheese to the left of her origin. Every point within the box, such as T, illustrates a possible sharing of the available bread and cheese between Mary and Norman. For any such point, Mary's consumption of bread and cheese is measured to the left and down from her origin. Norman's consumption of bread and cheese is measured to the right and up from his origin. It is obvious from inspection of the box that all bread produced and all cheese produced is consumed by one party or the other.

Mary's and Norman's tastes are represented within the box by sets of indifference curves like those in figures 3.3 and 3.4 above. These are shown in the right-hand version of the box. Measured from his origin at the south-west corner of the box, Norman's indifference curves are shown as solid lines, bowed inward toward the origin. Measured instead from her origin at the north-east corner of the box, Mary's indifference curves are the dashed lines which are appropriately shaped if you turn the page upside down.

The wavy line from Mary's origin, M, to Norman's origin, N, is the *efficiency locus* tracing all points of tangency between pairs of indifference curves, one for Mary and the other for Norman. The meaning of efficiency in this context is that no reallocation of bread and cheese between Mary and Norman can make both of them better off simultaneously. One person can always be made better off at the expense of the other; an unrequited transfer of either bread or cheese will always have that effect. An efficient allocation of bread and cheese is one from which no supplementary trade is mutually advantageous. The efficiency locus would be a straight line from M to N if Mary's and Norman's utility functions were in conformity with the utility function in equation (1). Otherwise the efficiency locus would be wavy as in figure 3.7, opening the possibility that efficient allocations of bread and cheese provide each party with relatively more of one good and relatively less of the other.

To see that points on the efficiency locus really are efficient, consider any point S which is not on the efficiency locus. Since each person's indifference curves cover the entire space in the box and since no two indifference curves are tangent at the point S, there must be a pair of indifference curves, one for Mary and the other for Norman, that cross at S, forming a lens with the point S at one end and another point S' at the other. It is immediately evident from the figure that S and S' lie on opposite sides of the efficiency locus, and that any point strictly inside the lens is superior to both S and S', for both Mary and Norman are better off at that point than they are at either S or S'. Norman is better off because he is on a higher indifference curve. Mary is on a higher indifference curve too, as long as higher is interpreted for Mary as a distance from her origin at the north-east corner of the box. For any point off the efficiency there must be some other point on the efficiency locus at which both Mary and Norman are both better off. Only for points on the efficiency locus is it impossible to find other points that are superior for both parties. A movement north-east along the efficiency locus makes Norman better off at the expense of Mary. A movement south-east makes Mary better off at the expense of Norman.

Among points within the box, any point off the efficiency locus is inferior for both parties to some point on the efficiency locus. Suppose, never mind how, Mary and Norman have traded cheese for bread, bringing them from the point E to the point S which is still off the efficiency locus. If so, Mary and Norman might be expected to continue trading – Norman supplying more bread to Mary and Mary supplying more cheese to Norman – to place themselves at a point on the efficiency locus within the lens formed by S and S'. All such points make both parties better off than they were at S, and any trade to a point within the lense but not on the efficiency locus leaves additional opportunities for new trades that make both parties better off. Recognizing this, Mary and Norman might be expected to trade from S to a point on the efficiency locus between S_α and S_β, where S_α is at once indifferent to S in Norman's assessment and the best point within the lense for Mary, and S_β is at once indifferent to S in Mary's assessment and the best point within the lens for Norman. But which point on the efficiency locus do the parties choose?

Obviously Mary wants S_α and Norman wants S_β. Somehow, they must agree on an efficient point in between, for failure to agree consigns both parties to their endowments at the point S where they are both worse off than they might become through trade. This is not an artificial problem. It is a paradigm for deals among nations. It is a paradigm for labor relations where management and union sit across the table allocating the earnings of the firm between themselves. It is a paradigm for commercial deals as when people with different assets and skills – such as a cook and a waiter opening a restaurant – establish a new firm and must determine each person's share of the ownership.

We know that people strike deals, and we know from experience that bargaining is frequently time-consuming and costly, but we cannot explain how one particular bargain emerges as the outcome of self-interested behavior on the part of all parties to the bargaining process. There is no solid explanation of how rational self-interested people choose among the many mutually advantageous bargains that might be struck. To the economist, pie division remains mysterious. By contrast, price will be shown below to clear large markets automatically, confining the realm of bargaining to unique transactions with only a few participants. We return to the bargaining problem later on in the book. For the remainder of this chapter, we concentrate on circumstances where piracy is suppressed, property is secure, and bargaining is circumvented by the price mechanism.

How Markets Coordinate Production

What can be expected of an economy occupied by many people, each seeking to maximize his own welfare by whatever means he can command? Our analysis so far would seem to suggest that the prospects are bleak. The fishermen and pirates story in chapter 2 was about how self-interested people free to do as they please would allocate themselves between the productive activity and the predatory activity, reducing income per head to well below what could be attained if predatory activity were somehow suppressed. The bargaining story in the preceding section was equally disheartening. Security of property was insufficient to generate an allocation of bread and cheese because there was no mechanism for securing a deal on the trade of bread for cheese. The allocation of people between fishing and piracy was at least determinate. The trade of bread for cheese was not. Even the Robinson Crusoe story was ultimately depressing because the "obvious" lesson was the need for a central authority who, like Robinson Crusoe, would decide how each plot of land is to be employed. Robinson Crusoe is an organizer who decides how each plot of land is to be employed, whether for bread or for cheese. It would stand to reason that organization is no less required in an economy with many people, especially as a decision would also be required on the all-important matter of how the total output is allocated among the occupants of the economy.

Protection of fishermen from pirates, the choice of what to produce and the allocation of the output among consumers would all seem to require a class of guardians and organizers to direct society in detail. But guardians are no less self-interested than anybody else. Once established, a class of guardians might be irresistibly drawn to employ the powers required to contain piracy, produce the right mix of goods and services and allocate the national income for their own ends at the expense of the rest of the population. Either way, the ordinary citizen is impoverished and oppressed.

To direct a modern economy with millions of people and millions of production processes, the organizer would need to assume vast powers over the disposition of resources, communication, the army, the police, and the ordinary citizen. Every person would have to be slotted into the industrial machine, and a wage would have to be assigned to each and every occupation. Each person's employment, remuneration, and livelihood would come to depend on the organizer's goodwill, and his wrath if crossed or criticized could be terrible indeed. The citizen's fear of impoverishment or worse would almost certainly invest the organizer with such complete authority over the rest of society as to place him beyond the control. The organizer might conceivably exercise his authority in the name of equality, but he would certainly be tempted to act in his own interest instead, and there are abundant examples throughout history of organizers who did just that. More will be said about this matter in the discussion of voting and public administration. For the present, take it as a working assumption that an organizer with as extensive control over the economy as Robinson Crusoe exercises over his five plots of land would act despotically. Nobody guards the guardians under those circumstances.

There is, however, another possibility. The central proposition of the science of economics is that, without central direction, something like the result in the Robinson Crusoe example can be attained in a large society as the outcome of self-interested but uncoordinated behavior. The proposition is that, to some extent and on certain conditions, private property substitutes for central planning, organizing the economy impersonally and without detailed control over the lives of citizens. To be sure, private property requires the support of the state, and a bureaucracy protecting private property has some of the ugly propensities of the central planner. The difference is in the scope of the authority of the bureaucracy. The organizer's reach is vast. The bureaucracy in an economy with private property is very much smaller and less intrusive on the life of the ordinary citizen. There remains some question as to whether this smaller corps of guardians may not be still too large to be restrained by the ordinary citizen, but that is a matter to be considered later on. For the moment, let us go to the other extreme of supposing that property needs no protection. Let it be assumed, as is customary in economic analysis, that property rights are secured costlessly. Our concern here is whether, to what extent, and under what circumstances secure property rights lead to an efficient economy.

Self-sufficiency in a five-person economy

Consider first an example where they do not. Imagine a community of five people, each of whom is the owner of one of the five plots of land described in table 3.1. Plot

Table 3.4   The inefficiency of self-sufficiency

Robinson Crusoe's usage of the five plots of land.

Plots of land	A	B	C	D	E	Total
Loaves of bread	16	6	0	0	12	34
Pounds of cheese	0	1	10	6	0	17

Usage of the five plots of land when each plot is owned by a different person, when there is no trade among the owners and when each owner produces a mix of bread and cheese to maximize his individual utility.

Plots of land	A	B	C	D	E	Total
Loaves of bread	8	4	2.5	3	6	23.5
Pounds of cheese	2	2	5	3	2	14

A is owned by person A, plot B is owned by person B, and so on. Everybody's tastes, as reflected in their indifference curves, are the same. Specifically, as between any two combinations of bread and cheese, the preferred combination is whichever yields the higher utility. Table 3.4 contrasts Robinson Crusoe's usage of the five plots of land with the usage when each plot is owned by a separate person, when each person's taste is represented by the utility function, $u = bc$, in equation (1), when there is no trade among people, and, consequently, when the mix of bread and cheese on each plot is chosen to maximize the welfare of its owner.

Robinson Crusoe's usage of each plot of land is shown in the top half of table 3.4. As explained in the discussion surrounding tables 3.2 and 3.3 above, he becomes as well off as possible with the technology at his disposal when he devotes plots C and D together with a quarter of plot B to the production of cheese, and the remainder of his land to bread. As shown in the top half of figure 3.4, he acquires 10 pounds of cheese from plot C and 6 pounds of cheese from plot D, but no bread from either plot. He also acquires 16 loaves of bread from plot A and 12 loaves of bread from plot E, but no cheese from either plot. A quarter of plot B is devoted to cheese and the remaining three-quarters is devoted to bread, yielding 6 loaves of bread and 1 pound of cheese. In accordance with equation (2), his demand price of cheese is b/c, equal to 2, where b and c are his total consumption of bread and cheese from the final column of table 3.4.

The bottom half of table 3.4 shows the usage of each plot of land for bread and for cheese when each of five people owns one of the five plots and employs his plot to supply himself with the best (utility-maximizing) attainable combination of bread and cheese. It follows from our, admittedly strong, assumptions about technology and taste that, with no trade among people and when every person uses his own plot to produce for himself the most desirable combination of bread and cheese, each of the five people would devote exactly half of his land to bread and half to cheese.

Consider person C. His plot of land yields 10 pounds of cheese, or 5 loaves of bread, or any combination such as 5 pounds of cheese together with 2.5 loaves of bread or 8 pounds of cheese together with 1 loaf of bread. The corresponding production

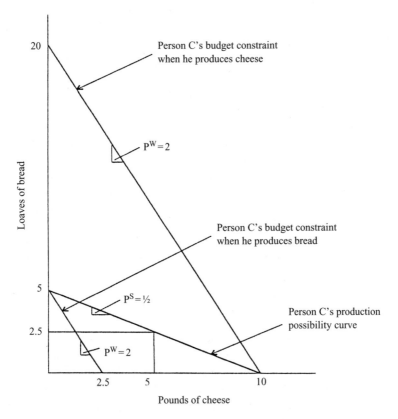

Figure 3.8 The production possibility curve and the budget constraint of person C.

possibility curve is a downward-sloping straight line represented by the equation[5]

$$10 = c + 2b \tag{13}$$

and illustrated by the middle curve in figure 3.8 cutting the vertical axis at 5 and the horizontal axis at 10. Wishing to consume some of both goods, person C subdivides his land into two parts, one for bread and the other for cheese. Since, by assumption, each square metre of land on plot C is like every other square metre of land in its capacity for cheese production or for bread production, person C's only concern in the division of the plot is with areas devoted to each good. Unlike Robinson Crusoe in his allocation of the five plots, person C does not care which bits of land are devoted to each good as long as the overall division is appropriate. (Ignore for the moment the two budget constraints made possible by trade.)

Like Robinson Crusoe in figure 3.5, person C chooses a point on his production possibility curve to place himself on the highest possible indifference curve. Think of the space in figure 3.8 as filled up with person C's indifference curves, exactly as in figure 3.5. An implication of the strong assumption about the form of the utility function in equation (1) is that shares of the land devoted to each good are exactly the same. As illustrated in figure 3.8 and table 3.4, person C (and the same is true of the other four people as well) splits his land into two equal parts, one yielding 2.5 loaves of bread and the other yielding 5 pounds of cheese.[6] Other, more realistic assumptions about the form of the utility function will be considered in the next chapter. On these alternative assumptions, the shares devoted to bread and to cheese need no longer be equal, but the story in this chapter about the role of prices in the economy would remain essentially the same.

The lesson in table 3.4 is that less of both goods are produced when each of the five landowners uses his own land to provide for himself than when Robinson Crusoe organizes production efficiently. Uncoordinated production yields outputs of 23.5 loaves of bread and 14 pounds of cheese as compared with 34 loaves of bread and 17 pounds of cheese when Robinson Crusoe utilizes the five plots of land efficiently to make himself as well off as possible. An organizer could replicate Robinson Crusoe's usage of land to yield more of both goods than when each person produced for his own use on his own land, but he would have to allocate the surplus among the five people in this example. What is true of this simple two-good economy is true a thousand times over of a modern economy with thousands of goods and thousands of industrial processes.

Trade at world prices

Our examination of the formation of domestic prices begins with a detour into international trade. Think of the five plots of land as situated on five small islands, each close to the mainland where bread and cheese may be traded at fixed-prices money of $P^{\$B}$ dollars per loaf and $P^{\$C}$ dollars per pound. These are like ordinary prices in the grocery store. Each of our five people can travel costlessly to the mainland to trade cheese for bread or bread for cheese as he pleases, as long as the value at mainland prices of what he buys is equal to the value of what he sells.

Consider person C once again. He retains the option of dividing his land between bread production and cheese production, but trade provides him with two new options. He can produce only cheese and trade some of his cheese for bread, or he can produce only bread and trade some of his bread for cheese.

Suppose, first, that he produces cheese. His output is 10 pounds of cheese of which he consumes c pounds and sells the rest. He sells $(10 - c)$ pounds of cheese for $(10 - c)P^{\$C}$ dollars, and he uses that money bread to buy $(10 - c)P^{\$C}/P^{\$B}$ loaves of bread. In other words,

$$b = (10 - c)(P^{\$C}/P^{\$B}) \tag{14}$$

which may be rewritten as

$$10p^W = b + p^W c \tag{15}$$

when the ratio $(P^{\$C}/P^{\$B})$ is replaced by p^W, the "world" relative price of cheese, the relative price on the mainland, which is what it is independently of the behavior of person C.

Equation (15) identifies all combinations of b and c attainable by person C if he chooses to produce only cheese and to acquire bread by trading bread for cheese on the mainland. Equation (15) becomes person C's budget constraint attainable by trading cheese for bread. Note particularly that money prices, $P^{\$B}$ and $P^{\$C}$, are in themselves of no interest to person C (or, for that matter, to anybody else). It makes no difference to person C whether he sells cheese at $2 per pound and buys bread at $1 per loaf, or if he sells cheese at $20 per pound and buys bread at $10 per loaf. All that matters to him is the relative price $(P^{\$C}/P^{\$B})$, the price of cheese in loaves per pound, which was indicated in equation (15) as p^W.

Person C might, instead, produce five loaves of bread, of which he would consume b loaves and sell the remaining $(5 - b)$ loaves for cheese. By the same reasoning that led to the budget constraint in equation (14), it may be shown that person C's new budget constraint would become

$$5 = b + p^W c \tag{16}$$

which is represented by the lower budget constraint in figure 3.8. Both equations, (15) and (16), are special cases of the general budget constraint

$$y = b + p^W c \tag{17}$$

where y is income in terms of bread, one's money income divided by the money price of bread. In equation (15), $y = 5$. In equation (14), $y = 10p^W$, the output of cheese evaluated at the relative price of bread.

Person C's opportunities – represented by equation (13) if he chooses not to trade, by equation (15) if he produces only cheese and trades some cheese for bread, and by equation (16) if he produces only bread and trades some bread for cheese – are illustrated by the three downward-sloping budget constraints in figure 3.8. It is immediately evident from figure 3.8 that trade is preferable to no-trade because one of the two trade-created budget constraints must lie entirely above the production possibility curve. Person C may be thought of as selecting the higher of the two trade-created budget constraints. He chooses whichever option yields the larger income at world prices, exporting whichever good is worth more (relative to the other good) abroad than at home. In the absence of trade, person C's supply price of cheese would be 0.5 loaves per pound. At any world price in excess of 0.5 loaves per pound, his better option is to sell cheese and buy bread.

Trade enlarges person C's options, placing him in exactly the same position as if, by magic, the productivity of his land for bread-making increased from 5 loaves to 20 loaves. Person C's trade-created budget constraint is like a new enlarged production possibility curve. Originally, he could produce either 10 pounds of cheese or 5 loaves of bread. Now he can "produce" either 10 pounds of cheese or 20 loaves of bread. In the absence of trade, he would choose to consume 5 pounds of cheese and 2.5 loaves of bread. With the opening of trade, he consumes 5 pounds of cheese and 10 loaves of bread. That his consumption of cheese remains unchanged is an accidental consequence of our assumptions: uniform productivity of land and a symmetry in the utility function in equation (1). That he is made better off by trade is a robust consequence, extending well beyond our special assumptions.

Generalizing somewhat, the story in figure 3.8 is that trade at world prices makes people unambiguously better off than they would be with no trade at all, as long as world prices differ from domestic prices as they would be in the absence of trade. Established rigorously for person C in his dealings with the mainland, this proposition remains valid in a wide range of circumstances. Person C sells cheese and buys bread if the world price of cheese is higher than his supply price. Alternatively, he sells bread and buys cheese if the world price of cheese is lower than his supply price. Either way, person C becomes better off than he would be in the absence of trade as long as the world price differs from the domestic price as it would be in the absence of trade and as long as some of both goods is consumed. That trade is better for everybody is a powerful proposition with strong implications for the organization of the world economy.

Located on their islands close to the mainland where bread and cheese are traded at fixed world prices, each of the five people is in essentially the same situation as person C. Each person's options can be represented on a separate diagram with the same general shape as figure 3.8 but with different numbers corresponding to the productivity of his land for bread and for cheese. Comparing his supply price of cheese with the world price, each person decides whether to sell bread and buy cheese or vice versa. If person C sells cheese and buys bread, he is said to have an *excess supply* of cheese. If he sells bread and buys cheese, he is said to have an excess supply of bread or, equivalently, an *excess demand* for cheese. The same may be said of all five people together. Depending on the world price of cheese in terms of bread, they may have a combined excess supply of cheese or a combined excess demand for cheese. If the world price of cheese is high, they would have a combined excess supply of cheese. If the world price of cheese is low, they would have a combined excess demand for cheese. Since each person's decision to become a net supplier or a net demander of cheese depends on a comparison of the world price of cheese with his supply price in the absence of trade, there must be some world price high enough that the five people together have an excess supply of cheese, there must be some world price low enough that the five people together have an excess demand for cheese, and there must be some world price in between at which there is neither excess demand nor excess supply. This is illustrated first in tables 3.5 and 3.6 and then in figure 3.9. Table 3.5 shows each person's production, consumption and excess demand at two possible world prices. Table 3.6 shows the combined excess demand for cheese at each of five prices. The supply and demand curves in figure 3.9 shows combined response to a range of possible world prices.

Table 3.5 is a comparison of production, consumption and excess demand at two possible world prices, a high price of cheese in terms of bread at which there is an excess supply of cheese from our five people together, and a lower price at which there is neither an excess supply nor an excess demand. The upper half of the table shows how each of the five people responds to a world relative price of cheese of 3.5 loaves per pound. As may be seen in the final column of table 3.2 above, a world price of 3.5 exceeds the supply prices of cheese of plots C, D, B, and E but not of plot A. Hence, persons B, C, D, and E are induced by that price to produce cheese, and person A is induced to produce bread. As shown in the final column of table 3.5, combined production of cheese by persons B, C, D, and E is 24 pounds. Computation of the total consumption of cheese is slightly more complicated. Given the world price of cheese in terms of bread, each person's income in terms of bread may be computed

Table 3.5 Production and consumption in response to the world price

Price of cheese = 3.5 loaves per pound.

Person	A	B	C	D	E	Total
Loaves of bread produced	16	0	0	0	0	16
Pounds of cheese produced	0	4	10	6	4	24
Loaves of bread consumed	8	7	17.5	10.5	7	50
Pounds of cheese consumed	2.3	2	5	3	2	14.3
Excess demand or supply (−) of cheese	2.3	−2	−5	−3	−2	−9.7

Price of cheese = 2 loaves per pound.

Person	A	B	C	D	E	Total
Loaves of bread produced	16	6	0	0	12	34
Pounds of cheese produced	0	1	10	6	0	17
Loaves of bread consumed	8	4	10	6	6	34
Pounds of cheese consumed	4	2	5	3	3	17
Excess demand or supply (−) of cheese	4	1	−5	−3	3	0

in accordance with equation (17). It is a convenient (though not always realistic) characteristic of the postulated utility function in equation (1) that, no matter what the price, expenditures on bread and cheese are the same.[7] Thus, at a world price of 3.5 loaves per pound, person C produces 10 pounds of cheese, consuming 5 pounds and selling the rest to acquire 17.5 loaves of bread. Everybody else's consumption of cheese is computed accordingly.

The lower half of table 3.5 contains the same information when the world price is 2 loaves of bread per pound of cheese rather than 3.5. Three features of this table should be noted. First, though each person has an excess demand or excess supply of cheese, the five people together have neither. At a price of cheese of 2 loaves per pound, the five people combined are neither net suppliers of cheese nor net demanders of cheese from the rest of the world. For all practical purposes, they do not trade with the rest of the world at all. From this it follows that a price of 2 loaves per pound would emerge if the five people constituted a closed market, trading with one another but with nobody else, where each person acted as though the market price were fixed and immutable and as though he could trade as much or as little as he pleased at that price without affecting the price itself. Second, person B alone has the misfortune of acquiring no gain from trade because the world price is the same as his equilibrium price would be if he could not trade at all. With or without trade, he consumes 4 loaves of bread and 2 pounds of cheese. Furthermore, he does not care whether he trades or not. He could acquire his 4 loaves of bread and 2 pounds of cheese by producing them, by producing only bread and trading some of his bread for cheese, or by producing only cheese and trading some of his cheese for bread. However, person B is shown in the lower half of table 3.2 as producing 6 loaves of bread and 1 pound of cheese because that is required to balance internal trade among the five people in a closed market where external trade is blocked. Third, at the market-clearing price of 2 loaves per pound of cheese, the usage of the five plots of land and the combined

Table 3.6 Excess demand and excess supply for the five people together depending on the world price of cheese

World price of cheese (loaves per pound)	Combined production of cheese (pounds)	Combined consumption of cheese (pounds)	Excess demand (+) or excess supply (−) of cheese (pounds)
3.5	24	14.3	−9.7
2.5	20	15.6	−4.4
2	17	17	0
1.5	16	20	4
0.75	10	33	23

production of bread and cheese by the five people together are exactly the same as Robinson Crusoe's utility maximizing usage in table 3.4. This is partly contingent on the specifics of the postulated utility function in equation (1) which requires that everybody's proportion between bread and cheese be the same for any given relative price of cheese, regardless of how well off or how badly off one happens to be. What is not contingent on the chosen form of the utility function or on the assumption that everybody's utility function is the same is that consumption guided by market prices is efficient in the sense that no planner could reorganize production and consumption to make everybody better off.

For five different prices, production, consumption, and excess demand (or supply) are shown in figure 3.6. The middle price of 2 loaves per pound is known in advance to be compatible with a balance of trade because it is Robinson Crusoe's equilibrium price when he is the sole owner of the five plots of land. Any higher price must generate an excess supply of cheese, and any lower price must generate an excess demand. The greater the disparity between the actual world price and the market-clearing price for the five people together, the greater the excess demand (or supply) must be. The construction of table 3.6 is straightforward. At any world price, the total quantity of cheese produced is the total production of cheese on all plots for which that world price exceeds the supply price in the absence of trade.

The dependence on the world price of the excess demand or excess supply of cheese for the five people together is illustrated on the demand-and-supply diagram in figure 3.9. As in figures 3.2 and figures 3.2 and 3.5, the price of cheese is graduated in loaves per pound and shown on the vertical axis, and quantities of cheese are shown on the horizontal axis. However, the price of cheese is now the world price, and the demand and supply curves show the response of quantity to the world price by all five people combined. The supply curve shows how much cheese would be produced at each price. The demand curve shows how much cheese would be consumed at each price. At every price the excess demand or supply is the horizontal distance between the demand and supply curves.

The supply curve in figure 3.9 is carried over unchanged from figures 3.2 and 3.5. It is a reflection of the community's production possibility curve which, by construction, is the same as when Robinson Crusoe occupied all five plots of land. The demand curve is different. Like Robinson Crusoe's demand curve in the bottom half of figure 3.5, it is downward-sloping and cuts the supply curve at a price of 2 loaves per pound, but it shows the five people consuming considerably more cheese than

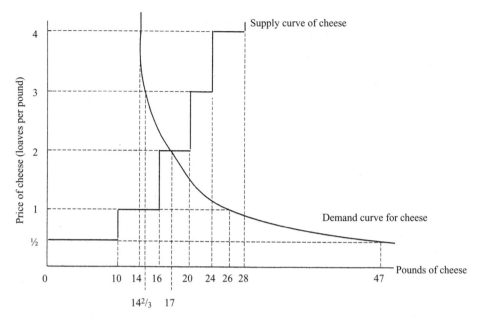

Figure 3.9   Demand and supply curves showing the combined response of the five people to the world price of cheese.

Robinson Crusoe was able to consume, both when the price of cheese is high and when the price of cheese is low. The reason for these differences is that trade lifts people off their production possibility curves whenever the world price differs from the domestic price as it would be in the absence of trade. At a high price of 4 loaves per pound, the five people consume 14 pounds of cheese where Robinson Crusoe would have consumed only 10 pounds. At a low price of 0.5 loaves per pound, the five people consume 47 pounds of cheese which is considerably more than Robinson Crusoe could provide for himself if he devoted all five plots to cheese.

Construction of the demand curve in figure 3.9 is facilitated by a particularly simple property of the postulated utility function in equation (1). At each world price, think of all five people as accumulating as much cheese as they can, by production or by trade, whichever supplies the most cheese, and then trading some of that cheese for bread. The convenient property of the postulated utility function is that, regardless of the world price, half of the accumulated cheese is consumed and the other half is sold for bread. At a price at or above 4 loaves per pound, all five plots of land would be devoted to cheese, total production would be 28 pounds (as shown in table 3.2), 14 pounds would be sold to finance the purchase of bread, and the remaining 14 pounds would be consumed. At a price of between 3 and 4 loaves per pound, everybody but person A would produce cheese, and person A would acquire cheese by producing bread for sale on the world market. Together, persons B, C, D, and E would produce 24 pounds of cheese, of which they would consume half. Person A would produce 16 loaves of bread, yielding him (depending on the price of cheese) between 4 and 5 1/3 pounds of cheese, of which he would consume half. (Alternatively, person A may be thought of as producing 16 loaves of bread, consuming 8 loaves and selling the rest to finance the purchase of, depending on the world price, between 2 and 2 2/3 pounds of cheese.) As soon as the price of cheese falls below 3 loaves per pound, person E joins person A in producing bread instead of cheese, and so on.[8] A demand curve like that in figure 3.9 could be constructed when people's utility functions differ and for any form of utility functions whatsoever. The utility function in equation (1) is convenient but not essential.

Figure 3.9 shows clearly that there is an excess supply of cheese when the world price exceeds 2 loaves per pound, that excess supply increases with the price of cheese over this range, that there is an excess demand for cheese when the world price is less than 2 loaves per pound, and that the excess demand increases as the world price falls. More importantly, from our point of view, figure 3.9 illustrates that, when excess demand or supply varies continuously with the world price, there must be some equilibrium price – not too high and not too low – for which there is neither an excess demand nor an excess supply of cheese for the five people together and at which the five people need not trade at all except with one another. In this example the equilibrium price is 2 loaves per pound, or, equivalently, any combination of money prices – such as $2 per loaf and $4 per pound, or 25 cents per loaf and 50 cents per pound – for which the money price of cheese is twice the money price of bread. The importance of this price is that it would emerge automatically in trade among the five people, as long as each person looks upon the price as market determined and beyond his control, buying or selling cheese at that price to make himself as well off as possible. Person B is something of an exception because his supply price turns out to be the same as the market equilibrium price and because he must apportion his land between bread and cheese. Trading in a world market, he would be indifferent between producing all bread or all cheese or any combination of the two. Trading in the market of five people, he must take cognizance of his effect on the market-clearing price. If he produced all bread, the market price of cheese would rise above his supply price and he would wish he had produced cheese instead. If he produced all cheese, the market price of cheese would fall below his supply price and he would wish he had produced bread instead. Only by dividing his land appropriately between bread and cheese – producing 6 loaves of bread and 1 pound of cheese – can he remain content with his choice.

An important general principle is illustrated in table 3.7 comparing each person's utility when all trade is blocked and he must consume what he produces on his own land with his utility when he can trade at various world prices. The first row reproduces each person's supply price from table 3.1. The principle is that each person becomes steadily better as the world price of cheese diverges in either direction from his own supply price reproduced from table 3.1 in the top row of table 3.7. For example, person A whose supply price of cheese is higher than any of the possible world prices considered in the table becomes progressively better off the lower the world price happens to be. Among all the prices in the table, he is best off, with a utility of 85.3, when the world price of cheese is 0.75, the lowest world price in table 3.1. By contrast person C whose supply price is lower than any of the world prices considered in the table is best off, with a utility of 87.5, at a world price of 4, the highest world price in the table. Person B, whose supply price is 2, is no better off when the world price is also 2 than he would be in the absence of trade, and he becomes progressively better off when the world price deviates from 2. Note, however, the dependence of the numbers in table 3.7 on the specification of the utility function. It has been

Table 3.7 Utility with and without trade

Person	A	B	C	D	E
Supply price (loaves per pound)	4	2	0.5	1	3
Utility without trade	16	8	12.5	9	12
Utility with trade at $p^W = 3.5$	18.3	14	87.5	31.5	14
Utility with trade at $p^W = 2.5$	25.6	10	62.5	22.5	14.4
Utility with trade at $p^W = 2$	32	8	50	18	18
Utility with trade at $p^W = 1.5$	42.7	10.7	37.5	13.5	24
Utility with trade at $p^W = .75$	85.3	21.3	18.8	12	48

Utilities measured in accordance with equation (1), $u = bc$, where b and c are can be computed from numbers in table 3.2.

argued above that, for any given set of indifference curves, the specification of the utility function is entirely arbitrary as long as points on the same indifference curve are endowed with the same utility and utility increases on passing from a lower to a higher indifference curve. Thus the numbers in table 3.7 are no more than indicators of the direction of change in people's well-being. Nor are they comparable from one person to another. A better measure of the gain from trade will be discussed in the next chapter.

The emergence of the market price

Up to this point in our story, the relative price of cheese is either implicit in Robinson Crusoe's choice of quantities of bread and cheese to make himself as well off as possible with the technology at his disposal, or externally given, allowing our five people in this chapter to trade as little or as much as they please at world prices. How prices get to be what they are in a market with many traders is a question that has not so far been discussed. We take up that question now.

Once again, there are five people, each person own a plots of land, and the five plots differ in productivity. Now, however, the five people constitute an isolated market. They can trade with one another, but there is no trade with outsiders and no world prices at which the five people may buy or sell. Instead a market price emerges from trade among the five people alone. It is immediately evident from the discussion surrounding figure 3.9 and table 3.5 that the market would clear – that the quantity of cheese demanded would equal the quantity of cheese supplied and that the quantity of bread demanded would equal the quantity of bread supplied – at a price of 2 loaves per pound as long as each person looks upon the market price as fixed independently of his own behavior and imagines himself able to buy or sell any amount of bread or cheese at the going market, provided only that the values of his purchases and sales be the same. In a closed society consisting of the five people consuming bread and cheese as described above, the *equilibrium* or *market-clearing* relative price of cheese is whatever world price of cheese would generate no excess demand or supply in the event that trade were permitted. Generalizing from two goods to many goods and from five people to many people, a complete set of equilibrium prices for all goods in the economy is whatever world prices would generate no excess demand or supply for any good. For a five-person two-good economy, the existence of an equilibrium price of cheese is adequately demonstrated in figure 3.9. The proof of the existence of a set of equilibrium prices for many goods at once is beyond the scope of this book but is treated in advanced courses in microeconomics.

Several questions arise at this point: (1) whether there *exist* market-clearing prices, (2) whether and in what sense trading at market-clearing prices is efficient, (3) whether and in what sense trading at market-clearing prices is socially desirable, and (4) whether and to what extent actual prices turn out to be market-clearing. I discuss these questions in turn.

"Existence" as applied to market prices is less ethereal than one unacquainted with economic discourse might suppose. It is a technical term with a very special meaning. Market-clearing prices – which, in our example, boil down to a market-clearing price of cheese in terms of bread – are said to exist when price-taking behavior by all of the actors in the economy clears all markets at those prices. One may think of market-clearing prices in a country or region closed to world trade as what world prices would have to be if the country or region were open to trade at world prices but did not, in fact, trade with the rest of the world because there was no excess supply and excess demand for any goods at those prices. That is why we examined international trade – trade between the five islands and the mainland where prices are invariant – before considering the formation of prices in a closed economy. Obviously, there exists a market-clearing relative price of cheese in our five-person economy, for we have found it. The market-clearing price is identified by the crossing of the excess demand curve with the vertical axis in figure 3.9. The market-clearing price is 2 loaves per pound because the quantity of cheese demanded by our five people together is just equal to the quantity supplied at that price. If our five people could trade abroad at any other price, they would find it advantageous to do so, but there is no advantage to trading abroad at a world price of 2 loaves per pound.

That there exist market-clearing prices is a proposition that remains true well beyond our simple example. Our simplifying assumptions about technology and taste are responsible for the transparency of the example and for the easy computation of the market price and of each person's consumption of bread and cheese. But the existence of a market-clearing relative price of cheese does not depend on those simplifying assumptions. It is sufficient for existence of some market-clearing price that the supply curve and the demand curve cross as shown in figure 3.9. The introduction of more than two goods presents more formidable problems. With just bread and cheese, we know that the clearing of one market implies the clearing of the other. With more than two goods, there would seem to be a possibility that prices which clear the market for cheese might create an excess demand, or supply as the case may be, in the market for beans, that new price clearing the market for beans might create an excess demand for cars, and so on ad infinitum. This is not the place to explain how the infinite regress can be circumvented. Suffice to say that the science of economics struggled with the problem for a hundred years, and that the existence of market-clearing prices in an economy with many people and many goods has been established. Our two-good example can be generalized.

The next question is whether trading at market-clearing prices is efficient in the limited technical sense that more of all goods – or more of some but not less of others – cannot be attained with the available technology of the economy. A five-person economy without trade and where each person produces for himself on his own land is not efficient, for total output of both goods was less than Robinson Crusoe would have obtained. Trade at market-clearing prices is efficient in our example because the outcome (34 loaves of bread and 17 pounds of cheese) is at a point on the production possibility curve as described in figure 3.1. Trade at market-clearing prices remains efficient in more realistic economies, but with one important qualification. In our example, each person produces bread, or cheese as the case may be, to maximize his income. In more realistic economies, income can only be maximized when many diverse resources – workers of all kinds, land, minerals, and machines – are organized to produce the goods people want to consume. Prices must be found not just for ordinary goods like bread and cheese but for all resources as well. Market-clearing wages, rents, house prices, and stock prices are all required. Price-taking behavior must guide the deployment of resources among different industries and in the production and distribution of goods. Prices are signals informing the actors in the economy how best to maximize revenue, ensuring that some point on the production possibility curve is attained.

Whether and in what sense trading at market-clearing prices is socially desirable is a more complex question. In the original Robinson Crusoe example, the crossing of the supply and demand curves signified at once that Robinson was acting as he pleased and that he was making himself as well off as possible with the technology at his command. Indeed, with only one person in the economy, there was not much point in distinguishing between these conditions. The distinction becomes important in an economy with five people. Acting as one pleases extends naturally to buying and selling at given market prices. Making oneself as well off as possible extends less readily to a community with five distinct people, for a criterion would seem to be required for balancing a gain to one person against a loss to another. There is however a subsidiary criterion that does not require interpersonal comparison of benefits. Extending the notion of efficiency in production, one might define efficiency in use to mean that no rearrangement of production or reallocation of goods to people could make everybody better off, or some people better off without making others worse off.

Turn back to table 3.5. The outcome with a market-clearing price of 2 is both technically efficient and efficient in use when the five people may trade with one another but not with outsiders, for there is no way to produce more of both goods and no additional trades among the five people could make everybody better off. Consider a trade in which person B supplies cheese to person A in return for bread. The exchange cannot be at a rate of 2 loaves per pound because both parties are already trading as much as it is in their interest to trade at that price. Nor can the exchange be at a different rate between bread and cheese because one party or the other would necessarily be accepting a worse deal than he could get from the market. For example, if the pound of cheese were exchanged for 3 loaves of bread, person A would be giving up more bread than would be required in ordinary trading at market prices. By contrast, disallowing trade with outsiders, the production of 16 loaves of bread and 24 pounds of cheese would be technically efficient but inefficient in use because there is *no* allocation of the 16 loaves of bread and 24 pounds of cheese among the five people for which they are not all worse off than they could be with *some* allocation of another technically feasible combination of bread and cheese, specifically 34 loaves of bread and 17 pounds of cheese. This must be true because the product of 34 and 17 exceeds the product of 16 and 24 and because it is characteristic of the postulated indifference curves in equation (1) that the larger product signifies the higher indifference curve.

Finally, even when market-clearing prices exist, there remains some question as to whether and to what extent such market-clearing prices will emerge from trading in actual markets. Recall the absence of equilibrium in the exchange of bread for cheese between Mary and Norman above. Is five really that different from two? With no equilibrium between two people, why should an equilibrium suddenly emerge from the addition of three more? The real difference between these examples lies not in the number of people, but in how they are assumed to behave. The five people are assumed to be price-takers. The two people are not. In fact, by playing about with figure 3.7, one can identify a market-clearing price if Mary and Norman are assumed to be price-takers too. And the nice equilibrium in the five-person example disappears if people begin to act strategically. Persons A and E who are the major sellers of bread may form a cartel, refusing to buy cheese at all, except at a price of 1.5 rather than 2 loaves per pound. What differentiated the stories is the absence in one and the presence in the other of universal price-taking behavior. The size of the market does matter. One person in a two-person economy can exert a considerable influence on the price. One person in a five-person economy is less influential. One person in an economy with millions of people has virtually no influence upon prices, and becomes for all practical purposes a thoroughgoing price-taker. The price of cheese at the grocery store really is determined by forces beyond my control. However, collusion among buyers or sellers remains a possibility. Monopoly will be discussed in the next chapter.

Money and money prices

Robinson Crusoe had no use for money. He had no use for little pieces of paper with portraits of George Washington or the Queen of England, and he had no use for gold because he consumed only bread and cheese and not jewelry. Nor, strictly speaking, is there any use for gold or paper money in the community described in this chapter where everyone produces bread or cheese, as the case may be, simultaneously, and then trades some of his produce for some of the other good. Think of the data in the top part of table 3.5 as describing production and consumption per week, and suppose there is a market every Sunday where the five people in this economy exchange their excess of the good they produce for some of the other good at whatever price – the relative price of cheese – emerges to clear the market. All trading is direct. If I produce only bread, you produce only cheese and we both want to consume both goods, we simply agree to trade some of my bread for some of your cheese. We may haggle over the price, but we have no need for currency to facilitate the transaction.

In practice, there are two principal uses for money, both of which are absent in the simple world we have constructed so far. The first and most important use of money is as a "medium of exchange." With only two goods, they can be exchanged for one another directly, and no medium is required. With many goods, a medium is required to circumvent the "double coincidence of barter" that people who supply what one wants do not necessarily want what one supplies. I supply lectures in economics. I consume, among other things, hamburgers. The person who supplies hamburgers may not want my lectures in economics. The person who wants my lectures does not supply hamburgers. As a medium of exchange, money conjures up a fictitious person who buys what I want to sell and sells what I want to buy, provided only that the values at going market prices of my sales and my purchases are the same. I sell lectures to the university, which resells them to students, who are, let us say, financed by their parents, who are farmers selling wheat to brewers, who sell whiskey to accountants, who, with the possible addition of a great many more steps, provide services to restaurants that provide hamburgers to many people, including me. This complex network of purchases is of no direct concern to me. Money is a vehicle that allows me to collect my pay cheque and to spend my income as I please as long as the value of what I purchase is no greater than the value of what I supply. I must be concerned about the markets for my lectures and for the goods I wish to buy, but not about the intermediate steps that connect the two. I supply lectures in return for gold or for little pieces of paper with pictures of George Washington or the Queen. I am content to do so because I know that other people require money for the same reason I do and will be prepared to accept my money in exchange for what I want to consume.

The other use of money is as a "store of value." A simple extension of the example in the lower portion of table 3.5 will show how this works. Imagine a community of 260 people, 52 like person A, 52 like person B, and so on. Each person's consumption per week is exactly as shown in the table. Each person's *average* weekly production is also as shown in table 3.5, but one's entire annual production is concentrated on a single day, though different people's production is staggered over the weeks of the year. Of the 52 people of type A, one brings his crop to market on the first Sunday of the year, another on the second Sunday, another on the third, and so on, and the same is true of the other four types, B, C, D, and E. Thus, 51 out of every 52 people bring nothing to market on any particular Sunday, but want to consume just the same. We might even suppose that bread and cheese cannot be stored for more than a week. Chaos can only be averted and the outcome described in the lower portion of table 3.5 can only be reproduced in these circumstances if there is a way for the sellers of bread and cheese on any given Sunday to acquire credits from the rest of the population, credits to be spent on bread and cheese over the rest of the year. With such credits and as long as everybody is a price-taker, the amounts for sale each Sunday are just as described in table 3.5, and the market-clearing relative price of cheese is the same as well.

The community consists of 52 groups, each with five people: one person of type A, one person of type B, one person of type C, and so on. Each group brings its produce to market on a different Sunday, so that the entire year of Sundays is provided for. At a market-clearing relative price of cheese of 2 loaves per pound, each group's weekly expenditure must be 68 loaves-worth (enough to purchase 34 loaves of bread and 17 pounds of cheese as shown in table 3.5). To finance that level of expenditure throughout the year, the group must provide the rest of the community with 3,536 loaves-worth (68×52) on the one day of the year when it comes to market, and in return the rest of the community must provide that group with credits that are run down gradually over the year until the group's next market day arrives. The group's average credit during the year is 1,768 loaves-worth, which is half the value of the annual production. Since market days are staggered, the credit at any given time of all 52 groups together is 91,936 loaves-worth ($1,768 \times 52$). Society requires 91,936 loaves-worth of credit if people are to live throughout the year on their earnings from their one annual sale of bread or cheese. In short, the economy needs money.

Think of a gold standard. Suppose this society has a stock of 9,193.6 ounces of gold. There is nothing special about this number; any other would serve just as well. The gold circulates. Each person acquires his annual supply of gold on the day he sells his crop, and he gradually spends the gold over the course of the year until he has none left on the day the next year's crop is brought to market. Since society requires a steady supply of 91,936 loaves-worth of accumulated credit and since, by assumption, it has 9,193.6 ounces of gold, the money price of bread must be exactly 1/10 ounces of gold per loaf. Since the market-clearing relative price of cheese is 2, the money price of cheese must be 1/5 ounces of gold per pound. In this example, the money supply must be half the annual income, and the *velocity of money* is 2. On average, a bit of gold changes hands twice a year.

Society requires a stock of money as a store of value and as a medium of exchange. In the store-of-value example above, the stock was exactly half the value of the goods and services traded each year. When other considerations are introduced, it may no longer be possible to infer from the technology of the economy the proportion between the stock of money and the value of the national income. Finance is intricate and complicated. However, one may say as a more or less accurate first approximation that there is some fixed proportion between the two. Define the "national income" as the value at money prices of the bread and cheese produced over the course of the year.

$$Y = P^{\$B}B + P^{\$C}C \tag{18}$$

where $P^{\$B}$ is the money price of bread, $P^{\$C}$ is the money price of cheese, B is the *total* output of bread in the economy as a whole, and C is the *total* output of cheese. The assumption we are making, called "the quantity theory of money", is that there is some constant k such that

$$M = kY = k(P^{\$B}B + P^{\$C}C) \tag{19}$$

where M is the stock of money in ounces of gold or in dollars and Y is the value of the annual produce. The theory is that, with quantities of goods and relative prices determined by the interaction of technology and taste as described earlier in this chapter, all money prices are then determined once the quantity of money is established. Once we know B and C and the relative price of cheese ($p = P^{\$C}/P^{\$B}$), the money prices, $P^{\$B}$ and $P^{\$C}$, are dependent on the money supply, M. In our example where $p = 2$, $B = 91,936$, $C = 47,468$, $M = 9,193.6$ ounces of gold and $k = 1/2$, the money prices of bread and cheese, $P^{\$B}$ and $P^{\$B}$, must be 1/10 ounces of gold per loaf and 1/5 ounces of gold per pound.

It is not our purpose to investigate money in depth. All we really need from the quantity theory of money to is complete our picture of the economy with an explanation, however crude, of how money prices are determined. Yet, it would be a shame to overlook a few simple and interesting propositions that flow directly from the theory.

(1) When taste and technology remain unchanged, an increase in the available stock of money leads to an equal proportional increase in *all* prices.

The essence of the quantity theory of money is that money prices are directly proportional to the stock of money in the economy. If the stock of money doubles, then all money prices must double too, though the real side of the economy remains unchanged. This follows immediately from equation (19) as long as k is invariant. A doubling of the money supply from 9,193.6 ounces to 18,387.2 ounces of gold has no effect on the required value of the stock of money in units of bread or on the relative price of cheese in terms of bread, but the price of bread must rise from 1/10 ounces to 1/5 ounces per loaf and the price of cheese must rise from 1/5 ounces per pound to 2/5 ounces per pound. Nobody's consumption of bread or cheese is affected as long as the new gold is distributed among people in proportion to their original holdings of gold. Thus,

(2) Though money is useful to society as a store of value and as a medium of exchange, the value of money to society is independent of the quantity of money available.

A gold standard may be autonomous in the sense that it works without the intervention of the government. The establishment of a gold standard may be spontaneous. No collective decision at a given time and place is required for people to accept gold as money. Of course, efficiency in the economy can only be maintained if the government protects people's entitlements to gold, but gold is no different in this respect from any other property. Thus,

(3) A gold standard does not require the intervention of the government in the money market.

A gold standard has some undesirable properties. Suppose one of the 260 people in this economy discovers a gold mine containing 919.36 ounces, equivalent to 10 percent of the original supply of gold in the entire market. The extra gold is worth 9,193.6 loaves of bread to the discoverer, but *nothing* to society as a whole because the discovery drives up all prices by about 10 percent, reducing by 10 percent the value in terms of bread of the original stock of gold before the extra gold was discovered. The discoverer gains gold worth 9,193.6 loaves of bread. The rest of society loses the equivalent of 9,193.6 loaves of bread from the diminution of the value in terms of bread of the gold it holds. The effect on society as a whole is a wash. It may nevertheless be advantageous for some people to devote their resources to the discovery of new gold. If a person can use his land for prospecting rather than to produce bread or cheese and if the value of the gold he discovers is greater than the value of the bread or cheese he might produce instead, it is advantageous for that person to become a prospector. The prospector becomes better off, but the rest of the population becomes worse off because the total output of bread and cheese must fall by whatever the prospector would have produced had he not become a prospector.

An increase in the money supply leads to an increase in the prices of bread and cheese making all holders of money worse off because their stocks of money are worth less bread and cheese than before. Though his activity may be quite legal, the prospector is at bottom a pirate, taking bread and cheese from the rest of the population. The conquistadores who stole the gold of the Incas in the sixteenth century were doubly pirates: once in stealing the gold from its original owners, and then again in exchanging their "worthless" gold for ordinary goods and services produced in Europe. Thus,

(4) The discovery of extra money is beneficial to the discoverer but not to society as a whole, and resources employed to increase the money supply are wasted.

Look once again at equation (19) connecting the stock of money, the velocity of money (k), money prices and outputs of goods, and suppose gold is the only money. Under a gold standard, one would expect prices to bounce up or down randomly as new gold fields are discovered (increasing M), or as outputs of goods (B an C) increase due to increases in population or the productivity of labor. Prices, $P^{\$B}$ and $P^{\$C}$, bounce up or down to equate the demand for and the supply of money. The discovery of new sources of gold or economic growth unaccompanied by new sources of gold give rise to long periods of inflation or deflation. Thus,

(5) An economy with a gold standard risks inflation or deflation as new gold is discovered or as more goods and services are produced.

Both defects of a pure gold standard – the waste of real resources in the production of gold and the variability of prices – can be circumvented by paper money. The government prints pieces of paper saying, "This is legal tender." In themselves the pieces of paper are worthless, but they serve as a medium of exchange and a store of value because people hold them for the same reasons they would hold gold under a gold standard. The government must maintain a monopoly of paper money because these specially marked pieces of paper are worth more as money than as paper. A government that chooses to do so can administer the money supply to hold prices constant, raising or lowering the money supply, M, in the equation (19) above to keep an average of prices, $P^{\$B}$ and $P^{\$C}$, unchanged over time. To say that a government *can* hold prices constant is not to say that actual governments are always prepared to do so. Revenue-hungry governments may print money as a substitute for taxation. The resulting inflation is a tax on the holders of money. Thus,

(6) Paper money has the potential advantages over gold as a medium of exchange that no resources are wasted in producing money and that the government can regulate the money supply to hold average prices constant.

Finally, the discrepancy between the cost of paper and the value of paper as money creates an incentive to produce money substitutes from ordinary durable assets. Bear in mind that money is not the only store of value. Among the other stores of value are real property, goods in process, stocks and bonds. Money differs from other stores of value in that it is quickly and cheaply traded for goods. Thus there emerges an incentive in the market to convert other stores of value into money. That is what banks do. Traditionally, banks create money out of goods in process. Stocks of goods in process are not money to begin with because the person from whom I want to buy a hamburger will not accept, for instance, title to a millionth part of the goods on the shelf at Sears as payment for his hamburger. He does not know what the goods are worth, he is not confident that I am really in possession of a millionth part of the goods on the shelf at Sears and he doubts whether he can use the piece of Sears paper I offer to buy what he wants. Banks facilitate that transaction. They borrow from a million people like me and they lend to a thousand firms like Sears, converting my "ultimate" ownership of a share of Sears goods in process into money that the seller of hamburgers can accept. Thus,

(7) Banks convert non-monetary assets into money.

The distribution of property and income

A key assumption with distinct implications for economies with private property was introduced quietly at the beginning of this chapter and has been maintained throughout. The assumption is that each plot of land is owned by a different person. Person A owns plot A, person B owns plot B, and so on. There are really two sides to the assumption, one innocuous and the other not. The innocuous side is that people own different kinds of resources. Some people own land that is best for bread, while others own land that is best for cheese, though the best usage of resources is not entirely independent of prices. This aspect of the assumption can be seen as representative of the division of labor in society. People are generalists in consumption but specialists in production. Most people consume some of most goods, but one man is a carpenter, another a doctor, another collects the garbage, another works on the assembly line, another grows wheat, another is prime minister, another gives piano lessons, another writes about economics. The market assimilates all their efforts to produce commodities for everybody to consume. Self-sufficiency would be as productive as the market if everybody owned equal shares of every plot of land, but no conceivable method of economic organization could assign all types of resources and skills to all people or could abandon completely the efficiencies in the specialization of production. The loss of potential output would be too great.

The other side of the assignment of land to people is that it was entirely arbitrary. There was no explanation, within the context of the model, of why, for instance, person A was assigned all of plot A rather than, say, half of it, or of why the assumed endowments of the five people were such that their incomes are not the same. Each person's income is the value at market-clearing prices of the returns to his resources. Suppose the market-clearing prices of bread and cheese are $3 per loaf and $6 per pound, which is consistent with the equilibrium in figure 3.9. With these prices, it is immediately evident from the lower portion of table 3.5 that the money incomes of the five people are $48 for person A, $24 for person B, $60 for person C, $36 for person D and $36 for person E. People's incomes differ because their endowments differ. The present distribution of property and income is the outcome of a long history in which violence and fraud as well as talent, effort, enterprise, and saving have all played a part. The arbitrary assignment of property to people in the example is not innocuous because inequality of endowments and incomes is an important consideration in the evaluation of alternative forms of industrial organization and because the lessening of inequality and reduction in the disparity of incomes and the elimination of dire poverty are major goals of social policy. We return to this matter in chapter 9.

THE VIRTUES OF THE COMPETITIVE ECONOMY

We began this chapter with an analogy between Robinson Crusoe and a central planner. Robinson Crusoe organizes the resources at his command to make himself as well off as possible. A community of people with different resources would seem to require an organizer or principle of organization to direct each person's efforts toward a common good, for self-sufficiency is at best inefficient, as illustrated in table 3.4, and at worst chaotic, as in the fishermen and pirates example. This chapter is about whether and to what extent private property and the impersonal price mechanism can do the job.

This much must be recognized at the outset: Private property cannot supplant government entirely because private property cannot protect itself. The postulated security of ownership in our five-person example is never automatic as we supposed. Private property requires the support of the law courts, the police, the prisons, and the army. The point at issue here is how much of the world's work can be undertaken by the market and whether the powers of government, which are inevitably extensive, can be pared down to the point where personal freedom and private enterprise are not squelched altogether.

The example in the previous section of this chapter is a comparison between two patterns of ownership of the five plots of land. In one pattern, all five plots are owned by Robinson Crusoe. In the other, each plot is owned by a different person with no coordination of production among the five owners except through the intermediary of prices. When everybody's tastes are the same and when indifference curves can be represented by equation (1), the outputs of bread and cheese are exactly the same under both patterns of ownership. When people's tastes differ, the output of goods and the assignment of goods to people depend in part on the distribution among people of the ownership of land. But, regardless of people's tastes, the outcome of the market is efficient in the sense that nothing is wasted; no reallocation of land among goods and no reallocation of goods among people can make everybody better off simultaneously. Whatever the distribution of property, the outcome appears as though it might have been arranged by an ideal economic planner, though that planner would have to be more knowledgeable and more benevolent than any actual planner in this imperfect world is ever likely to be. Specifically, five distinct virtues of the competitive market may be identified.

The first and fundamental virtue of the price mechanism is that it creates "order without orders" or "organization without an organizer," where all participants in the market behave as though they had deliberately coordinated their activities. Some people produce only bread. Others produce only cheese. The price mechanism creates an "equilibrium" where total supplies of bread and cheese are precisely what people wish to consume. No bread remains unconsumed for want of buyers. No cheese remains unconsumed for want of buyers. Markets clear in response to prices alone, and prices adjust accordingly. Not very surprising when there are only two goods, this feature of a competitive economy is quite remarkable in a world with thousands of goods and millions of traders who are unacquainted with one another and whose actions are coordinated by prices as though in conformity with one centrally woven design. There is, ideally, no hesitation or uncertainty about what to produce, and no looking over one's shoulder to see what others are doing before acting oneself. Most readers of this book will remember a children's game called one-finger-two-fingers where the winner is whoever guesses the other's actions correctly. Markets are not like that. Prices inform participants in the market with all they need to know in deciding what to produce and what to buy.

This beautiful property of the competitive model fits the world of work imperfectly. The fit is very close for the stock market and for large commodity markets. It is close enough for groceries, hardware and most consumer goods. It is less close for dealings among businessmen where bargaining is inevitable. It is less close in labor markets, for there could be no unemployment of labor if the model fit the world exactly. Nevertheless, the revelation on first acquaintance with economic ideas is not that markets sometimes fail to work as smoothly as the competitive model would suggest, but that markets work at all and that relations among people free to do as they please are anything other than chaotic. The unemployment of labor and the business cycle are not covered in this book. The student will encounter these topics in courses in macroeconomics.

A second virtue is efficiency. In our example, the price mechanism draws forth the most valuable bundle of goods and services from the resources and the technology at hand and it allocates that bundle of goods and services among people to make everyone as well off as possible in the limited, but nonetheless important, sense that no side-trades, no reallocation of resources to goods or of goods to people could make anybody better off without harming somebody else. This virtue of markets with private property extends, albeit imperfectly, from our five-person example to more realistic economies, though, as will be discussed in chapters to come, there are some quite significant exceptions to this rule. Prices substitute for commands. Prices generate incentives that would, in the absence of markets, have to be supplied by a central planner, whose control of the economy may not, in practice, be up to the task. Suppose that a certain effort is required on the part of the worker to obtain the maximal produce from the land, that each person knows the productivity of the land on which he works, that such information is unavailable to anybody else, and that the planner, in the name of equality, chooses to treat all five people alike. On these assumptions, the planner cannot know whether a particular cheese producer occupies land like plot C yielding 10 pounds of cheese or land like plot D yielding only 6 pounds. Consequently, there is nothing to stop an occupant of land like plot C from slacking off and producing only 6 pounds, for he has nothing personally to gain in return for the extra effort in producing the extra 4 pounds. The divorce of remuneration from effort destroys the incentive to work diligently. The incentive to innovate would also be suppressed, especially, as is often the case in bureaucracy, if failure is punished and success not significantly rewarded. The planner might pay the worker according to his product, but that would be a large step away from equality of income, and would, in any case, be difficult in real economies where production requires the cooperation of many workers with many different skills.

A third virtue is a special case of the second. Markets economize on knowledge. Hold to the assumptions in our example about the apportionment of land among people, but suppose that the owner of each plot of land is the only person who knows its productivity for bread or for cheese. For example, person A knows that plot A yields either 16 loaves of bread or 4 pounds of cheese, but that information is not available to another landowner or to the government that protects property rights. If agriculture were centrally planned, then some of the plots would be misallocated because the planner's best guess as to whether a particular plot should be used for bread or for cheese would sometimes be mistaken. But with agriculture in the private sector, the owner of each plot of land would be driven by prices to use his land to the best advantage, for he, personally, captures the full benefit of the produce. What matters in the example is whether a landowner can identify the most productive use of his land. It does not matter at all whether anybody else has that information. Person A must know a great deal about plot A, person B about plot B, and so on. A planner, on the other hand, has to know everything. Generalizing from the example to real economies with innumerable technologies and special situations requiring detailed information about local conditions, the argument becomes that profit maximization by owners of private property induces each person to make the best use of his own information about particular local situations in the economy and that the price mechanism automatically redirects each person's search for personal gain to the service of the common good, defined in the admittedly limited sense that the outcome for the economy is efficient in production and allocation. By contrast, a planner cannot solve the "thousands of equations" that are solved implicitly when market-clearing prices guide the allocation of resources to the production of goods. These sweeping statements will have to be modified somewhat to take account of aspects of the economy that we have overlooked so far, but there remains in them a good deal of truth.

"Who knows," Milton Friedman is fond of asking, "how to make a pencil?" The answer, oddly enough, is nobody. To be sure a pencil manufacturer knows how to place the graphite inside the wood, how to paint the pencil and how to attach the eraser with a bit of shiny metal. The pencil manufacturer does not know – considering just the wood – how to chop down a tree, how to convert trees into logs or how to dry the wood. The woodsman who knows these things does not know how to convert metal and wood into a saw. The maker of saws does not know how to smelt the ore into metal. The smelter does not know how to mine for ore. The miner does not know how to design and produce machinery. The designer of machinery does not know how to keep the books, or, for that matter, to convert wood and graphite into a pencil. The making of a pencil requires intermediate products, which in turn require other intermediate products, which in turn require still other intermediate products, back and back through technology after technology until the entire technology of the world is somehow engaged. Of that, nobody knows more than a small part.

Prices supply people at each stage of production with exactly the information they require about market conditions and the technology of the economy. The pencil-maker does not need to know how to chop down a tree. All he needs to know about forestry is contained within the price of wood. He knows he can purchase wood of the required quality at such-and-such a price, and no additional knowledge of forestry is needed for the task he is called upon to perform. Prices also signal scarcities that producers may know nothing about. House-builders in Peru may know nothing about the housing market in China, but they may nevertheless cut back on their usage of wood in response to a spate of house building in China because an increase in demand for wood in China raises the price of wood worldwide. The same is true of our bread and cheese model. Producers of bread need know nothing about the technology of cheese-making. It is sufficient for them to respond to price signals in their usage of land.

A forth virtue of markets with private property is to circumvent bargaining. As discussed above and as will be elaborated in later chapters, bargaining is not always circumvented and almost never completely. No market-clearing price can be identified in many unique person-to-person transactions. There is nevertheless a large domain of activities governed by prices, and the surplus over which people bargain is often small enough that bargains can be struck, not costlessly, but with little enough expenditure of time and money to keep the economy running. By contrast, a centrally planned economy would have to rely entirely on bargaining or command. The organizer is either a despot or a representative of the population at large. There is no need for bargaining if he is a despot because what he says goes. Bargaining may re-emerge among the members of a ruling class. Bargaining becomes unavoidable when the organizer is representative of the population at large and a balance must be struck among competing interests in society. The organizer must decide how practitioners of each and every trade are to be remunerated. He must specify the ranks in the different hierarchies of production, assign people to ranks, and decide how the occupants of every rank are to be rewarded. The organization of the economy becomes one vast multi-person bargaining problem that would have to be solved politically if at all. Little wonder that full-blown socialist economies where the entire means of production are owned collectively through the intermediary of the state are invariably dictatorial in practice.

The fifth virtue of the market is its compatibility with and support for democratic government. There are two aspects of this virtue, one psychological and the other political. The psychological aspect is somewhat problematic. It is often alleged that the experience of participation in the market endows citizens with the independence of mind, respect for others and mistrust of authority that is required for participation in a democratic society. All hierarchy breeds arrogance and subservience. A market economy cannot dispense with hierarchy altogether, but a society without markets must be organized as one vast hierarchy from top to bottom. Firms must be organized hierarchically, but their authority over their workers is tempered by the option of a dissatisfied worker to seek employment elsewhere or to go into business for himself. Competition among firms places bounds on the discretion of management. Stock markets punish arbitrary behavior. The political aspect focusses not upon the character of the citizen, but upon institutions themselves. As in virtually all economics, people are postulated to be greedy and selfish. The alleged political virtue of markets is that government by majority-rule voting can only be maintained in a society of such people when getting and spending is taken out of the political arena, so that voting for leaders need not at the same time be voting about who is to be rich and who is to be poor. The psychological aspect of this virtue seems plausible in the light of the descriptions of predatory government in chapter 2 and of markets in this chapter, but nothing more will be said about it in this book. The political aspect will be discussed in some detail in the chapters on voting, administration, and law.

The competitive economy has vices too. An important, though partially correctable, vice is a tendency to generate a wider distribution of income than many people would prefer, an inequality of income that an ideal organizer could easily correct. An organizer could collect all the bread and cheese produced in the optimal assignment of plots of land to goods and then divide up the total produce equally among the five people. As shown in table 3.4, each person would be supplied with 6.8 loaves (34/5) of bread and 3.4 pounds (17/5) of cheese. Reliance on an organizer becomes very much more problematic when people differ in skill and tastes, when inequality of remuneration is required as a goad to productivity and when the organizer's power over the economy may be misused in the interest of a ruling class. A degree of redistribution of income in an economy with private property may be the better bet.

Finally, a problem of method should be recognized before we turn to other matters. In comparing markets with central organization of the economy, it is important to avoid the error of weighing the ideal in one case against the actual in the other. It is important not to weigh, for example, the advantages of markets in our simplified model of the economy against central organization with all its defects in actual economies; and, of course, the opposite error is equally dangerous. We would like to weigh actual markets against actual organization. That may not be feasible because the mind has no direct pipeline to reality and one can only reason about the economy through the intermediary of models that correspond imperfectly to the economy itself. The best we can do is to try to identify as much as possible of the full political and economic consequences of any instance of public intervention in the economy and to judge how the common good might best be served.

Chapter **Four**

PUTTING DEMAND AND SUPPLY
CURVES TO WORK

*You can teach a parrot to be an economist. Just get it to repeat over and
over again: supply and demand, supply and demand.*

The simple model of demand and supply is at once a reminder of how resources are
guided by prices and a device for the analysis of public policy. The price mechanism was
the subject of chapter 3. This chapter is about the analysis of public policy. The chapter
begins with the technology of demand and supply curves, introducing the concepts
of *deadweight loss, surplus*, and *the full cost to the tax payer per additional dollar of tax
revenue*, all representable as areas on the demand and supply diagram. Deadweight
loss is the harm to society from the tax payer's diversion of consumption from more
taxed to less taxed goods. Surplus is the benefit of having access to a commodity
over and above the cost of producing it. The full cost to the tax payer per additional
dollar of tax revenue is central in determining whether public expenditure – on roads,
public buildings, education or anything else – is warranted. Economic arguments are
clarified when shapes of demand and supply curves are signified by their *elasticities*. The
second part of the chapter employs these concepts in expounding some of the lessons
of economics: the superiority of income taxation over excise taxation, the virtues of
free trade, the harm from monopoly, the logic of patents, identifying circumstances
where these lessons would seem to be valid together with important exceptions and
limitations. The chapter concludes with a close examination of some properties of
demand curves.

THE TECHNOLOGY OF DEMAND AND SUPPLY CURVES

The excess burden of taxation when the taxed good is costless to produce

Throughout most of this chapter, it will be assumed, as was assumed in chapter 3,
that there are only two goods and that those goods are bread and cheese. We begin,

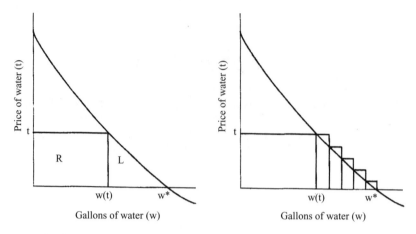

Figure 4.1   The deadweight loss from a tax on water.

however, with an even simpler assumption. Suppose people consume, not bread and cheese, but bread and water where the significant difference between cheese and water is that water is a free good with no alternative cost of production in terms of bread. Imagine an economy where people are either farmers or policemen. Each farmer produces b^{max} loaves of bread and nothing else. As in chapter 2, a police force is required to protect people from one another. A fixed number of police – no more, no less – is required to maintain order, and the police are paid enough that they are just as well off as farmers. Water is a free good in the sense that it is available in unlimited amounts – as much as anyone would ever want to drink – from a well in the town square. The key assumption is that water can be taxed but bread cannot. Think of farmers as widely dispersed throughout the land in places where the tax collector cannot find them. By contrast, as there is only one well, the tax collector has no difficulty in determining how much water each person takes or in collecting tax. Everybody, including the police, pays the tax on water. The tax is assessed in loaves per gallon. A tax revenue of R loaves per person is required to finance the police force.

The assumption that bread cannot be taxed is representative of the fact that some goods are taxable and others are not. The question at hand is whether this restriction matters. Given that a tax on water can be collected fairly and expeditiously, does it matter to the representative consumer that public revenue could not be acquired by a tax on bread instead? One might be inclined to suppose that the restriction is of no importance because one tax is as good as another as long as everybody is affected identically and the required revenue is obtained. That would be mistaken. To see why, consider the demand for water as illustrated in figure 4.1.

The demand curve for water is illustrated in figure 4.1 with the "price" of water, in loaves per gallon, on the vertical axis and gallons per person on the horizontal axis. For any given quantity of water, the corresponding demand price is the number of loaves of bread per gallon one would be prepared to pay for one extra glass of water. The demand curve is illustrated twice, side by side, to emphasize different aspects of the taxation of water. It cuts the horizontal axis at w^*, signifying that w^* gallons of water per head would be consumed if water were available free of charge. Strictly speaking, all demand curves must cut the vertical axis at a point of satiation for the person or group to which the demand curve refers, but that is normally of no practical importance unless goods are free.

A tax on water is more burdensome to the tax payer than an equivalent (in the sense of generating equal revenue) tax on bread. One way or another, R loaves of bread per person must be procured. When the R loaves of bread are procured by a tax on bread, everybody's consumption of bread is reduced by R loaves, but nobody's consumption of water is affected. Everybody consumes as much water as before. By contrast, when the R loaves of bread are procured by a tax on water, every person's consumption of bread is once again reduced by R loaves, but everybody's consumption of water is reduced as well. Taxation of water makes water expensive, reducing the amount of water each person chooses to drink. The amount of bread one would be prepared to give up to avoid this tax-induced reduction in the amount of water consumed is the excess burden, or deadweight loss, from the tax on water. It is a cost to the tax payer over and above the cost of the tax he actually pays. Thus the full burden of taxation to the tax payer includes not just the bread he actually pays as tax, but the water he is induced not to drink, despite the fact that his cutback in consumption of water is of no use to the policeman or anybody else. In short,

The full cost of taxation (measured in loaves of bread)
  = the reduction in the consumption bread (the tax revenue)
    + the value in terms of bread of the reduction in the
      consumption of water (deadweight loss)   (1)

For any given tax on water, the revenue from the tax and the deadweight loss from taxation can be represented as areas on figure 4.1. Since water would be free in the absence of the tax, the price of water and the tax on water are one and the same, and the demand curve for water can be represented by the equation $w = w(t)$ where t is the height of the demand curve when w gallons of water are consumed. Everybody, including the policeman, is taxed at a rate of t loaves of bread per gallon of water taken from the well. From the point of view of the user of water, the tax on water is a price. With a tax of t loaves per gallon, the revenue from the tax becomes $tw(t)$, represented on figure 4.1 by the rectangle R with base $w(t)$ and height t.

When the required revenue is extracted by a tax on bread, each person consumes $b^{max} - R$ loaves of bread and w^* gallons of water which is all anybody wants to drink when water is free. When the required revenue is extracted indirectly by a tax on water, each person consumes $b^{max} - R$ loaves of bread as before, but only $w(t)$ gallons of water. The source of deadweight loss is that what is in reality a transfer of bread from each tax payer to the rest of society – a transfer triggered by consumption of water – is seen by the tax payer as equivalent to a genuine cost of production. If water had to be produced and if the production of each gallon of water required the use of resources that might have been used to produce t loaves of bread instead, then people would be better off acquiring $w(t)$ rather than w^* gallons, for only when consumption of water is reduced to $w(t)$ would an extra gallon be worth the bread forgone to acquire it. Taxation induces people to look upon water as though it had been produced despite the fact that acquisition of water entails no loss of bread at all. The magnitude of the deadweight loss is the value in terms of bread of the tax-induced wastage of $w^* - w(t)$ gallons of water per tax payer when public revenue is acquired by the taxation of water rather than bread. The deadweight loss is an amount of bread just sufficient to compensate the representative consumer for the tax-induced wastage of water.

Deadweight loss is represented on the left-hand side of figure 4.1 as the triangular area L. To see why this is so, turn to the right-hand side of figure 4.1. The distance from $w(t)$ to w^* is divided into equal segments. In the figure, there are five such segments, but the choice of the number of segments is arbitrary. When there are n segments, the width, Δw, of each segment must be $[w^* - w(t)]/n$. Over each segment, a thin rectangle is constructed, equal in height to the demand curve at the beginning of the segment. By definition, the height of the demand curve over any point on the horizontal axis is the value of water – expressed as loaves per gallon – at that point. Thus the area of the thin rectangle constructed over the range from w to $w + \Delta w$ is the value of an extra Δw gallons of water, the amount of bread one would be prepared to give up in exchange for the extra water, when one has w gallons already. The height of the rectangle over the first segment to the right of $w(t)$ is the value of an extra gallon of water when one has $w(t)$ gallons already, the height of the rectangle over the next segment is the value in terms of bread of an extra gallon of water when one has $w(t) + \Delta w$ gallons already, and so on. The tiny triangles above the demand curve may be ignored because the sum of the areas of all these triangles approaches 0 when n becomes large. The sum of all the areas of all the rectangles from $w(t)$ to w^* is the triangular area L on the left-hand side of figure 4.1, the full value in terms of bread of an extra $w^* - w(t)$ gallons of water when one has $w(t)$ gallons already.

Taxation yielding a revenue of R imposes a cost on the tax payer of $R + L$. Since R and L are defined as amounts of bread, the ratio of L/R is dimensionless and may equally be thought of as loaves of deadweight loss per loaf of tax revenue, or as dollars of deadweight loss per dollar of tax revenue. On the latter interpretation, the full cost of taxation per dollar of tax revenue is $(R + L)/R$. If R is 1,000 loaves of bread and L is 200 loaves of bread, then the full cost per dollar of tax revenue becomes $1.20. The police force should be hired if and only if the benefit of the police force exceeds $1.20 for every dollar of taxation required to finance it.

Illustrating tax revenue, deadweight loss and surplus as areas on the demand and supply diagram

Return now to the bread and cheese economy, and suppose that cheese can be taxed but bread cannot. In principle, the tax on cheese could be assessed in pounds of cheese or in loaves of bread. Of every pound of cheese produced, one might be required to pay, for instance, an ounce of cheese or, alternatively, a half a loaf of bread to the tax collector. Assume for convenience that the numeraire in this economy is bread; the price of cheese is reckoned in loaves per pound and the tax on cheese is assessed in loaves per pound as well.

The impact of taxation is shown on figure 4.2, a standard demand and supply curve for cheese with price, p, graduated as loaves per pound on the vertical axis and quantity, c, graduated as pounds per person on the horizontal axis. Once again, the demand

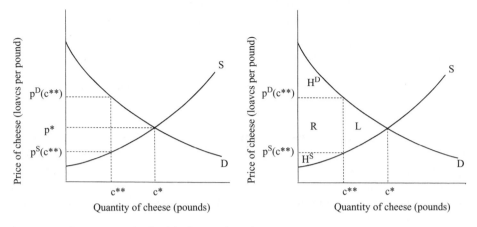

Figure 4.2   Tax revenue, deadweight loss, and surplus.

and supply curves are shown twice, side by side, each version conveying slightly different information. In the absence of taxation, the quantity of cheese produced and consumed would be c* where the demand and supply curves intersect and the price of cheese would be p*. With the imposition of a tax of t loaves per pound, the quantity of cheese falls from c* to c** at which the gap between the demand and supply prices is just equal to the tax. The demand price – the amount of bread people would be willing to give up to acquire an extra pound of cheese – rises from p* to $p^D(c^{**})$ and the supply price – the amount of bread that must be sacrificed to acquire an extra pound of cheese – falls from p* to $p^S(c^{**})$ where

$$p^D(c^{**}) - p^S(c^{**}) = t \tag{2}$$

The effect of the tax on cheese is to divert resources from the production of cheese to the production of bread, lowering the cost of cheese in terms of bread and raising its valuation as shown in figure 4.2.

All prices and quantities are shown on the left-hand side of figure 4.2. The right-hand side divides the area between the demand and supply curve into smaller areas – R, L, H^D and H^D – with important economic implications.

1 The area R is the revenue from the tax on cheese.
2 The area L is the deadweight loss, or excess burden, of taxation. It is the harm, assessed in loaves of bread, from the tax-induced diversion of production and consumption from taxed cheese to untaxed bread.
3 The area H^D is the remaining benefit to consumers from the availability of cheese, even though cheese is made more expensive by the imposition of the tax.
4 The area H^S is the remaining benefit of being able to produce cheese, even though the producer's price of cheese is reduced by the imposition of the tax.
5 The total area between the demand and supply curves – $R + L + H^D + H^S$ – is the benefit to people of being able to produce both bread and cheese rather than bread alone when production and consumption of cheese is not restricted by taxation.

Called the *surplus* from the availability of cheese, it is the amount of extra bread one would require, over and above what people could produce for themselves, to compensate for the loss of the option to produce cheese as well. The sum of H^D and H^S is the residual surplus when cheese is taxed. By definition,

$$\text{Total surplus} = \text{revenue} + \text{deadweight loss} + \text{residual surplus} \qquad (3)$$

These interpretations of the areas on the demand and supply diagram are not immediately obvious, but will be explained in the course of this chapter. Note, however, that the interpretation of areas on the demand and supply diagram as amounts of bread is an immediate consequence of the definition of price. Since the dimension of area is quantity × price, the dimension of quantity is pounds of cheese, and the dimension of price is loaves of bread per pound of cheese, the dimension of area must be loaves of bread – pounds × (loaves/pounds).

The interpretation of R as tax revenue is straightforward. The revenue from the tax is tc^{**} which, using equation (2), is equal to $[p^D(c^{**}) - p^S(c^{**})]c^{**}$ which is precisely R. The interpretation of the area L as waste requires some explanation.

Deadweight loss

A minor extension of the bread and water example establishes the area L in figure 4.2 as the deadweight loss from the tax on cheese. This is shown with the aid of figure 4.3 pertaining to the bread and cheese economy but combining features of both figure 4.1 and figure 4.2. Once again, a tax on cheese reduces consumption from c^* to c^{**}, increasing the output of bread accordingly, raising the demand price of cheese from p^* to $p^D(c^{**})$ and lowering the supply price of cheese from p^* to $p^S(c^{**})$. As in figure 4.1, the distance from c^{**} to c^* is divided into n equal segments. Then, above each segment constructs a pillar extending to the demand curve but originating not from the horizontal axis as in figure 4.1, but from the supply curve. One such pillar is shaded. It is the pillar over the segment from c to $c + \Delta c$. The height of that pillar is $p^D(c) - p^S(c)$, its width is Δc, and its area must therefore be $[p^D(c)\Delta c - p^S(c)\Delta c]$. From the definitions of demand and supply curves, it follows at once that the expression $p^D(c)\Delta c$ is the amount of extra bread that leaves a person as well off as before and the expression $p^S(c)\Delta c$ is the amount of extra bread produced when the output of cheese is reduced from $c + \Delta c$ pounds to c pounds per person and the output of bread is increased accordingly. The difference $[p^D(c) - p^S(c)]\Delta c$ must therefore be the net loss, measured in loaves of bread, from the reduction in the output of cheese when resources freed up from the production of cheese are devoted to the production of extra bread.

Since the area of each pillar in figure 4.3 is the bread-equivalent of the consumer's loss as the consumption of cheese is reduced along the segment at its base, the entire area between the demand curve and the supply curve over the range from c^{**} to c^*, being the sum of the areas of all the pillars, must equal the total loss defined as the amount of extra bread one would require to make the representative consumer

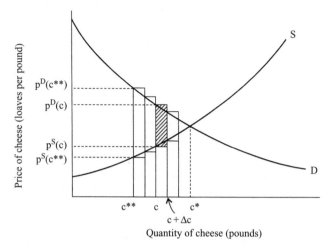

Figure 4.3 The deadweight loss from the taxation of cheese.

as well off as he would be without the tax-induced reduction in the production and consumption of cheese. Ignore the tiny triangles above the demand curve and below the supply curve in figure 4.3 because these shrink to insignificance as the number of segments placed between c^* and c^{**} becomes very large. Taxation provokes people to produce and consume less cheese and correspondingly more bread even though everybody would be better off if nobody responded that way.

Surplus: the discovery of cheese

The full surplus from cheese is defined as the amount of extra bread required, over and above the amount people could produce for themselves, to compensate for the loss of the option of producing and consuming cheese as well. It is measured by the entire area between the demand and the supply curves in figure 4.2 over the range of c from the origin to c^*. This can be demonstrated in two ways, an easy but slightly imprecise way and a more complex way that identifies the exact conditions under which the equivalence is valid. We shall consider both. The simple way involves nothing more than the observation that the deadweight loss L would occupy the entire area between the demand and supply curves if the tax on cheese were high enough to drive out consumption of cheese altogether. Also, having interpreted the total area between the demand and supply curves as the total surplus, the interpretations of H^D and H^S in figure 4.2 become obvious. Together, they must be the residual surplus after the loss of the tax revenue, R, and the deadweight loss, L. The consumers' surplus H^D is the full surplus as it would be if the supply curve were flat at a distance $p^D(c)$ above the horizontal axis. The producers' surplus, H^S, is the full surplus as it would be if the demand curve were flat at a distance $p^S(c)$ above the horizontal axis.

The other demonstration is a development of figure 3.5 explaining how demand and supply curves on the bottom part of the figure are derived from indifference curves and the production possibility curve on the top. For the purpose of exposition, it is convenient to begin with an economy where only bread can be produced and then to measure the gain from the discovery of how to make cheese.

The gain cannot be expressed as utility directly because utility is "ordinal." Recall the conceptual experiment in which Robinson Crusoe's indifference curves were discovered. He was asked a long series of questions of the general form, "Do you prefer this to that?" where this and that were bundles of bread and cheese. From the answers to such questions, there could be drawn boundary lines separating all bundles that are preferred to some given bundle from all bundles that are dispreferred. The boundary lines themselves were the indifference curves. What is important to emphasize now is that the process of questioning and answering that yielded the shapes of the indifference curves did not at the same time yield any natural numbering of indifference curves. Numbers had to be imposed arbitrarily if they were to be obtained at all, the only constraint being that higher numbers be attached to higher curves. Thus three indifference curves numbered as 1, 2, and 3 could equally well be numbered as 7, 8, and 100, or as any increasing sequence at all. Similarly, the postulated utility function in the last chapter, u = bc, should be interpreted as nothing more than an assumption about the shapes of indifference curves and no significance should be attached to the absolute value of utility. The functions $u = (bc)^2$ or $u = A(bc)$, where A is any positive parameter, or $u = bc + K$, where K is any parameter at all, would contain exactly the same information. Any transformation of the function u = bc would do as long as the transformed value of u is an increasing function of bc. A function is said to be ordinal when meaning can be attached to the direction but not the magnitude of change. Utility is ordinal in that sense. An increase in utility is an ambiguous measure of the gain from public policy. But to claim that utility is ordinal is not to claim that improvement cannot be measured at all or that utility has no bearing on such measurement. People's benefit from the discovery of cheese can be measured as a utility-equivalent amount of bread, the amount of extra bread required to make one as well off as one would become from the discovery of how to make cheese.

Construction of such a measure requires a change in our working assumption about the shapes of indifference curves. The postulated utility function u = bc served us well in the last chapter because it yielded important results simply and because its special properties did not lead us seriously astray. Now we run into trouble. The difficulty with this utility function is the implication that both goods are indispensable. No amount of bread could ever compensate people for the loss of the opportunity to consume cheese as well, for u = 0 whenever b = 0 or c = 0. This implication is sometimes quite realistic as, for instance, if c is interpreted as all food and b is interpreted as all clothing. Invented goods cannot be indispensable in that sense because people must have survived prior to the invention. To represent the gain from invention, a new representation of utility is required.

The new postulated utility function of the representative consumer is

$$u = \theta\sqrt{c} + (1 - \theta)\sqrt{b} \tag{4}$$

where b and c are his consumption of bread and cheese and where θ is a parameter assumed to lie between 0 and 1. Like the utility function u = bc, the new utility function in equation (4) is bowed inward implying that, if a person is indifferent between two slices of bread and two slices of cheese, he must prefer a combination of one slice of bread and one slice of cheese. It is easily shown that the associated demand price of cheese in terms of bread becomes[1]

$$p^D = [\theta/(1 - \theta)]\sqrt{(b/c)} \qquad (5)$$

The new utility function in equation (4) is a little more complicated than the utility function in the last chapter, but it has two properties that will prove useful here: (1) utility does not fall to 0 when one of the two goods is unavailable, and (2) the parameter θ is an indicator of the relative importance of cheese as compared with bread in the sense that, for any given production possibility curve, more cheese is consumed and less bread when θ is large than when θ is small.

Suppose, for example, that people originally consumed 9 loaves of bread and 9 pounds of cheese (that is, $b = 9$ and $c = 9$) and consider how much extra bread would be required to compensate for the loss of all cheese. We are seeking to discover an amount of bread, b, such that a combination of b loaves of bread and no cheese yields the same utility as a combination of 9 loaves of bread and 9 pounds of cheese. By equation (4), the utility of 9 loaves of bread and 9 pounds of cheese is 3, regardless of the value of the parameter θ. To acquire a utility of 3 with no cheese at all, the quantity of bread, b, must be such that $(1 - \theta)\sqrt{b} = 3$, or, equivalently, $b = [3/(1 - \theta)]^2$. It follows immediately that the larger θ, the greater is the amount of bread required to compensate for the total loss of cheese. If $\theta = \frac{1}{4}$, then $b = 16$ loaves. If $\theta = \frac{1}{2}$, then $b = 36$ loaves. If $\theta = \frac{3}{4}$, then $b = 144$ loaves. As θ increases, cheese becomes ever more important in one's preferences in the sense that ever more bread would be required as compensation for its absence.

Initially, people do not know how to make cheese and must subsist on bread. Eventually, it is discovered how to make cheese and, from then on, people may consume a combination of bread and cheese, rather than just bread. Our problem is to determine how much better off people become as a consequence of the discovery. Before the discovery, each person produced b^{max} loaves of bread per day, and consumed all that he produced. The discovery itself can he interpreted as the acquisition of a production possibility curve for bread and cheese. On learning how to make cheese, people do not forget how to make bread. If b^{max} loaves of bread could be produced before the discovery, they could be produced afterwards too if people chose not to produce some cheese instead. The new production possibility curve for bread and cheese together must be consistent with the original productivity at bread-making before the discovery. Suppose the new production possibility curve is

$$b^2 + c^2 = D \qquad (6)$$

where the value of D in equation (6) must be $(b^{max})^2$ if capacity for bread-making remains undiminished. As shown in the last chapter, the corresponding supply price becomes

$$p^S = c/b \qquad (7)$$

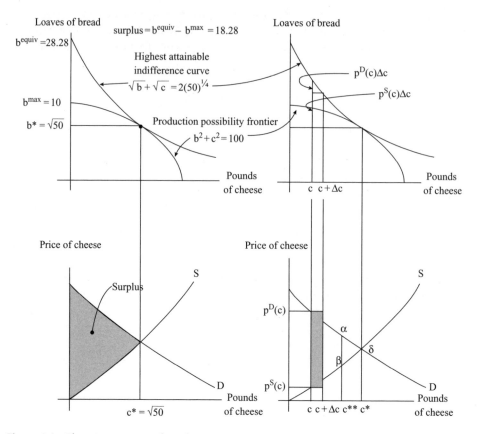

Figure 4.4   The measurement of surplus.

The gain from the discovery of how to produce cheese is illustrated in figure 4.4, which is a development of figure 3.5. In effect, a variant of figure 4.5 is reproduced twice, side by side, with different information in each replication. On both sides of figure 4.5, the production possibility curve in equation (6) is illustrated together with the highest attainable indifference curve in accordance with equation (4). As always, the chosen outputs of bread and cheese are represented by the point at which the two curves are tangent. This is the best people can do for themselves with the technology at their command. The chosen values of b and c depend on the shapes of the indifference curves which, in turn, depend on the chosen value of the parameter θ. For convenience of exposition, it is assumed in the construction of figure 4.5 that $\theta = \frac{1}{2}$ so that θ cancels out in the expression for the demand price in equation (5). It is also assumed that b^{max} equals 10 loaves of bread so that the value of D in equation (6) becomes 100.

Focus for the moment on the top left-hand portion of figure 4.5 showing the production possibility frontier *after* the discovery of how to make cheese, together with the best attainable indifference curves for bread and cheese together. People make themselves as well off as possible by choosing a combination of bread and cheese $\{b^*, c^*\}$ where the production possibility frontier is tangent to an indifference curve.

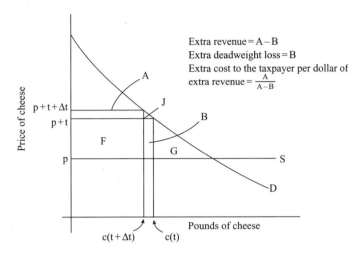

Figure 4.5   The full cost to the tax payer per additional dollar of tax revenue.

Together, equations (5) and (7) imply that the common value of p^S and p^D must be 1 loaf per pound. A different value of θ in the utility function or a differently shaped production possibility curve would have yielded a different equilibrium price. The symmetry in the assumptions about the shapes of the indifference curves and the production possibility frontier ensures that outputs of bread and cheese are equal. The chosen quantities of bread and cheese are $b^* = c^* = \sqrt{50}$. Employing the equation for the production possibility curve (6) to eliminate b in the equation for the supply price in equation (7), it is easily shown that the supply curve for cheese – the relation between quantity supplied and the relative supply price – becomes

$$c = 10\,p^S/\sqrt{[1 + (p^S)^2]} \tag{8}$$

Along the supply curve, the quantity of cheese, c, increases steadily with p^S, from 0 when $p^S = 0$, to $\sqrt{50}$ when $p^S = 1$, to 10 when p^S rises to infinity. With $c^* = b^* = \sqrt{50}$ and with θ set equal to $\frac{1}{2}$, the value of u in equation (4) become $(50)^{1/4}$ which is the highest attainable utility consistent with the production possibility curve in equation (6). Employing the utility function at those values of θ and u to eliminate b from the demand curve in equation (5), it is easily shown that the demand curve for cheese, the relation between the quantity demanded and the demand price of cheese, becomes

$$c = 4\sqrt{(50)}/(1 + p^D)^2 \tag{9}$$

Along the demand curve, the quantity of cheese, c, decreases steadily with p^D, from $4\sqrt{50}$ when $p^D = 0$, to $\sqrt{50}$ when $p^D = 1$, to 0 when p^D rises to infinity. These demand and supply curves are illustrated on the bottom left-hand portion of figure 4.4. They cross at $c = c^* = \sqrt{50}$ where people are as well off as possible with the technology at their command.

Surplus is the measure of how much better off one becomes by learning how to make cheese. It is the amount of bread that would compensate for *not* learning how to make cheese. It is the extra bread required, over and above the original ten loaves, to become as well off as one would be on learning how to make cheese. It is the difference between b^{equiv}, the intersection with the vertical axis of the indifference curve through the point $\{b^*, c^*\}$, and b^{max}, the original production of bread which was 10 loaves per day. By definition,

$$\sqrt{b^{equiv}} = \sqrt{b^*} + \sqrt{c^*} = (50)^{1/4} + (50)^{1/4} = 2(50)^{1/4}$$

so that $b^{equiv} = 4(50)^{1/2} = 28.28$. Thus

$$\text{Surplus} = b^{equiv} - b^{max} = 18.28$$

By learning how to make cheese, people becomes as well off as they would be if, instead, their production of bread increased from 10 loaves to 28.28 loaves per day.

In this example, the surplus from the invention is almost twice the original productive capacity (28.28 as compared with 10) and four times as large as the value ($\sqrt{50}$) in terms of bread of the cheese that is actually produced. Surplus is difficult to measure in practice, but there is reason to believe that it is often substantial. New products may convey benefits to the community well in excess of what people actually pay for them. Cars, air travel, television, and advances in medical technology have conveyed benefits to mankind far in excess of the cost of what we buy. Note that, like the equilibrium price, the surplus depends on taste as well as on technology. We have been assuming that the value of θ in equation (1) is equal to $\frac{1}{2}$, implying that bread and cheese are equally important as components of taste. Had it been assumed instead that θ is smaller than $\frac{1}{2}$, the surplus would have turned out smaller. Had it been assumed instead that θ is larger than $\frac{1}{2}$, the surplus would have been larger. If people did not like cheese there would be no surplus at all. The change in surplus becomes the indicator of gain or loss from the opening of trade, tariffs, taxation, monopolization, and patents as will be shown below.

Though we may not have access to direct measures of distance between indifference curves, we can measure surplus indirectly, making use of an equivalence between *distances* in the upper part of the left-hand side of figure 4.4 and *areas* in the lower part. Defined as the distance $b^{equiv} - b^{max}$ in the upper part of the figure, the surplus can be measured as the shaded area between the demand and supply curve in the lower part.

For an explanation of the equivalence, turn to the right-hand side of figure 4.4 which is identical to the left-hand side except for the removal of shading and the addition of a pipe over the range from c to $c + \Delta c$ where c is an arbitrarily chosen quantity of cheese within the span from the origin to c^* on the horizontal axis. The pipe extends upward through both parts of the figure, cutting the production possibility frontier and the indifference curves on the upper part of figure 4.4, and cutting the supply and demand curves on the lower part.

As shown on the upper part of the figure, the increase Δc in the output of cheese causes a *narrowing* of the gap between the indifference curve and the production possibility curve. From the definition of the demand price, it follows that the height of the indifference curve is reduced by an amount $p^D(c)\Delta c$. From the definition of the supply price, it follows that the height of the production possibility curve is reduced by an amount $p^S(c)\Delta c$. Thus, the gap between the heights of the indifference curve and the production possibility curve narrows by an amount $[p^D(c) - p^S(c)]\Delta c$. The expression $[p^D(c) - p^S(c)]\Delta c$ must be positive when c is less than c* because $p^D(c)$ is necessarily equal to $p^S(c)$ when c equals c* and because the opposite curvatures of the indifference curve and the production possibility curve force $p^D(c)$ to increase more rapidly than $p^S(c)$ as c is reduced.

But the expression $[p^D(c) - p^S(c)]$ has already been identified in figure 4.3 as the difference between the heights of the demand and supply curves at the point c, and the expression $[p^D(c) - p^S(c)]\Delta c$ must be the area of the shaded pipe in the bottom part of figure 4.4. To establish the equivalence between *distance* $b^{equiv} - b^{max}$ on the upper part of figure 4.4 and the shaded *area* between the demand and supply curves over the distance from 0 to c* on the lower part, divide the distance along the horizontal axis from the origin to c* into n equal segments, each of width Δc so that n Δc = c*. Over each segment, the narrowing of the distance between the indifference curve and the production possibility curve on the top part of the figure is equal to the area between the demand and supply curves on the bottom part. The sum of the narrowings is the distance $b^{equiv} - b^{max}$. The sum of the areas is the total shaded area between the demand and supply curves. The surplus can be interpreted either way.

A similar line of argument leads to a measure of the loss of surplus when cheese production is reduced but not eliminated altogether and when resources withdrawn from the production of cheese are reallocated to the production of bread in accordance with the production possibility curve. As the bottom right-hand side of figure 4.4 is a virtual replication of figure 4.3, it is immediately evident that the area $\alpha\beta\delta$ is the deadweight loss from the reduction in the output of cheese from c* to c**. Figure 4.4 identifies this loss as a vertical distance at the point c** between the production possibility curve and the highest attainable indifference curve.

There is a division of labor between these two essentially equivalent measures of surplus. The interpretation of surplus as a distance is best for establishing the meaning of the concept. The interpretation of surplus as an area is best for employing the concept in economic arguments and as a basis for measurement. Estimation based upon demand and supply curves requires information about price, quantity, and elasticities of demand and supply for the commodity in question. Estimation based upon indifference curves and the production possibility curve would require information about the entire apparatus of production and the shapes of indifference curves, a considerably more formidable requirement in a world with a virtually infinite variety of goods than in the simple bread and cheese world of this chapter.

The full cost to the tax payer per additional dollar of tax revenue

The full cost per dollar of taxation to the tax payer might be assessed as $(R + L)/R$, the sum of the tax actually paid and the deadweight loss from taxation expressed as a multiple of the tax paid, but for most purposes that ratio would be the right answer to the wrong question. When tax revenue is employed to pay for the police force, there is little advantage in knowing the full cost of the taxation required to pay for the police force because policemen must be hired regardless. The cost of anarchy in the absence of a police force would normally be far greater than the full cost of taxation to pay for the police force. The relevant question is not whether public services are costly, but when additional public projects, programs, or activities are warranted and how large the public sector ought to be.

Imagine a society that has already hired a certain number of policemen and is deciding whether to hire one more. The extra policeman would be helpful in reducing the incidence of crime but is not absolutely necessary for the preservation of society itself. Once again, all tax revenue is acquired by a tax on cheese. The extra revenue to hire the additional policeman would have to be acquired by a slight increase in the tax rate on cheese, and there would be a corresponding increase in the deadweight loss from taxation. Suppose the benefit of the extra policeman is assessed at \$x and the additional cost is assessed at \$y, where y is the cost as seen by the accountant, the dollar value of the extra expenditure excluding the extra deadweight loss associated with the required increase in the tax rate to obtain the extra revenue.

If the public decision were whether or not to have a police force at all, and if the financing of the police force were the only object of public expenditure, then the right criterion would be whether the total benefit of the entire police force exceeds the total cost inclusive of the total deadweight loss. Had x and y been defined as average benefit and average cost per policeman, then a police force should be established if and only if $x/y > (R + L)/R$. But when the decision is about the enlargement of the police force, the right criterion becomes whether the additional benefit of an *extra* policeman exceeds the additional cost by the value of the extra deadweight loss. In other words, the extra policeman should be hired if and only if

$$x/y > (\Delta R + \Delta L)/\Delta R \tag{10}$$

where x and y are interpreted as extra benefit and cost rather than as average benefit and cost, where ΔR is the extra revenue required, and where ΔL is the extra deadweight loss generated by the required increase in the tax rate to finance the extra expenditure.

Precisely the same criterion is appropriate for any additional public expenditure. An enlargement of the police force, a new tank for the army, a new school or a new hospital is worth acquiring if and only if its ratio of benefit to cost exceeds the critical ratio, $(\Delta R + \Delta L)/\Delta R$, of full cost to the tax payer, inclusive of deadweight loss, per additional dollar of tax revenue (or, equivalently, per additional dollar of public expenditure). As will be discussed in chapter 10, the economy-wide equilibrium value of this ratio – commonly referred to as the *marginal cost of public funds* – depends on the size of the public sector.

The meaning of this criterion is illustrated in figure 4.5 showing how revenue, R, and deadweight loss, L, change in response to the tax rate. To keep the story as simple as possible, the supply curve of cheese is assumed to be flat, indicating that the rate of substitution in production of bread for cheese is invariant no matter how much or how little cheese is produced. The analysis could be extended to allow for an upward-sloping supply curve.

As shown in figure 4.5, the supply price is invariant at p, that is, $p^S(c) = p$ for all c. The demand curve shows how the demand price, $p^D(c)$, varies with c. Since $p^D(c)$ is always equal to $p + t$ in equilibrium, there is no harm in representing c itself as a function of t. Thus c(t) is the amount of cheese produced and consumed at a tax of t loaves per pound of cheese, and $c(t + \Delta t)$ is the amount of cheese produced and consumed when the tax is raised to $t + \Delta t$. As functions of the tax rate, total revenue, total deadweight loss, and the increments in revenue and deadweight loss can be represented as areas on figure 4.5.

At the two tax rates, t and $t + \Delta t$, revenue and deadweight loss are:

$$R(t) = tc(t) = F + B \tag{11}$$

$$R(t + \Delta t) = (t + \Delta t)c(t + \Delta t) = F + A \tag{12}$$

$$L(t) = G \tag{13}$$

and

$$L(t + \Delta t) = G + B + J \tag{14}$$

where F, B, A, G and J are areas in figure 4.5. The area J is the triangular area at the meeting of the areas A and B. It may be ignored because it is very small compared to A or B, small enough that the ratios J/A and J/B approach 0 when Δt approaches 0. The area J will be ignored from now on.

It follows at once that

$$\Delta R(t) = R(t + \Delta t) - R(t) = A - B \tag{15}$$

$$\Delta L(t) = L(t + \Delta t) - L(t) = B \tag{16}$$

and

$$(\Delta R + \Delta L)/\Delta R = 1/(1 - B/A) \tag{17}$$

It is evident from inspection of figure 4.5 that, when the demand curve is approximately linear and as long as the ratio B/A remains less than 1, an increase in the tax rate leads to an increase in the ratio B/A which in turn leads to an increase in the full cost per additional dollar of public revenue.

The relation among tax rate, revenue and deadweight loss can now be illustrated in a simple example. In this example, it is convenient to express the price of cheese in money rather than in loaves of bread, so that revenue and deadweight loss can be expressed in money too. Fix the price of bread at $1 per loaf and let the supply price of cheese – the number of loaves of bread forgone per pound of cheese produced when resources are diverted from the production of bread to the production of cheese – be 2 loaves per pound or, equivalently, $2 per pound. The supply price is independent of the quantity of cheese produced because the supply curve of cheese is assumed to be flat.

Suppose the demand curve for cheese is

$$c = 5 - \tfrac{1}{2}p^{D} \tag{18}$$

In the absence of taxation, the demand and supply prices of cheese must be the same, so that $c(0)$ becomes equal to $5 - \tfrac{1}{2}p$. A tax on cheese of t dollars per pound raises the demand price of cheese from p to $p + t$. Thus, as a function of the tax rate, the demand for cheese becomes

$$c(t) = 5 - \tfrac{1}{2}(p + t) = 4 - \tfrac{1}{2}(t) \tag{19}$$

Table 4.1 How the full cost to the tax payer per dollar of tax paid increases with the tax rate when cheese can be taxed but bread cannot

Tax ($ per pound) t	Demand price ($ per pound) $p^D = 2+t$	Quantity demanded (pounds per person) $c(t) = 4 - \frac{1}{2}t$	Tax revenue ($ per person) $R(t) = tc(t)$	Deadweight loss ($ per person) $L(t) = \frac{1}{2}[c(0) - c(t)]t$	Additional tax revenue ($ per person)[a] $\Delta R(t) = R(t) - R(t-1)$	Additional deadweight loss ($ per person)[b] $\Delta L(t) = L(t) - L(t-1)$	Full cost to the taxpayer per additional dollar of tax revenue ($)[c] $[\Delta R(t) + \Delta L(t)]/\Delta R(t)$
0	2	4	0	0	—	—	—
1	3	$3\frac{1}{2}$	$3\frac{1}{2}$	$\frac{1}{4}$	$3\frac{1}{2}$	$\frac{1}{4}$	1.07
2	4	3	6	1	$2\frac{1}{2}$	$\frac{3}{4}$	1.30
3	5	$2\frac{1}{2}$	$7\frac{1}{2}$	$2\frac{1}{4}$	$1\frac{1}{2}$	$1\frac{1}{4}$	1.83
4	6	2	8	4	$\frac{1}{2}$	$1\frac{3}{4}$	4.50
5	7	$1\frac{1}{2}$	$7\frac{1}{2}$	$6\frac{1}{4}$	$-\frac{1}{2}$	$2\frac{1}{4}$	-3.50
6	8	1	6	9	$-1\frac{1}{2}$	$2\frac{3}{4}$	-0.83
7	9	$\frac{1}{2}$	$3\frac{1}{2}$	$12\frac{1}{4}$	$-2\frac{1}{2}$	$3\frac{1}{4}$	-0.30
8	10	0	0	16	$-3\frac{1}{2}$	$3\frac{3}{4}$	-0.07

[a] [area A less area B] in figure 4.5.
[b] area B in figure 4.5.
[c] [area A]/[area A less area B] in figure 4.5.

Table 4.1 is a comparison of quantity of cheese demanded, tax revenue, deadweight loss, additional tax revenue and additional deadweight loss at several tax rates from $1 per pound to $8 per pound. In constructing the table, it is assumed that the demand curve for cheese is in accordance with equation (19) above. As a function of t, the revenue from the tax on cheese becomes $R(t) = tc(t)$ and the deadweight loss becomes $L(t) = \frac{1}{2}[c(0) - c(t)]$ because the area L is a perfect triangle when, as assumed, the demand curve is a downward-sloping straight line. For any t, ΔR and ΔL can then be computed from equations (15) and (16).

Table 4.1 is largely self-explanatory. Alternative tax rates are listed in the first column. The next four columns show demand price, quantity demanded, tax revenue, and deadweight loss, all as functions of the tax rate. The last three columns show the increase in tax revenue resulting from a dollar increase in the tax rate, the increase in the deadweight loss resulting from a dollar increase in the tax rate, and the full cost to the tax payer per dollar of tax paid. The perverse result in the last four rows of the final column will be explained below.

Several features of this table are interesting in themselves and can be generalized well beyond the confines of our bread-and-cheese economy. First, the higher the tax rate, the larger the deadweight loss. Deadweight loss increases steadily from 25¢ per person when the tax is $1 per pound to $16 per person when the tax is $8 per pound. The larger t, the larger the gap between the demand price and the supply price, and the larger the tax-induced distortion of the pattern of consumption as people are induced to consume less and less cheese even though the value of cheese to the consumer exceeds the cost of production. Second, the relation between the tax rate and the tax revenue is humped. One might suppose that every increase in the tax rate would yield an increase in tax revenue, but that turns out not to be so. Eventually, as the tax rate gets higher and higher, the shrinkage of the tax base outweighs the rise in the tax rate. Revenue peaks at $8 per head when the tax rate is $4 per pound, and revenue declines steadily thereafter. Third, as an immediate consequence of the foregoing, the full cost per additional dollar of tax revenue increases steadily with the tax rate. With a tax on cheese of $1 per pound, the full cost is $1.07. With a tax of $2 per pound, the full cost rises to $1.30. With a tax of $4 per pound, the full cost becomes as high as $4.50. Beyond that, there is no extra revenue from an increases in the tax and the full cost per additional dollar of tax revenue is negative, indicating that the government can increase revenue by *lowering* the tax rate.

The gradual rise, together with the tax rate, in the full cost per additional dollar of tax revenue has immediate implications for public expenditure on new projects or programs. Suppose the government is contemplating a new project – the establishment of a new hospital, school, or road – that would cost $130 million and would yield benefits deemed to be worth $150 million dollars per year. Think of the benefits as spread out over the entire population so that distributional considerations may be ignored. Since the numbers in table 4.1 are per person and the costs and benefits of the project are for the nation as a whole, a conversion is required to bring the information in the table to bear on the problem at hand. Suppose that people consume only bread and cheese, that all public revenue is acquired by the taxation of cheese, and that the numbers in the table refer to purchases and revenues per person per *week* in a large economy with a million people whose demand for cheese is represented by equation (19). Suppose also that the initial tax on cheese is $1 per pound, so that as shown in the second row, tax revenue is $3.50 per person per week, for a total of $182 million per year ($3.5 \times 52 \times 1,000,000$). Extra revenue to finance the new project can only be obtained by increasing the tax rate.

One's first thoughts on the matter would be that (1) a program costing $130 million and yielding $150 million worth of benefits is clearly advantageous and should be undertaken, and (2) if a tax of $1 per pound of cheese yields a total revenue of $182 million, then an extra $130 million of expenditure could be raised by increasing the tax on cheese from $1.00 per pound to $1.71 per pound [because $(130/182) = 0.71$].

Both inferences would turn out to be wrong, and for the same reason. As the tax rate on cheese rises, people shift purchases from taxed cheese to untaxed bread, buying less cheese and more bread. The acquisition of an extra $130 million of revenue requires an increase in tax revenue per person from $3.50 to $6.00 [$(182 + 130)/52 = 6$] per week, requiring an increase in the tax rate on cheese not from $1.00 to $1.71, but from $1.00 to $2.00, as shown in the third row of the table. In other words, an increase in the tax on cheese from $1 per pound to $2 per pound raises revenue per head from $3.50 to $6.00 rather than to $7.00 as one who ignored the tax-induced diversion of purchasing power would automatically expect. The extra $2.50 per person per week is just sufficient to supply the extra $130 million ($2.5 \times 52$) required to finance the new project or program.

The extra tax-induced diversion of purchasing power imposes costs over and above the cost of the tax-financed project itself. With a tax of $1 per pound, people consume cheese only to the point where the value of the last pound is equal to $3, a cost of production of $2 plus an additional $1 of tax. A rise in the tax from $1 to $2 per pound raises the price of cheese from $3 to $4, leading to a reduction of consumption of cheese to the point where its value to the consumer is, once again, equal to its price. Extra taxation induces people to reduce consumption of a good that has become worth $4 per pound even though it costs only $2 to produce. As shown in the second to last column in the table, the additional deadweight loss from this diversion of purchasing power is 75¢ per pound. As shown in the last column, the full cost per additional dollar of tax revenue is 1.30 [$(2.5 + 0.75)/2.5$]. Together, the last three columns show that an additional expenditure of $2.50 per person per week generates an extra deadweight loss of 75¢ per person per week, raising the total cost to $3.75 per person per week, for a total of $1.30 per dollar of public expenditure. Thus, to be worth undertaking, a program or project must cover its cost scaled up by a factor of 1.3. A project costing $130 million must yield benefits of at least $169 ($130 \times 1.3$). A benefit of only $150 is not enough. The project ought to be rejected.

The relation between tax revenue and deadweight loss is illustrated on the top half of figure 4.6 with the tax rate on the horizontal axis and with dollars' worth on the vertical axis. The hive-shaped curve shows how tax revenue varies with the tax rate and tax revenue. The steadily rising curve shows how deadweight loss varies with the tax rate. The bottom half of figure 4.6 shows the full cost per additional dollar of tax revenue, $(\Delta R + \Delta L)/\Delta R$, as a function of the tax rate. The components of the expression, ΔR and ΔL, are read off the top half of figure 4.6. As long as $t < t^{max}$, the expression $(\Delta R + \Delta L)/\Delta R$ increases with t, rising to infinity at $t = t^{max}$ where, by

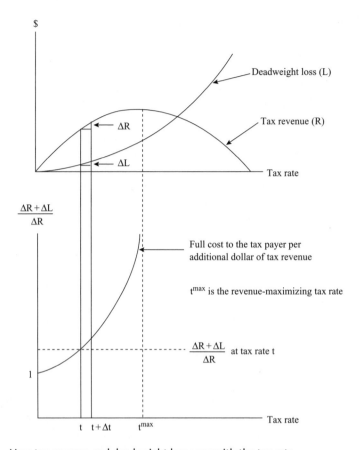

Figure 4.6   How tax revenue and deadweight loss vary with the tax rate.

definition, ΔR is equal to 0. These curves capture the essential features of table 4.1, but they are relevant to any and every tax system where the tax base shrinks because tax payers can divert effort from more taxed to less taxed activities.

The hive-shaped relation between tax revenue and tax rate, commonly referred to as the *Laffer* curve, is characteristic of all taxation: the taxation of cheese in this example, excise taxation, income taxation, tariffs, and so on. No tax-setter – not a monopoly, not a predatory government, and certainly not a government with the interests of the citizens in mind – would deliberately raise taxes beyond the point where the tax revenue is as large as possible. It has sometimes been alleged that countries have occasionally placed themselves on the wrong side of the Laffer curve by mistake. Particular taxes may be on the wrong side of the Laffer curve when some public purpose is served by reducing consumption of the taxed good. The tax on tobacco may be on the wrong side of the Laffer curve to deter smoking, as discussed in the next chapter.

Elasticity as a measure of the steepness of demand and supply curves

It is immediately evident from the inspection of figure 4.2 that the steeper the demand and supply curves, the smaller is the deadweight loss as a proportion of the tax revenue. Thus, for choosing among taxes or for estimating the full cost per additional dollar of public expenditure, it would seem helpful to have at hand a standard measure of the steepness of curves. One's first thought on the matter is that steepness could be measured by the slope, by the change in price per unit change in quantity, or, equivalently, by the change in quantity per unit change in price. Suppose the price of bread is fixed at one dollar per loaf, so that the price of cheese, defined in the first instance as "loaves per pound", can be reformulated as $ per pound. If a reduction of 100 pounds in the quantity of cheese leads to an increase of $2 in the demand price together with a decrease of $1 in the supply price, we would say that the demand curve is twice as steep, on average, as the supply curve, and we would infer that the greater part of the burden of taxation is borne by consumers.

There are, however, several difficulties with the slope as a measure of the steepness of demand or supply curves. First, the indicator of steepness is affected by the units of measurement. A steepness of 2 when the quantity of cheese is graduated in pounds translates into a steepness of 32 when the quantity of cheese is graduated in ounces and into a steepness of 1/4,000 when the quantity of cheese is graduated in tons. Second, the steepness of the demand curves for different goods could not be compared. There would seem to be no intuitively meaningful basis for deciding whether the demand for cheese is more price-sensitive than the demand for oranges. Third, and most important, we would like the steepness of a market demand curve to inherit the steepness of the demand curves of the individuals in that market. If the demand side of the market for cheese consists of 1,000 identical buyers and if the steepness of each buyer's demand curve for cheese is 2, then the steepness of the market demand curve for cheese would have to be 2/1,000. We would prefer an alternative measure of steepness for which these two numbers would have to be the same.

All three difficulties are circumvented when steepness is measured as an *elasticity* rather than as a slope. When two variables change together, the elasticity of one with respect to the other is defined as the percentage change in the former as a multiple of the percentage change in the latter. The elasticity of demand or supply – typically represented by the Greek letter ϵ – is defined as the *percentage* (or proportional) change in quantity in response to a *percentage* (or proportional) change in price along the demand curve or the supply curve as the case may be.

Formally, an elasticity, ϵ, of demand or supply is

$$\epsilon = (\Delta c/c) \div (\Delta p/p) \tag{20}$$

where c now refers to quantity (of any good, not just cheese), p refers to price, Δp is a change in price and Δq is the corresponding change in quantity along the curve. As the supply curve is upward sloping, we expect Δp and Δq to have the same sign and the corresponding elasticity to be positive. As the demand curve is downward sloping, we would expect changes along the curve to have different signs, but, by convention, we speak of elasticities of demand as positive. It follows immediately from the definition of elasticity that a flat demand curve has an infinite elasticity of demand, that a vertical demand curve has a zero elasticity of demand, and that a clockwise rotation of a demand curve around some point translates into an decrease in the elasticity of the curve at that point. The same is true of elasticities of supply, except that a clockwise rotation leads to an increase in the elasticity of supply. A useful distinction may be drawn between *arc* elasticities and *point* elasticities. Arc elasticities are defined over finite portions of demand or supply curves. Point elasticities are defined, as the name suggests, at particular points on demand or supply curves. The distinction is best clarified after demand and supply elasticities are formally defined.

Consider any two quantities of the good in question, c^1 and c^2. The elasticity of supply over the range from c^1 to c^2 is

$$\epsilon^S = [\Delta c/c^1]/[\Delta p^S/p^S] \tag{21}$$

where Δc means $[c^1 - c^2]$, p^S means $p^S(c^1)$, and Δp^S means $[p^S(c^1) - p^S(c^2)]$. Similarly the elasticity of demand over the range from c^1 to c^2 is

$$\epsilon^D = -[\Delta c/c^1]/[\Delta p^D/p^D] \tag{22}$$

where Δc means $[c^1 - c^2]$, p^D means $p^D(c^1)$, and Δp^D means $[p^D(c^2) - p^D(c^1)]$, ensuring that the elasticity of demand is positive even though the slope of the demand curve is negative. These are automatically arc elasticities when there is a finite distance between c^1 and c^2. They become point elasticities when c^1 and c^2 are placed very close together. When c^2 is close to c^1, the numerator, $[\Delta c/c^1]$, and the denominators, $[\Delta p^S/p^S]$ and $[\Delta p^D/p^D]$, of the expressions for elasticity become very small, but the point elasticities themselves remain finite. Elasticities can be estimated from time series of prices, quantities and other variables governing the shifts of the curves over time. The measurement of elasticities is part of econometrics, a subject outside the range of this book but almost always included in undergraduate programs in economics. Though the concept of elasticity is most commonly employed in connection with demand and supply curves, the concept itself is more general. Whenever a variable x is a function of another variable y, an elasticity of x to y may be defined.

Suppose an increase in price of cheese from $2 per pound to $3 per pound leads to a decrease in a person's demand for cheese from 4 pounds to 3.5 pounds. The elasticity of demand over that range is 0.25 $[(\frac{1}{2}/4) \div (\frac{1}{2})]$. The numerator of the expression, $(\frac{1}{2}/4)$, is the proportional change in quantity demanded, and the denominator, $(\frac{1}{2})$, is the proportional change in price. Quantity units cancel out in the numerator, and price units cancel out in the denominator, leaving the elasticity itself with no dimension at all. Extending the example from one person to a market with 1,000 such people, the elasticity of demand remains equal to 0.25 because a decrease in each person's demand for cheese from 4 pounds to 3.5 pounds is a decrease in the market demand from 2 tons to $1\frac{3}{4}$ tons, which is exactly the same percentage change. Being dimensionless, the elasticity is comparable between goods. It is meaningful to say, if that be the case, that the elasticity of demand for cheese is greater than the elasticity of demand for potatoes.

A number of questions are best framed with reference to elasticities.

1   How is the burden of taxation divided between producers and consumers? As shown in figure 4.2 above, a tax on cheese of t loaves per pound reduces production and consumption of cheese from c^* to c^{**} pounds, raises the demand price of cheese from p^* to $p^D(c^{**})$ and lowers the supply price of cheese from p^* to $p^S(c^{**})$. Denote the fall in the output of cheese by Δc, the rise in the price of cheese by Δp^D and the fall in the price of cheese by Δp^S where, by construction,

$$\Delta c = c^* - c^{**}, \quad \Delta p^D = \Delta p^D(c^{**}) - p^* \quad \text{and} \quad \Delta p^S = p^* - p^S(c^{**}) \quad (23)$$

and

$$\Delta p^D + \Delta p^D = t \quad (24)$$

Thus the consumers' share of the burden of the tax becomes $\Delta p^D/t$ and the producers' share becomes $\Delta p^S/t$. It is easily shown that consumers' and producers' shares depend on elasticities of demand and supply. Specifically,

$$\Delta p^D/t = \epsilon^S/(\epsilon^S + \epsilon^D) \quad \text{and} \quad \Delta p^S/t = \epsilon^D/(\epsilon^S + \epsilon^D) \quad (25)$$

where ϵ^D and ϵ^S are the arc elasticities of demand and supply over the range from c^{**} to c^*.[2]

2   How large is the deadweight loss as a proportion of the tax revenue? Referring again to figure 4.2 and using linear approximations to demand and supply curves over the range from c^{**} to c^*, the tax revenue, R, is tc^{**} and the deadweight loss, L, is $\frac{1}{2}t\Delta c$. The deadweight loss as a proportion of tax revenue becomes

$$L/R = \frac{1}{2}\Delta c/c^{**} = \frac{1}{2}\tau\epsilon^D\epsilon^S(\epsilon^D + \epsilon^S) \quad (26)$$

where τ is the tax rate expressed as a proportion of the price of cheese as it would be in the absence of taxation.[3] Whatever the elasticities of demand and supply, an increase in the tax rate increases the deadweight loss as a proportion of the tax revenue. With a tax on cheese of 50 percent, the deadweight loss becomes one-eighth of the tax revenue when the elasticities of demand and supply are both equal to 1. The ratio of deadweight loss to tax revenue rises from an eighth to a quarter when the elasticities of demand and supply rise from 1 to 2. Note also that if the elasticity of supply were infinite as assumed in figure 4.4, the ratio of deadweight loss to revenue, L/R, reduces to $\frac{1}{2}\tau\epsilon^D$.

3   What is the full cost to the tax payer per additional dollar of tax revenue? Like the ratio of total deadweight loss to total tax revenue, this turns out to depend straightforwardly on the tax rate and the elasticities. Continue to assume, as in figure 4.4, that the supply curve of cheese is flat. It then turns out that

$$(\Delta R + \Delta L)/\Delta R = 1/(1 - \epsilon_{ct}) = 1/(1 - \tau\epsilon^D) \quad (27)$$

where ϵ_{ct} is the elasticity of tax base to tax rate and is just equal to $\tau\epsilon^D$.[4]

Equation (27) also identifies the appropriate mix of tax rates on some commodities when taxation of other commodities is blocked. If there were three goods, bread, cheese, and oranges, if only cheese and oranges could be taxed, and if each tax shifted consumption away from the taxed good toward untaxed bread rather than toward the other taxed good, then a government seeking to minimize the total cost of taxation to the tax payer would choose rates of tax on cheese and oranges so that their full costs per additional dollar of tax revenue – indicated as $1/(1 - \epsilon^D \tau)$ in equation (27) – would be the same. That in turn requires the tax rate on each good to be inversely proportional to its elasticity of demand; the higher the elasticity of demand, the lower the rate of tax. This rule is consistent with the general principle from the preceding section that, if all goods can be taxed, then their rates of tax should be the same. The absence of the elasticity of supply in equation (27) is because, for convenience of exposition, the supply curve in figure 4.5 has been assumed to be flat. Let the supply curve be upward sloping, and equation (27) must be modified to account for both the elasticity of demand and the elasticity of supply.

THE INCOME TAX, MONOPOLY, PATENTS, TARIFFS, AND THE GAIN FROM TRADE

The superiority of the income tax over the excise tax

The incautious reader might suppose that, if the taxation of cheese causes a deadweight loss, the imposition of a tax on bread as well would magnify the loss, increasing the gap between the cost of taxation to the tax payer and the revenue from the tax. That is not so. Deadweight loss arises not because cheese is taxed, but because bread is exempt from tax. Deadweight vanishes when all goods are taxed at the same rate. Furthermore, in so far as the income tax is equivalent to a set of excise taxes at equal rates on all goods consumed, the income tax must be free of deadweight loss.

To illustrate these propositions, consider a society where (1) a proportion T of the population is required to serve on the police force, (2) everybody else is a farmer who can produce either b^{max} loaves of bread per day, or c^{max} pounds of cheese per day, or any combination of the two, and (3) the salary of the police is financed by taxation of farmers at a level just high enough that policemen and farmers are equally well off. Assumption 2 ensures that the production possibility curve identifying all feasible outputs of bread and cheese is a downward-sloping straight line and that the supply curve of cheese is horizontal as shown in figure 4.5.

Diversion of a proportion T of the population from farming to policing reduces total outputs of bread and cheese accordingly. The maximal output of bread *per person* falls from b^{max} to $b^{max}(1 - T)$. The maximal output of cheese *per person* falls from c^{max} to $c^{max}(1 - T)$. The production possibility curve identifying all feasible outputs of bread and cheese *per person* (not per farmer) becomes

$$P^{\$B}b + P^{\$C}c = Y(1 - T) \tag{28}$$

where $P^{\$B}$ and $P^{\$C}$ are the money prices of bread and cheese, graduated as dollars per loaf and dollars per pound, Y is the value of a farmer's production, the common value of $b^{max}P^{\$B}$ which is the amount of money a farmer could earn by producing all bread and $c^{max}P^{\$C}$ which is the amount of money a farmer could earn by producing all cheese. As explained in the last chapter, money prices may be high or low depending on the money supply. But whatever money prices turn out to be, the proportion between them must be invariant as shown in equation (29).

$$p = b^{max}/c^{max} = P^{\$C}/P^{\$B} \tag{29}$$

where p is the supply price of cheese (the rate of trade-off in production between bread and cheese regardless of how much of each good is produced) and where $P^{\$B}$ and $P^{\$C}$ are the money prices of bread and cheese.

When public revenue is raised by an income tax, the required tax rate must be equal to the proportion, T, of the economy's resources transferred from the tax payer to the government. Though equation (28) was constructed as a production possibility curve, it can equally well be seen as a person's post-tax budget constraint displaying the set of options for the consumption of bread and cheese. From among all combinations of bread and cheese consistent with equation (28), a person chooses a combination to place himself on the highest attainable indifference curve, a combination of bread and cheese at which an indifference curve is tangent to the budget constraint, the demand price is just equal to the supply price, and there is no tax-induced distortion in the consumer's allocation of production and consumption between bread and cheese. Income taxation generates no deadweight loss because the productive capacity remaining after the diversion of some workers from farming to policing is employed to make the representative consumer as well off as possible with the resources at hand.

Suppose instead that public revenue is raised by a pair of excise taxes at rates τ_B and τ_C on bread and cheese. A distinction must now be drawn between producer prices and consumer prices. Redefine $P^{\$B}$ and $P^{\$C}$ as pre-tax money prices of bread and cheese received by producers, prices for which equation (29) must remain valid. The excise tax on bread raises the money price of bread to the consumer from $P^{\$B}$ to $P^{\$B}(1+\tau_B)$. The excise tax on cheese raises the price of money cheese to the consumer from $P^{\$C}$ to $P^{\$C}(1+\tau_C)$. Together, these taxes generate a demand price of cheese – the consumers' rate of trade-off between bread and cheese – of $[P^{\$C}(1+\tau_C)]/[P^{\$B}(1+\tau_B)]$. The demand price is either higher or lower than the supply price depending on whether or not $\tau_B < \tau_C$.

In the discussion surrounding the demand curve for cheese in figure 4.5, a tax on cheese was graduated in loaves per pound. By contrast, the excise taxes τ_B and τ_C are expressed as proportions of demand prices. Look once again at figure 4.5 where a deadweight loss emerges because of the imposition of a tax on cheese of t loaves per pound. The deadweight loss may be thought of as arising because of a divergence between the *true* supply curve of cheese represented by the flat line at a height p above the horizontal axis and the consumers' *perceived* supply curve represented by a flat line at a height p+t above the horizontal axis. With an income tax there would be no such divergence because the demand and supply prices of cheese are the same. With a pair of excise taxes, the implicit tax on cheese, assessed in loaves per pound, in accordance with equation (2), becomes

$$t = p^D - p = [P^{\$C}(1 + \tau_C)]/[P^{\$B}(1 + \tau_B)] - P^{\$C}/P^{\$B}$$

$$= [P^{\$C}/P^{\$B}][(1 + \tau_C)/(1 + \tau_B) - 1] \tag{30}$$

which is positive if $\tau_C > \tau_B$, which is negative if $\tau_C < \tau_B$ and which is zero if $\tau_C = \tau_B$. A pair of equal excise taxes is equivalent to an income tax and gives rise to no deadweight loss because no gap is interposed between the demand and supply prices of cheese in terms of bread.

Another way of thinking about excise taxation is that it may create a divergence between the *true* production possibility curve in equation (28) and the consumers' *perceived* options as represented by their budget constraint,

$$P^{\$B}(1 + \tau_B)b + P^{\$C}(1 + \tau_C) = Y \tag{31}$$

As long as the excise taxes are imposed on all consumption of bread and cheese, including what the farmer reserves for his own use, the farmer may be thought of as producing Y dollars worth of bread or cheese and then using his income to buy bread or cheese at market prices $P^{\$B}(1+\tau_B)$ and $P^{\$C}(1+\tau_C)$. To provide the required public revenue for the police force, excise taxes must be set high enough to force consumers to choose a combination of bread and cheese on the net production possibility curve in equation (28). If in addition the excise tax rates are the same, equations (28) and (31) become identical, the excise taxes become equivalent to an income tax, and there can be no deadweight loss. On the other hand, if the excise tax rates differ, the budget constraint in equation (31) cuts the production possibility curve in equation (28), the perceived supply price of cheese differs from the true supply price, and the consumer is induced by taxation to choose the wrong point on the production possibility curve. If only one of the two goods is taxed or if the goods are taxed at different rates, the consumer is driven to an inferior point on the production possibility curve where an indifference curve is tangent not to the production possibility curve itself, but to the perceived budget constraint in equation (31).

The core of the "proof" of the superiority of the income tax over the excise tax is the avoidance under the income tax of a tax-induced diversion of consumption from taxed to untaxed goods. The proof is subject to qualifications. As discussed above, the proof becomes irrelevant when excise taxes are imposed at equal rates on all goods, for, in that case, income taxation and excise taxation are indistinguishable. More importantly, the income tax becomes like an excise tax when some goods are excluded from the tax base. Just as the tax on cheese diverts consumption from cheese to bread, so too does the income tax divert consumption from taxed commodities to untaxed leisure, from paid work to do-it-yourself activities, and from investment to consumption. The tax-induced shift from labor to do-it-yourself activity will be discussed in detail in chapter 9 where it becomes a major impediment to the redistribution of income. The tax-induced shift from investment to consumption can be explained by example. Suppose I earn a dollar in circumstances where the tax rate on earned income is 50 percent, leaving me 50¢ to spend today or to save as I please. If I spend the dollar immediately, my initial 50¢ of tax is all that I have to pay. If I save the remaining 50¢ at, say, a rate of interest of 10 percent, I trade my 50¢ today for an income of 5¢ a year forever on which I must pay an additional tax of 2.5¢ per year. Spending today entails tax of 50¢ immediately. Saving to spend tomorrow entails the same 50¢ of tax today plus an extra tax of 2.5¢ per year forever. That is called the *double taxation of saving*. Spending today is like consuming bread, though with low tax rather than with no tax. Saving to spend tomorrow is like consuming cheese. A rise in the rate of the income tax diverts purchasing power to one from the other. In fact, deadweight loss reemerges under the income tax whenever the tax base shrinks in response to an increase in the tax rate not just because expenditure is diverted from more taxed to less taxed goods, but because resources are diverted from the production of goods to the concealment of taxable income and to the investigation and punishment of tax evasion.

Virtually all taxation induces the tax payer to alter his behavior in ways that are advantageous to the tax payer himself but disadvantageous to society as a whole. Taxation is an involuntary contribution from the tax payer to the rest of the community. As citizen and as voter, a person recognizes that his contribution is reciprocated. As self-interested consumer, a person seeks to minimize his own contribution if and to the extent that others' contributions are what they are regardless of how he personally behaves. One way or another, the acquisition of public revenue requires that goods be taxed. Taxes induce diversion of purchasing power from taxed to untaxed goods, lowering one's tax bill at any given rate of tax, but mandating higher-than-otherwise tax rates for the acquisition of any given amount of public revenue, and making everybody worse off than if everybody could agree not to alter their consumption patterns.

The gain from trade

International trade is a substitute for invention. The surplus from the invention of cheese, illustrated in figure 4.4, is equally attainable when cheese can be purchased abroad. Consider a "small" country – small in the sense that its trade is too small a part of the world market to have a significant effect on world prices – where people's taste for bread and cheese is in accordance with the utility function in equation (4) above, where the parameter θ in the utility function is set equal to $\frac{1}{2}$, where people can produce nothing but bread and where the output of bread is b^{max} per person. People never learn to make cheese, but can buy cheese instead. The country is situated in a worldwide market where bread can be sold and cheese can be bought at fixed money prices, $P^{\$B}$ dollars per loaf of bread and $P^{\$C}$ dollars per pound of cheese. To say that prices are fixed is to say that people can buy as much cheese as they please as long as the values at world prices of their imports and their exports are the same.

$$b^{ex}P^{\$B} = c^{im}P^{\$C} \qquad (32)$$

where b^{ex} and c^{im} are exports of bread and imports of cheese per head. Consumption of bread and cheese become

$$b = b^{max} - b^{ex} \quad \text{and} \quad c = c^{im} \qquad (33)$$

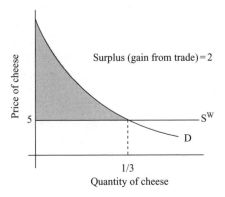

Figure 4.7   The gain from trade.

From equations (33) and (34) together, it follows that

$$b^{max} = b + pc \qquad (34)$$

where $p = P^{\$C}/P^{\$B}$, the relative price of cheese on the world market. Equation (34) is, in effect, the trade-created equivalent of a production possibility curve for bread and cheese together. The only difference between the trade-created equivalent and the actual production possibility curve in figure 4.6 is in the shape of the curve. The trade-created equivalent curve is a downward-sloping straight line rather than a quarter circle, implying that the corresponding supply curve of cheese is flat. With that qualification, the shaded area in figure 4.7 can be equally well interpreted as the surplus from invention or the gain from trade.

Suppose that production of bread is 10 loaves, and that world prices of bread and cheese are $2 per loaf and $10 per pound, so that the relative price, p, of cheese is 5 loaves per pound. Options for the consumption of bread and cheese become

$$10 = b + 5c \qquad (35)$$

which is a special case of equation (34) above. With the parameter θ in the utility function of equation (4) set equal to $\frac{1}{2}$, the demand price of cheese becomes

$$p^D = \sqrt{(b/c)} \qquad (36)$$

The chosen quantities of bread and cheese, b* and c*, are identified by equating the domestic demand price to the world price, and then substituting for b or c in equation (35). Since the world relative price of cheese is 5 and the demand price is $\sqrt{(b/c)}$, it must be the case that $b = 25c$. Substituting for b in equation (35), we see that the chosen consumption of cheese, c*, is $\frac{1}{3}$ pounds, and that the chosen consumption of bread, b*, is 25/3 loaves. Utility in accordance with equation (4) becomes $6/\sqrt{3}$, $[\sqrt{(1/3)} + \sqrt{(25/3)}]$, and the amount of bread, b^{equiv}, that would compensate for the loss of the opportunity to trade bread for cheese is $(6/\sqrt{3})^2 = 36/3 = 12$ loaves. The gain from trade, $b^{equiv} - b^{max}$, is 2 loaves of bread per person.

The gain from trade is represented as an area in figure 4.7, showing demand and supply curves for cheese when only bread can be produced but cheese may be acquired by trade. The demand curve, D, may be thought of as carried over from figure 4.4 because taste for cheese, as represented by the postulated utility function, is the same. The supply curve is S^W where the superscript is mnemonic for "world trade." It differs from the supply curve in figure 4.4 in two respects: It is a reflection of opportunities for transforming bread into cheese through trade rather than through production. It is flat rather than upward sloping because opportunities for acquiring cheese are as represented by the linear production possibility curve in equation (34) rather than by the bowed out production possibility curve in equation (6). Nevertheless, as in figure 4.4, the surplus from the availability of cheese is the shaded area between the demand curve and the supply curve. Note that the surplus from the acquisition of cheese exceeds the value of the cheese acquired. As computed above the surplus is 2 loaves. As is immediately evident from figure 4.7, the value of the cheese (the amount of bread forgone in trade to acquire the cheese) is only 5/3 which is slightly less than 2.

The magnitude of the surplus from trade depends upon the world price. If the world relative price of cheese were higher, the supply curve of cheese would be higher too and the surplus would be less than 2. If the world relative price of cheese were lower, the supply curve of cheese would be lower too and the surplus would be greater than 2.

The gain has been described so far for the import of goods that a country cannot make for itself at all. Though the magnitude of the gain diminishes, a gain from trade remains when imports become a supplement rather than a substitute for domestic production. It assumed above that cheese cannot be produced domestically. Now assume instead that both bread and cheese can be produced domestically in accordance with the protection possibility curve in figure 4.4. In the absence of the opportunity to trade, the surplus would once again be the shaded area between the demand curve and the supply curve in the bottom left-hand portion of figure 4.4. These demand and supply curves are reproduced as the curves D and S in figure 4.8. Once again, the supply curve shows opportunities for acquiring cheese through production rather than trade. Without the opportunity to trade, people would produce c* pounds of cheese per head, and the surplus per head from the availability of cheese would be the triangular area GAH.

Trade provides a second supply curve, allowing people to convert bread to cheese through either or both of two routes represented by their supply curve in production, S, and by their supply curve in world trade, S^W. The best strategy is to go some distance along both routes. Consume c^D pounds of cheese, for which the demand price (the height of the demand curve) is just equal to the world price of cheese, p^W. Produce c^S, pounds of cheese, for which the supply price (the height of the supply curve) is just equal to the world price of cheese, p^W. Buy $c^D - c^S$ pounds of cheese on the world market.

This strategy may be looked upon as combining the two supply curves into a single new supply curve, the kinked curve HEJF, tracing S until c^S and tracing S^W thereafter. This strategy increases consumption from c*, as it would be in the absence of trade, to c^D, enlarging the surplus from the availability of cheese from GAH, as it would be in the absence of the opportunity to trade, to GFEH. The additional surplus acquired by trade is the shaded area EAD. That is the new gain from trade.

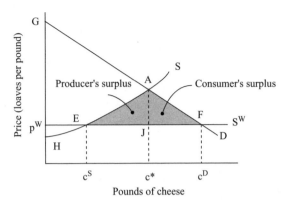

Figure 4.8 The gain from trade when both goods can be produced at home.

When trade supplements production, the gain from trade may be thought of as composed of two parts. One part, the area AEJ, is the saving of bread by the substitution purchase for production, buying $c^* - c^S$ pounds of cheese on the world market rather than producing it at home. The other part, the area AJD, is the gain from the acquisition of an extra $c^D - c^*$ pounds of cheese, worth more than the cost of acquisition if and only if it can be acquired through trade rather than through production. This demonstration of the gain from trade is constructed on the assumption that the world relative price of cheese is lower than the domestic price (the height of the point A) as it would be without the opportunity to trade. There is a similar gain from trade in the opposite case where the world relative price of cheese exceeds the domestic price as it would be in the absence of trade. Cheese would be exported rather than bread. Either way, trade is advantageous.

That trade is beneficial is as true for countries in a world market as for people in a local market. People produce a few things and they want many. People specialize in production to maximize income, and then spend their income on a great variety of goods they require. One person grows peas, another sells cosmetics at the local drug store, another delivers babies, another lectures on economics. Everybody consumes an almost infinite variety of goods and services, drawing on the entire technology and all of the available resources in every country in the world. Trade makes this possible. Trade remains advantageous even when autarchy is feasible – when all of the goods one wants to consume could be produced at home – as long as world relative prices differ from relative prices as they would be if all goods consumed had to be produced at home.

Tarrifs

Figure 4.8 showed the gain from trade when the world price of cheese, p^W, is less than the domestic price – indicated by the crossing of the demand curve and the supply curve at A – as it would be if all foreign trade were blocked. In the absence of trade, c^* pounds of cheese would be produced and consumed. Unrestricted trade led to a reduction in domestic production to c^S, an increase in consumption to c^D, and

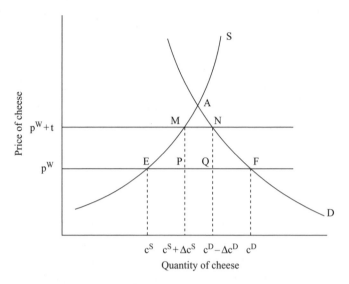

Figure 4.9   A tariff on the import of cheese.

a surplus to the representative consumer represented by the shaded area, AEF. The imposition of a tariff on the import of cheese has three effects upon the economy: It diminishes the gain from trade by raising the domestic price above the world price, it yields revenue, and it may (but need not) lead to a reduction in the world price itself. Concentrate for the moment on the first two effects.

When the world price of cheese is invariant, the impact of the tariff upon the domestic economy is illustrated in figure 4.9, which is an extension of figure 4.8 above. The tariff is set at t loaves of bread per pound of cheese (or \$t per pound when the price of bread is held invariant at \$1 per loaf), and the domestic price of cheese rises from p^W to $p^W + t$. Responding to the rise in the domestic price, domestic suppliers increase production of cheese from c^S to $c^S + \Delta c^S$ and domestic consumers reduce consumption of cheese from c^D to $c^D - \Delta c^D$. The import of cheese is reduced from $c^D - c^S$ to $(c^D - \Delta c^D) - (c^S + \Delta c^S)$, which is equal to the distance PQ (or MN) in figure 4.9. The revenue from the tariff is t loaves per pound imported, equal to the area of the box PQMN in figure 4.9. The impact of the tariff on domestic producers and consumers of cheese is as though the world price of cheese had risen from p^W to $p^W + t$.

By raising the domestic price of cheese, the tariff reduces the gain from trade from AEF to AMN. The reduction in the gain from trade is represented by the area MNFE. Balancing the reduction in the gain from trade (area MNFE) against the revenue from the tariff (area PQNM), we see that there is a net loss equal to the sum of the two triangles, MPE and NFQ. The tariff would seem to be unambiguously harmful because the loss of surplus exceeds the gain in tax revenue.

In short, tariffs chuck away a significant portion of the gain from trade. When the import of cheese is taxed at a rate t, the benefit, or surplus, to the tax payer from the availability of cheese is doubly reduced, once by the revenue from the tariff and again by the deadweight loss from the tariff-induced reductions in the production of bread and in the consumption of cheese. The first of these costs of the tariff is balanced by the acquisition of public revenue to pay for police, roads, schools, and other public facilities. The second is pure waste.

The moral of the story would seem to be that trade taxes should be avoided altogether because citizens are better off when public revenue is acquired by income taxation or by taxing consumption of all goods at the same rate, regardless of whether goods are produced at home or abroad. That is part of the reason why most federal countries forbid states or provinces from levying taxes on inter-state or inter-provincial trade. That is part of the rationale for the European Union and the North American Free Trade Agreement where taxes on trade flows between signatories are limited or banned altogether.

However, one hesitates to accept this sweeping condemnation of all tariffs because tariffs were once the principal source of revenue in many countries and are still imposed by almost every country today. Why, it may be asked, are tariffs and other impediments to trade ever imposed if they are harmful to the countries that impose them? There would seem to be three main reasons.

The first is that tariffs may be relatively inexpensive to collect. Recall the explanation for the tax on water in the discussion surrounding figure 4.1. Throughout most of history, it was difficult and expensive for the tax collector to measure each person's production, and it was virtually impossible to determine each person's income as a basis for the imposition of an income tax. Better to rely for public revenue on the taxation of imports and exports which could at least be observed with some degree of accuracy. All things considered, trade taxes may have been less burdensome than any other form of public revenue.

The second reason is that the excess burden of a moderate tariff may not exceed the excess burden of other taxes the government might collect. Recall the discussion surrounding figure 4.5 and table 4.1 above of the full cost to the tax payer per additional dollar of tax revenue from a tax on cheese, as illustrated in figure 4.4 and expressed by the ratio $(\Delta R + \Delta L)/\Delta R$ where R is revenue and L is deadweight loss. A comparable ratio may be identified for the tariff with revenue measured by the area PQNM in figure 4.9 and deadweight loss measured by the sum of the areas MPE and NFQ. It should be evident from the diagram that as the tariff increases from 0 to something high enough to choke off imports altogether, the ratio of deadweight loss to revenue varies between 0 and infinity. There must then be some rate low enough that the full cost per additional dollar of tax revenue acquired by the tariff is no greater than the full cost of revenue acquired through other methods of taxation.

The third reason is to shift the burden of taxation abroad. Tariffs may be beneficial to the countries that levy them if and to the extent that the burden of the tax is borne by one's trading partners. This consideration was deliberately abstracted away by the assumption that the home country is too small a player in the world market to affect the price of cheese. The assumption was that the world price of cheese was fixed at p^W loaves per pound regardless of how much or how little cheese people in the home country choose to buy. But world prices need not be invariant. A tariff on cheese reduces the import of cheese. If, contrary to what we have been assuming, the home country were a large player in the world market, the tariff-induced reduction in the demand for cheese abroad might lead to a fall in the world price of cheese as suppliers of cheese abroad compete vigorously with one another over shares of the diminished volume of business. Were that so, the imposition of a tariff at a rate t could cause a fall in the pre-tariff price of cheese and a correspondingly smaller rise in the domestic price, $p^W + t$, than if the world price were invariant. If a tariff of t causes the world price to fall by x from p^W to $p^W - x$, then the tariff-inclusive domestic price of cheese becomes $p^W - x + t$. Think of figure 4.9 as it would be if the price of cheese rose from p^W to only $p^W - x + t$. Imports would be somewhat larger than MN, the revenue from the tariff would be somewhat larger too, and the loss of surplus, MNFE, would be somewhat less. Depending on the magnitude of x, the gain in revenue may or may not be sufficient to overbalance the remaining loss of surplus. A tariff may be advantageous to the country that imposes it as long as other countries do not retaliate.

But that is exactly what other countries would be inclined to do. If there is to be a tax on international trade, I want it to be levied by my country rather than by yours. Effects of trade taxes on the volume of trade, on prices in both our countries and on both countries' residual surplus are the same no matter where trade taxes are levied, but the revenue from a tax on trade accrues to the country that levies it. I want to turn prices in my favor. You want to turn prices in yours. When we both act on such considerations, we may both end up worse off than if we agreed between ourselves to keep our tariffs low. Furthermore, from an initial position where we have both levied optimal trade taxes in response to the other trade taxes, there may be a wide range of bargains we might strike – some bargains relatively advantageous to you and others relatively advantageous to me – that make us both better off. Countries bargaining over tariff reduction are like Mary and Norman in the last chapter. The determinacy of the price mechanism gives way to the indeterminacy of negotiation.

Monopoly and patents

In competition, firms respond to prices looked upon by each and every firm as invariant regardless of how little or how much the firm chooses to produce. By contrast, a monopolist – defined as the one and only producer of some good – knows that it can affect prices through its choice of how much to produce, and it acts accordingly to maximize its profit. Monopoly profit is like a private excise tax levied for the benefit of the monopolist. Figure 4.2 above can be reinterpreted as describing a monopoly of the market for cheese. The height of the supply curve is the cost in terms of bread of an extra pound of cheese. The height of the demand curve becomes the monopolist's attainable price of cheese as dependent on the quantity supplied. The area R is the monopoly profit. The monopolist need not tax cheese directly. Instead, monopoly revenue is maximized by the choice of either c (the quantity of cheese produced) or p^D (the price at which cheese is offered for sale) to make the monopoly profit, R, as large as possible. Monopoly is inefficient in exactly the same way that an excise tax is inefficient, by creating a deadweight loss, L, which is harmful to consumers without at the same time yielding any corresponding benefit to the monopolist. The benefit of the monopoly to the monopolist is the monopoly profit, R. The cost to users of the monopolized product is the sum of R and L. In addition, monopoly is deemed harmful to society because the transfer of income, R, to the monopolist from the rest of society is unbalanced by any social gain and because competition among would-be monopolists to acquire monopoly power may turn out to be wasteful. Patents are an exception to the rule for reasons to be discussed below.

Monopoly power may arise naturally, may be conferred by the state, or may be acquired privately. A road or railroad sufficient to accommodate all traffic is a natural monopoly and would for that reason be normally owned or heavily regulated by the state. A monopolist road-owner would charge a revenue-maximizing fee for the use of the road, reducing the flow of traffic in circumstances where the deterred traffic would impose no burden on anybody. (Tolls imposed to reduce congestion are another matter, but there is no presumption that the revenue-maximizing toll and the appropriate congestion-reducing toll are the same.) Monopoly may be conferred by the state for a variety of reasons. Monarchs have sold monopoly rights to raise money for wars, or have granted monopolies to their relatives, courtiers, and friends. Patents and trade unions are monopolies conferred by the state for various reasons. Monopoly may be acquired without the connivance of the state through voluntary coordination among firms within an industry or by one firm replacing all the rest. A firm may acquire title to all known sources of a raw material by buying up rival firms or driving them out of business. Sellers may collude to drive up prices by restricting supply without any one firm acquiring all the rest. Standard Oil's acquisition of a monopoly of petroleum in the United States during the late nineteenth century is an example of monopoly by acquisition. OPEC is an example of collusion to drive up prices. In most countries, deliberate monopolization by acquisition or by collusion is illegal. Governments maintain anti-trust departments that break up monopoly and punish monopolists for certain kinds of behavior.

A patent is a special kind of monopoly. It is a monopoly granted by the state to an inventor on the use of his invention. Typically, a patent is valid for a fixed term of years and subject to a battery of subsidiary conditions such as, for example, that the patent-holder of a very beneficial drug may not, willingly and capriciously, keep the drug off the market altogether until the patent runs out. The justification for the granting of this special kind of monopoly is that it may be the only feasible, or least expensive, way of providing an incentive for invention, and that the consumer is better off having the newly invented product monopolized than if he did not have the newly invented product at all. Once the invention appears, the patent is inefficient for the same reason that any monopoly may be inefficient: the full cost of the patent to the user of the invention exceeds the revenue to the patent-holder. Despite this cost, patents are awarded as inducements to invention, for, even when the revenue from the patent is maximized, there always remains a residual surplus for the users and the producers of the new product. The residual surplus is represented by the sum of the areas H^D and H^S in figure 4.2 when R is reinterpreted as the largest attainable revenue of the patent-holder whose income from the patent is just like an ordinary tax on the parented product and who is entitled by the patent to choose the revenue-maximizing tax.

A patent is a monopoly conferred by the government on an inventor to make invention profitable. Consider once again the discovery of cheese. Whoever makes the discovery must first devote resources to invention, resources which would otherwise be devoted to the production of bread. To induce the invention of cheese, the rest of the community must compensate the inventor. The market does not compensate him automatically because, once cheese has been invented and the knowledge of how to make cheese becomes readily available, the inventor has no edge over anybody else in its manufacture and he can expect no reward for his effort in creating it. He requires some special privilege as a reward for the invention. The inventor might be compensated with a salary financed by taxation. That is how basic scientific research is financed in universities and in government labs. Alternatively, the inventor might be compensated by a prize set in accordance with an estimate of the value to society of the invention. Such compensation would be difficult to administer, unfair and capricious because nobody can be sure what a discovery is worth. Where the invention consists of the discovery of a well-specified product or process, the granting of a patent rewards the inventor without the government having to decide on the value to society of the invention. If the invention turns out to be highly beneficial in the sense of leading to a large surplus, then the revenue from the patent is likely to be large too. Otherwise the revenue will be small. In practice, patents are issued for a term of years after which the monopoly to the inventor is rescinded and anybody is free to use the invention without compensating the inventor.

There is a great deal at stake here. People are better off today than they were two hundred years ago in part because we have learned to make goods with a smaller input of labor, but primarily because we have learned to make new types of goods that our ancestors did not have at all, including electricity, aeroplanes, cars, telephones, radios, television, and the medicines that make our lives longer and more comfortable. Innovation may not have been forthcoming if inventors were not rewarded for their inventions. We return to the subject in the chapter on technology.

Alternative Interpretations of the Demand Curve

The constant money income demand curve

The demand curve was defined in the last chapter for an isolated person constrained by a production possibility curve. A similar though not quite identical curve may be constructed for a person with a given income and confronted with given market prices. For such a person, the demand curve for cheese shows how his purchase of cheese changes in response to changes in the price of cheese when his money income and all other prices remain constant. Consider a person in an economy with many people but only two goods, bread and cheese. He has a money income of Y dollars, and he is confronted with market prices of $P^{\$C}$ dollars per pound of cheese and $P^{\$B}$ dollars per loaf of bread to be spent on the purchase of bread and cheese. He chooses quantities, c pounds of cheese and b loaves of bread, to make himself as well off as possible with the money at his disposal. In other words, he maximizes his utility, u(c, b), subject to his budget constraint

$$bP^{\$B} + cP^{\$C} = Y \qquad (28)$$

which, dividing through by $P^{\$B}$, can be rewritten as

$$b + pc = y \qquad (37)$$

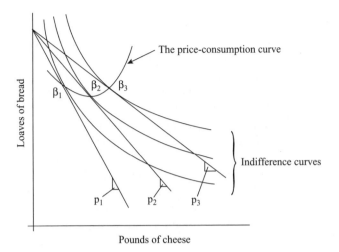

Figure 4.10 The price-consumption curve for the constant income demand curve. The downward-sloping straight lines originating at y are alternative budget constraints.

where p, defined as $P^{\$C}/P^{\$B}$ is the market-determined relative price of cheese, and y, defined as $Y/P^{\$B}$, is the amount of bread the person can buy when he spends all his money on bread.

Consider a person with a money income, Y, of $20,000 per year when the price of bread, $P^{\$B}$, is $4 per loaf and the price of cheese, $P^{\$C}$, is $8 per pound. That person may equally well be said to have an income, y, of 5,000 loaves from which he may purchase cheese at a price of 2 loaves per pound. The advantage of this second version of the budget constraint is that it can be represented together with indifference curves on the bread-and-cheese diagram we have been using throughout this chapter, and a person choosing b and c can be represented as placing himself on the highest indifference curve attainable within his budget constraint.

Now the demand curve shows how a person's purchase of cheese varies when the price of cheese varies but his income and the price of bread remain the same. His behavior is illustrated on the bread and cheese diagram in figure 4.10. Income (in units of bread) is shown as a distance, y, on the vertical axis. For any given relative price of cheese, all attainable bundles of bread and cheese are represented by a "budget constraint," a downward-sloping straight line beginning at y and with slope equal to p, the relative price of cheese. As long as the money price of bread is assumed constant, any change in the money price of cheese, $P^{\$C}$, is a change in its relative price, p, as well, but only the latter can be illustrated on figure 4.10. Three budget constraints are shown for three distinct relative prices of cheese, p_1, p_2, and p_3. Three indifference curves are also shown, each tangent one of the three indifference curves. Points of tangency are labeled β_1, β_2, and β_3. Each point of tangency represents the person's best (utility maximizing) combination of bread and cheese when his income and the price of bread are held constant. A curve, called the "price-consumption" curve, is drawn through all points such as β_1, β_2, and β_3.

As will be explained in the next section, this demand curve is slightly different from the demand curves employed earlier in the book. It is relatively easy to estimate from data on prices, quantities, and income. It is useful as a component of a large model of the economy where changes in income can be accounted for within the rest of the model. It is easily generalized from the bread-and-cheese economy to a many-good economy where a person's demand curve for any particular good shows how his quantity demanded of that good varies in response to its price when his income and all other prices remain invariant. It may be interpreted as showing how the quantity demanded of some good responds to a change in the technology of the economy in the special case where the production possibility curve is a downward-sloping straight line and where the change in technology can be represented by a rotation of that line from its intersection with the vertical axis. A straight-line production possibility curve may be characterized completely by its slope (represented by p) and the height of its intersection with the vertical axis (represented equivalently by b^{max} or y). Any technical change can be represented as a change in one or both of these parameters.

As quantity is assumed to depend on price and income, the consumer's behavior may be summarized in two key elasticities, the price elasticity of demand and the income elasticity of demand. For our bread-and-cheese economy, the *price elasticity of demand* for cheese is

$$\epsilon^{cp} = \frac{\text{percentage change in quantity of cheese consumed}}{\text{percentage change in price}}$$

$$= \frac{\Delta c^p / c}{\Delta p / p} \tag{38}$$

where Δc^p is the number of extra pounds of cheese consumed in response to an increase in the price of cheese from p to $p + \Delta p$ and where income remains constant, and the *income elasticity of demand* for cheese is

$$\epsilon^{cy} = \frac{\text{percentage change in quantity of cheese consumed}}{\text{percentage change in income}}$$

$$= \frac{\Delta c^y / c}{\Delta y / y} \tag{39}$$

where Δc^y is the number of extra pounds of cheese consumed in response to an increase in income from y to $y + \Delta y$ and where the price of cheese remains constant. The first of these elasticities is defined for a given income and the second is defined for a given price. In an economy with many goods, a price elasticity of demand for any particular good is the percentage change in quantity demanded in response to a percentage change in its price when income and all other prices remain constant.

The meanings of these changes in quantity, price and income are illustrated in the two sides of figure 4.11. The left-hand side of figure 4.1 shows price changing when income remains the same, and the right-hand side shows income changing when price remains the same. The changes in the relevant variables – Δp, Δy, Δc and Δc^y – can all be read off figure 4.1. In principle, price and income elasticities of demand can be measured from observations of changes in prices, quantities, and incomes. Consider a person whose income is invariant at $50,000 per year. This week when the price

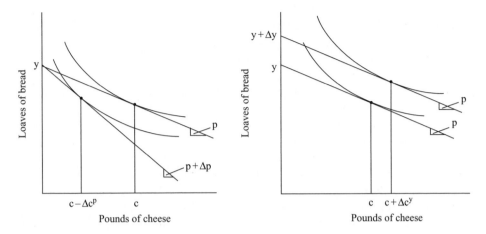

Figure 4.11 Price and income elasticities of demand for cheese.

of cheese is $2 per pound, he buys 3 pounds. Next week when the price has fallen to $1.75 a pound, he buys 3.5 pounds. His implied price elasticity of demand for cheese is $1\frac{1}{3}$, the absolute value of $[(3\frac{1}{2} - 3)/3]/[(2 - 1.75)/2]$. His income elasticity of demand for cheese could be determined accordingly from evidence about how his quantity consumed changed when his income changed but the price of cheese remained invariant. Something more sophisticated than this would be required if quantities consumed changed randomly from time to time for reasons that had nothing to do with changes in prices or incomes. Estimation allowing for a degree of random behavior would be discussed in a course on econometrics. Note that elasticities may vary along the demand curve. The price elasticity of demand may be high at low prices and low at high prices, or vice versa.

A family of demand curves

In this chapter and in the preceding chapter, we have employed four distinct types of demand curves with marked similarities, but with some differences too. Every demand curve connects the quantity consumed of some good to its demand price, defined as the rate of trade-off in use between that good and a chosen numeraire good, and represented as the slope of the appropriately chosen indifference curve. For any particular good, types of demand curves may differ in their assumptions about variations along the curve in the quantities of other goods. In the last chapter, the demand curve was read off the production possibility frontier. That demand curve, which might be called the *constant technology demand curve*, showed how the demand price and quantity of cheese changed together as Robinson Crusoe altered amounts of bread and cheese produced in accordance with his technically given production possibility frontier. In this chapter, the demand curve was read off an indifference curve. To measure surplus and deadweight loss, it was appropriate to construct a demand curve, which might be called the *constant utility demand curve*, connecting demand price and quantity consumed where quantities of other goods were assumed to vary so as to keep the representative consumer on the highest attainable indifference curve. A third demand curve, which might be called the *constant income demand curve*, was discussed in the preceding section. Its focus is not upon the representative consumer, but upon the individual within a competitive market, who earns a certain income, who looks upon prices as externally given and whose preferences, as represented by the shapes of his indifference curves, may differ from those of other people in his community. The fourth type of demand curve, which might be called the *trade demand curve*, shows a country's response to changes in the world price. Exemplified by the demand curve for cheese in figure 4.9 of the last chapter, a country's trade demand curve would be a scaled-up version of a person's constant income demand curve, if the country produced only bread and imported all its cheese regardless of the world price, and if everybody's taste were in conformity with the utility function in equation (1) of the last chapter.

Each of the four demand curves – the constant technology demand curve, the constant utility demand curve, the constant money income demand curve, and the trade demand curve – has its own sphere of application. The constant technology demand curve may be the right demand curve from the vantage point of the policy-maker evaluating the impact of taxes, tariffs, restrictions on the outputs of certain goods or other aspects of economic policy upon the welfare of citizens and upon the economy as a whole. The constant utility demand curve may be the right demand curve from the vantage point of a historian trying to assess the benefit of technical change. The constant income demand curve may be the right demand curve from the vantage point of the consumer in a large economy looking up at prices seen as fixed independently of their individual behavior. The constant income demand curve would also be appropriate in estimating the change in quantity demanded of some good in response to a change in price brought about by technical change, where, for all practical purposes, the economy-wide production possibility curve may be thought of as a multidimensional plane that tilts appropriately when a good becomes relatively inexpensive to produce. As the name implies, the trade demand curve shows the response to world prices of a country engaged in international trade.

The four demand curves, and other types of demand curves as well, are differentiated from one another by what might be called their *auxiliary functions* showing how quantities of goods change together along the demand curve. For any set of indifference curves in our bread-and-cheese economy, there is a well-defined demand *function*, $p(c, b)$, showing the demand price of cheese in terms of bread, p, as a function of the quantities of bread and cheese consumed. That there must be some such function is immediately evident from the representations of indifference curves in figures 4.3, 4.4, and the top half of figure 4.5 of the last chapter. At any point (c, b) in the top half of figure 4.5 of the last chapter, the demand price of cheese is the slope of the indifference curve at that point, and one might reasonably expect that slope to be a function of both b and c rather than of c alone. But the demand *curve*, as illustrated in the bottom half of the figure, shows the demand price of cheese as dependent on the quantity of cheese alone, with no reference to the quantity of bread at all. The demand curve represents a relation of the form $p(c)$, not $p(c, b)$ as in the demand function. Somehow, the demand function $p(c, b)$ must be transformed into a demand curve $p(c)$.

Any such transformation can be represented as an auxiliary function, $b(c)$, which, when plugged into the demand function for cheese, $p(c, b)$, yields the demand curve, $p(c)$, showing demand price dependent on c alone. For the constant technology demand curve, the auxiliary function is the production possibility curve. For the constant utility demand curve, the auxiliary function is an indifference curve, typically the highest indifference curve attainable with the technology at hand. For the constant income demand curve, the auxiliary function is the price consumption curve in figure 4.9. In principle, the choice of auxiliary functions is entirely unlimited, and every auxiliary function gives rise to its own unique demand curve. But the choice among demand curves is not entirely arbitrary. The appropriate demand curve and its auxiliary function are inherent in the problem at hand.

Recognition of the existence of conceptually distinct demand curves leads naturally to the question of magnitudes. Are the different types of demand curves close enough to one another that estimates of elasticities for one type of demand curve can be assumed for all practical purposes to be valid for other types of demand curves as well? Suppose a price elasticity of demand for cheese for the constant income demand curve has been estimated from data of prices, incomes, and quantities. The question is whether that elasticity can be appropriately employed in estimating the effect of a tariff on the quantity of cheese demanded in the nation as a whole (a problem for which the constant technology demand curve would seem most appropriate) or for estimating the corresponding deadweight loss (for which a constant utility demand curve would seem most appropriate)? The answer to this question is broadly speaking "yes" if and to the extent that cheese occupies a small share of the budget of the consumer, but "no" otherwise.

There are circumstances where all types of demand curves fuse into one unique demand curve or where the different types of demand curves become close enough that remaining variations among them can be ignored. Consider the different types of demand curves for cheese in a bread-and-cheese economy. All such curves fuse and the auxiliary functions become irrelevant in the special case where indifference curves are stacked up, one on top of the other, so that their slopes depend on c but not on b. Since the price of cheese, $p(c, b)$, is the slope of the indifference at the point (c, b), a vertical stacking of indifference curves means that $p(c, b^1) = p(c, b^2)$ for every b^1 and b^2. In effect, $p(c, b)$ becomes independent of b, the auxiliary function becomes irrelevant and all types of demand curve become the same. However, vertical stacking of indifference curves, though not impossible, is quite unlikely and unusual. Neither of the two utility functions discussed in this chapter – $u = bc$ and $u = \sqrt{b} + \sqrt{c}$ – conform to that pattern. As shown in equation (2) of chapter 3 and equation (5) of this chapter, both utility functions require the price of cheese to be an increasing function of the ratio of b to c. The price of cheese is b/c in one case and $[\theta/(1 - 0)]\sqrt{(b/c)}$ in the other.

But the different demand curves do fuse together – not completely but sufficiently for most contexts where demand and supply curves are employed – for goods occupying a small part of the budget of the consumer. This will be demonstrated for two of the four demand curves we have examined, the constant income demand curve and the constant utility demand curve. That these curves fuse for goods occupying a small part of the budget can be shown analytically or by example. An example will be presented first, to be followed by a general demonstration yielding a formula for converting one price elasticity to another. The example is a comparison between food and pears, one constituting a large share of the budget of the representative consumer and the other constituting a small share of the budget of the representative consumer. Suppose food and pears are alike in their income elasticities of demand and in their price elasticities along the constant utility demand curve, but very different in their shares of the budget of the consumer. It will be shown that the price elasticity of demand for food along the constant money income demand curve differs significantly from the price elasticity of demand for food along the constant utility demand curve, but that the corresponding elasticities for pears are approximately the same.

Their common income elasticity is 2. Their common price elasticity along the constant utility demand curve is $\frac{1}{2}$. The share of food in the budget of the consumer is 30 percent. The share of pears in the budget of the consumer is only $1/100$ percent. The representative consumer has an annual income of $50,000 of which $15,000 (30%) is spent on food and $5 (1/100%) is spent on pears. To keep matters simple, suppose that the supply prices of food and pears are both invariant at $1 per pound, so that the preceding values are immediately translatable into quantities. Finally, imagine that the price of a commodity (food or pears as the case may be) is increased by 10 percent by an excise tax of 10¢ per pound, raising the price of the commodity in question from $1.00 to $1.10. Demand curves can be said to fuse if the resulting changes in quantity along both demand curves are the same. That is nearly so for pears, but not for food.

Consider food first. Since the price elasticity of demand along the constant utility demand curve is $\frac{1}{2}$, a 10 percent increase in the price of food must induce a 5 percent, or 750 pounds, reduction in the quantity of food consumed, from 15,000 pounds to 14,250 pounds. To keep the representative consumer on the same indifference curve, he must be compensated by *at least* the value of the tax he pays. The revenue from the tax is 10 percent of the value of the new quantity consumed – (0.1) (15,000–750) – equal to $1,425. If the revenue from the tax is not returned to the consumer, as is assumed to be the case in the construction of the constant money income demand curve, then, in effect, his income is reduced by 2.85 percent, [(1,425/50,000)(100)]. With an assumed income elasticity of 2, his consumption of food must be reduced by an additional 5.7 percent, or 855 pounds (0.057)(15,000) over and above the direct reduction from the 10 percent increase in price. Thus the total reduction in the quantity of food consumed from an uncompensated tax-induced 10 percent increase in price must be 1,605 pounds (750 + 855). Along the constant utility demand curve, the price-induced reduction in the quantity of food consumed is 750 pounds, or 5 percent of its original amount. Along the constant money income demand curve, the price-induced reduction in quantity of food consumed is 1,605 pounds or 10.7 percent of its original amount. A 10 percent increase in the price of food reduces the amount of food consumed by 5 percent along the constant utility demand curve and by 10.7 percent along the constant money income demand curve. The implied price elasticity of the constant money income demand curve is 1.07.

Now consider pears. Since the price elasticity of demand along the constant utility demand curve is equal to $\frac{1}{2}$, a 10 percent increase in the price must lead to a 5 percent reduction, or 0.25 pound reduction in quantity of salt consumed, from 5 pounds to 4.75 pounds. Once again the revenue from the tax is 10 percent of the value of the new quantity consumed – (0.1)(5–4.75) – equal to 12.5¢. If the revenue from the tax is not returned to the consumer, as is assumed to be the case in the construction of the constant money income demand curve, then, in effect, his income is reduced by only 0.00025 percent, $[(0.125/50,000)(100)]$. With an assumed income elasticity of 2, his consumption of pears must be reduced by an additional 0.00025 percent, or 0.0000125 pounds $[(0.0000125)(5)]$ over and above the direct reduction from the 10 percent increase in price. Thus the total reduction in the quantity of pears consumed from an uncompensated tax-induced 10 percent increase in price must be 0.2500125 pounds $(0.25 + 0.0000125)$. Along the constant utility demand curve, the price-induced reduction in the quantity of pears is 0.25 pounds, or 5 percent of its original amount. Along the constant money income demand curve, the price-induced reduction in quantity of food consumed is 0.2500125 pounds or 5.00025 percent of its original amount. A 10 percent increase in the price of pears reduces the amount consumed by 5 percent along the constant utility demand curve and by 5.00025 percent along the constant money income demand curve. Unlike food, the reductions along the two demand curves are virtually the same. The implied elasticity of the constant money income demand curve is 0.500025.

For any commodity, the formula connecting the three elasticities of demand – the price elasticity along the constant utility demand curve, the price elasticity along the constant money income demand curve, and the income elasticity of demand – is

$$\epsilon^M - \epsilon^U = s\epsilon^Y \tag{40}$$

where

   ϵ^M is the price elasticity of demand along the constant income demand curve,
   ϵ^U is the price elasticity of demand along the constant utility demand curve,
   s is the share of the commodity in the budget of the consumer, and
   ϵ^Y is the income elasticity of demand.

Equation (89) is established with the aid of figure 4.12, which is an extension of figures 4.10 and 4.11. Once again, the representative consumer has an income of y loaves of bread and he can buy cheese at a price of p loaves per pound. He consumes quantities of bread and cheese represented by the point α_1. His consumption of cheese is $c(p,y)$. When the price rises to $p + \Delta p$, his budget constraint swings clockwise around the point y on the vertical axis, and he consumes quantities of bread and cheese represented by the point α_2. So far, the diagram is exactly like the left-hand side of figure 4.11.

A distinction must be drawn among three price-induced changes in the quantity of cheese. When the price of cheese rises from p to $p + \Delta p$,

   Δc^p is the reduction in the quantity of cheese consumed when income, y, remains unchanged,
   Δc^u is the reduction in the quantity of cheese consumed when income increases by an amount Δy which is just sufficient to keep the consumer on the same indifference curve, and
   Δc^y is the reduction in the quantity of cheese consumed when income is decreased from $y + \Delta y$ to y while the price of cheese remains constant at $p + \Delta p$.

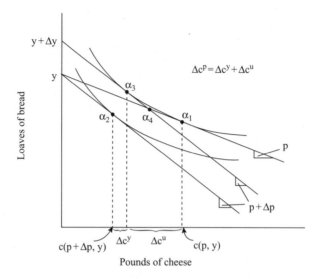

Figure 4.12   Comparison of the price elasticities on the constant income demand curve and the constant utility demand curve.

By construction,

$$\Delta c^p = c(p,y) - c(p + \Delta p, y) = \Delta c^y + \Delta c^u \qquad (41)$$

Consumption of cheese falls by an amount Δc^p which is represented in the diagram by the *sum* of Δc^y and Δc^u. The key step in the demonstration of equation (40) is the representation of Δy, the amount of extra bread one would need to be as well off after the rise in the price of cheese as before. The increase, Δy, is just sufficient to ensure that one's utility on choosing the best available combination of bread and cheese, represented by the point α_3, at the new higher price, $p + \Delta p$, and the new augmented income, $y + \Delta y$, is just equal to one's original utility at the original price, p, and the original income, y. In short, Δy is such that α_3 and α_1 lie on the same indifference curve.

With income held constant, the price increase, Δp, induces a shift in consumption from the point α_1 to the point α_3, reducing consumption of cheese from $c(p, y)$ to $c(p + \Delta y, y)$. By definition, Δc^p is the fall in consumption of cheese along the constant money income demand curve in response to an increase of Δp in the price of cheese. As is evident from the figure, Δc^p is the sum of two parts, Δc^u, the reduction in consumption of cheese between α_1 and α_3, and Δc^y, the reduction in consumption of cheese between α_3 and α_2. Δc^u may be interpreted as the fall in consumption of cheese along the constant utility demand curve in response to an increase of Δp in the price of cheese because the points α_1 and α_3 lie on the very same indifference curve. Δc^y may be interpreted as the fall in consumption of cheese in response to a fall in income from $y + \Delta y$ to y because the slope of the indifference curves at the points α_1 and α_3 are exactly the same. With these interpretations of the terms Δc^u and Δc^y, equation (40) can now be derived from equation (41).[5]

From here on all distinctions among types of demand curves will be ignored on the supposition that the good in question occupies a small share of the resources of the economy or that the errors in inferences from demand and supply curves are not large enough to overshadow the main story in the analysis. One cannot think about society without the intermediation of gross simplifications, but neither can one desist from analysis. All one can do is to be aware of one's simplifications so as to recognize circumstances where one might be led seriously astray. Analysis of public policy with demand and supply curves is no exception.

Chapter Five

TASTE

The tragedy of the commons develops in this way. Picture a pasture open to all. It is to be expected that each man will try to keep as many cattle as possible on the commons. Such an arrangement may work reasonably satisfactorily for centuries because tribal wars, poaching and disease keep numbers of both man and beast well below the carrying capacity of the land. Finally, however, comes the day of reckoning ... the only sensible course for him is to add another animal to his herd. And another; and another. This is the conclusion reached by each and every rational herdsman sharing a commons. Therein is the tragedy. Each man is locked into a system that compels him to increase his herd without limit – in a world that is limited. Ruin is the destination toward which all men rush in a society that believes in the freedom of the commons. Freedom in a commons brings ruin to all.

Garrett Hardin, 1968

The main story in chapter 3 can be summarized in two propositions: that there exists a competitive equilibrium and that it is efficient. Existence of a competitive equilibrium means that there is some set of prices at which the total amount of each good that all consumers want to buy is just equal to the total amount of that good that all producers want to sell, as long as everybody looks upon prices as determined by the market and as independent of his own actions. Efficiency of a competitive equilibrium means that no planner, however knowledgeable, however powerful, however benevolent, could rearrange the economy to make everybody better off simultaneously. These propositions are far from obvious and are generally disbelieved by non-economists. Together, they constitute a significant part of the contribution of economics to the understanding of the world. The propositions have strong political implications. They suggest that the government might best stay out of the running of the economy, restricting itself to the protection of property rights and the broad redistribution of income from rich to poor. The main preoccupation in this chapter is whether and to what extent these implications of the simple model are sustained when account is taken of important aspects of the world that have so far been assumed away.

Concealed in the demonstration of the virtues of the competitive economy were four critical assumptions: that all goods are *private*, that utility is timeless, that information is complete, and that everybody is unreservedly selfish. The main task of this chapter is to relax the first of these assumptions. Ordinary private goods are contrasted with public goods, externalities, and personal goods to be defined presently. There is some discussion of risk. Preferences among goods available at different times are considered by replacing the bread and cheese in the utility function with consumption today and consumption tomorrow. Information and advertising are discussed briefly at the end of the chapter. Altruism is put off until chapter 8.

A private good is a good such that its total output is allocated among people, where each person benefits from his own portion exclusively with no impact, favorable or unfavorable, of one person's consumption upon the rest of the population. With only two goods, bread and cheese, total outputs, B and C, are divided up among the N people in the economy. Person j consumes b^j loaves of bread and c^j pounds of cheese. His utility is $u^j(b^j, c^j)$. The sum of all b^j is equal to B and the sum of all c^j is equal to C. This characteristic of private goods – that total output is divided up among people, each of whom consumes his portion exclusively – extends easily from a world with only two goods to a world with many goods, as long as we adhere to the assumption that all goods are private.

Cheese is a private good in that the pound of cheese I consume is necessarily denied to you. We can share a piece of cheese, but we cannot eat the same mouthful. That is true of bread as well, but not of all goods. We can both watch the same television program, you on your set and I on mine, without interfering with one another. We are both protected simultaneously by the army and by the police. There is a class of *public* goods that people can consume together, all at once. The distinction between private and public goods is important because the virtues of a competitive economy do not extend to the provision of public goods. The market cannot be relied upon to supply the right amount of public goods. Typically though not invariably, public goods have to be supplied collectively by the government if they are to be supplied at all.

Half way between private goods and public goods are *externalities*. One and the same good may convey some benefits to its owner, while at the same time conveying other benefits or harm to the rest of the community. My car is a private good in the sense that you and I cannot both drive the same car at the same time, but my use of the car harms everybody at once when exhaust fumes are released into the atmosphere. The term externalities implies that the harm to society is external to my purpose in using the car, an undesirable but unintended consequence of driving.

There was no provision for risk in the economy as described in chapters 3 and 4. There was no uncertainty about how much bread and cheese each person would consume or about how consumption would be affected by one's choices in production and trade. The world is not like that at all. The future is intrinsically uncertain. Looking ahead, one must recognize that actions today can influence consumption tomorrow but cannot determine consumption exactly. Representation of taste by a utility function can be reconstituted to allow for uncertainty. Utility can be made to depend not just on amounts of different goods, but on amounts of income in equally likely *states of the world*. The accounting for risk gives rise to a utility of income function incorporating a person's degree of risk aversion.

The assumption about time in chapters 3 and 4 was that everything happens simultaneously. Utility was defined in an instantaneous world with no past and no future, or, equivalently, in a world without change, where past, present, and future are all identical. That is implied when we assume that u = u(b, c). Later on in the chapter, the notion of utility will be enlarged to cover goods consumed at different times. An intertemporal utility function will treat bread consumed at different dates as distinct commodities. This reinterpretation of the utility function does not overturn the demonstration of the virtues of the competitive economy.

There follows brief discussions of personal goods and advertising. Personal goods – notably leisure and life expectancy – are private goods like bread and cheese except that their valuations differ from one person to the next. There was no place for advertising in the world of chapters 3 and 4 where taste was not malleable, people were fully rational and all relevant information was available automatically to everybody in the economy. Advertising becomes profitable to the advertiser when that is not completely so. Advertising may provide knowledge about products, certify quality, influence taste, and supply an incentive for the private provision of some public goods.

The chapter concludes with an explanation of the concept of *real income*. Real income was exemplified in chapter 1 by the time series of gross national product per head in Canada, interpreted as indicating the improvement in the Canadian standard of living over a long period of time. In chapters 3 and 4, utility and income were treated as distinct concepts. In statistics of real income, these concepts are fused. The discussion of real income explains how this is done.

TYPES OF GOODS

The utility function is considerably more flexible than has been supposed so far. It can be made to encompass many kinds of goods: private goods which have been the exclusive focus of our analysis so far, public goods, such as the army, that convey benefits to everybody simultaneously, externalities, exemplified by exhaust fumes from automobiles, where one person's consumption harms another person or the rest of society, goods consumed at different times, and risk. Types of goods will be discussed in turn, with emphasis on how each type can be fitted into the utility function, on the extent to which the strong propositions about the existence and efficiency of the competitive equilibrium carry over from a world where all goods are private to a world where other types of goods are important, and on the implications for the role of government.

Many private goods: [u = u(b, c, d, e, f, g, h. . .)]

Though the utility function has been looked upon so far as representing a person's tastes in an economy with only two goods, the function is easily expanded to account for the virtually infinite array of goods and services that people consume: bread, cheese, dates, electric bulbs, fruit, games, houses, and so on. Though not demonstrated here, it can be shown that the nice properties of the competitive economy extend from two to many goods. A demand curve for any good whatsoever shows how the amount of that good consumed is affected by changes in its price when prices of all other goods remain the same. All of the types of demand curves discussed at the end of the last chapter can be reformulated in a multi-good context. The extension of the constant income demand curve requires only that money income remain unchanged as the price of some good varies. The production demand curve and the compensated demand curve can be extended to a multi-good context by combining the change in the price of some good with a change in money income just sufficient to keep the consumer on the production possibility frontier or on the same indifference curve as the case may be.

Public goods and private goods: [u = u(b, G) where b is butter and G is guns]

As discussed in chapters 3 and 4, bread and cheese were *private* goods, defined by the property that society's total supply of these goods must somehow be apportioned among all consumers and that each person's utility is affected by his consumption of these goods, regardless of the amounts consumed by anybody else. Not all goods are like that. Some goods, such as television signals and protection by the army and the police, carry benefits to everybody at once. Such goods are called *public*.

The distinction between public goods and private goods is exemplified by guns and butter. Guns (shorthand for national defense as a whole) are public because each person's benefit depends on the total supply of the nation as a whole. Butter is a private good because each person's benefit depends not on the total supply, but on the portion assigned to him exclusively. Public goods are non-rivalrous; one person's benefit from a public good does not detract from the benefit of any other person. Private goods are rivalrous; the more that accrues to me the less left over for you when total production is invariant. When the army buys a tank, that tank protects us all. When one of us consumes a pound of butter, the rest of us are automatically deprived of the pound of butter he consumes. To account for public goods, the arguments in the utility function are transformed from "b and c" into "b and G" where b, now mnemonic for butter rather than bread, is a person's consumption of a private good, and G, mnemonic for guns, is the total output of a public good.

Consider tanks rather than guns. A country with a population of 30 million buys tanks at a cost of $1.5 million each. When a tank is purchased by the government on behalf of the entire population, the cost of a tank per person is 5 cents [1.5 million/30 million]. A government acting on behalf of its citizens buys the tank if and only if the value to the typical citizen of the extra protection that the tank provides against the enemies of one's country is at least 5 cents. Value in this context is the amount of money the citizen would be prepared to pay for the extra protection that the tank supplies. If the citizen is prepared to pay in 5 cents, the tank should be purchased. Otherwise not.

The value of the tank to the typical citizen would presumably depend on the number of tanks the army has already. If the army is well supplied with tanks, the extra tank may not add much to the safety of the citizen. If the supply of tanks on hand is small, the value of the citizen of an extra tank may be quite large. The right procedure for the government buying tanks in the interest of its citizens is to acquire tanks up to the point where the value to the typical citizen of the last tank bought is just a nickel.

It would, on the other hand, be ludicrous for a citizen to supply tanks for the army all by himself. He might perhaps do so as an act of charity, but never in his own self-interest, for the disparity between the cost of a tank ($1.5 million) and the benefit he, personally, can expect from the tank (5 cents) is just too large. When he can spend his income as he pleases on guns (that is, on tanks) or butter, the citizen spends his entire income on butter even though he can be made better off when the government takes some of his money in taxation for the purchase of guns. The rational citizen votes for the compulsory purchase of items he would never buy on his own.

In sharp contrast to the bread-and-cheese economy in chapter 3 where the government can never rearrange production to make everybody better off, the guns-and-butter economy requires the active intervention of the government in determining what to produce. In one economy, it is sufficient for the government to enforce property rights. In the other, the government must intervene in production as well.

To formalize this example, imagine a society where everybody is just like everybody else and where supply prices are invariant so that the production possibility curve is a downward-sloping straight line and all supply curves are flat. In a bread-and-cheese economy with N identical people, the economic problem is to place the typical person on the highest possible indifference curve, maximizing his utility $u(b,c)$ where b and c are consumption of bread and cheese per person. When, in addition, the production possibility curve is a downward-sloping straight line, each person can be thought of as producing y loaves of bread which he can convert to cheese at a rate of trade-off in production of p. His choice of b and c is then confined by the equation

$$b + pc = y \tag{1}$$

As the nation is the individual writ large, the national production possibility curve becomes

$$B + pC = I \tag{2}$$

where $B = Nb, C = Nc$ and $I = Ny$ which can be thought of as the national income in units of bread. Equivalently,

$$BP^{\$B} + CP^{\$C} = Y \tag{3}$$

where $P^{\$B}$ and $P^{\$C}$ are money prices of bread and cheese, and Y is the national income in units of money where, by definition, $Y = IP^{\$B}$.

By contrast, in a guns and butter economy, the economic problem is to maximize the typical person's utility $u(b,G)$ when b and G are consumption per person of butter and the total supply of guns, and when the economy may be represented by the national production possibility curve

$$BP^{\$B} + GP^{\$G} = Y \tag{4}$$

where B is now the total production of butter, $P^{\$B}$ and $P^{\$G}$ are invariant supply prices of butter and guns, and Y is, once again, the national income. Equation (4)

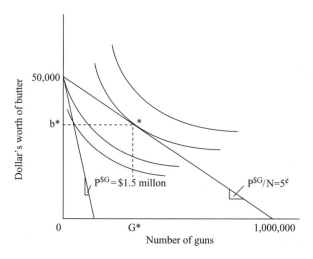

Figure 5.1 Guns and butter.

shows the options in production for the nation as a whole. Suppose, for convenience, that $P^{\$B}$ equals $1 per pound so that the term $P^{\$B}$ drops out of equation (4) and $P^{\$G}$ can be interpreted equally well as the money price of guns and as the relative price of guns. The equivalent set of options for the individual, obtained by dividing all terms by N, becomes

$$b + G(P^{\$G}/N) = y \qquad (5)$$

where y is a person's income in units of butter, and $(P^{\$G}/N)$ is the price of guns as seen by the individual who can share the cost of guns with the rest of the population. Without collective provision of guns, each person would have to pay the full price of guns if he wished to add guns to the nation's stock. His options in productions become

$$b + GP^{\$G} = y \qquad (6)$$

which is the same as equation (5) except that *his* price of guns rises from $P^{\$B}/N$ to $P^{\$G}$.

Replacing tanks with guns in our example, the price of butter, $P^{\$B}$, is $1 per pound, the price of guns, $P^{\$G}$, is $1.5 million per gun and the population, N, is 30 million. Assume each person's income to be $50,000. He produces 50,000 pounds of butter which can be converted to guns at a rate of $P^{\$G}$ pounds of butter per gun. On these assumptions, a person's options in production are represented by the two production possibility curves in figure 5.1. The lower and steeper production possibility curve shows a person's options for the purchase of guns and butter all by himself. The higher and flatter production possibility curve shows that person's options when he buys butter privately and buys guns collectively. All by himself, this person could acquire no more than a than one-thirtieth of a gun, even if he devoted his entire income to the purchase of guns. Collectively, he could acquire as many as a million guns [50,000×30 million/1.5 million] if he, along with everybody else, devoted all of his income to the purchase of guns. Presumably, society would choose many fewer guns than that.

Each person's preference is represented in figure 5.1 by a set of indifference curves, comparable to the indifference curves for bread and cheese in chapter 3. A society of identical people unanimously chooses a combination of guns and butter, shown in figure 5.1 as b* and G*, to place each person on the highest possible indifference curve. Public choice when people have different preferences and different incomes is discussed under the general heading of voting in chapter 9. As the indifference curves are drawn, a person with a stock of 50,000 pounds of butter – representative, of course, of all private goods – cannot make himself better off by buying guns individually, but he can do so by buying guns collectively.

Externalities: u = u(b, c, C) where b and c are a person's consumption of bread and cheese and C is society's total consumption of cheese

The general form of an externality is that one person's activity is harmful or beneficial to somebody else where the harm or benefit is not reflected by the price mechanism. A person's consumption of cheese might convey some harm to the rest of society if manure from cattle farms polluted the drinking water. A person's consumption of cheese might convey some benefit to the rest of society if cheese production gave out a delicious smell that everybody enjoyed. In either case, each person's utility would be affected by the total consumption of cheese. A somewhat different example illustrates what may be at stake.

Fifty students in a lecture hall. Every student likes to smoke but dislikes sitting in a smoky room. All students are alike. Each student who smokes emits 1,000 particles of smoke into the room. In deciding to smoke, a student acquires the pleasure of smoking together with the displeasure of occupying a slightly more smoky room, and his decision to smoke or not to smoke is necessarily a balancing of these considerations.

Every student values the pleasure of smoking at one dollar. Every student values the displeasure of smoky rooms at $(1/100)$¢ per particle of smoke. To say that the student values the pleasure of smoking at $1 is to say that – taking account of the price of cigarettes and the risk to health – he would pay up to $1 for the right to smoke if, miraculously, his own smoking had no effect on the amount of smoke in the room, that is, if the amount of smoke in the room were the same regardless of whether he smokes or not.

Two social arrangements are to be compared. In the first, each student smokes or desists from smoking as he pleases. In the second, students vote to permit smoking or to forbid it altogether. Voting is by majority rule, but the details of the voting mechanism do not matter here because identical students would vote identically as long as voting is restricted to rules treating everybody alike. Students are assumed to be entirely selfish, full-fledged "economic men" who maximize their own welfare exclusively, in choosing to smoke or not to smoke or in voting to allow or disallow smoking.

Suppose, first, that each student smokes or desists from smoking as he pleases. In deciding whether to smoke, a student must weigh the pleasure of smoking against the extra unpleasantness in the lecture hall from the additional smokiness he would create. The monetary equivalent of the pleasure of smoking is $1.00. The monetary equivalent of his displeasure from the extra smokiness he generates by smoking is 10¢, [1,000 particles @1/100¢ per particle]. His net gain from smoking is therefore 900¢, and he chooses to smoke.

Suppose instead that smoking is permitted or forbidden altogether in accordance with the outcome of a vote. There is a proposal to ban smoking, and each of the fifty students must vote yes or no. How does a student vote? Once again, he compares the benefit and cost of smoking, but now it is on the understanding that, by giving up his own right to smoke, he is stopping his classmates from smoking as well. In voting to ban smoking, a student forgoes the pleasure of smoking in return for an entirely smoke-free room. He values the loss of the pleasure of smoking at $1. He values a smoke-free room as compared with a room where all 50 students smoke at $5.00. [When each of 50 students emits 1,000 particles of smoke, there are 50,000 particles of smoke in the room. A student who values the harm from each particle at $(1/100)$¢ must value the harm to himself from 50,000 particles at $5.00.] Since every student's gain from a smoke-free room ($5.00) exceeds his benefit from smoking ($1.00), the students vote unanimously to have smoking banned. In his own self-interest, a rational person votes to ban smoking though he personally would smoke if the ban were not enacted! The moral of the story is that selfish people may vote to prohibit behavior that would be advantageous were it not prohibited.

This is no great paradox. It is a commonplace example of an "externality." The bread and cheese story in the last two chapters was about goods that convey benefits to consumers without affecting anybody else. Other goods or actions convey costs (such as smokiness in our example) or benefits (such as the security from the presence of an army) to people without compensation. Such benefits or costs to other people are called externalities because they are external to the price mechanism. The market does not require the purveyor of a negative externality to compensate his victims, or provide the purveyor of a beneficial externality with compensation from his beneficiaries. Smoke in the air exemplifies a great many types of pollution where some common, nationwide or worldwide aspect of life is adversely affected by actions of people who are not held responsible for the consequences of their behavior. Depletion of fish stocks by fishermen, the effect of hydrofluorocarbons on the ozone layer of the atmosphere, smog in cities, the greenhouse effect of carbon dioxide in the atmosphere, the extinction of species of plants and animals and the destruction of rainforests are all, with individual variations, negative externalities of private actions. Positive externalities are conveyed by a beautiful garden that gives pleasure to passers-by, by television programs that may be watched by anybody who chooses to turn on his set, or by education that increases the taxable earnings of the student.

Returning to smoking and smokiness, note that, when smoking is allowed, it is individually advantageous for each person to smoke no matter how many or how few others do so. If n out of N students choose to smoke, the net benefit or cost, of smoking and smokiness together, to a student who chooses to smoke is the monetary values of his pleasure in smoking less his displeasure when n students smoke. As each smoker imposes a cost of 10¢ on every student in the room, the net benefit or cost to a student who smokes is $(1 − n/10)$. A student who chooses not to smoke bears the

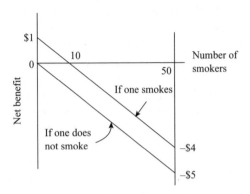

Figure 5.2   How universal selfishness may be worse than cooperation.

same cost of smokiness without the pleasure of smoking himself. He bears a cost of $(n/10)$ and is always worse off than a student who smokes regardless of the number of students who smoke. This is illustrated in figure 5.2 with the number of smokers on the horizontal axis and the net benefit per person on the vertical axis. The two lines in figure 5.2 show the net benefit per student, if he smokes and if he does not smoke, depending on the number of smokers in the class. Net benefit if one smokes falls steadily with the number of smokers from $1 if it were somehow possible to smoke without smoking up the room at all, to −$4.00 if all 50 students smoked. Net benefit if one does not smoke falls steadily from 0 to −$5.00. Figure 5.2 shows that one is always better off smoking than not smoking, though everybody would be better off if nobody smoked at all. The "tragedy of the commons" in the quotation at the outset of this chapter is that uncoordinated self-interested behavior makes everyone worse off than he might be if the students could coordinate their behaviour in the common interest. The tragedy is that Adam Smith's invisible hand – referred to in the quotation at the beginning of the introduction of this book – may sometimes be unreliable.

The conclusion is dependent on the parameters of the example. It was assumed that the harm per particle of smoke in the room was $1/100$¢ per particle. Had it been assumed instead that the harm is only $(1/1,000)$¢ per particle, the harm per student from smoke in the air when all 50 students emit 1,000 particles each would have been only 50¢ rather than $5.00, and every student would be better off when everybody smokes than when nobody smokes. Not all externalities should be banned or even curtailed. It is sometimes in the common interest to ignore externalities because the private gain from an externality-bearing activity exceeds the social cost. My neighbor may resent my neglect of my front lawn, but, within limits, we think it best for each person to look after his lawn as he pleases.

Alternatively, the common interest might best be served by a reduction in smoking rather than by a total ban. Suppose a student's benefit from smoking depends on how many cigarettes he smokes. Let p represent the student's valuation of his pleasure from smoking one extra cigarette; p is a student's demand price per cigarette, excluding the monetary equivalent of his displeasure from the extra smokiness brought about by his own smoking. Suppose p diminishes with q, the number of cigarettes smoked, in

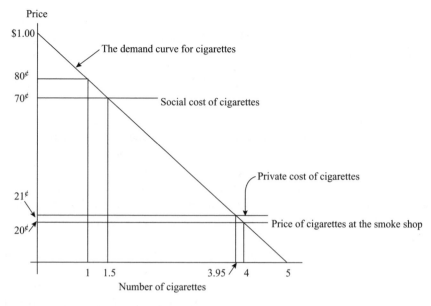

Figure 5.3   Private and social cost of smoking.

accordance with the demand curve

$$q = 5 - 5p \tag{7}$$

For convenience, the quantity of cigarettes is assumed to be continuous rather than discrete, as though one could buy fractions of a cigarette. The student smokes five cigarettes if they are free, no cigarettes if they cost a dollar each, 1 cigarette if they cost 80¢ each, and 3.95 cigarettes if they cost 21¢ each.

The demand and supply sides of the market for cigarettes are illustrated in figure 5.3 on the assumptions that the price of a cigarette at the smoke shop is 20¢, that each cigarette emits 100 particles of smoke and that the monetary value of each person's displeasure from smokiness is (1/100)¢ per particle. The demand curve is a direct representation of equation (7), but there are three distinct supply curves, corresponding to different interpretations of the price of cigarettes. All three curves are flat because prices per cigarette are independent of the number of cigarettes smoked. The height of the lowest supply curve is 20¢, the price of cigarettes at the smoke shop. The height of the next supply curve up is 21¢, the full cost of a cigarette to the smoker: the sum of the price at the smoke shop and the cost to the smoker himself $[100 \times (1/100)¢]$ of the extra smokiness in the lecture hall. The height of the top curve is 70¢, the entire cost of a cigarette to society: the sum of the cost of the cigarette at the smoke shop and the combined cost to all 50 students $[50 \times 100 \times (1/100)¢]$ of the extra smokiness when one student smokes one extra cigarette.

A student whose smoking is unconstrained chooses to smoke 3.95 cigarettes for which private benefit from one's very last puff is just equal to private cost. By contrast with the preceding variant of this example, the class would not now vote to ban smoking altogether. Consider a vote to allow each student to smoke one cigarette but no more. The benefit to the smoker is 90¢[half way between the value of the first puff which, as may be seen from the demand curve, is worth $1.00 per cigarette, and the last puff which is worth only 80¢]. The cost to each person of the smoke generated when everybody smokes one cigarette is 50¢ and the cost of the cigarette itself is 20¢. The benefit per person when everybody smokes one cigarette, and no more, is 95¢. The corresponding cost is only 70¢. Thus everybody is better off smoking one cigarette than no cigarettes, and students vote unanimously to allow the first cigarette.

Self-interested students vote to allow one another to smoke one and a half cigarettes. Imagine a vote between two bills in the student parliament. The first bill allows all students to smoke 1.5 cigarettes. The second bill allows students to smoke a number, q^*, of cigarettes, where q^* is different from 1.5. Students vote unanimously for the first bill. When $q = 1.5$, the corresponding p in accordance with equation (7) is 70¢ which is precisely the full social cost of a cigarette. Below 1.5, the benefit of an extra puff exceeds the social cost. Above that, the benefit of an extra puff falls short of the social cost.

In the original version of this example, all students, left to themselves, would smoke, but the appropriate public policy was to ban smoking because everybody was better off when nobody smoked than when everybody smoked. Now all students, left to themselves, would smoke 3.95 cigarettes, but the appropriate public policy is to reduce smoking to 1.5 cigarettes. Students would vote unanimously to reduce smoking to 1.5 cigarettes. The question now arises of how such a rule might be policed. When smoking was banned altogether, it would presumably be obvious to everybody when the ban was violated. It may be less obvious whether a particular student is exceeding his quota.

The standard remedy is taxation. Suppose the class party costs $150 in total or $3 per student. The class might vote to impose a tax of $3 per student to finance the party. Alternatively, it could levy a tax of 49¢ per cigarette, raising the tax-inclusive cost of a cigarette 70¢ [20¢ at the smoke shop, plus 1 cent for the cost of smokiness to the smoker, plus 49¢ tax to compensate other students for the harm from the smoke emitted by a cigarette]. With this tax in place, each student reduces his smoking to 1.5 cigarettes, the income from the cigarette tax is $36.75 [49¢ × 50 × 1.5] or 73.5¢ per student. The extra $2.26 per student to pay for the party could be acquired by direct taxation. The revenue to finance the party remains at $3 per student, but the change in the form of the tax alters smoking patterns, making everybody better off than he would be if smoking were unconstrained. [While it is true that taxing students may be cumbersome in the context of this example, it should be evident to the reader that what we are really talking about is an excise tax on the producer of an externality-bearing activity.]

The moral of the new version of the story is that it is better to tax than to ban when the common good is best served by a reduction, rather than a complete termination, of the externality-bearing activity.

Now consider once again our bread-and-cheese economy with the additional assumption that there is an externality in the production of cheese. Cheese factories belch smoke which pollute the atmosphere, and each person's well-being depends upon his own consumption of bread and cheese and upon the total amount of smoke in the atmosphere. There are N people in the economy, production of a pound of cheese emits s particles of smoke, and the cost to each person of a particle of smoke

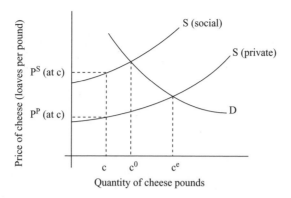

Figure 5.4 How the equilibrium quantity of cheese differs from the optimal quantity when there is an uncorrected externality.

(the amount of bread he would give up to procure a reduction of one particle of smoke in the atmosphere) is k. Then the "private" supply price of cheese to the buyer of cheese is

$$P^p = (\Delta b + sk)/\Delta c \tag{8}$$

where the superscript p is mnemonic for private, where Δb is the number of loaves of bread that must be sacrificed when resources are diverted to make Δc extra pounds of cheese, and where sk is the cost (to the buyer of cheese alone) of the extra smokiness in the atmosphere that he generates in arranging for the production of one extra pound of cheese. The "social" supply price of cheese is different. It incorporates the cost to every person when any person consumes one extra pound of cheese. It is

$$p^s = (\Delta b + skN)\Delta c \tag{9}$$

where the superscript s is mnemonic for social and where N is introduced because everybody has to put up with extra smoke when anybody consumes an extra pound of cheese. The story is illustrated in figure 5.4 which, like figure 5.3 above, shows demand and supply curves with price on the vertical axis and quantity on the horizontal axis. The important difference between the two figures is that the price in figure 5.3 was a money price (cents per cigarette) while the price in figure 5.4 is a relative price (loaves of bread per pound of cheese as in the demand and supply curves in chapter 4). The demand curve for cheese in figure 5.4 is just like the demand curves in the last two chapters. Now, however, there are two supply curves: the private supply curve shows the cost of cheese in terms of bread as the sum of the ordinary cost of production and the cost to the consumer himself of the smoke from his extra consumption of cheese, and the social supply curve shows the cost of cheese in terms of bread as the sum of the ordinary cost of production and the cost to everybody of the smoke from some person's extra consumption of cheese. The heights of the supply curves above any arbitrarily chosen point c are shown. If the externality is uncorrected, then the equilibrium, market-clearing consumption of cheese is c^e pounds (where the superscript e is mnemonic for equilibrium). This is too large because everybody would become better off if each person reduced his consumption of cheese to c^o pounds (where the superscript o is mnemonic for optimal) which is what a society of identical people would vote for unanimously. As in the classroom example, the optimal outcome could be obtained by taxing the externality-bearing activity.

On the face of it, the moral of the smoke and smoking story told here appears to be the exact opposite of the taxation story in chapter 4. There, it was shown that, if an amount of money is to be extracted from Robinson Crusoe by taxation, he is better off when that money is taken as a lump sum regardless of how he spends his remaining income, or when both goods are taxed at equal rates, when cheese is taxed but not bread. The discrepancy is only apparent. In the context of chapter 4, taxation of cheese but not bread created a distortion in an otherwise distortion-free economy. Here, taxation of cheese corrects for an externality-borne distortion. The overriding moral is to use taxation to correct distortions in the market, but, otherwise, to tax all goods alike, perhaps by means of an income tax. In either case, the welfare of the typical citizen is the appropriate guide to public policy.

Finally, an important aspect of many externalities is abstracted from, and even hidden by, the smoke-and-smoking story. The story is strictly *atemporal*. Actual externalities are often *intertemporal*. The distinction is best introduced by an extension of the story. In telling the story, it was implicitly supposed that the private benefits from smoking and the common harm occur all at once. The quality of the air today depended on how many people smoke today regardless of whether or not people smoked yesterday or at any time in the past. Nor does smoking today affect the quality of the air tomorrow. It is as though air quality restores itself automatically overnight. The assumption was atemporal (without time) in the sense that cause and effect are simultaneous. In this example as in many others, the atemporal assumption is very convenient and effective in conveying the essence of a problem clearly. It may nevertheless conceal important considerations.

The smoke-and-smoking story could have been told differently. It might have been supposed that smoke hangs in the air for days or even years. The harm from smoking today would then linger on and on, perhaps forever. This would be an intertemporal (among different times) variant of the story, more difficult to tell but capturing aspects of the world that might turn out to be important. Many actual environmental problems have a crucial intertemporal dimension. Grazing of my cattle on the commons today diminished the nutrition available for your cattle not just today but for years to come as the soil is, perhaps permanently, depleted. Overfishing today depletes the stock of fish tomorrow. Greenhouse gasses emitted today do little harm immediately but hang in the atmosphere for centuries gradually warming the planet. Extraction of minerals today has no impact on human welfare until such time as the world's mineral resources become more expensive to extract or run out altogether. All of these phenomena are like the smoke-and-smoking example in that private gain yields public loss, but their timing is not the same.

The next section passes from atemporal to intertemporal analysis. Externalities from population growth are discussed in some detail in the next chapter.

Consumption today and consumption tomorrow: [u = u(b$_1$, b$_2$) where b$_1$ and b$_2$ are loaves of bread consumed at different periods of time]

The models in chapters 2, 3, and 4 were strictly atemporal. Production and consumption took place in an isolated moment of time with no links to the future or to the past. One can think of those models as either abstracting from connections between moments of time or pertaining to a world where every yesterday and every tomorrow is just like today, and where people's actions remain the same forever. The simplest way to introduce time into the model is to replace "bread and cheese today" with "bread today and bread tomorrow," and to replace the relative price of cheese with the rate of interest as the mediator between the quantities of the two goods consumed. There is a straightforward analogy between (1) the relative price of cheese as a mediator between the demand for and supply of cheese at a moment of time and (2) the rate of interest as a mediator between consumption of bread today and consumption of bread tomorrow.

To see this, it may be helpful to begin with the ordinary rate of interest on money. Consider the deposit of money in a bank. I deposit $1,000 at 5 percent interest. In doing so, I am trading $1,000 today for $1,050 next year, or, equivalently, I am buying dollars next year with dollars this year at a price of approximately 95¢. Recall that the price of cheese in terms of bread is $\Delta b/\Delta c$ where Δb is the amount of bread I must give up to acquire an amount of Δc of cheese. By analogy, the price of dollars next year in terms of dollars this year has to be (Δ dollars this year)/(Δ dollars next year) which in our example is $(1000)/(1050) \simeq 0.95$. That is how much money I must give up this year to acquire a dollar next year. More generally, when the rate of interest is r ($r = 0.05$ means a rate of interest of 5 %), a dollar this year exchanges for $(1 + r)$ dollars next year, and the price of a dollar next year in terms of dollars this year is $1/(1 + r)$. The rate of interest is not some mysterious entity that is altogether different from prices. It is just an ordinary price transformed. Similarly, if I leave money in the bank indefinitely and collect the interest each year, then $1/r$ becomes the price in terms of current dollars of a stream of $1 per year forever.

Our main concern here is not with the relative prices of money available at different periods of time, but with the comparable prices of goods. We are concerned here with the relative price of bread next year and bread today. To buy a pound of cheese with money is to exchange dollars for cheese. To buy a pound of cheese with bread is to exchange bread for cheese. To buy a loaf of bread next year with bread today is to give up as many loaves of bread today as the market requires in exchange for a loaf of bread next year. Designate this year by 1 and next year by 2. Suppose the price of bread this year is $P^{\$B}(1)$, the price of bread next year will be $P^{\$B}(2)$ and the ordinary rate of interest on money is r, or, equivalently, 100r percent. To exchange a loaf of bread today for bread available next year, here is what I must do. I sell the loaf for $P^{\$B}(1)$, the going price of bread today, and then I lend the $P^{\$B}(1)$ dollars at the going rate of interest. At the end of the year, I receive back $P^{\$B}(1)(1 + r)$ dollars with which I purchase bread at the going price at that time, acquiring $P^{\$B}(1)(1 + r)/P^{\$B}(2)$ loaves of bread next year. If, by this process, one loaf of bread today can be exchanged for $P^{\$B}(1)(1 + r)/P^{\$B}(2)$ loaves delivered next year, then, by definition, the relative price of bread next year, with the bread this year as the numeraire, must be the inverse of that fraction. With bread this year as the numeraire, the price today of bread available next year – the number of loaves one must give up this year in order to acquire one extra loaf next year – becomes $P^{\$B}(2)/[P^{\$B}(1)(1+r)]$.

Now define the *own rate of interest on bread*, r_B, as the amount of extra bread I can acquire next year by postponing the consumption of one loaf by one year. From the definition r_B, it follows at once that a loaf today exchanges for $1 + r_B$ loaves next year, and that the relative price of bread next year in terms of bread this year is $1/(1 + r_B)$. It then follows immediately that

$$1/(1 + r_B) = P^{\$B}(2)/[P^{\$B}(1)(1+r)] \tag{10}$$

for the two sides of the equation are different expressions for one and the same thing. Equation (10) has two straightforward but important consequences. First, if the price of bread is the same in both years – if $P^{\$B}(2) = P^{\$B}(1)$ – then the money rate of interest and the own rate of interest on bread must be the same, i.e.

$$r_B = r \tag{11}$$

Second, when the rate of inflation of the price of bread is i, that is, when $[P^{\$B}(2)/P^{\$B}(1)] = 1 + i$, then

$$(1 + r) = (1 + r_B)(1 + i) \tag{12}$$

or, equivalently, when the cross-product, $r_B i$, is considered small enough to ignore,

$$r = r_B + i \tag{13}$$

If prices of goods are changing over time at different rates, then each good has its own forward price and its own rate of inflation, but equation (13) remains valid for each good individually as long as the term r_B is reinterpreted as the own rate of interest for the good in question.

Equation (13) can be reinterpreted as pretaining to the economy as a whole. Think of i as the common rate of inflation measured, for example, by the change in the consumer price index, and think of r_B as the "real rate of interest" defined as the average of the own rates of interest on all goods together. On these interpretations of i and r_B, equation (13) becomes the proposition that

"the money rate of interest" equals "the real rate of interest"
plus "the rate of inflation." $\tag{14}$

If the money rate of interest is 5 percent and if prices of goods and services are rising at 3 percent, then a dollar invested today yields me 2 percent more goods next year than I must give up this year to acquire them. A person saving for his old age is of course concerned with the real rate of interest on his money, rather than with the money rate of interest.

The introduction of time requires us to differentiate between *flow* prices and *stock* prices. The relative price of cheese is a flow price, a rate of exchange between two goods produced and consumed at a moment of time. Money prices of bread and cheese are also flow prices because bread and cheese are short-lived even though money is not. The price of land is a stock price because land persists through time and because the purchase of a plot of land today is really the purchase of the stream of goods produced by that land every year until the end of time. Stock prices are connected to flow prices by interest rates. If a plot of land yields $1,500 per year forever and if the money rate of interest is 5 percent, then the price of land must be $30, 000[1,500 × 1/(0.05)]. If a plot of land yields 500 loaves of bread each year forever, if the price of bread today is $3 a loaf, and if the own rate of interest on bread is 2 percent, then the price of that land – the stock price – has to be $75,000[500 × 3/(0.02)]. Note that the own rate of interest on bread can only differ from the money rate of interest when the price of bread is expected to increase over time, so that a constant flow of bread becomes the equivalent of a steadily increasing flow of money. At these interest rates, one would need to deposit $30,000 in the bank to provide oneself with an annual income of $1,500, but one would need $75,000 to provide oneself with an annual flow of 500 loaves of bread.

Though interest rates are usually positive, they are not always so. Money rates of interest cannot be negative as long as gold or paper money can be stored cost-lessly. Real rates of interest are usually positive because land and machinery are productive. Expenditure on machinery today can be expected to yield a positive return, after provision for depreciation, for as long ahead as one can see. But real rates of interest can be negative in some circumstances. The five-year own rate of interest on grain was negative in ancient Egypt at the end of the seven fat years, when the seven lean years were due to begin, and when pharaoh, on the advice of Joseph with his flair for economic planning, had accumulated stocks of grain some of which would surely be eaten by mice or accidentally burned from time to time. If, of every bushel of grain stored, only half a bushel remains available to be consumed in five years time, then the own rate of interest on grain would be -13%, the solution to the equation $(1 + r_B)^5 = 1/2$. Similarly and for the same reason, the own rate of interest on grain is typically negative over the six months after the harvest.

Nothing has been said so far about how the rate of interest is determined. As the rate of interest is a price, one would expect it to be determined by the same interactions between taste and technology that determine the relative price of cheese. So it is, but the mechanism is complex because the rate of interest today is conditioned by anticipations of future for as far ahead as one can see.

A simplified version of the mechanism determining the rate of interest is illustrated in a reinterpretation of the Robinson Crusoe story as set out in chapter 3. Now, Robinson Crusoe consumes only bread, not bread and cheese as had been assumed. Instead, he lives for two years, youth and age, produces 10 loaves of bread when he is young, and invests of his produce so that he has something to consume when he is old. In chapter 3, Robinson Crusoe was confronted with a trade-off in production between bread and cheese. He could produce more cheese and less bread or more bread and less cheese. Now he is confronted with a similar trade-off between quantities of bread at two periods of time. Suppose – no matter how – he can transform 1 loaf of bread in the first year for 1.1 loaves of bread in the second, so that his technologically determined rate of interest on bread is 10 percent. There is no explanation within the model of why the technologically given rate of interest is 10 percent or of why it is positive at all. One might think of this as representative of more elaborate economies where investment – the giving up of consumption this year to acquire consumption in the future – is productive.

Robinson Crusoe's options for consumption in the two years can be represented by the intertemporal production possibility curve

$$10 = b_1 + (1/1.1)b_2 \tag{15}$$

where b_1 is his production of bread in the first year and b_2 is his production of bread in the second. Among his options are to consume 10 loaves per day in the first year and nothing in the second, to consume 5 loaves per day in the first year and 5.5 loaves in the second, or to consume nothing in the first year and 11 loaves in the second. It follows immediately that the supply price of bread next year in terms of bread this year is ratio $\Delta b_1/\Delta b_2$ where Δb_1 is a small decrease in consumption of bread this year and Δb_2 is the resulting increase in consumption of bread next year in accordance with equation (15), and that $\Delta b_1/\Delta b_2 = 1/1.1$. Note also that $\Delta b_1/\Delta b_2$ is the same for all consistent values of b_1 and b_2 because equation (15) is a downward-sloping straight line.

Robinson Crusoe's tastes, or preferences, can be represented by a set of indifference curves with a corresponding utility function

$$u = u(b_1, b_2) \tag{16}$$

analogous to his earlier choice of bread and cheese. He chooses consumption each year, b_1 and b_2, to place himself on the highest possible indifference curve, as specified in equation (16), attainable with the available technology, as specified by the production possibility curve in equation (15). His chosen combination of bread this year and bread next is illustrated in figure 5.5, analogous to figure 3.5, with technology and taste in part A and with demand and supply in part B.

Indifference curves and the production possibility curve are shown in Part A of figure 5.5 with b_1 on the vertical axis and b_2 on the horizontal axis. Clearly, Robinson Crusoe has attained the highest possible indifference curve at a combination of b_1 and b_2 for which that indifference curve is just tangent to the production possibility curve. In the special case where indifference curves can be represented by the simple function $u = b_1 b_2$, the slope of the indifference curve is equal (by analogy with the earlier demonstration for bread and cheese) to b_1/b_2. Equating the slope of the indifference curve to the slope of the production possibility curve, we see that $b_1/b_2 = 1/1.1$. Since any combination of b_1 and b_2 must lie on the production possibility curve, the two equations $b_1/b_2 = 1/1.1$ and $10 = b_1 + 1/1.1 b_2$ imply that $b_1 = 5$ and $b_2 = 5.5$.

Exactly the same story is told in part B with b_2 (consumption in the second year) and the price of b_2 in terms of b_1 on the vertical axis. The price of b_2 in terms of b_1 is the ratio $\Delta b_1/\Delta b_2$, the amount of bread this year that must be given up to acquire a loaf of bread next year. The supply curve, S, shows the supply price of bread in year 2 as a function of the quantity supplied, where the supply price is, as in earlier chapters, the rate of substitution in production as indicated by the slope of the production possibility curve in part A. Here the supply curve is flat because the

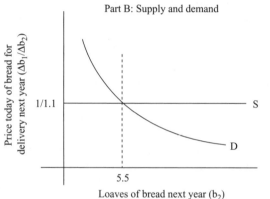

Part A: Technology and taste

Part B: Supply and demand

Figure 5.5 Intertemporal choice.

production possibility curve is a downward sloping straight line. The demand curve shows the slope of the indifference curve along the production possibility curve for various values of b_2. The demand curve is downward sloping reflecting the assumed curvature of the indifference curves. The intersection of the demand and supply curves shows the amount of bread produced and consumed in the second year together with the relative price of bread in the second year from which the real rate of interest (i.e. the own rate of interest on bread) can be determined.

The rate of interest and the allocation of consumption over time are determined by the same market forces that determine the prices of goods and the choice of a mix of goods at a moment of time. Just as the atemporal story was told about an economy with only two goods, so that intertemporal story is told about an economy with only two periods of time. Both stories can be generalized to many goods and many periods of time.

Risk: [u = u(Y$_V$, Y$_M$, Y$_U$) where Y$_V$, Y$_M$ and Y$_U$ are income in different states of the world.]

A person is choosing a career. He has narrowed his options to law and medicine, and his only concern in this choice is his annual income once his career is under way. If he knew for certain what his annual incomes would be in the two careers, he would automatically choose the career with the higher income, but both careers are somewhat risky. Specifically, in each career, he is equally likely to be very successful, moderately successful, or unsuccessful. His incomes in each career and in each eventuality are shown in table 5.1. The main difference between these careers is that the expected income is higher in law than in medicine ($110,000 as compared with $100,000), but law is more risky. One may earn as little as $30,000 or as much as $190,000 in law, as compared with $90,000 and $110,000 in medicine. What does this person do?

The person's choice between law and medicine depends on his attitude toward risk. If he is indifferent to risk or only slightly risk averse, he chooses law which provides him with the higher expected income. If he is quite risk averse, he chooses medicine with a lower expected income but a smaller gap between the best and the worst outcome. Our object here is to describe this choice precisely.

An uncertain world can be modeled precisely as consisting of a number of *states of the world*, each of which will occur with a certain probability. In the toss of a coin, there are two states of the world, heads and tails, each of which will occur with a probability of one-half. In the toss of a dice, there are six states of the world, each of which will occur with a probability of one-sixth. In each profession as described above, there are three states of the world, unsuccessful, moderately successful, and very successful, each of which will occur with a probability of one-third.

To compare professions, each yielding a different set of incomes depending on the state of the world, we would like to construct a utility function – over incomes in different states of the world rather than over different amounts of bread and cheese – such that the preferred profession yields the greater utility. We would like to construct a utility function

$$u = u(Y_V, Y_M, Y_U) \tag{17}$$

where Y_V, Y_M and Y_U are a person's incomes in equally likely "states of the world," that the person is very successful (V), moderately successful (M) and unsuccessful (U). We would hope that the function which reflects choice among risky prospects with

Table 5.1 Annual incomes in law and medicine depending on whether one is very successful, moderately successful, or unsuccessful

	Unsuccessful	Moderately successful	Very successful	Expected income	Dispersion of income
Medicine	$90,000	$100,000	$110,000	$100,000	$10,000
Law	$30,000	$110,000	$190,000	$110,000	$80,000

three states of the world can be generalized to any number of equally likely states of the world.

Suppose initially that the person is risk neutral. To say that a person is risk neutral is to say that, in any choice between gambles or between a gamble and a sure thing, he always chooses the option with the largest *expected income*, E, defined with reference to our example as

$$E = (1/3)Y_V + (1/3)Y_M + (1/3)Y_U \qquad (18)$$

The expected income of doctors is what every doctor would obtain under an agreement among all doctors to share their incomes, whatever they turn out to be. The expected income of lawyers is defined accordingly. If incomes in each profession were to be shared among all practitioners, then everybody would choose law over medicine. A person who is risk neutral chooses law regardless, even when income is not shared. A person who is strongly risk averse might choose medicine over law because the larger expected income in law does not compensate such people for the one-third chance of an income of only $30,000, which is only a third of the lowest possible income in medicine.

Corresponding to every risky prospect is a *certainty equivalent* that differs from one person to the next according to their degrees of risk aversion. Consider the choice between a risky prospect with expected income E and a sure thing with an income of Y. A risk-neutral person chooses whichever is the larger. A risk-averse person might choose the sure thing even when Y is less than E. A person's certainty equivalent of a risky prospect is an income Y^c (where c is mnemonic for certainty) such that the person is indifferent between the risky prospect and the sure thing. If one is risk neutral then $Y^c = E$ where Y^c is the certainty equivalent and E is the expected income of the risky prospect. If one is risk averse, then $Y^c < E$. The size of the gap depends on the person's degree of his risk aversion. The greater his risk aversion, the greater the gap. When the risky prospect is law or medicine and when the person choosing a profession is risk averse,

$$Y^c < E = (1/3)Y_V + (1/3)Y_M + (1/3)Y_U \qquad (19)$$

Consistency of choice requires that one choose the profession with the higher certainty equivalent as assessed in accordance with one's taste for risk

Since all choice can be interpreted as maximizing something and since a risk-averse person does not maximize expected income in his choice among risky prospects, there must be some function of income that a risk-averse person does maximize. We call that function the *utility of income*, u(Y), which may be thought of as a measure of utility to account for risk. Recall that, in the world without uncertainty in chapters 3 and 4 where people consume only bread and cheese, money income is a completely satisfactory measure of utility as long as prices are invariant, for, no matter what the shape of one's indifference curves, one is better off at any given set of prices with more money rather than less. Recall also the discussion of the numbering of indifference curves at the beginning of this chapter where it was shown that *any* numbering of indifference curves is satisfactory as an indicator of utility as long as higher curves are assigned higher numbers, and that any monotonicly increasing function of a satisfactory utility indicator is itself a satisfactory utility indicator. For example, if indifference curves conform to the function u = bc, so that the product bc is a satisfactory utility indicator, then so too are (bc)^2 and $10(bc)^{12}$. The utility of income function we seek is a renumbering of utility to account for a person's behavior toward risk.

Utility is initially represented by income. What we are seeking in a utility of income function, u(Y), is a monotonic transformation of income such that, if Y^c is the certainty equivalent of equal chances of incomes of Y_U, Y_M and Y_V, then

$$u(Y^c = (1/3)u(Y_V) + (1/3)u(Y_M) + (1/3)u(Y_U) \tag{20}$$

Having to choose between any two risky prospects, a person always chooses the prospect with the larger expected utility of income. For a risk neutral person, this means no more than that he chooses the prospect with the higher expected income, for u(Y) = Y, the inequality in equation (19) becomes an equality, and equations (18) and (20) are essentially the same. Otherwise the shape of u(Y) has to be discovered.

Since the utility of income function is designed to represent a person's willingness to bear risk, and since one's willingness to bear risk is an aspect of taste, the only way to discover a person's utility of income function is to ask him, directly or indirectly, to tell you what it is. A person's utility function is discovered in essentially the same process that was used to discover his ordinary indifference curves over different combinations of bread and cheese. He must be asked a long series of questions of the general form, "Do you prefer this to that?" until the entire shape of his utility of income function is revealed. The trick is to ask a person about his preferences in a simple, well-specified risky situation, and then to rely upon the assumed consistency of "economic man" to infer his behavior in more complex risky situations.

The demonstration is a bit complex but can be broken down into stages: (1) A person's attitude toward risk is elicited in a long series of questions not about preferences among combinations of bread and cheese, but about preferences between a standard gamble and a sure thing. The sure thing is a fixed income attained with certainty. The gamble yields a big prize or a little prize, with a given probability of each. A sort of indifference curve will be derived connecting the probability of winning the big prize and the size of the income as a sure thing. This curve encapsulates a person's attitude toward risk. (2) Along this curve, the probability of the big prize must be an increasing function of income as a sure thing. Since income is a valid indicator of utility in a world of invariant prices and since any increasing function of a utility indicator is a utility indicator too, the probabilities along this curve can be interpreted as utilities of the corresponding incomes. This is the utility of income function we seek if it can be shown that the person to whom the curve refers always seeks to maximize expected utility in accordance with this curve, not just in the simple context where the curve is derived, but in more complex risky situations. That turns out to be so. (3) Once identified through the linking of utility and probability, the utility of income function can be employed to rationalize choice in complex situations. The prospects of law and medicine can be equated to simple gambles that can at once be ranked in accordance with their expected utilities. The higher the expected utility, the more desirable the gamble in the assessment of the person to whom the utility of income function refers.

By these steps, there is established a utility of income function encapsulating a person's degree of risk aversion, while at the same time ranking all risky prospects. Knowing a person's utility of income function, one knows how he will behave in any risky situation such as the choice between law and medicine in table 5.1.

The questions are framed as follows: A person is confronted with a choice between a sure thing and a simple risky prospect. The sure thing is an annual income of Y for the whole of one's working life. The risky prospect has two possible outcomes: one relatively good, the other relatively bad. The good outcome is an annual income of $250,000 for the whole of one's working life. The bad outcome is an annual income of $20,000 for the whole of one's working life. The probability of the good outcome is π.

The person is asked to choose between Y and π. He may, for instance, be asked to choose between a sure income of $100,000 and a risky prospect where π = 1/2, that is, with a 50 percent chance of an annual income of $250,000 and a 50 percent chance of an annual income of $20,000. Whatever he chooses, the value of π can then be adjusted, up or down as need be, until the person is indifferent between the risky prospect and the sure thing. If, for example, he is indifferent between a sure income of $100,000 and a 73 percent chance of the good outcome, we say that $\pi(100,000) = 0.73$. Then we change the value of the sure income (for example, from $100,000 to $110,000) and repeat the process over and over again until we know $\pi(Y)$ for every value of Y from $20,000 to $250,000.

Necessarily, $\pi(250,000) = 1$ because, otherwise, one could only lose by choosing the risky prospect over the sure thing when Y is as high as $250,000. Similarly, $\pi(20,000) = 0$ because, otherwise, one could only lose by choosing the sure thing over the risky prospect when Y is as low as $20,000. The function $\pi(Y)$ must increase with Y because a risky prospect with a higher probability of the good outcome is preferred to a risky prospect with a lower probability of the good outcome as long as the outcomes themselves remain the same.

The function $\pi(Y)$ connecting each income Y to a probability of winning the big prize in the standard lottery is precisely the utility of income function we seek, an increasing function of income capturing a person's deportment toward risk. The function $\pi(Y)$ is defined so that, if a person is indifferent between a sure income and a gamble, the utility of the sure income and the expected utility of the gamble are necessarily the same. It follows that equation (20) is automatically valid for this utility function, that is, when the general utility function u(Y) is replaced by the specific utility function $\pi(Y)$ as defined here. Each of the three utilities on the right hand side of equation (20) – $u(Y_V), u(Y_M)$ and $u(Y_U)$ – becomes a probability of winning the big prize rather than the small one, and, since the events V, M, and U are mutually exclusive, the entire right hand side of equation (20) is the probability of winning the big prize that is implicit in the gamble with equal probabilities of the three events. To say that a rational self-interested person seeks to maximize the expected probability of the big prize in any choice among alternative gambles, is to say that he maximizes expected utility as defined in equation (20) with $\pi(Y)$ as the utility of income function.

Shapes of alternative utility of income functions $\pi(Y)$ are illustrated in figure 5.6 with Y on the horizontal axis and π on the vertical axis. Two utility of income functions are shown, one for a risk neutral person and the other for a risk averse person. A risk neutral

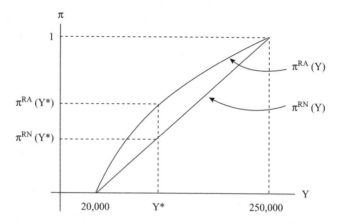

Figure 5.6 The utility of income function when a person is risk neutral and when a person is risk averse.

person is indifferent between "a sure income of y" and "a probability p of winning the big prize of $250,000 where the alternative is winning a small prize of $20,000" if and only if

$$Y = p(250,000) + (1 - p)(20,000) = 20,000 + p(230,000) \qquad (21)$$

or, replacing p with the function $\pi^{RN}(Y)$ where the superscript RN stands for risk neutral,

$$\pi^{RN}(Y) = Y/230,000 - 20,000/230,000 \qquad (22)$$

as shown in the upward-sloping straight line in figure 5.6. On the other hand, if a person is risk averse, it must be the case that

$$Y < 20,000 + p(230,000) \qquad (23)$$

or, replacing p with $\pi^{RA}(Y)$ where the superscript RA stands for risk averse,

$$\pi^{RA}(Y) > Y/230,000 - 20,000/230,000 \qquad (24)$$

A utility of income function of a risk averse person – a utility function consistent with equations (23) and (24) – is illustrated by the curved line in figure 5.6. For any point Y^* that is greater than $20,000 but less than $250,000, $\pi^{RA}(Y^*)$ must be greater than $\pi^{RN}(Y^*)$. Thus, since $\pi^{RA}(Y)$ and $\pi^{RN}(Y)$ have to be the same at the upper and lower limits, the function $\pi^{RA}(Y)$ must be concave as shown in figure 5.6.

As constructed, the function $\pi(Y)$ is *a* satisfactory utility of income function but not the *only* satisfactory function. Obviously, our choice of limits, $250,000 and $20,000, was entirely arbitrary. Any other limits would have done as well. It can be shown that any increasing linear function of $\pi(Y)$ would be equally acceptable as a utility of income function reflecting a person's behavior toward risk.

Table 5.2 Utility as probability

[The utility of income is interpreted as the minimal probability of a good outcome required to induce a person to accept a risky prospect in preference to a sure thing.]

Income, Y ($ thousands)	Utility of income: risk neutrality, $\alpha = 1$	Utility of income: moderate risk aversion, $\alpha = 3/4$	Utility of income: strong risk aversion, $\alpha = 1/4$
20	0	0	0
30	0.0435	0.0629	0.1212
50	0.1304	0.1744	0.2924
90	0.3034	0.3610	0.5185
100	0.3478	0.4150	0.5627
110	0.3913	0.4588	0.6037
150	0.5652	0.6254	0.7439
190	0.7391	0.7810	0.8584
250	1	1	1

Sources: Utility and income are related by the general formula, $\pi(Y) = AY^\alpha + B$ where A and B are selected for each value of α to ensure that $\pi(250,000) = 1$ and $\pi(20,000) = 0$. One can easily check that $A = 1/[(250,000)^\alpha - (20,000)^\alpha]$ and $B = (20,000)^\alpha/[(250,000)^\alpha - (20,000)^\alpha]$. With risk neutrality, the values of A and B must be 0.434783×10^{-5} and -0.0869565. With moderate risk aversion such that $\alpha = 3/4$, the values of A and B must be 0.1052793×10^{-3} and -0.1770579. With strong risk aversion such that $\alpha = 1/4$, the values of A and B must be 0.09552368 and -1.1359734.

Since the utility of income function, $\pi(Y)$, is discovered in a conceptual experiment, one cannot say *a priori* that it will conform to any arbitrarily chosen functional form. Nevertheless, just as indifference curves in a bread and cheese economy were illustrated by the function $u = bc$, so too can taste for risk be illustrated by supposing that a person's choice under uncertainty just happens to conform to the function

$$\pi(Y) = AY^\alpha + B \qquad (25)$$

where α is an indicator of a person's risk aversion and the parameters A and B are chosen for each value of α so that $\pi(20,000) = 0$ and $\pi(250,000) = 1$. This function has the right limits, the right general shape for risk aversion, and is easy to manipulate. If $\alpha = 1$, the person to whom the function $\pi(Y)$ belongs is risk neutral because the expected value of $\pi(Y)$ would automatically be maximized whenever the expected value of Y is maximized. Otherwise, if $\alpha < 1$, a person is risk averse, the more so the smaller the value of α. Note, however, that there is nothing in the conceptual experiment requiring a person's risk aversion to be representable by an exponential function. A person's aversion to risk might be representable by that function, but need not be. The exponential function is just useful for exposition.

For Y varying from a low of $20,000 to a high of $250,000, the $\pi(Y)$ is shown in table 5.2 for three possible values of α signifying risk neutrality ($\alpha = 1$), moderate risk aversion ($\alpha = 3/4$), and strong risk aversion ($\alpha = 1/4$). The first column lists alternative incomes. The second, third, and fourth columns show the corresponding

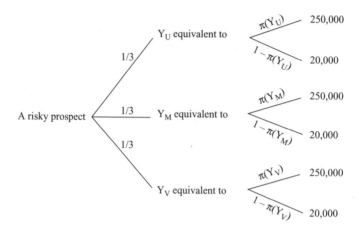

Figure 5.7 The expected utility of a risky prospect.

minimal probabilities of success in the gamble required to induce a person with the indicated degree of risk aversion to accept the gamble rather than the sure thing.

A person's choice between law and medicine can now be modeled as the maximization of expected utility where the utility of income function is deemed to represent that person's behavior toward risk in a simple experiment. Each occupation yields equal probabilities of incomes Y_V, Y_M, and Y_U as shown in table 5.1 above. Expected utility of these prospects becomes

$$\text{Exp}(\pi) = (1/3)\pi(Y_V) + (1/3)\pi(Y_M) + (1/3)\pi(Y_U) \tag{26}$$

and one chooses between law and medicine according to the values of $\text{Exp}(\pi)$ in equation (26). Consistency requires that one choose the prospect with the larger value of $\text{Exp}(\pi)$. One chooses the prospect with the larger value of $\text{Exp}(\pi)$ because $\text{Exp}(\pi)$ is equivalent in every respect to a probability of the good outcome in the simple conceptual experiment as described above. As explained in the discussion of equation (20), the crux of the matter is that a risky prospect with equal chances of incomes Y_V, Y_M, and Y_U – or any other risky prospect, no matter how complex – is necessarily equivalent to a simple risky prospect where the good outcome is $250,000, the bad outcome is $20,000. The logic of this assertion can be seen with the aid of figure 5.7. Each of the three possible values of Y is equivalent in a person's assessment to a probability of the good outcome in our simple conceptual experiment. That being so, equal chances of each of the three outcomes must be equivalent in that person's assessment to a compound probability of the good outcome of $\text{Exp}(\pi)$ as shown in equation (26) above.

The choice between law and medicine is a choice between risky prospects with different outcomes in each of three equally likely states of the world. A person's choice between these prospects can be predicted from his utility of income function, summarizing his supposedly observed behavior in the conceptual experiment from which the function was derived. The key to the reduction is consistency. Each risky prospect can be reduced to a simple choice between a standard gamble and a sure thing. Within this framework, there is imposed the assumption that a person's utility of income function conforms to equation (25) for some value of α. For that value of α, each of the three "prizes" in medicine – \$90,000, \$100,000, and \$110,000 – is itself equivalent in the person's assessment to a lottery with a certain probability of the big prize of \$250,000, and where to lose is to acquire the small prize of \$20,000. For instance, as may be read off table 5.2, an income of \$90,000 is equivalent in the assessment of a person for whom $\alpha = 3/4$ to a lottery with a probability of 0.361 of winning the big prize. Thus, equal chances of incomes of \$90,000, \$100,000, and \$110,000 in the medical profession are like equal chances of entering one of three lotteries with the same prizes – \$250,000 and \$20,000 – but different probabilities of attaining the big prize, probabilities dependent, as shown in table 5.2, on one's degree of risk aversion. That in turn is equivalent in every respect to entering one grand lottery with the same prizes and a probability of winning, π(medicine), which is the average of the probabilities attached to the grand lottery with the same prizes and a probability of winning, π(medicine), which is the average of the probabilities attached to the three possible incomes.

The choice boils down to a comparison between π(medicine) and π(law), each defined as expected utility in accordance with equation (25). For three values of $\alpha - 1$, 3/4, and 1/4 – the expected utility of each profession can be determined from the information in table 5.2. If one is risk neutral so that $\alpha = 1$, the appropriate values of π (Y) can be read off the second column of the table.

$$\pi(\text{medicine}) = (1/3)(0.3034) + (1/3)(0.3478) + (1/3)(0.3913) = 0.3475 \quad (27)$$

and

$$\pi(\text{law}) = (1/3)(0.0435) + (1/3)(0.3913) + (1/3)(0.7391) = 0.3913 \quad (28)$$

With risk neutrality, π(law) $>$ π(medicine), and one chooses the profession of law. If one is moderately risk averse ($\alpha = 3/4$), the appropriate values of π(Y) can be read off the third column.

$$\pi(\text{medicine}) = (1/3)(0.3610) + (1/3)(0.4150) + (1/3)(0.4588) = 0.4116 \quad (29)$$

and

$$\pi(\text{law}) = (1/3)(0.0629) + (1/3)(0.4588) + (1/3)(0.7810) = 0.4342 \quad (30)$$

and law is still the preferred profession. But if one is strongly risk averse ($\alpha = 1/4$), the appropriate values of π(Y) can be read off the last column.

$$\pi(\text{medicine}) = (1/3)(0.5185) + (1/3)(0.5627) + (1/3)(0.6037) = 0.5614 \quad (31)$$

and

$$\pi(\text{law}) = (1/3)(0.1212) + (1/3)(0.6037) + (1/3)(0.8584) = 0.5278 \quad (32)$$

and one chooses medicine instead. The choice between the professions depends on one's degree of risk aversion as represented by the curvature of the utility of income function. By asking himself about his preferences between risky and riskless options, the reader may discover his utility of income function and may discover whether he prefers law or medicine in the circumstances of table 5.1.

Almost everybody is risk averse, though some people are more risk averse than others. Consider a family of four people assessing a risky prospect with a 50 percent chance of $190,000 per year and a 50 percent chance of $30,000 per year. Though its expected income is $110,000 per year, it would almost always prefer a sure income of $110,000 to the risky prospect. One can live comfortably with an income $110,000. A 50 percent chance of earning an extra $80,000 would not normally be worth the risk of poverty at an income of $30,000. Suppose the family's degree of risk aversion could be represented by a value of α of $\frac{1}{4}$ in equation (25). If so, the certainty equivalent of the risky prospect is $83,907, over $26,000 less than the expected income. [This may be deduced from equation (25) and the data in table 5.2. The family's expected utility is 0.4898, that is, $\frac{1}{2}$ (0.1212 + 0.8584). As explained above, the parameters A and B of the utility function in equation (25) are determinate for any given value of α, and, as indicated in the note to table 5.2, A = 0.09552368 and B = −1.1359744 when $\alpha = \frac{1}{4}$. Plugging these numbers into equation (24), we see that the certainty equivalent of the risky prospect with an expected utility of 0.4898 is $83,907.] Confronted by a risky prospect with a 50 percent chance of an income of $30,000 and a 50 percent chance of an income of $190,000, a family with a value of α of $\frac{1}{4}$ would be prepared to pay about $106,000 in the fortunate state in return for a grant of only $54,000 in the unfortunate state, these amounts being just sufficient to convert the risky prospect into its certainty equivalent. If that family could take out fair insurance – costing one dollar in the good state for one dollar in the bad state – it would certainly do so. Conversion of the risky prospect with an expected value of $110,000 into a sure income of $100,000 would be clearly advantageous. If necessary, the family would be willing to pay a "risk premium" of up to $26,000 for the right to take out fair insurance. Insurance companies convert risk into certainty, or reduce the intensity of risk, by pooling where the misfortune of one family is set against the good fortune of another. Insurance companies cannot offer "fair" insurance because they must cover a cost of administration. Insurance remains advantageous as long as the cost of administration is less than the risk premium.

People cover risks with insurance when they can. We insure houses and personal property against fire and theft. We insure against illness. We insure against unemployment. Pensions and annuities insure us against poverty through survival beyond what our accumulated assets can finance. Programs of welfare for the very poor are insurance against destitution. Sometimes insurance is private. Sometimes it is undertaken through the intermediary of the government.

Recognition that insurance is sometimes private and sometimes public raises the general question of whether insurance is a commodity like bread and cheese that is supplied efficiently by the market, or a commodity like guns for the army that must be provided by the government if they are to be provided at all. Fire insurance is invariably private. Insurance against unemployment, destitution, and natural disasters is invariably supplied through the intermediary of the government. Insurance against illness and against poverty on surviving to a very old age are partly public and partly private, the mix varying at different times and places. Our concern here is not so much with what we do, but with our reasons for doing so. To what extent do the virtues of the competitive economy extend to the provision of insurance? Is there something about insurance that calls for collective action?

There are three major impediments to insurance in a competitive economy: (1) We learn too soon about impending misfortune; (2) insurance destroys the incentive to avert misfortune; (3) the insured may have private information that is concealed from the insurer.

It is normally supposed that information is desirable. The more we learn, the better off we become. That is true of most kinds of information, but there is at least one important exception. As an example, consider the date of your death. Suppose an angel offered to announce the date of your death not just privately to you, but to everybody who might want to know. The information would be advantageous by helping you to plan the rest of your life. The information may be disadvantageous by condemning you to poverty in the event that you will live to a ripe old age. Whether public or private, pensions have an aspect of insurance. One's annual income from a pension is set in accordance with the average life expectancy of the participants in the pension fund, so that people who live long lives automatically gain at the expense of people who do not. Participants are content with that arrangement as long as nobody knows in advance who the long-lived people will turn out to be. But if the angel announced the date of your death, you would not participate in the pension fund. If you are to have a short life, you would not wish to participate. If you are to have a long life, you would not be allowed to do so.

Similarly, if every doctor's prospects are as indicated in table 5.1, if nobody knows in advance who the very successful doctors and who the unsuccessful doctors will be and if the difficulties discussed in the next two paragraphs can be ignored, all doctors would wish to pool their incomes, transforming the risky prospect into a sure income of $100,000 per year. But if it is known in advance who will fall into each category, then pooling of incomes becomes impossible. All medical students agree to pool their incomes at any time prior to the moment when their incomes as doctors are revealed. Afterwards, once incomes are revealed, it is too late for pooling because the wealthy doctors will no longer participate. To destroy insurance, knowledge need not be complete. It may be sufficient to know that some people have a better than average chance of being successful.

The problem is compounded by *adverse selection* when information is private. Suppose there were two types of medical students, those with a 60 percent chance of being very successful and those with a 20 percent chance of being very successful, and suppose everybody knew who belonged to each type. Incomes could still be pooled within each type separately. People with a 20 percent chance of success would want to enter a pool with people with a 60 percent chance of success, but they would not be allowed to do so. Pooling could break down completely if each person knew his type and if the information were private, so that potentially successful people could not identify themselves as a basis for excluding people of the less successful type.

Another impediment to pooling is that *moral hazard* may destroy the incentive to work and save. Pooling may be destroyed even though there is no telling at the time of the insurance contract who the prosperous or fortunate people will be. Consider the doctors once again, but with a slight change in the interpretation of table 5.1. Suppose the numbers in table 5.1 refer to the incomes of doctors who work hard. A doctor who does not work hard is guaranteed an income of $90,000 (the income of an unsuccessful doctor) regardless. A doctor who works hard has equal chances of each of the three incomes in the table. Doctors work hard because they consider the chance of higher incomes to be worth the sacrifice. Under these circumstances, it is likely that pooling of incomes would destroy the incentive to work hard unless doctors could compel one another to do so. Without pooling, hard work is worth a one-third chance of an extra income of $10,000 and a one-third chance of an extra income of $20,000. With pooling and with many doctors in the pool, hard work gets you nothing because the gains from your hard work are shared equally among all the doctors in the pool. Analogously to the smoke and smoking example, nobody works hard and everybody is worse off in expectation than he would be without pooling. Pooling tends to emerge in sectors of the economy where disincentives are small. Pooling may be thwarted when disincentives are large.

The moral of the story is that people may favour public insurance in circumstances where the market supplies no private insurance or where they themselves would not take out private insurance if it were available. Public insurance cannot circumvent disincentives. Public insurance can, in effect, be contracted "earlier" than private insurance. Public provision of health care, of assistance for the unemployed and of pensions for the old and destitute, can be thought of as a contract established by our grandparents on our behalf, signed in our names well before any of us knows what his circumstances will be and long before we could arrange a contract for ourselves. Insurance is not the only motive for public provision of services. Other motives will be discussed in the chapters ahead.

Personal goods: [u = u (b, c, L, s) where b is bread, c is cheese, L is hours of leisure and s is survival probability]

Leisure and life expectancy are like ordinary private goods in that they belong to one person exclusively, but they differ from other private goods in that they cannot be purchased at a uniform price that is the same for everybody. My leisure and my life expectancy are mine alone, but I cannot trade them as I can trade bread or cheese. Consider leisure first. A person's utility function may be written as $U = u(b, c, L)$ signifying that his well-being depends upon his consumption of bread, b, per day, his consumption of cheese, c, per day, and his hours of leisure, L per day. Endowed with 24 hours in the day and confronted with prices $P^{\$b}$ and $P^{\$c}$ of bread and cheese and with a wage w, he chooses b, c, and L to maximize U subject to his budget constraint

$$bP^{\$b} + cP^{\$c} = w(24 - L) \tag{33}$$

The value at market prices of his consumption of bread and cheese equals the value at his wage of his supply of hours of work, $24 - L$. What differentiates leisure from bread and cheese is that the competition churns up market-wide prices, $P^{\$b}$ and $P^{\$c}$, of bread and cheese but not leisure. The wage would serve as a market-wide price of leisure if everybody were equally skilled, but that is not normally the case. Highly skilled people have high prices of leisure. Less-skilled people have low prices of leisure. You give up more bread per extra hour of leisure when your wage is high than when when your wage is low. That is the sense in which leisure is a personal good while bread and cheese are not. Each person's wage becomes his own personal price of leisure in terms of goods.

Life expectancy is like bread and cheese in two important respects. We strive to have more of it, and we are prepared to trade life expectancy for other goods or for money as, for example, when we desist from buying a safer car because it is too expensive. Life expectancy could be incorporated into the utility function, but only if the atemporal (without reference to the passage of time) function that we have been employing were generalized to account for goods consumed in different years with due allowance for the probability of being alive in each future year. We can avoid these complications and still account for survival probability by postulating an atemporal utility function $U = u(b, c, L, s)$ where, once again, b, c, and L are bread, cheese, and leisure, where s is one's probability of survival over the course of the current year, and where U is an increasing function of all four terms. What makes survival probability into a personal good like leisure rather than an ordinary private good like bread or cheese is the form of the budget constraint.

$$bP^{\$b} + cP^{\$c} + V(s)s = w(24 - L) \tag{34}$$

where the price of survival, $V(s)$, unlike prices of bread and cheese, is an increasing function of s. To see why $V(s)$ is an increasing function, note first that

$$s + m = 1 \tag{35}$$

where m is one's mortality rate. Survival would be an ordinary private good like bread and cheese if everybody could buy reductions in mortality rates at a uniform market-determined price. Were that so, the function we are calling $V(s)$ would reduce to a constant like $P^{\$b}$ and $P^{\$c}$.

The function $V(s)$ is increasing with s rather than constant because we buy reductions in mortality rates indirectly. Why this is so is best explained by an example. Consider a person whose base mortality rate – if he takes no steps to reduce it – is 2 percent; there would be a 1-in-50 chance of his dying over the course of the year. However, as shown in table 5.3, he can reduce his mortality rate in various ways.

Table 5.3 must be taken with a grain of salt. First, all the numbers are made up, with only the slightest connection to actual market costs. Second, and more importantly, many safety expenditures are joint products. For instance, one may trade in one's jalopy for a Ford, not just because the Ford is safer, but because it is more pleasant to drive. One visits a doctor not just to prolong one's life, but to make one's life more comfortable and disease free. Think of the numbers in the table as costs net of other benefits from the purchase in question. Third, not all expenditure to reduce mortality rates is in the form of money. For instance, the decision whether or not to wear a seat belt on any particular trip is a trade-off between time and mortality in the first instance, though the evaluation of time can convert trade-off into one between mortality and money. Since leisure is a personal good too, the exact terms of the trade-off between mortality and money would vary from one person to the next, but there is some determinate rate of trade-off for each and every person. Typically though not invariably, the monetary value of time is higher for the rich than for the poor. Fourth, certain expenditures may be appropriate for some people but not for

Table 5.3   The cost of survival and the value of life

Ways to reduce one's mortality rate	(1) cost ($)	(2) reduction in mortality rate (%)	(3) cost per life saved ($) 100(1)/(2)
Visit doctor once a year	1,000	0.4	250,000
Trade in one's jalopy for a new Ford	1,000	0.2	500,000
Install a fire alarm in one's house	200	0.02	1,000,000
Test for cancer	1,000	0.05	2,000,000
Trade in one's Ford for a Cadillac	10,000	0.2	5,000,000
Put a radio in one's yacht	800	0.004	20,000,000
Hire a co-pilot for one's private plane	30,000	0.06	50,000,000

The mortality rate with no expenditure on safety is 2%.

others. For instance, the option of putting a radio in one's yacht is of no significance to somebody who cannot afford or does not want to own a yacht. Fifth, one's base mortality rate is not constant as we have supposed but depends on how one conducts one's life. For instance, with reference to the last row of the table, one's mortality rate may be higher if one flies one's own plane than if one does not, but that mortality rate is reduced nonetheless by having a co-pilot.

What remains valid and instructive in table 5.3 is that everybody is presented with an array of mortality-reducing options, that each option has a well-specified market price, and that there is a limit on how much mortality-reduction one can buy with each option. For instance, one can buy a 0.4 percent reduction in mortality by visiting the doctor once a year, but one cannot buy an extra 0.4 percent reduction in one's mortality rate by visiting the doctor a second time. Indeed, if one could acquire the same reduction in mortality rate with each trip to the doctor, there would be no need for any of the other, more expensive means of mortality reduction shown in the other rows of the table. One would go to the doctor over and over again until one's mortality rate is reduced to 0 and one lives forever. It is this unhappy feature of mortality reduction that makes it a personal good rather than an ordinary good like bread and cheese.

The important feature of table 5.3 is the third column showing the cost per life saved of each type of mortality-reducing expenditure as shown in column (3). The cost per life saved is the amount of money a group of people would need to spend to save one life among them. For instance, if one person's trip to the doctor reduced his mortality rate by 0.4 percent, then the expectation is that one life would be saved per 250 people [100/(0.4) = 250] who visit the doctor. Their combined cost would be $250,000 [$1000 × 250]. The different ways of reducing one's mortality rate are ordered in table 5.3 from the lowest to the highest cost per life saved. One may think of the cost of life column (3) as a numerical correspondence to V(s) in equation (34). Specifically, the cost per life saved is the increase in V required for a given increase in s.

Taking table 5.3 at face value, supposing that the mortality-reducing expenditures in table 5.3 are the only such expenditures available, and ignoring the qualifications in the preceding paragraphs, we may think of each person as choosing his preferred place in the table. For each person, there is a cut-off expenditure such that he buys all cheaper reductions in his mortality rate and desists from buying all more expensive reductions. For instance, one may install a fire alarm but not test for cancer, in which case one would also visit a doctor once a year and buy a Ford rather than a jalopy, but not buy a Cadillac, put a radio in one's yacht or hire a co-pilot.

Generalizing the example, we may suppose each person to be confronted with a schedule of ways of buying reductions in mortality rates, and each person may be said to have a *value of life* defined as the most money he is prepared to pay *per life saved* to decrease his overall mortality rate. Typically but not invariably, the value of life of the rich would exceed the value of life of the poor, meaning not that the life of a rich person is worth more than the life of a poor person in some absolute sense or that the government, in choosing among public projects, should pay more to save the life of a rich person than it is prepared to pay to save the life of a poor person, but simply that the rich are prepared to spend more than the poor are prepared to spend to reduce their own mortality rates. We shall return to this matter in the chapter on public administration.

QUALITY, INFORMATION, AND ADVERTISING

It has been implicitly assumed so far, and will be assumed again in subsequent chapters, that people have full knowledge of their options, of the nature of the commodities they buy or might buy, and of their own preferences. These assumptions are all partly true, but not completely so. When there is only one kind of bread, one kind of cheese, and no other commodities, as was assumed in previous chapters, it is reasonable to suppose that choice is in conformity with a well-specified utility function. With thousands of different goods, each with an unlimited variety of qualities and textures, that is no longer so. I buy pills at a drug store not because I know by my own experience and expertise that they are on balance beneficial, but because I have been advised to do so by a doctor who, in turn, relies on the local medical journal reporting on research by the Food and Drug Administration whose scientists have come to believe that the good effects of the pills probably, for there may be no absolute certainty, outweigh the possible harm. I choose a brand of soap not because I have tested all brands, but by habit or because I was influenced by advertising on television. Neither the advice nor the advertising could be influential if the economist's model of taste were an accurate description of the world. There would be no advertising because no producer would have a financial incentive to advertise. A vast industry occupies the territory which the model postulates away.

The virtues of the competitive economy were demonstrated in chapter 3 for a model with perfect and complete knowledge of all products. Recognition of this limitation of the model raises the question of whether and to what extent these virtues carry over from the world in the model to the world at large. Does advertising promote efficiency in the economy, or could people become better off if advertising were curtailed? Does advertising foster the production of useful goods and the allocation of goods to people who need them most, or is advertising like piracy in the fishermen and pirates model, benefiting advertisers at the expense of consumers who pay the cost of advertising in the price of the goods they buy. Advertising is a complex phenomenon. The most that can be undertaken here is to list some of its impacts on society, without attempting to draw a balance between benefits and costs.

Advertising provides knowledge: A new product comes onto the market. There may be many people who would buy the product – and become better off by doing so – if they knew of its existence. Advertisements in newspapers and on television inform such people that the product has arrived and describe the product in enough detail that potential users are inclined to try it.

Advertising certifies quality: Consider a new brand of tomato juice. I may like it or I may not. Ordinarily, I might not be inclined to try it. But if the new tomato juice is heavily advertised, I may think to myself that it is probably quite good because the producer would not otherwise go to the expense of advertising. Let x be the percentage of those who try the new tomato juice who will like it and continue to use it. Presumably, the better the tomato juice, the higher x will turn out to be. Initially, the producer can be expected to know enough about the quality of the new tomato juice to make a shrewd guess about the magnitude of x, but potential consumers are entirely uninformed. Advertising may be the producer's only way of conveying to potential consumers the advertiser's true belief that x is rather high, for if x were low so that most people who tried the new tomato juice disliked it and resolved never to buy it again, the producer's expenditure on advertising would be wasted.

Both of these explanations would seem to be at least partly correct, and, in so far as either is correct, advertising promotes the welfare of the consumer. Though there is no role for advertising in the world of perfect knowledge as described in chapter 3, a role emerges when knowledge is imperfect and incomplete. Advertising transmits knowledge credibly from producer to potential consumer, causing actual markets to be closer than otherwise to the perfect markets we have postulated. In that role, advertising is fishing rather than piracy, productive rather than predatory. Yet it is hard to believe that the transmission of information is the whole of the matter. Too much of the advertising we encounter is for well-known products and adds nothing to our information about the products themselves.

Advertising transforms taste, creating a false association of the advertised product with happy times or conveying an aura of pleasure with no basis in the quality of the advertised product. A brand of cigarettes identifies the smoker with a cowboy riding a horse on the open range. Kids are encouraged to eat seriously twisted fries. We enjoy the antics of the energizer bunny. The province of Ontario associates gambling with wholesome small-town life around the country store. No watcher of television can suppose that the hour or so of commercials to which he is subjected each day is anything but a play on his emotions, an attempt to influence his behavior and a waste of his time. There is surely more here than the mere provision of information or assurance of quality.

Advertising is a waste of resources in inter-brand rivalry. Producers of different brands of essentially identical soap, cola, cigarettes, or financial services each tout the virtues of its brand and the superiority of its brand over all the rest. My advertising persuades consumers to buy my brand rather than yours. Your advertising persuades consumers to buy your brand rather than mine. Total sales of whatever it is we produce may be very little affected by the commotion, but resources that could be devoted to making things or to providing useful services are devoted instead to persuasion in circumstances where the net effect of each advertiser may be to neutralize the impact of its rivals. Advertising in this context is largely piracy, where the pirates take not just from fishermen, but from one another. There may be a prisoners' dilemma among advertisers within an industry. It may be profitable for each firm to advertise as long as other firms are free to advertise or not as they please, but every firms's profit might be higher if no firm advertised at all. Tobacco companies may secretly welcome a government-imposed ban on cigarette advertising, a ban that would be illegal collusion if the cigarette companies arranged it themselves.

Advertising finances public goods: The discussion of public goods earlier in this chapter began by citing the army and television as examples, but then focussed upon the army alone in the explanation of why public goods have to be supplied by the government if they are to be supplied at all. Television and the army are public goods because the entire expenditure on each of these goods conveys actual or potential benefits to a great many people at once, because each person's benefit from public goods flows from the entire expenditure rather than from a part reserved specially for him, and because beneficiaries do not interfere with one another. If you are protected by the army, then so too am I. Your pleasure from watching a television program is not diminished if I watch it too. But the army is provided by the government, while television is not. The army is provided by the government because nobody has an incentive to contribute to the cost of the army without some guarantee that other people will pay their share as well, a guarantee that can only be provided by compulsion. We vote for a government that forces each of us to pay for the army through our taxes. That is not true of television because there is an alternative source of finance. Television programs are provided free by firms as a vehicle for advertising. The programs are an inducement to watch ads we would never consent to watch if they were provided alone. It is difficult to say whether this is fishing or piracy: television programs offered in exchange for an opportunity to condition our tastes for the goods that the sponsors produce.

It is easier to list impacts of advertising – provision of information, certification of quality, creating artificial preferences, financing communicative public goods, distorting the quality of the public goods they finance – than to assess its overall impact upon the economy. Though a distinction can be drawn between commercial free speech and political free speech, a right of free expression blends at the edges into a right to advertise in that the latter cannot be abrogated altogether without affecting the former significantly. Yet the two are by no means identical. A right to advertise cigarettes may be denied without, at the same time, denying a right to discuss cigarettes, and to persuade people that cigarettes are not harmful to one's health or that the pleasure of smoking is worth the cost. All advertising could be taxed (or advertising could be reclassified as investment rather than as a cost of production) without violating the right of free speech.

REAL INCOME AS AN INDICATOR OF UTILITY

Time series of income per person were a substantial part of the evidence in chapter 1 of how dreadful life used to be. Table 1.9 showed the Canadian "real" national income per head to have increased from $2,554 in the year 1870 to $11,343 in the year 1950 and then to $34,492 in the year 2000. The term "real" implies comparability of incomes over time. Incomes each year had to be expressed in dollars of a common *base* year, so that, for instance, the income in the year 1950 would not appear small for no other reason than that prices of most goods have increased over time. The choice of a base year was arbitrary. The year 2000 was chosen because it is the most recent year in the series. People alive today can best relate to that year and can be expected to have a sense of what it means for a person to have an income of $2,554, $11,343, or $34,492 in the year 2000. These numbers signify that, over the entire 130-year time span between 1870 and 2000, the rate of economic growth – assessed as the solution, r, to the equation $2,554e^{r130} = 34,492$ – has been almost exactly 2 percent.

Most readers of this book will be familiar with statistics of real income and economic growth. Newspapers regularly quote such statistics as evidence of how much better off the nation is today than it was in some former year or of how much better off one country is than another. In presenting the numbers, it was simply assumed that the reader would have a general sense of what they mean. As already mentioned in chapter 1, real income each year would be the quantity of bread consumed if people consumed only bread. It is when many goods are consumed and when their prices change at different rates from year to year that the concept of real income becomes problematic. There was no attempt in chapter 1 to define real income precisely or to explain how the numbers were produced. We consider this matter now.

Statistics of real income are based on an analogy between a country and a person. If your annual income rises from $11,343 to $34,492, you have no difficulty in saying that you have become just over three times (3.05) as prosperous as you were before. The core meaning of the statement that Canadian real income per head grew from $11,343 in the year 1950 to $34,492 in the year 2000, is that people in the year 1950 were on average as prosperous as you would be today with an income of $11,343 and that people in the year 2000 were on average as prosperous as you would be today with an income of $34,492. Without that analogy, the statistics in table 1.9 would be devoid of implications about our lives. Once the analogy is recognized, real income each year assessed with reference to prices in the year 2000 becomes the amount of money one would require in the year 2000 to be as well off as the typical person in that year.

To pin down the meaning of "as well off as," imagine a comparison between yourself today (presumed to be the year 2000) and your grandfather at about the same age in the year 1950, where both you and grandfather are representatives of the people of your times, where you are presumed to be enough of a chip off the old block that both of your preferences can be represented by one and the same set of indifference curves. What has changed between 1950 and 2000 is the technology of production.

To sharpen the analysis, consider an economy with only two goods, bread and cheese, where everybody is identical to everybody else so that an unambiguous representative consumer can be identified, where taste (the set of indifference curves) remains invariant over time, but where technology is changing so that more of both goods can be produced in the year 2000 than could be produced in the year 1950. The technology in each of the two years is illustrated in figure 5.8 as a pair of production possibility curves, the lower curve showing all possible combinations of bread and cheese that could be produced in the year 1950, and the higher curve showing all possible combinations of bread and cheese that could be produced in the year 2000.

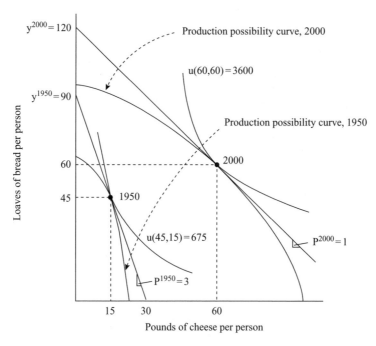

Figure 5.8 Different technologies and common tastes in the years 1950 and 2000.

A common set of indifference curves in the two years is assumed to conform to the utility function u = bc where b and c are loaves of bread per person and pounds of cheese per person. Recall from the discussion surrounding equation (2) of chapter 3 that the demand price of cheese, $p^D(b,c)$, the slope of the indifference curve at any combination of b and c, is just equal to b/c. Two indifference curves are shown, one tangent to the production possibility curve in the year 1950 and the other tangent to the production possibility curve in the year 2000.

The chosen outputs of bread and cheese in the two years are labeled "1950" and "2000." As in chapter 3, these are characterized by the tangency between an indifference curve and the production possibility curve, signifying that people make themselves as well off as possible with the available technology. The common slopes of indifference curves and production possibility curves at these points are the relative prices of cheese in terms of bread in the two years. Had the production possibility curve in the year 2000 been a scaled-up version of the production possibility curve in the year 1950, the relative price of cheese would have been the same in both years, for the postulated indifference curves are all scaled-up or scaled-down versions of one another. Prices are not the same because the shapes of the production possibility curves are different. As the curves are drawn, technical change between the year 1950 and the year 2000 was biased toward cheese. The percentage increase in the output of cheese as it would be if only cheese were produced exceeds the percentage increase in the output of bread as it would be if only bread were produced. Consequently, the increase in cheese production exceeded the increase in bread production, and the relative price of cheese declined. As shown in the figure, production of cheese

Table 5.4 Prices, quantities, and incomes

[Money incomes and real incomes computed from prices and quantities.]

	1950	2000	Growth rate (%)
Quantity of bread (loaves per head)	45	60	0.6
Quantity of cheese (pounds per head)	15	60	2.8
Price of cheese (loaves per pound)	3	1	—
Price of bread ($ per loaf)	40¢	$4.00	4.6
Price of cheese ($ per pound)	$1.20	$4.00	2.4
Money income ($ per head)	$36.00	$480.00	5.0
Quantities revalued at prices in the year 2000	$240.00	$480.00	1.4
Real income at prices in the year 2000 ($ per head)	$207.84	$480.00	1.7

increased from 15 pounds to 60 pounds per person, production of bread increased from 45 loaves to 60 loaves per head, and the relative price of cheese fell from 3 loaves of bread per pound to 1 loaf of bread per pound. This information is also listed in the first three rows of table 5.4.

In every year t, the income of the representative consumer is the amount of money required to buy the bread and cheese consumed per person in that year at the going market prices. Money income per person in the year t is

$$Y^{\$t} = P^{\$Bt}b^t + P^{\$Ct}c^t \qquad (36)$$

where b^t and c^t are amounts of bread and cheese consumed per person, and where $P^{\$Bt}$ and $P^{\$Ct}$ are money prices of bread and cheese in the year t. For the years 1950 and 2000, money prices and money incomes are shown in table 5.4.

Money income cannot be represented on a bread and cheese diagram such as figure 5.8. What can be represented is income with bread rather than money as the numeraire, the amount of bread that would be acquired if one devoted one's entire money income to the purchase of bread. With an income of $Y^{\$t}$ dollars, one could purchase $Y^{\$t}/P^{\$Bt}$ loaves of bread. Dividing both sides of equation (36) by the price of bread, we obtain the income of the representative consumer with bread rather than money as the numeraire,

$$y^t = b^t + p^t c^t \qquad (37)$$

where y^t is defined equal to $Y^{\$t}/P^{\$Bt}$ and p^t is defined equal to $P^{\$Ct}/P^{\$Bt}$, the price of cheese expressed as loaves (rather than dollars) per pound. For the years 1950 and 2000, income with bread as the numeraire is shown as a distance on the vertical axis of figure 5.8. It is the sum of actual consumption of bread and the amount of extra bread one could acquire by exchanging cheese for bread at the current relative price of cheese. It is the height of the projection onto the vertical axis of the point representing consumption of bread and cheese by a line with slope equal to the current relative price of cheese. Income in terms of bread is 90 loaves [45 + (15 × 3)] in the year 1950, and is 120 loaves [60 + (60 × 1)] in the year 2000.

With this machinery in place, we return to the original problem of measuring real income each year for the simple economy we have constructed. Set the year 2000 as the base year or standard of comparison, so that real income in the year 2000 and money income in the year 2000 are one and the same. Define real income per head in any other year t as the amount of money one would need in the year 2000 – and confronted with prices as they were in the year 2000 – to be as well off as one was in the year t with the average income and confronted with prices as they were in the year t.

Since real income is a measure of utility, one might suppose that real income could be measured as utility itself when, as assumed, $u = bc$. With the numbers we have chosen, the utility, u, of the representative consumer increases from 675 [15×45] in the year 1950 to 3,600 [60×60] in the year 2000. These numbers are clearly unsatisfactory measures of real income in 1950 and 2000 because the percentage increase in real income between any two years must lie within the range of the percentage increases of the different commodities. Bread consumption increases by a third (from 45 loaves to 60 loaves), cheese consumption increases four-fold (from 15 pounds to 60 pounds), but utility increases by more than five-fold.

The reason for the anomaly is that utility is *ordinal*. Recall the construction of Robinson Crusoe's indifference curves in chapter 3. Robinson Crusoe was asked a long series of questions of the general form "Do you prefer this to that?" He was never asked questions of the form, "By how much do you prefer this to that?" He could not be expected to answer such questions because there was no scale against which "by how much" could be determined. That is why utility is said to be *ordinal* (recognizing more or less) rather than *cardinal* (placing numbers on how much more or less). Only the shapes of indifference curves could be identified and their numbering was entirely artificial. A set of indifference curves conforming to the utility function $u = bc$ would conform equally well to the function $u = (bc)^2$ or to the function $u = \sqrt{(bc)}$. In this respect, utility is like temperature before the invention of the thermometer. It is often said that you cannot attach numbers to indifference curves, but that is not quite right. A more accurate statement is that you can attach numbers too easily. Any numbering system will do as long as higher curves get higher numbers. However, just as the height of a column of mercury quantifies temperature, so too may one particular quantification of utility take precedence over the rest because it focuses on some special concern or supplies a unique answer to some precise question. What we are seeking is a thermometer of utility, a choice of one of the many possible cardinalizations to indicate in a natural and humanly meaningful way how much better off people are becoming over time.

One might suppose that real income in any year t could be measured by repricing goods consumed in the year t at prices as they became in the year 2000. For any year t and expressing income in terms of bread rather than money, this measure becomes

$$y(b^t, c^t, p^{2000}) = b^t + p^{2000}c^t \tag{38}$$

The income, $y(b^t, c^t, p^{2000})$, is what would be required to purchase the bread and the cheese actually consumed in the year t at prices as they became in the year 2000. For $t = 1950$, this measure of income is illustrated as $y(b^{1950}, c^{1950}, p^{2000})$ on the vertical axis of figure 5.9 which is a reproduction of figure 5.8 with the production possibility curves removed to avoid cluttering the diagram and with additional information. It is the projection of the point "1950" onto the vertical axis by means of a line with slope

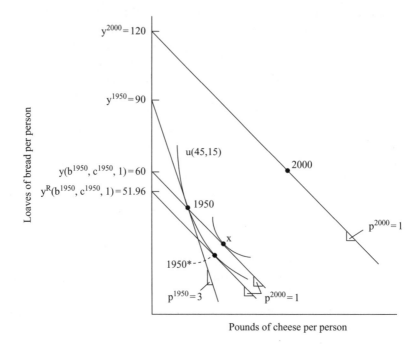

Figure 5.9   Income at current prices, income at prices in the year 2000, and real income.

equal to 1 (rather than 3) because the relative price of cheese in terms of bread in the year 2000 was equal to 1. As shown in the figure, the value of $y(b^{1950}, c^{1950}, p^{2000})$ is 60 loaves of bread. Converted from loaves of bread into dollars, the value of 1950 quantities at 2000 prices becomes $240[60 × 4] because the price of bread in the year 2000 was $4.00 per loaf.

The value at prices in the year 2000 of quantities consumed in the year 1950 turns out to be a good approximation to the measure of real income we are seeking, and it is often employed in practice because the primary data are readily available. But it is not quite right. It is an overestimate of real income in the year 1950 with the year 2000 as the base year because a person provided with enough money at prices in the year 2000 to buy the bundle of goods actually purchased in the year 1950 could make himself somewhat better off than the representative consumer in the year 1950. He would buy a bit more cheese which has become relatively cheap and a bit less bread which has become relatively dear, moving to a point such as x on a somewhat higher indifference curve. With an income sufficient to buy 45 loaves of bread and 15 pounds of cheese when the price of cheese is 1 pound per loaf – an income of 60 loaves of bread – a person whose taste is represented by the utility function u = bc would devote equal amounts of income to each good. He would buy 30 loaves of bread and 30 pounds of cheese, yielding him a utility of 900 [30 × 30] as compared with a utility of only 675 [15 × 45] acquired by the representative consumer in the year 1950. At prices in the year 2000, an income of 60 loaves is a bit too high.

With the year 2000 as the base year and with bread as the numeraire, the true measure of real income in 1950 is shown in figure 5.9 as the height on the vertical axis of the point $y_R(b^{1950}, c^{1950}, p^{2000})$. With that income and confronted with the relative price of cheese as it was in the year 2000, a person places himself on the highest attainable indifference curve by purchasing quantities of bread and cheese represented by the point 1950*. Real income $y^R(b^{1950}, c^{1950}, p^{2000})$ is a valid indicator of utility because, by construction, utilities at the points 1950 and 1950* are the same.

$$y^R(b^{1950}, c^{1950}, p^{2000}) = y(b^{1950*}, c^{1950*}, p^{2000}) \tag{39}$$

With our simple utility function, $u = bc$, we can easily compute the quantities b^{1950*} and c^{1950*} and the real income $y^R(b^{1950}, c^{1950}, p^{2000})$. These may be derived from two equations:

$$b^{1950*}c^{1950*} = b^{1950}c^{1950} \tag{40}$$

indicating that the two combinations of bread and cheese – b^{1950*} and c^{1950*}, and b^{1950} and c^{1950} – lie on the same indifference curve, and

$$b^{1950*}/c^{1950*} = p^{2000} = 1 \tag{41}$$

indicating a tangency between the notional budget constraint and an indifference curve – an equality between the demand price and slope of the budget constraint – when the consumer places himself on the highest attainable indifference curve. Together, equations (40) and (41) imply that real income in the year 1950 must be 51.96 loaves of bread.[1] Expressed in dollars rather than loaves of bread and with a price of bread of $4.00 per loaf in the year 2000, real income in the year 1950 becomes $207.84 [51.96 × 4] as shown in the bottom row of table 5.4.

For any year t and with the year 2000 as the base year, real income becomes

$$y^R(b^t, c^t, p^{2000}) = y(b^{t*}, c^{t*}, p^{2000}) \tag{42}$$

where b^{t*} and c^{t*} are determined by the procedure we have employed to determine b^{1950*} and c^{1950*}. This is a genuine utility indicator. Real income is the same for all points on the same indifference curve. It increases in passing from a lower to a higher indifference curve. As mentioned above, the choice of the year 2000 as the base year for a time series of real income is entirely arbitrary in that any other base year would have yielded equally valid measures of real income as an indicator of utility, but it is entirely appropriate in that the most recent year is "our" natural standard of comparison, telling us what we want to learn from the data.

Defined precisely for a person whose indifference curves are presumed to remain invariant, the concept of real income is put to work for comparisons between entire countries where people within each country have different preferences and where preferences differ from one time or one place to another. In constructing statistics of real income, such as the series for Canada in table 1.9, the statistician has no option except to proceed as though the time series of prices and quantities from which statistics of real income are to be constructed reflect the preferences of a representative consumer whose circumstances change but whose tastes remain invariant over time. Without that presumption, the weighting of quantities by prices would be meaningless. Furthermore, even in circumstances where everybody's taste is the same (in the sense of having the same set of indifference curves) and even if tastes remained invariant over time, the statistician cannot observe what the representative consumer would buy at some arbitrarily chosen set of prices. Quantities per head of bread, cheese, and other goods consumed are averages over many people whose tastes are never quite the same and whose incomes differ substantially. The rich may consume relatively more bread and the poor may consume relatively more cheese, even though their tastes are the same in the sense that each would adopt the same consumption pattern at any given income. At best, the shapes of indifference curves can be estimated, never observed directly. In practice, the statistician may have to rely on a repricing of quantities as the best available approximation to real income, on a measure of $y(b^t, c^t, p^{2000})$ in equation (38) as the best available approximation to $y^R(b^t, c^t, p^{2000})$ in equation (39).

The most formidable difficulty in construction of a time series of real income per head is in accommodating the virtually infinite range of goods and services consumed. Any measure of real income must account for a greater diversity of goods than the statistician can ever hope to observe. Bread is not a uniform substance as we have so far assumed. It is a collective noun incorporating hundreds of varieties and qualities of rye bread, bagels, muffins, baguettes, sliced white bread, onion bread, pita bread, and so on. Cheese is a collective noun incorporating hundreds of varieties and qualities of cheddar, Swiss, camembert, stilton, feta, cream cheese, cottage cheese, and so on. And, believe it or not, consumption encompasses more than bread and cheese. Qualities as well as quantities are changing all the time. What is the poor statistician to do? His only recourse is to estimate quantities of broad classes of goods by value deflated prices of selected items.

At the statistician's disposal each year are current money values of the purchases of the different classes of goods – such as groceries, clothing, and housing – and prices of a list of goods specified in great detail. Broad categories of expenditure may be broken down into somewhat finer categories such as vegetables, bread and cheese, but without direct measures of quality change over time. Prices on the other hand may be very specific, but only for a selection of goods. For example, the price of a certain quality of cheddar cheese may be tracked over time, but prices of many varieties of cheese may not be tracked at all. Quantities may be inferred by "deflation" of categories of goods or of the national income as a whole. Suppose that, between 1950 and 2000, the dollar value of sales of cheese per head rose by a factor of 324 percent and that the price of a specific quality of cheddar cheese rose by a factor of 152 percent. If we knew that prices of all varieties of cheese rise and fall in step, we would infer that the quantity of cheese per head increased by a factor of 213 percent. Comparable information about quantities could be inferred for each and every category of goods. If all prices rose or fell proportionally over time, an accurate time series of real income could be obtained by deflating money income each year with the price of tooth picks.

But prices do not rise or fall proportionally. The price of tooth picks soared over the last fifty years by comparison with the price of personal computers, which is to say that computing power has become dramatically cheaper. Since prices of different goods change at different rates, statistics of real income are computed by deflating money income with a price index, a weighted average of prices. High weighting for prices of goods becoming relatively more expensive over time yields a relatively low rate of economic growth. High weighting for prices of goods becoming relatively less expensive over time yields a relatively high rate of economic growth. The problem of how to measure real income can be reformulated as a problem of choosing the appropriate price index.

Repricing quantities and deflating money income with a price index are two sides of the same coin, and all of the problems discussed above in the choice of price weights reappear in the choice of the appropriate price index. Conceptually, these procedures are identical. In practice, statistics of real national income, such as the Canadian time series in table 1.9, are constructed by deflating money income with a price index because adequate data on income and prices are available but adequate data on quantities are not. The usual procedure for the construction of price indices is to weigh price changes by observed value shares of the different goods, and to change weights about once per decade to ensure that the estimated rate of economic growth each year does not depart too much from current valuations. This has the additional advantage of capturing some of the surplus from the introduction of new types of goods that tend to be expensive when first introduced and to become progressively less expensive over time. A unit of such goods is automatically given more weight at first and progressively less and less later on.

Statistics of real income must also take account of investment, depreciation, public expenditure, exports, and imports. We have so far been discussing real income as though the world were entirely static. To focus on the core meaning of statistics of economic growth, each year was looked upon as though it were entirely self-contained with no influence from the past and no preparation for tomorrow. By contrast, national statistical agencies construct income statistics as snapshots of economic activity each year. In table 1.9, the concept of real income was referred to as "Gross Domestic Product at 2000 Prices." *Product* refers to all goods and services produced in the current year by the government as well as by the private sector, inclusive of goods for consumption, such as bread, health care, and cheese, and goods for investment, such as factories, roads, and machines. *Gross* means that there is no deduction for depreciation. A new machine counts as part of gross domestic product even if an identical old machine is taken out of service. The reason for the asymmetry is that real depreciation is difficult to measure accurately. *Domestic* refers to production in Canada regardless of the owners of the factors of production. The study of how data are collected and compiled for the construction of time series of real national income is beyond the scope of this book, but would be covered in a text on the national accounts.

Chapter **Six**

TECHNOLOGY

Famine seems to be the last, the most dreadful resource of nature. The power of population is so superior to the power in the earth to produce subsistence for man, that premature death must in some shape or other visit the human race. The vices of mankind are active and able ministers of depopulation. They are the precursors in the great army of destruction; and often finish the dreadful work themselves. But should they fail in this war of extermination, sickly seasons, epidemics, pestilence, advance in terrific array, and sweep off their thousands and ten thousands. Should success still be incomplete; gigantic inevitable famine stalks in the rear, and with one mighty blow, levels the population with the food of the world.

Thomas Malthus, 1798

Among the oldest arguments in political economy is that mankind is destined to perpetual poverty because poverty alone can check the growth of population. Families are biologically programmed to bear about ten children, and most of our great grandparents did just that. If, of these ten births, four children survive to bear children themselves and if the average age of the mother at childbirth is twenty-five, then population doubles every twenty-five years. A million people in 1800 becomes two million in 1825, becomes four million in 1850, and so on. Sooner or later, population outruns the food supply and the standard of living falls to whatever level is necessary to check population growth. Starvation, poverty-born disease and malnutrition may be required to suppress the survival rate and to balance births and deaths. When people become prosperous through good harvests or technical change, their prosperity is soon eaten away by population growth and the old conditions of poverty are restored on a larger scale. A small ruling class might remain prosperous, but the great majority of people can never do so. Only within the last hundred years has technical change outdistanced population growth in much of the world, allowing ordinary people to become prosperous beyond the wildest dreams of our ancestors.

The model of technology in chapters 3 and 4 was adequate for explaining how markets work, but it is not adequate for expounding the Malthusian argument. In that model, bread and cheese were produced on lands of different productivities, with no recognition of the role of labor in production or of population growth. These are introduced here. The organization of the chapter is as follows: First, technology is represented as a simple *production function* in which bread is produced with land and labor. There follows a discussion of the optimal size of firm. The Malthusian story is then retold with the aid of an aggregate production function for the economy as a whole. Several aspects of production are then examined briefly: the determination of wages and rents, a multiplicity of goods and investment. Finally, technical change is introduced and the Malthusian story is modified accordingly.

THE PRODUCTION FUNCTION

Consider the technology of a farm where bread is produced by the application of labor to land. Specifically (supposing for simplicity that farmers grow loaves of bread rather than bushels of wheat), a farm of d acres of land and employing l workers produces b loaves of bread per day in accordance with the farm's production function, f,

$$b = f(l, d) \tag{1}$$

For a given input of land, $\bar{d}$, the production function is illustrated in figure 6.1. If the input of land were greater than $\bar{d}$, the entire production function would swing counter-clockwise, indicating that a larger output of bread would be obtained with any given input of labor. The principal assumption about the form of the production function can be expressed in two equivalent ways: that the production function bends forward, and that an *increase* in the input of labor *decreases* the output of bread per worker. The bending forward of the production function, as shown in figure 6.1, is referred to as concavity. Diminishing output per worker is illustrated in figure 6.2, which is identical to figure 6.1 except for the addition of new information. For any input of labor, such as l_1, the output of bread per worker, b_1/l_1, is shown in figure 6.1 as the slope of the line from the origin to the production function above l_1. It is immediately evident that output per worker would be constant if the production function were an upward-sloping straight line, but that output per worker decreases because the production function bends forward. Specifically, if

$$l_3 > l_2 > l_1 \tag{2}$$

then,

$$\frac{b_3}{l_3} < \frac{b_2}{l_2} < \frac{b_1}{l_1} \tag{3}$$

The farm owner's demand for labor – the number of workers hired at any given wage – and his residual rent on land – output of bread over and above the cost of

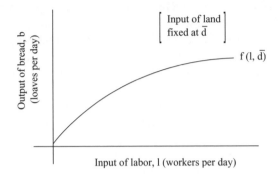

Figure 6.1   The production function.

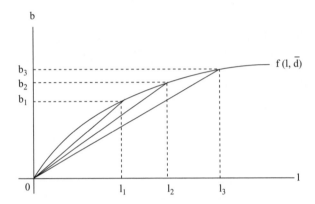

Figure 6.2   How an increase in the input of labor lowers the output of bread per worker.

labor – are illustrated in figure 6.3 which is another extension of the production function in figure 6.1. The farm owner hires workers at a market-determined wage, w, graduated in loaves of bread rather than money. He can hire any number of workers at a wage of w loaves of bread per day. [One can equally well think of the wage as $w per day when the price of bread is $1 per loaf, or as $wp per day when the price of bread is $p per loaf.] His options are represented in figure 6.3 by a "cost of labor," the line, 0β, with slope w, showing total payment to labor, wl, for any given number, l, of workers employed.

In choosing how many workers to hire, the farm owner seeks to obtain the largest possible *rent*, defined as the difference between the amount of bread produced and the amount of bread the farm owner must pay out in wages. For any input of labor, rent is represented in figure 6.3 by the vertical distance between the production function and the cost of labor line. As is evident from figure 6.3, this distance is as large as possible when the farm owner hires l* workers, where the slope of the production function is parallel to the cost of labor line. Equivalently, the rent-maximizing number of workers is that for which the *marginal product of labor* is just equal to the wage rate. The marginal product of labor is the slope of the production function. It is the

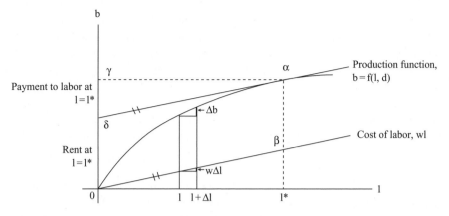

Figure 6.3   How the farm's demand for labor responds to the wage rate.

increase in output per unit increase in labor. It is the ratio $\Delta b/\Delta l$, where Δb is the increase in the production of bread brought about by a small increase, Δl, in the number of workers. When l workers have been hired, the change in rent from a small increase, Δl, in the number of workers is $\Delta b - w\Delta l$. If the change in rent is positive, the increase in the number of workers is advantageous to the farm owner and the original number of workers, l, must be too small. Similarly, if the change in rent is negative, the original number of workers must be too large. Only if there is no change – if $\Delta b - w\Delta l = 0$ when the number of workers is increased slightly – is the farm owner's rent maximized. But if $\Delta b - w\Delta l = 0$, then $(\Delta b/\Delta l) = w$ which is precisely the condition that the marginal product of labor is equal to the wage. [Notice that the word "rent" is employed here in a somewhat unusual sense. It refers here not to the amount of money one must pay for the use of someone else's land, but to the amount of money (or bread in this example) one acquires from the usage of one's own land. In the next section, we shall revert to the ordinary usage of the word. It turns out both usages of the term "rent" are virtually identical within the model of the agricultural economy in this chapter.]

The line $\delta\alpha$ in figure 6.3 is drawn parallel to the cost of labor line, touching the production function at α and intersecting the vertical axis at δ. The point α has to be directly above l* on the horizontal axis. It is immediately evident from the geometry of figure 6.3 that, when the farm owner hires the rent-maximizing number of workers, l*, his payment to labor becomes βl^*, equal to $\gamma\delta$ on the vertical axis, and that his rent becomes $\alpha\beta$, equal to $\delta\alpha$ on the vertical axis. The total output of bread, 0γ, is allocated $\gamma\delta$ to labor and 0δ to land.

THE ORGANIZATION OF PRODUCTION BY FARMS

Concentrating, as it has, on the individual farm, the analysis of production has as yet yielded no explanation of the size of farms (or, more generally, of the size of firms no matter what they produce). Suppose an economy contains L workers (each assumed to work a fixed number of hours per day) and D acres of land. We still require an explanation of how the land is divided up into farms. Bread might be produced by a vast number of small farms (as many farms as there are people, so that each farm contains D/L acres of land), by one great collective farm comprising the entire land of the nation, or by something in between. Bread, cheese, and most vegetables are typically produced by family farms. Cars, ships, and TV sets are typically produced by large firms hiring thousands of workers.

The production function in equation (1) has been looked upon as representing the technology of an isolated farm with a fixed acreage of land. It may also be looked upon as the technology of farming available to anybody and everybody who wishes to establish a farm. Think of an economy where bread, b, is produced with labor, l, and land, d, in accordance with the production function in equation (1), and where land and labor are for hire at market-determined *factor prices*: labor at a wage of w and land at a rent of r, both denominated in loaves per day. In this economy, entrepreneurs hire labor and land to maximize profit, expressed as a quantity of bread and defined as the difference between the quantity of bread produced and the quantity of bread paid out as wages and rents. Specifically,

$$\text{cost of production} = wl + rd \tag{4}$$

and

$$\text{profit} = b - (wl + rd) = f(l, d) - (wl + rd) \tag{5}$$

Our problem in this section is to explain the formation of wages, rents, and the size of farms in an agricultural economy with fixed supplies of labor and land. Profit maximization may be considered in two stages: the choice of l and d for any given b, and the choice of b on the understanding that l and d are optimal for any given b. The production function allows a given quantity of bread to be produced with many different combinations of labor and land. The first stage of profit maximization is to find the least expensive combination of labor and land for the production of a given amount of bread at a given wage and a given rent. The second stage is to choose the best size of farm on the understanding that the mix of land and labor is best for any given size output.

In the first stage, l and d are chosen to minimize the cost of production when output is fixed at b loaves of bread. Though the b loaves of bread could be produced with various combinations of labor and land (more land and less labor, or more labor and less land), there must be some best combination of l and d at which the average cost of bread (given w and r) is as low as possible. A profit-maximizing entrepreneur seeks to minimize the *average cost* of production, $T(b, w, r)$, where the average cost must, of course, be dependent on the wage, w, and the rent, d, and would normally be dependent on the output of bread, b, as well. The best proportion is whatever minimizes the cost of production in equation (4). As it is advantageous for the farm to minimize its cost of production at each and every possible quantity of bread produced, there may be defined a minimum average cost, $T(b, w, r)$, of producing b loaves of

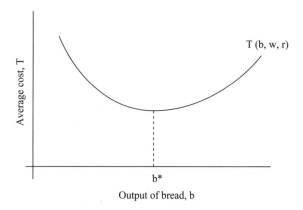

Figure 6.4   The average cost curve.

bread when the wage is w and the rent is r. Specifically, for any, b, w, and r,

$$T(b, w, r) = \min_{l,d} \left[\frac{wl + rd}{f(l, d)} \right] \quad \text{where } f(l, d) = b \tag{6}$$

and where the term $\min_{l,d}$ means "the combination of l and d that minimizes the value of the term in square brackets."

Since average cost is minimized for each and every combination of w, r, and b, all cost-minimizing combinations of l and d can be represented by a pair of functions,

$$l = l(w, r, b) \tag{7}$$

and

$$d = d(w, r, b) \tag{8}$$

with the property that

$$T(b, w, r) = [wl(w, r, b) + rd(w, r, b)]/b \tag{9}$$

It could happen that the average cost of bread is independent of scale so that $T(b, w, r)$ is the same regardless of whether the firm's output of bread, b, is large or small. If so, there would be no technological explanation of the size of firms. Otherwise, for any w and r, there is some optimal size of farm, b^*, for which

$$T(b^*, w, r) < T(b, w, r) \tag{10}$$

where b is any other quantity of bread. As illustrated in figure 6.4, the average cost of bread for given values of w and r would be U-shaped with a minimum at $b = b^*$.

The postulated shape of the average cost curve in figure 6.4 requires some explanation. There is reason for supposing it might be flat rather than U-shaped. The reason is that experiments can be replicated. If you can produce 5 tons of bread with 1 acre of land and 2 workers, then you should be able to produce 10 tons of bread with 2 acres and 4 workers. On the other hand, if cost curves of all products were flat, there would be no explanation of the size of firms and no reason why all the nation's goods and services are not produced together by one huge firm. To explain why average cost curves might be U-shaped is to explain why increases in output lower average cost up to some optimal output b*, but raise average cost thereafter. The fall in average cost below b* is typically explained by "indivisibilities." A farm requires at least one farmer, just as an automobile company needs a complete assembly line whether it produces one car or ten thousand. The rise in average cost beyond some b* is typically explained by limitations in the span of control. The larger the farm, the larger the hierarchy, and the greater cost of communication between the center and the periphery and the greater the risk of malfeasance at all ranks in the hierarchy. Optimal scale – the exact position of b* – depends on the technology of production. Once food was distributed by many thousands of small independent grocery stores. Now it is distributed by a few large grocery chains.

Generalizing from the farm to the firm in any industry whatsoever, the principal source of economies of scale is the division of labor. A thousand men working together can produce more cars per year than if each of them attempted to build an entire car all by himself. Modern production requires more knowledge and skill than any one person can be expected to master. The accountant, the lawyer, the marketing agent, the machinist, and specialized workers attending to each of the many stages in the making of a car must somehow coordinate their activity to produce cars in the right amounts and at the lowest possible cost. Sometimes stages in production can be separated by prices, as when a car company buys auto parts or material from other firms. The greater the importance of detailed coordination among stages in production, the greater the advantage of placing labor in one large firm that owns the means of production. Typically though not invariably, the optimal size of firm is substantially less than the total output of the good in the economy as a whole. Excessively large firms become unwieldy as initiative and flexibility are lost in a vast administrative bureaucracy. We shall have more to say about the organization of the economy in the next chapter.

Competition destroys profit. As long as every farm's technology is the same and as long as everybody is free to start up a farm by renting land and hiring labor at the going market prices, the only possible outcome in the market is for wages and rents to adjust to eliminate profit altogether, directing the entire output of the economy to workers and to owners of land. If profit, as defined in equation (5), were anything in excess of zero, more and more new entrepreneurs would establish new farms until such time as the scarcity of land and labor drives up wages and rent in a process that must continue until all profit is wiped out. Profit greater than zero is inconsistent with a competitive economy. Profit less than zero would drive farms out of business. Profit must be zero, and that can only occur when farms are producing at minimum average cost. Of course, profit can only be zero when l and d are chosen to minimize average cost of production in equation (6). Otherwise profit would have to be negative.

To say that pure profit (as defined in equation (4)) is wiped out in a competitive economy, is to say that

$$b^* = wl(w, r, b^*) + rd(w, r, b^*) \tag{11}$$

but

$$b < wl(w, r, b) + rd(w, r, b) \tag{12}$$

for any b other than b*. Competition among entrepreneurs requires w and r to be such that the cost (when wages and rents are denominated in loaves of bread) of producing b loaves of bread must be exactly b loaves of bread.

The reader may well balk at this implication of our model of the competitive economy. Surely, the entrepreneurs cannot be left with zero profits because businessmen who make no money would not remain in business at all. The reason why this story seems so peculiar is that real live entrepreneurs exert effort in contributing to the success of their firms, and they are compensated accordingly. They contribute a special kind of labor. By contrast, entrepreneurs in this description of the market contribute nothing, earn nothing, and are only useful as a rhetorical device to explain how the cost-minimizing farm emerges in the market.

The word "profit" is used here in a very special sense. Frequently the word profit is used to refer to the return to capital (so far not discussed) and entrepreneurship; on that definition, farms must earn profit. Here profit refers to the return to the farm over and above the earnings of all inputs; on this definition the equilibrium profit must be zero, and a non-zero profit portends some change in prices or production. The rock bottom meaning of the zero profit condition is that competition governs the returns to the talents of businessmen, just as it governs prices of goods and the returns to ordinary factors of production, with nothing left over as a free gift to the entrepreneur. A more realistic model of production would allow entrepreneurs to differ in ability; in effect, each entrepreneur would have his own production function linking output to all other inputs. In that case, all but the least efficient among the entrepreneurs who are actually operating firms would earn some profit. This case is usually covered in ordinary textbooks of microeconomics.

Finally, the market determines wages and rents to equate the sums of all farms' demands for labor and land to the available supplies.

$$Nl = L \tag{13}$$

and

$$Nd = D \tag{14}$$

where N is the number of farms, l and d are each farm's usage of labor and land, and L and D are the total supplies of labor and land in the economy as a whole.

Pulling all this together, we can represent this agricultural economy by six equations:

technology:

$$b = f(l, d) \tag{1}$$

the farm's demand for labor:

$$l = l(w, r, b) \tag{7}$$

the farm's demand for land:

$$d = d(w, r, b) \tag{8}$$

disposition of the supply of bread:

$$b = wl(w, r, h) + rd(w, r, h) \tag{11}$$

market for labor:

$$Nl = L \tag{13}$$

market for land:

$$Nd = D \tag{14}$$

These six equations determine market-clearing values of six unknowns: b, w, r, l, r, and N. Markets and technology determine wages, rents and the size of farms, just as they determined the outputs and prices of bread and cheese in chapter 3.

The same general principles govern the allocation of the various resources of the nation into firms producing the entire spectrum of goods that people consume. It is essential for a competitive economy that the cost-minimizing size of firms in any industry be small relative to industry as a whole. Small firms are price-takers, like the owners of the five plots of land in the latter part of chapter 3. Firms too small for their behavior to affect prices, wages, or rents look upon all such prices as market-determined and invariant, and they make their production decisions accordingly. By contrast, large firms exercise a degree of monopoly power and must bargain with one another over prices of inputs and outputs.

THE AGGREGATE PRODUCTION FUNCTION AND THE IMPOVERISHMENT OF MANKIND

When the productive resources of the economy are allocated appropriately among farms, one can pass from the production function of the farm – $b = f(l, d)$ in equation (1) – to an *aggregate production function* for the economy as a whole

$$B = F(L, D) \tag{15}$$

where B is total output of bread, L is the total supply of labor, D is the total acreage of land, and the function F for the entire economy is a magnification of the function f for the farm. The aggregate function F inherits the general shape of the function f, so that output per worker, B/L, diminishes steadily as L increases when D remains constant, and the slope of the function F(L, D) – like that of the farm in figure 6.3 – becomes the wage of labor in the economy as a whole. In short, figures 6.1, 6.2, and 6.3 can be reinterpreted as pertaining to F, L, and D rather than f, l, and d, on the understanding that the scale of production is appropriately chosen.

It is often helpful to give the production function a specific algebraic form. A useful specification for the purposes of this chapter is

$$B = F(L, D) = AL^{\alpha}D^{(1-\alpha)} \tag{16}$$

where A is a parameter representing the efficiency of the economy. This specification of the production function has three very convenient properties: constant returns to scale, constant share of output accruing to labor, and a simple specification of the rate of growth of output per worker. These will be considered in turn.[1]

Constant returns to scale means that a proportional increase in the inputs, L and D, generates the same proportional increase in output, B. If inputs of L and D yield an output B in accordance with equation (16), then, for any x whatsoever, inputs of xL and xD yield an output of xB.[2] If it just so happens that 10 workers and 5 acres of land can produce 1 million loaves of bread per year, then 30 workers and 15 acres of land can produce 3 million loaves of bread per year. Note that there is no contradiction between constant returns to scale in the aggregate production function and variable returns to scale – increasing returns to scale up to some output b* and decreasing returns to scale afterwards – for the farm. The reason is that farms can be replicated. A U-shape cost curve for the firm is consistent with a flat cost curve for the entire industry to which the firm belongs.

The parameter α in equation (16) turns out to be the share of output accruing to labor.[3] This remains true regardless of whether the input of labor is large or small. Specifically, it follows from equation (16) that

$$wL = \alpha B \tag{17}$$

and

$$rD = (1 - \alpha)B \tag{18}$$

If the input of labor is large, the equilibrium wage of labor must be small. If the input of labor is small, the equilibrium wage of labor must be large. Adjustments in w within a competitive economy are just sufficient to keep wL constant and equal to αB. From equations (17) and (18) together, it follows that

$$wL + rD = B \tag{19}$$

Constant returns to scale in the production function guarantees that the returns to land and labor exhaust the product with nothing left over.

Malthus' pessimistic prediction in the quotation at the beginning of this chapter can be translated into the language of the production function. The prediction is that there is no escape from perpetual poverty because all income over and above bare subsistence is eaten away by population growth. It is that, if population grows steadily at some fixed percentage per year whenever output per worker, B/L, exceeds the subsistence level, then output per worker can never exceed the subsistence level for any length of time. Technical change or a great epidemic, such as the Black Death, may lift output per worker temporarily, but population growth always returns output per worker to a biologically predetermined level.

To establish this proposition, rewrite equation (16) as

$$Y(t) = AL(t)^{\alpha}D^{(1-\alpha)} \tag{20}$$

where Y replaces B in designating the total output of bread (because Y is the usual symbol in economics for the national income), where Y and L are dependent on time, and where A (representing the state of technology in the economy) and D (the total output of land) are assumed to be invariant. The implications of technical change, allowing A to vary over time, will be examined later in the chapter. Now suppose the labor force grows steadily at a rate of n, or 100n percent per year, so that the number of workers, $L(t)$, in each year t becomes

$$L(t) = L(0)e^{nt} \tag{21}$$

where $L(0)$ is the input of labor in some reference year 0 which may be thought of as the present.[4]

Dividing both sides of equation (20) by $L(t)$, we acquire an indicator of output of bread per worker, $Y(t)/L(t)$, each year

$$B(t)/L(t) = A[D/L(t)]^{(1-\alpha)} = A[D/L(0)]^{(1-\alpha)}e^{-(1-\alpha)nt} \tag{22}$$

Since A, D, and $L(0)$ are invariant, it follows that output of bread per person must decline over time at a rate of $(1-\alpha)n$ per year.

$$\text{The rate of growth of output per head} = -(1-\alpha)n \tag{23}$$

If the labor force grows at 3 percent per year (i.e. $n = 0.03$) and if labor's share of the national income is two-thirds (i.e. if $\alpha = 2/3$), then the output of bread per person *declines* at a rate of 1 percent per year (i.e. $-(1-\alpha)n = -(1/3)(0.03) = -0.01$). Of course output per head cannot decline at a constant rate forever. Eventually, the fall in output per head checks population growth because people reduce birth rates voluntarily or because death rates rise as a consequence of impoverization.

With this machinery in hand, we can now tell the Malthusian story numerically. The numbers are chosen to represent an imaginary agricultural Canada where the entire national income consists of one great pile of bread produced with land and labor. Designate the year 2000 as the current year for which the value of t in equation (20) is equal to 0. There are 30 million people, of whom half are in the labor force. The national income is $900 billion. The area of land is 300,000 square miles (a strip of land 3,000 miles long and 100 miles high, on the assumption that all land more than 100 miles from the US border is barren). Labor's share of the national income is 2/3, but people's income derives in part from the ownership of land. Thus, $Y(0) = 900$, $L(0) = 15$, $D = 3$, and $\alpha = 2/3$ where Y is expressed in billions of dollars, L is expressed in millions of workers, and D is expressed in hundreds of thousands of square miles. To be consistent with these numbers,[5] the value of A in equation (20) must be 102.6. It follows immediately that, with half the population at work, a doubling of the population from 30 million to 60 million leads simultaneously to a rise in the national income from $900 billion to $1,429 billion and to a fall in income per worker from $60,000 to $47,622, or a fall in income per head from $30,000 to $23,811.

Obviously, population cannot grow forever. Eventually, population growth at any given rate per year drives income per head down to the subsistence level where people are so impoverished that population growth stops, either because the birth rate falls or because the death rate from starvation or disease increases to match the existing population growth. Suppose current population growth is 3 percent per year and the subsistence income is $15,000 per head (or $30,000 per worker), exactly half the income per head in the year 2000. Designating t as the year when income per head falls to the subsistence level, it follows immediately from equation (20) that L(t) equals 120 million workers and population in the year t must have grown to 240 million people.[6] When the year 0 is 2000, the year t must be 2069 because t = 69 is the solution to the equation

$$L(t) = L(0)e^{(0.03)t} \qquad\qquad (24)$$

where $L(0) = 15,000$ and $L(t) = 120,000$. If the production function in equation (20) were the true representation of the technology of the Canadian economy and if the assumed parameters were strictly correct, population growth would continue for the next 69 years and then stop, while income per head would decline steadily over this period until it becomes half what it is today.

It is interesting to consider what happens when population growth is not invariant, but varies in accordance with the standard of living. The greater the income per head the higher the rate of population growth up to some critical limit beyond which population growth remains constant. Realistic demographic models can be quite complicated because account must be taken of birth and death rates at every age of a person's life. It is sufficient for our purposes to adopt the radically simplified demography incorporated in the following assumptions:

1   Everybody works, so that population and labor force are the same.
2   Property is equally distributed, so that everybody's income, y, is the same.
3   On surviving to age 30, half the population gives birth to quintuplets. Childbearing occurs at no other time in a person's life.
4   The proportion of the population surviving to age 30 is as indicated by the curve in figure 6.5, showing that one's probability of living to age 30 increases steadily up to 100 percent at a standard of living of y^1 and that only two-fifths of the population survives to age 30 if the standard of living falls as low as y^0. [A survival rate of two-fifths is just sufficient to keep the population constant when half the population surviving to age 30 gives birth to 5 children and when no births occur at any other age.]

On these assumptions, the only mortality rate that matters is the probability of not surviving to age 30. Since all births occur at age 30 and since each and every birth is of quintuplets, the population would grow two and a half times per generation – or at an annual rate of 3 percent per year – if the standard of living were high enough that people's survival rate to age 30 were 100 percent. But the standard of living cannot remain above subsistence permanently. As shown in figure 6.2, a steady rise in population with a fixed supply of land causes a steady fall in the standard of living.

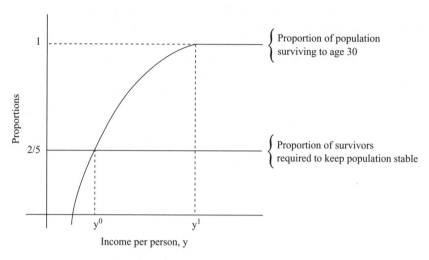

Figure 6.5   Births, deaths, and the standard of living.

Eventually, the standard of living drops to y^0, causing a high enough mortality rate to stop population growth. From then on, the standard of living remains low enough that the birth rate and death rate are the same. Actual population dynamics can be quite complex, but our simple assumptions require the economy to evolve into a steady state where only two-fifths of all children born survive until age 30 to give birth to children of their own. As shown in chapter 1, the world was somewhat like that until about a hundred years ago. If y^1 were $25,000 per year and y^0 were $15,000, then the population would eventually stabilize at the lower income. The Malthusian story is not that population keeps growing forever but that it stops growing at some level of income low enough to increase the death rate or reduce the birth rate sufficiently that they become the same.

The pessimistic account of the human condition in this chapter stands in sharp contrast to the glowing account of economic progress in chapter 1, especially the historic rise in both population and national income per head as exemplified by the Canadian time series in table 1.9. A ten-fold rise in national income per head was accompanied by a ten-fold increase in population. Can we therefore dismiss the Malthusian story as unrealistic fiction that need not trouble us today? There are several reasons why the story may still be interesting. It does seem relevant for many countries where potential prosperity has been thwarted by population growth. It may point to environmental risks down the road where the scarcity may be minerals, water, or air as well as land. By focussing on a very simple but internally consistent model of production, it supplies a framework for the introduction and analysis of additional considerations that may account for the observed coexistence of population growth and increase in the standard of living over a long period of time. The rest of this chapter is an examination and extension of the simple Malthusian model.

Why aren't Canadians starving? There are at least four possible answers. The first is that Canadians have carved out for themselves a very large and sparsely populated chunk of the world's territory and are actively keeping others out. The second is that people have learned to control population, reducing the average size of family even when the standard of living is high. The third is that investment can compensate for population growth. The fourth is that productivity per worker has been buoyed up by technical change. The first answer is undoubtedly right, but may not be the whole story. The second may be very much more important, not just to Canada but to many countries close to the margin of subsistence. One of the reasons why couples have traditionally wanted large families was to ensure that some of their children survive to care for them in their old age or to preserve the family name. As discussed in chapter 1, very large families were once necessary to preserve communities from extinction and to ensure parents that some children would survive to care for them in their old age. The rapid decline in mortality rates as a consequence of prosperity and of advances in medical care brings forth huge increases in population until such time as people learn to reduce the size of their families, as they may be inclined to do in order to afford to educate their children well. The third and fourth considerations will be discussed below.

PRODUCED MEANS OF PRODUCTION: CAN SOCIETY INVEST ITS WAY OUT OF CATASTROPHE?

We have reasoned so far as though production and consumption occurred timelessly and simultaneously. In chapter 3, each day's bread and cheese were produced by land on that very day. In this chapter, each day's bread is produced with current supplies of labor and land. Nothing done yesterday could augment the area of land today. Nothing done today can augment the area of land tomorrow. To reason from a model of goods produced with labor and land is to abstract from the many factors of production that are themselves produced. Even land is augmentable in that fertilization today affects the productivity of land tomorrow. Other factors of production – such as factories and machines – are not supplied by nature, must themselves be built, and depreciate or become obsolete in the course of time.

To capture this aspect of technology we introduce a new factor of production called *capital* defined as the summation of all non-human resources: land, factories, machines, trains, ships, roads, airplanes, and so on. What differentiates capital from land in our model of production is reproducibility. Capital can be produced: land cannot. Think of capital as a number of machines, though the nation's stock of capital is in reality much more comprehensive. The stock of capital in the year t is designated as K(t).[7] The role of capital in the economy can be modeled by three key assumptions.

(a) Capital replaces land in the economy-wide production function, so that

$$Y(t) = F(L(t), K(t)) \qquad\qquad (25)$$

where $L(t)$ is the input of labor in the year t, $K(t)$ is the input of capital in the year t, and $Y(t)$ is income in the year t, best thought of in this context as the quantity of some all-purposes good.

(b) Income may be consumed or invested in new capital.

$$Y(t) = C(t) + I(t) \tag{26}$$

where $C(t)$ is consumption in the year t and $I(t)$ is investment in the year t.

Equation (26) is the production possibility curve for consumption goods and investment goods together. With bread as the only consumption good and machines as the only capital good, equation (26) shows what combinations of bread and machines can be produced in the year t. This production possibility frontier is comparable to the production possibility frontier for bread and cheese in chapter 3, but linear rather than curved. The critical assumption in equation (26) is that the relative price of bread and machines is independent of how many of each are produced, that the supply curve of machines in terms of bread is flat. There is an additional assumption that, with Y measured in dollars, the prices of bread and machines are both equal to 1; this additional assumption is innocuous because units of bread and cheese can be appropriately defined. If a loaf of bread costs $2 and a new machine costs $100, then a loaf of bread counts as two units of income and a machine counts as 100 units of income.

(c) Investment this year augments capital next year through the equation

$$K(t + 1) = K(t)(1 - d) + I(t) \tag{27}$$

where d is the rate of depreciation per year. The capital stock available for use in the year $t + 1$ is the sum of the undepreciated portion of the capital stock from the previous year plus the extra capital produced in that year.

The replacement of irreducible land with reproducible capital alters the Malthusian story significantly. Inevitable impoverishment is replaced by a possibility of consumption per head remaining permanently above the subsistence level, but not of permanent growth. Impoverishment can sometimes be warded off indefinitely, and consumption per person held permanently above the subsistence level when the rate of population growth is not too large.

To show this, replace the general production function in equation (25) with the specific function

$$Y(t) = AL(t)^{\alpha}K(t)^{1-\alpha} \tag{28}$$

and assume that (1) population grows at a rate of n per year, (2) the rate of investment is constant at i year after year. In other words,

$$\Delta L(t)/L(t) = n \tag{29}$$

and

$$I(t)/Y(t) = i \tag{30}$$

Equation (29) is the same as equation (24) except for the representation of time. In equation (24), the variable t is continuous. In equation (29), t refers to a chunk of time such as a day or a year and $\Delta L(t)$ refers to the changing population of the labor force during that year. Together, equations (29) and (30) ensure that society

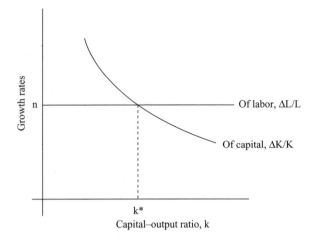

Figure 6.6 Growth rates of labor and capital.

evolves automatically to a *steady state* at which consumption per head does not decline, but remains the same, year after year, forever. The steady state is characterized by a permanent capital–output ratio, k^*, at which Y and K grow at the same rate as L. From equations (27) and (30), it follows immediately that

$$\Delta K(t)/K(t) = I(t)/K(t) - d = i/k(t) - d \qquad (31)$$

where $\Delta K(t)$ is defined as $K(t+1) - K(t)$, and $k(t)$ is the capital–output ratio, $K(t)/Y(t)$. The meaning of equation (31) is that the rate of growth of capital is high when the capital–output ratio is low, and is low when the capital–output ratio is high, as illustrated in figure 6.6. One can see from the figure that as there is no upper or lower limit to $\Delta K(t)/K(t)$, there must be some value, k^*, of the capital–output ratio for which $\Delta K(t)/K(t) = \Delta L(t)/L(t) = n$, signifying that the growth rates of labor and capital are the same. From equation (28) it follows that if L and K both grow at a rate n, then Y must grow at that rate as well, ensuring that consumption per head remains constant.

The permanent, steady-state value of the capital–output ratio must be

$$k^* = i/(n+d) \qquad (32)$$

and the steady-state value of consumption per head becomes[8]

$$C/L = A^{1/\alpha}[(1-i)i^{(1-\alpha)/\alpha}]/[(n+d)]^{(1-\alpha)/\alpha} \qquad (33)$$

The steady-state value of consumption per person (the value of C/L that can be maintained year after year) depends on the parameters i (the rate of investment), n (the rate of population growth), d (the rate of depreciation), α (labor's share of the national income when the aggregate production function is as shown in equation (28)), and A, the constant term in the production function. The lower the rate of depreciation, the lower the rate of population growth and the higher the rate of investment (as long as the rate of investment remains below some critical level), the higher the steady-state consumption per head will turn out to be. Depending on the magnitudes of the parameters, the steady-state consumption per head may or may not exceed the subsistence level, and, if not, disease or malnutrition can be expected to lower the rate of population growth. But under no circumstances can consumption per head increase indefinitely. Eventually, some steady-state consumption per head is attained, beyond which there can be no additional growth in consumption per head. For no values of the parameters is consumption per head permanently increasing. For long-term economic growth, there must be technical change.

TECHNICAL CHANGE

As sketched in chapter 1, the twentieth century has witnessed a vast increase in the standard of living for much of the world's population coupled with an equally vast increase in population itself, a combination that would have been impossible if technology had conformed to the production functions we have described so far. Even with full allowance for the role of reproducible capital in the production function, the increase in population per acre of arable land would have reduced the standard of living drastically, or starvation would have choked off population growth long before the present population was attained.

In practice, technical change and capital formation interact in complex ways, but, to introduce the economics of technical change, it is expeditious to abstract from capital, reverting to the simple production function in equation (16) where income is produced with land and labor. There are several ways to incorporate technical change into this aggregate production function. The simplest, and perhaps most instructive, is to convert the term A in the production from a constant to a variable that increases over time reflecting the accumulation of knowledge, spontaneously or as a consequence of deliberate research. The production function becomes

$$Y(t) = A(t)L(t)^{\alpha}D^{(1-\alpha)} \tag{34}$$

where D is constant, L(t) grows steadily over time at a rate n, there are constant returns to scale in L and D (doubling L and D leads to a doubling of Y as well), and technical change is at a steady rate g, that is

$$A(t) = \overline{A}e^{gt} \tag{35}$$

On this specification of technology, the standard of living may rise or fall over time as the outcome of a balance between population growth and technical change. Other things being equal, population growth reduces output per head. Other things being equal, technical change increases output per head. The balance could go either way, depending on the rate of technical change, the rate of population growth, and the precise form of the production function.

Let y(t) represent income per person in the year t, that is $y(t) = Y(t)/L(t)$. When population grows at a rate n, income per person in the year t becomes

$$y(t) = Y(t)/L(t) = \overline{A}e^{gt}[D/L(t)]^{1-\alpha} = \overline{A}[D/L(0)]^{1-\alpha}e^{[g-(1-\alpha)n]} \tag{36}$$

where L(t) grows steadily at a rate g in accordance with equation (21) and where $\overline{A}[D/L(0)]^{1-\alpha}$ is invariant. It follows immediately from equation (36) that

$$\text{Growth rate of income per head} = g - n(1 - \alpha) \qquad (37)$$

Equation (37) shows that income per head may be positive or negative depending on the balance between population growth and technical change. In our example, where population grows at 3 percent and labor's share of the national income is $\frac{2}{3}$, a rate of technical change of 2 percent generates a rate of growth of income per head of 1 percent per year. There is no guarantee that technical change is sufficient to offset population growth in the determination of output per head. The balance depends on the magnitudes of g, n, and α. Presumably, the Canadian parameters have been sufficient to maintain a steady rise in output per head.

INVESTMENT, TECHNICAL CHANGE, AND RETURNS TO SCALE

Increasing or decreasing returns to scale are easily incorporated into the aggregate production function. It is sufficient to rewrite equation (16) as

$$B = AL^{\alpha}D^{\beta} \qquad (38)$$

where the parameters α and β need not add up to 1. Returns to scale depend on the sum of α and β. The aggregate production function shows

constant returns to scale if α and $\beta = 1$,

increasing returns to scale if α and $\beta > 1$

and

decreasing returns to scale if α and $\beta < 1$.[9]

Except where α is greater than 1, increasing returns to scale cannot, all by itself, stave off the decline in output per head, but it can reinforce or dampen other effects.[10] We saw above how investment can stabilize output per head in the presence of population growth. Some growth of output per head can be attained when there are increasing returns to scale. In that case, a steady rate of investment preserves the capital–labor ratio, allowing increasing returns to scale to buoy up output per head. The mechanics of the interaction among investment, technical change and returns to scale are beyond the scope of this book, but would be covered in texts on economic growth.

Investment and technical change reinforce one another, investment preserving the capital–labor ratio and technical change lifting output per unit of input of labor and capital together. Nor is it necessary, as we have so far supposed, that technical change be attached to the constant term, A, in the aggregate production function. To attach technical change to the constant term is to envision technical change as falling like manna from heaven regardless of what people do or how they behave. It might instead be assumed that technical change attaches itself to capital, investment, or even population. To attach technical change to investment is to suppose not only that new technology is incorporated in new machines, but that, the more society invests, the greater the impact of technology must be. That assumption might be incorporated into the model of investment above by allowing A to remain constant and replacing the term I(t) in equation (27) with the term I(t)e^{gt} where g is the rate of technical change. To attach technical change to labor or population is to suppose each person is as likely as any other to discover a way to increase productivity, so that the more people there are, the greater the overall change in productivity will be.

THE ENVIRONMENT OF TECHNICAL CHANGE

From a distance, aggregate technical change can be looked upon as a steady, almost autonomous, increase in productivity represented by the growth over time in the "constant term" of the aggregate production function. Up close, aggregate technical change consists of a thousand small, deliberate, man-made changes in the economy. People create technical change by scientific research into the laws of nature, by tinkering with products to improve them, and by developing new kinds of goods and services. Recognition that technical change is deliberate raises questions about whether the right amount of resources is being devoted to technical change, about whether the competitive market deploys those resources expeditiously and about the proper role, if any, of the collectivity in sponsoring and directing discovery.

Research is like investment in that expenditure of money and effort today yields a stream of benefits tomorrow. Research differs from most ordinary investment because knowledge is a public good, like television, roads, or guns, yielding benefits to large numbers of people simultaneously. No two people can eat the same slice of bread or own the same machine; but any two people can watch the same television program, drive on the same road or possess the same knowledge of the laws of nature without one person's activities interfering with the activities of the other. Your understanding of a theorem does not block me from understanding that theorem as well. Reverting to the example in chapter 4, imagine a society where everybody has a plot of land and where, until people learn how to make cheese, every plot yields 20 loaves of bread and nothing else. Once people discover how to make cheese, every plot yields 20 loaves of bread or 10 pounds of cheese or any linear combination of the two, such as 10 loaves *and* 5 pounds of cheese, or 16 loaves *and* $2\frac{1}{2}$ pounds of cheese. Each person chooses a combination of bread and cheese to make himself as well off as possible, and my choice of a combination of bread and cheese imposes no restriction on yours. Any restriction on the production of cheese is inefficient in the sense that an appropriate reorganization of production and distribution could make everybody better off.

An unfortunate attribute of public goods – not excluding knowledge – is that nobody produces them voluntarily and at his own expense. Though everybody gains from being defended by the army, people must be compelled to contribute a share of the cost. People vote to finance the army through taxation, though nobody would be prepared to pay any tax unless compelled by the community to do so. The same is true of the acquisition of knowledge. If the cost of learning how to make cheese is more than any one person's benefit from the discovery but less than the sum of everybody's benefits from the discovery, and without a collective arrangement for sharing the cost or rewarding the inventor, the secret of how to make cheese may never be discovered, though everybody would gain from the discovery.

The acquisition of knowledge confronts society with a trade-off between efficiency in the acquisition of knowledge and efficiency in use. As knowledge is a public good, efficiency in use warrants that information be made freely available to everybody; but if knowledge were free there would be no private incentive to create it. There are two ways around this dilemma. Like roads and the army, the acquisition of knowledge might be administered by the government and financed by taxation. Alternatively, creators of knowledge might be awarded property rights to their discoveries, in the belief that society's gain from providing an incentive to create knowledge outweighs its loss from restricting subsequent use. The first procedure is followed when research is conducted in publicly funded research labs or universities. The second is followed when patents are awarded for invention.

A patent is a grant to the inventor by the state of a monopoly on the use of his invention. By making invention profitable, patents draw forth inventions from every corner of society, mobilizing talent and ideas that no centrally directed agency would be able to identify and coordinate. Among the virtues of the competitive economy listed at the end of chapter 5 was that markets economize on knowledge. Prices are signals to each and every participant in the market about how his resources may be employed not just to enhance his own income, but to produce what the rest of society values and is prepared to pay for. Profit-seeking in response to prices induces people with special knowledge of local conditions to act as though coordinated by an all-seeing central planner, though no actual flesh-and-blood planner could ever recognize and employ all the information that traders collectively command. This is so not just for local opportunities (such as where to locate and how to design a restaurant or grocery store), but, much more importantly, for invention. Invention is almost always problematic. People disagree about whether this or that prospective invention is likely to materialize. Companies with solid records of achievement make what is subsequently recognized as huge mistakes in judgment. No planner could ever be expected to know in advance what is worth developing and which routes lead to a deadend. Here, above all, it is important to cull ideas from everywhere and to draw upon a diversity of experience and expectations. Patents do this, albeit imperfectly, by enabling a person with an idea for invention to proceed all by himself if he has the funds or if he can persuade a few rich people or firms that his idea has merit, as exemplified by the now-famous garages of Menlo Park. Patents draw forth invention that no planner could be expected to recognize.

There are social costs to the patent system. Among these costs is the restriction on the use of the newly invented product. A patent is a monopoly, and, like any monopoly, can only supply revenue to its possessor by enabling him to raise the price of the monopolized product above what the price would be in a competitive market.

As was discussed in chapter 4, this tax-like feature of patents imposes a deadweight loss on society as a whole, for the cost of patent protection to the users of the patented product exceeds the revenue to the patent-holder. The deadweight loss is, nevertheless, a price worth paying for access to a product which, but for the patent system, would not be available at all. As was also discussed in chapter 4, the newly invented product yields a surplus to the community, even when the newly invented product is monopolized.

Revenue from a patent may be insufficient or excessive. It is insufficient when the cost of inventing is less than the full benefit of the invention to society as a whole but more than the return to the investor from the patent. This situation can arise because patents are granted for a fixed term of years and because there remains a surplus to consumers that cannot be appropriated by the patent-holder. Revenue from a patent is excessive if, for example, a shorter patent life would have been sufficient to draw forth the invention. The progress of science has a dynamic of its own. As science evolves, there appear from time to time prospects for new inventions that are easily developed against a background of the science of the day, but that would have been virtually impossible to develop earlier. In these circumstances, the reward goes to the person who wins the race to the patent office. Small effort in discovery may generate huge profit to the patent-holder and huge monopoly-induced distortions in production and consumption, though the discovery itself was virtually pre-ordained. Patents supply the same reward – monopoly power to all inventions, though many inventions would be forthcoming for less. Even without patents, the prospect of being first to produce a newly invented product may be sufficient inducement to invention, though this incentive is significantly weaker, and likely to draw forth fewer inventions, than the patent system.

Where the prospective income from a patent is substantially in excess of the cost of invention, there may emerge a patent race among potential inventors, multiplying the cost of invention without significantly affecting the quality or the timing of the discovery itself. Suppose the progress of science suddenly churns out a potential invention that costs $1 million to develop to the point where it can be patented and yields $10 million to the patent-holder. As many as ten potential inventors may go for the prize. All potential inventors are sure they can create the invention, but there remains some uncertainty about when the invention will be completed and who among them will win the patent race by inventing first. In these circumstances, the only advantage to the consumer in having ten contenders rather than one is that the invention might appear a little sooner than otherwise, an advantage that may not be worth the extra $9 million payment to the patent-holder. One must be careful with this argument. When the returns to a patent are large, the benefit from the invention would be large too, and a small reduction in the length of time before an invention appears may be quite valuable. Furthermore, potential inventors may adapt different strategies of discovery where nobody knows in advance which strategy or strategies will be successful. Duplication of invention actively is wasteful in some circumstances, but socially advantageous in others.

The patent office and the courts must decide when a patent is warranted and what exactly is to be covered by the patent. Patents are often awarded when the process of discovery is far enough along that one can be sure the invention is feasible, but before a new product is actually produced. Fine judgment is required to determine the exact moment of feasibility. In the patenting of the computer chip, a higher court reversed the decision of a lower court to award the patent to an early applicant with a less specific invention rather than to a later applicant with a more detailed plan. The scope of a patent is equally contentious. Firm A invents product A. Then firm B invents product B that is only useful in the presence of product A, or firm B makes use of the technology in product A to develop product B which is superior to product A. Should firm B be entitled to a patent on product B? If not, the patent on product A destroys the incentive for anybody other than firm A to develop extensions or improvements in product A. If the patent on product A covered product B as well, firm A would be able to squeeze out most of the potential profit from product B, rendering the invention by firm B unprofitable. But if the patent-holder of product B owes nothing to the patent-holder of product A, then the profit from the patent on product A might be insufficient to induce firm A to undertake the invention, in which case neither product A nor product B might have appeared. There is no obviously correct resolution to these problems.

There is an international dimension. Knowledge benefits everybody worldwide. In so far as patents are required to procure invention, it may be in the common interest of people everywhere to respect patent rights. There may, nevertheless, be a prisoners' dilemma among countries deciding how extensive patent protection should be. A small country or a country with very little research of its own may have an incentive not to recognize patents granted abroad, enabling its firms to produce patented goods cheaply and to compete effectively with firms in other countries where patents are enforced. International treaties have attempted to curb such behaviour, but major disputes remain over the range of discoveries that can be patented.

A distinction is drawn between science and invention. Science uncovers the laws of nature. Invention creates new machines and new goods. Society declines to grant patents on scientific laws because every discovery rests on previous discoveries, so that it would be virtually impossible to determine the value of the extra contribution of scientific discovery to subsequent changes in products or processes. Instead, scientific research is conducted at public expense in government laboratories and in government-funded research by universities. Within universities, each researcher is expected to choose and direct his own research, in the belief that modest rewards for publication and each researcher's pride in discovery supplies a better guide for the conduct of research than could be supplied by any central administration. Frequently, this consideration predominates. Sometimes not, as in the Manhattan project to develop the atomic bomb where researchers with different skills were directed to a common goal.

No bright line separates unpatentable science from patentable technology. Inevitably, the demarcation of the boundary between science and invention is open to dispute. The patenting of life forms is especially contentious. Some believe that life forms – genes, genetically engineered seeds, and genetically engineered species of animals – should be patentable. Others believe that all knowledge about life forms belongs within the domain of science and should be available to all mankind.

MALTHUS AGAIN

Malthus's gloomy prediction that mankind is condemned to poverty bordering on starvation remains of great significance today not for its accuracy, but for its logic and for calling attention to the reasons why it turned out wrong. As shown in table 1.4, world population grew over seven-fold from 1750 to 1994, but standards of living did not decline as Malthus would have predicted. Instead, as shown in table 1.8, income per head grew from three-fold in some regions of the world to almost twenty-fold in others. In the course of the chapter, we clarified Malthus' prediction with reference to an aggregate production function without technical change, and then went on to show how technical change may buoy up the standard of living indefinitely.

Economic history can be seen as perpetual war between technical change and population growth, a war that technical change has been winning for some time, but not everywhere and not necessarily forever. The war may be changing its character. Malthus saw impoverishment as a consequence of population growth in the presence of a fixed and unchangeable supply of land. Scarcity of land remains an important consideration, but science has increased the productivity of land considerably, and new scarcities are appearing. In some countries, the scarcity is water rather than land. Stocks of minerals and petroleum are limited. So too is the capacity of the biosphere to accommodate human activities. Some fish stocks are running out, and the atmosphere cannot absorb an unlimited amount of domestic and industrial waste. In parts of Africa and elsewhere, the crude Malthusian story remains largely true, with substantial population growth creating widespread famine in years when agricultural output is reduced by drought.

Though the world may be over-crowded, a community may see itself as too small. Every religion, every linguistic group, acquires an incentive to expand its population as a means of dominating society through strength of arms or by majority rule voting. The suspicious may even be inclined to see this consideration as a source of opposition to abortion and birth control, though, were that so, the emphasis would be on opposing these practices in one's own community, but not elsewhere. Population control may confront us with a classic prisoners' dilemma. It may be in every faction's interest to increase its share of the population, but in the interest of the community as a whole to avoid substantial population growth.

Population growth remains an impediment to prosperity, in some countries because of new scarcities of water, minerals and the capacity of the biosphere, in other countries for the old Malthusian reason that a fixed endowment of land has to be divided into smaller and smaller plots per person. In western Europe, America and parts of Asia, birth control alone may be sufficient to check the growth of population, though the practice of abortion is widespread. No longer dependent on the support of one's children in old age and confident that almost all children survive to adulthood, people respond to the fall in mortality rates by reducing birth rates accordingly. In other countries, birth control may be inadequate to check population growth, and there may be no escape from the grim choice between tolerance of abortion and the starvation of live children later on. Once a requirement for the preservation of the tribe, the biblical injunction "be fruitful and multiply" may be lethal today.

ADDENDUM: MANY GOODS, MANY INPUTS

When people consume bread and cheese, instead of just bread, there would be separate production functions for each good, specifically,

$$B = F(L_B, D_B) \tag{39}$$

and

$$C = G(L_C, D_C) \tag{40}$$

where B and C are total outputs of bread and cheese, where F and G are the corresponding production functions, where L_B, L_C, D_B, and D_C are inputs of labor and land in the two industries, where

$$L_B + L_C = L \tag{41}$$

and

$$D_B + D_C = D \tag{42}$$

where L and D are total supplies of labor and land in the economy as a whole. From these four equations there can be derived a production possibility frontier, such as is shown in figure 3.1, where points on the frontier show the largest possible output of one good for each and every output of the other. Then, combining goods markets as described in chapter 3 with the factor markets as described above, we arrive at a determination of total outputs – B and C – together with the inputs of land and labor for each good – L_B, L_C, D_B, and D_C – and the corresponding prices – p, w, and r, the relative prices of cheese in terms of bread, the wage of labor and the rent of land. Typically, when resources are organized to maximize the output of cheese for any given output of bread, the resulting ratio of land to labor would be different for cheese than for bread (L_C/D_C differs from L_B/D_B) reflecting differences in the shapes of the production function G and F. This explanation of the emergence of the market "equilibrium" values of p, w, r, B, C, L_B, L_C, D_B, and D_C is to say the least sketchy and intuitive, just sufficient to give the reader a sense of the process and some confidence that the market "works." Our excuse is that these matters are discussed much more thoroughly and at greater length in standard textbooks on microeconomics.

Generalizing once again, we can think of the economy as churning out thousands of different goods (bread, cheese, apples, sweaters, shoes, cars, train rides, movies, and so on), each with its own production function summarizing the contributions of thousands of different inputs (labour of many different skills, managers, factories, machines, legal services, marketing services, and so on), together with prices just sufficient to clear the markets for every good and every input. Nevertheless, for some purposes, the entire process can be represented by *one* production function such as that in equation (24), where Y is aggregate output of all consumable goods and services, L is the total input of labor, and D is the total input of non-human factors of production.

When many goods and many factors of production are recognized, three types of prices can be distinguished: *flow* prices of goods, such as bread and cheese, produced and consumed at a moment of time, *factor* prices for the use of resources, such as land and labor, in the production of goods, and *stock* prices for the ownership of resources, such as land and shares on the stock market, expected to yield a return for a long time ahead. Most of the analysis in this book pertains to flow prices in an economy that does not change over time. Economic dynamics would be discussed in an advanced course in economic theory or economic growth. Stock prices are central to the economics of finance.

Chapter **Seven**

ASSOCIATIONS

Firms are "islands of conscious power in this ocean of unconscious cooperation like lumps of butter coagulating in a pail of buttermilk."
D. H. Robertson

The endowments of schools and colleges have . . . not only corrupted the diligence of public teachers, but have rendered it almost impossible to have any good private ones.

Adam Smith

The picture of the market in chapter 3 was of people interacting with prices but not with one another. Each person buys or sells what he pleases in an impersonal market with no argument, no bargaining, no subordination of inferior to superior, no law suits, no conflict, no politics, and no fighting. People supply labor and the services of other factors of production to acquire income for the goods they wish to consume, in an environment where all wages, rents, and prices are determined by the market automatically and beyond the capacity of any person or small group of people to influence to any significant extent. *Perfect competition*, as this process is called, is the perfect absence of competition in the everyday meaning of the term. The extraordinary feature of the price mechanism is that a degree of order emerges from the apparent chaos. Each person acts in his own interest entirely, yet the outcome is not chaos or gross inefficiency as in the model of fishermen and pirates in chapter 2. The outcome is efficient in the admittedly limited sense that no rearrangement of resources and reallocation among people of the goods and services produced could make everybody better off. Some people could be made better off but only at the cost of making others worse off.

Life in the market is lonely but free. The impersonal market provides everyone, rich or poor, with a sphere of independence within which he may conduct his life as he pleases. For centuries, the capacity of perfect competition to supply "order without orders" has captured the imagination and the admiration of thoughtful people, limiting the role of the government in the economy, leaving room for personal liberty, without which democracy would be impossible, and establishing an essential link between liberty and prosperity.

This picture of the price mechanism is at once enormously compelling, accurate in the aggregate but inaccurate in detail. From a distance, people's actions appear to be governed by market-determined prices exclusively. At the grocery store, you are confronted with prices which you can do nothing to change, and you may buy what you please at those prices. Prices may differ slightly from one store to another, but there are limits on how much prices can differ because a grocery store that charges more than other grocery stores, and that does not supply its customers with compensating services, will soon lose its business. In the daily newspaper, you can find bid and ask prices of all stocks of all major stock companies, prices that gyrate wildly from time to time, but are what they are regardless of whether you trade or not. Commodity markets are equally impersonal. Even labor markets are impersonal to the extent that average earnings of different skills and occupations are determined by broad economic conditions beyond anybody's ability to control. Prices are affected by broad trends in the market as a whole, but, at the grocery store or in the stock market, the individual trader is typically too small a player to affect prices all by himself.

Up close, a different picture emerges. Businessmen are constantly bargaining with one another about prices or contracts. Deals break down in acrimony and recrimination. Output is wasted in maneuvers that are profitable to the actor but wasteful of resources and detrimental to society as a whole. Disagreements often find their way to court, where they are resolved at great trouble and expense to all concerned. Workers are organized in hierarchies where the relation between superior and inferior is similar in kind, though not in degree, to the relation between lord and peasant in the middle ages. The market remains as the enemy of subordination, providing workers with the opportunity of changing employment or of working for themselves, but the cost of quitting a job is often high enough that the sting of command cannot be eliminated altogether.

This chapter is a look beneath the price mechanism at associations among people not guided by prices exclusively. We begin with bargaining which was discussed briefly in chapter 3 but only as a foil for the market, as an apparently intractable problem that the market circumvents. Now we recognize that bargaining is not circumvented completely and that people do strike deals, sometimes quickly and easily, sometimes slowly, painfully, and expensively. Though bargaining is ubiquitous in the economy, the science of economics has no entirely satisfactory explanation of how bargains are struck. There are theories of bargaining, but no compelling model of how rational people bargain, comparable to the model of rational people responding self-interestedly to prices churned up by the market. Next we discuss contracts. We have reasoned so far as though the protective role of the state were limited to the defense of fishermen against pirates or, more generally, the assurance to each person that his land and capital will not be appropriated by others. That is necessary but by no means sufficient as the foundation of a well-functioning economy. The protective role of the state must extend from the protection of property to the enforcement of promises. There is no other way to supply each person with sufficient assurance that others' promises will be kept and that his own promises will be believed. Though the protection of ordinary property is less straightforward than we have supposed so far, the enforcement of contracts is considerably more problematic, for promises are typically ambiguous at the edges, and not all promises are enforced by the state. The labor contract is especially complex and will be discussed separately. Voluntary associations are then considered. Corporations, labor unions, and political parties can be looked upon as complex contracts with rights and obligations specified by the state. The chapter ends with a review of the boundaries of property rights.

PRICE-TAKING AND DEAL-MAKING

A house is for sale. Eventually, the market narrows down to a most enthusiastic buyer who would be prepared to pay as much as $300,000 and the next most enthusiastic buyer who would be prepared to pay no more than $250,000. The seller would rather dispose of the house for $250,000 than leave it on the market. There is, therefore, a surplus of $50,000 between the highest price that an enthusiastic buyer would be prepared to pay and the lowest price that the seller would be prepared to accept from the most enthusiastic buyer. The market places upper and lower limits on the deal, but within these limits the buyer and the seller must somehow agree upon the price. Whatever price they agree upon is, in effect, a division of the surplus between them.

A firm hires a worker. Employment requires an understanding about the number of hours of work, the right of the employer to demand overtime, payment for overtime, and what exactly the employer may require the employee to do. Once the employee has acquired some experience at the job, there is likely to be a gap between the most an employer can demand without inducing the employee to quit and the least the employee can supply without inducing the employer to fire him. The gap is a surplus that employee and employer must divide between them.

An accountant and a biologist come together with a good idea for a new business. The enterprise provides them with a combined income of $500,000 per year, but, to run the business, they must give up their old jobs that provided the accountant with a salary of $225,000 per year and provided the biologist with a salary of $175,000 per year. Before embarking on the new enterprise, the accountant and the biologist must first agree on how to allocate the $500,000 between themselves. Clearly, whatever the allocation, it must supply the accountant with at least $225,000 and the biologist with at least $175,000, for otherwise one of them would be better off at his old job. The bargaining problem is how to allocate the $100,000 per year of *surplus* from the enterprise, the difference between the income from the enterprise, $500,000, and the sum, $175,000 + $225,000, of the participants' *outside options* forgone. Bargaining takes place over the surplus. Once again, the market places limits on the deal, reducing the range over which people must bargain, but, within these limits, the participants must agree upon a division of the pie.

In all three cases – the sale of a house, the employment of labor, and the formation of a new business – the market churns up a surplus that must somehow be divided between associates. The third cases may serve as a paradigm for all three and for a host of similar situations. The case is illustrated in figure 7.1 with the accountant's income

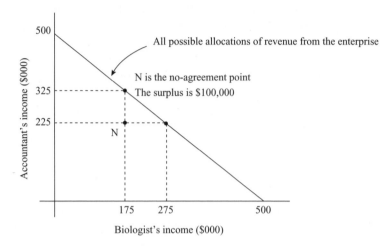

Figure 7.1   The context of bargaining.

on the vertical axis and the biologist's income on the horizontal axis. The downward-sloping line, at 45 degrees to both axes and cutting each axis at $500,000, shows all possible allocations of ownership between the accountant and the biologist. The point N, mnemonic for no-agreement point, shows each party's income in the event that they fail to reach an agreement and must earn incomes in some other way. It is immediately evident from the figure that each party would acquire $100,000 over and above his outside option – $325,000 instead of $225,000 for the accountant, or $275,000 instead of $175,000 for the biologist – if the other party were prepared to participate in the enterprise for no more than his outside option. The portion of the line between the two dots, one directly above and the other to the right of the no-agreement point, shows the locus of all allocations that make both parties better off than they would be if the business did not get off the ground because the parties failed to agree on an allocation of the profit. The little triangle formed by these two dots and the non-agreement point itself shows all net allocations (actual allocations less the part of the potential profit used up in bargaining) for which both parties are better off agreeing than disagreeing. Bargaining takes place over the surplus. Bargaining models are explanations of how the surplus might be allocated.[1]

Before considering how bargains may be struck, note two important situations where the need for bargaining does not arise. The first is where the accountant and the biologist come together to create a standardized product to be sold in a market where other accountants and other biologists are combining to produce identical products and where remuneration of accountants and biologists is determined in a wider labor market for the economy as a whole. In these conditions, there can be no surplus for the accountant and the biologist to divide. Suppose that the going incomes of accountants and biologists are Y_A and Y_B per year, and that, together, an accountant and a biologist produce one unit of the product per year. If so, the forces of demand and supply would generate prices of the products of such enterprises just sufficient to supply accountants and engineers with their outside options. The combined income from the enterprise would be $Y_A + Y_B$, and there would be no surplus to bargain about. Competition eliminates much potential bargaining, but not all. Bargaining remains in bilateral monopoly when, for instance, the management of a firm confronts a unionized labor force, when a monopolist of software confronts a monopolist of hardware, or when, as we have been supposing, an accountant and a biologist must divide the profit in a unique enterprise in which they are both essential if the enterprise is to be conducted at all.

The other situation where bargaining need not arise is if one party "owns" the common venture and the other party is hired at a market-determined wage. If the surplus of $500,000 is from a product or process that is patented by the biologist and if satisfactory accountants can be hired at the going wage of $225,000, then the biologist need not offer "his" account more than $225,000, and he can keep the remaining $275,000 for himself. Bargaining becomes necessary when a particular accountant and a particular biologist need one another if the project is to be undertaken at all. The surplus may be looked upon as the cost of abandoning long-term collaboration.

HOW PEOPLE BARGAIN

A bargain is the splitting of the surplus between two claimants called person A and person B, who might be the accountant and the biologist in the discussion surrounding figure 7.1. The "stake" in the bargain is a sum of money, Y, to be allocated by agreement between person A and person B,

$$Y = Y_A + Y_B \tag{1}$$

where Y_A is the income assigned to person A and Y_B is the income assigned to person B. If a bargain is struck, the parties lose their outside options consisting of an income of N_A to person A and income of N_B to person B. The bargain is only worthwhile when the income to be allocated in the bargain exceeds the sum of the outside options, that is, when $Y > (N_A + N_B)$. Since the agreement is voluntary, no bargain can be struck unless both parties' incomes exceed their outside options, that is, unless $Y_A > N_A$ and $Y_B > N_B$. The surplus from the bargain is the value of the stake over and above the outside options.

$$S = Y - (N_A + N_B) = (Y_A - N_A) + (Y_B - N_B) \tag{2}$$

Any bargain is an allocation of the surplus, $Y_A - N_A$ to person A and $Y_B - N_B$ to person B. The bargain is illustrated in figure 7.1 with $Y = 500, N_A = 255, N_B = 175$ and, therefore, $S = 100$. The bargaining problem is to explain how a deal on the allocation of the surplus is struck.

Bargaining may be modeled as arbitration or as negotiation. When bargaining is seen as arbitration, the outcome of a dispute becomes a reflection of the arbitrator's sense of fairness or of the sense of fairness of the parties to the dispute. When bargaining is seen as negotiation, the outcome of a dispute emerges from a sequence of offers and counter-offers that continue until some offer by one party is accepted by the other. In either case, the ideal is to identify an equilibrium resolution to the dispute, a bargaining equilibrium comparable to the competitive equilibrium allocation of bread and cheese among the five people in chapter 3. The ideal is to predict the resolution of a dispute from its circumstances, just as the allocation of bread and cheese is predicted from the initial distribution of the ownership of property. Much is riding on this enterprise. Businessmen and politicians strike bargains all the time. Neither commerce nor government could otherwise be maintained. If bargaining cannot be explained satisfactorily, then we have to recognize that much of the detail of the world escapes our net and cannot be explained with the tools of economic analysis. Recognizing that people often bargain successfully, we would have to treat people's willingness to strike a bargain as an empirical, unexplained fact of life.

Though the models of arbitration and negotiation to be discussed below are both determinate, they require such strong restrictions on the context of bargaining as to constitute an admission that there really is no satisfactory explanation within the confines of economic analysis of how bargains are struck. The models are insightful nonetheless. Important features of bargaining are highlighted by the strong assumptions required to make bargaining determinate. Both of the models to be discussed are representative simplifications of a large literature on how deals are struck.

The arbitration model prescribes an allocation in accordance with the arbitrator's sense of what is right, just, fitting, or appropriate as a resolution of the dispute. There may or may not be an actual arbitrator whose decision the parties to the dispute have agreed to accept. If not, the arbitration model would reflect a common understanding by the parties to the dispute of what is appropriate and fair. The underlying principle in the arbitration model is equality. When nothing is known about the circumstances of the parties to the dispute, the only conceivable allocation is a fifty-fifty split. This solution might be modified when there is information about the nature of the dispute and the consequences of a failure to agree. A fifty-fifty split makes no sense when one of the parties' outside options is preferable. For example, if the revenue from a new enterprise is $500,000 and if the parties' outside options forgone are $300,000 and $100,000 (rather than $225,000 and $175,000 as assumed in figure 7.1), a fifty-fifty split of the revenue from the new enterprise would leave one party worse off than he had been before. The only reasonable interpretation of a fifty-fifty split in this context pertains to the surplus rather than to the combined income from the enterprise. With outside options of $300,000 and $100,000, a fifty-fifty split of the surplus would supply the parties with incomes of $350,000 and $150,000.

There are additional problems. Bargainers may differ in their attitude to money. One party may have little use for more than, say, $200,000; his utilities of all sums in excess of $200,000 may be almost the same. Another party may have a critical target income; his life's ambition may require at least, say, $275,000, but, if he cannot obtain that, he may not much care whether he gets, say, $175,000 or $200,000. Bargains may be struck over matters other than money. The employment contract takes account of all aspects of the job: hours of work, obligation to work overtime, overtime pay, safety standards, time off, the right to join a union, or rules for promotion, as well the rate of pay. Bargainers' attitudes toward money and non-monetary aspects of disputes should somehow be recognized in any rule of arbitration.

The rule requiring a fifty-fifty split is generalized in equation (3) to account for such considerations. Define $u^A(Y_A)$ and $u^B(Y_B)$ to be the utility functions of person A and person B where Y_A and Y_B could be incomes as supposed above but could also be the entire set of benefits to person A and person B under the terms of an agreement. The outside options, N_A and N_B, could be specified accordingly. The utility functions, u^A and u^B, may be discovered by the conceptual experiment discussed in chapter 5 for identifying risk aversion. A possible rule of arbitration is to provide the parties with incomes or benefits, Y_A and Y_B, to maximize the product

$$W = [u^A(Y_A) - u^A(N_A)][u^B(Y_B) - u^B(N_B)] \tag{3}$$

where $Y_A + Y_B = Y$ (because the sum of the payments cannot exceed the total amount to be shared) and where W must be greater than zero as long as there is anything to bargain about.[2]

The bargain is determinate within the model. One can always find some combination of Y_A and Y_B to maximize the value of W in equation (3). It is obvious from the symmetry that the maximization of W in equation (3) prescribes a fifty-fifty split when N_A and N_B are equal (possibly 0) and when the claimants' utility functions are the same. With identical utility functions, the maximization of W supplies person A with the larger income if and only if $N_A > N_B$. There is however some question about how closely the model fits the real world of negotiation. Bargaining breaks down if each party exaggerates its claim on the other as a means of raising its return from the bargaining process or, more importantly, if one or the other party simply refuses to accept the outcome of the model as binding on himself. One's sense of fairness may not correspond to equation (3). One may refuse to play fair. One may just say no.

Models of negotiation are more interesting and insightful. With no arbitrator and no common understanding of what is fair, a bargain may nevertheless be struck. A bargain between person A and person B over the allocation of a sum of money Y is rendered determinate by four assumptions about the bargaining process:

(1) *A prescribed sequence of offers.* The parties make alternate offers separated by prescribed periods of time. Each offer is a proposed allocation of the stake, so much for person A and the remainder for person B. Suppose the process begins in the year 2000. On January 1, 2000, one person is entitled to make a take-it-or-leave-it offer, and immediately the other person says either "yes" or "no." If the answer is "yes," a bargain is struck and there is nothing more to discuss. If the answer is "no," all communication ceases until January 1 of the following year, 2001, when the parties switch roles. Then it is the other person's turn to make a take-it-or-leave-it offer. The process continues with the parties alternating roles year after year until somebody's offer is finally accepted.

(2) *A gag rule.* No communication between the parties is allowed during the prescribed time from the rejection of one offer and the appearance of the next.

(3) *The cost of delay.* The stake diminishes over time. A business venture that seems promising if undertaken today may not be quite so promising if delayed until tomorrow. Suppose the opportunity that gives rise to the bargain becomes available on January 1, 2000, with an initial stake of Y(2000). By January 1, 2001, the stake has shrunk to Y(2001) which is somewhat less than Y(2000), and so on. For every

Table 7.1   How the allocation of the surplus depends on the timing of the loss from delay in bargaining

[Incomes and surpluses in thousands of dollars.]

Year (t)	The remaining stake on January 1 of the year t	The remaining surplus on January 1 of the year t	Loss of surplus during the year t	Party entitled to make the offer in the year t	Offered allocation of the remaining surplus in year t $\{Y_A(t) - N_A, Y_B(t) - N_B\}$	Offered allocation of total income in the year t $\{Y_A(t), Y_B(t)\}$
2000	500	100	20	A	$\{80, 20\}$	$\{305, 195\}$
2001	480	80	10	B	$\{60, 20\}$	$\{285, 195\}$
2002	470	70	40	A	$\{60, 10\}$	$\{285, 185\}$
2003	430	30	10	B	$\{20, 10\}$	$\{245, 185\}$
2004	420	20	20	A	$\{20, 0\}$	$\{245, 175\}$
2005	400	0	—	B	$\{0, 0\}$	$\{225, 175\}$

year t, $Y(t + 1) > Y(t)$. As the outside options, N_A and N_B, remain invariant, the surplus each year, $Y(t) - N_A - N_B$, diminishes accordingly. Any feasible and mutually advantageous allocation of the available income in the year $t - Y_A(t)$ to person A, and $Y_B(t)$ to person B – entails an allocation of the surplus, providing $[Y_A(t) - N_A]$ to person A and $[Y_B(t) - N_B]$ to person B. The shrinkage of the stake supplies both parties with an incentive to strike a bargain quickly.

(4) *Sequential rationality.*   At no time does party A refuse an offer if he cannot expect party B to accept another offer more advantageous to party A later on. Nor does party B refuse an offer if he cannot expect the party A to accept another offer more advantageous to party B later on.

Under these rules, bargaining terminates when an agreement is reached or in the event that there is nothing left to bargain about because the surplus available when the negotiation began has all been wasted in delay.

   To see how this might work out in practice, consider the example of negotiation in table 7.1 above which is based on the bargain between the accountant and the biologist in figure 7.1. Originally, on January 1 of the year 2000, the stake to be allocated is $500,000 and outside options forgone are $225,000 for person A and $175,000 for person B, so that the surplus is $100,000. As the years go by, the stake diminishes but the outside options remain the same. By the year 2005, total income has shrunk to $400,000 which is no larger than the sum of the parties' outside options, and there is no surplus left. The bargaining begins on January 1, 2000, with an offer $\{Y_A(2000), Y_B(2000)\}$ from person A to person B, meaning that of the available income, $Y(2000)$, person A gets an amount $Y_A(2000)$ and person B gets an amount $Y_B(2000)$. If person B accepts the offer, the bargaining process has come to an end. Otherwise, neither party is allowed to speak to the other until January 1, 2001 when it is person B's turn to make an offer, indicated by $\{Y_A(2001), Y_B(2001)\}$. The process continues, person A making the offer in even years and person B making the offer in odd years until either somebody's offer is accepted or the surplus is dissipated by delay until there is nothing left to bargain about.

The first five columns of the table show the situation confronting the two parties to the bargain. The first column indicates the date, from the year 2000 to the year 2005. The second column shows how the stake diminishes over time from $500,000 to $400,000. The next column shows the corresponding diminution of the surplus each year from $100,000 on January 1, 2000, to $80,000 on January 1, 2001, to nothing by January 1, 2005. The next column shows the loss of the surplus from one year to the next. The next column shows which of the two parties is entitled to make the offer each year. The sixth column is different. Assuming sequential rationality, it shows the offer that would be made each year by the person entitled to make it, in the event that bargaining has not been terminated already by agreement. The final column shows the offered allocation of the remaining stake.

The four assumptions about the nature of the bargaining process are sufficient to establish a unique and determinate bargain in the circumstances described in table 7.1. A bargain is struck at the very first opportunity. On January 1, 2000, person A proposes an allocation of $305,000 to himself and $295,000 to person B, and person B accepts. Other allocations in the final column of the table show what the outcome of bargaining would have been if bargaining had continued beyond January 1, 2000, but those bargains are entirely hypothetical.

The explanation is obtained by reasoning backwards. Suppose no agreement was reached prior to January 1, 2004, the last day when a mutually advantageous deal could be struck. By that time, the stake would have fallen to $420,000 and the corresponding surplus would be $20,000. It would be person A's turn to make an offer which person B must accept or reject immediately. Since person B can obtain no more than his outside option by waiting for his turn to make an offer the following year, it would be rational for him to accept anything over and above his outside option immediately, even as little as one penny. Knowing that, person A keeps the entire surplus of $20,000 for himself. He proposes an allocation of $\{245, 175\}$, meaning $245,000 for himself and $175,000 for person B – strictly speaking $245,000 less one penny for himself and $175,000 plus one penny for person B. Person B would have to accept, for, being rational, he would rather have a surplus of one penny than no surplus at all.

Step back a year to January 1, 2003. The stake would then be $430,000, the corresponding surplus would be $30,000, and it would be person B's turn to make an offer. Both parties know that person A can assure himself of no more than $245,000, or $20,000 of surplus, by refusing person B's offer and waiting for his own chance to make an offer in the year 2004. Recognizing this, person B offers party A $20,000 of surplus immediately, keeping $10,000 of the surplus for himself. Person B would offer person A an allocation $\{20, 10\}$ of the surplus, or equivalently $\{245,185\}$ of the stake, and his offer would be accepted.

The sequence of offers of surplus and of total income that each person would be prepared to make when his turn comes around is shown in the two last columns of table 7.1. These columns should be read from the bottom up, for the rationality of each offer stems from the knowledge by the party making the offer of what he can expect in the following year. From this line of reasoning, it follows immediately that each year's offer would be accepted if, for some reason, no bargain had been struck already. In particular, the first year's offer is accepted and the bargaining stops immediately, and none of the surplus is wasted by attrition over time. When both parties bargain rationally, each party's share of the surplus is the sum of the reductions in the surplus during all of the years when that party is entitled to propose the bargain. The actual bargain is {305, 195} as shown at the top of the final column in table 7.1.

The model of negotiation is forward looking. The bargain struck today is determined by what would otherwise happen tomorrow, and that in turn depends on what would happen the day after tomorrow, and so on into the indefinite future or until there is nothing left to bargain about. Bargains that would otherwise have been struck in subsequent years influence the content of the bargain that is actually struck as soon as the bargaining process begins. The bargaining process makes the outcome of the bargain determinate. On the strength of the four assumptions above, there is a unique bargaining equilibrium comparable to the equilibrium market-clearing prices discussed in chapter 3.

The model can be modified in several ways: Instead of supposing that the surplus diminishes over time, it might be supposed that the surplus remains the same but that the parties place a smaller value on a given sum tomorrow than they place on the same sum today. On that supposition, the less impatient person (the person with the lower rate of discount) would get the larger share of the pie. The reader may have noticed that the outcome of the bargain in table 7.1 depends critically on which of the two parties is entitled to make the first offer. That advantage gradually disappears with more frequent offers, for instance every week rather than every year, and when the parties' time preferences are substituted for the shrinkage of the stake. There may also be uncertainty about the size of the stake in the dispute. Parties may have private information. In a dispute between labor and management, the management may be the better informed about the profitability of the firm as a function of the wage rate.

The solution is correct, but very fragile. All of the four assumptions as set out above are essential. If, for example, silence is not maintained between offers, the bargaining process breaks down in a cacophony of nearly simultaneous offers, counter-offers and threats with no hint of an equilibrium in sight.

The final assumption, sequential rationality, is especially dubious. Suppose, knowing his share of the $100,000 of surplus is to be no more than $20,000 in the circumstances of table 7.1, person B contracts with the local notary to accept nothing less than, say, $60,000 and to pay the notary $100,000 if he does. Now person A is stuck, for, in these new circumstances, he must accept $40,000 of surplus or nothing. Being rational, person A accepts the $40,000 of surplus, even though he could have had twice that much if person B had behaved differently. Of course person A could play the same game, so that whoever plays the game first would seem to win. If they both made credible take-it-or-leave-it demands and if the sum of their demands exceeded $500,000, there could be no agreement at all and the surplus in the bargain could be wasted altogether. In practice, not all mutually advantageous bargains are struck. The accountant and the biologist may fail to come to an agreement even though they are both made worse off by their failure than they would be under any allocation of the surplus. Some large bargains are struck easily. Some mutually advantageous agreements are thwarted over trifles. Typical outcomes of bargaining can be observed. Outcomes in specific disputes cannot be predicted.

Rationality may be disadvantageous; irrationality may be advantageous. If person B is rational in the circumstances of table 7.1, he accepts the $20,000 of surplus in the bargaining solution. If he is irrationally attached, for example, to a fifty-fifty split and unwilling to accept any other regardless of the consequences to himself when the bargaining process is complete, then person A, if he is rational, might as well accede to person B's demand. That is not just true for a fifty-fifty split but for any split whatsoever as long as person B can be expected to hold fast whatever the consequences to himself. A standard maxim of bargaining is to "Make yourself into a force of nature," compelling your opponent to concede today by denying yourself the option of conceding tomorrow. One says to one's opponent that "One of us has got to be rational, and it won't be me." The strategy often works, but it is dangerous. One's opponent may be as irrational as oneself, mutually advantageous trades may be lost and a person with a reputation as an unreasonable bargainer may be unwelcome as a participant in associations where bargaining over shares is inevitable.

There is no denying that people do make deals. Bargains are struck. Just how bargains are struck in practice, and when bargaining breaks down, remains mysterious.

SALES AND CONTRACTS

It was supposed in the description of the market in chapter 3 that all transactions are instantaneous. In the model of barter, the bread producer hands over the agreed-upon amount of bread to the cheese producer at precisely the moment that the cheese producer hands over the agreed-upon amount of cheese to the bread producer. Nobody need trust anybody else because each party releases his goods at exactly the same instant of time. Nothing is altered when bread and cheese are exchanged for money rather than for each other. Bread is exchanged for money instantaneously. Cheese is exchanged for money instantaneously. Sometimes actual transactions are like that, but many transactions in business and investment are of the form, "You do this for me today and I will do that for you tomorrow." An essential requirement for transactions over time is that the parties trust one another. Promises must be believed, either because parties are intrinsically trustworthy or because the law makes them so.

Contracts differ from sales in several respects:

(1) *Timing.* An ordinary sale of cheese is instantaneous not just in the sense that the sale occurs at a moment of time, but in the more interesting sense that there is no lingering obligation once the purchase is complete. Admittedly, even an ordinary sale has something of the character of a contract if the seller preserves responsibility for defective products. The seller may be required under the customs of trade to refund one's money in the event that the bread is stale or the cheese is rotten. There are in practice gradations between sales without lingering obligations and contracts binding parties to actions in the future.

(2) *The written document.*   A promise is easier to enforce when it is written down. A grocery store may give me a sales slip when I pay for the cheese, but there is no need for me to provide comparable documentation to the grocery store because it has my money already. A written document might also be dispensed with in more complex arrangements if both parties to the transaction have established reputations for honesty that might be jeopardized in a dispute. One may, alas, have a long-term connection with one's doctor, but no formal contract. But the less parties to a trans-action know about one another and the more complex the terms of contract, the greater the need for a written document, if only to provide the law with a statement of obligations in the event of a dispute. When there is no written contract but it is generally understood what parties to a contract must do, we say that the contract is "implicit."

(3) *Public enforcement.*   Public protection of private property goes beyond the defense of the fisherman against the pirate. It is more than the protection of things. It encompasses the public support of private promises. An inventor discovers how to make a new and useful product, but he does not have the money to finance its development, manufacture, and distribution of the product. The inventor joins forces with a lender who supplies the money up front in return for a share of the profit from the enterprise. Everybody gains from the arrangement. The inventor and the lender acquire shares of the surplus from the enterprise. The general pub-lic gains access to a product that was not available before. Essential to the enterprise is that the inventor's promise is believed. The lender must have confidence that his agreed-upon share of the profit from the enterprise will actually be forthcoming. He must trust the inventor to give up a part of the profit as he promised. The inven-tor has every incentive to make the promise in order to acquire the lender's funds, but he acquires an incentive to welch on his promise and to take the entire profit from the enterprise for himself. The inventor may or may not be honest. Moti-vated by greed, and by greed alone, *homo economicus* would surely break his promise. There is enough truth in the economist's caricature of mankind that many poten-tially beneficial ventures are lost because people in circumstances like that of the inventor cannot bind themselves, or be bound by the state, to keep their promises. Enterprise, prosperity, and progress are only possible when such promises can be believed.

Sometimes promises can be relied upon because of the concern of the promisor for his reputation. He keeps promises today to ensure he will be welcome as a partner in future transactions. The threat of ostracism may be sufficient enforcement in dealings among small groups of traders who expect to continue dealing with one another for a long time to come. That is a common explanation of the trading success of tight ethnic groups – the Jews of medieval Europe, the Chinese in South-east Asia and the Parsees of India – within societies where the law is lax and inefficient. Allegedly, the diamond trade still operates without legally binding contracts. These are exceptions. In general, and especially in transactions among strangers, promises require enforcement by the state. As long as the inventor's promise to the lender was made in the proper manner, the lender can sue the inventor for breach of promise and the courts will supply redress. Then and only then is the inventor believed.

Just as the local policeman stops me from stealing a pound of cheese, so too does he stop me from reneging on my contract. The policeman supplies the trust without which most mutually advantageous contracts would in practice be blocked. But, by invoking the protection of the state, a contract engages the entire society and creates a universal interest in what would otherwise be a private arrangement between two parties. I gain from public enforcement of contracts not just so that I can rely on your promises, but so that you can rely on mine. Economies run on trust which can only be secured by public enforcement. Enforcement of contracts can be seen as an aspect of the protection of property rights without which neither prosperity nor economic growth can be attained.

(4) *Limits to public enforcement.* Not all private promises can or should be enforced by the state. The state cannot place itself so completely at the service of each and every person that all private agreements acquire the force of law and are treated as property rights. "I'll stick up the bank teller and you drive the get-away car" is a promise that is obviously not in the public interest to enforce. The state does not enforce contracts to violate the law. The state does not enforce my promise to supply you with a pound of my flesh in the event that I fail to pay back a loan. The state does not enforce my promise to sell myself or my children into slavery, though at other times and in other societies such promises would be enforced. Nor does the state enforce a contract to engage in prostitution or, among firms with similar products, to restrict output to raise the market price. There is considerable dispute today about whether and in what circumstances a pregnant woman may consign her child for adoption. Human blood and organs are saleable commodities in some societies but not in others. Rules about the governance of corporations can be interpreted as bounds on the state's enforcement of promises. The prohibition on insider trading by executives and directors of corporations is a kind of public enforcement of the contract between management and shareholders in which management promises to desist from actions reducing the value of the firm.

(5) *Ambiguity at the edges.* It is difficult, often impossible, to specify the terms of a contract completely. Some contracts are so well specified that no dispute over their meanings can arise. An agreement to buy a number of shares of stock at a given price at some designated date in the future may be a contract of that kind. Most contracts are different. They are well defined at their core but ill defined at the edges. You are to rent me a hall for a wedding. Have you honored your side of the bargain if one of the curtains is torn or missing, if some of the tables are smaller than I, in good faith, had believed they would be, or if there is a rock band playing in the next room? Have I honored my side of the bargain if I pay less than we had agreed upon as a consequence of some of these conditions? Even as simple a contract as the renting of a hall is somewhat ambiguous. Or, I am a contractor who has agreed to build you a house at some specified price. Have I complied with the contract if I fail to complete the house on time, employ what you claim to be inferior materials or demand extra payment for features of the house you now claim were covered by the original agreed-upon price? Important contracts among large corporations can be a mine-field of ambiguities. Billions of dollars turned on a court's decision whether

a handshake constituted a contract to sell the Getty Oil Corporation to Penzoil rather than to Texaco. Fortunes have been spent on legal fees in disputes over whether a contract is valid, what it means, and who must pay what to whom when a contract is breached. The simple fact of the matter is that it is frequently impossible to write so complete a contract that every possible eventuality is covered. Almost all contracts are somewhat incomplete. Disputes can arise no matter how carefully a contract is drafted.

(6) *Adjudication of disputes.*   There are two sides to public oversight of private contracts: enforcement and adjudication. Enforcement is required when non-compliance by one party to a contract is tantamount to theft, when, for example, a contractor absconds with the money he has accepted in payment for building a house. Adjudication is required to settle disputes where parties disagree in good faith about the interpretation of the terms of a contract. You demand a discount on the price of your house because I, the contractor, failed to complete construction by an agreed-upon date. I contend that the delay was not my fault because an ice storm had made it impossible to complete the building on time and that our contract has an implied waiver for acts of God. Either of us may take the other to court, but that route to dispute resolution is sometimes capricious and always expensive. It is capricious because judges and juries are likely to know less about the relevant commercial customs than do the parties to the dispute. It is expensive to litigants even though the cost of the court itself is usually born by the state. To avoid the expense and uncertainty of litigation, parties to a dispute acquire a special incentive to "bargain in the shadow of the law," to agree privately to whatever they guess the courts will decree. Thus, the real social benefit of litigation lies not so much in the resolution of disputes that are actually before the court but in the resolution of other similar disputes without litigation. More will be said about this in the last chapter of the book.

Markets and Hierarchies

Every country requires an army and a civil service which must inevitably be organized as hierarchies. Privates are commanded by sergeants, who are commanded by majors, who are commanded by colonels, who are commanded by generals who are commanded by the supreme commander. The hierarchy may be more or less rigid, more or less oppressive, but there must be a hierarchy. There is simply no other way to run an army. More relevant to our main concerns in this book is that firms must have hierarchies too. There were no firms in chapters 3 and 4 because each person connected to the market, as seller and as buyer, individually. Some markets are really like that. Others are not because production requires large factories, complex machinery, and many workers with different and complementary skills to be directed toward a common goal. Firms had a shadowy existence in chapter 6 as a reflection of the optimal scale of organization identified by the base of the U-shaped cost curve, but hierarchy was hardly mentioned.

The economy can be looked upon as a complex interaction between two modes of organization of production: a command structure within the firm and a price

mechanism among firms and between firms and people. Both modes are indispensable. The models in chapters 3 and 4 were of governance by prices. Organization
within the firm is governance by direct command that is similar to but less rigid than
the army, for workers may quit while soldiers may not. The boundary between pric-
ing and command, between markets and hierarchy, is a trade-off between the costs
and advantages of each. Recall the discussion in chapter 6 of the optimal size of firm.
Sometimes, as in most farming, the optimal size of firm is whatever can be managed
by one farmer and his family. Sometimes, as in most modern industry, the optimal size
of firm requires an army of employees whose work can only be coordinated within
a hierarchy.

One way or another, the profit motive guides the formation, size and dissolution
of firms. If one thousand cars can be produced more cheaply in one large firm than
in ten small firms, then one large firm will emerge from the merger of smaller firms
or from the expansion of one of the ten small firms driving the rest out of business. If
the balance were the other way round, the owners of the one large firm would acquire
an incentive to break it up, or the large firm would be driven out of business by its
smaller competitors. Prices guide firms, large and small, in choosing what to produce
and what factors of production to employ, but prices cannot coordinate an assembly
line, decide when to hire the lawyer, pass judgment on the potential usefulness to
the firm of two job candidates with equal paper qualifications, choose where and
how to invest, or administer research and innovation. Like the army, business has
to be administered. The boundary between firms and markets is the outcome of a
trade-off between the advantages of information supplied by prices and the advantages
of coordination within the firm. Difficult though it may be to explain the location
of the boundary in detail, there is no doubt that profit-maximization by the actors in
the economy does resolve the problem in practice.

The enormous improvement in the means of communication over the last few
hundred years – from the pony express, to the telegraph, to the telephone, to email –
coupled with our capacity to keep track of massive amounts of data, has greatly
enhanced the comparative advantage of deliberate coordination over the price mechanism, and has led both to the internationalization of firms and to an increase in their
absolute size. There was a time when, for all practical purposes, the firm was synony-
mous with the shop that could be, quite literally, watched over by its owner. That, of
course, is no longer true. Conglomerates grow dangerously large, threatening monopolization of their industries and wielding disturbingly large political influence. Yet, at
the same time, innovation churns out thousands and thousands of tiny independent
firms that operate quite profitably within a niche. The corner grocery and the local
café give way to massive chains, but new independent biotech firms are starting every
day. Inevitably, there is concern about whether and to what extent the virtues of the
competitive market can be preserved in this environment.

The hiring of labor by the firm is like the purchase of ordinary goods and services
if and to the extent that workers are as substitutable one for another as, for example, boxes of cornflakes on the shelf at the grocery store. The hiring of labor becomes
more problematic when the employer cannot specify the worker's job in detail or readily observe the amount of work performed. Worker and employer may agree upon the
wage per hour, but they cannot always agree upon the intensity or quality of worker

because there is no publicly available gauge of quality. Is the teacher's performance sat-isfactory? Typically, there is no objective standard to which the teacher and the school board may appeal. Even when there is a standard – such as the percentage of students passing a certain exam – one party may claim that the standard is inappropriate in his case because, for example, the teacher's students are atypical. It may be a matter of judgment whether or not the teacher is doing his job well. In other kinds of work, it may be impossible to say with certainty how much time is required to complete the job, whether a poor crop is due to bad weather or to a want of diligence by the tenant farmer, or the extent to which the profitability of the firm is attributable to the ability and diligence of management. Ordinarily, the more skilful the worker and the greater the responsibility of the worker, the harder it becomes to tell if the worker is doing his job well.

In the absence of an objective standard of performance and where remuneration must be set per hour, or per year, rather than per unit of goods produced, there arises a *principal–agent* problem. The principal hires the agent. Principal and agent may be the owner of a firm and his workers, or the school board and the teachers, or the stockholders and the chief executive officer. The principal–agent problem is that the agent works less diligently, and for less pay, than would be in the interest of prin-cipal and agent together if they could agree on a standard of performance that could be observed and enforced. In the absence of an objective standard, the agent lacks the incentive to be as diligent as he would otherwise be. Anticipating the correspond-ingly lower output per worker, the principal knows that he must offer a lower wage to maintain any given level of profit, and the market-clearing wage would be correspond-ingly reduced. The less observable the performance of the worker, the more serious does the principal–agent problem become. Adam Smith alluded to the problem in the matter at the outset of this chapter, arguing in effect that the principal–agent problem is more acute when the principal is a publicly owned or endowed school than when education is purchased privately by parents for their children, and schools are likely to go bankrupt unless incompetent teachers are dismissed. The corresponding case for public schools rests upon externalities similar in some respects to the smoke and smoking problem discussed in chapter 5. Public provision of schooling may inculcate civic virtues because children from every stratum of society are educated together. The principal–agent problem is especially acute in socialist societies where prices need not reflect scarcities, where firms need not be profitable, and where the principal–agent problem between workers and management is compounded by a principal–agent prob-lem between managers and the government. In the words of the Russian joke, "You pretend to pay us, and we pretend to work."

There is another closely connected problem. Non-observability of the quality of the labor supplied leads inexorably to some involuntary unemployment of labor. If the output of the worker could be observed perfectly, the labor contract would dissolve into a sale of goods. All work would become piece-work, there would be established a market-clearing rate of pay per unit of work done and it would be a matter of indifference to the employer how little or how much any given worker chooses to do. Otherwise, when payment is per hour rather than according to the amount of work accomplished, there is an incentive to shirk. Dismissal for shoddy workmanship may be the principal's only weapon to enforce diligence. But dismissal is no threat when there is a uniform market-clearing wage because a person dismissed from one firm can expect the same wage from another. Somehow, if the threat of dismissal is to be a goad to diligence, the worker must become worse off when he is dismissed. A blacklist among employers may be sufficient. Otherwise, since all firms are in the same boat, the wage of employed workers must be high enough that a dismissed worker must wait longer for re-employment than he would prefer.

Where want of diligence by the worker is especially costly to the firm, and where diligence is difficult to observe, a profit-maximizing employer may wish to provide some workers with "trust wages": wages high enough that dismissal constitutes a substantial penalty to the malfeasant worker. If, as an employee, I have a 50 percent chance of getting caught and being dismissed for malfeasance – anything from laziness to outright theft – and if my gain from undetected malfeasance is $1,000, then my employer acquires an incentive to pay me a wage high enough that I am at least $500 worse off seeking a new job than I am working for him. The greater the cost of my malfeasance to my employer, the greater his incentive to deter malfeasance by whatever means he can. Trust wages may be an effective option. Workers in the diamond trade might earn trust wages. Salaries of judges may depend as much on the harm a corrupt or inattentive judge may do than on the skill that he brings to his office, though the prospect of loss of honour may go a long way in keeping judges in line. Huge salaries for chief executive officers of large corporations – which can be thousands of times greater than the average wage in the population as a whole – may be due in part to their special skills, but may also reflect the cost to their corporations of negligence at the top of the industrial hierarchy or their opportunities for personal profit in dealings with other firms. Occupants of such positions are fortunate because they are paid more than their skills would fetch in less sensitive jobs.

To a greater or lesser extent depending on the specifics of the law and peculiarities of the labor market, the labor contract entails a humiliating subordination of the worker to his boss. Ideally, there would be no such subordination. If the market for labor were like the market for cheese, then a worker dismissed from one job could instantaneously find another commensurate with his skill and experience, placing boss and worker on equal footing. The worker's threat to quit would be no less potent than the boss's threat to fire him, and there would be no sense in which either party could be said to exert power over the other. In reality, losing a job is costly and unpleasant. At a minimum, one is deprived of his wage until another job is found, a cost that is reduced but not eliminated altogether by severance pay and unemployment insurance. If the new job is in another town, one must sell one's house and buy another. The new job may be at a lower wage. Searching for work is intrinsically unpleasant, especially if one is not quite sure that one will ever get a new job at all. By contrast, the stress on the boss who fires you is more bearable, especially if there is a large pool of the unemployed from which replacements can be drawn. A boss or supervisor may even take pleasure in acquiring a reputation for being hard-nosed, in concentrating on the bottom line or in exercising authority over the lives of other people. The asymmetry between boss and worker is likely to be greater in a company town than in a large city, in a factory than in a university, and in a non-unionized firm than in a firm where there is a union, though, as will be discussed presently, unions present problems of their own.

Voluntary Associations

Voluntary associations are like elaborate contracts, among their members in the first instances, but also between their members and the rest of society. Marriages, condominium associations, corporations, unions, charities, and political parties are voluntary associations established to achieve objectives collectively that cannot be achieved individually through the price mechanism. Such associations are established in accordance with patterns or templates recognized by the law as manifested in thousands of court decisions resolving points of dispute about who owes what to whom. Such associations may convey privileges and obligations not just among the members of the association, but to society as a whole. The public interest in private associations may be no more than to facilitate the common purposes of a group of citizens, but some associations confer benefits upon the community at large.

It is of little importance to the rest of society whether a group of people occupying apartments in the same building do so as tenants or as members of a condominium association. As it is of importance to the occupants themselves, the state provides a framework of law for the enforcement of their promises to one another and for the resolution of disputes. Typically, an explicit condominium agreement would specify the broad purposes of the condominium and the general terms of the agreement. The agreement would implicate the state as the ultimate enforcer in the event that one party violates the terms of the agreement and as the final interpreter of the contract in the event of disputes as to its meaning. No agreement, no written document, can provide for every contingency and for every dispute that may arise. The full meaning of the words of the agreement can only be understood against a background of law. Ultimately, the terms of the agreement are whatever the courts are prepared to enforce.

A marriage is like a condominium association in that the terms of both agreements must be enforced and interpreted by the courts. A marriage differs from a condominium association by the presence in a marriage of a distinct public interest going well beyond the interests of the parties to the contract and manifest in the privileges and obligations that marriage conveys. The state's principal interest is in next generation. Marriage laws are to a large extent about the raising of children to become good citizens. On marrying, a couple may write a marriage contract, but most marriages are without explicit contracts because a contract is implicit in the law of marriage and in the traditions of the courts as revealed in the entire history of the courts' resolution of marital disputes about the obligation of spouses to one another, the dissolution of marriage, the custody of children, the responsibilities of parents to children and the responsibilities of children to parents.

The Corporation

The corporation combines a unity of organization with a diversity of ownership. The unity of organization is required to cope with economies of scale and with the multitude of small decisions that must be coordinated if modern industry is to work at all. An industrial hierarchy is required to direct the research, locate the factories, hire workers with the appropriate mix of skills, prepare the accounts, arrange advertising, sue one's competitors over patents and other matters, buy raw material and parts, and organize the assembly line to direct the flow of cars, radios, aeroplanes, computers, food, clothing or whatever the firm produces. Assets worth billions and billions of dollars must be brought under one authority and used to promote the profit of the whole.

Few people are wealthy enough to acquire sole ownership of a large corporation. Instead, the corporation issues shares held in relatively small amounts by many people, most of whom would prefer not to risk their entire fortunes in a single enterprise. Shareholders are at once the claimants to the earnings of the corporation and bearers of the risk in the event that the earnings are not forthcoming. Like the condominium, the corporation may in the first instance be established by a single entrepreneur who sells shares to raise capital or to divest himself of the entire firm as profitably as possible. Initially, the entrepreneur may have a good deal of discretion in establishing the rights of shareholders. He might prefer, for example, to issue non-voting shares, but may desist from doing so because prospective buyers would be unwilling to pay much for shares in a corporation where the original owner can, by one means or another, deflect the profit of the corporation from the non-voting shareholders to himself. Occasionally, the original owner is trustworthy or can be bound by the constitution of the corporation to treat non-voting shareholders well. Usually not. Non-voting shares are legal in some countries but not in others.

The corporation is at once a network of contracts and a set of legally established privileges and obligations that a person or group of people may choose to assume. Shareholders contract with one another over the governance of the firm, with bondholders to return their initial payments with interest, with workers to accept the authority of the management of the firm (within certain limits) in return for their wages, with suppliers of parts and raw materials, with customers to supply goods of a certain quality. There is sometimes alleged to be an implicit contract between the stockholders of a firm and its stakeholders: bondholders, workers, suppliers, and even the general public. The implicit contract would require management to take account of all these interests – and not just the shareholders' interest in profitability – in the running of the business. Though this is often said, it is unclear how the different interests are to be balanced, one against another, and the entire distinction between stockholders and stakeholders may be little more than propaganda to justify managerial incompetence or to the keep the regulators away.

The greatest privilege of the corporation is limited liability. No matter how unprofitable the corporation, the stockholder is never liable for its debts. If I invest $100 in the stock of a corporation and if the corporation goes bankrupt, I can lose my entire investment but can never be obliged to pay an extra $50, for example, if the uncovered financial obligation of the bankrupt corporation is $50 per share. Losses of the bankrupt corporation may be borne by its suppliers, by bondholders and by workers whose wages remain unpaid, but the worst that can happen to me, as a stockholder, is that my shares become worthless. The stockholder's other assets are not in jeopardy. Corporations are different in this respect from partnerships; partners are fully liable for all debts of the partnership. Partners may not even want limited liability because of the greater assurance that unlimited liability provides to their associates that the debts of the partnership will be paid. The public interest in limited liability is to allow small investors to participate in the ownership of large aggregations of capital without at the same time risking their homes and their retirement incomes on the chance that, through miscalculation or chicanery by the executives of the corporation, the corporation acquires large debts that it cannot pay.

The corporation is bound by an elaborate framework of law. It must establish a board of directors to whom the officers of the firm are ultimately responsible. If its shares are traded on the stock market, it must produce an annual report with financial information certified by a chartered accountant. There are rules restricting "insider trading," the purchase or sale of stock by officials of the corporation to profit from information unavailable to the general public. There are rules about the government of the corporation, mandating, for example, that there must be an annual meeting of the stockholders, that decisions at the annual meeting are binding on the firm and that such decisions are to be based on majority rule voting, one share one vote. There are rules about fairness among stockholders, such as the rule that all shareholders receive the same dividend per share.

There are rules protecting the rights of minority shareholders in a takeover of a corporation. Corporation law must specify whether, for example, an offer to buy shares at a certain price can be limited to just enough stocks to secure control of the firm for the buyer and whether all current stockholders must be treated alike. There are rules about transactions with other businesses. Corporation law must specify whether and in what circumstances a party with a controlling interest in a corporation may buy up some or all of its assets. An unlimited right to do so would provide a majority shareholder with a way to expropriate the minority shareholders. An unrestricted prohibition would block mutually advantageous transactions. A balance has to be drawn, but no balance can be entirely satisfactory in all circumstances.

Control of the corporation is especially problematic. A controlling hand is required to direct resources coherently. This presents no difficulty for a small firm with a single owner whose income depends on how efficiently he manages his resources. With ownership shared among thousands of stockholders, the corporation must be governed by voting, with one vote per share rather than per person as in voting for Members of Parliament. The law requires two stages of control: shareholders vote for the board of directors at an annual meeting, and the board of directors takes ultimate responsibility for the running of the firm including the appointment of the chief executive officer and other executives down the line. A majority stockholder can control the firm by electing his nominees to the board of directors. A large shareholder with less than a majority of the shares may do so too if other shareholders are passive, as many shareholders tend to be. Control of a corporation may be desirable for its own sake, for the authority it conveys over other people and for the access it conveys to politicians and to the civil service. Whoever controls the corporation is empowered to appoint its executives, set the wages of employees, choose the recipients of trust wages, provide jobs for relatives or friends, or arrange large compensation for himself. Control may also supply opportunities to manipulate, expand, or reorganize the corporation to one's advantage.

There is on the other hand a "free-rider problem" in the participation of minority shareholders. Suppose all stockholders know that their corporation is badly managed. Suppose that there are 1,000 shares outstanding, that an expenditure of $10,000 would be sufficient to mount a takeover of the corporation to displace the old management and that the efficiencies of the new management would raise the present value of the corporation by $20,000. An expenditure of $10 per share would lead to a rise of $20 in the stock price. Whether the return to the would-be raider exceeds the cost of the raid depends on how many shares, and at what price, the raider acquires. If he can acquire 70 percent of the shares at the original price before the take-over is anticipated, then the take-over is profitable, yielding him $14,000 ($20 per share for each of 700 shares) at a cost of only $10,000. But if the raider can acquire no more that 40 percent of the shares at the original price, then the take-over becomes unprofitable, for the gain in the value of his shares is only $8,000 ($20 per share for each of the 400 shares he acquires) which does not cover the cost of reorganization. Worse still, if a successful raid were anticipated by the market, the cost of the shares to the raider would include the value of his anticipated reorganization, rendering the take-over unprofitable no matter how many or how few shares the raider acquires. The nub of the free-rider problem is that the raider bears the full cost of the raid even though a successful raid raises the value of everybody's shares by $20.

Control is an elusive concept. It is obvious enough what it means when one stockholder owns more than 50 percent of the shares, but the perquisites of control can frequently be obtained with very much less. Control can be maintained with 25 percent of the shares if 50 percent of the shareholders are unwilling to monitor the conduct of the corporation or to vote in proxy contests. Control can be maintained by leveraging. A corporation with assets of $1 million can be controlled with as little as $100,000 of one's own capital by issuing, say, $800,000 of bonds and then selling just under half of the stock of the corporation. Control can be maintained by pyramiding. A corporation worth $1 million can be controlled absolutely with assets of as little as $250,000 by setting up an intermediary corporation which holds just over 50 percent of the stock in the primary corporation. To play this game, one must, of course, persuade others to hold just under 50 percent of the shares of both corporations, but that can be effected gradually by buying control of existing firms and moulding them to one's purposes. Ten stages of pyramiding, which would be bizarre but is not actually illegal in some countries, could secure control of a corporation worth $1 million by means of an investment of less than $1,000. Better still, one can control a corporation with no assets of one's own at all by establishing two corporations, A and B, each of which owns over 50 percent of the shares of the other. Both corporations have the same directors who meet twice every year, once on January 1 in their capacity as the board of directors of corporation A and again on June 1 in their capacity as the board of directors of corporation B. As representatives of corporation A, they re-elect themselves as directors of corporation B. As representatives of corporation B, they re-elect themselves as directors of corporation A. It does not matter which corporation actually controls the productive assets and generates the revenue for the two corporations together. The scheme is foolproof, or would be if it were not illegal. I understand that such a scheme was once maintained with the connivance of the government of South Africa to preserve the diamond cartel.

In practice, control may lie with the management of the firm, with banks, with pension funds or with wealthy individuals, depending in no small measure on the legal framework of corporate finance. Fearing the emergence of monopoly and of the domination of industry by large banks, the United States and Canada established a complex network of rules – about the composition of the assets of banks, the holding of equity by the banks, the placing of representatives of banks on the board of directors of corporations, interlocking directorates, and a multitude of other matters – to place a wall between the control of banks and the control of corporations. Similarly, among financial institutions, it was until quite recently thought appropriate to separate banks, insurance companies, stockbrokers, and trust companies, forbidding each type of firm from encroaching on the business of the others. Now, as financial business becomes more complex and more international, the lines are dissolving and corporations may be in all four businesses at once. Not all countries shared these concerns. In particular, Germany and Japan were content to allow a much closer association between banks and corporations.

The danger in prohibiting banks and other financial corporations from controlling manufacturing corporations is that control may revert to a self-perpetuating oligarchy of the managers or to financial pirates who find ways of diverting revenue from ordinary stockholders. Regardless, control of large corporations is the Achilles heel of capitalism. Modern industry requires large aggregations of capital. The revolution in computing technology generates ever larger economies of scale and facilitates a far greater span of control, over diverse production processes and among many countries, than anything we have seen in the past. The national income and the rate of economic growth are both significantly higher when some firms are very large than if all firms could somehow be kept tiny. Economies with large, privately owned corporations have proved infinitely more productive than economies where the means of production are publicly owned. There is, nevertheless, a major drain of resources in the contest for control and a disturbing influence of large corporations on the conduct of government.

Unions

Like the corporation, the union is a legally established pattern of association, with well-specified privileges and obligations, that people can choose to adopt or not to adopt as they see fit. Like a corporation, the union is bound by an intricate web of laws specifying how a union is certified, how elections are conducted, the authority of a union over its members, when a union may strike, when the union, or the firm with which it bargains, can demand compulsory arbitration of disputes, whether or not all workers in a unionized firm are obliged to join the union, and many other matters. Unions may be permitted in some industries but not in others. Typically, unions are prohibited in essential services where a strike may do a great deal of harm to the community at large, or, if permitted, their range of activity might be considerably circumscribed.

A union is a workers' cartel or monopoly over the supply of labor in some trade or industry to raise incomes by restricting the supply of labor. As discussed in chapter 4, there is a general presumption that monopoly is detrimental to society as a whole, but most countries make an exception for trade unions. Though one cannot rule out naked political influence, a rationale for this exemption is to be found in the special circumstances of the labor market. A worker would normally be hired by a firm for an extended period of time on the understanding that the relationship may be terminated by either party on short notice. Employment may be more or less precarious for the worker depending on the circumstances of the labour market. A worker fired from his job bears a cost, varying from negligible to catastrophic. There may be a flourishing labor market where he can find another job easily and at little inconvenience to himself. He may be confronted with a period of unemployment until a new job appears. He may be required to sell his house and move his family to unfamiliar surroundings if the only available job is in another town. He may have to take a cut in pay. He may not find a new job at all. A union may supply a degree of security in employment.

Unionization may raise the wages of unionized workers, but higher wages must be at somebody else's expense. Unionized workers may gain at the expense of the owners of the firms with which the union bargains, of consumers who pay higher prices for the products of unionized industries and of non-unionized workers whose wages are forced down by the presence of extra workers who would otherwise be employed in unionized industries. On the other hand, where the circumstances of the worker in the absence of a union conveys a degree of monopoly power on the firm over its workers, the establishment of a union may transform a simple monopoly of the firm over its workers into a *bilateral monopoly* of a market for labor. In such circumstances, a union may supply a workforce with a monopoly over the firm to balance the firm's monopoly over its workforce. The situation of unionized workers and their employers may be more like the confrontation between Norman and Mary in the discussion of bargaining in chapter 3 than like ordinary monopoly as described in chapter 4.

A union may defend the dignity of labor, but does not always do so. A union subjects the worker to a second hierarchy that may be every bit as oppressive as the first. The dignity of labor may be undermined by the union's bureaucratization of employment, blocking the connection between worker and boss with a hierarchy of union officials and destroying the worker's incentive to innovate in the workplace or to work with extra diligence for extra pay. Unions may turn corrupt, trading high incomes for union officials at the expense of the workers they are supposed to represent and confronting ordinary workers with a situation not unlike the fishermen with public as well as private predators in chapter 2. A free market in labor may be the best defense of the dignity of labor. Good prospects for finding another job may be the worker's best remedy for the officiousness of the boss and the string of command. In segregating the labor market, unions may render the life of the worker less independent on balance. Unionization may even confront workers with a prisoners' dilemma in which union members are better off than other workers, but both classes of workers become worse off with every increase in the proportion of workers unionized so that workers in a fully unionized economy would be worse off than if there had been no unions at all.

The balance of gain and loss depends on the circumstances of the industry. One would guess that a union of migrant fruit pickers would raise the incomes and social status of its members and would limit the ability of farm owners to lord it over their workforce, as a modicum of procedure is established for the resolution of disputes. By contrast, a union of university professors is designed to raise professors' wages by threatening to cancel lectures and exams if, depending on how the university is financed, the students, their parents, or the taxpayers refuse to pay professors what they insist they deserve. A professors' union may increase their incomes, but does nothing for the dignity of ordinary professors who lose access to the administration and must contend with the petty regulations of a union which, in the nature of things, comes to be dominated by those least interested in research or students. Nor is a union much help to would-be professors working as waiters or taxi drivers when the number of jobs is cut to augment the salaries of union members already employed.

CHARITIES

A charity is a private organization supplying what its members see as a public good. It is an association of fund raisers who collect money from the public and pass it on, as services or as cash, to the ultimate recipients: the poor, the blind or the homeless, medical researchers or whoever the focus of the charity happens to be. Fund raising may be voluntary or for pay. Few charities can avoid paid employment altogether, but charities differ in the extent of employment. Some charities make do, almost entirely, with volunteers to publicize the aims of the charity, to collect funds and provide services to the recipients. Other charities are organized like telemarketing firms, with salaried officials, advertising agencies to manage solicitation and house-to-house collectors working on commission.

The government sets rules for charities, specifying the requirements for recognition as a charity, offering tax advantages for donors, matching grants and defending the public against fraud. Governments may contribute as well, directly as in grants to the Red Cross, or indirectly as in the tax exemption for charitable contributions. If one's tax rate is 30 percent, a tax-deductible donation of $100 to a registered charity costs $70 to the giver and $30 to the government (and ultimately to the population at large) in the form of reduced tax revenue. There need be no clear line between a charity and a department of government. Formally, the Red Cross is a charity that solicits contributions from the government as well as from people. As the only collector of blood for medical purposes, the Red Cross participates in the public provision of medical care, and could not in practice deviate to any significant extent from the role the government expects it to play.

Charity is puzzling to the economist because, as discussed in chapter 5, public goods cannot ordinarily be financed by the private sector. Just as society cannot rely on private donations to finance guns and tanks for the army, neither – or so one would suppose – can it rely on private donations to finance the Red Cross, the cancer foundation or the Public Broadcasting System. *Homo economicus*, the citizen as modeled in standard economic theory and as personified by Robinson Crusoe in chapter 3, is utterly selfish and would donate nothing to charity at all. Yet there are private charities and voluntary non-governmental organizations.

Consider, for example, the Public Broadcasting System. This is a standard public good because, once on the air, it is available for everybody to watch. If publicly financed, the cost would be covered by a special tax on television sets or out of general tax revenue, and expenditure would be chosen to make the typical person as well off as possible. Ideally, the government decides how much to spend by a cost-benefit rule, spending up to but not beyond the point where the sum of every person's benefit from the last dollar of expenditure per head is just equal to one dollar. Suppose the total population of tax payers is one million people and the appropriate expenditure on PBS turns out to be $100 per person, or $100 million in total.

Compare the financing by private donations. As a voter, the typical citizen favored a total expenditure of $100 million, requiring a tax of $100, on himself and everybody else as well. But when donations are voluntary, the typical citizen reasons as follows: If I donate $100, my consumption of other goods and services is reduced by $100 and PBS's total expenditure on television programming is increased from $9.9999 million to $10 million, a percentage increase too small to have any significant effect on the quality of the programming I receive. I would certainly donate if my donation triggered equal donations from everybody else, but there is no point in my donating if everybody else is going to donate (or not as the case may be) regardless of what I do. Everybody reasons that way, and nothing is contributed. PBS's appeal for funds is ignored and the network goes off the air, even though everybody would be better off if it continued to broadcast and each person were obliged to pay his share of the cost. Voluntary provision to PBS confronts people with a classic "prisoners' dilemma." Nobody contributes voluntarily, even though everybody would be better off if everybody did so.

Notwithstanding the economist's proof to the contrary, people do contribute voluntarily to PBS and to many other charities as well! There is a major discrepancy here between the predictions of the economic model and the facts of the world. Part of the discrepancy can be attributed to altruism – a concern for the welfare of other people as well as for one's own comfort and satisfaction – which has so far been assumed away altogether but will be discussed briefly in the next chapter. Altruism could have been incorporated into the model of behavior in chapter 3 but only at the cost of muddying the waters when the model is employed in other contexts where the simple behavioral assumptions have proved effective in explaining phenomena and as a guide to public policy. On the other hand, the commonly heard argument that one contributes to PBS or the cancer foundation or the institute for the blind because one likes PBS television or fears cancer or may become blind oneself is simply false, unsatisfactory because all but a minute fraction of the benefit one can expect as a recipient of charity would accrue regardless of whether one contributes oneself. Nor is it sufficient to invoke altruism because that does not alter the fundamental problem, which is that no person's contribution to a public good can make a significant difference in the total amount provided.

Something more is required. Giving to charity may provide personal rewards or personal satisfaction beyond mere approval of the work of the charity itself. Names of university buildings are, quite simply, for sale to anybody prepared to make a sufficient contribution. People may feel morally compelled to give time and money to their communities. The size of one's own contribution may be important regardless of the impact of one's contribution on the total activity of the charity in question. Motives may be mixed. One's satisfaction from attaching one's name to a building may depend on the usefulness to society of the activity within.

POLITICAL PARTIES

Political parties occupy a special niche, partly voluntary associations and partly components of the government. They are voluntary because people need not, and most people do not, belong to political parties at all. They are components of government because they are indispensable if democratic government is to function at all. Democratic government could survive without the Red Cross and without the cancer society, but not without political parties. Democratic government requires removable peaks. The electorate must be able to displace the occupants of the commanding heights of government and to choose periodically among contenders for office. Voting per se will be discussed in the next chapter. Suffice to say here that the replacement of the executive and the legislature can only be effected when candidates for office and their supporters are organized in political parties with the resources to fight an election and with more or less well-specified policies that voters can recognize when they cast their ballots.

Like all of the other voluntary associations we have examined, political parties must operate within a framework that is partly custom and partly law. The party's nomination of leader and the leader's authority over the rest of the party are to a large extent determined by custom, which the law might nevertheless choose to enforce. Parties operate within a legal framework specifying who gets his name on the ballot, what penalty is to be imposed upon a nuisance party that acquires a minuscule proportion of the vote, from whom the party may accept contributions, the tax treatment of private contributions to political parties, how much money may be spent on advertising, which party leaders get to debate on public television, when the prime minister must step down because he has lost the confidence of the House of Commons, who the governor-general appoints in his place, and when elections are required.

THE BOUNDARIES OF PROPERTY RIGHTS

Property has so far been largely unproblematic. In chapter 2, it was the fisherman's catch which belonged to him but might be wrongfully appropriated by pirates. In chapter 3, it was the farmer's land which yielded him crops that he could consume himself or trade. In this chapter, it has been less clear what property entails. The introduction of bargaining, contracts, and associations of many kinds requires a reconsideration of the meaning of property. We have claimed private property to be essential for the maintenance of an efficient economy, and we shall go on to argue that it is equally indispensable for the maintenance of democratic government, but, like so many concepts, the concept of property turns out on close inspection to be well specified at the core but fuzzy at the edges. Two aspects of the specification of property will be considered in turn: the content of property rights and the transfer of property from one person to another.

Property "is a relation not between an owner and a thing, but between an owner and other individuals in reference to things." The chief significance of the distinction is that one cannot do whatever one pleases with one's property. One may do with one's property what the law allows, and is protected from invasion by others only in so far as the law constrains them. The most straightforward of all property rights is a person's ownership of his house, but that is by no means unlimited. Yes, the property is mine. Yes, the swimming pool is entirely on my land. But the pool must, by law, be fenced, for the rights of ownership are subordinate in this case to the rights of little children to wander where they please and to be physically constrained from placing themselves in danger. The right of ownership does not include the right to endanger little children, regardless of how naughty they happen to be. Ownership of a cabin in the woods does not include the right to deny access or food to the stranger who would otherwise perish. Ownership of residential property is bound by an infinity of zoning laws covering such matters as the minimal distance from the house to the street, the height of the building on the land, the distance between buildings and whether the building can be used as a shop.

Ownership of shares of a corporation is at the mercy of a myriad of rules governing the conduct of the corporation: rules about the obligations of the board of directors to the shareholders, about executive compensation, about political contributions, about mergers with other corporations, about insider trading by the executives of the corporation, about minority rights in the event of takeovers by large shareholders, about the types of stocks and bonds the corporation is allowed to issue, about devices to maintain control of the corporation, about the rights of unions. When person A owned plot A in chapter 3, there was no question as to what that ownership entailed. When a person owns shares, the significance of his ownership depends on a vast array of rules and is affected by changes in the rules that occur from time to time.

Ownership may not be of things at all. Ownership may be no more than another's promise to do something at some time in the future. A contract with a builder to erect a house or a contract between partners in a law firm about the division of the earnings is not the possession of things but it can be as valuable as the possession of things. It is property in so far as the law is prepared to protect entitlements. As enforcement is always costly, the law must specify when a contract is valid and what rights remain with the beneficiary of a contract in the event that the contract is breached. Is a handshake sufficient? Must there be a written document? Can a contract be one-sided in the sense that you give me something but get nothing in return? What about a pact between thieves? The closer one looks at the matter, the more intricate and complex does the law of contracts become.

Ownership may be the right to prohibit. The ownership of land normally includes the right to prohibit trespass on that land, but the right to prohibit may entail no possession of things at all. A patent is a right to block anybody from making, selling or using the patented process or machine. Copyright is the right to block the printing and sale of novels or other texts. Patents and copyrights are valuable property because and in so far as their owners can induce people to pay for the use of the restricted technology or literature. As discussed toward the end of the last chapter there is no bright and unmistakable line between unpatentable scientific discovery and patentable invention.

Ownership blends into civil rights. People hold different amounts of property, but enjoy the same civil rights. Everyone has the same right to vote, the same right to free speech, the same right to hold a passport, the same right to protection from the police, and the same right not to be harassed by one's government in the event that one becomes unpopular with the government of the day. Civil rights impinge on property rights when, for instance, a publicly supplied old age pension or publicly supplied medical care is provided equally to all citizens, becoming for many people the most valuable property they possess. Such "new property" tends to be constitutionally protected. The government of the day may abolish the old age pension or public provision of medical care, but it may not withdraw these rights from particular people who become unpopular without actually breaking the law. Property rights impinge on civil rights when, for instance, the outcome of an election is influenced by campaign contributions that the rich can afford but the poor cannot, or when money buys access to politicians or civil servants with favors to dispense. The boundary between civil rights and property rights is guarded by an intricate web of rules specifying in detail what money can and cannot buy. As mentioned above, one cannot buy or sell slaves. Nor can one buy or sell votes explicitly. Campaign contributions to political parties are allowed in some circumstances but forbidden in others. Politicians running for office cannot accept contributions from non-citizens. The value of property to the property-holder depends critically on what the rights of property turn out to be.

Beyond that, the meaning of property depends very much on the rules by which property may be acquired or divested. Property may change hands by sale or by inheritance. Nowadays there are few restrictions imposed by the state on either transaction, but that has not always been so. In the middle ages, when property-owners were requires to provide the king with troops in the event of war, the inheritance of property was circumscribed by the rules of primogeniture. A property-owner could not bequeath to whomever he pleased. Property was passed down undivided from father to eldest son, to ensure the persistence of large enough blocks of property that the surplus could cover the owner's obligation to the state. Daughters might receive dowries. Younger sons could be out of luck. There may at that time have been no better way to finance the government in time of war. Today ordinary taxation is usually sufficient.

There is no clear line between the rights of property and the powers of the state. The state's monopoly of the means of violence empowers it to take anybody's property at will, but a state prepared to exercise that power to the full would, in effect, be abolishing all property rights and would be very much poorer than if it exercised restraint. The English common law and the constitution of the United States both prohibit the taking of private property by state, except where compensation is provided. The government can expropriate my land for a road or a school, but the law requires that I be compensated. Yet I may lose some or all of the value of my property as a consequence of regulations where no compensation is required. My business may be ruined if my street is designated as one-way or if a bus route is changed or by new parking laws. These may be just as costly to me as the outright expropriation of my land, but one is compensatable while the other is not. The attempt to compensate the losers, and perhaps to tax the gainers, of each and every public decision would be too costly to society, too error-prone and too subject to chicanery. The state compensates owners for the outright expropriation of land and for some other publicly imposed harms, but it cannot compensate for everything. Inevitably, the property-owner bears some risk of loss from a change in the rules.

Chapter 3 concluded with a list of the virtues and vices of the competitive economy. Chapters 2, 4, 5, and 6 listed tasks that cannot normally be entrusted to the market and that only the government can perform. From our brief review of bargaining, contracts, associations, and property in this chapter, there emerges one more broadly defined task for the government. As explained in chapter 2, government must protect property rights if there is to be a market at all. Now we see that protection alone is not sufficient. One way or another, government must define property rights, for the market only works when each person knows the scope and the boundaries of his entitlements. Simple ownership gives way to a vast web of rules that only the government can supply.

Chapter Eight

THE COMMON GOOD

Value judgments concerning social welfare are a special case of judgments of preference . . . if the person who made this judgment had to choose a particular income distribution in complete ignorance of what his own relative position would be in the system chosen . . . if he had exactly the same chance of obtaining the first position (corresponding to the highest income) or the second, or the third, etc., up to the last position (corresponding to the lowest income) available within that scheme.

John Harsanyi, 1953

They steal and steal and steal. They are stealing absolutely everything and it is impossible to stop them. But let them steal and take their property. They will become the owners and decent administrators of this property.

Anatoly Chubais, 2000

What do economists economize?

D. H. Robertson, 1956

Political argument must appeal to some notion of the common good. Consider the choice between public and private provision of medical care. You favor public provision. I favor private provision. Each of us may hold the view he does because of the impact of medical care on his own life, but, to persuade others, one must appeal to something beyond his own personal interest. Each of us must argue that his preferred method of provision is best for the nation as a whole. Recognizing that no policy is ideal for everybody, we try to show that the gains to some people outweigh the losses to others. To do so is to appeal, implicitly or explicitly, to a commonly accepted scale. Notions of better off and worse off, so far restricted to the well-being of the individual, must somehow be extended from the individual to the community. A common good must be recognized as a criterion for the evaluation of public policy. Economists call that a *social welfare function*.

The social welfare function has a special role to play in the conduct of government. People's preferences may to some extent be aggregated into public policy by voting. A public decision may emerge in a straight, up-or-down vote between public and private medical care when each person votes selfishly and without anybody having to weigh benefits to different people on a common scale. Not all public policy can be determined that way. It will be shown in the next two chapters how only the broad lines of public policy may be shaped by voting, leaving the detail to be administered by the civil service. The legislature can never vote on more than a few laws each year. Sometimes the detail of administration is implicit in the law. More often, civil servants must act within the confines of the law to do what they (and hopefully others too) see as best for the community as a whole. Pharmaceutical products may be sold over the counter, provided only by prescription or banned altogether. I, along with almost all other voters, am not well enough informed about the properties of drugs to vote intelligently on which drugs belong in which category. Recognizing our ignorance, we vote for the establishment of a food and drug administration to make such decisions on our behalf. Some drugs are so dangerous that it is obvious to any informed person they should be banned. Some drugs are so beneficial on balance and have so few side-effects that it is obvious they should be available without prescription. In between, a standard of what is best for the community is required to weigh the benefits to some people against the potential harm to others.

The legislature may establish a food and drug agency; civil servants must decide on the status of each and every drug. The legislature may decide how much money is to be devoted to road-building; civil servants must decide which roads to build. The legislature may decide how much money to devote to medical care and on the apportionment of medical care between the public and private sectors of the economy; civil servants must run the hospitals and decide in detail how available services are to be allocated among people in need. Just as individual decision-making may be modeled as the maximization of private utility, so too may public decision-making be modeled as the maximization of a social welfare function.

A great deal is riding on this enterprise. Social science in general and economics in particular are not much use unless they can be made to yield prescriptions, however tenuous, for public policy. Virtually everything economists claim to derive from their discipline – rules for the establishment of property rights, for the scope and conduct of the public sector, for the design of tax systems or for the governance of international trade – disintegrate unless some notion of the common good can be identified. This ill-defined but indispensable notion will have a large role to play in the chapters to follow on voting, administration, and law.

The chapter opens with a discussion of how altruism may be incorporated into the utility function. Then the social welfare function is introduced as the grand utility function for the community as a whole, incorporating every person's utility, just as every person's utility incorporates his quantities of goods consumed. There follows a discussion of how and to what extent one's sense of social welfare may serve as a guide to public policy, with special emphasis on the redistribution of income. Next, an apparent contradiction between concern for the common good and the defense of property rights is dismissed as groundless. The chapter concludes with a reassessment of the virtues and vices of the competitive economy.

Altruism

On first encountering the economist's description of human motivation and behavior, exemplified by Robinson Crusoe in chapter 3, the sensitive reader may object that *homo economicus* is an insulting, degrading, even slanderous caricature of *homo sapiens*. *Homo sapiens* is the biologists' name for people as distinct from other species. *Homo economicus* is the somewhat satirical name for people as conceived in economic analysis. It is the name given by economists and detractors of economics to the people whose sole purpose in life is to maximize utility as a function of amounts of goods and services consumed. Sometimes hours of leisure is included in the list of goods, implying that people seek a nirvana of idleness with an unlimited flow of goods and services. *Homo economicus* has no friends, takes no pleasure in conversation, craves no association with others, has no concern for the welfare of others, is a stranger to ambition, reputation and revenge, and is content to enjoy his goods in idleness and isolation. Gorillas, elephants, and bees show more affection for their fellow creatures and are more willing to sacrifice for the common good of their species. How, it may be asked, can any truth be expected to emerge from a science grounded upon such a shallow and unrealistic conception of human nature?

Against this charge of callousness and inhumanity, economics might be defended by three lines of argument among which the third is most relevant here. First, *homo economicus* is a conceptual device for dealing with a range of problems where the selfishness assumption is broadly speaking efficacious. What is the effect of an increase in the progressivity of the income tax on amount of investment and the supply of labor? By how much is the quantity of cheese reduced by a sales tax of 20 percent? What is the effect of rent control on the supply of new houses and apartment buildings? What is the effect of an increase in the money supply on employment today and on the price level in the long run? What fosters prosperity? Who guards the guardians? Experience in dealing with such questions suggests that little is to be gained by incorporating altruism into the utility function. Typically, though not invariably, that would only serve to muddy the waters, without improving the analysis at all.

Second, utility functions of supposedly selfish people may be looked upon as the building blocks for an indicator of the common good. If the welfare of the community is seen as an aggregate, then one would want the utilities of individuals to reflect their own selfish interests exclusively, lest concern for others be double-counted, once in the measure of individual utility and again in the aggregation of utilities to represent the common good.

Third, the utility function can be extended to incorporate altruism. Consider parents and children in circumstances where prices are invariant so that each person's utility can be reflected unambiguously by his income. By analogy with the utility of the individual in a bread-and-cheese economy, the welfare, w^P, of a parent who cares about his children may be looked upon as incorporating expenditure for the benefit of the parent, Y_P, and expenditure for the benefit of the child, Y_C, on the assumption that all goods prices are invariant so that more expenditure implies higher utility defined in the usual non-altruistic sense of the term. Specifically,

$$w^P = w^P(Y_P, Y_C) \tag{1}$$

where the function w^P is any assignment of numbers to indifference curves of the parent's preferences among bundles of Y_P and Y_C and where the shapes of the indifference curves are as shown in figure 3.3. These indifference curves may be thought of as summarizing the parent's answers to a long series of questions of the general form, "Do you prefer this to that?" The conceptual experiment would be like that used to elicit a person's indifference curves for bundles of bread and cheese, except that bread and cheese would be replaced by Y_P and Y_C. Were prices of goods not invariant, the money incomes Y_P and Y_C may be replaced by indicators of real income as defined at the end of chapter 5. While this formulation may not capture the essence of the parent-child relation, it does serve to demonstrate that the concept of utility can be extended from the isolated individual to social relations.

Nor need altruism be confined to parents' concern for children. Redefining P as "prosperous" rather than parent, and C as "castaways" (or poor people) rather than child, we may think of equation (1) as the utility function of a prosperous person prepared to sacrifice some of his own income to help the poor. Think of Y_P as a rich person's expenditure on himself and of Y_C as the average income, inclusive of transfer payments and charity, of all poor people or of some class of poor people about whom the rich person is concerned. When formulated that way, utility, W, would normally be supposed to depend in part on Y_C if and only if $Y_P > Y_C$, (that is, if the group whose average income is designated as Y_C is really poor). Otherwise W would depend on Y_P alone. The assumption here is not that rich people are fundamentally nicer or more generous than poor people. It is that everybody is conditionally altruistic, altruistic only to people poorer than oneself. Furthermore, if each rich person's generosity were directed to all poor people together, we might expect the altruistic rich to favor publicly mandated redistribution where each rich person is required to pay his share, but to desist from private charity because, by itself, no person's contribution is large enough to have any significant effect on the average income of the poor.

Concern for other people may be graduated by "social distance." Your utility function may take the form

$$w^0 = w^0(Y_0, Y_1, Y_2, Y_3 \ldots) \tag{2}$$

where you are person 0, where the utility function, w^0, represents your preferences and concerns, where Y_0 is your income, where $Y_1, Y_2,$ and $Y_3 \ldots$ are incomes of other people or groups of people. A function like equation (2) allows for the possibility that one is willing to sacrifice more for a person of his own language group or religion than for a person of another language group or religion.

THE SOCIAL WELFARE FUNCTION

Social welfare is something more than altruism. It is one's sense of what is best for society as a whole with no priority for one's own income over the income of anybody else. Consider an N-person community where all prices are invariant. For such a community, a social welfare function can be written as

$$W = W(Y_1, Y_2, \ldots, Y_N) \tag{3}$$

where W is social welfare and where Y_i is the income of person i. Typically, we think of social welfare as *anonymous*, so that a reordering of the N incomes in equation (3) would leave W unchanged. If society consists of only Joe and Charlie, then an income of $50,000 for Joe and an income of $100,000 for Charlie would be assigned the same social welfare as an income of $50,000 for Charlie and an income of $100,000 for Joe. On most people's assessments, social welfare is greater: (1) the higher the average income for any given variance, and (2) the lower the variance of income for any given average. In a society of two people, the criteria imply that the social welfare attached to the pair of incomes {$100,000, $50,000} exceeds both the social welfare attached to the pair {$99,000, $49,000} and the social welfare attached to the pair {$101,000, $49,000}, the first case because the average income is higher while the variance is about the same, and the second case because the variance is lower while the average income is the same. Public policy is often described as a trade-off between the two criteria. The common good is achieved when, from among all feasible distributions of income, the distribution with the highest social welfare is chosen.

The altruistic utility function in equation (2) and the social welfare function in equation (3) look very much alike, but anonymity sets them apart. Formally, the difference lies in the distinction between the personal function, w^0, in equation (2) and the impersonal function, W, in equation (3). People may or may not differ in their assessment of the common good. If everybody's conception of the common good is the same, then the function w in equation (3) is the same too. Otherwise, each person has his own conception of W, but each person's W may still be anonymous.

Words do not necessarily refer to things. We can speak of the common good without at the same time guaranteeing that there really is a common good, just as we can speak of angels (disconcertingly similar to the common good) without at the same time guaranteeing that there really are angels. We can write down a social welfare function without at the same time guaranteeing that such a function *exists* as a characteristic of social life. There are really two questions here: "Has each of us a sense of the common good?" and "To what extent, if at all, are our conceptions of the common good the same?" We shall consider these questions in turn.

Whether people have a sense of the common good and whether people's sense of the common good can be represented by a social welfare function along the lines of equation (3) are questions each person must ask of himself. These questions can nevertheless be framed in a conceptual experiment out of which a person's social welfare function, if there is one, might be expected to emerge. The conceptual experiment is a first cousin of the conceptual experiment by which "your" indifference curves were discovered. Both involve a long series of questions, questions of the form "Do you prefer this to that?" rather than "By how much do you prefer this to that?" because only the former questions are answerable.

Suppose the community of which you are a part must choose between two mutually exclusive policies: between monarchy and democracy, between the death penalty and long imprisonment as punishment for murder, between more or less progressivity in the income tax or between public and private provision of medical care. Now imagine that you, and you alone, can choose between these policies on the understanding that, whichever policy you choose, *your position in society will be assigned randomly.* Whichever policy you choose, you have an equal chance of occupying the circumstances of each and every person in the society where that policy applies. If society consists of a king and 999 serfs, then you have a 1 in 1,000 chance of being the king and a 999 out of a 1,000 chance of being a serf. If everybody is equal, you are like everybody else. You are said, in this experiment, to be located behind a *veil of ignorance* where you are assumed to know a great deal about the technology of the economy and the organization of society but nothing about your place in that society once the veil is lifted. It may then be said that, as between the two policies, the common good, as you see it, is best served by whichever policy you choose *in your own interest but from behind the veil of ignorance.* The "veil of ignorance" test enlists self-interest in identification of the common good.

Consider the choice between public and private provision of medical care, looked upon as well-specified alternatives. You must choose between them from behind a veil of ignorance, knowing a great deal about the conditions of society as it would be with each system of medical care, but knowing nothing about your particular place in society. You may be old; you may be young. You may be rich; you may be poor. You may be male; you may be female. Your chances of each are a reflection of proportions in society as a whole. A doctor who expects to enjoy a higher income and a better life under private provision of medical care than under public provision may nonetheless believe that the common good is best served by public provision. With equal chances of filling the shoes of each and every person in society, he might trade away the advantages of private provision to doctors for the advantages of public provision to people other than doctors. Behind the veil of ignorance, every policy is a gamble. The gamble in public provision might be preferred to the gamble in private provision, even to one who would prefer private provision if he knew for certain he would become a doctor.

Imagine yourself behind the veil of ignorance choosing between public and private provision of medical care for a society with just three people, 1, 2, and 3. You do not know who you will turn out to be when the veil is lifted, or, equivalently, you may be able to suppress and ignore that information in your assessment of the common good. Your choice is all-encompassing. Each policy is assumed to determine the annual incomes of each person for the rest of his life. For each policy, the three incomes are shown in the second, third, and fourth columns of table 8.1. The last two columns show average income and dispersion of income where dispersion is represented by standard deviation. Table 8.1 is constructed so that the average income is larger under public provision ($110 thousand as compared with $100 thousand), but the dispersion of incomes is larger too ($80 thousand compared with $10 thousand).

The numbers in table 8.1 are chosen to draw out the analogy between social choice behind the veil of ignorance and private choice when confronted with ordinary risk. One's choice between policies behind the veil of ignorance is just like one's choice of professions when one cannot predict how successful in one's profession one will turn out to be. In fact the numbers in table 8.1 are reproduced from the example on risk in table 5.1. Medicine and law become public and private medical care. The

Table 8.1 Comparison of public and private medical care

Provision of medical care	Person 1	Person 2	Person 3	Average income	Dispersion of incomes
Public	$90,000	$100,000	$110,000	$100,000	$10,000
Private	$30,000	$110,000	$190,000	$110,000	$80,000

randomly determined outcomes, "very successful," "moderately successful" and "not successful" become persons 1, 2, and 3 whose incomes a person behind the veil of ignorance might eventually acquire. The choice between two gambles – on professions with uncertain incomes, and on policies behind the veil of ignorance – is the same.

On the strength of this comparison, your utility function, u(Y) derived to reflect your deportment toward risk, becomes the basis of your social welfare function. Just as you can be said to maximize expected utility in choosing among risky options, so too, behind the veil of ignorance, can you be said to maximize expected utility for the community as a whole, where incomes of different people replace incomes of the same person in different situations. You choose between the policies to maximize expected utility, or, equivalently, to maximize the sum of the utilities of every person in society. You maximize social welfare, or the common good, which on the assumptions we are making, can be represented as the sum, W, of the utilities of income of each and every person in society. With only three people, equation (3) becomes

$$W = u(Y_1) + u(Y_2) + u(Y_3) \qquad (4)$$

where Y_1, Y_2, and Y_3 are their incomes, and where the derivation of the utility of income function, u(Y), is as explained in chapter 5. If you are a risk-neutral person, the common good is promoted – that is, the value of W in equation (4) is made as large as possible – by choosing private medical care with the larger average income. If you are very risk-averse, the common good is promoted by choosing public medical care with the smaller dispersion of income. If your observed utility of income function just happens to conform to the postulated utility of income function in equation (25) of chapter 5 ($u = AY^{\alpha} + B$ where α is a parameter signifying your degree of risk aversion), the common good is promoted by public provision when your value of α is close to 1 and by private medical care when your value of α is close to 0.

Regardless of the assumed form of the individual utility function, the doctrine that the common good is the *sum* of the utilities of every person in society is called *utilitarianism*. With a population of N, the doctrine is that

$$W = u(Y_1) + u(Y_2) + \cdots + u(Y_N) \qquad (5)$$

Philosophers have attached the veil of ignorance test to the maximization of the income of the worst-off person in the community. On this criterion, a program, policy, or institution promotes the common good if and only if the worst-off person when this program, policy or institution is adopted is better off than the worst-off person under any alternative. That is just plain wrong. One would never opt for such a rule behind the veil of ignorance. Consider a society of four people whose incomes would be $19,900, $100,000, $100,000, and $100,000 under private medical care and $20,000, $20,000, $20,000, and $20,000 under public medical care. Ask yourself which option you would choose behind the veil of ignorance with equal chances of becoming any of the four people in whichever option you choose. You would have to be absurdly and pathologically risk averse to choose the second option (forgoing a 75 percent chance of an $80,000 gain to avoid a 25 percent chance of a $100 loss), but that is what the maximization of the income of the worst-off person would lead you to do. Behind the veil of ignorance and with these consequences of the two systems of medical care, any reasonable person would choose private provision.

Several objections can be raised to the identification of the social welfare with the welfare of the individual behind the veil of ignorance. The test is corrupted to some extent by differences in taste. Even behind the veil of ignorance, people may differ in their ranking of societies according to their weighting of average income and variance of income, but people's tastes may differ in other respects as well. One person's vision of a good life is a big house in the fashionable part of town and foreign vacations on his private yacht. Another's vision of the good life is a snug cell in a monastery with plenty of time for private contemplation. Their rankings of methods of providing medical care need not be the same. The veil of ignorance test cannot be relied upon to supply a unique vantage point for the evaluation of public policy because, even with equal chances of filling the shoes of every person in society, people's conceptions of the common good differ in accordance with their visions of the good life. On the other hand, the veil of ignorance does successfully abstract from differences in income which may, in practice, be the largest source of disagreement over public policy. To account for other differences among people's tastes, it would have to be imagined that tastes as well as material advantages are randomly assigned.

One might also object to the alleged identity in the veil of ignorance test between one's concern for other people and one's willingness to bear risk oneself. Strictly speaking, a risk-neutral person would prefer private over public medical care because his sense of the common good takes account of average income exclusively, and no weight whatsoever is placed upon the dispersion of income in his community. That may not be true. A person willing to take large gambles in his own life may nonetheless favour public medical care over private medical care. He may adhere to a conception of social welfare that takes account of the variance of income as well as average income, and he may favor substantial redistribution of income to the poor. Though inconsistent with the assumptions in the veil of ignorance test, and perhaps unlikely, such behavior is by no means impossible. It is even arguable that the juxtaposition of risk aversion and altruism is just coincidental, and that risk aversion plays no necessary role to ensure a place for equality, in addition to efficiency, as part of people's conception of the common good.

One might assert instead that the common good is independent of computations of gain and loss. I might simply "know" that public medical care is right, or wrong as the case may be, almost regardless of its consequences. I might know that through direct intuition or because it is decreed in the holy book. You cannot prove that I do not have such knowledge and you cannot budge me from views by vulgar calculation. On the other hand, if recognition of the common good falls upon our consciousness like manna from heaven, what possible counter-argument can one put forward against the fundamentalist who sees a mandate in his holy book for inherited privilege, slavery, capital punishment, the cutting off of the hands of a thief, the stoning of women taken in adultery, or the destruction of infidels? A common understanding of the common good is always difficult to acquire. It is virtually impossible to acquire unless the common good is understood as an aggregate of utilities or unless conformity is imposed by a priestly class empowered to punish heresy. The gods may well be utilitarians, concerned about the consequences for humankind of policies, programs, and institutions. Even so, decrees transcribed yesterday may no longer be appropriate today. Disagreeing, we may have no recourse short of violence to determine whose god is the stronger or whose intuition is right.

The notion of the common good may be dismissed as superfluous or illusory because political disputes are resolved and society is preserved by people's self-interested support for the rules of society. On this view, I do not try to persuade you that my preferred system of medical care is best for society as a whole. I try to persuade you that it is best for *you*. Once democratic institutions are established, we are content to resolve disputes by voting because we fear the consequences to ourselves if the outcome of the vote is overturned by violence or trickery. Enough people reasoning that way can compel others to abide by the rules too. The whole process takes place without anybody behaving in a way that, all things considered, is not best for himself. In fact, voting is examined in the next chapter on precisely this view of the world.

On the other hand, political arguments are framed with reference to what is best for society as a whole, and it is hard to believe that such talk is entirely hypocritical. There would be no such talk unless somebody, speaker or audience, believed there to be a common good and was prepared to temper self-interest accordingly. Concern for one's children, one's relatives, one's friends and so on, with diminishing weight for an ever-widening circle of people, transforms one's individual utility function into something more and more like a social welfare function. Seen in this light, people's social welfare functions differ, but differences among social welfare functions are less pronounced than differences in ordinary utility functions.

It is doubtful whether society could get on without some residue of concern for the common good. At a minimum, a significant portion of the population must be willing to vote even though voting is never advantageous from a purely selfish point of view. The private benefit of voting is always less than the private cost. The cost of voting is the time and trouble required to inform oneself about the candidates and to cast one's ballot. The expected benefit of voting is the gain to oneself from having one's preferred candidate win the election weighted by the probability that one's vote will swing the election. That probability is minute. Consider an election with two candidates and a million and one voters. The only way for any particular voter's participation to affect the outcome of the election is for all other voters to split evenly between the two candidates, with 500,000 votes for each. It is all but impossible for an election to be that close. A decision to vote voluntarily is like a decision not to smoke voluntarily in the smoke-and-smoking example in chapter 5. There, my smoking was assumed to be beneficial to me despite the fact that everybody would be better off if nobody smoked. Each person's gain from a smoke-free room was assumed to outweigh his loss from not smoking himself. Here, my decision not to vote is beneficial to me despite the fact that everybody is better off when everybody (or a significant proportion of the population) chooses to vote, for the continuance of democratic government is at stake. In both cases, there are externalities associated with individually costly actions, externalities large enough that everybody is better off when everybody bears the private cost than when nobody does, though it is in no person's interest to do so when all other people's actions are what they are independently of one's own. People vote because they enjoy participation in elections or because they feel a duty to do so. D. H. Robinson's answer to the question posed in the quotation at the beginning of this chapter was that economists economize love. By love, he meant altruism, a willingness to forgo one's own personal advantage for the common good. Love is a scarce commodity. Economists postulate a society where everybody is entirely self-interested not because "greed is good," but in the hope of transacting as large a share as possible of the world's business by means of greed, to avoid squandering love unnecessarily and to preserve that scarce and precious commodity for domains of life where love, and love alone, will suffice.

The real problem, in my opinion, in the evaluation of alternatives for public policy is not so much that people differ in their assessments of the common good, but that they, naturally enough, favor policies likely to benefit themselves, regardless of the effects on other people. There are many considerations in the choice between public and private provision of medical care. With private provision, the best physicians command the highest fees to allocate their services to those who value them most. With public provision, it is difficult not to pay all physicians in accordance with their formal qualifications and with the number of patient visits. Public provision may induce especially capable doctors to emigrate to countries where medical care is still private and remuneration is more in accordance with the physicians' diligence ability. Resources may be wasted in *rent seeking*. If some physicians are better than others and if physicians are assigned to patients by the state, then, one way or another, people pressure the state to supply them with the best physicians and the best medical services. Workers in unions may have the edge in this process over unorganized workers. Rent seeking is costly to supplicants, to the administration which must cope with competing claims to the services at its disposal, and in the temptation to corruption when what should be allocated evenly is, in practice, sold. Politics may be destabilized to some extent as the party in office is tempted to direct the best medical care to its supporters. Health or life itself may be at stake if failure to support the party in power comes to mean that fewer hospitals and less competent doctors are provided for one's region or social class. On the other hand, private medical care requires insurance which is by no means problem-free. Without insurance, each person's anticipated cost of medical care is like a gamble in which some people are bankrupted and others get away free. Insurance imposes a considerable administrative cost in deciding whether any given medical procedure is warranted in the case at hand and it places people at the mercy of insurance companies with an incentive to reject clients who are especially likely to become ill and to terminate very ill people with large medical bills. Beyond these considerations are others based on wealth. The rich can be expected to favor private provision of medical care because with progressive income taxation (anything more progressive than a head tax) the cost of public provision of medical care is borne disproportionately by the rich and because private medical care enables the rich to purchase the services of the better doctors.

The poor can be expected to favor public medical care for much the same reasons and because many poor people, unable to afford the cost of medical care or medical insurance, are obliged to rely on charity or are denied medical care altogether.

To take a different example, consider the death penalty when one's probability of being executed for murder is correlated, as seems to be the case in most societies where the death penalty is imposed, with one's income or one's class in society. If I am rich or a member of the upper classes, I may favor the death penalty, secure in the knowledge that I am very unlikely to be executed because the rich need not commit murder or because they can usually manipulate the legal system to impose a lesser penalty. If I am poor or a member of the lower classes, I may oppose the death penalty, being only too well aware that I stand a substantially higher than average chance of being executed because the poor commit more than their share of murders or because they cannot afford the expertise to manipulate the legal system to impose a lesser penalty. Behind the veil, these considerations balance out because I am assumed not to know who I shall become when the veil is lifted. In actual judgments, that information may be difficult to conceal.

Finally, it is worth mentioning that this discussion of the common good has not crossed the barrier between *is* and *ought*. The purpose of this chapter has not been to impose a notion of the common good upon the reader, but to analyze his sense of the common good and to show what his premises must be in favoring this or that policy, program, or institution. Much, though by no means all, of economic analysis is what might be called conditional prescription: "If this is your objective and these are your options, then this is what you ought to do." The role of economics in this context is to facilitate reasoning by spelling out the consequences of any given set of premises.

Social Welfare in Practice

The social welfare function ranks alternative institutions, policies, or programs such as public vs. private medical care and the infinite gradations in between. To do so, it must be translated from a summation of every person's utility into a weighting of broadly defined objectives of public policy. We cannot rank private and public medical care by subtracting Bill's loss of utility from Carol's gain. The best we can do is to reformulate social welfare as dependent on the size of the national income, the degree of inequality in the distribution of income, average life expectancy, the dispersion of life expectancy between rich and poor and between other groups in society, leisure, political freedom and so on, including, but not restricted to, the entire range of considerations discussed in chapter 1.

For purposes of exposition, utility, u, has been defined as a function of money income, Y, as though nothing else mattered. There are circumstances where that formulation is useful and where a more realistic representation of the components of a person's well-being would be counter-productive by diverting attention from the essence of the problem at hand. The simple formulation might be best for identifying the appropriate degree of progressivity in the income tax, progressivity being the gap between the rate of income tax levied on the rich and the rate of income tax levied on the poor. In other circumstances, that interpretation of u would be ridiculous. The choice between private and public provision of medical care has more to do with life expectancy and health than with income per se.

The term Y in the utility function may be stretched to cover many aspects of life. It may incorporate non-monetary aspects of well-being such as leisure, longevity, and health. It may allow for the impact tomorrow of public policy today. Most of the analysis in this book is *static*, as though the world we see today were to replicate itself in every detail forever. For many purposes, this simplification is convenient. Sometimes it is too far from the truth to be useful, as when preventive medicine today improves our lives tomorrow or when roads built today remain in use for a long time to come. The term Y may be reinterpreted as wealth rather than money income. Non-monetary considerations may be combined with ordinary goods and services in an enlargement of the measure of real income discussed at the end of chapter 5, or income may be reconstructed as a vector with income (as ordinarily defined) and non-monetary considerations as components.

Social welfare function may be adequately represented in some contexts by the national income, more or less as measured in the time series in table 1.8. As will be discussed in greater detail in the next two chapters, national income may be the best available surrogate for social welfare for use by the Ministry of Transport in deciding which roads to build and which roads to desist from building. All roads are of some benefit to everybody but each road is especially beneficial to identifiable sub-groups of the population. A rule is required to defend society from costly bickering over who is to be favored and at whose expense. A prior agreement to choose among roads so as to make the national income as large as possible has the double virtue that, with the usual uncertainty about what the future may bring, nobody may know at the time the rule is adopted who the ultimate beneficiaries of the rule will be and that everybody's expected net gain – the difference between one's benefits from all roads together and one's taxes to pay for them – is larger than it would be under any other rule. The common name for that rule is *cost-benefit analysis*.

Generalizing somewhat, public policy can be designed for efficiency, defined in economics as "the absence of waste." Three levels of efficiency might be identified: productive, allocative and distributive. These are most easily distinguished with reference to the bread-and-cheese economy in chapters 3 and 4. An economy is *productively* efficient when outputs of bread and cheese lie on, rather than below, the production possibility curve. An economy is productively efficient when it cannot be reorganized to yield more of some goods without yielding less of others. As a first approximation, an economy is productively efficient when the national income is as large as possible. An economy is *allocatively* efficient when the utility-maximizing combination of bread and cheese is chosen from among all possible combinations on the production possibility curve or among all attainable combinations. Consider a many-person economy where everybody is identical in every respect. For such an economy, there is one, unique, combination of bread and cheese – from among the set of combinations along the production possibility curve – at which everybody is better off than he would be with any other feasible combination. Output corresponding to any other mix of bread and cheese would be allocatively inefficient. This notion of efficiency is useful in the analysis of taxation. Allocative inefficiency may arise when some goods are heavily taxed and other goods are lightly taxed or untaxed altogether. An economy is *distributionally* efficient when the available bread and cheese cannot be reapportioned to make everybody better off simultaneously. In a society of two people who like to eat cheese sandwiches, an apportionment where one person consumes all the bread and another consumes all the cheese is distributionally inefficient in this sense. Distributional efficiency is entirely distinct from equality in the distribution of income. The apportionment of bread and cheese may be efficient even though some people are very well off and others are very badly off. Distributional efficiency requires that no trade can make all parties better off simultaneously. Full efficiency is a combination of productive, allocative, and distributive efficiency. The absence of waste means more than that the consumption of some goods is less than it might be. It also means that potential utility is not forgone through production of the wrong mix of goods or through the misapportionment of goods among people such that everybody could gain from trade. Public policy is efficient when nobody could be made better off without at the same time making somebody else worse off.

Desirable as it is, efficiency cannot be the only criterion for public policy, programs, or institutions because efficiency is not unique and because a somewhat wasteful policy may be preferred to a less wasteful policy with a significantly less equal distribution of income. Recall, for example, the distribution of 100 loaves of bread and 50 pounds of cheese between Mary and Norman as described in figure 3.7. Many possible distributions are not efficient, but there is a wide range of efficient distributions along the "efficiency locus," from the assignment of everything to Mary at one extreme to the assignment of everything to Norman at the other. Something beyond efficiency is required for choosing among points on the efficiency locus.

The significance of distribution as a component of social welfare is illustrated in a standard utilitarian argument not just for a degree of redistribution of income, but for full and complete equality. The argument presupposes a given national income, a utilitarian social welfare function (consistent with the veil of ignorance test) and *concavity* of the common utility of income function. A concave utility of income function bends forward so that each additional dollar of income yields progressively less utility. Concavity of the utility of income function was introduced in chapter 5 as an indicator of risk aversion, but, as shown in the discussion surrounding table 8.1, can be extended to the weighting of the incomes of different people, some prosperous, others not, in assessing the costs and benefits of public projects. Consider an economy with just two people, one rich and the other poor, whose incomes prior to redistribution are Y_R and Y_P (where of course $Y_R > Y_P$) and whose utilities are $u(Y_R)$ and $u(Y_P)$ for some common utility function $u(Y)$ as illustrated in figure 8.1. A transfer of income, ΔY, from the rich person to the poor person reduces the income of the rich person from Y_R to $Y_R - \Delta Y$ and increases the income of the poor person from Y_P to $Y_P + \Delta Y$, lowering the utility of the one by Δu_R and raising the utility of the other by Δu_P, where

$$\Delta u_R \equiv u(Y_R) - u(Y_R - \Delta Y) \quad \text{and} \quad \Delta u_P \equiv u(Y_P + \Delta Y) - u(Y_P) \qquad (6)$$

It follows at once from the concavity of the utility function in figure 8.1 – and is immediately evident from inspection of the figure – that $\Delta u_P > \Delta u_R$. Though total income remains unchanged, the gain of utility to the poor exceeds the loss of utility

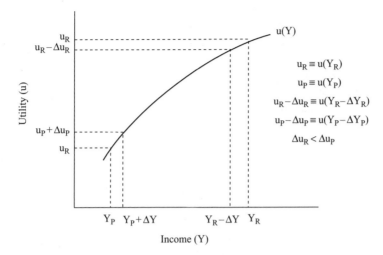

Figure 8.1 The effects on the utilities of a rich man and a poor man of a transfer of income from one to the other.

to the rich, so that the sum of the utilities of the rich and the poor together – which is our measure of social welfare – must be increased. Specifically,

$$u(Y_R - \Delta Y) + u(Y_P + \Delta Y) = u(Y_R) - \Delta u_R + u(Y_P) + \Delta u_P > u(Y_R) + u(Y_P) \quad (7)$$

Gains and losses of incomes balance out, but gains and losses of utilities do not. Each additional transfer of income from rich to poor increases total utility until incomes are equalized. The argument travels from the assumed risk aversion of the citizen, to the concavity of his utility of income function, to the gain in social welfare from a redistribution of income. This line of reasoning would seem to imply that any inequality of income is too much and that redistribution of income is always socially advantageous no matter how small the inequality happens to be.

There is a standard objection to this proposition: If we tried to share the national income equally, there would soon be nothing to share. If we are all to receive equal incomes no matter how hard we work or how much we have saved in the past, the incentive to work and save would quickly be destroyed and the national income would fall precipitously. Such perverse incentives have been waved away by supposing that total income remains constant. On that supposition, the increase in the income of the poor would just equal the decrease in the income of the rich, and the original incomes, Y_R and Y_P, would be converted by redistribution into the new incomes, $Y_R - \Delta Y$ and $Y_P - \Delta Y$, leaving total income, $Y_R + Y_P$, unchanged. The objection to redistribution is that total income would not remain unchanged.

To say that 100 percent redistribution would destroy the entire national income (defined as the sum of the incomes over the entire population) and that, by extension, any redistribution destroys some of the national income, is not to say that no redistribution is ever warranted. Where the disparity between the incomes of rich and poor is large, a modest reduction in the national income may be a fair price to pay for a partial narrowing of the distribution of income. Or, to express the point in the language we have developed, a partial redistribution of income may increase social welfare even at the cost of reducing the sum of the incomes of all citizens and despite the fact that a massive redistribution of income could be expected to reduce social welfare.

The basic idea is that the pie shrinks as you share it. Knowing income is to be redistributed, people work less, save less and devote more of their resources to the hiding of their incomes from the tax collector, so that the national income becomes less than it might otherwise be. A useful way to think about this is to suppose that, one way or another, a transfer of income that increases the net income of the poor by T would decrease the net income of the rich by θT where θ is greater than 1 and where the value of θ typically increases with T. For example if θ were 2, the income of the rich would have to be decreased by \$2,000 to bring about an increase of \$1,000 in the income of the poor. Social welfare, W, is maximized when the increase, Δu_P, in the utility of the poor from the last dollar of transfer from the rich is just equal to the decrease, Δu_R, in the utility of the rich caused by whatever reduction in income is necessary to procure that extra dollar for the poor. Specifically, redistribution has gone far enough when an additional transfer of income yielding \$1 to the poor affects the utilities of the rich and the poor so that

$$\Delta u_P = \Delta u_R \quad \text{where} \quad \Delta u_P = u_P(Y_P + 1) - u_P(Y_P) \quad \text{and}$$

$$\Delta u_R = u_R(Y_R) - u_R(Y_R - \theta) \tag{8}$$

When $\Delta u_P = \Delta u_R$, no feasible redistribution can increase one party's utility without decreasing the other's utility just as much, which is another way of saying that the sum of their utilities is as large as possible. Properly interpreted, the utilitarian social welfare function typically warrants some redistribution but never, in realistic conditions, as much as 100 percent. How to determine the value of θ will be discussed in chapters 9 and 10.

An economy with huge disparities between rich and poor may be efficient. As will be discussed in the next two chapters, an economy with substantial redistribution of income is typically somewhat inefficient (in the sense that an omnipotent planner could rearrange the economy to make everybody better off), but this may be considered a fair price to pay for the greater equality in the distribution of income. The story in chapter 3 is that a competitive economy is efficient in all three senses of the term. The utilitarian criterion interpretation of social welfare boils down in practice to the amalgamation of efficiency and equality into one higher criterion to provide "the greatest good for the greatest number," where the trade-off between these two "greats" is a reflection of the specification of welfare and of the utility of income function in equation (3).

PROPERTY, EQUALITY AND THE COMMON GOOD

One can think of social welfare as a person's ranking of entire distributions of income for society as a whole. Just as one is presumed able to rank alternative bundles of bread and cheese as better, worse or equal in the construction of indifference curves, so too is one presumed able to rank bundles of incomes of different people as better, worse, or equal in one's assessment of the common good of the community, though, to do so, one must somehow abstract both from his own place in the income distribution and from the identities of the occupants of each and every slot. As mentioned above, we normally think of social welfare as anonymous, so that an income of $100,000 a year to Charlie and an income of $50,000 a year to Joe is deemed neither better nor worse than an income of $100,000 a year to Joe and an income of $50,000 a year to Charlie.

To reason this way is to sweep an important question under the rug. If one person is to have an income of $100,000 and the other person is to have an income of $50,000, why does Charlie get to enjoy the higher income and not the other way round? Why in the example in chapter 3 does person A consume twice as much bread and cheese as person B? Why might the head of a major corporation earn, literally, thousands of times the income of the lowest paid worker? At one level the question is easily answered. People's incomes are a reflection of their resources in land, shares of companies, skills, and situations in society. The answer is true but unsatisfactory, for the real question is why resources, broadly defined, are allocated unevenly. Why, referring again to the example in chapter 3, does person A get plot A and person B get plot B, rather than some more even distribution of land between them? No explanation was provided. An allocation of resources to people was simply assumed.

We speak of people "earning" incomes, but earnings themselves are the outcomes of social conventions that might have been other than they are, and not all routes to high incomes are admirable or advantageous to society as a whole. Fortunes are often acquired by invention and industry, but not always so. Much wealth is acquired by chicanery, political influence, speculation (where the gain to the speculator is at the expense of the rest of society), or outright theft that somehow escapes the law. Ownership may be the loot of a thief made secure by a conspiracy of thieves. North America was stolen by the Europeans from the native people. Land occupied by tribes of native people at the time of the European conquest had been stolen by their ancestors from other tribes whose members rarely survived to claim their historic rights. The respectable landed fortunes of England originate in the banditry of William the Conqueror. Trace back the origins of "old wealth" today, and you will often find evidence of plunder. The claim that "property is theft" is at least partially true. If that be so, why should people tolerate the gross disparities of income that are to be found in almost any capitalist society with a degree of private ownership of the means of production?

The question is sometimes answered by an appeal to a "right of property." "Life, liberty and property" are seen as inalienable rights that no government may abrogate. In the late nineteenth century, an assumed right of property led the American Supreme Court to ban income tax as unconstitutional. A constitutional amendment was required before income tax could be reinstated. Some people see property rights as god given, or profess to find warrant for property rights in the Bible. Others see property rights as derived from a right to one's own labor or from a principle of "first possession," exemplified by the settler who gets to own the plot of land he clears from the wilderness.

This line of argument is not wrong, but back to front. Society upholds property rights not for their own sake, but because property rights are a requirement for other things we value, for general prosperity and, as we shall argue in the remaining chapters of this book, for democratic government. We protect property not though the heavens fall, but because the heavens will fall if we do not. Justification of wide disparities of income with reference to an absolute right of property may be persuasive to the wealthy. It is less likely to be persuasive to the poor. More in keeping with the spirit of economic analysis is the pragmatic justification from need. Property *is* theft in so far as some great fortunes do originate in plunder. We accept property rights as we find them because that is what we need to make society work.

The law recognizes a principle of *adverse possession* according to which a person who has been in possession of property for a long time is deemed to own it, regardless of how the property was first acquired. If I occupy a piece of land, if I build a fence around it, and if my occupation is unchallenged for a certain number of years, that land becomes mine, though it may have belonged to somebody else when I first occupied it. My house inherited from my father and grandfather is mine, even if grandpa acquired it by trickery or by theft. The logic of adverse possession is that the community as a whole is better off with secure title than if each person's property could be taken from him on the basis of some obscure transaction long ago.

So too, with all property. We respect property rights, not because of any abstract right, not because all property is discovered, created, or purchased by its owner and, not because inheritance *per se* is sacrosanct, but because we need them. Having established an apportionment among people of society's resources, we can maintain a market economy with the virtues listed at the end of chapter 3 and with the additional virtue, to be examined in the next three chapters, that a degree of private property is a requirement for personal liberty and a prerequisite of democratic government. Without private property, the community must allocate the national income politically. Each person's income would have to be determined individually by a central authority. Political allocation of the entire national income leaves no private sphere to serve as a check on the ruling class. Justification for disparities of income flows not from the rights or virtues of the occupants of the wealthier ranks of society, but rather from society's need for some non-political allocation of property and income in an economy where industry and innovation are rewarded. Unjustifiable in themselves, property rights can be seen as part of the overhead capital of the nation.

A country with a recognized allocation of property is fortunate. A country with no recognized allocation of property is unfortunate, destined to waste resources in conflict over the apportionment of income among citizens, as in the Soviet Union after the breakdown of communism where the resources of the nation were stolen or extracted through political manipulation by the former officials of the old Communist Party and the old industrial administration. With luck, the children and grandchildren of today's crooks and swindlers will become respected businessmen tomorrow, just as children and grandchildren of crooks and swindlers occupy many honorable positions in Europe and North America today.

Even as a reward for industry and invention, property rights are what they are on the strength of society's rules, some rules supplying property rights, other rules delimiting those rights, prohibiting certain uses of property as anti-social, obliging property-holders to pay tax and imposing whatever redistribution of income – increasing the net income of the poor and, correspondingly, reducing the net income of the rich – is deemed appropriate by the government of the day. The real justification of disparities of income and wealth is to be found not in the rights or virtues of the wealthy themselves, but in the belief that disparities of wealth are an inescapable by-product of rules deemed best in the long run for society as a whole. The virtues of the market justify the present distribution of wealth, but only in so far as disparities of wealth are really required for the virtues of the market to be realized.

REASSESSING MARKETS

This chapter is a transition from the study of markets to the study of government on the premise that the proper role of government in the economy depends on what the market can be expected to do. A list of the virtues of the market was presented at the end of chapter 3. To that list may now be added a list of vices that have come to light in the last four chapters. The list of virtues identified at the end of chapter 3 is recapitulated as follows:

- *The competitive market creates "order without orders."* Self-interested and uncoordinated actions by a great flock of decision-makers fit together as though by design, as though organized by a single will or a planning commission that arranged everything. Instead, there emerges a market-clearing price (the relative price of one good in terms of the other when there are only two goods) or prices (when there are many goods) at which whatever one wants to sell finds a buyer and whatever one wants to buy finds a seller. That much of the world's work can be done without direction by any central authority is of great political significance, establishing markets as a requirement for the maintenance of democratic government.
- *The competitive market is efficient.* The prices generated by a competitive market induce efficient production and allocation. The outcome of the market is efficient in that there is nothing wasted. No planning commission – however knowledgeable, however extensive its capacity to deploy the resources of the economy as it sees fit, and however benevolent – can rearrange production and reallocate goods to people to make everybody better off at once or to make anybody better off without at the same time making somebody else worse off.
- *The competitive market economizes on knowledge.* Market prices tell producers and consumers what they need to know about the technology and the tastes of other people throughout the world, allowing specialists in each line of production to slot their activities appropriately into the world economy without detailed information about what other people are doing. Prices lead markets to replicate the ideal planning commission in possession of more information about the economy than any actual planning commission could ever process or comprehend.
- *The competitive market circumvents bargaining.* As long as markets are large enough that nobody imagines himself to exert an independent influence on the price, people are enabled to trade with the market rather than with one another and there need be no wastage of resources in negotiation, trading and the abandonment of profitable deals because folks cannot agree on the sharing of the surplus.

The chapters on taste, technology, and associations yielded a comparable list of vices:

- *The market requires the protection of the state.* In chapter 2, the protection of property was the defense of fishermen against pirates. In chapter 5, land was possessed securely, and with no explanation within the model of how security of property was maintained. In chapter 8, the definition of property and the task of protecting property were broadened considerably. Protection of property came to include the enforcement of private contracts, with the inevitable requirement for the society to interpret the language of contracts in the resolution of disputes and to decide which contracts are to be enforceable and which not. The virtues of the market cannot be realized without public enforcement of private contracts, but the weight of government cannot be brought to bear on behalf of any and every private arrangement. The definition of property itself tends to blur at the edges, leaving some question of what exactly it is the task of government to protect.

- *The competitive market will not supply public goods.* The proof that a competitive equilibrium exists and is efficient depended critically on the assumption that all goods are "private" like bread and cheese. As shown in chapter 5, the proof breaks down completely for "public" goods like the army and the police because people want to be free riders on society's provision of public goods. Benefiting as much from your contribution to the financing of the army as from my own, I choose not to contribute at all and rely instead on the contribution of others. When everyone behaves that way, nothing is provided, and we are all worse off than if we compelled one another to contribute. The odd exception is television where advertising fulfills the role of taxation.

- *The competitive economy takes no account of externalities, of public benefits or harms that are somehow linked to the provision of private goods.* The example in chapter 5 was of smoking and smoke, looked upon as a paradigm of pollution of all sorts associated with the production of private goods. The principal remedy is taxation to bring private and social values into line.

- *The competitive economy may subject people to risks that cannot be entirely insured away but that can be reduced or pooled by public action.* The risk of being born unhealthy or incompetent cannot be pooled privately because too much is known about people when an insurance contract is signed. Nor can the market insure against unemployment or poverty because such insurance is only likely to be valuable to the insured when everybody is obliged to participate. The extent to which public insurance can fill the gap has for decades been the subject of considerable debate.

One extra vice and one extra virtue have emerged in this chapter and will play a large role in the chapters to come. *The extra vice is that the distribution in a competitive economy may turn out to be very unequal.* Care must be taken in drawing out the political implications of this vice of competitive markets. In principle, a government can arrange for a more equal distribution of income than what appears spontaneously in the market. In practice, the distribution on income can be, and is, equalized to some extent. Nevertheless, there is always some risk that a government empowered to redistribute income from rich to poor will in the end redistribute income from the ordinary citizen to the administrative classes or to favored social classes, corporations, or individuals.

The extra virtue of the competitive market is its compatibility with democratic government. It is no accident that virtually all reasonably democratic societies have economies based on the private ownership of the means of production. There is a technical, or mechanical, connection between the two. Capitalism is a prerequisite to democracy, not in the extreme sense that any modification of thoroughgoing, all-encompassing, capitalism spells the death of democracy, but in the sense that a somewhat ill-defined core of the economy has to be entrusted to the market if democracy is to be preserved. This proposition will be discussed under the general heading of voting in the next chapter.

Chapter Nine

VOTING

. . . a pure democracy, by which I mean a society consisting of a small group of citizens, who assemble and administer the government in person, can admit of no cure from the mischiefs of faction. A common passion or interest will, in almost every case, be felt by the majority of the whole; a communication and concert results from the form of government itself; and there is nothing to check the inducements to sacrifice the weaker party or an obnoxious individual. Hence it is, that such democracies have ever been spectacles of turbulence and contention; have been ever found incompatible with personal security, or the rights of property; and have, in general, been as short in their lives, as they have been violent in their deaths.

James Madison, *The Federalist Papers*, 1787

So deep is the respect for democratic government, and so manifest is the evidence that democratic countries provide freer and more prosperous lives for their citizens, that democracy itself is now seen as almost self-evidently desirable. Everybody is in favour of democracy; so much so that the word has found its way into the names of some of the ugliest and most undemocratic, in the ordinary sense of the word, regimes on earth, notably the Democratic Republic of Kampuchea and the now dissolved German Democratic Republic. Democracy is a complex term with many meanings and many more connotations, but at its core is majority-rule voting about the choice of leaders and the passage of bills in the legislature. Democracy may be more than just voting, but government without voting is not democracy. We are all brought up to think of majority-rule voting as unreservedly good.

That has not always been so. Until the eighteenth century, it was firmly believed by most thoughtful and well-intentioned people that democracy, interpreted as public decision-making by majority-rule voting, is a system of government which, whatever its virtues "in theory," simply does not work. Like the ancient Israelites, most people took it for granted that countries required a king with extensive powers over ordinary people. On that view, government by majority rule is destined to self-destruct because it contains no equilibrium comparable to the equilibrium prices in a competitive economy with well-specified property rights. On that view, democracy is inevitably a step on the road to despotism or to anarchy, to autocracy or to chaos. In Madison's words in the quotation at the beginning of this chapter, "democracies have ever been spectacles of turbulence and contention; have ever been found incompatible with personal security, or the rights of property; and have, in general, been as short in their lives as they have been violent in their deaths." The context of the quotation is extraordinary. Madison was one of the designers, some say the principal designer, of the constitution of the United States. The quotation itself is from *The Federalist Papers*, a series of tracts intended to persuade American voters to accept the constitution, replacing a loose confederation of semi-sovereign ex-colonies by a considerably tighter federal system of government. Madison accepts the anti-democratic argument as it applies to "a pure democracy" with "a small group of citizens" but he goes on to argue in defense of the new United States where factions might be expected to neutralize one another in a larger "compound republic." The argument retains some validity today not as a prediction of the demise of democracy or as reason for rejecting democratic government altogether, but as a vehicle for identifying weakness in democratic government and designing rules and subsidiary institutions by which democratic government can be sustained. The main task of this chapter is to study the mechanics of voting as a doctor studies diseases in the attempt to keep people well. The old view that voting cannot work carries within it lessons about what can be determined by voting and what cannot.

HOW WE VOTE AND WHAT WE VOTE ABOUT

Our society maintains two systems of rights: property rights which are intrinsically unequal, and voting rights which are intrinsically equal. Property rights are, in practice, unequal, for people hold different amounts of property. Property should be understood in this context to include *human capital* in skills (such as the ability to practice medicine or to run an efficient business) enabling their possessors to earn high incomes, as well as *physical capital* in the ownership of land and other resources. Voting rights are intrinsically equal, for each person has one and only one vote. In speaking here about rights, I am not suggesting that the rights are God-given or established in the sky independently of human interests or human will. I am merely asserting that many societies maintain both systems of rights simultaneously, despite the inevitable conflict at the edges. We maintain these rights because we believe them to be useful in the broadest sense of the term. We maintain these rights because we believe a society where both of these rights are not protected would be a dreadful place to live.

Each system of rights has a core domain of application, with a disputed boundary in between. Politics is to a large extent about the boundaries between rights. Consider medical care. Medical care could be entirely within the domain of property, as it was in Canada until well after the Second World War. People could be left to buy as much or as little medical care as they choose, just as they buy bread and cheese. Alternatively, medical care could be entirely within the domain of voting, as it is for the most part in Canada today, where the amount and composition of medical care are determined by the legislature in the first instance with extensive delegation to the administration. Provision of drugs remains partly within the domain of property.

To vote is to choose among laws, policies, or leaders in accordance with the preferences of the majority in the community. Consider a simple variant of an example that will be developed later in this chapter. A class of students is ordering sandwiches for lunch. The only choice is between ham sandwiches and tuna sandwiches. The cafeteria can supply only one type of sandwich, either ham or tuna, for everybody. To vote is to ask those who want ham rather than tuna sandwiches to raise their hands. If more than half the class do so, the choice is for ham. Otherwise the choice is for tuna. With only two options to choose from, the preference of the majority is identified unambiguously, and is invariably selected. With more than two options to choose from, the outcome of voting is, as we shall see, not entirely determinate.

Three contexts of voting may be usefully distinguished: the choice among candidates for office, the choice of bills in the legislature, and the passage of laws by referendum. For the choice among candidates for office, it is the practice in Canada to divide the territory into constituencies with equal numbers of people, to allow as many candidates as wish to run in any constituency, and to declare as winner in each constituency the candidate who is *first-past-the-post* with the largest number of votes, regardless of whether he obtains a majority (more than 50 percent) or just a plurality (more than any other candidate) of the votes. First-past-the-post voting is used for electing Members of Parliament in Canada and for electing Senators, Congressmen and the President in the United States. With ten candidates, the winner might have as little as 11 percent of the votes, and one of the losing candidates might have beaten the winner by as much as 89 to 11 if no candidates other than these two had entered the race. One fanatic could beat out 9 moderates if the moderate candidates split the moderate vote. Of course, for this to happen, the moderate candidates and their supporters would have to be very stubborn or very stupid; otherwise they would arrange for some (perhaps as many as 8) of the moderate candidates to drop out of the race.

To avoid this outcome, other countries have adopted different electoral rules. Under pure *proportional representation*, there need be no subdivision of the country into constituencies. Political parties order their candidates on lists, people vote for parties rather than candidates, seats in the legislature are assigned to parties in accordance with their votes, and parties assign seats to candidates in accordance with their lists. For example, under proportional representation and with 600 seats in Parliament, if the Liberals get two-thirds of the votes and Conservatives get one third, then the first 400 candidates on the Liberal list and the first 200 candidates on the Conservative list become the Members of Parliament.

Alternatively, elections may be designed to take cognizance of voters' orders of preference among all candidates, so that, for example, a candidate who is every voter's second choice may win over a candidate who is ranked first by a small plurality of voters but who is detested by the rest. One such voting mechanism is the *Borda method*. Each voter orders all candidates, the candidates are awarded points accordingly, and the candidate with the most votes wins. With three candidates, a first place would be worth two points, a second place would be worth two points and a third place would be worth nothing. Another way of accounting for voters' orders of preference is the *single transferrable vote*. Each voter orders all candidates. Then, in single-candidate constituencies, any candidate with over 50 percent of first-place votes is declared the winner. If there is no such candidate, the candidate with the lowest number of first-place votes is dropped, and his votes are reassigned among the remaining candidates in accordance with his supporters' second preferences. If the first preference of voter A is dropped, then voter A's second preference is elevated to a first preference, his third to a second, and so on. The process is repeated as many times as is necessary for a candidate to emerge with 50 percent of the total vote. The single transferable vote is designed to avoid the situation described above where a small percentage of the vote (11 percent in our example) is sufficient to procure a victory because voters opposing the winning candidate are split among many similar candidates. Members of Parliament in New Zealand are chosen in a single transferrable vote.

A different set of problems arises in voting on bills within the legislature. On any given issue, the legislature must choose among many possible courses of action, and the legislators would normally differ in their rankings of the available options. Suppose there is a general consensus that the old age pension is becoming too expensive. Some legislators may favor raising the retirement age from 65 to, say, 67. Others may prefer an even higher retirement age. Others may prefer to lower the dollar value of the old age pension. Others may prefer the pension to become contingent on income. Others may prefer to leave the current program untouched. Somehow, one policy, or combination of policies, must be chosen. With a clear majority in Parliament and with adequate party discipline, the party in power could presumably do as it pleased, constrained only by the possibility of a revolt of its backbenchers if its actions were too unpopular, and by concern about the next election. With no clear majority for any course of action or with some degree of independence on the part of the legislators (as in the Congress of the United States), the situation becomes more complex.

A bill is proposed, perhaps by the party in office, perhaps by an individual legislator. Then an amendment is proposed. Then a second amendment is proposed. Then a third, or perhaps an amendment to an amendment, and so on. With only two mutually exclusive amendments, the legislature would be confronted with four options – reject the bill, pass the bill unamended, pass the bill with the first amendment and pass the bill with the second amendment – options from which one must be selected. The selection procedure could, in principle, be comparable to first-past-the-post in the choice of Members of Parliament. All options might be voted simultaneously on the understanding that the option with the most votes wins. To the best of my knowledge, this procedure has never been adopted in any country, presumably because it is too readily open to manipulation to ensure that any innovation – a bill with or without amendments – is preferred by a majority of the legislators to the status quo.

Instead, parliamentary procedure is based upon *sequential voting* in which all votes are between pairs of options (never more than two) with new options introduced one by one against the survivor of the preceding vote. Sequential voting requires a subsidiary rule for the ordering of votes. In parliamentary procedure, the sequence of options is in reverse order of their appearance in the legislature. In our four-option example, the first vote would be between the two amendments, the second would be between the winner of the first vote (the bill as amended by the winner of the first vote) and the bill unamended, and the third vote would be between the winner of the second vote and the status quo. The decision of the legislature would then be the winner of the final vote.

Sequential voting is somewhat strategy-proof but does not block strategy altogether. It is strategy-proof to the extent that any option commanding more than 50 percent of the votes in a pair-wise contest with any other option must necessarily triumph regardless of the ordering of the votes in the sequence. However, where there is no such commanding option, options introduced later on in the sequence have an edge over options introduced earlier. An option can be knocked out early in the sequence even though it would have won in a pair-wise vote against the option that is ultimately victorious. This cannot happen to the status quo under parliamentary procedure because the status quo is always placed at the end of the sequence of votes. Parliamentary procedure gives the edge to the status quo by placing it at the end of the voting chain, guaranteeing that no bill, however amended, can become law unless preferred to the status quo by a majority of the Members of Parliament. Nor does sequential voting block *log rolling* in which two bills that would otherwise be rejected are both passed because you agree to vote for my bill and I, in return, agree to vote for yours. It does not block strategic amendments. Suppose a bill to build a road in district A would win on a straight up-or-down vote. Those who oppose the bill might attempt to defeat it with a strategic amendment to build a road in district B as well. The strategic amendment works as intended if the amendment is passed and then the bill as amended is defeated because some legislators, who would be willing to fund a road in district A only, are unwilling to fund two roads in districts A and B. The ploy may work when some legislators vote sincerely at each stage, while other legislators do not.

Our final context is the *referendum*. Normally, citizens vote for legislators, and legislators vote for laws. A referendum breaks this pattern, allowing citizens to vote for laws or policies directly. In California, a referendum is initiated by a petition with the appropriate number of signatures, and the outcome of a referendum is binding on the legislature. Some years ago, the people of California voted by referendum to limit the rate of the property tax. Recently, California voted by referendum to eliminate reverse discrimination, changing dramatically the racial composition of college students in the state. In Canada, where mere citizens have less control over their governments, a referendum can only be initiated by the government and the outcome of a referendum is not binding. Quebec held a referendum on separation in 1995. Newfoundland has held two referendums on transferring control of education from religious groups to the provincial government, though the actual transfer could only be effected by a constitutional amendment requiring approval by the Legislature of Newfoundland and the Parliament of Canada.

THE DISEASES OF DEMOCRACY

It is not within the scope of this book to describe democratic politics in detail. Our object is instead to identify common difficulties in all democratic government, to show how these difficulties may be confronted, and, especially, to identify connections between the organization of the economy and the stability of democratic government.

Several diseases of democracy can be identified, some relatively mild, others potentially fatal. Among the diseases of democracy are its failure to reflect intensity of preference, its capriciousness, the paradox of voting, the threat to private property, and the exploitation problem. These will be discussed in turn.

Intensity of preference

Consider once again the students' choice between ham sandwiches and cheese sandwiches, but now suppose some students are kosher. Suppose the 80 percent of the students who are not kosher prefer ham to tuna, and the 20 percent of the students who are kosher prefer tuna to ham. Obviously, ham wins four-to-one in a straight vote. Suppose also that the non-kosher students, though they prefer ham to tuna, do not care very much about the matter and would be content to eat tuna if only tuna were available, while the kosher students would forgo lunch altogether rather than eat ham. Were that so, the common good as described in chapter 8 might be best served by the choice of tuna sandwiches, even though the vote is for ham. Consider a person "behind the veil of ignorance" not knowing whether he is kosher but expecting a one-in-five chance of turning out to be kosher when the veil is lifted and his place in the world is finally revealed. That person may choose tuna sandwiches, notwithstanding the four-to-five chance that he will eventually prefer ham. Alternatively, adopting a utilitarian criterion and treating each person's utility as dependent on the type of sandwich, it may turn out that the sum of everybody's utility is higher when tuna is served than when ham is served.

The general problem exemplified here is that voting takes no account of *intensity of preference*. Voting recognizes whether one prefers this to that, but not by how much, if indeed "how much" can be specified at all. Within the strict confines of this example, ham wins and the kosher students are out of luck. On the other hand, it is hard to see how intensity of preference could be measured or compared objectively. If you prefer ham and I prefer tuna, it is easy enough for me to claim that my preference is more intense than yours, but it is rarely possible for me to prove that claim or for you to disprove it. Sometimes one can produce evidence of religious conviction or medical allergy, but more often one's intensity of preference is unobservable.

A crude substitute for evidence on intensity of preference might emerge in voting about several matters at once. Tuna may prevail over ham as part of a menu or platform. Suppose students vote on two matters, the choice of sandwiches and the choice of dessert, where the choice of sandwiches is between tuna and ham and the choice of dessert is between apple pie and cherry pie. Once again, everybody's lunch must be the same: all tuna or all ham, all apple pie or all cherry pie. If the non-kosher students are evenly split between apple pie and cherry pie, there may be room for a deal in which kosher students vote for one or the other dessert in return for a vote for tuna over ham. Voting deals may or may not be socially advantageous. The deal about sandwiches and dessert seems harmless enough. Other deals are less innocuous. In practice, deals are struck among legislators and in the formation of platforms of political parties. More will be said about this matter below.

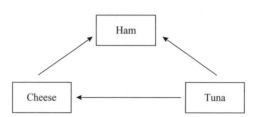

Figure 9.1 A directed graph of the outcomes of pair-wise votes between ham, cheese, and tuna. The arrow from, for example, cheese to ham, means that cheese beats ham in a pair-wise vote.

The capriciousness of voting

Voting becomes capricious when the outcome depends more upon the intricacies of the voting rules or upon side deals among voters than upon the preferences of the voters themselves. To show how the outcome of voting depends on voting rules, we construct an example with three options in a community composed of three groups of voters where preferences among the options are identical within each group but different from one group to another. Suppose once again that the class must choose one and only one type of sandwich for everybody, but that now there are three types of sandwiches to choose from: ham, tuna and cheese. With these three options, there can be six preference orderings: "ham preferred to cheese preferred to tuna," "ham preferred to tuna preferred to cheese," "cheese preferred to ham preferred to tuna," "cheese preferred to tuna preferred to ham," "tuna preferred to cheese preferred to ham," and "tuna preferred to ham preferred to cheese." Every student's preference ordering must be one of the six, though not every possible ordering need be represented among students' preferences. Suppose all students have one of the three preference orderings in table 9.1, so that outcomes of all pair-wise votes are as shown in figure 9.1. In a class of 100 students, there are 35 students (called group I) who prefer ham to tuna to cheese as shown in the first row of table 9.1, 33 students (called group II) who prefer tuna to cheese to ham as shown in the second row, and 32 students (called group III) who prefer cheese to tuna to ham as shown in the third row. To emphasize how public choice may be affected by the voting mechanism, the preferences are chosen so that ham has more first preferences than either cheese or tuna, but ham loses to both cheese and tuna in a pair-wise vote. This constellation of preferences is odd but by no means impossible. The voting methods to be compared are first-past-the-post, sequential voting, the single transferable vote, the Borda method, and proportional representation.

First-past-the-post

Each person votes for one of the three sandwiches, and the sandwich with the most votes wins. Ham gets 35 votes; tuna gets 32 votes; cheese gets 33 votes. With first-past-the-post voting and with tastes as shown in table 9.1, ham wins because it gets the largest number of votes. If sandwiches were political parties, if the entire country were

Table 9.1 Preferences among ham, cheese, and tuna sandwiches

Group	Number of students in the group	Orders of preference		
		First	Second	Last
I	35	Ham	Tuna	Cheese
II	32	Tuna	Cheese	Ham
III	33	Cheese	Tuna	Ham

divided into constituencies each electing one Member of Parliament, and if preferences of voters in each constituency were as shown in table 9.1, the ham party would win every seat in Parliament, even though it commands no more than 35 percent of the total vote.

First-past-the-post voting is especially susceptible to vote-splitting. Think of the ham party as "right wing" and of the cheese and tuna parties as "left wing". The situation in table 9.1 is where the left is split between two parties, both of which could beat the right-wing party in a straight pair-wise vote, but both of which lose to the right-wing party when neither is prepared to abandon the field to the other. Ambition, jealousy, minor differences in political views, or mere inertia may keep both candidates in the running though they each know they will both lose the election. In Canada today, the "conservative" vote is split between the Progressive Conservative Party and the Alliance Party, and it is at least conceivable that a combined conservative party could defeat the Liberals, though the Liberals would always emerge victorious in a three-way contest.

Supporters of first-past-the-post argue in its defense that vote-splitting is less important in practice than extreme and fanciful examples might suggest because recognition of the possibility of vote-splitting provokes parties with similar programs to fuse before the election and because the really important consideration in societies where voters are not too diverse is that voting yields a majority party in Parliament with the ability to govern the country. Recognition of the possibility of vote splitting pressures political parties with similar programs to coalesce before the election. Typically, though by no means invariably, elections are contested by two major parties with platforms hammered out as a compromise among their supporters before the election. The very terms left wing and right wing are a reflection of this possibility.

Yet there is something peculiar about the implicit assumption that people's views on all political issues can be categorized as left or right, so that a person who holds a left view on one issue can be expected to hold a left view on the rest. One would like to think that people are more independent than that. The original reference of these terms was to the French National Assembly of 1789 where the seating arrangement was a reflection of how nasty one was prepared to be to King Louis XVI. It is hard to imagine a correspondence between that seating arrangement and anything of importance today. The only sense I can make of these terms is as convenient labels for broad coalitions of politicians seeking office, with perhaps some reference to the extent of government influence over the economy.

First-past-the-post rules can have dangerous consequences for a society that is deeply divided by language, race, or religion and where the division is within constituencies, not among them. First-past-the-post voting rules would simply not be respected in a society where religion is divisive and where, for example, 51 percent of each constituency is Muslim and the remaining 49 percent is Hindu, or vice versa. Some other political accommodation would have to be devised.

Sequential voting

Though ham wins in first-past-the-post voting, it must necessarily lose to tuna in sequential voting because tuna is preferred to either of the other sandwiches in a pairwise vote. Frequently, the outcome of sequential voting depends on the order of the sequence, but not in this case.

The single transferrable vote

Voters are instructed to list all candidates in order of preference, so that, for example, a voter in group 1 of table 1 would write, "ham, tuna, cheese." If any option has more than 50 percent of the first-place votes, that option wins. Otherwise, the option with the lowest number of first places is deleted from everybody's list, and the votes are recounted. Once again, if any option has more than 50 percent of the first-place votes, that option wins. The process is repeated as many times as is necessary for one of the options to emerge with over 50 percent of the first-place votes. The process must eventually supply a winner because one candidate must have over 50 percent of the vote when the number of contenders is reduced to two and because a tie is virtually impossible when there are millions of voters. In our example, no option gets 50 percent of the vote on the first round, tuna is deleted from the contest because it has the smallest number (32) of first places, and then cheese gets 65 out of 100 votes in the contest with ham. Though ham wins under first-past-the-post and tuna wins in sequential voting, cheese wins in the single transferrable vote.

The Borda method

Voters are instructed to list all candidates in order of preference. With three options, an option gets 2 points for each first place, 1 point for each second, and 0 points for each third place. With 35 first places and no seconds, ham gets 70 points [35 × 2]. With 32 first places and 68 second places, tuna gets 132 points [(32 × 2) + 68]. With 33 first places and 32 seconds, cheese gets 101 points [(33 × 2) + 32]. With voting by the Borda method and with tastes as shown in table 1, tuna wins.

All three sandwiches are chosen in at least one of these four methods of voting. Voting is capricious, in the sense that the outcome is dependent on the method of voting, when there is no single overwhelming winner with enough support in the electorate to prevail in all of the methods of voting we have examined.

Proportional representation

Members of Parliament may be selected not in one constituency at a time but altogether. Think of ham, tuna, and cheese as names of political parties (no sillier than donkeys and elephants) rather than as names of sandwiches. Think of the numbers in the second column of table 1 as percentages of the electorate, and suppose 100 Members of Parliament have to be chosen. Under proportional representation, seats in parliament are proportional to votes in the nation, 35 seats for the ham party, 32 for the tuna party and 33 for the cheese party. Legislators in Germany and Israel are chosen by proportional representation.

Another aspect of the capriciousness of voting is that the outcome may depend upon deals among voters when two or more matters have to be resolved together. Suppose that 10 percent of the population favors the support by the state of the "one true religion," and that the 90 percent of the population who oppose support by the state of the one true religion are divided equally between liberals and conservatives, distinguished, for example, by their preferences about state control of industry. If those in favor of the state support of the one true religion do not care one way or another about the control of industry, or if their concern about industry is entirely subordinate to their concern about religion, then the religious group can ally itself, and form a majority, with either the liberals or the conservatives. A majority coalition of the religious folk and the conservatives would implement a platform of conservative economic policy and state support of the one true religion. A majority coalition of the religious folk and the liberals would implement a platform of liberal economic policy and state support of the one true religion. There is no basis for predicting which of the two alliances will be formed. We will return to this problem in the discussion of bargaining at the end of this chapter.

The paradox of voting

The constellation of preferences in table 9.1 and figure 9.1 has been chosen so that tuna beats either cheese or ham in a pair-wise vote. From this fact alone, one might be inclined to say that tuna is the right choice for the class and that the outcome of first-past-the-post voting is an aberration. The inference would be that sequential voting is preferable because tuna emerges victorious in any sequence of votes. Suppose, for example, that the sequence is tuna against cheese in the first round of voting, followed by the winner against ham in the second. Tuna is "elected" because it wins both rounds, and would continue to do so in any other sequence. Unfortunately, sequential voting has its own equally troublesome problems.

Consider a slight modification of the constellation of preference orderings in table 9.1. Preferences in table 9.2 are the same as in table 9.1 except for a reversal of the second and last preferences of group III, as shown in the bottom row. Once

Table 9.2 An example of a paradox of voting

| | Number of students | Orders of preference | | |
Group	in the group	First	Second	Last
I	35	Ham	Tuna	Cheese
II	32	Tuna	Cheese	Ham
III	33	Cheese	Ham	Tuna

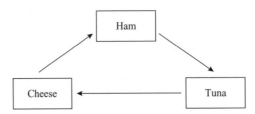

Figure 9.2 A directed graph of the paradox of voting.

again, ham wins in a three-way contest, though a slight change in proportions of voters would alter that. However, with this pattern of preferences, sequential voting turns perverse, giving rise to what is called a "paradox of voting." One can see immediately from table 9.2 that ham beats tuna and that tuna beats cheese. Both wins are substantial. Ham beats tuna with 68 percent of the votes, and tuna beats cheese with 67 percent of the votes. If the outcome of the vote can be thought of as representing the preferences of society, then, to be consistent, society would have to prefer ham to cheese as well. One would naturally expect ham to beat cheese in any pair-wise vote. The essence of rationality is consistency. If a person tells you that he prefers ham to tuna and that he prefers tuna to cheese, but that, nevertheless, he prefers cheese to ham, it would be hard to escape the conclusion that this person is irrational, even insane. Collective decisions by majority rule voting may be just like that! With the constellation of individual preferences in table 9.2 and with collective decision-making by voting, cheese is preferred to ham – by a vote of 66 percent – despite the fact that ham is collectively preferred to tuna and tuna is collectively preferred to cheese. Depending on the pattern of preferences, a community of people may vote inconsistently without any individual being inconsistent or insane. The paradox of voting is that though each voter is rational, the community as expressed by voting need not be. For the pattern of preferences in table 9.2, the outcomes of all pair-wise votes are shown in the directed graph in figure 9.2.

An immediate consequence of this potential irrationality is that the "agenda setter" can sometimes determine the outcome of voting through his authority to choose the sequence of votes. With three options to choose from, there are three possible sequences of pair-wise votes: (1) ham against tuna, followed by the winner against cheese, (2) ham against cheese, followed by the winner against tuna, and (3) cheese against tuna, followed by the winner against ham. The agenda setter is the person who chooses among these sequences. When preference orderings are as shown in table 9.1, the agenda setter is powerless because tuna wins regardless. But when preference orderings are as shown in table 9.2, the agenda setter can rig the outcome of the vote in his choice among the three possible sequences. The trick is that, with the preference orderings in table 9.2, the option introduced in the last vote always wins. If the agenda setter wants ham to win, he need only choose the third of the three sequences above.

The agenda setter can be foiled by *sophisticated*, as distinct from *sincere* voting. Voting is said to be sincere when, for example, I always vote for ham over cheese if I really prefer ham to cheese and regardless of what I expect to be the outcome of a sequence of votes to be. Voting is said to be sophisticated when I vote against my preferences now in order to get a better outcome in the end. Suppose the agenda setter favours ham, and consider the strategy of the third group of students whose preferences, as shown in the bottom row of table 2, are for tuna, cheese and ham in that order. Hoping to maneuver students to vote for ham, the agenda setter arranges a first round of voting between tuna and cheese, anticipating that tuna wins the first round and is then beaten by ham in the second. That is exactly what happens if everybody votes sincerely. The agenda setter gets his way at the expense of the third group of students for whom ham is the least desirable sandwich. Understanding this, these students may vote for cheese rather than tuna in the first round, anticipating that cheese beats ham in the second. These students would prefer tuna, but they cannot get it. The best they can do is to vote against their first preference, tuna, to obtain cheese which is at least preferable in their estimation to ham. The moral of the story is that voting is unpredictable and dependent on the strategies of the voters.

The poor dispossess the rich

A classic argument against democratic government runs more or less as follows: With universal franchise, there is nothing to stop the poor from employing the power of the vote to expropriate the rich. As nobody's wealth would be safe from predation by voting, it would be in nobody's interest to work hard, to educate himself or to invest in order to become rich. Enterprise would cease. Society would sink into poverty until such time as majority-rule voting with universal franchise is replaced by some other form of government. Perhaps society could get by with a property qualification for voting, as favored by the classical economists and as was the practice in most democratic countries until the end of the nineteenth century. Otherwise monarchy or dictatorship would seem to be required.

The argument that the voting allows the poor to dispossess the rich can be framed with reference to the choice of a rate for a *negative income tax*. A negative income tax is a universal lump sum transfer of income financed by a proportional income tax. Suppose for convenience of exposition that the government undertakes no expenditure other than the transfer of income. The government levies proportional income tax at a rate t to pay for a transfer of T dollars per person. Thus, if a person's gross (pre-tax-and-transfer) income is y^G, his net (post-tax-and-transfer) income becomes y^N where

$$y^N = T + (1 - t)y^G \tag{1}$$

Suppose also that tax collection is costless in two respects: (1) There is no administration cost to tax collection, no tax inspectors to be paid, no tax evasion and no need for police to detect and prosecute tax fraud. (2) There is no inefficiency or wastage of resources as people rearrange their affairs to reduce their tax bills, switching expenditure from taxed to untaxed goods or from taxed work to untaxed leisure and do-it-yourself activities. Thus, regardless of the tax rate, the national income remains invariant. With no administrative cost or wastage of resources in taxation, the government balances its budget as shown in equation (2).

$$NT = t[y_1^G + y_2^G + \cdots + y_{N-1}^G + y_N^G] \tag{2}$$

where N is the total population of tax-payers, y_i^G is the gross income of person i, the left-hand side of the equation is total public expenditure, and the right-hand side of the equation is total public revenue. Substituting the government's budget constraint, equation (2), into equation (1), we see immediately that each person's net income, y_i^N, is connected to his gross income, y_i^G, as follows

$$y_i^N = t\bar{y} + (1 - t)y_i^G \tag{3}$$

where t is the tax rate and $\bar{y}$ is average gross income of all tax payers together

$$\bar{y} \equiv [y_1^G + y_2^G + \cdots + y_{N-1}^G + y_N^G]/N \tag{4}$$

A natural interpretation of equation (3) is that a person's net income is a tax-weighted average of his gross income and the average income in the population as a whole. The higher the tax rate, the closer to the average does each person's net income become. Thus, an increase in the transfer per head financed by an increase in the tax rate is beneficial to everybody with a gross income below the average, and is detrimental to everybody with a gross income above the average.

The tax rate is determined by voting. Since everybody seeks to maximize his net income, it follows from equation (3) that everybody with below-average pre-tax income favors maximal redistribution, while everybody with above-average pre-tax income opposes redistribution altogether. The one group wants t = 100 percent. The other group wants t = 0 percent. In a vote, the option of setting t = 100 percent wins if more than half the voters have below-average pre-tax incomes, and the option of setting t = 0 wins otherwise. In fact, all electorates have majorities with less than average incomes. At virtually every time and place where the income distribution has been observed, there have been more people with below-average incomes than with above-average incomes, reflecting a skewed distribution of income with a few exceptionally wealthy folk and a great clustering of ordinary folk with incomes somewhat below the mean. For example, in a community of five people whose incomes are $1, $2, $3, $5, and $9, the average income per head is $4 but three out of the five people have incomes below $4. A majority of three of these five people votes for a tax rate of

100 percent. On our assumptions so far, a majority would always vote for a tax rate of 100 percent in a one-to-one contest with any other rate. All income is confiscated and redistributed equally among all citizens. The incentives to work and save are wiped out completely. Whether the assumptions required to derive this gloomy prognosis are reasonable, and what becomes of the proposition when the assumptions are modified, will be discussed below.

The exploitation problem

Seven people sit around a table. On the table is $700,000 which is theirs as soon as they can decide how to allocate the money among themselves. All decisions are by majority-rule voting. What happens? Whatever the outcome, it can be represented as a platform $\{y_1, y_2, y_3, y_4, y_5, y_6, y_7\}$ where y_1 is the allocation to the first person, y_2 is the allocation to the second person, and so on, and where the sum of the seven allocations has to be $700,000.

The obvious procedure is to divide the money equally, $100,000 per person. The platform would be $\{100, 100, 100, 100, 100, 100, 100\}$ where the numbers refer to thousands of dollars. If people are considerate, that is how the sum might be divided. But economics is the calculus of greed, and greedy people might hit upon a more advantageous allocation. Suppose four of the seven are men and the remaining three are women. The four men might strike a deal to take the entire sum for themselves, excluding the women altogether. They might agree to vote for the platform $\{175, 175, 175, 175, 0, 0, 0\}$ which provides $175,000 for each man and nothing for any of the women. This greedy platform defeats the original platform $\{100, 100, 100, 100, 100, 100, 100\}$ in a pair-wise vote. Nor is it essential to this example that people differ by gender. The seven people may differ by race. Four blue people might form a coalition to dispossess three green people. Four western people might form a coalition to dispossess three eastern people. Majority rule voting allows any four people to establish a coalition to exploit the remaining three.

The allocation of $175,000 to each of four people is not an electoral equilibrium in the sense that it can defeat every other allocation in a pair-wise vote. Though it can beat the platform $\{100, 100, 100, 100, 100, 100, 100\}$, the platform $\{175, 175, 175, 175, 0, 0, 0\}$ cannot beat *every* other platform. It is beaten by the platform $\{200, 200, 200, 0, 100, 0, 0\}$ which could emerge as follows: The first woman (person 5) might propose to the first three men that they join her in a coalition where they each get $200 thousand, she gets $100 thousand and the fourth man is displaced altogether. Everybody in the new coalition is better off than in the old coalition, and the first three men would be inclined to accept the proposal if they could be certain that the coalition would hold. But the new coalition is no more stable than its predecessor. For example, the second woman might offer to accept $25 thousand in a new coalition excluding the second man and providing an extra $25 thousand to each of the three remaining members of the old coalition. That platform could be defeated by yet another platform, and so on, ad infinitum. There is no electoral equilibrium at all. There is no platform that cannot be defeated by some other platform in a pair-wise vote.

The nice platform {100, 100, 100, 100, 100, 100, 100} may be especially vulnerable and unstable as a consequence of mistrust. I may be prepared to accept my fair share, $100,000, of the income as long as I am confident of your good faith. But, if I begin to doubt you, if I begin to fear you may be about to form a coalition behind my back and from which I am excluded, then I may begin negotiations of my own, and you, in turn, may be provoked to act more aggressively than if you trusted me. The nasty platform {175, 175, 175, 175, 0, 0, 0}, while not a full electoral equilibrium, may be more stable in practice than the nice platform because each beneficiary, each of the four men in this example, knows that he has more to lose in the end – 175 rather than 100 – if the nasty platform is overturned.

The exploitation of minorities by majorities and the dispossession of the rich by the poor, as discussed in the preceding section, are similar in that one group suffers at the hands of another, but they differ in the manner and consequences of discrimination. In the exploitation example, there are no prior rights to shares of the $700,000. There is no generally accepted rule for the voters to follow. (Equality might constitute such a rule in some societies, but not in societies with market-based economies where incomes differ markedly from one person to the next.) In the dispossession of the rich by the poor, there are two rules which conflict to some extent. There is a prior allocation of income (or, equivalently, of property rights), and there is a prior agreement not to reassign people's incomes arbitrarily – so much for you, so much for me depending on how favorable a deal each of us can make within the majority coalition. There is one tax rate for everybody, and the vote is confined to determining what that tax rate is to be.

An important moral can be drawn. Democracy – by which I mean no more than that major public decisions are taken by majority rule voting – works best in societies not too sharply divided between identifiable groups with opposing interests. Current rhetoric notwithstanding, democracy is hardly threatened by the division of mankind into men and women because men and women have too many interests in common, not least of which is their common concern for their children of both genders. Language is potentially more divisive. Most bilingual or multilingual countries establish federal governments with constitutionally protected powers for states or provinces where minority languages are geographically concentrated. Church and state are rigidly separated in democratic countries for fear that religion may become politically significant. Hindu and Muslim coexisted peacefully enough within greater India as long as India was a colony, but ceased to coexist on the establishment of democratic government after independence. Location, social class, or industry will do as a basis for expropriation when nothing better is available.

The argument is not that different languages, races or religions are incompatible in themselves, but that they supply people with the badges that facilitate exploitation by voting. How do you know in practice who belongs to the majority coalition and who is to be exploited? You know because people are identifiable by language, religion, or race. The sharper the division in society, the more stable a majority coalition is likely to be. Exploitation by language, religion, or race originates in the pathology of democratic politics rather than in the pathology of language, religion, or race.

THE DEFENSES OF DEMOCRACY

Defenses of democracy can be classified under three headings which might be called natural, procedural, and institutional. Natural defenses are circumstances where majority rule voting works very well and the diseases of democracy do not threaten at all. Voting about some topics gives rise to a paradox of voting or the expropriation of minorities by majorities. Voting about other topics is free of these defects. Procedural defenses are subsidiary voting rules, imposed regardless of what people vote about. People do not just vote, on and on, with amendment after amendment ad infinitum as our exposition of the exploitation problem might suggest. Voting is framed by subsidiary procedures that supply a degree of determinacy which might otherwise be absent. Institutional defenses are man-made constraints upon the content of voting. Matters that would otherwise prove divisive are removed from the domain of voting and consigned instead to the domains of non-political institutions, to markets with private property, and to civil rights. These three defenses of democracy will be discussed in turn. As we proceed, the reader should bear in mind that the world of voting is more various and complex than the models we employ to describe it. Models can be useful as guideposts without at the same time describing the terrain completely or marking each and every pitfall along the way.

Natural defenses

Two kinds of natural defenses may be distinguished. The first might be called matters of common concern, among them the choice of executives and administrators, foreign affairs, monetary policy, fiscal policy, measures to reduce unemployment of labor, administration of the police, transport, and communication. Citizens differ in their opinions about these matters, but the great majority of citizens gain or lose together according to whether policy is chosen and administered well. Other things being equal, most people are better off when a country is at peace with its neighbors, when alliances are formed judiciously and when the crime rate is low Though there is no bright line separating matters of common concern from matters giving rise to conflict of interest among voters – as when high-paid and low-paid workers differ about the appropriate weighting of employment and price stability as objectives of financial policy – there may be enough of a distinction to explain why voting can sometimes proceed without much bitterness or controversy.

The second natural defense is that people's preferences – however different they may be – can sometimes be lined up on a common scale. Interests may differ markedly, but the constellation of preferences may nevertheless be such that an *electoral equilibrium* does arise. The essence of the paradox of voting, exemplified by the vote about ham, cheese and tuna sandwiches as discussed above, is the absence of an electoral equilibrium comparable to the equilibrium in competitive markets. Not all divergences among preferences are like that.

Imagine a less peaceful university than the university to which you are accustomed, a university where the different classes fight one another with spears. Consider a class of 11 students who decide collectively how many spears to buy. Spears cost $550 each, and there is a firm agreement among the students in the class that (1) total expenditure on spears is to be borne equally by every student (so that, if the class decides to buy 5 spears altogether, the cost to each student is $250 [(5 × 550) ÷ 11] and that (2) the number of spears purchased is to be determined by majority rule voting. Each student's preferred number of spears for the class is a trade-off in his assessment of the cost of spears – the loss of other goods from his share of the expenditure on spears – and the benefit of fighting effectively. Students can then be lined up – "doves" to the left and "hawks" to the right – in accordance with the number of spears they want the class to buy. Suppose it just so happens that the first and least-hawkish student wants the class to buy 1 spear, the second wants the class to buy 2 spears, the third to buy 3, and so on until the eleventh and most hawkish student wants the class to buy 11 spears. Suppose also that, in a choice between two numbers of spears, a person always prefers the number of spears that is closest to his first preference.

The outcome of the vote is now determinate. As long as each student votes his true preference in any pair-wise vote, the class votes to buy 6 spears, for the number 6 wins against any other number. To see why this is so, suppose person six proposes 6 spears and person nine proposes 9 spears. In this contest, everybody who wants 9 or more spears votes for 9 against 6; everybody who wants 6 or less spears votes for 6 over 9. Person seven votes for 6 spears, and person eight votes for 9 spears. Six spears wins because the six people who want 6 spears or less (and who therefore vote for 6 six spears over 9 spears) constitute a majority of the eleven voters. An analogous argument establishes that 6 spears also wins in a pair-wise vote against any smaller number because more than half the voters want 6 or more spears and are therefore prepared to vote for 6 over any smaller number. Six spears wins because it is the first preference of the median voter, the voter in the middle, when all voters are lined up according to their first preferences on some common scale.

This example immediately generalizes to all public goods, defined in chapter 5 as yielding benefits that accrue to everybody simultaneously, as long as each person's share of the total cost is set in accordance with an agreed-upon rule of taxation. Total expenditure on roads, police, public education, public transport or public health usually conform, more or less, to this pattern. People differ in their preferences for public goods, but an electoral equilibrium emerges regardless.

The marked contrast between the determinacy in voting about the number of spears and the indeterminacy in voting about ham, cheese, and tuna sandwiches calls for a general explanation of why the examples differ and of the relevance of the examples to the stability of voting in actual democratic societies. What is it about the one example that avoids the pitfalls of the other? The main difference between the spears example and the ham, cheese, and tuna example lies in the possibility of ordering options on an electorally meaningful scale. In the spears example, people need not agree about which option is best, but their preferences for spears can be ordered in a way that voters' preferences for ham, tuna, and cheese sandwiches cannot. To see what this means, simplify the spears example by reducing the size of the class from eleven students to three students called A, B, and C, and consider only three military options – large expenditure, medium expenditure, and small expenditure. Person A

Table 9.3 Two constellations of preferences for military expenditure

	There exists an equilibrium of voting				There exists no equilibrium of voting		
People	First preference	Second preference	Last preference	People	First preference	Second preference	Last preference
A	Large	Medium	Small	A	Large	Medium	Small
B	Medium	Small	Large	B	Medium	Small	Large
C	Small	Medium	Large	C	Small	Large	Medium

is a hawk whose preferences are for large, medium, and small military expenditure in that order. Person C is a dove whose preferences are just the opposite, for small, medium, and large military expenditure in that order. Person B is a slightly dovish moderate whose preferences are for medium, small and large military expenditure in that order. Their preferences are set out in the left-hand side of table 9.3.

The outcome of the vote is immediately obvious from inspection of table 9.3. Person B's preference prevails. Medium expenditure wins in a pair-wise vote with either of the other two options. Person B combines with person A to vote for medium expenditure against small expenditure, and person B combines with person C to vote for medium expenditure against large expenditure. With this constellation of preferences, the three-person example is exactly analogous to the eleven-person example we examined before.

The right-hand side of table 9.3 is almost the same. Preferences of persons A and B are exactly the same. The first preference of person C is the same as well, but his second and third preferences are reversed. Now, though person C's first preference is for small expenditure, he is nevertheless assumed to prefer large to medium expenditure. One might imagine that person C, and person C alone, is of the opinion that the extra expenditure in passing from small to medium is useless because the extra spears would be insufficient to attain victory over one's enemies, but that large expenditure would be effective though still not worth the price. Regardless, the small change in the preferences of person C upsets the voting equilibrium completely. Formerly, medium expenditure won in a pair-wise vote with either large or small expenditure because medium expenditure was always the first preference of one voter and the second preference of the other two. Now, that is no longer so, though neither of the other two options can displace medium expenditure altogether. All three options are on equal footing, and none can win in both pair-wise votes with the other two. There is, in fact, an exact correspondence between the right-hand side of table 9.3 and the ham, tuna, and cheese example in table 9.2 above: large replacing ham, medium replacing tuna, and small replacing cheese. The ordering of options on a common scale that created an electoral equilibrium in the original spear example is missing in the example illustrated on the left-hand side of table 9.3. A natural ordering is sometimes present in actual voting, and sometimes not.

A more precise specification of the conditions for an electoral equilibrium can be obtained from a generalization of our example. Consider once again the guns and butter economy discussed in chapter 5. Suppose everybody works the same number of hours per day, but people differ in their tastes and in their productivities of labor.

Think of each person i as producing y_i^G units of output in that time, where a unit of output consists of either one pound of butter or one gun. The output, y_i^G, of person i is his *gross*, pre-tax income. As there is no investment in this guns and butter economy, a person's *net*, post-tax income can only be spent on butter.[1] The net post-tax income, y_i^N, of person i and his consumption of butter are one and the same. Each person i has a unique utility function $u^i(y_i^N, G)$ where y_i^N is his consumption of butter and G is society's total production of guns. From a person's utility function, there may be constructed a set of indifference curves, with the same general shape as the indifference curves in figure 5.1. Suppose, finally, that there is an inflexible rule in this society that all taxation is directly proportional to income, so that a person's consumption of butter is equal to

$$y_i^N = y_i^G(1 - t) \tag{5}$$

where t is society's chosen rate of taxation. Total tax revenue is tyN where t is the tax rate, y is *average* pre-tax income in the economy as a whole, and N is total population. The government uses the revenue from taxation to employ people to produce guns. Since, by assumption, one unit of labor is required to produce one gun, the total supply of guns, G, is just equal to total revenue. The government's budget constraint is

$$G = tyN \tag{6}$$

Utility functions can now be reconstructed as dependent on the total output of guns.

$$u^i(y_i^N, G) = u^i(y_i^G(1 - t), G) = u^i(y_i^G(1 - G/yN), G) = u^i(G) \tag{7}$$

The utility, welfare, or well-being of person i depends in the first instance on both the quantity of butter he consumes and the number of guns his government acquires for the defense of the realm. His utility can nevertheless be expressed as dependent on the number of guns alone because average income, population, and his own pre-tax income are what they are regardless of society's choice of the number of guns, but his consumption of butter (his post-tax income) is determined by the number of guns when the tax rate is just sufficient to finance the guns that the government chooses to buy. Utility depends upon G alone not because the other terms have suddenly become irrelevant, but because the other terms are either invariant or determined once G is chosen. The terms y_i^G (gross income of person i), y (average income), and N (population) have been assumed invariant. The tax rate, t, depends on the choice of G.

It is critical in what follows that every person's utility function, $u^i(G)$, be hive-shaped as illustrated in figure 9.3 rather than wavy, in other words, that the utility function be *single peaked*. Every person i must have a preferred value of G, called G_i in figure 9.3. Extra guns would not be worth the extra tax he would have to pay to finance them. Fewer guns would reduce his security by more than the value of the corresponding reduction in taxation. To assume preferences are single-peaked is to suppose that every person's utility diminishes steadily the farther away society's choice of G happens to be from his first preference G_i. To use a different example, a person whose political preference is in the center of the political spectrum prefers policies on

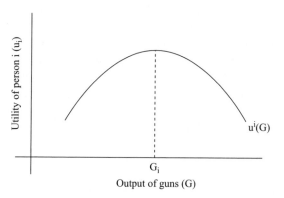

Figure 9.3   Person i's preference for guns.

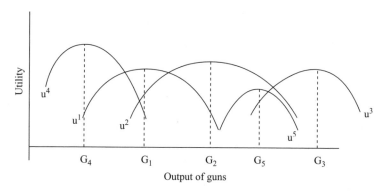

Figure 9.4   Identifying the median voter.

the moderate right to policies on the extreme right. All preferences on the left-hand side of table 9.3 and the preferences of persons A and B on the right-hand side are single peaked. The preference of person C on the right-hand side of table 9.3 is not. While by no means impossible, person C's preference ordering is unusual and will be ignored in the analysis to follow. The assumption that all preferences are single peaked is important because, without it, the electoral equilibrium may fail to appear.

People need not agree upon the best number of guns for their government to procure, but disagreement can be resolved by voting. Imagine a society of five people with different utility functions, $u^i(x_i, G)$ for $i = 1$ to 5, and different gross incomes, y_i^G. A distinct hive-shaped utility function like that in figure 9.3 can be constructed for each person. Since incomes and utility functions differ among the five people, the functions $u^i(G)$ would differ as well. Each person i has a different preferred quantity of guns, G_i, corresponding to the top of his utility function. Suppose preferences turn out to be as shown in figure 9.4. Person 3 wants the most guns, person 5 next, person 2 next, person 1 next, and person 4 least.

The outcome of voting about the number of guns in this five-person society is very different from the outcome of voting in the examples of the paradox of voting and the exploitation problem as discussed above. There an electoral equilibrium eluded us. Here a unique equilibrium emerges. An electoral equilibrium, if there is one, is a number of guns chosen over any other number of guns in a pair-wise vote. It is immediately evident there is an electoral equilibrium number of guns, and that it is G_2, the first preference of person 2. The reason is exactly the same as in the spears example. In fact, the guns and butter example is the spears example with each person's preference about the number of spears grounded in the circumstances of the economy and his utility function for spears and for whatever else money can buy. When the five voters' preferred numbers of guns are lined up from smallest to largest as shown on the horizontal axis of figure 9.4, the first preference of person 2, G_2, is in the middle of the line with as many first preferences to the left as to the right. Person 2 is said to be the *median voter*. A majority of voters can always be found to vote for G_2 against any other option. G_2 guns wins in any pair-wise vote against any larger number of guns because everybody who would prefer fewer than G_2 guns votes together with person 2 for G_2. Similarly, G_2 wins in any pair-wise vote against any smaller number of guns because everybody who would prefer more guns than G_2 votes together with person 2 for G_2. Generalizing from this example, it may be said that "the first preference of the median voter is an electoral equilibrium when all preferences are single peaked." [A minor adjustment to this statement is required if the number of voters is even rather than odd.] Many issues are single-peaked.

A critical assumption in the spear example was that, however many spears are purchased, the total expenditure on spears is allocated equally among all voters. The corresponding assumption in the guns and butter example was that, high or low, the tax *rate* is the same for everybody. In both examples, the tax convention was the outcome of a prior agreement that everybody continues to respect. Either convention (and a number of other conventions besides) would do, but *one* convention must somehow be chosen to keep the exploitation problem at bay, for the choice by voting of each person's tax bill, one by one, is analogous to the allocation of $700,000 by voting, with the unimportant exception that people receive in one case and the government takes in the other. Voting on tax shares would automatically create a classic exploitation problem, as described above in the discussion of the diseases of democracy. If tax shares were determined by majority rule voting, a majority coalition might well form – based on gender or language or religion or race or anything else – to shift the entire burden of the cost of spears onto the excluded minority. That outcome can only be blocked by a prior agreement restricting the scope of voting so that the problem does not arise.

A unique electoral equilibrium may also emerge in voting about the redistribution of income. Voting about the redistribution of income may be more like voting about the number of spears than like voting about the allocation of a fixed sum of money, but, to avoid the pitfalls of faction, the vote must be about one number representing the degree of redistribution and governing the entire pattern of redistribution in the economy as a whole. Consider once again the negative income tax which was the vehicle in an earlier example for the expropriation of the rich by the poor. Continue to suppose that the income of the median voter (the voter half way along the scale from the very poorest person to the very richest person) is less than the average income (total income divided by the number of people), as is the case in actual societies where the income distribution is always skewed. In the earlier example, the median voter favored 100 percent redistribution, destroying all incentive to work and save.

There was something fishy about that example. Surely, if 100 percent redistribution is destructive, it would be in everyone's interest to desist from 100 percent redistribution. Nobody would vote for complete redistribution of income for fear of killing the goose that lays the golden eggs. The weak point in the argument is the assumption that income per head remains invariant regardless of whether or to what extent the income is shared through the intermediary of taxation. The argument breaks down when the pie contracts as you share it or when redistribution of income diminishes total income by weakening the tax payer's incentive to work and to save and by diverting the energies of the taxpayer from production to tax evasion. With complete redistribution of income, there would soon be little income left to redistribute, and even the very poor would become worse off than if there had been no redistribution at all. Another way of expressing this concern is to say that taxation is costly, not just in the sense that the tax collector has to be paid, but in the more important sense that taxation provides tax payers with incentives to take actions yielding small benefits to themselves while generating large harms to others. The "proof" that the poorer half of the population would vote for 100 percent redistribution required that taxation be costless. That is never so, and the proposition disintegrates when the costliness of taxation is taken into account.

The disintegration is not complete, and a residue of the proposition remains even when the tax-induced contraction of the national income is recognized. Consider a community of three people who all work 12 hours a day, who differ in their earnings per hour, who redistribute income through a negative income tax and who choose the tax rate by majority rule voting. The first person earns $20 per hour, the second earns $10 per hour, and the third earns $6 per hour, and their daily incomes are $240, $120, and $72 respectively. Their average income is $144 a day, and their median income is $120 a day. The community votes for a tax rate, t, to finance a lump sum transfer, T, for everybody. There is no other government expenditure. A tax rate of 0 percent means that there is no redistribution. A tax rate of 100 percent would ensure that everybody's post-tax, post-transfer income is the same. As long as the average income remains invariant no matter what tax rate is chosen, the community votes two-to-one for a negative income tax at a rate of 100 percent because the low-wage person earning $72 per day and the middle-wage person earning $120 per day are both better off than they would be at any other tax rate. The high-wage person is correspondingly worse off, but, as long as the mean income is greater than the median, he is consistently outvoted. So far, the pessimistic conclusion of our earlier example is borne out.

The key assumption generating this inference is that everybody's pre-tax income is independent of the tax rate. The assumption is that the declared taxable incomes of $24, $120, and $72 per day are what they are regardless of whether and at what rate they are taxed. There are several reasons why this might not be so. As the tax rate increases, tax payers might switch from taxed work for pay to untaxed leisure or do-it-yourself activities. They might resort to untaxed barter or might find ways of concealing ever-larger shares of their incomes from the tax collector. Tax payers' allocation of time would be irrelevant if taxation could be levied as a fixed amount per head, or made dependent upon the taxpayer's ability as indicated by his wage per hour, or set in

Table 9.4   The productivity of do-it-yourself activities

[A person can devote at most 1 hour to each activity. Time not devoted to do-it-yourself activities is devoted to work for pay.]

Activity	Rank of activity	Value of output per hour ($)
Cooking	I	18
House cleaning	II	16
Flower gardening	III	14
Vegetable gardening	IV	12
Washing clothes	V	10
Snow removal	VI	8
Window cleaning	VII	6
Home repair	VIII	5
Mending clothes	IX	4
Wood chopping	X	3
Plumbing	XI	2
Electrical repair	XII	1

accordance with any attribute of the taxpayer that is unaffected by the tax rate. A head tax is technically feasible, but obviously unsuitable as a source of income for redistribution. An ability tax is infeasible because the tax collector has no accurate measure of people's abilities. Nor can the government observe and evaluate people's do-it-yourself activities. In practice, there is really no alternative to an income tax exempting leisure, barter, and do-it-yourself activities.

To explain why a majority of self-interested voters prefer redistribution well short of 100 percent, it is sufficient to consider the switch from taxed work for pay to untaxed do-it-yourself activities. Continue to assume that each person works for exactly 12 hours a day, but suppose the available 12 hours can be allocated between work for pay which is taxed and do-it-yourself activities which are not. Assume also that, though they earn different wages per hour, the three people have the same options for do-it-yourself activities. Each person may devote up to one hour to each of the twelve do-it-yourself activities in table 9.4. The do-it-yourself activities are listed in the left-hand column and numbered with Roman numerals in the middle column according to their productivities. The right-hand column shows the productivity of each do-it-yourself activity, measured as the number of dollars it would cost to purchase an hour's worth of that activity in the market. Thus, the number 12 for vegetable gardening means that it would cost $12 to buy the equivalent of what one grows for oneself in one hour of vegetable gardening.

Every person requires all of the services listed in table 9.4, but each person produces for himself only those services that he cannot acquire from the market at an expenditure of less than an hour of work. If my after-tax income from paid work is $15 per hour, I do an hour of cooking and an hour of house-cleaning but no other do-it-yourself activities, leaving 10 hours for paid work. If my after-tax income from work is $13 per hour, I do an hour of flower gardening as well, and an hour less paid work. If my after-tax wage exceeds $18, I engage in no do-it-yourself activities at all. If my after-tax wage is less than $1, I engage in 12 hours of do-it-yourself activities and do no paid work. Every person has a critical do-it-yourself activity; he engages in that activity and all lower-numbered activities, but no higher-numbered activities.

For each of the three people – whose earnings are $20, $10, and $6 per hour – and for every tax rate from 0 to 100 percent, one can tell which do-it-yourself activities are advantageous for that person, and, consequently, what his income from do-it-yourself activities, his income from paid work, his tax paid, his total after-tax income, and his total production will be. This information, which is easily computed, is presented in the three parts of table 9.5. The story for the high-wage person is told in table 9.5a. The story for the middle-wage person is told in table 9.5b. The story for the low-wage person is told in table 9.5c. In all three tables, the gradual rise in the tax rate from 0 to 100 percent has two principal effects: (1) The amount of tax paid begins at 0 when the tax rate is 0 percent, gradually increases together with the tax rate, reaches a peak at a tax rate that is well short of 100 percent, and then declines, falling to 0 again when the tax rate reaches 100 percent. (2) The value of total production – inclusive of the output of paid work and the value of do-it-yourself activities – falls steadily as the tax rate rises from 0 to 100 percent.

Though the tax rate could be anything from 0 to 100 percent, it is sufficient for our purposes to tabulate the effects of taxation on each tax payer for eleven rates, including a rate of 0 percent and a rate of 1 percent, which is too low to affect anybody's choice of do-it-yourself activities. For each tax rate, the after-tax earning per hour of work is shown in column (2) and the choice of do-it-yourself activities is listed in column (3). For example, at a tax rate of 41 percent, a person with a wage of $20 per hour has an after-tax income of $11.80 per hour [(1 − 0.41) × 20 = 11.8]. From table 9.4 above, one can see that a person can earn more than $11.80 at the first four do-it-yourself activities – cooking, cleaning, flower gardening, and vegetable gardening – but at no others. He is shown in figure 9.5a as engaging in those activities, yielding him benefits worth $60[18 + 16 + 14 + 12]. As he has 12 hours of time in total, he devotes only 8 hours to paid work, earning $160 per day as shown in column (5). The high-wage person pays $65.60 tax as shown in column (6). As shown in the final column, his total production, from paid work and do-it-yourself activities, falls steadily from a maximum of $240 when the tax rate is 0 percent to a minimum of $99 when the tax rate reaches 100 percent, the $99 being the sum of the returns from all twelve do-it-yourself activities.

The cause of the fall in production is the tax-induced substitution of less productive but untaxed activities for more productive but taxed activities. At paid work, a high-wage person who can earn $20 per hour before tax must be producing goods worth $20 per hour. When the tax rate is 41 percent, his net, after-tax earnings are only $11.80 per hour. At that rate of remuneration, it becomes advantageous for him to divert four hours from paid work to the four most productive do-it-yourself activities: cooking, house cleaning, flower gardening and vegetable gardening. For the high-wage person himself, the diversion is advantageous, the acquisition of $60 worth of output from do-it-yourself in exchange for $47.20 [11.80 × 4] of income from paid work. For society as a whole, the diversion is harmful, the acquisition of $60 of

Table 9.5a The high-wage tax payer's response to taxation

[This person's wage is $20 per hour.]

(1) Tax rate (%)	(2) After-tax earnings per hour ($)	(3) Do-it-yourself activities	(4) Income from do-it-yourself activities ($)	(5) Income from paid work ($)	(6) Tax paid ($)	(7) Total after-tax income (4) + (5) − (6) ($)	(8) Total production (4) + (5) ($)
0	20	None	0	240	0	240	240
1	19.8	None	0	240	2.4	237.6	240
11	17.8	I	18	220	24.2	213.8	238
21	15.8	I and II	34	200	42	192	234
31	13.8	I to III	48	180	55.8	172.2	228
41	11.8	I to IV	60	160	65.6	154.5	220
51	9.8	I to V	70	140	71.4	138.6	210
61	7.8	I to VI	78	120	73.2	124.8	198
71	5.8	I to VII	84	100	71	113	184
81	3.8	I to IX	93	60	48.6	104.4	153
100	0	All	99	0	0	99	99

Table 9.5b The middle-wage tax payer's response to taxation

[This person's wage is $10 per hour.]

(1) Tax rate (%)	(2) After-tax earnings per hour ($)	(3) Do-it-yourself activities	(4) Income from do-it-yourself activities ($)	(5) Income from paid work ($)	(6) Tax paid ($)	(7) Total after-tax income (4) + (5) − (6) ($)	(8) Total production (4) + (5) ($)
0	10	I to V	70	70	0	140	140
1	9.9	I to V	70	70	0.7	139.3	140
11	8.9	I to V	70	70	7.7	132.3	140
21	7.9	I to VI	78	60	12.6	125.4	138
31	6.9	I to VI	78	60	18.6	119.4	138
41	5.9	I to VII	84	50	20.5	113.5	134
51	4.9	I to VIII	89	40	20.4	108.6	129
61	3.9	I to IX	93	30	18.3	104.7	123
71	2.9	I to X	96	20	14.2	101.8	116
81	1.9	I to XI	98	10	8.1	99.9	108
100	0	all	99	0	0	99	99

do-it-yourself activities in exchange for $80 of output from paid work. The cause of the discrepancy is the sharing through taxation of every tax payer's gross income with the rest of the community. The loss of output arises from the tax payer's tax-induced choice of less productive activities for which the returns need not be shared.

Table 9.5c The low-wage tax payer's response to taxation

[This person's wage is $6 per hour.]

(1) Tax rate (%)	(2) After-tax earnings per hour ($)	(3) Do-it-yourself activities	(4) Income from do-it-yourself activities ($)	(5) Income from paid work ($)	(6) Tax paid ($)	(7) Total after-tax income (4) + (5) − (6) ($)	(8) Total production (4) + (5) ($)
0	6	I to VII	84	30	0	114	114
1	5.94	I to VII	84	30	0.3	113.7	114
11	5.34	I to VII	84	30	3.3	110.7	114
21	4.74	I to VIII	89	24	5.04	107.96	113
31	4.14	I to VIII	89	24	7.44	105.56	113
41	3.54	I to IX	93	18	7.38	103.62	111
51	2.94	I to X	96	12	6.12	101.88	108
61	2.34	I to X	96	12	7.32	100.68	108
71	1.74	I to XI	98	6	4.26	99.74	104
81	1.14	I to XI	98	6	4.86	99.14	104
100	0	all	99	0	0	99	99

Since the largest tax revenue from the high-wage tax payer is $473.20 per day obtained at a rate of 61 percent, no higher rate could ever be in the interest of the middle-wage tax payer who is the median voter. In fact, the median voters' preferred tax rate is lower still. The electoral equilibrium tax rate is shown in table 6 which is constructed from the three parts of table 9.5. Recall that a negative income tax is a method of redistribution in which tax is collected in proportion to peoples' incomes, so that the richer you are the more tax you pay, and the revenue is redistributed in equal amounts per head, so that income is fully equalized when the tax rate rises to 100 percent. The list of tax rates in the left-hand column of table 9.6 is the same as that in table 9.5. Total tax revenue in column (2) is the sum for all three people of taxes paid as shown in column (6) of table 9.5. Total tax revenue per person in column (3) is the amount redistributed to each person in a negative income tax. At each tax rate and for each of the three people, the post-tax post-transfer income is the sum of that person's post-tax income (from column 6 in table 9.5) and his transfer (from column 2 of table 9.6). The post-tax post-transfer incomes of the high-wage person, the middle-wage person, and the low-wage person are shown in columns (4), (5), and (6). The sum of their post-tax, post-transfer incomes is shown in column (7).

The story in these tables is told by the three starred (*) numbers in table 9.6. Suppose that one of the three people were entitled, all by himself, to choose the rate of a negative income tax from among the rates listed at the left-hand side of table 9.6. That person would choose whatever rate yields him the largest post-tax post-transfer income because the higher one's post-tax post-transfer income, the larger his consumption of goods and services will be. He would scan the appropriate column of table 9.6 for the largest number. For each of the three people, these numbers are indicated by a star. For the high-wage person, the star appears at a 0 percent tax rate because he

Table 9.6 The impact on voters of the redistribution of income in a community with three voters where taxable income may shrink in response to taxation

(1) Tax rate (%)	(2) Total tax revenue ($)	(3) Tax revenue per person (2)/3($)	(4) Post-tax, post-transfer income of the high-wage person ($)	(5) Post-tax, post-transfer income of the middle-wage person ($)	(6) Post-tax, post-transfer income of the low-wage person ($)	(7) Total post-tax, post-transfer income, (all three people) ($)
0	0	0	240.0*	140.0	114.0	494
1	3.40	1.1	238.7	140.4	114.8	494
11	35.20	11.7	225.5	144.0	122.4	492
21	59.64	19.9	211.9	145.3	127.9	485
31	81.84	27.3	199.5	146.7*	132.9	479
41	93.38	31.1	185.6	144.6	134.7	465
51	97.92	32.4	171.0	140.8	135.3*	447
61	98.82	32.9	157.7	137.6	133.6	429
71	89.46	29.8	142.8	131.6	129.5	404
81	61.56	20.5	124.9	120.4	119.6	365
100	0	0	99.0	99.0	99.0	297

always pays more in tax than he gets back from the transfer. His personal interest is in having no redistribution at all. For the middle-wage person, the star appears at 31 percent. His post-tax post-transfer income is less at any lower or at any higher rate of tax. Recall that he is the person with the median wage ($10 per hour) which is less than the average wage ($12 per hour). As explained above, this discrepancy would lead him to favour a tax rate of 100 percent if all pre-tax incomes were invariant. But they are not invariant. The switch to do-it-yourself activities causes all taxable incomes to shrink as the tax rate increases, so that the middle wage person is best off not at a tax rate of 100 percent, but at a tax rate of only 31 percent. The low-wage person would prefer a tax rate of 51 percent.

Note in passing that the relation between tax rate and tax revenue in column (3) of table 9.6 is similar to the relation between tax rate and tax revenue in table 4.1. In both tables, tax revenue begins at 0 when the tax rate is 0 percent, rises to a peak at some tax rate well short of 100 percent, and gradually falls to 0 again as the tax rate approaches 100 percent. In both tables, the relation between rate and revenue is hive-shaped because the tax base shrinks as the tax rate increases. In chapter 4, the tax base was the consumption of cheese in a bread-and-cheese economy where only cheese could be taxed. Here, the tax base is earned income where do-it-yourself activities cannot be taxed. The example in table 9.6 is generalized in the next chapter, and other similarities to the story in chapter 4 will be examined.

Since the middle-wage person is the median voter, his preference prevails. The electoral equilibrium tax rate is 31 percent, yielding a net transfer of $27.30 per person, causing a net loss of $40.50 to the high-wage person, a net gain of about $6.70 to the middle-wage person, a net gain of about $18.90 to the low-wage person, and a net reduction of $15 worth of goods and services [$494–$479] to the three people together. Majority rule voting results in some redistribution of income, but not at confiscatory rates. The gap between rich and poor is narrowed, but not eliminated altogether. The rich remain relatively rich. The poor remain relatively poor. It is in nobody's interest to close the gap completely.

Though the example is made up, the main conclusion extends, with qualifications, to more realistic environments. First, it was essential to the example that the average wage exceed the median wage, for, otherwise, the median voter would have opposed redistribution altogether. The median voter would have opposed all redistribution if, for example, the wages had been $20, $15, and $7 per hour instead of $20, $10, and $6 per hour as we assumed. With wages of $20, $15, and $7 per hour, the median wage is $15 an hour, the average wage is only $12 per hour, and the median voter is made worse off, not better off, by redistribution. But the assumption in the tables that the average wage exceeds the median wage is entirely realistic, a reflection of the fact that all income distributions ever observed have been skewed with a few rich and many poor.

Second, the flight from paid work to do-it-yourself activities is only one of several incentives generated by taxation. As the tax rate increases, people tend increasingly to divert time from work to leisure, to substitute barter for the market, to participate in the underground economy, and to employ lawyers and accountants to discover ingenious ways of minimizing their tax bill. All this tends to reinforce the story in our example of do-it-yourself activities that the pie shrinks as you share it, limiting the extent of sharing in the interest of the recipients of redistribution. A somewhat uncharacteristic feature of the example is that the alternative to earning taxable income is the same for everybody, rich and poor alike. Everybody is supposed to be equally adept at do-it-yourself activities. Other opportunities for reducing tax paid, notably legal tax avoidance, are likely to be more available to the rich than to the poor.

Third and most important, the redistribution of income, depicted here as the choice of a rate for a negative income tax, is in practice very much more complicated. There is no single rate of tax. Instead, there is a progression of tax rates, a basic exemption, a low rate on additional income up to some amount, a higher rate on the next chunk of income, and so on. There is no single source of income. Instead, there are different kinds of income – wages, dividends, rent, capital gains – each with its own tax rates and tax exemptions. There is no uniform transfer of income. Instead, the transfer is targeted in many programs including welfare to the demonstrably poor, unemployment insurance, the old age pension, and public provision of health and education financed by taxation but provided equally to everybody in the appropriate circumstances. It is nevertheless possible to make a crude assessment of the degree of redistribution in tax and expenditure together, and there is some counterpart in real politics to the median voter whose sense of the appropriate degree of redistribution is a basis for public choice among the possible redistributive programs. More will be said about this in the next chapter.

The ordered and self-limited redistribution in this example is in sharp contrast to the exploitation problem as discussed above under the general heading of the diseases of democracy. In the exploitation problem, voting about the allocation of income yielded no equilibrium or stopping place, and the impact of voting on people's incomes was so dramatic – transporting people from very rich to very poor at the whim of the electorate – that people would soon cease to respect the outcome of the vote or, in one last vote or by coup d'etat, would replace government by voting with some more stable form of government. By contrast, in the present example, there is a unique electorial equilibrium and the people's incomes are less drastically affected by the outcome of the vote. The rich, though poorer, remain relatively rich. The poor, though richer, remain relatively poor.

The principal difference between the exploitation problem exemplified by voting about the allocation of $700,000 and the redistribution of income in our three-person example is that the transfer of income in the latter is systematic. Though people vote on the magnitude of redistribution (on the value of t), there is a prior agreement about the form of taxation that is completely absent in the specification of the exploitation problem. The ordering of incomes on the scale of rich and poor is taken off the agenda because people choose not to vote about it. In actual politics, voting is substantially less constrained, but is not unconstrained altogether. Democratic societies avoid ad hominem taxation. Though taxation may be redistributive, there is some respect for the principle of *horizontal equity* according to which people with equal incomes are to be equally taxed.

A variant of the anti-democratic argument, referred to by James Madison in the quotation at the beginning of this chapter, is that the poor cannot be entitled to vote because they would use the vote to expropriate the rich, removing the incentive to become rich or to invest one's wealth productively and, in the end, impoverishing the nation as a whole. On this argument, property rights can only be maintained by restricting franchise to the well-to-do. Our example of redistribution in a three-person society suggests that universal franchise may have less dramatic consequences. To be sure, the poor do use the vote to expropriate the rich to some extent, narrowing the gap between the rich and the poor, but there is a natural stopping place to redistribution, a stopping place well short of 100 percent confiscation of wealth, where the median voter is content. There is an electoral equilibrium where the rich get to keep enough of their income to induce a substantial degree of enterprise and thrift. It may even be that improvements in accounting over the last century have made possible a self-limiting redistribution of income – through progressive taxation, welfare, the old age pension and other measures – as distinct from the free-for-all that might have been the outcome of universal franchise in years gone by when systemic redistribution was infeasible.

Procedural defenses

Procedural defenses of majority rule voting are subsidiary conventions about how voting is conducted. We do not just vote. We vote in context, and the context matters. Voting for bills in the legislature is conducted according to parliamentary procedure, a set of rules about when amendments are permitted, who may propose amendments, the order of voting once all amendments are on the table, the length of debate, and a host of other matters. Legislators may be chosen by plurality voting (the candidate with the most votes wins) in single-member constituencies, by proportional representation in multi-member constituencies, or by two-stage elections in which the two candidates with the most votes in the first round become the only candidates in the second. There is inevitably some residue of the paradox of voting and the exploitation problem in any and every method of voting, but, as we shall see, the virulence of these diseases of voting can be reduced considerably.

James Madison himself placed considerable weight on the division of powers between the central government and the state government, among legislature, executive and judiciary within the central government, and between the Senate and the House of Representatives. The hope was that factions or coalitions of factions within one branch of government would be neutralized by other factions within other branches of government. If the agricultural interests come to dominate the Senate, then perhaps the manufacturing interests will come to dominate the House of Representatives. If assent of both houses is required for the passage of a bill, then competing factions in the two houses may give rise to a compromise that is not too bad for either faction or for the country as a whole. Outcomes are determined to some extent by the constellation of voters' preferences, but not entirely so. Just as bargaining and deal-making supplement the price mechanism in guiding the economy, so too do bargaining and deal-making supplement the voting mechanism in public decision-making. It might even be said that actual democratic government is designed to be inefficient, to move slowly, and to frustrate a party in office with a clear vision of how society ought to be redesigned, curbing the power of factions or coalitions of factions to change society today in ways that cannot be reversed tomorrow.

To see how political outcomes can depend on subsidiary voting rules, consider a simple society without private property where three people, called A, B, and C, vote about the allocation of the national income, Y, among themselves[2]. An allocation of income, written as $\{y_A, y_B, y_C\}$, is an assignment of incomes y_A to person A, y_B to person B, and y_C to person C, where $y_A + y_B + y_C = Y$. Voting about such an assignment collapsed into incoherence in the seven-person example above where all voters were free to propose amendments indefinitely. Suppose instead that there is a prior agreement among the three people that the voting will be conducted as follows:

Step 1

The three people draw lots to determine who among them may propose a bill specifying the allocation among themselves of a fixed national income, Y. The bill proposed by the winner of the draw is designated as $\{y_A^0, y_B^0, y_C^0\}$. This bill is chosen to provide the proposer with the highest possible income, not immediately, but in the final outcome of the voting process.

Step 2

Once a bill $\{y_A^0, y_B^0, y_C^0\}$ has been proposed, there is automatically a vote on fast-track consideration. If fast-track consideration is approved, no amendment to the bill is allowed and voting proceeds to step 3. If fast-track consideration is denied, voting proceeds to step 4 where an amendment is allowed. Approval of fast-track consideration may require either unanimity or acceptance by a majority of the voters. It will be shown below that the requirement has a marked influence upon the allocation of the national income among the three voters.

Step 3

There is a vote on the original bill. If a majority favors the bill, it becomes law and the allocation $\{y_A^0, y_B^0, y_C^0\}$ prevails. If a majority opposes the bill, it does not become law and voting proceeds to step 4.

Step 4

The three people draw lots once again to determine who among them may propose an amendment designated as $\{y_A^a, y_B^a, y_C^a\}$. If the author of the original bill wins the lottery to propose the amendment as well, he may, but need not, choose to repeat the original bill as an amendment. A vote is conducted between the original bill $\{y_A^0, y_B^0, y_C^0\}$ and the amendment $\{y_A^a, y_B^a, y_C^a\}$. The winner of that vote becomes law, and the allocation of income is determined accordingly. No additional amendments are allowed.

Voting always ends at step 3 or step 4. The outcome of voting at step 3 is either the original bill or a decision to permit an amendment. The outcome of voting at step 4 is either the original bill or the amendment. At both steps, voting is by majority rule, which, in a society of three people, means that whichever option is favored by two out of the three voters becomes law. The voting rule at stage 2 – on whether to grant fast-track consideration for the original bill – may be by majority rule or by unanimity. In fact, the entire point of the example is to show how the outcome of the voting process can be radically different depending how voting at stage 2 – on whether to grant fast-track consideration for the original bill – is conducted. One of the following two rules is adopted.

1 Fast track consideration (proceeding to step 3) is only granted if approved by voters *unanimously*.
2 Fast track consideration is granted if approved *by a majority*, two out of three voters.

But for the special voting rules we have imposed, this situation would have all the hallmarks of a standard exploitation problem with no electoral equilibrium. From our discussion of the exploitation problem, we might expect a deal between two of the three people, providing each with half the income and excluding the third altogether. If the deal is between person A and person B, then the outcome becomes $y_A = y_B = Y/2$ and $y_C = 0$. As long as the deal holds, any other outcome is voted down. We assume instead that there can be no deals among voters, that each voter behaves rationally and selfishly at each step of the voting procedure (an assumption that yielded no outcome when every proposal could be outvoted by some other proposal put forward as an amendment) but that voting is circumscribed by strong procedures.

We also assume that everybody is somewhat risk averse. In a choice among gambles, each person acts to maximize his expected utility, where the utility of income, y, is assumed to be $\sqrt{y}$. For example, a person would be indifferent between an income of 4 for sure and equal chances of incomes of 1 and 9, even though the expected income associated with equal chances of incomes of 1 and 9 is 5 rather than 4. With equal chances of incomes 1 and 9, a person's expected income is $5, [\frac{1}{2}(1) + \frac{1}{2}(9)]$, but his expected utility is $2, [\frac{1}{2}\sqrt{1} + \frac{1}{2}\sqrt{9}]$, while the utility of a sure income of 4 is also equal to $2, [\sqrt{4}]$. With these assumptions – no coalitions, pure selfishness and restricted voting – the outcome of voting becomes determinate.

Consider first what happens when voting about fast-track consideration is by *majority rule*. There is no harm in assuming that person A wins the draw to propose the original bill. The outcomes when B or C win are analogous. Person A would like to take the entire national income for himself, setting $y_A^0 = Y, y_B^0 = 0$ and $y_C^0 = 0$. The bill would be $\{Y, 0, 0\}$. He dare not propose that bill because it would surely lose the vote over fast-track consideration at stage 2, and person A would have a two-thirds chance of ending up with nothing at the end of stage 4. If, by chance, person A wins the draw to propose the amendment as well, he could acquire the national income by proposing an amendment that supplies a penny to person B, and nothing at all to person C. With the original bill as the alternative, persons A and B vote for the amendment at stage 4, and it becomes law. But if either person B or person C wins the draw to propose the amendment, he would propose an income of Y less a penny for himself, a penny for the other, and nothing for person A.

A better course for person A is to offer one of the other two people, say person B, enough income to induce him, in his own self-interest, to vote for fast-track consideration and then to support the original proposal at step 3. Person A's original proposal becomes $\{Y - y_B^0, y_B^0, 0\}$ where y_B^0 is just high enough to induce person B to vote as person A requires. How large must y_B^0 be? That depends on what person B anticipates in the event of an amendment. Person B compares the certainty of y_B^0 if he votes for fast-track consideration with equal chances of incomes y_B^{aA}, y_B^{aB}, and y_B^{aC} depending on who wins the draw to propose the amendment. If person A wins, his amendment provides a penny for person C, Y less a penny for himself, and nothing for person B. Thus, $y_B^{aA} = 0$. If person B wins, his amendment provides nothing for person A, a penny for person C, and Y less a penny for himself. Thus, since a penny is virtually nothing, $y_B^{aB} = Y$. If person C wins, his amendment provides nothing for person A, y_B^0 plus a penny for person B, and $Y - y_B^0$ less a penny for himself. Thus, $y_B^{aC} = y_B^0$. The amendment always wins over the original proposal because the amendment is designed to provide the proposer of the amendment with the largest possible income consistent with one other person being better off with the amendment than with the original bill.

Pulling all this together, we see that person A's original proposal contains the smallest y_B^0 such that

$$\sqrt{y_B^0} > \frac{1}{3}\sqrt{y_B^{aA}} + \frac{1}{3}\sqrt{y_B^{aB}} + \frac{1}{3}\sqrt{y_B^{aC}} = \frac{1}{3}\sqrt{0} + \frac{1}{3}\sqrt{Y} + \frac{1}{3}\sqrt{y_B^0} \qquad (8)$$

Thus, $2\sqrt{y_B^0} = \sqrt{Y}$ or $y_B^0 - Y/4$. Person A's original bill must be $y_A^0 = 3Y/4, y_B^0 = Y/4$, and $y_C^0 = 0$. With majority rule voting on fast-track consideration, the fortunate person who wins the draw to make the original proposal gets to keep three-quarters of the income for himself, offers a quarter of total income to one of the other two persons and offers the remaining person nothing.

Now consider the other voting rule for the granting of fast-track consideration. Suppose fast-track consideration is denied unless the vote in favor is unanimous. If person A wins the draw for the right to propose a bill for the allocation of the national income among the three people, he must be more accommodating to persons B and C because *either* of them can force an amendment by voting against fast-track consideration. Person A's bill must provide incomes of y^0 to both person B and person C, leaving an income of $Y - 2y^0$ for himself, where y^0 must be large enough that nobody wants to vote against fast-track consideration.

Consider person B's calculation of his options, bearing in mind that the circumstances of person C are identical. If person B approves fast-track consideration and on the understanding that the proposal will be adopted in the vote to follow, person B's income becomes y^0 and his expected utility becomes $\sqrt{y^0}$. Alternatively, if fast-track consideration is denied, his expected utility depends on who wins the draw to propose the amendment. If person B wins, he proposes an amendment providing person C with y^0 plus a penny, providing person A with nothing, and leaving an income of $Y - (y^0$ plus a penny) for himself. If person C wins, his proposal is analogous, providing person B with y^0 plus a penny, providing person A nothing and leaving $Y - (y^0$ plus a penny) for himself. If person A wins, the calculation is a bit more complex. It would be in person A's interest to cut out either person B or person C. Person A does not care which of the two is excluded, though he does not announce his decision prior to the vote on fast-track consideration for fear of antagonizing the excluded party. He flips a coin. If the coin comes up heads, he provides an income of y^0 plus a penny to person B, and nothing to person C, leaving an income of Y (y^0 plus a penny) for himself. If the coin comes up tails, he substitutes person C for person B.

Thus, in the event of an amendment (and recognizing that a penny is virtually nothing) person B acquires a one-third chance of an income of $Y - y^0$, a one-third chance of an income of y^0, an additional one-sixth chance of an income of y^0, and a one-sixth chance of an income of 0. Now person A's original proposal contains the smallest y^0 such that

$$\sqrt{y^0} > \tfrac{1}{3}\sqrt{Y - y^0} + \tfrac{1}{3}\sqrt{y^0} + \tfrac{1}{6}\sqrt{y^0} + \tfrac{1}{6}\sqrt{0} \qquad (9)$$

It follows at once that

$$\tfrac{1}{2}\sqrt{y^0} = \tfrac{1}{3}\sqrt{Y - y^0} \qquad (10)$$

so that $y^0 = (\tfrac{4}{13})Y$. When the motion for fast track consideration of the original proposal requires unanimous assent, the proposer of the original motion offers each of the other two parties an income of $\tfrac{4}{13}Y$ and takes an income of $\tfrac{5}{13}Y$ for himself. It is still advantageous to win the draw to make the original proposal, but for less so than when fast-track consideration required only a majority of votes.

The moral of the story is that voting rules matter. On the critical assumption that everybody votes selfishly and with no side deals among voters, the outcome of the vote over the allocation of the national income is very skewed when fast-track consideration requires the assent of a majority of voters – $\frac{3}{4}Y$ to one person, $\frac{1}{4}Y$ to a second, and nothing to a third – but is almost equal when fast-track consideration requires unanimity. It must be borne in mind, however, that side deals are often feasible in practice and that the outcome of voting then depends critically on which group of voters comes together to vote as a block.

The reader should be wary of this example. Though instructive about how subsidiary rules can affect the outcome of the vote, the example is misleading in several respects. First, actual parliamentary procedure is very much more intricate than the voting rules in this example. In particular, the right to propose bills lies primarily with the party in office and not with randomly chosen legislators. At best, the rules about private members' bills bear some resemblance to our example. Second, rules of actual parliamentary procedure are very much more elastic and more open to negotiation than our example would suggest. Third, there is an inextricable component of bargaining in parliamentary procedure. Though more nearly determinate than our discussion of the paradox of voting and of the exploitation problem would suggest, the outcome of voting is less determinate and the electoral equilibrium is less well grounded than one might infer from our example of voting procedures.

Institutional defenses

Procedural constraints on majority rule voting place restrictions upon how we vote. By contrast, institutional constraints place restrictions upon what we vote about. We do not vote about fining, imprisonment, disenfranchisement, or expropriation of particular people or groups of people because everybody – or a substantial majority of citizens – understands that he himself might be placed in jeopardy if such ad hominem voting were allowed. We do not vote about who owns what, in the sense of establishing a complete, brand-new allocation of property among citizens. We refrain from voting about people's civil rights or property rights, and we protect these domains from the authority of the civil service. Civil rights are protected in a written or unwritten constitution that the great majority of citizens is prepared to respect and defend because the alternative is despotism or chaos. Property rights are protected in part by the constitution but primarily because of a general understanding that, without security of property, neither prosperity nor democracy itself could be sustained. These institutional constraints defend democracy by relying upon institutions other than voting, on the market and on the constitution, to resolve disputes that would prove dangerous and divisive in the hands of the legislature.

The Charter of Rights and Freedoms in the Canadian constitution and the Bill of Rights in the American constitution set bounds that no government, federal or state, can overstep without at the same time signaling to citizens and to public officials that loyalty toward one's government, and obedience of inferior to superior within the government, may be dissolved. Among the provisions of the Bill of

Rights are that "Congress shall make no law respecting the establishment of religion," that a person may not "be deprived of life, liberty, or property, without due process of law," and that "private property shall (not) be taken for public use without just compensation." The separation of church and state is to prevent a majority of one religion from using the authority of the government to impose that religion on others or to acquire special privileges for its adherents. "Due process of law" blocks the legislature, the courts and the administration from punishing a person – no matter how greatly they may disapprove of his actions and no matter how unpopular he may be – unless that person has actually broken the law. The prohibition of *taking* without compensation means that the legislature may not expropriate a person's property, although it may take property *with* compensation as when a person's land is in the path of a new road or is needed for a school. In such cases, the government may expropriate a person's property but must compensate that person at market value. Similar constraints on voting are included in the constitutions of virtually every democratic country, though, as in the UK, the constraints may reside in the "unwritten" constitution rather than in an officially sanctioned text. Entrenchment of civil rights in a constitution cannot guarantee that civil rights will always be respected, but it increases the likelihood that civil rights will be respected by providing each citizen with an extra degree of assurance that his respect for civil rights, and for the constraints they impose upon political behavior, will be reciprocated by his fellow citizens.

Expectations play a major role in the institutional defense of democracy. The duly elected government today desists from the disenfranchisement of its opponents as long as the personnel of the government and their supporters among the electorate are confident that they themselves will not be disenfranchised tomorrow when they find themselves excluded from a new majority coalition. Were that not so, if I as a member of a majority coalition today expect to be disenfranchised when I am excluded from the new majority coalition tomorrow, then I had better abandon all restraint and entrench my privileges while I can. Nobody can be 100 percent confident that the constraints will always be respected, but constraints are more likely to be respected when entrenched in a constitution.

Another institutional defense is equally important. Democracy needs private ownership of the means of production. Recall the principal example in chapter 3 where five people – called A, B, C, D, and E – each owned land that could be used to make bread or to make cheese. In that economy, the production of bread and cheese, the return to each plot of land and the allocation of all produce among the five people were guided by prices in an impersonal market. A unique outcome emerged automatically, and that outcome was efficient as long as each person maximized his income at market clearing prices. A fundamental assumption in that example was that ownership was secure. No explanation was provided of how people acquired land or of how property rights were maintained. Secure ownership was simply taken for granted.

Now suppose these five people live in a civil society where public decisions are by majority rule voting and where, for the sake of the argument, there are no constraints whatsoever on what people may vote about. That being so, the five people might choose to hold all land collectively rather than privately. Collective ownership would constitute no violation of civil rights, but it is extremely unlikely that majority rule voting could at the same time be maintained. Without private ownership of the means of production, a political mechanism would be required to determine how much bread and cheese to produce and, more importantly, how to allocate the produce among the five people. The allocation of the national income would have to be determined by voting. Allocation by voting would confront society with a standard exploitation problem. In such a society, there would be nothing to stop three out of the five voters from expropriating the land of the other two. It would be convenient, though by no means necessary, for the members of the majority coalition to have something in common. Three of the five people might differ from the other two by race, language, religion, or occupation. Any characteristic of voters might serve as a badge to distinguish the majority of the exploiters from the minority of the exploited. The minority might be disproportionally taxed, dispossessed of its land, disenfranchised, enslaved, or executed.

Why not? If people are unlimitedly greedy, as they are assumed in the study of economics to be, why should not a majority employ the vote to take the land of the minority? This question has been posed for centuries as an argument against democracy itself. The only answer would seem to be that voters desist from these extremes of predatory behavior for fear of destroying democratic government. No government in office would risk defeat at the ballot box, no temporary majority would risk the loss of its privileges in an election, and no political party, on losing an election, would accept defeat gracefully if the loss of an election meant the loss of one's property or one's life. Governments risk loss of office, their supporters risk loss of privileges and political parties accept defeat gracefully because the institution of voting is expected to persist, so that a person who finds himself in a minority today has a reasonable chance of finding himself in a majority in a new vote on a different issue tomorrow. The substitution of allocation by markets with allocations by voting automatically raises the stakes of an election beyond what citizens can tolerate and ultimately corrodes the electoral process.

Property protects voting by attending to a task that voting cannot perform. The moral of our discussion of the exploitation problem was that the national income cannot be allocated by voting because there is no unique electoral equilibrium allocation when each voter behaves selfishly and because the most likely form of cooperation in voting about the allocation of income is for some majority to vote as a block to dispossess the remaining minority. Understanding how voting works, citizens would cease to respect the rules. Sooner or later, a party in power would abolish voting rather than risk the privileges of office at the ballot box. A market mechanism based on private ownership of the means of production (including one's own skill and labor power) circumvents the exploitation by placing the allocation of the national income among citizens outside the political arena.

Markets determine wages, rents, land prices, and returns to the ownership of capital, as well as prices of ordinary consumption goods, like bread and cheese. Formally, the price mechanism stops at the door of the public sector, so that wages of public servants have to be determined politically, but the market supplies a standard that the government may choose to respect, just as the incomes of the police could, but need not, be set to equal the incomes of fishermen in the model of predatory behavior in chapter 2. Workers in the public sector can be paid what their skills would command in the private sector of the economy. Governments may, of course, choose not to respect the standard, but without private ownership of the means of production there is no standard at all. The problem is compounded enormously when everybody becomes an employee of the state. With public ownership of the means of production, each person's remuneration and status in the industrial hierarchy must in the end be determined by the state. The placement of people in hierarchies, the salaries and privileges at each rung in the ladder and the disposition of funds for investment to this or that region or industry must ultimately be chosen by a planning commission, appointed and assigned criteria by the legislature. With such authority over the entire distribution of income, legislators must be tempted to reserve high paying jobs and influential positions for themselves and their supporters, and to take steps to protect their advantages from the whims of a fickle majority of the voters. Sooner or later, that temptation would prove irresistible. Sooner or later, a government in office would employ the army and the police to preserve its privileges and the privileges of its supporters and clients when loss at the ballot box appears imminent. A vibrant private sector is a refuge for politicians out of office as well as for public servants who resign or are fired because they disagree with superiors in the hierarchy. Otherwise, there would be nowhere for dissidents to go, and politicians removed from office in an election would become the employees of their successors. With too much at stake, the outcome of an election would no longer be accepted peacefully.

Democracy can withstand the systematic redistribution of income, reducing the income of the rich and increasing the income of the poor according to a simple rule such as negative income tax, because, as shown above, there is a natural stopping place to the redistribution, well short of complete expropriation of wealth, at which the median voter is content. With complete assignment of income by the state – so much to Joe, so much to Charlie – at the whim of the party in office, no median voter can be identified, and there is no stopping place in the public allocation of income short of total impoverishment of an unfortunate minority. It is no accident that, among countries where laws and leaders are chosen by genuine majority-rule voting, there is no country where the means of production are not to a large extent privately owned and where people's incomes are not to a large extent dependent on returns to their property and skills, their material, and human capital.

Majority-rule voting cannot allocate the entire national income without at the same time destroying the willingness among citizens – losers as well as winners – to accept the outcome of the vote. The legislature can safely redistribute income to some extent and cannot avoid influencing the allocation of income as a by-product of public decisions of all kinds. The legislature cannot safely prescribe the entire allocation of the national income, as would be required if the means of production were owned collectively by the state. The citizen can accept the loss of an election by the candidate or political party he favors and can acquiesce quietly when adversely affected by decisions of the government of the day as long as he is confident there will in time be another election, and perhaps a more sympathetic government, and as long as the greater part of his income flows from his ownership of property and skill. Otherwise, if everything depends on the state, one is drawn irresistibly to an electoral coalition with others of one's religion, race, language, region, or industry to ensure that the state is favorably disposed. The market must allocate enough of the national income apolitically to allow democratic government to continue. The market automatically supplies what the legislature lacks, compensating for the major weakness in democratic government and preserving the economic substratum of democratic government. Private property defends democracy because, without private property, government by majority rule voting would be virtually impossible.

BARGAINING, FACTIONS, AND POLITICAL PARTIES

An important lesson from our examination of the natural defenses of democracy is that faction is a considerably smaller threat to majority rule voting when issues are single peaked than when they are not. In single-peaked issues, options can be lined up on a scale from one extreme to another, each voter has a preferred outcome on the scale, and preferences are such that, from the right or from the left, a voter always prefers an option that is closer to his first preference to another option farther away. Preferences conformed to that pattern in our discussion of the negative income tax as a vehicle for the redistribution of income. A person whose preferred tax rate was 20 percent would always vote for 18 percent over 15 percent, or for 30 percent over 35 percent.

Single-peaked preferences would be reflected first in platforms of political parties and then in decisions of the legislature. Consider a society composed of three equal-sized groups of voters whose wage rates and preferences are as shown in table 9.5, with two political parties whose only objective is to be elected, and where the one and only task of government is to redistribute income in accordance with a negative income tax. In such a society, the platform of a political party can be nothing other than the rate of tax (and the corresponding universal transfer of income) that it promises to levy if elected. Then, to maximize their chances of being elected, both political parties must adopt the same platform. Both parties promise to establish a tax rate of 31 percent which, as shown in table 9.6, is the first preference of the median voter. For instance, if one party promises 31 percent and the other promises 35 percent, the first party attracts the votes of both high-wage people and medium-wage people who together constitute a majority of two-thirds of the electorate, winning the election and establishing a tax rate of 31 percent. The outcome would be the same if the second party promised a tax rate of only 20 percent, except that low-wage people would displace high-wage people in the majority coalition. Understanding the dynamics of voting, the two parties converge toward the center, each promising a tax rate of 31 percent and, with any randomness in voting, each acquiring a 50 percent chance of being elected. Regardless of whether the parties call themselves Liberal and Conservative or Republican and Democratic, the outcome of voting is the same, determined by the underlying preferences of the voters.

This proposition has to be qualified in several respects. No account has been taken of voters' assessments of the quality of the leadership of the two political parties, of the role of advertising in politics or of the political preferences of the personnel of the parties themselves, all of which affect the choice of platforms and the outcome of the vote. More importantly, the proposition rests on the premise that voters' preferences over all possible platforms of parties are single-peaked. Preferences are single-peaked with regard to the rate for the negative income tax, but there are other issues – such as the choice among ham, cheese, and tuna sandwiches where there was no way to line up all the available options on a common scale such that a median voter could be identified – for which this need not be so. In the absence of a median voter, one might expect political parties to become the vehicles by which majorities coalesce to exploit the corresponding minorities. In a society with three industries, farming, fishing and manufacturing, and with equal numbers of voters in each industry, one would expect political parties to seek the loyalty and support of two rather than all three industries because each of two industries can be better served by ignoring the interests of the third and because voters in any two industries constitute a majority of the electorate. There is no telling in advance which the two favored industries will be.

The danger of faction is compounded by the unfortunate feature of voting that the juxtaposition of two single-peaked issues is not necessarily single-peaked. In demonstrating the existence of the median voter, we have so far postulated what might be called single-issue politics. Society must choose the number of spears and nothing else, or the degree of redistribution of income and nothing else, with the tax rate set just high enough to finance the chosen level of expenditure. Now assume instead that two issues must be settled simultaneously. Specifically, society must choose a level of military expenditure *and* a degree of redistribution. To make the example more forceful, assume that both issues, considered one at a time, are single-peaked with well-specified median voters. There would be a median voter on military expenditure if military expenditure were the only item on the agenda. There would be a median voter on redistribution if redistribution were the only item on the agenda. The question is whether there is a median voter on platforms of military expenditure and redistribution when both issues are considered together.

Suppose for simplicity that each issue allows only three options and that voters' preferences for each issue separately are single-peaked. Military expenditure may be high (H), moderate (M), or low (L). Redistribution may be extensive (E), limited to the alleviation of destitution (D), or absent altogether (A). Single-peakedness requires that a voter who prefers, for example, H to M on military expenditure must prefer M to L and vice versa, though a voter whose first preference is M may prefer H to L or L to H. Similarly, a voter who prefers E to D on the redistribution of income must prefer D to A and vice versa, though a voter whose first preference is D may prefer E to A or A to E. With two issues and three options for each issue, there are exactly nine distinct platforms or combinations: {H, E}, {H, D}, {H, A}, {M, E}, {M, D}, {M, A}, {L, E}, {L, D}, and {L, A}, where, for example, {H, E} means high military expenditure *coupled with* extreme redistribution of income. The eight other platforms are interpreted accordingly. A voter's political stance is his ordering of the nine platforms, from most preferred to least preferred with the possibility of ties along the way. Political parties adopt platforms, each party promising to implement its platform if elected.

On each issue, the electorate is divided into three distinct groups with equal numbers of voters in each group. These preferences are shown in table 9.7. For military expenditure, the groups are I, II, and III, with preferences as shown in part (a). For the redistribution of income, the groups are 1, 2, and 3 with preferences as shown in part (b). It is convenient to suppose that people who want moderate military expenditure are indifferent between high and low, and that people who want redistribution

Table 9.7   The structure of preferences

Groups	Share of electorate	First preference	Second preference	Least preferred
(a) *Military expenditure*				
I	$\frac{1}{3}$	H	M	L
II	$\frac{1}{3}$	M	H,L	H,L
III	$\frac{1}{3}$	L	M	H
(b) *Redistribution of income*				
1	$\frac{1}{3}$	E	D	A
2	$\frac{1}{3}$	D	A,E	A,E
3	$\frac{1}{3}$	A	D	E

restricted to the destitute are indifferent between extreme redistribution and none at all; these assumptions are harmless and could be relaxed without changing the story significantly. Indifference is signified by the expressions H, L, and A, E repeated in the last two columns of the middle rows of part a and part b respectively. As the issues are single-peaked, there must for each issue be an option (M for military expenditure and D for redistribution) that beats any other option in a pair-wise vote, and there must be a median voter (II for military expenditure and 2 for redistribution) whose first preference prevails. Moderate military expenditure wins over high and low. Redistribution restricted to the destitute wins over extreme redistribution and the absence of redistribution. In pair-wise votes, M wins over H or L, and D wins over E or A. Our problem is whether and under what conditions voting among platforms is single-peaked. If so, then the platform {M, D} – where M beats all other military options and D beats all other redistributive options – must be the first preference of the median voter, but we have no assurance as yet that there is a median voter at all when issues are bundled into platforms of political parties. It turns out that there may or may not be an electoral equilibrium platform depending upon aspects of preferences we have not yet considered.

To focus on the presence or absence of an electoral equilibrium, we contrast two alternative society-wide patterns of preferences that have a good deal in common, but with one critical difference that will determine whether there is an electoral equilibrium or not. These are called "the left-right continuum" and "a world of extremists," and are shown in tables 9.8 and 9.9. Both patterns are chosen to be consistent with society's preferences for military expenditure and for redistribution when these are considered one at a time. For military expenditure, the entire population divides into groups I, II, and III as shown in part a of table 9.7. For redistribution, the entire population divides into groups 1, 2, and 3 as shown in part b of table 9.7. In principle, occupants of these groups may or may not be the same. For instance, people in group II might divide in any proportions whatsoever among groups 1, 2, and 3. To focus on the relative importance of military expenditure and redistribution in the preferences of each group, it is assumed instead that there is a one-to-one correspondence between

Table 9.8 A left–right continuum

	Right wing	Center	Left wing
Proportion of voters	$\frac{1}{3}$	$\frac{1}{3}$	$\frac{1}{3}$
First preference	{H, A}	{M, D}	{L, E}
Second preference	{H, D}	{M, A}	{L, D}
	{M, A}	{M, E}	{M, E}
		{H, D}	
		{L, D}	
Third preference	{M, D}	{L, A}	{M, D}
	{H, E}	{L, E}	{H, E}
	{L, A}	{H, A}	{L, A}
		{H, E}	
Fourth preference	{L, D}	—	{H, D}
	{M, E}		{M, A}
Worst	{L, E}	—	{H, A}

Platforms in the same box are assumed equally preferred.

the two groupings. Occupants of group I and group 1 are the very same people. So too are the occupants of groups II and 2, and of groups III and 3. With this fusion of groups, preferences over platforms in tables 9.8 and 9.9 are inherited from table 9.7. Each group's best platform and worst platform are determined. For example, the first group – consisting of group I in part a of table 9.7 and of group 1 in part b – must prefer the platform {H, A} to all others because H and A are its first preferences on military expenditure and redistribution, and, similarly, its worst platform must be {L, E}. Furthermore, the preferences of the first and third groups are opposites, the best platform in one group being the worst for the other, and the preferences of the second group are in between.

But the groups' preferences over platforms are not fully determined from their preferences over issues one at a time. For example, nothing in table 9.7 predetermines whether the first group prefers the platform {H, E} to the platform {L, A}, both of which supply the first group with its most preferred outcome on one issue and least preferred outcome on the other. It turns out that the presence or absence of an electoral equilibrium among the nine platforms depends critically on the entire pattern of preferences – second preference, third preference and so on – of the three groups. Tables 9.8 and 9.9 show two strongly contrasting possibilities.

The pattern in table 9.8 is called a left–right continuum and the three groups are renamed right wing, center, and left wing. Each group's preferences among platforms are based on a principle of impartiality between military expenditure and redistribution. For each group, a platform yielding its first preference on military expenditure and its second preference on redistribution is treated as equivalent to a platform yielding its first preference on redistribution and its second preference on military expenditure, and so on over the entire scale of preferences. Thus, the right-wing group must be indifferent between the platforms {H, E} and {L, A} because both platforms supply one first preference and one third preference, and the table shows this to be so.

Table 9.9 A world of extremists

	Militarists	Center	Egalitarians
Proportion of voters	$\frac{1}{3}$	$\frac{1}{3}$	$\frac{1}{3}$
First preference	{H, A}	{M, D}	{L, E}
Second preference	{H, D}	{M, A} {M, E} {H, D} {L, D}	{M, E}
Third preference	{H, E}	{L, A} {L, E} {H, A} {H, E}	{H, E}
Fourth preference	{M, A}	—	{L, D}
Fifth preference	{M, D}	—	{M, D}
Sixth preference	{M, E}	—	{H, D}
Seventh preference	{L, A}	—	{L, A}
Eighth preference	{L, D}	—	{M, A}
Worst	{L, E}	—	{H, A}

Platforms in the same box are assumed to be equally preferred.

From inspection of table 9.8, it is evident that the platform {M, D} beats every other platform in a pair-wise vote. The center group always votes for {M, D} because {M, D} is its first preference, and {M, D} must be preferred to any other option by *one* of the other two groups because an option that is high on the preference scale of one of these groups is correspondingly low on the preference scale of the other. The three platforms preferred to {M, D} by the right wing – {H, A}, {H, D}, and {M, A} – are all strictly dispreferred by the left wing. The three combinations preferred to {M, D} by the left wing – {L, E}, {L, D}, and {M, E} – are all strictly dispreferred by the right wing. The combination {M, D} commands the support of the center group and, depending on the alternative, either the right wing or the left wing in a contest with any other platform. The essence of the left–right continuum is that all platforms can be strung out on one and the same linear scale representing, depending whether you read the scale from the right or from the left, the order of preferences of the right-wing group or the left-wing group. The first preference of the center group lies in the middle of the scale. A pair of single-peaked issues fuses into one single-peaked issue for which a median voter can be identified. A political party with a combination {M, D} as its platform can count on a majority of voters in a head-to-head electoral contest with another political party with a different platform.

Note in passing that, though we have chosen to call the combination {H, A} right and the combination {L, E} left, the existence of a two-dimensional electoral equilibrium is independent of which issues are aligned. Preferences might have been such that the scale of combinations runs from {H, E} at one extreme to {L, A} on the other. The important consideration is that there be some correspondence between preferences on different issues. Preferences conforming to a left–right continuum provoke political parties to choose a platform at or near the center. In a two-party race, both parties are inclined to adopt {M, D} as their platform and politics becomes more a contest of personalities than of policy. Parties dare not stray too far from the center if a median platform can be identified and if that platform would win in a pair-wise vote against any other.

All this changes in a world of extremists exemplified by the pattern of preferences in table 9.9 with the groups renamed as militarists, center, and egalitarians. Extremism in this context refers to a group's intensity of concern for one issue over another, rather than to a group's location at one end of a scale of preferences. Extremists care about one issue over and above every other, about defense above all, about redistribution above all, or, more generally, about religion, a region of the country, language, or any other issue predominantly. Preferences of the extremists are lexigraphic. Extreme militarists prefer platforms with larger military expenditure to platforms with smaller military expenditure, regardless of the extent of redistribution, though, between two platforms with the same military expenditure, their choice depends on the amount of redistribution. Extreme egalitarians prefer platforms with more redistribution to platforms with less redistribution, regardless of the amount of military expenditure, though, between two platforms with the same redistribution, their choice depends on the amount of military expenditure.

With voters' preferences on a left–right continuum as in table 9.8, there was a unique electoral equilibrium platform {M, D} that defeated any other platform in a pair-wise vote. A political party adopting the electoral equilibrium as its platform could count on winning an election in a two-party race with another political party that adopts a different platform. In a world of extremists, as in table 9.9, that is no longer so. The platform {M, D} remains the first preference of the center group, but it can now be defeated by the platform {H, E}, preferred to the platform {M, D} by a coalition of extreme militarists and extreme egalitarians, both of whom obtain their first preferences on the one issue which is their primary concern. Notice that the platform {H, E} supplies both militarists and egalitarians with their most favored option on one issue together with their least favored option on the other. Both groups vote for {H, E} because the advantage of the one outweighs the disadvantage of the other in a head-to-head vote with the platform {M, D}. A world of extremists in table 9.9 has very much in common with the exploitation problem where each voter is concerned with his own income exclusively and any number of majority coalitions might form to grab the entire national income for their members.

Though the platform {M, D} was an electoral equilibrium when voters, preferences formed a left–right continuum, and though the platform {H, E} beats the platform {M, D} in a world of extremists, the platform {H, E} fails to displace the platform {M, D} as the new electoral equilibrium. Instead, there is now no electoral equilibrium at all. The combination {H, E} defeats the combination {M, D}, but is, in turn, defeated by either {H, D} or {M, E}. For example, {H, D} defeats {H, E} because {H, D} is preferred by militarists and centrists, while {M, E} defeats {H, E} because {M, E} is preferred by both egalitarians and centrists. But both {H, D} and {M, E} can be defeated by {M, D} which is in turn defeated by {H, E}, completing

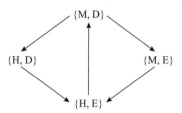

Figure 9.5 The instability of voting in a world of extremists.

the paradox of voting as shown in figure 9.5 where, as in figure 9.1 above, an arrow from one combination to another signifies that the first beats the second in a pair-wise vote. Each triplet in figure 9.5 – the left-hand triplet of {M, D}, {H, D}, and {H, E}, and the right-hand triplet) of {M, D}, {M, E}, and {H, E} – yields a paradox of voting analogous to that in the ham, cheese and tuna example. Each triplet represents the three ways for two out of three parties – in this case militarists, center, and extremists – to outvote the third.

When issues are single-peaked, one at a time, and in the absence of collusion among voters or of vote-trading (where I vote contrary to my preferences on a matter of special concern to you, and you, in return, vote contrary to your preferences on a matter of special concern to me), the first preference of the median voter on each issue is likely to prevail. When people's preferences on different issues tend to line up on a left–right continuum, then the combination of first preferences of the median voter becomes an electoral equilibrium and is likely to be reflected in the platforms of competing political parties. But when the electorate is divided into many minorities, each passionately concerned about a separate issue which would be voted down in a straightforward vote on that issue alone, then several minority groups may combine to form a majority of minorities, based on vote-trading where each minority agrees to support all the others in the coalition in voting on its issue of primary concern. A collection of policies that would be voted down one by one may yet prevail together.

Political parties may cement such coalitions, providing an institutional environment where the promises of the different groups may be trusted. Returning to our example of military expenditure and redistribution, suppose the vote on military expenditures comes first and the vote on redistribution comes afterwards. A coalition of egalitarians and militarists might prevail if they trust one another, but egalitarians may refuse to support large military expenditure in the first vote because they do not trust the militarists to support redistribution in the second vote. A political party that adopts large military expenditure and substantial redistribution of income as its platform may be trusted to deliver both because it cannot afford to acquire the reputation as a promise-breaker.

The double paradox of voting among the four platforms – {M, D}, {M, E}, {H, E}, and {H, D} – arises because and only because voting between each pair of combinations is assumed to be sincere. The assumption is that each voter opts for his preferred platform in the vote at hand, ignoring the possibility that he may be out-manuevered in the very next vote. The apparently endless process is short-circuited, and a combination that beats all other combinations emerges in practice, once two of the three groups – militarists, egalitarians, and centrists – form a binding coalition to vote for whichever political party adopts the agreed-upon platform: {H, E} for the militarists and egalitarians, {M, E} for centrists and egalitarians, and {H, D} for centrists and militarists.

The founding fathers who drafted the constitution of the United States had hoped and expected there would be no political parties in the new country they were creating. Legislators and executives would be chosen as individuals rather than as members of competing groups. That was not to be. The lure of office soon led to the creation of permanent associations designed, on the one hand, to win elections for their members, and, on the other hand, to promote policies that would appeal to their supporters among the electorate. Majority coalitions of voters could have coalesced without the intermediation of political parties, but such coalitions could prove fragile. Political parties provide the glue that holds factions together.

There remains some question about which factions will coalesce into a majority party. In a society with three distinct factions, a bargain may be struck between any two factions to acquire advantages at the expense of the third, but there is no way to tell which of the three possible coalitions will emerge. In practical politics, a great many issues have to be resolved simultaneously. Some issues are more or less single-peaked; others are of special interest to distinct communities. There is no neat and exclusive division of all voters into well-specified categories. The formation of political parties and the determination of each party's platform is a complex process where the underlying preferences of voters count for something but where there is an inextricable element of bargaining and unpredictability. Platforms of political parties are in part the outcomes of bargains that cannot be entirely predicted from the underlying preferences of voters.

Democratic politics is not just voting. It is an intermingling of voting with custom, bargaining, and strategy. Custom is the elaborate framework of rules within which voting takes place, rules prescribing the method of voting for leaders and for bills (methods such as first past the-post or proportional representation), the privileges and responsibilities of political parties, the formation of political parties, the apportionment of the powers of government among legislature, executive and judiciary, procedures for proposing and amending bills in the legislature, sequencing of votes required for the passage of bills into law, a sphere of individual liberty, spheres of authority of the different levels of government, and procedures (usually requiring a supermajority) for replacing old rules with new rules. Bargaining is required to determine which interests are to be fused into a working majority through the establishment of the platforms of political parties or by vote-trading within the legislature, and to determine how the privileges accruing to the majority coalition are to be allocated among its factions. For example, if domestic bread producers and domestic cheese producers are part of a majority coalition and if their interests within the majority coalition are to obtain tariff protection, a bargain must necessarily be struck to establish how high the tariff on each good shall be. Strategy is ubiquitous as leaders and would-be leaders forge coalitions in the legislature and balance the legislators' interests and preferences to secure favourable votes.

With voting unconstrained, the voting mechanism would self-destruct because the privileges of belonging to the majority coalition would be too great to risk in an election. Politicians in office and their supporters in the population at large cannot be expected to divest themselves of the powers of government if divestment at the hands of the electorate brings destitution and impoverization. Voting is only sustainable as a method of public decision-making if and in so far as the perquisites of office and privileges of membership in a majority coalition are somehow constrained. The required constraint is supplied in part by the surrounding customs and traditions which restrict majorities in their acquisition of privilege at the expense of the rest of the population. Exploitation by voting is constrained by civil rights that politicians in office and majorities in the legislature cannot easily ignore for fear of losing support among the electorate. Exploitation by voting is constrained by a blurring of the lines between interest groups (so that, for instance, children of the rich may become poor, children of Easterners may become Westerners, and children of farmers may become business executives) and by the citizen's sense of the common good. In general, the less rigid are the lines between social classes, the less does the minority have to fear at the hands of the majority. Recognition of the potential divisiveness of religion lies behind the strict separation in many democratic countries between church and state. Exploitation by voting is constrained especially by the determination of the greater part of most peoples' incomes within a market that is to some extent, if not entirely, autonomous and outside the political arena. Voters respect the constraints on the perquisites of office and of majority status in the realization that democracy itself is at stake and that the loss of these perquisites is inconsequential by comparison with the risk of placing oneself at the mercy of the king, great helmsman, or an unconstrained ruling class.

Two hundred years ago, it was commonly believed that majority rule voting with universal franchise was destined to self-destruct. Our discussion of the diseases of democracy reveals why thoughtful people might have held that view. On the strength of that belief, most countries restricted franchise to property-holders. Today, majority-rule voting takes hold in some countries but not in others. Identification of the preconditions for majority-rule voting – and of the natural, procedural, and insti tutional defenses – may facilitate the introduction of democracy where it is absent and the preservation of democracy where it exists.

Chapter Ten

ADMINISTRATION

The statesman who should attempt to direct private people in what manner they ought to employ their capitals, would not only load himself with the most unnecessary attention, but would assume an authority which could not be safely trusted, not only to no single person, but to no council of state whatever, and which would no-where be so dangerous as in the hands of a man who had folly and presumption enough to fancy himself fit to exercise it.

... The sovereign has only three duties to attend to; three duties of great importance, indeed, but plain and intelligible to common understandings: first, the duty of protecting the society from the violence and invasion of other independent societies; second, the duty of protecting, as far as possible, every member of society from the injustice and oppression of every other member of it, or the duty of establishing an exact administration of justice; and, third, the duty of erecting and maintaining certain public works and certain public institutions, which it can never be in the interest of any individual, or small number of individuals to erect and maintain ... though it may do much more than repay it to a great society.

Adam Smith, *The Wealth of Nations*, 1776

Every modern society, no matter how suspicious of government or how devoted to the ideal of the competitive market, maintains, as it must, a large public sector. Adam Smith's tasks of government are no less indispensable now than they were in his day. Defense can only be provided collectively. The police – together with the whole paraphernalia of courts and prisons – can only be provided collectively. Large public works are still required, and can only be acquired collectively. Government must provide roads, bridges, ports, airports, public buildings, clean water, supervision of food and drugs, and defense against epidemics. Beyond that, contemporary governments socialize some risk, provide a mechanism for the resolution of private disputes, specify the rights and obligations of corporations and other legal entities, impose taxes or regulations upon privately advantageous behavior that is harmful to the environment or to society at large, and redistribute income, reducing the gap between rich and poor through progressive income taxation, welfare, and other measures.

Every modern society needs a vast bureaucracy to administer the public sector. Cadres of soldiers, police, judges, prison guards, tax collectors, diplomats, and administers are required to collect taxes, regulate the economy, monitor food, drugs, and industrial pollution, arrange basic research, control fraud in the stock market, supervise public lands, guard against monopoly, oversee money and public debt, write legislation, supply police protection, punish crimes, run the army, maintain roads and public buildings, and supervise the provision of social services including education, health care, the old age pension, unemployment insurance, welfare for the poor, and subsidies to firms. If the market is the realm of prices, the administration is the realm of command. The entire bureaucracy must be organized hierarchically. There is no other way to organize, though the chain of command may be more or less rigid: more rigid in the army and the police, less rigid in universities because a major task of the universities is to promote independent research which, almost by definition, requires the ordinary professor to choose the subject of his research and to conduct that research as he sees fit. Corporations are hierarchical too, but they are disciplined by prices and have no legitimate recourse to violence.

The governments of Canada employ about a sixth of the labor force, purchase about a sixth of the nation's goods and services, and allocate just under half of the national income. In the year 2000, government expenditure on goods and services in Canada – federal, provincial, and local, with intergovernmental transfers canceled out – amounted to $228 billion out of a total gross domestic product (the value of all goods and services produced) of $1,056 billion. To conduct its business, the Canadian government employed 2.8 million people out of a total labor force of 16 million, plus another million, mostly doctors and other medical personnel, who were nominally independent but paid by the government per unit of service. Throughout history, less extensive bureaucracies were able to dominate their societies completely. A principal concern in this chapter is how our public officials may be subordinated to the voter and directed toward the attainment of the common good.

The growth of government since the 1920s is shown in table 10.1. Column headings are percentages of gross domestic product devoted to the different components of public expenditure: government expenditure on goods and services, transfers to persons, transfers to business, and interest on the public debt. As in virtually every country in the world, total government expenditure increased substantially. Even as a percentage of gross domestic product, the expenditure of the Canadian government grew over three fold, from 15 percent of gross domestic product in 1926 to 50 percent in 1944 at the height of the Second World War. It fell back to just over 20 percent after the war, then rose steadily to 45 percent in 1990 and then fell back to 40 percent in the year 2000. Since the Second World War, the growth of public expenditure was largely in transfers to people and firms and in the interest on the national debt. Expenditure on goods and services grew more modestly from 9 percent in 1926 to 12 percent in 1950 and then to 22 percent in 1990.

Ideally, the bureaucracy is entirely subordinate to the elected representatives of the people. The legislature formulates policy and the administration executes that policy

Table 10.1   The size of government as a percentage of gross domestic product

[Canada, all levels of government combined, selected years from 1926 to 2000.]

Year	Government expenditure on goods and services	Transfers to persons	Transfers to business	Interest on the public debt	Total public expenditure
1926	9.26	1.38	0.04	4.31	14.99
1930	12.15	1.53	0.12	4.06	17.86
1940	16.44	2.92	0.76	3.91	24.03
1944	41.66	2.11	2.21	3.50	49.48
1950	12.68	5.35	0.33	2.84	21.20
1960	17.09	7.83	0.80	2.77	28.49
1970	22.00	7.83	0.93	3.65	34.41
1980	21.80	9.83	2.66	5.42	39.71
1990	22.19	11.45	1.48	9.48	44.60
2000	21.57	10.64	1.05	7.23	40.49

*Sources: **Statistics Canada:** National Income and Expenditure Accounts, Annual estimates, 1926–86 (13-531) and subsequent annual volumes (13-001-XPB).*

under the direct authority of an elected President or Prime Minister who appoints the occupants of the top ranks of the civil and military hierarchy. In practice, legislative control of the administration may be less than complete, for the legislature can never cope with the multitude of decisions that have to be made. A few large decisions each year is as much as a legislature can be expected to accomplish. The legislature must pass the budget specifying how much money is to be spent and how money is to be allocated among the departments of government. It cannot supervise administration in detail. It must approve total expenditure on schooling, but it cannot write the curriculum of each and every subject taught, decide who within the school system is to be hired, promoted, or fired, or specify the locations of every net school. The authority of the bureaucracy over the economy depends on what citizens assign their government to do. Payment of interest on public debt requires little more than the writing of the appropriate cheques. Public provision of schooling and medical care require a cadre of civil servants and detailed supervision over a great deal of expenditure. The armed forces require a rigid hierarchy and an unambiguous chain of command.

With its monopoly of legitimate organized violence and its tentacles deep into the economy, the military and civilian bureaucracy would seem well equipped to establish a predatory ruling class as described in the fishermen–pirates–policemen story of chapter 2. Throughout history, from the praetorian guards of ancient Rome to the nomenklatura of contemporary communist societies, that is exactly how bureaucracies tended to behave. Difficulties in the legislative supervision of bureaucracy are compounded by the problem of faction discussed in the last chapter. Control of the bureaucracy may become the means by which a majority faction or governing plurality of legislators consolidates its authority. More will be said about the administration as a ruling class at the end of this chapter. For the present, it is sufficient to observe that delegation requires subsidiary rules – rules supplied by custom, courts or the legislature itself – to guide the bureaucracy in its conduct of day-to-day business, for in no other way can the intention of the legislature be realized or the power of the administration over the rest of society be contained.

Within the bounds of its delegated authority, the bureaucracy must seek to promote the common good. In effect, the legislature says to the bureaucracy, "Take this sum of money and use it wisely within the confines of your legislated authority." The National Research Council is told to do what it sees as the most appropriate research. The Ministry of Transport is told to build the most appropriate roads. Universities are told to strike the right balance between teaching and research, and to make available the appropriate selection of courses. The army is provided with a certain revenue, assigned tasks (which may be as broadly specified as keeping the country safe from invasion or as narrow as an instruction to buy such-and-such weapons that the legislature thinks appropriate), subjected to some *ex post* oversight, and told to get on with its business as best it can. Of course, departments of government are restricted in the range of their activities. The Ministry of Defence directs the army to fight wars or undertake peace-keeping missions abroad, but may not redistribute income among citizens, even if, in the opinion of the principals in the ministry, it would be in the national interest do so. There are jurisdictional disputes at the edges of each ministry's authority, but no ministry can stray too far from its core territory in pursuit of its vision of the good of the nation as a whole.

Within its domain of authority, the administration is constrained by a principle of equality. That people in like circumstances be treated alike is a constitutional restriction, binding on legislature and administration and supervised by the courts. Public schooling and public provision of health care are to be the same for all. No child is to be less well educated than other children. No ill person is to be less well treated than other ill people. The principle is difficult to apply in practice because people differ in their needs and in the cost of the public services they require. It is one thing to say that two people with the same disease ought to be provided with equal medical service. It is another to allocate resources for medical care between pre-natal care and lung cancer. There is also a conflict between equality of expenditure and equality of service.

It costs a great deal more to treat any given illness in sparsely populated regions than in the big cities where nobody lives very far from a hospital. With equal expenditure per head, people in sparsely populated regions would be much less well cared for than people in the big cities. With equal care for all, expenditure on people in sparsely populated regions would be much larger per head than expenditure on people in the big cities. As a guide for the administration, the principle of equality subdivides into two competing principles, and there is, inevitably, a trade-off between them. Normally, expenditure per head on medical care would be larger but the standard of care would be lower in sparsely populated regions than in the big cities.

A second principle is efficiency. Like equality, efficiency may be thought of as a dimension of the common good. Efficiency boils down in practice to the maximization of the national income broadly defined to include all benefits "to whomsoever they may accrue." On this *cost–benefit* principle and with only enough money to build one of two equally expensive roads, the Ministry of Transport should build road A rather than road B if the value of all services to the users of road A exceeds the value of the services to the users of road B. The procedure may be justified on the grounds that the typical person can expect to be better off with this procedure than with any other *in the long run* when the procedure is used consistently, over and over again.

Normally, the legislature would want the administration to transact its business efficiently, doing what it is assigned to do at the lowest cost to the tax payer and creating as large a bundle of services as it can with the resources at its disposal. There are exceptions. As discussed in the last chapter, there is a trade-off between efficiency and equality in the redistribution of income. The legislature may favor one faction, or coalition of factions, over the rest of society. Small benefits for some people may impose large costs on others.

Cost–benefit analysis – the pursuit of efficiency in the public service – has a double role to play. Its primary purpose is prosperity, making people collectively as well off as possible with the resources at the disposal of the administration and devoting just enough resources to the public sector to undertake those tasks, and only those tasks, that are more than worth the cost. Cost–benefit analysis has a political purpose as well, to supply rules for the administration to follow, limiting its discretion and reducing the likelihood that the vast powers of the bureaucracy will foster conflict in the legislature or destabilize democratic government.

ASPECTS OF COST–BENEFIT RULES

Vote-trading as the foundation of cost-benefit analysis

Imagine a country of five million people living in five regions, A, B, C, D, and E, with one million people in each region. Every region elects a member of parliament who votes in accordance with the interests of his constituents. Three votes constitute a majority. Suppose parliament is voting about road building. Five roads are under consideration, one in each of the five regions. Parliament must decide whether to build all five roads, some of the roads or none at all. As shown in table 10.2, every road costs $100 million to build, conveys total benefits of $80 million to the people in *its* region, and conveys benefits of $10 million to the people in each of the other four regions. There is an established rule in this country that all public expenditure is financed by a head tax on everybody in the entire country. No matter where one lives, one's tax bill is one five-millionth of total public expenditure. Thus, the building of each and every one of the five possible roads imposes a cost of $20 [100 million/5 million] on every person, no matter where he lives, conveys a benefit of $80 [80 million/1 million] to each person in the region where the road is built, and conveys benefits of $10 [10 million/1 million] to each person in each of the other four regions. The five roads in our example are public goods, like guns in the guns-and-butter example in chapter 5, but, though they benefit everybody simultaneously, they do not do so equally. Each road conveys large benefits to some people and small benefits to others.

The legislature might vote about each road, one at a time, or it might vote about several roads, perhaps all five, together. Suppose, first, that voting is about one road

Table 10.2 The costs and benefits of five similar roads in different regions

	In total ($ million)	Per head ($)
Cost of each road	100	20
Benefit of each road to people in its region	80	80
Benefit of each road to people in any other region	10	10
Total benefits of all five roads in each region	120	120
Tax bill for all five roads in each region	100	100

at a time. Since the regions are identical, it is sufficient to consider the road intended for region A. No matter where one lives, the tax bill per head must be $20. The corresponding benefit per head is $80 for a resident of region A and $10 for a resident of any other region. Thus, everybody living in region A gains $60 [80 − 20], and everybody living in any of the other four regions – B, C, D, and E – loses $10 [20 − 10]. The net gain to people in region A exceeds the sum of the losses in the other regions, but ordinary voting takes no account of that. Each member of parliament votes for or against the building of the road in region A depending on the effect of the road upon voters in his region alone. Since the value of benefits falls short of the cost of taxation in four out of the five regions, four out of the five members of parliament vote against the proposal to build a road in region A, and it is not built. As the calculation is the same for the roads in the other four regions, no roads are built at all.

Nor would any road be built if road-building were the responsibility of the regional governments. People in region A would be left to build their road, or to desist from building it, on the understanding that the road would be financed by local taxation within region A. The benefit would be $80 per head, the cost of taxation would be $100 per head, and the road would not be built.

The outcome is entirely different when all five roads are considered together. Total expenditure would be $500 million. Tax per head would be $100. Benefit per head would be $80 from the road in one's own region plus $10 from each of the roads in the other four regions, for a total of $120. Benefits worth $120 per head are obtained for a tax bill of $100 per head. All five members of parliament vote for the omnibus bill, and all five roads are built. Local authority over road-building would be adequate if (1) the benefits of each road accrued *entirely* within the region where that road is built, and (2) tax collection were sufficiently decentralized that residents in each region could pay for their road by region-wide, rather than country-wide, taxation. The first of these requirements is violated in our example because each road conveys some benefit in every region. The second requirement would be violated if the example were about diseases rather than about roads because, for example, there is no mechanism for taxing men rather than women for the cost of research on prostate cancer, or taxing women rather than men for the cost of research on breast cancer.

None of the five roads is built when they are considered separately. All of the five roads are built when they are considered together. This is a common situation. Public services – highways, hospitals, police, schools, universities – are often like the five roads in our example. Benefits accrue simultaneously to large numbers of people, these benefits are concentrated in one region or upon one subgroup of the population, but they not so are completely concentrated that people outside the region are unaffected altogether. The combined benefits of a collection of projects may exceed their combined costs, though none of these projects would be undertaken if considered one at a time and if all voters looked to their immediate self-interest in every vote. A vote trade among people in all five regions together to build all five roads – in circumstances where none of the roads would have been built had the legislature voted about each road separately – can be looked upon as an appeal by the legislature to cost–benefit analysis: the principle that a project should be undertaken if and only if the sum of its benefits exceeds its cost to whomsoever the benefits and costs accrue.

Exploitation of minorities through project selection

The exploitation by the majority of the minority was discussed in the last chapter in the context of the allocation by voting of a sum of money or of the entire national income. Exploitation may sometimes be arranged by project selection. Projects of value to the majority may be accepted and projects of value to the minority rejected regardless of the balance of costs and benefits. Though the spread between total benefit and total cost is greatest when all five roads are built, it may still be advantageous for any three members of parliament to form a majority coalition to vote *for* the roads in their regions and *against* the roads in the other two. Everybody has a net gain of $20 when all five roads are built. For the three regions in the coalition, the net gain per person is increased to $40 [80 + 10 + 10 − 20 − 20 − 20]. For the other two regions, the net gain is converted to a net loss per person of $30 [10 + 10 + 10 − 20 − 20 − 20]. The coalition is advantageous to its members, though the sum of the gains to the majority falls short of the sum of the losses of the excluded majority.

Cost–benefit analysis has a pronounced political dimension. It may be looked upon as a rule for circumventing the exploitation problem. Legislators and their supporters in the general population may be willing to desist from forming coalitions in support of projects in their regions when there is an understanding that other legislators will show equal restraint. A decision to respect the outcome of cost–benefit analysis may be the basis for such an understanding.

Diverse projects

The neat symmetry of the five-roads example is entirely artificial. Not all projects are alike. Some are worthwhile. Others are not. Road projects may be large or small, profitable or unprofitable, relatively concentrated in one region or relatively unconcentrated. Cost–benefit analysis discriminates among roads or other projects, signifying which roads ought to be built and which roads ought not to be built. Consider a modification of the five-roads example: Suppose, once again, that each of the five roads is designated for one of the five regions, and that each road conveys benefits of $80 per head to every person in its regions and $10 per head to every person in the other four regions, for an average benefit of $24 in all five regions together. Now, drop the assumption that every road costs $100 million (or $20 per head in all five regions together), and suppose instead (1) that the roads cost different amounts to build and (2) that voters do not know at the time the vote is taken which roads will be expensive and which roads will be cheap.

Suppose, specifically, that all roads yield combined benefits of $120 million allocated among regions as indicated in table 10.2, that one road will cost $50 million, another $100 million, another $150 million, another $200 million, and another $250 million (equivalent to $10, $20, $30, $40, and $50 per head), but that nobody in parliament knows which road is which. That information will be discovered before any roads are built but after voting is finished. By adopting a cost–benefit rule, the legislature supplies the administration with a procedure for choosing whether or not to build any particular road, removing administrative discretion without at the same time specifying which roads are to be built. To adopt a cost–benefit rule is to instruct the Ministry of Transport to build all roads for which total benefit exceeds total cost regardless of the identities of the beneficiaries. With such a rule, the roads costing $50 million and $100 million are built, but the roads costing $150 million, $200 million, and $250 million are not.

Discounting

Cost–benefit analysis must compare projects with benefits and costs accruing at different times. Just as the market churns out prices for bread, cheese, and every other good today, so too, as explained in chapter 5, does it churn out prices for the same good, and for money, available at different times. The price today of money payable tomorrow is indicated by the rate of interest, though, as we shall see, the two concepts are not quite identical. Suppose the interest rate on savings deposits is 8 percent. When I deposit $1,000 in the bank at that rate, I am, in effect, buying money next year at a price which is a transformation of the rate of interest. I buy $1,080 next year at a price of 92.590¢ [1,000/1,080] per dollar. Generalizing, when the rate of interest is r percent, the going price is $1/(1 + r)$ per dollar delivered next year, $1/(1 + r)^2$ per dollar delivered two years hence, $1/(1 + r)^3$ per dollar delivered today for each dollar delivered three years hence and so on. In our discussion of cost–benefit analysis, we ignore the gap between lending rates and borrowing rates, all variations among year-to-year rates of interest at different times in the future, inflation and changes over time in the relative prices of goods, matters that would normally be covered in textbooks of macroeconomics or money and banking. Here there is one market-wide rate of interest by which values of costs and benefits accruing at different times may be compared. A cost C to be incurred in five years time is equivalent to a cost of $C/(1 + r)^5$ incurred today. A benefit B accruing in three years time is equivalent to a benefit $B/(1 + r)^3$ accruing today.

Discounting allows costs and benefits accruing at different times to be compared on a common scale of "present values." Consider a project with costs C_1, C_2, and C_3 in years 1, 2, and 3 and then with benefits B_4, B_5, and B_6 accruing in years 4, 5, and 6. With a rate of interest of r, the total cost, TC, of the project assessed as a present value in the year 0 is

$$TC = [C_1/(1 + r)] + [C_2/(1 + r)^2] + [C_3/(1 + r)^3] \qquad (1)$$

while the total benefit, TB, assessed as a present value in the year 0 is

$$TB = [B_4/(1 + r)^4] + [B_5/(1 + r)^5] + [B_6/(1 + r)^6] \qquad (2)$$

The cost–benefit analysis certifies a project as worthy if and only if TB > TC, if the present value of total benefits exceeds the present value of total costs assessed at the going rate of interest.

A generalization of equation (2) will prove useful in the analysis to follow. If a project yields benefits every year forever and if the values of those benefits each year are the same, then the total benefit, TB, expressed as the present value of the stream of annual benefit, B, becomes

$$TB = B/r \qquad (3)$$

when the rate of interest, r, is invariant over time.[1] For each project, there may be defined a "rate of return," the rate of interest for which the total benefit of the project would be just equal to its total cost. When benefits are constant every year forever, the project's rate of return becomes B/TC. The cost–benefit rule to undertake a project if and only if TB > TC becomes equivalent to the rule that a project is worth undertaking if and only if (B/TC) > r, that is, if its rate of return exceeds the target, or market-determined, rate of interest.

Consider the six roads described in table 10.3. Each road has a fixed cost of construction today and yields an annual flow of benefits each year forever. Roads are listed in the first column, their fixed costs are shown in the second, their annual benefits (assumed constant in perpetuity) are shown in the third and their rates of return, the ratio of annual return to fixed cost, are shown in the final column. Suppose the rate of interest is 8 percent, meaning that the market is prepared to exchange $100 today for an income of $8 in perpetuity. In choosing among roads, the Ministry of Transport can rely upon the market rate of interest for comparing costs and benefits, building all roads yielding at least 8 percent and rejecting all roads yielding less than 8 percent. The Ministry of Transport builds roads A, C, E, and F, and it desists from

Table 10.3 Costs and benefits of six roads

Roads	Total cost, TC ($ million)	Annual benefit, B ($ million)	Rate of return, B/TC (%)
A	100	12	12
B	30	2.1	7
C	400	44	11
D	600	30	5
E	500	100	20
F	30	3.9	13

building roads B and D, reflecting citizens' preferences in the choice between present and future consumption.

Nothing need be said about where the roads are located or about the identity of the users of the roads. All roads might be used equally by everybody, or each road might be specially beneficial to people in one of five distinct regions as was supposed above. Cost–benefit analysis recognizes no such distinction because benefits and costs are compared "to whomsoever they may accrue." Invariably, a strict application of cost–benefit rules will turn out to favor some regions over others when projects are financed by taxes levied uniformly on the population as a whole. Only by accident will all regions gain equally.

Though cost–benefit analysis may yield unequal net advantages among regions and among people, there are several strong reasons why it is employed: (1) If benefits exceed costs, then everybody could be made better off by combining the project in question with an appropriate set of transfers from gainers to losers. While that is true, it may be cold comfort to the losers in any given project if, in fact, the transfers are not forthcoming. (2) Even without compensatory transfers, each person may expect to become better off in the long run from a series of projects, some favoring one group of people, some favoring another, as long as all projects for which benefits exceed cost are undertaken and all projects for which benefits fail to exceed cost are not. A long series of public projects would be like a long series of gambles at favorable odds. One can expect to come out ahead in the end. (3) A benefit–cost rule may be the only rule in sight and the citizen's only protection against arbitrary and discriminatory behavior by the civil service. The rule to build all roads for which benefits exceed cost by some specified margin is, at least, a rule. Abandon that, and the allocation of funds for road-building becomes like the allocation of money in the exploitation problem of majority rule voting. With no objective basis for choosing among projects, bureaucracies are exposed to the temptation to serve clients who can be expected to return favors. Political parties coalesce around groups of people – identified by region, occupation, language, or religion – who expect to be rewarded for their support by favorable treatment in the allocation of public expenditure.

Admittedly, the choice of a target rate of interest is somewhat problematic. There are many rates of interest in the economy, and it is not always evident which rate of return ought to be applied. Should it be the rate of return on government bonds, on consumer borrowing, on bank deposits, on commercial loans or on some other transaction? There is no solid consensus on this matter, but the weight of opinion seems to be that the rate on bonds is probably the most appropriate.

THE MARGINAL COST OF PUBLIC FUNDS, THE REDISTRIBUTION OF INCOME, AND TOTAL PUBLIC EXPENDITURE

Governments require a rule for choosing the size of the public sector, deciding which projects, programs, and activities to undertake and which to reject as too expensive. There is no end to the things governments might usefully do in providing for the army, the police, health care, education, basic research, support for the old, alleviation of poverty, and so on. The entire national income would not be sufficient to cover

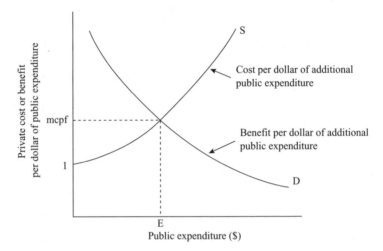

Figure 10.1 How the demand and supply for public expenditure determine the size of the public sector and the marginal cost of public funds.

every desirable undertaking. In the service of the citizen, governments must balance the benefits of public expenditure against the cost in private consumption forgone. An omnipotent, omniscient and benevolent government – a government that could levy personalized lump sum taxes and could align each person's share of the cost of every project to that person's share of the benefit – would undertake all projects, programs, and activities for which the combined benefits to all citizens are sufficient to outweigh the cost of consumption goods forgone.

A less than omnipotent government that must finance public expenditure by ordinary taxation would alter the rule, undertaking only those projects, programs, and activities for which benefits exceed the full cost of taxation inclusive of the excess burden of taxation, the cost of taxation to the tax payer over and above the revenue acquired by the government. In choosing which projects to undertake and which to reject as too expensive, due allowance must be given for the harm in the tax-induced diversion of resources and purchasing power from more productive but more taxed uses to less productive but less taxed uses, as well as in privately advantageous but socially disadvantageous maneuvers to reduce one's tax bill.

An additional project requires additional public expenditure that can only be acquired by an increase in tax rates. Increases in tax rates lead to increases in the excess burden of taxation which must be included as part of the cost of any additional project. The determination of total public expenditure can be represented by the crossing of appropriately defined demand and supply curves. These are shown in figure 10.1 with total public expenditure on the horizontal axis and the cost to the tax payer per additional dollar of public expenditure on the vertical axis. The height of the intersection of the demand and supply curves, called the *marginal cost of public funds* and designated by "mcpf," is the common value in equilibrium of the benefit and cost per additional dollar of public expenditure. The corresponding public expenditure is designated by E.

The demand curve is based on an ordering of projects, programs, and activities, from best to worst, according to their benefit per dollar of public expenditure, where "benefit" refers to the sum of all benefits to whomsoever they may accrue. For any given expenditure, E, the height of the demand curve is the highest attainable benefit per dollar of expenditure among all projects, programs, or activities that remain when E has already been spent on other more advantageous projects. The demand curve is downward sloping by construction. It cannot be otherwise when projects, programs, and activities are ordered by their benefit per dollar of expenditure.

The supply curve shows the full cost to the tax payer per dollar of additional public expenditure as an increasing function of total public expenditure. For any expenditure, E, the height of the supply curve is $(\Delta R + \Delta L)/\Delta R$ as defined in equation (17) of chapter 4 where ΔR is the extra revenue acquired, where ΔL is the additional excess burden of taxation and where public revenue and expenditure are necessarily the same. Such a supply curve has already been developed in two different contexts. In chapter 4, the height of the supply curve of public expenditure was reflection of the loss of surplus associated with the tax-induced shift in consumption from taxed cheese to untaxed bread. The extra bread consumed was worth less to the tax payer than the cheese he might have consumed instead, the tax each person saved by switching from cheese to bread had to be paid by somebody else, the required tax rate was slightly higher than it would otherwise have been, and there was a less than optimal mix of bread and cheese consumed. In chapter 9, the deadweight loss in taxation was a reflection of the reduction in total output from the tax-induced switch from paid work to untaxable do-it-yourself activities. Since do-it-yourself activities were exempted from tax, each person was inclined, in his own interest to do less work for pay and more do-it-yourself activities than would be appropriate if all sources of income could be taxed.

The switch in consumption from more taxed to less taxed goods and the switch from paid work to do-it-yourself activities are not the only sources of the excess burden of taxation. As mentioned in chapter 4, the income tax entails a double taxation of saving, inducing a switch from investment to consumption not unlike the switch from cheese to bread. Taxation also provokes a diversion of private resources from the production of goods to legal tax avoidance and illegal tax evasion, together with a diversion of public expenditure from the provision of benefits like roads, schools, and hospitals to the detection and punishment of tax evasion. There is a compounding of the different sources of the excess burden of taxation. As shown in equation (27) of chapter 4, the marginal cost of public funds is a reflection of the shrinkage of the tax base in response to an increase in the tax rate. Demonstrated for a bread and cheese economy, this remains true of any and every source of the tax-induced shrinkage of the tax base.

The supply curve begins at a height of 1 because, when public expenditure is tiny, the required tax rate is tiny as well, and there is virtually no excess burden per dollar of public revenue. The supply curve rises steadily as additional public expenditure requires ever-higher tax rates and generates an ever-increasing excess burden of taxation. Along the supply curve for the bread and cheese economy in table 4.1, the full cost to the tax payer per additional dollar of public expenditure rose steadily from 1.07 when public revenue is $3.50 per person per week, to 1.3 when public revenue is $6.00 dollars per person per week, to $1.83 when public revenue is $7.50 per person per week. A similar story could be told about the choice in chapter 9 between paid labor and

Table 10.4   Recalculation of costs and rates of return when the marginal cost of public funds is 1.5

Roads	Cost as seen by the Ministry of Transport ($ million)	Cost borne by the tax payer ($ million)	Annual benefit ($ million)	Rate of return as assessed by the tax payer (%)
A	100	150	12	8.00
B	30	45	2.1	4.60
C	400	600	44	7.30
D	600	900	30	3.33
E	500	750	100	13.33
F	30	45	3.9	8.60

do-it-yourself activities. In general, the supply curve would reflect a compounding of all sources of the excess burden of taxation.

The economy-wide marginal cost of public funds (indicated as mcpf on figure 10.1) identifies the cut-off for public projects, programs, and policies. Those with benefit–cost ratios above the marginal cost of public funds are undertaken. Those with benefit–cost ratios below the marginal cost of public funds are not. In practice, the economy-wide marginal cost of public funds varies from time to time and from place to place in accordance with the characteristics of the economy and the share of the government in the national income. The determination of the marginal cost of public funds is complex and judgmental because every facet of taxation must be taken into account. Estimates at various times and places suggest that the marginal cost of public funds might be in the order of 1.5, and we shall suppose that to be so. A marginal cost of public funds of 1.5 means that the cost to the tax payer of any program or project is $1.50 per extra dollar of tax revenue acquired. Table 10.3 above shows the costs and benefits of the five roads as they appear to the accountant in the Ministry of Transport. To say that the marginal cost of public funds is 1.5 is to say that all costs should be marked up by 50 percent to account for the excess burden of taxation. With this rule in place, the recalculation of costs and benefits of the five roads is as shown in table 10.4.

Ignoring deadweight loss and postulating a market-wide rate of interest of 8 percent, we tentatively inferred from the information in table 10.3 that roads A, C, E, and F are worth building while roads B and D are not. A marginal cost of public funds of 1.5 raises all costs accordingly. Now, of the six roads, only roads E and F yield more than the required 8 percent, though a third road, A, is just on the margin.

The simultaneous determination in figure 10.1 of total public expenditure and the marginal cost of public funds is based on the assumptions that society's only concern in choosing projects, programs, and policies is to ensure that the benefit exceeds the full cost inclusive of the deadweight loss in taxation, and that the allocation of cost and benefit among people can be safely ignored. The analysis suggests a simple rule of thumb for the government to follow. Undertake projects, programs, and activities if and only if the benefit–cost ratio (where cost is measured net of the deadweight loss in taxation) exceeds the marginal cost of public funds. Admittedly, projects, programs, and policies are not neutral in their impacts on different people. One project is especially beneficial to the rich. Another is especially beneficial to the poor. Another is especially beneficial to people in the east. Another is especially beneficial to people in the west. The rationale for this rule of thumb is that it makes most people better off in the long run than any other procedure the government might adopt.

The rule requires justification. To argue that the rule is appropriate, one would need, at a minimum, to identify simple cases where it is unambiguously right. Two such cases are especially interesting. The first is where people are identical in every respect, so that everybody's benefit and cost from any given project are the same. The rule is clearly appropriate in this case as long as projects are financed by ordinary taxation, but it is open to the objection that, if people really were identical, projects would be financed by lump sum taxes instead. Consider the derivation of the full cost of additional public expenditure in chapter 4. If people really were identical, it would be silly for the government to raise public revenue, denominated in bread, by a tax on cheese. Far better to impose a uniform head tax of a certain number of loaves of bread, eliminating all deadweight loss because the tax-induced wedge between the demand price and the supply price of cheese would be removed. To look upon the rule of thumb as being strictly correct for a society of identical people, it would be necessary to forbid lump sum taxation, recognizing by the back door that people are not really identical at all.

Another simple interpretation of the rule of thumb links the discussion of costs and benefits of projects in this section with the discussion in the last chapter of the determination by the median voter of the rate of the negative income tax. The rule of thumb is strictly valid for a community of people whose incomes differ but whose benefits and costs of each and every project are proportional to their incomes. The assumption is that if a project costs $100 per head and yields benefits of $200 per head, the benefit and cost to a person with the average income are $200 and $100, the benefit and cost to a person with twice the average income are $400 and $200, the benefit and cost to a person with half the average income are $100 and $50, and so on.

Generalizing, the simplification is that a project yielding total benefits of $B in an economy with N people would yield an average benefit per person of (B/N), but its benefit to person i with income y_i becomes $(y_i/y_{av})(B/N)$ where y_{av} is the average income per person. Similarly, a project with a total cost of $C, inclusive of the excess burden of taxation, would entail an average cost of (C/N), but its cost to person i becomes $(y_i/y_{av})(C/N)$. This is obviously so for the proportional income tax. Assume this allocation holds for the additional excess burden as well. Think of the allocation of benefits and cost in accordance with people's incomes as a paradigm case, against which other possibilities may be compared. Wealthier people are assumed to place higher valuations on the benefits of public undertakings, but to bear proportionately more of the tax and the associated deadweight loss.

This assumption eliminates all conflict of interest in the choice of public projects, programs and activities, for, if one of two projects has the higher benefit–cost ratio for me, it must have the higher benefit–cost ratio for you as well. The assumption has an important bearing on the meaning of the scale of the vertical axis for the demand

and supply curves in figure 10.1. Now, the height of the demand curve is not just the benefit per dollar of additional public expenditure. It is the benefit per dollar of additional public expenditure on the understanding that benefit is allocated among people in proportion to their incomes. The height of the supply curve is not just the full cost to the tax payer per additional dollar of public revenue. It is the full cost to the taxpayer on the understanding that taxes and the excess burden of taxation are borne by different people in proportion to their incomes. For any particular person, a benefit or cost is higher or lower than indicated by the demand and supply curves of figure 10.1 depending on whether his income is greater or less than the average.

This restriction on the allocation among people of the benefits and costs of projects permits a sharp distinction to be drawn between "ordinary" taxation and expenditure with costs and benefits accruing to people in proportion to their incomes and "lump sum" taxation and transfers with costs and benefits that are always the same for everybody. A lump sum tax is a fixed dollar value of tax per person, rich or poor. A lump sum transfer is a fixed payment by the government to every person, rich or poor. The lump sum transfer was exemplified by the demogrant in the negative income tax discussed in the last chapter. Of course, these instruments cannot be employed simultaneously because they would cancel out.

The new, more structured scaling of the vertical axis allows lump sum taxes and transfers to be linked to ordinary expenditure, but the equivalence varies from one person to the next in accordance with one's income. For example, for a person whose income is twice the national average, a lump sum tax of $1.00 per head is equivalent to only 50¢ per head of ordinary taxation because the cost to that person of 50¢ per head of ordinary taxation is a full dollar. When 50¢ per head is raised by ordinary taxation and when each person's burden of taxation is proportional to his income, that person's burden of taxation must be a full dollar which is equivalent in his assessment to a lump sum tax of $1.00. Similarly, for a person whose income is half the national average, a lump sum tax of $1.00 per head is linked on the vertical axis of figure 10.1 to ordinary taxation of $2.00 per head because that person's share of $2.00 of ordinary taxation is only $1.00.

Now consider the median voter whose preferences are assumed to determine all expenditure and taxation. In this analysis, two cases must be carefully distinguished. In the first case, the government can raise a lump sum tax or supply a lump sum subsidy to each and every person, without exception, and the median voter is utterly self-interested in his choice of public revenue and taxation. In the second case, poverty limits the scope of lump sum taxation and the median voter may be somewhat altruistic. Begin with the first case.

The median voter is considering whether to allocate an extra dollar of public expenditure per person to increasing the demogrant or to undertaking an ordinary public expenditure yielding a benefit per person of b dollars where, as we have assumed, the benefit is allocated among people in accordance with their incomes. Ignoring any extra administrative cost of taxation, an extra dollar per person spent to increase the demogrant provides the median voter with exactly $1. An extra dollar per person spent on the additional project yields an average benefit of $b but a benefit to the median voter of only $b(y_{med}/y_{av})$. The median voter is indifferent between an addition to the demogrant and equally costly additional provision of ordinary public services – extra

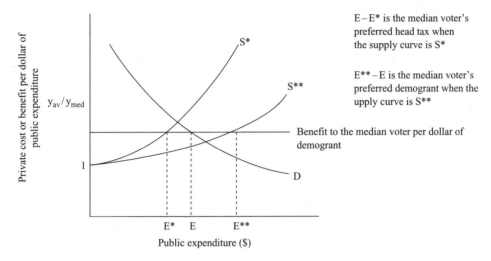

Figure 10.2 Redistribution of income and the marginal cost of public funds.

expenditure on the army, education, health care and so on – when the benefits to himself of the two options are the same, that is when $b(y_{med}/y_{av}) = 1$. That being so, the median voter can only be content with the apportionment of public expenditure between ordinary public projects and the demogrant when

$$b = (y_{av}/y_{med}) \qquad (4)$$

A demogrant or head tax is equivalent in the eyes of the median voter to an extra tax or benefit (allocated among people in proportion to their incomes) of y_{av}/y_{med} dollars. The median voter sees an equivalence between one dollar per head allocated equally to everybody and y_{av}/y_{med} dollars per head allocated among people in proportion to their original incomes. As represented by the units on the vertical axis of figure 10.1, the benefit to the median voter of an additional dollar of demogrant is not one dollar, but y_{av}/y_{med} dollars.

The simultaneous choice by the median voter of dollar values of ordinary public expenditure and the demogrant or head tax is illustrated in figure 10.2 which is a reproduction of figure 10.1 with additional information. His valuation per dollar of head tax or demogrant is represented by the height of the flat line a distance y_{av}/y_{med} above the horizontal axis. The median voter may or may not favor the redistribution of income depending, primarily, on the shape of the supply curve for public funds. Figure 10.2 shows two alternative supply curves of public funds, a steeper supply curve, S^*, and a flatter supply curve, S^{**}. Figure 10.2 illustrates how a demogrant or head tax drives the equilibrium marginal cost of public funds up or down toward the ratio y_{av}/y_{med}. Precisely the same argument can be made about the head tax. The median voter wants additional public revenue to be acquired by a head tax rather than by ordinary taxation as soon as the full cost per dollar of additional public revenue exceeds y_{av}/y_{med}.

The equilibrium marginal cost of public funds cannot be less than y_{av}/y_{med} because, if it were, the median voter would favor an increase in the demogrant, and the equilibrium marginal cost of public funds cannot be more than y_{av}/y_{med} because, if it were, the median voter would favor a decrease in the lump tax. If public expenditure lifts the marginal cost of public funds substantially as indicated by the supply curve S*, the crossing of the demand and supply curves occurs above the flat line at a height representing the cost or benefit to the median voter per dollar of head tax or demogrant. In that event, the median voter wants the government to undertake E dollars of public expenditure financed by E* dollars of ordinary taxation and a head tax of $E - E^*$ dollars. If public expenditure lifts the marginal cost of public funds moderately as indicated by the supply curve S**, the crossing of the demand and supply curves occurs below the flat line at a height representing the cost or benefit to the median voter per dollar of head tax or demogrant. In that event, the median voter would want the government to raise E** dollars of revenue by ordinary taxation, to undertake E dollars of ordinary public expenditure and to supply a demogrant of $E^{**} - E$ dollars. In either case, the equilibrium marginal cost of public funds must be y_{av}/y_{med}.[2]

For Canada in the year 1998, the ratio of average family income to median family income was about 1.2 [all family units, 1998]. If the marginal cost of public funds would exceed 1.2 in the absence of a lump sum tax, the median voter would favor the introduction of a lump sum tax. If the marginal cost of public funds would be less than 1.2 in the absence of a lump sum transfer, the median voter would favor the introduction of a lump sum transfer. In either case the marginal cost of public funds settles down at 1.2.

This explanation of how lump sum taxes or transfers constrain the marginal cost of public funds depends critically on the assumption that each and every person, without exception, can be subsidized or taxed alike. Drop that assumption and the clean results of the preceding paragraph begin to disintegrate. As the assumption is not unreasonable for a lump sum transfer, the estimate in the preceding paragraph may be reasonable as a lower limit to the marginal cost of public funds when the supply curve in figure 10.2 rises slowly enough that a lump sum transfer is warranted. Lump sum taxation is different because some people are deemed too poor to pay the tax. This constraint may raise the marginal cost of public funds considerably. For example, if 25 percent of the population were deemed too poor to pay the lump sum tax, then the cost to the median voter per dollar of tax revenue (per person) raised by the lump sum taxation must rise from \$1 (which is what the median voter actually pays) to \$1.33 (equal to $1/(0.75)$ which is what the median voter must pay to increase the revenue from the lump sum tax by \$1 per person in the population as a whole). Furthermore, since the median voter pays only 83¢ $(1/1.2)$ per dollar of ordinary tax revenue, the full cost per dollar of additional public revenue must rise to \$1.60 (1.33×1.2) before it becomes in the interest of the median voter to raise additional public revenue by a head tax instead. The exemption from the head tax of 25 percent of the population raises the marginal cost of public funds from \$1.20 per dollar of public expenditure to \$1.60. Generalizing, it may be said that the median voter is only content with the mix of ordinary taxation and lump sum taxation once the marginal cost of public funds has risen not to y_{av}/y_{med} but to $(y_{av}/y_{med})/s$ where s is the proportion of the population paying the head tax.

That is not the end of our difficulties. The exemption from the head tax must be based on some minimal income. Suppose the minimal income is $20,000 and the head tax is $1,000 per person. In these circumstances, anybody who, in the absence of the head tax, would have a taxable income between $20,000 and $21,000 is provided by the tax with an incentive to lower his declared taxable income – working less or evading more – below the critical threshold at which the exemption takes effect. Even people whose incomes are somewhat higher than $21,000 might be inclined to take steps to drive taxable income below $20,000 to avoid the head tax. This contraction of taxable income is a kind of deadweight loss that must be taken into account when assessing the effect of lump sum taxation, and the equilibrium marginal cost of public funds must rise accordingly. The flat line in figure 10.2 begins to curve upward soon after the transition from lump sum transfer to lump sum tax. The ratio of median to average income becomes a lower bound to the marginal cost of public funds, effective in the event that the supply curve of public funds is low enough for a lump sum subsidy to be warranted, but not binding when a lump sum tax is imposed. These difficulties would normally rule out the lump sum tax as a practical proposition. The simple story in figure 10.1 may be essentially right except when the supply curve of public funds is low enough to warrant a lump sum subsidy.

There is also a political reason why it is neither possible nor desirable for the government to trace the beneficiaries of each and every project. An omniscient, omnipotent, and benevolent planner would maximize the value of some social welfare function by weighing the benefits of all projects according to the incomes of the people to whom those benefits accrue. A democratic society must eschew such fine computations. A great virtue of benefit–cost analysis is that it is blind. Costs are weighed against benefits, to whomsoever the benefits accrue. A simple rule suppresses conflict among potential recipients, avoiding the scramble for public largess and the vast potential conflict among would-be beneficiaries that would otherwise occur. The best rule in the circumstances is whatever is likely to benefit most people in the long run. The question is how and to what extent, in forming such a rule, the marginal cost of public funds should be taken into account. The "right" marginal cost of public funds is the most appropriate mark-up cost in this context. Even so, the weighing of benefits might be slanted to take account of their apportionment among people and of the incentives they generate. Other things being equal, a project favoring the poor might be preferred over a project favoring the rich, or, where the excess burden of taxation arises from the diversion of effort from labour to leisure, a project, such as a training school, that encourages people to work might be favored over a project, such as a park, that encourages people to take more leisure.

Finally, it should be stressed that the excess burden of taxation only arises because, and only because, of people's individually advantageous but socially disadvantageous maneuvers to reduce the amount of tax they pay. There could be no excess burden if each person's tax assessment could be set independently of his behavior. A head tax would do, but that would impose a very great burden upon the poor. A skill tax would do as well. There could be no maneuvering to reduce one's tax bill if the government could observe each person's ability and impose taxes accordingly. That will not do, in practice, because skill cannot be observed or assessed objectively as a tax base.

The closest observable counterpart to skill is income which can be influenced by working less, by diverting labor time from taxable work for pay to untaxable do-it-yourself activities or by diverting effort from production of goods to tax avoidance or tax evasion. Starting from any tax system whatsoever, all deadweight loss could be eliminated by an agreement or contract among tax payers to abolish the system by which each person's tax is determined but to continue paying the same tax as before. Such an agreement would allow each person to make the best use of his resources without at the same time reducing total public revenue. The excess burden arises because no such agreement could be enforced.

THE EVALUATION OF PERSONAL GOODS

Most goods – like bread and cheese in the models of the economy in chapters 3 and 4 – have market prices which are the same for everybody, but there are exceptions. Some goods cannot be traded between people at uniform market-wide prices because they are attached to their users. Eggs are ordinary goods because everybody, old and young, rich and poor, pays the same price for a dozen eggs at the grocery store. Leisure is a personal good because people place different values on an hour of leisure. A highly skilled person who earns $300 per hour and who may work as many or as few hours as he pleases places a value of $300 on an hour of leisure because, if his value of leisure were less than $300, he would work more, and, if his value of leisure were more than $300, he would work less. An unskilled person who earns a minimum wage of $6 an hour and who can also work as many or as few hours as he pleases places a value of about $6 on an hour of leisure. There can be no uniform economy-wide price of leisure because there is no mechanism enabling people with low valuations of leisure relative to goods to sell leisure at a uniform market-wide price to people with high valuations of leisure relative to goods. Mortality rates are also personal goods because people differ in their willingness to pay for small reductions in their mortality rates. Typically, a rich person is willing to pay a relatively high price for a given reduction in his mortality rate, as, for instance, when he buys a safe but expensive car that the poor cannot afford.

Personal goods create two sorts of problems for cost–benefit analysis: (1) how to value personal goods, such as time saved or lives saved due to improvements in transport, when people may or may not differ in their valuations of personal goods, but decision-makers have no information whatsoever about whether or to what extent beneficiaries' valuations differ from one project to the next, and, (2) how to compare projects when the beneficiaries of one project are known to place higher values on personal goods than the beneficiaries of another project. The latter question is whether a higher value should be placed on an hour of time saved or a life saved in the avoidance of road accidents in a project where the beneficiaries are rich (and therefore likely to place high valuations on time saved and lives saved) than in another project where the beneficiaries are poor. We shall discuss these matters in turn, with special reference not to leisure, but to the value of life. The remainder of this section is about the choice of a value of life for cost–benefit analysis on the working assumption that everybody's

Table 10.5 Number of lives saved and cost per life saved in eight road safety projects

Road safety projects	Cost of the project ($ millions)	Number of lives saved	Cost per life saved ($ millions)
a	30	20	1.5
b	120	200	0.6
c	150	50	3
d	20	40	0.5
e	500	250	2
f	60	2	30
g	48	6	8
h	80	100	0.8

value of life is the same. Differences among beneficiaries of projects will be discussed in the following section.

The Ministry of Transport is contemplating a number of projects to improve the safety of roads. Eight projects are under consideration. Their costs in millions of dollars and their expected numbers of lives saved are as shown in table 10.5. (Assume for convenience that the projects have no benefits other than lives saved, and that the saving of lives occurs over a short enough period of time that the discounting of costs and benefits accruing at different times can be ignored.)

What ought the Ministry of Transport to do? We cannot slough off the problem with platitudes about the pricelessness of life because the trade-off between money and life is inescapable. We routinely trade money for lives in decisions about medical care when, for instance, we decide whether or not to adopt expensive but potentially life-saving procedures, or whether or not to undertake expensive research which may in time give rise to live-saving discoveries. We could spend the entire national income on medical care before exhausting all the opportunities to save lives at a price. If lives were priceless, we would never build tall buildings, send sailors to sea or collect ore in mines. Implicitly or explicitly, we must place a value on life, saying, in effect, that a life is worth saving if it can be saved for less than some dollar amount, but not otherwise. We must do so because the alternative is to throw lives away, for instance, in spending ten million dollars to save a life in one highly visible project but refusing to spend five million dollars to save two other lives elsewhere.

A distinction must be drawn in this context between an actual life and a statistical life. To say that one's value of life is, for instance, five million dollars is not to say that one would voluntarily give up one's life for five million dollars. That is not what the statement means. To say that one's value of life is five million dollars is to say how much he would be prepared to spend to avoid a small risk of losing his life. It is to say one would spend up to $100 to avoid a one in 50,000 chance of losing his life, or would spend up to $1,000 to avoid a one in 5,000 chance of losing his life, or that 1,000 people just like him would together pay $5,000,000 to save one randomly chosen life among them. We make such calculations all the time in deciding when to use a

Table 10.6   Projects reordered by cost per life saved

Road safety projects	Cost of the project ($ millions)	Number of lives saved	Cost per life saved ($ millions)	Cumulative expenditure ($ millions)	Cumulative number of lives saved
d	20	40	0.5	20	40
b	120	200	0.6	140	240
h	80	100	0.8	220	340
a	30	20	1.5	250	360
e	500	250	2	750	610
c	150	50	3	900	660
g	48	6	8	948	666
f	60	2	30	1,008	668

seat belt, when to undergo expensive medical tests, how fast to drive, and whether to take a dangerous job. (The decision about how fast to drive is a trade-off between mortality and time in the first instance, but time itself is valued in money.) There is, furthermore, a natural transition between the small and the large. If each person in a community of one million people would spend $100 to avoid a one in 50,000 chance of losing his life, then the entire community would spend $100 million for the virtual certainty of saving 20 lives (1,000,000/50,000), at a cost of $5,000,000 per life. Risk to the individual is a certainty to the community as a whole.

Suppose Parliament supplies the Ministry of Transport with a budget for road safety, and instructs the ministry to use the available funds to save as many lives as it can. With these instructions, there is a best way for the ministry to proceed. On the working assumption that a life is a life is a life regardless of whose life is saved, the ministry allocates its budget among projects to maximize the number of lives saved. The simplest procedure is to reorder the projects in table 10.5 according to the cost per life saved as shown in table 10.6. The logic of the reordering is that with a budget of only $20 million, the efficient procedure for the Ministry of Transport is to undertake the first project, d. When the budget is increased to $140 million, the Ministry of Transport should undertake the first two projects, d and b. When the budget is increased to $400 million, the Ministry of Transport should undertake the first three projects, and so on. The first four columns in table 10.6 are the same as in table 10.5. Each row in the fifth column in table 10.6 shows the cumulative cost when the project in that row and all preceding projects are undertaken. Each row in the final column in table 10.6 shows the cumulative number of lives saved when the project in that row and all preceding projects are undertaken. Thus, for example with a budget of $750 million, the Ministry of Transport would undertake projects d, b, h, a, and e which together save 610 lives. No other combination of safety projects saves more lives at that cost.

There is another possibility. Parliament may supply the Ministry of Transport with a "value of life." The ministry would be instructed to undertake those, and only those, projects for which the cost per life saved is less than the prescribed value of life. The value of life in this context is the amount of money the government is prepared to spend to save a randomly chosen life. For example, a value of life of $2 million means that the government stands ready to spend up to, but not beyond, $2 million per life saved. With a value of life of $2 million, road safety projects d, b, h, a, and e would be undertaken, but not projects c, g, and f. Notice the correspondence between the value of life and the budget for road safety of the Ministry of Transport. To set a budget of $750 million is, implicitly, to set a value of life of $2 million, and vice versa. However, Parliament may prefer to present the ministry with a value of life rather than with a budget to maintain a balance between life-saving expenditures of different kinds. Just as it would be inefficient for the Ministry of Transport to spend $150 million on project c rather than on projects b and d, so too would it be inefficient to maintain different values of life in, for example, road safety and medical care. Other things being equal, a discrepancy between the values of life in the two departments of government would constitute a waste of lives. For any total expenditure on life-saving in the two departments together, fewer lives would be saved when the values of life are allowed to differ than when they are required to be the same.

What value of life might the government choose for this purpose? In approaching this question, the reader might consider his own value of life not as a reflection of his willingness to pay for the avoidance of certain death, but as a reflection of his willingness to purchase the avoidance of a small risk of losing his life in any of the many decisions we make every day – care in crossing the street, using or not using a seat belt, taking a more or less dangerous job, or deciding how fast to drive. To discover *your own* value of life, imagine yourself confronted with the Angel of Death who holds an urn in one hand and a scythe in the other. The urn contains 999 blue balls and one red ball. At a price, the Angel of Death will ignore you for the present. Otherwise, if you refuse to pay the price, the Angel of Death reaches into the urn and pulls out a ball at random. If that ball turns out to be blue you escape. If that ball turns out to be red, the Angel of Death makes an end of you with his scythe. Your value of life is a reflection of what you would be prepared to pay to the Angel of Death to ignore you. If, for example, you would be prepared to pay up to $2,000, then your value of life must be $2,000,000 [2,000 × (1/1,000)]. The value of life is the amount that a group of people just like you would be prepared to pay to save one life for certain, where nobody knows who among you would be the one to perish.

In principle, the Ministry of Transport could determine a value of life by asking people directly and adopting the average of the respondents' valuations as the appropriate guide for cost–benefit analysis. That procedure is unlikely to be satisfactory in practice because people have difficulty deciding how they would behave in hypothetical situations. Instead, the ministry might observe the value of life implicit in actual behavior in the market. A value of life is implicit in "danger pay," the additional wage one requires to accept a risky job. Suppose that jobs in mining are "above ground" and "below ground," that both types of jobs are equally skilled and equally onerous, but that the risk of losing one's life at work is 1 in 2,000 per year above ground and 1 in 1,000 per year below ground. If the equilibrium wages of miners are $50,000 per year above ground and $52,000 per year below ground, then miners' value of life must be $4,000,000. A group of 2,000 miners receives an extra $4,000,000 [(52,000 − 50,000) × 2,000] as payment for an expected loss of one life among them. If all citizens were exactly like the miners in this respect, they would require their government to spend up to $4,000,000 per life saved in public projects. In our road safety example, they would want all projects but g and f to be undertaken. Of course, citizens are not alike in this respect, and the government must draw a balance between the interests of people with high values of life and people with low values of life.

A bias against the poor

Valuation of life or leisure become especially problematic when public projects have different impacts upon the rich and upon the poor. Some projects are especially beneficial to the rich. Other projects are especially beneficial to the poor. In assessing costs and benefits of two projects, should the administrator value lives saved in each project according to the value of life of its beneficiaries exclusively, or should the decision-maker adopt a common value of lives saved for both projects together? Respect for private valuation would mirror the market where, for instance, the rich buy expensive safe cars and the poor get by with relatively unsafe jalopies. In fact, in North America today, the average length of life of the wealthiest fifth of the population is a full ten years more than the average length of life of the poorest fifth.

Consider two projects, one to improve the safety of buses used by the poor, and the other to improve the safety of aeroplanes used by the rich. Assume (1) that the projects must be undertaken and financed by the public sector or not at all, (2) that each project costs $25 million, (3) that the project for safety on buses is expected to save the lives of 20 travellers, (4) that the project for safety on aeroplanes is expected to save the lives of 10 travellers, and (5) that the value of life of the rich is $3 million, while the value of life of the poor is only $1 million. How do we evaluate these projects? If the public sector treats all lives as equally valuable, regardless of differences among people's own values of life, then the project for safety on buses would be placed ahead of the project for safety on aeroplanes. Both projects would be undertaken if the prescribed value of life were greater than $2.5 million. Neither project would be undertaken if the prescribed value of life were less than $1.25 million. Between these limits, the bus project would be undertaken but the aeroplane project would not. Alternatively, if the administrator respects people's own valuation of life as revealed in the market, he would undertake the aeroplane project but not the bus project. The aeroplane project costs $25 million and yields benefits assessed at $30 million. The bus project costs $25 million and yields benefits assessed at only $20 million. The value of life of the rich who use aeroplanes is $1 million which is above maximal value of life – $2.5 million – at which an expenditure of $25 million to save 10 lives is justified. The value of life of the poor who use buses is $1 million which is below the minimal value of life – $1.25 million – at which an expenditure of $25 million to save 20 lives is justified. Valuing beneficiaries' lives at their own valuations, cost–benefit analysis would pass the project for the rich and fail the project for the poor, even though both projects cost the same and more lives are saved in the latter project.

Should private valuations of personal goods be respected in public decision-making? Bear in mind that this outcome of rigid cost–benefit analysis is precisely what the rich and the poor would each arrange for themselves if the projects were financed by their beneficiaries. A legislature of the rich would choose to finance the project for safety in aeroplanes. A legislature of the poor would choose not to finance the project for safety in buses. A cost–benefit rule respecting private valuations could make everybody better off if projects were combined with transfers from beneficiaries to non-beneficiaries.

There is, on the other hand, something distinctly unpleasant about the government saying, in effect, that the lives of the rich are worth more than the lives of the poor, as would implicitly be said if more public resources were spent to save the life of a rich person than to save the life of a poor person. Though society cannot escape from having to trade money for lives and though rates of trade-off in the public sector are usually arranged to reflect rates of trade-off in the private sector, most people are unwilling to follow the market completely when lives are at stake. Perhaps, like the right to vote, public-sector projects are placed in the domain of equality. We allow unequal ownership of property and unequal enjoyment of the goods that private income may procure, but we maintain equal civil rights including people's rights as beneficiaries of public projects. We recognize that public facilities will be used unequally, that a particular road, for example, conveys more benefit to some people than to others, but we balk at rules that seem to favor one class over another. In practice, the government may treat all lives as equal even though the market would do otherwise. In the market where all dollars are equal, the high value of life of the rich automatically takes precedence over the low value of life of the poor. In the public sector where all people are equal, all lives may be equal too.

Judgment versus calculation

Not all public administration can be reduced to the acceptance or rejection of projects on the strength of the well-specified rules of cost–benefit analysis. Many aspects of public administration and public expenditure require the administrator to judge what is best for society within the domain of his authority. Such judgment cannot always be reduced to precise calculation. Consider the university. The university is, in effect if not in law, a department of government granted substantial independence in teaching and research because voters and legislators know that *their* purposes for the university are best served by leaving the university alone or by limiting public supervision to broad guidelines for the use of public money. Within the university, administrators and professors are expected to direct their time and resources to the acquisition and transmission of knowledge. They choose research projects, write articles and books, decide what courses to offer, arrange the content of each course, set reading lists, hire new professors, and so on. In doing so, they are expected to serve what they see as the common good, but there is no accurate *quantitative* measure of whether and to what extent this amorphous goal is achieved. Some aspects of academic life are amenable to precise evaluation, but it would be silly to suppose that the whole of academic life can be subsumed within the domain of cost–benefit analysis. There is no substitute for the practitioner's judgment of what is best, where "best" in this context must ultimately refer to the common good of society as a whole.

The same is true of other branches of public administration. The maximization of life expectancy may serve as a rough and provisional criterion for public expenditure on medical care, but that criterion cannot be applied mechanically and cannot displace personal judgment altogether. The maximization of life expectancy is insufficient as a guide for weighting reductions in mortality rates at different ages. The life of an old person should count less than the life of a child but not necessarily in direct proportion to their life expectancies. Pain, suffering and the quality of life must be considered along with longevity. Fundamental research is expected to contribute to social welfare in the long run, but the outcome of medical research is too uncertain for any meaningful measure of benefits to be attached to each and every project. There is also a complex trade-off between efficiency and equality when, for example, the cost of medical procedures is higher in the sparsely populated north than in the densely populated south. A balance must be drawn in public provision of medical care between the risk of gross wastefulness and inefficiency in the complete absence of measurement, however inexact, and the opposite risk of wastefulness and inefficiency when only measurable benefits are recognized.

Efficiency and Redistribution

The redistribution of income was introduced in the last chapter in a world where narrowly self-interested voters determine the rate of the negative income tax. The analysis was focused on why a majority of the poor do not employ the vote to expropriate the rich altogether. For that purpose and to explain the emergence of an electoral equilibrium tax rate well short of 100 percent, it was useful to assume that each voter's only concern was to maximize his own post-tax, post-transfer income. At least three other concerns might be identified: altruism, insurance, and fear. We may favor the redistribution of income because we are good Samaritans not wishing to see other people starving on the streets, or, less dramatically, willing to give up some of our own income to improve the lot of people very much worse off than ourselves. As a vehicle for such altruism, public redistribution may be preferable to private charity because all prosperous people are compelled to contribute a share. If I am one of 1,000 rich people, my contribution of a dollar of private charity augments the total income of the poor by one dollar, but my contribution of one dollar through taxation imposed on all rich people augments the income of the poor by $1,000. We may favor the redistribution of income because, in this uncertain world, we ourselves might one day become poor – or our children or grandchildren might become poor – and we want there to be a safety net when we need it. People rich enough to be net contributors to a system of redistribution of income may favor it out of fear that the poor, if denied a safety net, would rise up and destroy the system of private property on which the good fortune of the rich depends. The multiplicity of motives complicates the picture of voting in the last chapter, but it need not destroy the electoral equilibrium altogether. Actual redistribution, as practiced in most societies, is much more complex and imposes substantially more responsibility upon the government. Actual redistribution is typically a combination of *progressive* taxation, *targeted* transfers of income, and provision of specific public services.

The negative income tax has never been adopted by any country, but almost all tax systems are, at least in principle, progressive. Progressivity may be with respect to *average* tax rates or with respect to *marginal* tax rates. Average tax rates are said to be progressive when, the higher one's income, the larger is the ratio of one's tax bill to one's pre-tax income. Marginal tax rates are said to be progressive when, the higher one's income, the higher the tax rate on each additional dollar of income. Consider a tax schedule with no tax on the first $15,000 of income, a 10 percent tax on the next $15,000, a 25 percent tax on the next $20,000, and a 50 percent tax on the rest. A person earning $40,000 would pay $4,000 of tax (nothing on the first $15,000 of income, $1,500 of tax on the next $15,000 of income, and $2,500 of tax on the remaining $10,000). His marginal tax rate would be 25 percent, but his average tax rate would be only 10 percent. A person earning $100,000 would pay $33,000 of tax. His average tax rate would be 33 percent, but his marginal tax rate would be 50 percent. When the lump sum transfer is taken into account, the average tax rate in the negative income tax is progressive even though the marginal tax rate is not. Actual tax codes are typically complex, and overall progressivity is correspondingly difficult to assess. Mortgage payments may or may not be deducted from taxable income. Corporation income tax may or may not be credited against the tax liabilities of the shareholders of the corporation. The line between personal expenses and business expenses is notoriously hard to draw. Some but not all savings may be deducted from taxable income. Progressivity of the income tax begins to look like a negative income tax when a large chunk of services is supplied equally to all citizens by the government. It is more like a negative income tax when medical care is provided by the government than when each person provides for his own medical care through the market.

Disbursement of public revenue to citizens is typically targeted rather than universal. The demogrant in the negative income tax is provided to everybody, young or old, rich or poor. In practice, redistribution is directed to specific groups of people: the disabled, the unemployed, the old. Targeting requires an administrative procedure to insure that the appropriate people, and nobody else, are subsidized. It automatically transforms the targeted groups of people into factions, each seeking to enlarge its grants at the expense of the rest of the population. Just as taxation creates an incentive on the part of the tax payer to shift from more tax to less taxed goods or activities, so too does targeting induce people to alter their activities to become eligible for grants. For example, people become less anxious to remain employed when there is unemployment insurance than when there is not. On the other hand, targeting concentrates public largess on people deemed in need of it, lowering the overall tax bill and reducing every tax payer's incentive to divert effort from taxed to untaxed activities.

Universal programs tend to provide services rather than money, the two most important services being public education and public medical care. A natural starting place for the examinations of such programs is the general argument that transfers to people should always be in cash rather than in kind. If the government is going to spend $100 per head on transfers to people, that $100 should be in cash rather than, for example, in providing everybody with a woolen sweater because, useful as a sweater may be, we are all better off with cash we can spend either on a sweater or on something else we value more. The question becomes what, if anything, differentiates public education and public medical care from public sweaters. Some say that there is no difference and that public provision of services is never warranted. Others justify public provision of education and health care as the purveyors of externalities. The justification is that the unaided market which would supply the appropriate number of sweaters would supply too little and inappropriate kinds of education and health care, or that each person's education and health care is of concern to everybody else in a way that each person's purchase of sweaters is not. Public provision would then become a fusion of redistribution and of corrections for externalities. For education, the argument is that we are all concerned about the next generation, through pure altruism or to provide an environment where our own children may flourish. Selfish as we may be in relation to people who are poor now, we may look upon all children as to some extent our children and we may wish them all a more or less equal start in life.

The rationale for public provision of medical care may be a mixture of commodity-specific altruism and insurance. People who do not care whether their fellow citizens live in big houses or little houses may, nevertheless, be prepared to sacrifice a part of their incomes to ensure that their fellow citizens get adequate medical treatment. People may also favor public provision of medical care as insurance because they fear that they themselves may become sick. The insurance argument must come to terms with the possibility of private insurance. If I can insure against the cost of illness, then public provision of medical care becomes like public provision of sweaters, something I can provide for myself though I may not choose to do so. On the other hand, as discussed above in the section on risk and with reference to the choice between the professions of law and medicine, there are risks against which one cannot adequately insure. Law would have been everybody's preferred profession if the risk of low income could have been insured away. That was not possible because too much was assumed to be known about each person's prospects as a lawyer at the time he would have applied for insurance and because of the moral hazard problem that people insured against low income lose the incentive to work hard, educate themselves or invest and because of the adverse selection problem that people who know themselves to be potential low-earners but are not known as such by the insurance company take out income-insurances, while people who know themselves to be potential high-earners do not. There are analogous problems with the private provision of medical care. Private insurance is invariably incomplete because illness is not entirely random. Insurance companies can segregate people according to their risk of becoming ill, charging high rates to people with greater risk and denying insurance altogether to people with the highest risk of all. Private insurance would only be complete if embryos could buy themselves lifetime insurance and if nothing could be inferred about their health status from the circumstances of their parents. Once insurance has been granted, the insurance company acquires an incentive to minimize the cost of treatment by discarding customers who become ill or by letting ill patients die. Such behavior by insurance companies is constrained to some extent by the requirements of the law and by the companies' concern to persevere a reputation for honesty, without which new customers could not be attracted. Private insurance entails a substantial overhead cost in choosing subscribers and vetting claims.

Public provision of medical care is universal, but has problems of its own. The full cost of publicly provided medical care may exceed the cost of medical care in the private sector because the extra tax that must be levied to finance public medical care adds to the overall deadweight loss in taxation. The greater the full cost per dollar of public revenue, the weaker the case for public provision becomes. All insurance, public and private, creates a moral hazard. Paid for out of general tax revenue rather than by fee-for-service, insured medical care provokes over-use of medical services. When medical care is free, patients might be inclined to visit doctors too frequently, to use too many drugs or to devote too little effort to maintaining good health. Private insurers may be better than a public insurer at constraining the demand for health services, but that is not always advantageous. Though the ideal of public provision is to treat everyone equally, that ideal is attained to a greater or lesser extent depending on the integrity of the public sector, and is never attained completely. The rich and well connected get some priority of service, are funneled to the best doctors, pushed to the head of the queue, and given the benefit of the doubt when there is some question of whether this or that service is contained in the standard health-care package. This last consideration might easily tip the balance between public and private health care. Countries weigh these considerations differently. In Canada, medical care is mostly public. In the United Kingdom, it is public but with a private fringe for those who can afford it. In the United States, it is provided only to the old and to the very poor.

CONTESTS

For the most part, governments buy what they need. Education is supplied by buying school buildings and hiring teachers. Health care is supplied by buying hospitals and hiring doctors. Defence is supplied by buying military equipment and hiring soldiers. But some public objectives are sought by contests rather than by purchase. For example, in 1713, the British government offered a great prize of £20,000, a fortune in those days, to the first person to invent a chronometer that would be accurate at sea within about a third of a second per day, and a board of longitude was established to judge when the required accuracy had been attained. The purpose of the chronometer was to enable ships to locate their positions at sea. Latitude was easy; that could be determined from angle between the north star and the horizon. Longitude could be determined from the time of sunrise or of high noon, but only if time could be measured absolutely as, for instance, Greenwich mean time. In establishing the great prize, the British Parliament did not actually buy anything or commission anybody to do anything. It arranged a contest where the activities of the competitors were expected to be beneficial to society at large.

There are many kinds of publicly sponsored contests. Some are deliberately established; others not. Some are socially beneficial; others not.

- *The contest to invent an accurate chronometer.*
- *Patent races.* As discussed in chapter 4, the patent system induces invention by providing the inventor with a monopoly on his invention. A patent race occurs when two or more firms realize that there is something useful to be invented and that the patent will be awarded to whichever firm invents first.
- *Quotas on imports.* Domestic industry could be protected equally well by tariffs or by quotas. Tariffs yield revenue for the government. Quotas yield no public

revenue. Instead, they increase the profitability of firms that are fortunate enough to receive a share of the quota. Suppose, for example, a tariff of $1 per unit of some imported good would reduce total imports from whatever they would have been in the absence of the tariff to 1 million units. If a quota of 1 million units were established instead, there would automatically be created a $1 million prize to be shared among those domestic importers fortunate enough to be assigned shares of the quota. Would-be importers compete for the prize, though no such competition may have been intended or expected when the quota was established. Competition for quotas is expensive for competitors, in wastage of time soliciting favors from officials empowered to dispense quotas, in reorganizing one's firm to make it appear quota-worthy, or in outright bribes. With free entry into the race for quotas and with many essentially identical risk-neutral contestants, the prize would normally be used up in such expenses.

- *Investment grants.* Many governments subsidize investment selectively. An investment might be subsidized because it is expected to promote a new industry or to promote employment in a poor region of the country. Government agencies are established to distinguish the worthy from the unworthy applications for grants. Ideally, grants would be awarded so judiciously that no firm's profitability is enhanced. Each recipient firm would be induced by the grant to act differently than it would otherwise be inclined to do – to hire more workers, to locate its plant in a socially desirable but less profitable part of the country, or to make investments that would otherwise be unprofitable – and these changes in the behavior of the recipient firm would be worth more to the country as a whole than the cost of the subsidies that procured them. That objective is never fully attainable in practice. Receipt of a grant is profitable to the recipient. Grants become prizes for which firms compete in ways that are privately advantageous but socially wasteful.

- *Trials.* You claim I owe you $1,000. I claim I do not. You sue me. Our dispute is then resolved in court. If judges were omniscient, no expenditure by either of us could influence the outcome of the trial. If judges are merely wise, the trial becomes expensive for both of us – in time, effort, and legal fees – for we both know that expenditure in support of one's position increases one's chance of winning the case. From one point of view, the expense of the trial, to plaintiff, to defendant and to the state, is a waste that could be avoided by bargaining in the shadow of the law, replicating privately what we predict the court will decree. In fact, most civil disputes are settled out of court. From another point of view, the expense of the trial is a necessary cost of maintenance of a civil society, for, without the law as the ultimate resolution of disputes, bargaining degenerates into vengeance and retribution with a cost to society not unlike the cost of predation in the world of fishermen and pirates in chapter 2.

- *Lobbying.* When a bill under consideration by the legislature has a special, positive or negative, impact on the profitability of particular industries, the representatives of those industries converge on legislators to persuade them to vote "correctly." The prize in this contest is a gain or an avoidance of harm. Contestants may be industries differently affected by proposed legislation, or one industry against the rest of society.

Participation in publicly sponsored contests may be classified under three headings: socially useful activities that the contest is intended to promote, bribes to public officials sponsoring or directing the contest, and pure waste. The development of an accurate chronometer, the emergence of new products in a patent race, investments which would not have been undertaken but for the offer of investment grants and which have valuable spin-offs for the community as a whole, and the maintenance of civil order through the resolution of disputes are all examples of beneficial outcomes of contests, outcomes that might not have been procurable in any other way. Contests may become the vehicle for bribery directly – as when recipients of import quotas or investment grants compensate public officials or politicians to direct public largess in their direction – or indirectly – as when would-be recipients of public favors contribute to politicians running for office or let it be known that public officials who behave reasonably can expect to be hired at lucrative salaries on retirement from public service. Contest-induced expenditure becomes wasteful when efforts to win the contest carry no public spin-off at all. A patent race can be wasteful when developments in pure science make it evident to several firms at once that a profitable invention is just over the horizon and the winner of the race is the firm that gets to the patent office a few days ahead of the rest. Import quotas and investment grants can be wasteful when the way to obtain a quota is to build excess capacity in plant and equipment, to advertise the virtues of one's firm or to redirect administrative talent from administration of production to grovelling before politicians or bureaucrats.

It is difficult to say *a priori* how to divide expenditures to win contests among the three categories. Expenditure to procure import quotas would seem to be almost entirely bribery or waste because whatever effect on the economy can be obtained by import quotas can usually be obtained equally well with tariffs yielding public revenue rather than private profit. The consequences of investment subsidies are more difficult to assess, but that difficulty itself suggests that investment subsidies are corruption-prone. There is no precise and universally recognizable test, comparable to students' grades in exams, to which the public official can appeal in deciding between two requests for investment subsidies. It is in the nature of the situation that he must exercise his own judgment in weighing the pros and cons of the options before him. In this context, there is an ongoing risk of bribery as bureaucrats are corrupted by their circumstances or as circumstances draw forth bureaucrats prone to be corrupted.

Regardless of the nature of the contestants' expenditures – whether they be socially useful or corruption or waste – these expenditures are determined in a complex process where contestants respond to one another rather than to market-determined prices. Suppose the government sets a prize of $P where, never mind why, there are only two eligible contestants called A and B, and where each contestant's probability of winning the prize depends on both contestants' *rent-seeking* expenditures. Let π_A be contestant A's probability of success and let π_B be contestant B's probability of success, where, of course, $\pi_A + \pi_B = 1$. To quantify the cost of rent-seeking, it is necessary to postulate *contest success functions* showing how each contestant's probability of attaining the prize depends upon both contestants' rent-seeking expenditures. A serviceable contest success function for a two-party contest is

$$\pi_A = E_A/(E_A + E_B) \quad \text{and} \quad \pi_B = E_B/(E_A + E_B) \tag{5}$$

where E_A is the rent-seeking expenditure of contestant A and E_B is the rent-seeking expenditure of contestant B. The contest success function is intended to represent the behavior of the government as prize-giver. Any and every reasonable contest success function must have the characteristics that (1) with only two contestants, the sum of their probabilities of success must add up to 1, and (2) the larger each party's expenditure to attain the prize, and the smaller the expenditure of its competitor, the greater is that party's probability of winning. The specific contest success function in equation (5) has these properties, but so too do other plausible functions that will not be discussed here. No explanation is being offered of why the government acts in accordance with any particular conflict success function. It is sufficient for our purposes to note that governments must respond somehow to contestants' expenditures to attain the prize and that the response in equation (5) is intended to be representative of what governments actually do.[3]

It follows at once that the expected profits of the two contestants, R_A and R_B, are

$$R_A = \pi_A P - E_A = [E_A/(E_A + E_B)]P - E_A \quad \text{and}$$
$$R_B = \pi_B P - E_B = [E_B/(E_A + E_B)]P - E_B \tag{6}$$

Each contestant's expected profit is the difference between his expected prize and his rent-seeking expenditure, where his expected prize is the prize itself weighted by his probability of winning it, and his probability of winning the prize is a function both of his rent-seeking expenditure and of that of his opponent. In equation (6), the two contestants' probabilities of attaining the prize are $E_A/(E_A + E_B)$ and $E_B/(E_A + E_B)$. Note how each contestant's optimal expenditure depends on the other contestant's expenditure. If contestant B drops out of the race and spends nothing (that is, if $E_B = 0$), then contestant A can win the race by spending next to nothing. No matter how large the prize, contestant A can win the prize for sure by spending no more than a penny as long as contestant B spends nothing at all. A larger expenditure by contestant A would be warranted to maximize his expected profit once contestant B gets back in the game. Note also that the contestants could collude to cheat the government. They could agree to spend no more than one penny each, or for one contestant to drop out of the race and the other to share the prize once it has been obtained. Such collusion would presumably be illegal and would be difficult in real situations where there may be many contestants and potential contestants.

Behavior of rational self-interested contestants can be quite complicated because each contestant's preferred expenditure depends not only on the actual expenditure of the other but on how the other can be expected to respond to one's own behavior. To derive specific results, we have recourse to a strong simplifying assumption. Suppose each party chooses his rent-seeking expenditure – contestant A chooses E_A and contestant B chooses E_B – to maximize his own expected profit on the assumption that the rent-seeking expenditure of his competitor is invariant.[3] Whatever the expenditure of contestant B, contestant A chooses his expenditure to maximize his expected profit. Whatever the expenditure of contestant A, contestant B chooses his expenditure to maximize his expected profit. For the contest success function in equation (6), a unique pair, E_A and E_B, can be found when both parties can behave in that way.

Table 10.7   Expected profits of two contestants, A and B, for a prize of $100,000

[The prize-seeking expenditure of contestant B is $25,000. Alternative prize-seeking expenditures of contestant A are listed in the first column.]

Prize-seeking expenditure of contestant A, E_A ($)	Expected profit of contestant A, R_A ($)	Expected profit of contestant B, R_B ($)	Total prize-seeking expenditure, $E_A + E_B$ ($)
0	0	75,000	25,000
10,000	18,571	46,429	35,000
20,000	24,444	30,556	45,000
25,000	25,000	25,000	50,000
30,000	24,545	20,455	55,000
50,000	16,667	8,333	75,000
75,000	0	0	100,000

Obviously, the symmetry of the problem ensures that both contestants' expenditures are the same.

It turns out that, with a prize P, the equilibrium profit-maximizing expenditures of the two parties are both $P/4$, so that half the prize accrues as net profit to the contestants and the other half is used up in seeking the prize, regardless of whether rent-seeking expenditure is socially beneficial, bribery, or waste.[4] If the prize is $100,000, then contestant A spends $25,000 to increase his probability of winning the prize, contestant B also spends $25,000, and each contestant acquires an expected net gain from the contest of $25,000. The larger the number of contestants, the larger the share of the prize that is wasted in rent-seeking expenditure.

To demonstrate that this is the outcome of the contest, suppose contestant B has chosen to invest $25,000 in the contest and contestant A is deciding how to respond. By construction, the best response of contestant A is whatever maximizes its expected profit, R_A, as specified in equation (5) where E_B is set at $25,000. Alternative values of E_A are shown in the first column of table 10.7. For each expenditure by contestant A, the expected profit of contestant A is shown in the second column, the expected profit of contestant B is shown in the third column, and total expenditure by both contestants – the total waste in the event that all rent-seeking expenditure is wasteful – is shown in the last column.

The main story in table 10.7 is that, if one contestant chooses a rent-seeking expenditure of $25,000, it becomes profitable for the other to do so too. When both contestants choose rent-seeking expenditures of $25,000, it is in the interest of neither to change his behavior. As long as contestant B maintains an expenditure of $25,000, any change, up or down, in contestant A's expenditure leads to a fall in contestant A's expected profit. As shown in the third column, the expected profit of contestant B decreases steadily from $75,000 to nothing as contestant A increases his expenditure from nothing to $75,000, but that is of no concern to contestant A. His only concern is with his own expected profit, and that is maximized at a rent-seeking expenditure of $25,000.

The contestants are locked into a prisoners' dilemma. Both can increase their expected pay-offs by colluding to reduce their rent-seeking expenditures from $25,000 to, say, $10,000 each. The maneuver would raise both contestants' expected pay-offs from $25,000 to $40,000. Though advantageous to both contestants, this collusive outcome of the rent-seeking contest is fragile because it provides both parties with an incentive to cheat. When both contestants spend $25,000, there is no incentive for either to change his behavior, for any deviation would reduce the net profit of the deviator. But when both contestants spend only $10,000, it becomes advantageous for either party to raise his rent-seeking expenditure surreptitiously, so long as the other can be entrusted to abide by his agreement and not follow suit. Suppose contestant B cheats, raising his expenditure to $25,000 while contestant A holds fast at $10,000. Such a situation might arise if contestant A must move first and if his rent-seeking expenditure is locked in regardless of how much contestant B subsequently chooses to spend. Then as one can see from table 10.7, the expected pay-off of the cheater, B, rises from $40,000 to $46,429, while the expected pay-off of the sucker, A, falls from $40,000 to $18,571. An equilibrium outcome where both contestants spend $25,000 is stable in that neither party has an incentive to cheat, even when moves are sequential rather than simultaneous. A collusive outcome where both parties spend only $10,000 is more profitable to the contestants, but unstable.

There are two interpretations of the story in table 10.7. In so far as expenditure to win the contest is socially desirable, the story becomes that only 50 percent of the public revenue devoted to the contest (the prize P) is converted into a socially desirable activity while the other 50 percent becomes a pure subsidy to the contestants. In so far as expenditure to win the contest is wasteful or bribery, the contest becomes an expensive and inexpedient way of subsidizing firms. Of course, the exact fifty-fifty split of the prize arises from an arbitrary choice of the parameters in the example. That there is some splitting is characteristic of all contests.

Ideally, governments arrange contests when rent-seeking activities are socially desirable and cannot be induced in any cheaper way. Only a contest could draw forth an accurate chronometer when nobody in government could predict who would be able to develop it and where no other method of remuneration seemed appropriate to induce the required inventive activity. But to choose import quotas over tariffs, or to offer investment grants to selected applicants when an appropriate tax reduction would have approximately the same effect upon the economy, is to set up an unnecessary contest which is likely to be wasteful and corruptive. Legal contests can be wasteful too, but there would seem to be no alternative for the resolution of disputes. Such "waste" may be unavoidable in any democratic society.

Of all the contests that the government may allow or disallow, none is more potentially divisive among citizens than the contest to avoid taxation by shifting the burden of taxation onto somebody else. Let it be known that each group's tax burden is to be determined individually by the civil service or by the legislature, and every citizen – as voter, as lobbyist, and as supplicant before the bureaucracy – is drawn into a vast contest that is at once very expensive and corruptive of democratic government. The specter of such a contest is the ultimate justification for the principle of "horizontal equity," that people with equal incomes should be taxed equally. The butcher who earns $50,000 a year should not, because he is a butcher, be more heavily, or less heavily, taxed than the baker who also earns $50,000 a year. There is much debate within the field of public finance over the appropriate tax base, the two main contenders being the income tax and the consumption tax. (If you earn $50,000 a year and if, of that $50,000, you save $10,000 and consume the remaining $40,000, then you would be taxed on $50,000 under an income tax and on $40,000 under a consumption tax. That being so, the tax rate on consumption must be higher than the tax rate on income when the amount of revenue procured is the same. The difference between these tax systems is that the high saver pays relatively more under an income tax and relatively less under a consumption tax.) However, the principle of horizontal equity is not about the choice of the tax base. It is about the establishment of firm and simple rules for all tax payers at once. It is as applicable to one tax base as to the other. Its purpose is to forestall the great scramble for tax concessions among every trade, race, language group, and region that would inevitably occur if the allocation among people of the tax burden were entirely unconstrained. To be sure, the scramble occurs now, but not to the extent that would be expected if the principle of horizontal equity were abandoned altogether.

Another way of looking at the negative income tax – the vehicle for the redistribution of income in the last chapter – is that it projects horizontal equity from the tax side onto the expenditure side of the public accounts. A negative income tax could displace a variety of social programs, among them welfare, unemployment insurance, the old age pension, public housing, personal exemptions under the income tax, and child tax credits. One rule would replace a vast range of political discretion about who the beneficiaries of redistribution should be and how generously each group should be treated. The tax system is as simple as a tax system can be, the role of the bureaucracy is limited to cheque-writing, and the tax rate itself is chosen by the legislature. That is part of the attractiveness of the negative income tax to economists and others who fear the authority of the government over the economy.

A ruling class

As the public sector grows, accumulating one task after another, a series of problems becomes more and more troublesome and complex, as follows.

The larger the public sector, the higher the private cost of public funds. More public expenditure requires higher tax rates which, in turn, provoke ever-greater diversion of output from less taxed to more taxed goods, ever-greater effort to conceal income from the tax collector and ever-greater diversion of public expenditure to the detection and punishment of tax evasion. Every society must set an agenda for its government, specifying what the government is to do and what to refrain from doing. The agenda should be smaller, perhaps very much smaller, when the private cost of public funds is taken into account than would be warranted in the absence of deadweight loss.

The larger the public sector, the more difficult it becomes to subsume public policy under well-defined criteria and the more likely are the different criteria to conflict. The larger the public sector, the greater the conflict between efficiency and equality, between maximization of the value per dollar of the services that government provides and the principle that governments should treat everybody alike. Should the police force be distributed throughout the city to minimize the number of people robbed or to minimize the dollar value of theft? Should more money be devoted per sick day to preventing the ulcers of the rich than the back injuries of the poor? Should educational expenditure be slanted to promoting the bright kids or to encouraging the less fortunate? Should subsidies to firms be directed to firms in poor regions of the country or to firms, wherever located, in high-tech industries? Should a large stadium in a major city be subsidized by the central government? When the government's role in the economy is limited to the provision of well-specified public goods, such choices may be few and relatively unproblematic. When the government's role expands, these choices become increasingly burdensome.

The larger the public sector, the looser the tie of public sector wages to wages in the surrounding private sector market for labor and the more judgmental does the setting of public sector wages become. When provision of medical care is primarily in the private sector, the market can be expected to establish a wage for doctors (or a schedule of wages depending on skill), and the few doctors in the public sector can be paid what they would earn if they worked in the private sector instead. When provision of medical care is primarily in the public sector, the government acquires considerable scope in choosing doctors' wages. In such an environment, doctors' wages may be high or low depending on the policy of the government in office and upon the outcome of negotiation between the doctors and the government. The larger the share of the output of goods and services produced in the public sector, the greater the role of administrative discretion in the choice of prices and wages not just within government, but in the private sector as well, and the more politically determined and dependent on the goodwill of the administration does each person's income become.

The larger the public sector, the greater the scope for corruption within the bureaucracy and the more difficult does the detection of corruption become. There are two kinds of corruption. An official may cheat individually, accepting bribes or favoring clients who can be expected to offer lucrative jobs on his retirement from the bureaucracy. Officials may cheat collectively by quietly overlooking one another's misdeeds, acquiring income and privileges over and above their legally established remuneration. Every public service – every import permit, every visit to the publicly financed doctor, every application for a license to conduct business – may require a bribe, part of which is passed up from the immediate bribe-taker to his superiors. The system can be more or less overt. Expecting civil servants to accept bribes, the legislature may set their wages artificially low or may wink at privileges not available to ordinary citizens. Punishment for crimes may be dependent on one's social class as discussed in chapter 1. In Canada today where medical care is provided in the public sector, top politicians, civil servants, and generals can expect substantially better and more timely medical care than is available to ordinary citizens. Privileges within the gift of the administration become instruments for keeping ordinary citizens acquiescent. Subsidies to business may or may not be forthcoming on the basis of criteria that become increasingly imprecise with every increase in the government's role in the economy. Television frequencies get allocated to government channels or to businesses with a healthy point of view.

Newsprint becomes scarce when newspapers prove obstreperous. The administration's spin on public affairs becomes the received truth.

As opportunities in the private sector diminish, civil servants may lose capacity or inclination to disobey the commands of their superiors in the hierarchy, no matter how unjust, predatory, illegal, or vicious those commands may be. In the discussion of hierarchical organization in chapter 7, it was supposed that the problem of obedience was the propensity of the subordinate to serve his own interest within the context of the employment contract rather than the interest of his employer. Workers cheat bosses. Executives cheat stockholders. The opposite malfeasance was largely ignored because the subordinate in the private sector can usually terminate the relation if the superior behaves unreasonably. Obedience within the civil service becomes more problematic. The civil servant serves two masters: his immediate superior and the general public, where service to the general public is within the framework of broad constitutional rules that the civil service is expected to respect. How faithfully the general public is served – by whistle-blowing where public wrongdoing is observed, by resignation or outright disobedience – depends on the consequence of disobedience. Where the punishment for disobedience is nothing worse than dismissal and where jobs are readily available in the private sector, one might expect a degree of independence within the civil service. Where the punishment for disobedience is harsh and where the alternative to employment in the bureaucracy is impoverishment for oneself and one's family, one might expect all but saints and heroes to obey orders quietly.

The decision to obey or to disobey one's superiors may depend critically on how one expects others in the hierarchy to behave. If I expect others to be obedient and to turn savagely against me when I am not, I may be inclined to obey regardless of my private reservations about the probity of my actions. If I anticipate widespread disobedience, then I need have less fear of retribution in the event that I disobey also. It is common, though by no means universal among societies with strong private sectors that obedience of the civil service is conditional. The President of the United States, as head of the administration and commander-in-chief of the armed forces has greater nominal power than any pharaoh or Roman emperor could ever command. Yet that vast power disintegrates when the president oversteps the bounds of his authority. I obey the policeman when his commands are within the law because I know that he is backed up in his demands by the rest of the police force, the judiciary, and the prisons. I need not obey the policeman when his commands are not within the law because I know that, in that event, the rest of the police force, the judiciary, and the prisons will oppose him and defend me. That is, at least, how society is intended to work, not just for the policeman but for the President of the United States and the Prime Minister of Canada as well.

All government requires bureaucracy, and all bureaucracy is in varying degrees honest and corrupt, an impersonal instrument in the hands of elected officials and pawn of interest groups in the private sector, selflessly devoted to the common good and a ruling class in its own right. In chapter 2, bureaucracy was personified as the policeman with a monopoly of organized violence who might use his authority for his own gain, as a ruling class, or to promote the common good on the understanding that policemen's wages are to be set equal to the wages of fishermen. A contrast was drawn between predatory and benevolent bureaucracy, but nothing was said about the innards of bureaucracy or about conditions under which each type of bureaucracy is likely to arise. Hierarchy in the corporations was discussed in chapter 7 with particular reference to the principal–agent problem and to the role of trust wages as a defense against malfeasance. Predatory voting – the propensity under majority-rule voting for exploitation of minorities by majorities – was discussed in the last chapter. The working assumption in preceding sections of this chapter has been that the policeman is benevolent. Bureaucracy has been portrayed as using whatever discretion it is allowed in the conduct of public policy to promote the common good to the best of its knowledge and ability. Whether and to what extent that portrayal is valid depends critically on the size of the bureaucracy, what the bureaucracy is required to do, its range of discretion, and the willingness of bureaucrats to oppose the commands of their superiors – by speaking-out, by resignation or by plain disobedience – when those commands are venal, illegal, unconstitutional, or manifestly contrary to the common good.

Recognition of these propensities of bureaucracy adds weight to the arguments in the last chapter about the role of the market as a constraint on exploitation by majority-rule voting. It was argued there that the stability of democratic government depends in part upon the extent of the privileges conferred by the winning of an election upon the personnel of the winning party and upon their supporters in the electorate. The greater these privileges, the greater is the prize at stake in an election and the less willing does the party in office become to risk that prize in subsequent elections. A significant part of the privileges of office is the control of the bureaucracy: the authority to make senior appointments and, directly or indirectly, to choose the beneficiaries of bureaucratic discretion. When the bureaucracy is small and its authority is circumscribed, one might expect the party in office to call elections at the appropriate time and to vacate office when an election is lost. When the bureaucracy is large and its authority over the rest of society is considerable, the party in office may be tempted to bend the rules to avoid losing its privileges in an election. A party in office might invoke its authority over the bureaucracy to remain in office indefinitely. The bureaucracy itself, especially the army, might stage a coup d'etat. In either case, the bureaucratic hierarchy could become self-perpetuating with a king, an emperor, a first secretary of the communist party, a pharaoh, a fuhrer, or a great helmsman as the final source of authority.

Now that communism in Russia has collapsed and communism in China has degenerated to the rule of an utterly self-serving political party, it is worth remembering that the doctrine began life in a great profusion of idealism. The early communists were not evil men. On the contrary, many, if not all, were genuinely prepared to dedicate their lives to the betterment of humankind. The glowing accounts of the early Russian communists in John Reed's *Ten Days that Shook the World* and of the early Chinese communists in Edgar Snow's *Red Star over China*, while perhaps a bit sentimental, are by no means entirely false. Yet ten millions of people have been allowed to starve because Stalin wished to regiment agriculture or because Mao Zedong fancied himself an economist. It is important not to vilify the early communists on the basis of what became of them, for an important lesson in social science, perhaps the most important lesson, would be lost. The lesson is that systems of political and economic organization have implications of their own quite apart from the intentions of their founders. Good men with the best of intentions may create monstrosities.

It is difficult to say how large the government may safely be. Much depends on what the government is required to do. For example, though a negative income tax churns a great deal of money through the public sector, it is almost innocuous because it is the easiest of all modes of redistribution to administer. It requires virtually no discretion on the part of the administrator. As discussed in the last chapter, the tax rate and corresponding lump sum transfer can be chosen by the legislature in circumstances where the first preference of the median voter is identified and can be expected to prevail. At the other extreme, *ad hominem* taxation turns every man against his neighbor in a great scramble to shift the burden of taxation onto somebody else, a situation comparable to the allocation by voting of the entire national income. In between are grants to specific businesses or local governments on criteria so vague that discretion, by politicians or civil servants, cannot be avoided in deciding who gets what and potential recipients are induced to grovel or threaten in the hope of acquiring the largest possible slice of the pie.

In the days before widespread literacy, a tiny cohesive ruling class of soldiers and administrators might dominate a large society of peasants. Contemporary capitalist economies can bear large public sectors without ceasing to be capitalist or placing democracy in jeopardy. In Canada, as shown in table 10.1 above, the share of government in the national income grew three-fold over the course of the twentieth century, from about 15 percent in the year 1900 to a peak of about 45 percent in the year 1990. The experience of many other countries was similar. The expansion was not a conspiracy of evil bureaucrats seeking to enhance their authority over the rest of us. It was primarily a reflection of what informed citizens wanted their government to do on their behalf in health care, education, and science as well as in the provision of the infrastructure of roads, public buildings, protection, and the regulation of the economy that only government could supply.

The unprecedentedly large bureaucracies in most Western societies have remained subservient to elected officials in the legislature and the executive, and many democratic countries do manage to avoid becoming captives of their bureaucracies. Several explanations have been proposed, all partly true in my opinion, but none uniquely correct. Some authors emphasize checks and balances within the government: the division of government into legislature, executive, and judiciary, the splitting of the American legislature into two houses with different electoral procedures and somewhat different constituencies, and the complex allocation of powers among the branches of government, so that, for example, the President appoints judges subject to the approval of Congress, Congress passes bills subject to a presidential veto, a presidential veto can be overturned by two-thirds of Congress and Congress can impeach the President. Others emphasize federalism which dilutes authority differently: the splitting of powers between the federal government and the provincial governments, with enough ambiguity to keep the two levels of government at loggerheads, too preoccupied squabbling with one another and too anxious to enlist public opinion in support of the expansion of their powers to oppress ordinary citizens as they would like. Others emphasize the free press: the ever greater access by the citizen to information in newspapers, television, and the Internet, automatically breaking what once was a monopoly of information by the ruling class. Rebellion becomes difficult if not impossible when communication among citizens is restricted and when the virtues of humble obedience to one's betters are promulgated without competition by court and pulpit. A few years ago, a popular revolt in Thailand was nicknamed the cellular phone revolution. Others emphasize the constitutional prescription of individual rights and of limits to the powers of government. Perhaps otherwise unconstrained officials are prepared to respect the constitution. Others emphasize democracy itself: the choice of leaders by voting, the rivalry among political parties vying for office, and the periodic replacement of the top of the bureaucracy in elections. The emphasis here is on markets with endogenous prices and wages as a defense against the excesses of the bureaucracy. The larger the market, the smaller the dependence of each person's income and status on the goodwill of the legislature and the civil service, and the more completely can the administration be bound by rules governing the conduct of the civil service and protecting the rights and obligations of citizens.

As government grows, acquiring one new function after another, there must come a time when further expansion places democratic government in jeopardy. There is a line that cannot be safely crossed. It is difficult to locate the line precisely. What does seem clear is that, wherever the line may be, it was crossed by the communist governments of Russia, China, Vietnam, Cuba, and Cambodia but has not yet been crossed in Canada and many other western countries, large though the public sector may be by historical standards. Recognition of the danger in unlimited expansion of government may be part of the explanation of why the growth of government seems to have stopped at the end of the twentieth century and why the share of government in the Canadian economy has fallen about 5 percent from its peak in the year 1990.

Chapter **Eleven**

LAW

Courts of law are established for the express purpose of limiting public authority in its conduct toward individuals.

Sir James Stevens, quoted in J. Dickinson,
Administrative Justice and the Supremacy
of the Law in the United States

It is more important that a rule be settled than that it be settled correctly.

Lord Mansfield, quoted in M. J. Horwitz,
The Transformation of American Law,
1780–1860

The "rule of law" is "the absolute supremacy or predominance of the regular law as opposed to the influence of arbitrary power" or to "wide discretionary authority on the part of the government. . . . A man may be punished for a breach of the law, but he can be punished for nothing else." . . . The rule of law means "equality before the law, or the equal subjugation of all classes to the ordinary law of the land administered by the ordinary Law Courts."

A. V. Dicey,
The Law of the Constitution

The role of law in the economy has been implicit throughout this book. The law present in one sense but absent altogether in another from the story of the fishermen and the pirates in chapter 2. The law present in that the story was about crime and punishment. The model without police focussed upon the equilibrium when people choose self-interestedly between crime and ordinary work, an equilibrium in which everybody, criminal and victim alike, is distinctly worse off than if crime were somehow prohibited. The introduction of the police dramatized the logic of deterrence. Punishment of criminals decreases the incidence of crime, making everybody better off, though the cost of detection and punishment of any particular crime may exceed the cost of the harm from the crime itself.

The law was absent from the fishermen and pirates story in that there were no lawyers, no judges, no courts and nothing of the profusion of rules that characterizes the law in any modern society. What exactly is a crime? How in practice do we distinguish among self-interested acts between those we treat as legitimate and those we designate as criminal? On what principles do we choose the severity of punishment? Who is to determine when a crime has been committed? What constrains people empowered to enforce law from using their authority for their own advantage? How can citizens be protected from victimization in the name of the law? The police say, "you are a pirate." You deny it. How is the matter to be resolved? None of these questions were considered. They were all abstracted out of sight by the simple assumptions that there is one crime, theft, and that there is no doubt in anyone's mind about the appropriate punishment or about when punishment is warranted. A criminal law is required to designate crimes, prescribe punishments and determine whether or not an accused person is guilty.

Though nothing was said about the law in the discussion of taste, technology, and markets in chapters 3 to 6, the law was implicit in the assumption that all property is unambiguous and secure. The law was closer to the surface in the analysis of associations in chapter 7 where the emphasis was on the complexities of the market, on bargaining, on deal-making as opposed to price-taking and on contracts that are inevitably somewhat vague at the edges. A civil law is required for the resolution of disputes over the boundaries between people's property rights and the interpretation of contracts.

An additional role for the law was suggested in the discussions of predatory government in chapter 2, of exploitation by voting in chapter 9, and of administrative discretion in chapter 10. The state's monopoly of organized violence may be employed for the benefit of a ruling class, regardless of the welfare of the rest of society. Majority rule voting may be employed to exploit or expropriate an identifiable minority of the population. Administrative discretion in the interpretation of laws may be employed to victimize particular people or classes of people. The primary defence against these tendencies is the realization by citizens that voting and public administration must be conducted within certain bounds if democratic government is to be preserved. Constitutional and administrative law are required to specify the bounds precisely, prescribing the limits of acceptable legislation, restricting the scope of the authority of the administration, and dissolving the bonds of obedience within the governmental hierarchy if the rules are not respected.

The study of the overlap between law and economics in this chapter is focussed upon three topics: bringing abstract economic concepts down to earth by reference to laws and law cases where the scope of property rights is in dispute, showing how, and to what extent, the principles employed in the choice of public projects and policies can be extended to the choice of laws, and explaining how property, voting, and the law are intertwined in the defense against predatory government. The chapter is organized accordingly.

THE WEB OF RULES AND THE BRANCHES OF THE LAW

Our study of the economy has focussed upon simple models, or stories, claimed to be helpful in explaining how people interact and what the outcomes of various interactions might be. Stories about fishermen and pirates, Robinson Crusoe, the five plots of land, paid work and do-it-yourself activities, and exploitation by voting all conform reasonably well to that pattern. The stories are informative because they are not just stories. They are representative of aspects of the world. They flag social interactions which, but for the stories, might be misunderstood or overlooked in a maze of "inessential" detail.

Such stories employ concepts that never fit the world exactly. We speak of property, price, buying, selling, voting, making, and taking as though we know exactly what such terms mean as applied to the ebb and flow of life. We know no such thing. Our concepts serve as signposts for inquiry and as guides to action, but nice judgment is required to recognize when policies derived from simple models must be modified in the light of discrepancies between the assumptions of the model and the detail of the economy.

From a distance, society can be looked upon as composed of a few large institutions: markets, voting, public administration, marriage, the criminal justice system. Up close, society becomes a virtual infinity of rules governing every aspect of life as broad rules subdivide into narrower and narrower rules when the rules are put into practice. Among the rules that have been in force at various times and places are these:

- A person may vote in elections for Parliament if he is male, is over 18 years of age and earns over 40 shillings a year.
- A candidate is elected if and only if he gets more votes than any other candidate.
- The prime minister is the established leader of a political party with a majority of seats in parliament.
- A bill is passed into law if it wins a majority of both houses of parliament, or if it passes in the House of Commons, fails in the Senate and is passed again in the House.
- A quorum is required to pass a bill in the House of Commons.
- I may evict a trespasser from my house.
- A sale of a house may be invalid if the seller conceals from the buyer that the house is infested by termites.
- A husband has complete authority over the disposition of the property of his wife.
- I must compensate the victim in a motor accident if the law judges me to be at fault.
- I may not sell myself into slavery, but I may rent my labor for a day.
- A marriage may be contracted between two people of opposite sexes but not between two people of the same sex.
- I am deemed married if I undertake the appropriate ceremony.
- I must pay tax in accordance with the appropriate schedule.
- Shareholders in a corporation have limited liability, but Lloyd's names do not.
- One is admitted to university if one has the appropriate grades, or at the discretion of the officers of the university.

- Land that I occupy for, say, ten years uncontested is deemed by the law to be mine.
- A jury consists of nine members who are sequestered during the trial.
- I may not build an unfenced swimming pool on my land.
- I and my fellow workers may vote to establish a union.
- A union may go on strike, and, if it does, the employer may (or may not as the case may be) hire substitute workers.
- I may not steal.
- The discoverer of base metals – iron, copper, or zinc – becomes their owner and he is entitled to mine them for profit, but the noble metals – gold and silver – belong automatically to the king.
- The inventor of a new product is entitled to a patent conveying a monopoly over the use of the product for a number of years.
- Telephone rates are set by an administrative tribunal with no judicial review.
- Contributions to political parties are tax deductible.
- One may be executed for murder.
- Carriers of dangerous diseases may be involuntarily quarantined.
- Potentially dangerous substances may not be produced without specific permission of the appropriate regulatory body.

Rules can be classified according to the domain of life to which they apply. There are *legal rules*: rules of criminal law, specifying punishment for a long list of crimes; rules of tort law, identifying compensatable harm and providing for redress; rules of contract, prohibiting some contracts (such as contracts to sell oneself into slavery), allowing others and indicating which the courts are prepared to enforce; elaborate rules of court procedure specifying who must do what to determine that a law has been violated and how punishment is meted out. There are *property rules*: rules about what may or may not be owned by individuals, the administration of common property, who owns what, how title is verified, how property may be acquired, when, and under what terms, property may be taken by the state; rules governing the conduct of business, what goods may be produced, standards of quality and the limits of permissible advertising; rules about the governance of the firm, limited liability, poison pills and take-overs. There are *political rules*: electoral rules about who may run for office, what candidates may or may not do during elections and how to identify the winner in an election; procedural rules about how a bill must be presented to parliament, quorum, the role of the senate and when a bill can be said to have passed into law; jurisdictional rules allocating powers to tax and spend between levels of government. There are *administrative rules*: rules specifying when one is liable for tax and how much tax one must pay in a wide variety of circumstances; rules of entitlement to public services and transfers; rules about the appointment of judges and other public officials. There are *constitutional rules*: rules limiting the powers of elected government; rules about civil rights, freedom of speech, of association, of religion and from arbitrary arrest; rules specifying how the constitution itself may be changed.

Most, perhaps all, rules are two sided. They specify what one must do, what one may do or what one must not do, as the case may be. They also impose an obligation on the rest of society to ensure that one's rights are maintained, that one is not harmed by another's violation of the rules and that rule-breakers are adequately deterred by punishment, for a rule without sanction for disobedience is really no rule at all. "Thou shalt not steal" is addressed to the would-be thief and to society at large. It is an injunction to all of us to ensure that thieves are punished. Everybody is involved in every rule, though one's involvement is often delegated to some extent.

Rules can also be classified as *rules of substance* and *rules for changing other rules*. "Thou shall not steal," speed laws, and the obligation to pay income tax are rules of substance. Political rules in a democratic society can be looked upon, at least in part, as rules for changing other rules. Changing rules is the first business of parliament. Even the most primitive society manages to change rules from time to time, and there must be a written or unwritten procedure for doing so.

Rules require interpretation. Ideally, laws should be so carefully drafted that there can be no doubt whatsoever as to their meaning. It should be immediately evident to everyone whether such and such an act is in conformity with my property rights, whether a crime has been committed, whether a contract has been breached and, if so, what remedy is required. Trials should be unnecessary, except possibly to decide who is telling the truth when different people's accounts of an event conflict. (You say I was present at the scene of the crime. I claim I was not.) The world, alas, is not like that. Regardless of how carefully a law is drafted, there is inevitably a fringe of indeterminacy with room for dispute among honorable and disinterested people about whether the law means this or that. There is a considerably wider range within which rogues or partisans may tilt the law in their own interest. Lawyers speak in this connection of the "open texture of the law." Laws are drafted with words, and it is in the very nature of words to be less than completely precise.

The ideal is a "government of laws, not of men." Rules govern our conduct, providing a framework within which people are able to look after themselves without destroying one another in the competition for political office and material advantage. The ideal is attained, at best, imperfectly, but that may be sufficient.

The law can be looked upon as a tree with many branches and cases hanging like leaves on each branch. The two principal branches pertain to the conduct of the citizen and to the conduct of governments. As illustrated in figure 11.1, the branch pertaining to the conduct of the citizen divides into criminal law and civil law, and then the civil law divides into property, contracts, and torts. The branch pertaining to the conduct of government divides into administrative law and constitutional law.

The civil law is about the resolution of disputes. I claim you owe me $100. You claim to owe only $50, and refuse to pay anything unless I agree that $50 is sufficient to discharge the debt. What do we do? In the absence of law, we fight. Trial by combat, which was not uncommon in ancient times, is a huge deterrent to economic association and a great impediment to general prosperity as the gains from trade, discussed in detail in chapters 3 and 4, are wasted in conflict and mistrust. The civil law is a substitute for violence. By contrast with the criminal law to be discussed presently, the civil law invokes the state as referee in disputes between plaintiff and defendant, and is not a participant in its own right. (Of course, a citizen may be sued by a department of government, but the government in that event becomes schizophrenic, part judge and part litigant.) Typically, there is no punishment under

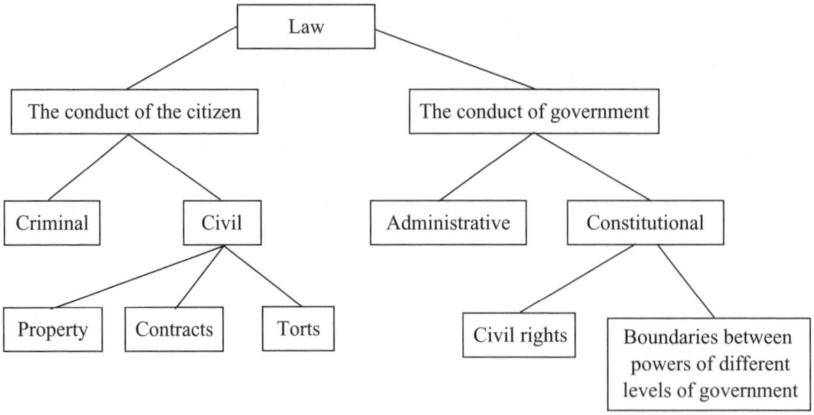

Figure 11.1   The branches of the law.

the civil law, only the restoration to each person of "his own" when one's property or one's rights are violated by another.

Within the civil law, the law of property law is about who owns what. Who is entitled to a deer that I have been chasing through the woods and that you come upon and shoot once the deer is exhausted? Who owns a piece of land that is registered in my name but that you have fenced and farmed for some years with no objection from me? Can I claim compensation from the city if my land is expropriated to make way for a new road? Can I claim compensation if my land is rendered valueless because a road that was formerly one-way in one direction becomes one-way in the other? (In practice, the answers to these last two questions may differ, though my loss may be the same.) What are the boundaries of ownership? To say that I own my house is not to say that I can do exactly as I please with it, for I am bound, as is every other house owner, by a maze of rules specifying what I may, and may not, do with it. I may not be allowed to convert my house to a store because my neighborhood is not zoned for commercial property. I may build a swimming pool in my backyard, but only if adequately fenced because the right of little children to wander takes precedence over my right to enjoy my property as I please.

Contract law is about the public enforcement of promises. Markets require public enforcement of promises not just to protect the promisee from malfeasance on the part of the promise-maker, but to render promises credible for the benefit of the promise-maker himself. Rules of property extend beyond the protection of land, buildings and tangible goods from predation by one's fellow citizens, corrupt officials or an acquisitive majority in the legislature. They also protect lenders, bond-holders, and creditors from malfeasance on the part of the borrower. The law supplies a surrogate for honesty, inducing others to treat the promise-maker as an honest man, whether he be so or not. An entrepreneur needs capital to start a new venture. Potential investors might fear that the entrepreneur will refuse to reimburse them once the venture is profitable. Potential investors need not be afraid if and in so far as the law compels the entrepreneur to honour his contracts. This consideration could be ignored in the bread and cheese economy of chapter 3 where all transactions were supposed to take place simultaneously. Trust is essential for markets where I do this for you today so that you will do that for me tomorrow. The law of contracts imparts a trust between participants in the market without which business could not be conducted at all.

There has evolved an elaborate network of rules specifying when a contract is valid and what compensation is warranted if a contract is breached: May I sell myself or my children into slavery as was permitted in many countries not long ago? Is a promise legally binding when the promisee has offered nothing in return? What do I owe you if I simply cannot keep my part of a bargain? When, if ever, is a transaction unconscionable? One often reads in the financial pages of the newspaper about disputes between people or between firms over the exact content of a sale. I buy a car. Have I simply bought the object, or have I bought the assurance by the manufacturer that it will perform to certain standards? Driving is always risky. The risk to life and limb depends in part on the whim of the gods, in part on how carefully I drive and in part on how safe my car was made. The manufacturer and I both understand that the intrinsic safety of the car depends on how much the manufacturer is prepared to pay to make it safe. In a sense, the customer does not require a car to be too safe because it would become too expensive. But how unsafe should the car be, and at what point can the victim of an accident sue the manufacturer of the car because it was less safe than the buyer had a right to expect?

Tort law is about compensation when one person harms another and is required "to make the victim whole". When and from whom is compensation required for the victim in a traffic accident? Are cigarette companies liable to the families of smokers who died from lung cancer or to the government to compensate for the cost of treatment of lung cancer victims? Does it matter that some non-smokers also die of lung cancer? Each of these questions has to be answered one way or another. Disputes are resolved in court or by bargaining in the light of what we believe a court would decree. The "plaintiff" demands what he believes to be his rights against the "defendant" who seeks to persuade judge or jury that the plaintiff's rights have not been violated and that no compensation is warranted.

Criminal law differs from civil law in the role of the state. In civil law, the alleged harm is to a person who must be compensated if his claim is valid, and the role of the state is limited to the adjudication of disputes. In criminal law, the alleged harm may be to a person in the first instance, but it is deemed to be against the state as well. The law seeks out the guilty party to inflict punishment by fine, imprisonment or worse. The criminal law involves the state not just as umpire between disputants, but as a participant in the dispute. Theft and murder are acts against the state as well as the immediate victims of the crimes. To kill a person deliberately is murder, a breach of the criminal law. To kill a person accidentally may, depending on the circumstances, be a breach of the civil law. The perpetrator of a traffic accident may be required to compensate the wife and children of the deceased for the loss of income but would not be punished by the state unless the accident were accompanied by criminal activity such as driving while drunk or with exceeding recklessness. One who carelessly causes death in a traffic accident may escape penalty altogether if there is nobody with a financial interest in the victim's survival.

Every society must draw a line between legitimate actions and actions prohib-ited under the criminal law. Sometimes it is obvious where the line should be drawn; sometimes not. There is not much dispute about reading newspapers, buying lunch at the local restaurant, murder or bank robbery, but there is no clear line between what most people would have the law allow and what most people would have the law prohibit. Society cannot permit indiscriminate theft, but would make allowances for the person lost in the woods who might starve unless he is prepared to steal food from a cabin he happens to discover. Owning a hand gun is a crime in some societies but not in others. Adultery is punished by stoning in some societies and unpunished altogether in others. Causing a traffic accident may or may not be a crime depending on the circumstances. Patricide is a heinous crime in some societies and a civic duty in others.

The criminal law requires a schedule of punishments. The primary consideration is deterrence. Imagine a person deciding whether or not to steal in circumstances where there are many opportunities for theft each yielding $200 if undetected, where, in each instance of theft, the police have a 5 percent chance of discovering the identity of the thief and where theft is punishable by a fine. To deter theft, the fine must exceed $4,000. If the thief cannot afford the fine or if the $4,000 cannot be extracted from him one way or another, then theft must be punished by imprisonment. The cost of detection and imprisonment is typically well in excess of the cost of the crime itself, but society must bear that cost, for the punishment of a few detected crimes deters many crimes that would otherwise be committed. The schedule of punishments is a trade-off between the full cost of crimes committed and the benefit of crimes deterred.

The principal criterion for classifying harmful acts as torts or as crimes is identifiability. Typically, though perhaps not invariably, a tort is identified costlessly. The creditor knows the identity of the recalcitrant debtor. The perpetrator of an automobile accident remains on the spot waiting for the police to arrive, and he is guilty of a crime if he does not. The perpetrator of a crime normally seeks to evade detection and not infrequently succeeds. It is usually characteristic of harmful acts classified as crimes that (1) such acts can only be deterred if the severity of punishment is sufficient to overbalance the possibility that the criminal remains undetected and unpunished, (2) the expected cost of detection is high enough that the victim would be unwilling to bear the cost himself, and (3) detection requires investigation by an agency of the government rather than by an investigatory firm in the private sector of the economy.

The state must involve itself in the detection, prosecution, and punishment of crimes as part of its general monopoly of the use of legitimate violence. Deterrence requires an authority to search, interrogate, and arrest people who are suspected of crime but who may in the end turn out to be innocent, an authority unpleasant enough when undertaken by the state but completely intolerable in private hands. In the absence of a central police force, private investigation would quickly degenerate into private crime or private war. Deterrence also generates an externality in crime detection, not unlike the externality in the smoking example in chapter 5. The victim of theft today may be prepared to devote resources in the attempt to recover his property, but he may instead prefer to accept his loss and get on with his normal business because he is unconcerned about other crimes perpetrated on other people tomorrow. If everybody reasoned that way, few crimes would ever be investigated and nobody's property would be secure. These considerations do not apply to acts classified as torts because the perpetrator is immediately identifiable and the role of the state can be limited to judging claims and specifying appropriate redress.

Administrative law is about judicial supervision of the officials of the government in dealings with the public. Modern industrial society cannot dispense with a degree of bureaucratic discretion. Try as we may, we cannot write rules so comprehensively and so precisely that it is immediately obvious to everybody who is entitled to what. Administrative judgment is required to determine who is a valid refugee, whether there has been insider trading of stocks or who is entitled to a research grant. On the other hand, some judicial oversight is necessary because an entirely unconstrained administration could destroy anybody who happens to be disliked by, or a threat to, the party in office. Democracy could not withstand such unlimited authority in the hands of the government. A substantial body of law stands guard over the vague boundary between what the administration may and may not do.

Constitutional law stands guard over a somewhat different boundary. The Charter of Rights in the Canadian constitution of 1982 codifies long-established principles in the common law for the protection of civil rights. A special tax on Dan Usher and nobody else would, I hope, be struck down by the courts as unconstitutional. In a federal system of government, each level of government has its own constitutionally protected domain of jurisdiction which may not be encroached upon by other levels of government. Administrative law and constitutional law will be discussed at the end of this chapter.

NATURAL LAW

Law may evolve gradually through custom or through adjudication by the courts. This "common law" evolved – first in England, then in the United States, Canada, and other common law countries – through centuries of accumulation, case after case, of court decisions. Laws may also be promulgated by an act of the legislature, the king, or the dictator depending on the type of government in force. Most of tort law and contract law has no foundation in legislation, and has evolved as principles within the common law in the course of adjudication. Normally, legislation takes precedence over the common law. In England during the nineteenth century, the common law denied married women control over the disposition of property, subordinating women to their husbands completely. Legislation was required in the latter part of the century to set matters right. There is a doctrine among some students of the law that the cumulation of judgments in case upon case from time out of mind has yielded a perfection in the common law that can only be sullied by innovative legislation. The doctrine emerged at its most extreme in seventeenth-century England where the common law stood as a defense against the absolutist claims of the monarch. Nowadays, the doctrine tends to be tinged with mistrust of normal politics and with the belief that judges are more adept, and more to be trusted, than legislatures in identifying the common good and designing rules accordingly.

An even older tradition posits a "natural law" to which the actual law in force at any given time may be a poor approximation. True law, on one version of the doctrine of natural law, is what is best for mankind. True law, on another version, is God's law, but as God is seen as benevolent, the two versions may amount in practice to more or less the same thing. The idea of natural law is simply that there is a best law, where the meaning of "best" in this context is whatever serves to promote some conception of the common good. As discussed in chapter 8, the common good may be interpreted as whatever rules, policies and institutions I would choose, in my own interest exclusively, for a hypothetical community that I am destined to enter with an equal chance of occupying the circumstances of each and every person there. Natural law would then be the laws I would choose in those circumstances. The common good may also be interpreted more broadly as contributing to whatever one sees as the good of society, as distinct from one's own immediate self-interest, regardless of how one's conception of the good of society is formed. The common good some-times boils down to efficiency. Where the distribution among people of the costs and benefits of laws is unpredictable, the best law, like the best among a set of alternative public projects, may be whatever serves to maximize the national income, suitably modified to account for leisure and life expectancy in so far as these are affected by the law.

Of course, to speak of a natural law is not to say that I ought to obey the law as it should be when some other law is actually in force. That would be a recipe for chaos. Nor can the law be changed all at once. There is a sense in which the law is found, not made. We are born into a society with the rules already in place, and we have reason to believe that the attempt to overturn all rules, root and branch, would be disastrous. We can and do change this or that, but not everything at once. Perhaps the rules embody an ancient wisdom we now no longer fully understand. Perhaps the habit of obedience to law, on which all civilized life depends, requires a degree of continuance. Perhaps rules are too many and too connected to established institutions to be changed all at once. Changing the law has been compared to replacing rotten planks on a boat while staying afloat: possible, even necessary, but always difficult.

Responding to changes in the economy and in the organization of society, we change our laws from time to time and we would like to think that, in doing so, we are replacing worse laws (in the current circumstances) with better ones. The concept of natural law is a reflection of the belief that better and worse are meaningful in this context. Whether and to what extent a natural law can be identified at any time and place will now be considered with reference to the law of product liability and to the law of murder. For the law of product liability, it is at least arguable that a natural law can be identified. For the law of murder, the ideal of natural law is instructive but not always sufficient as a guide for deciding what the law should be. In both areas, the law has changed decisively over the years. A hundred years ago, the law of product liability adhered closely to the principle of *caveat emptor* (let the buyer beware). Buyers were expected to find out if goods were defective, and the maker had no responsibility for goods once they left his shop. Now, the law imposes much more responsibility on the maker for the quality and performance of his product. A hundred years ago, the death penalty was standard punishment for murder in every country in the world. Now most countries impose a long prison sentence instead.

One might argue that there can be no natural law if the appropriate law is changing over time. That argument would have to be correct if natural law is seen as rules that remain valid forever because they are dictated from on high, for example in the

Ten Commandments. On that interpretation, the old law may be natural, or the new law may be natural, or neither, but not both. On the other hand, if natural means "appropriate" or "best" rather than God-given and eternal, the content of natural law may change together with changes in technology and society. The interpretation of natural law as whatever serves to promote the common good should suggest an explanation of why the laws have changed over time.

Product liability

A new stove may be reliable or defective. Suppose the stove costs the stove-maker $209 to build and there is an invariant and unalterable risk of 5 percent (no matter how careful the stove-maker chooses to be) that a stove turns out to be defective. Suppose also that a defective stove can never be repaired, and that the replacement of a defective stove requires a "transaction cost" – the ruined dinner, perhaps some personal injury, and the nuisance of having to return and destroy the old stove and to replace it with a new one – of $200 over and above the cost of a new stove.

If the replacement stove were guaranteed to work perfectly, and if the maker bore no responsibility for the defective product, the expected cost of a working stove to the purchaser would be $229.45, $[209 + (0.05)(209 + 200)]$, which is the sum of the purchase price of the stove and the expected cost of replacing it if defective. If, as would normally be the case, the replacement stove was like the original in every respect, there would be a risk of $(0.05)^2$ that both the original and the replacement turn out to be defective, together with a risk of $(0.05)^3$ of three defects in a row, and so on. The expected cost of a working stove would then have to be slightly higher. The full expected cost of a working stove rises from $229.45 to $230.51, $[209 + (0.05)(209 + 200) + (0.05)^3(209 + 200) + (0.05)^4(209 + 200) + \cdots =$ $\{209 + [(0.05)/(1 - (0.05)](209 + 200)]$, as shown in the second to last column of table 11.1. In general,

$$\text{Expected average cost of a working stove} = C + [d/(1 - d)][C + T] \qquad (1)$$

where C is the bare cost of production, T is the transaction cost of replacing a defective stove (over and above the cost of the replacement itself), d is the percentage of defective stoves, and the expected proportion of replacements to initial purchases is $d + d^2 + d^3 + d^4 + \cdots = d/(1 - d)$. In our example, $C = \$209$, $T = \$200$ and $d = 0.05$ or 5 percent.

What should the law be in this case? Should the buyer be held responsible in the event that the stove is defective and has to be replaced, should the maker be held responsible, or should responsibility be somehow divided between them, with, for instance, the maker held responsible for the cost of replacing the stove and the buyer held responsible for the transaction cost in the event a stove turns out to be defective? The instructive feature of this example is that, *on the assumptions we have made so far*, it makes no difference to anybody what the law requires. There are two reasons. First, with competition among stove-makers, the price of stoves adjusts to the law, leaving both parties in the same position no matter what the law requires. If the law requires

Table 11.1   Efficient percentage of defective stoves as dependent upon the transaction cost of replacement

[At each transaction cost, the lowest average cost of stoves, inclusive of the expected cost of replacing defective stoves, is indicated by*.]

Percent of defective stoves (%)	Cost of production ($)	Cost of reducing the probability of defects by 1% ($)	Expected average cost ($)		
			With *no* transaction cost of replacement	With $200 transaction cost of replacement	With $600 transaction cost of replacement
0	244	—	244.00	244.00	244.00
1	235	9	237.37	239.39	243.43*
2	227	8	231.63	235.71	243.87
3	220	7	226.80	232.98	245.39
4	214	6	222.92	231.26	247.94
5	209	5	220.00	230.51*	251.55
6	205	4	218.09	230.84	256.36
7	202	3	217.20*	232.27	262.39
8	200	2	217.39	234.80	269.60
9	199	1	218.68	238.46	278.02
10	199	0	221.11	243.29	287.69

With no transaction cost, with a transaction cost of $200, and with a transaction cost of $600, the efficient percentages of defective stoves are 7%, 5%, and 1% respectively.

the maker to compensate the buyer for the full cost of replacing a defective stove, then the price of the stove becomes $230.51 for which the maker just covers the full cost of production and replacement. Stove-makers would not enter the business at any lower price, and competition among them stops the price from rising any higher. If the law places the full cost of a defective stove on the buyer, the price of a stove falls to $209 which is just sufficient to induce stove-makers to enter the business. Regardless, the cost of a stove to the buyer is $230.51, paid altogether in one case, and in two distinct parts – one part to the stove-maker and the other part as the assumption of risk or as a premium to the insurance company to cover that risk – in the other.

Second, whatever the law requires, the maker and the buyer can *contract around the law*. If the law holds the maker responsible for defects, but, contrary to what has been assumed so far, the transaction cost is lower for the buyer than for the maker, a clause exempting the maker from responsibility could be included in the contract of sale. Or if the law holds the buyer responsible for defects, but the transaction cost is lower for the maker than for the buyer, a clause requiring the maker to bear the full cost of defects could be included in the contract of sale. Regardless of the letter of the law, the market would seek out the lowest average cost, all things considered.

This example is useful as a starting point for discussion of the law of liability because it abstracts from the reasons why the law is important, allowing those reasons to be introduced and examined one by one. Before beginning this inquiry, it should be noted the market does more than assigning responsibility for defects. The market also determines the optimal percentage of defects when a reduction in the percentage of defects is feasible but costly. Optimality in this context is defined unambiguously as whatever serves to minimize the full cost (paid one way or another by the user) of a working stove. There is a unique cost-minimizing percentage of defects, and the market supplies that percentage automatically regardless of who – the maker or the buyer – bears the legal responsibility for defects.

To establish this proposition, it is necessary to give the maker a choice between a larger and a smaller number of defects. The cost of production has to increase as the percentage of defective products declines, for otherwise it would be in nobody's interest to make products that are less than completely defect free. Suppose the relation between the percentage of defective stoves and the cost of production is as shown in the first two columns of table 11.1. It would cost $244 per stove to make stoves that are entirely defect free. It would cost $199 per stove to make stoves that are 10 percent defective. As shown in the third column, there is a steadily rising cost of reducing the percentage of defective stoves. Stove-makers would never allow more than 9 percent defects because it costs nothing to reduce defects from 10 to 9 percent. Thereafter, the cost of reducing the percentage of defective stoves increases steadily from $1 per stove to reduce the rate of defects from 9 to 8 percent, all the way up to $9 to reduce the rate of defects from 1 percent to nothing. The efficient proportion of defects minimizes the expected average cost of a working stove, inclusive of the cost of production and the expected cost of replacement.

As shown in table 11.1, the efficient rate of defects depends on both the cost of production and the transaction cost of replacement. The last three columns of the table show expected average cost, in accordance with equation (1) above, with no transaction cost, with transaction cost of $200 (as assumed in the example above) and with transaction cost of $600. In each column, the lowest average cost is indicated by *. It turns out that the efficient percentage of defects is 7 percent in the absence of transaction cost, 5 percent when the transaction cost is $200, and 1 percent when the transaction cost is as high as $600. Transaction cost could be high if, as might well happen, a defective stove causes an accident, perhaps a fire, that is more costly than the stove itself. In the circumstances of table 11.1, risk is like an ordinary commodity. The market churns out a quantity and price of risk, just as it churns out quantities and prices of bread and cheese.

The stove example is intended to be representative of a large class of mishaps including accidents as well as faulty products. Care by one party affects the risk of misfortune to another. The driver of a car is killed when the gas tank of his car explodes in a collision, and the heirs of the driver sue the manufacturer of the car, claiming that extra expenditure on strengthening the gas tank would have prevented the explosion. Producers of asbestos are sued when it is discovered that asbestos insulation of houses causes the occupants to become ill. Tobacco companies are sued by smokers dying of lung cancer. A customer at a restaurant accidentally overturns a cup of coffee, is scalded and sues the restaurant because the coffee was too hot. In these cases, the law must assign the cost of the harm, leaving it with the ultimate victim – the person whose stove has to be replaced, the person burned up in his car, the person whose house is insulated with asbestos, the person dying of lung cancer, the person scalded by hot coffee – or reassigning the responsibility and the cost of the harm to somebody else who must then compensate the victim.

In the latter case, the law has two principal objectives which sometimes fit together nicely and sometimes conflict. The law is intended to "make the victim whole" and to induce the efficient, cost-minimizing level of care by the perpetrator of the harm. The ultimate objective in making the victim whole is to substitute publicly enforced compensation for private retribution. In ancient times, clans defended themselves from one another, an eye for an eye and a tooth for a tooth because a clan not prepared to reciprocate injury would be victimized and exploited. Such primitive justice might be no worse than contemporary civil law if the parties could agree on the appropriate restitution. Otherwise, private vengeance could escalate into feuding, where each party believes himself to be victimized by the other and the initial harm is multiplied without end. The civil law provides a remedy for harm and, what is more important, a termination to private disputes.

In the stove example, both objectives of the law are obtained simultaneously, regardless of where the legal responsibility for accidents is assigned. The price mechanism can be relied upon to supply the efficient level of care as long as it is clear to everybody *either* that the stove-maker is obliged to compensate the buyer in the event a purchased stove is defective *or* that the stove-maker is exempt from responsibility. Making the victim whole is somewhat more complex, for the designation of the buyer as "victim" depends on the original understanding between the buyer and the seller. The buyer of a defective stove becomes a victim if and only if there was an understanding that the stove would be in good working order. The buyer would then need to be made whole (supplied with a new stove) as the law requires. On the other hand, the buyer could hardly be considered a victim if he understood and agreed to bear the risk as part of the sale. The buyer of a stove is no more victimized in that case than is the buyer of a stock which subsequently falls in price.

In practice, the two objectives of the law do not always fit so well together, and the efficiency of the market may be conditional on the assignment between buyer and seller of responsibility for defects. The real purpose of the stove example is as a foil for identifying reasons why one legal regime might be preferable to another. The example is based on simple assumptions, and reasons why the law might assign liability for harm from defective products to the buyer or to the maker as the case may be (and why the principle of *caveat emptor* has gradually been overturned), emerge as these assumptions are relaxed and as special features of the market for risky products are introduced. These special features may be described under the headings of damages, adjudication, observability and fault, which will be discussed in turn.

Damages

The cost of replacing a defective stove was assumed to be known indisputably by the maker, the buyer and, if necessary, the courts. The world is not always like that. A person is injured by a defective stove, an exploding car, the spilling of an excessively hot cup of coffee, or misinformation by tobacco companies that induced him to smoke when he would not otherwise have done so. Medical expenses can probably be assessed with tolerable accuracy, though doctors may be inclined to bill generously when they know the patient will be reimbursed. Pain and suffering are immensely more difficult to evaluate. The victim may claim – and the claim may well be true – that no amount of money, however large, would compensate him for his injury or induce him to accept the injury voluntarily. The court must choose a figure if the victim is to be compensated, but the derivation of the figure is often mysterious. Perhaps the appropriate procedure is for the courts to give up trying to make the victim whole, and to concentrate instead on inducing the perpetrator of the harm to exercise optimal care. Regardless, the court's estimation of harm cannot be other than subjective, varying from one judge to another or upon the whim of the jury.

Injury resulting in death is especially problematic. Obviously, the victim cannot be made whole. Heirs or dependants may be compensated instead, but the amount of compensation deemed appropriate by the courts may differ from the amount of compensation required to induce optimal care by potential injurers, and there would be nobody to compensate if the deceased had no heirs or dependants at all. The potential victim may not want to be compensated. It was supposed in the stove example that the cost of a defective stove is the original price plus a transaction cost. Suppose instead that there is a tiny risk of a stove blowing up and killing its owners. If the risk is small enough, people might still buy stoves. Not being around to collect compensation, buyers might prefer a legal regime where the manufacturer is not held responsible for defects. Compensation in the event of accidents might add significantly to the price of stoves. Trusting in competition among stove-makers to force the price of stoves down to the average cost (inclusive of the expected cost per stove of compensation in the event of accidents), the buyer may prefer a lower price without compensation for his heirs and dependants to a higher price when the law requires that compensation be paid. The example is not as fanciful as it may appear. Workers in very dangerous jobs, such as extinguishing fires in oil rigs, may prefer to earn high wages if they survive than to be compensated vicariously if they do not. Typically, such workers would be men without dependants trying to build up a stake. For obvious reasons, such workers would have to be knowledgable enough about their business to be sure their employer is taking appropriate precautions for their survival.

Adjudication

Uncertainty about the magnitude of damages generates substantial legal costs over and above the other costs of defects or accidents. My stove explodes, causing some property damage and some injury. If the law exempts the maker from responsibility, I bear the full cost of the accident, whatever it turns out to be. If the law requires the maker to compensate me for the damage, then a dispute typically arises about the magnitude of the harm. I claim damages of $200,000. The maker recognizes damages of only $50,000. Society requires a mechanism for resolving the dispute. That mechanism is the civil law. I, the plaintiff, sue the maker for $200,000. The maker of the stove, as defendant, claims the harm to be no more than $50,000. A judge or jury has to decide between us, specifying the appropriate award in this case. The maker and I each hire lawyers who, between them, use up a significant proportion of the $150,000 in dispute. The combined cost to us of the two lawyers and to the state for conducting the trial would typically be about half the money in dispute, but could in some circumstances eat up the surplus entirely.

Suppose, for instance, that the gap between claims is $150,000, that each party's legal fee in the event of a trial is $50,000, and that each party has a 50 percent chance of winning his suit (where, for simplicity, there is assumed to be no chance of an intermediate verdict with, say, two-thirds of the sum under the dispute to me and one-third to the maker of the defective product). The legal fees can be avoided if one party backs off, but neither party does so because there is an expected gain from going to court. Each party's expected gain from the trial would be $25,000 (50 percent of $150,000 less legal fees of $50,000). In these circumstances, there would be room for a deal. Parties to the dispute may *bargain in the shadow of the law*. For both parties, the bargain must be preferable to a trial. I must receive something more than $75,000 (the sum of the stove-maker's initial offer and my expected additional gain from going to trial). The stove-maker must pay me no more than $175,000 (the difference between my initial demand and his expected saving from going to trial). For instance, the stove-maker might agree to pay me $125,000, which is half way between my claim of $200,000 and the maker's claim of $50,000, to avoid the trial. That would be mutually advantageous, but such a bargain is not always negotiated. The parties may disagree about the division of the surplus. Knowing that the maker will offer to split the difference, I may raise my initial claim for damages above what I know the true damages to be. Or the maker may hang tough, doing whatever he can to raise my cost of litigation to deter future claims. Tobacco companies are alleged to have adopted this "General Patton" strategy to deter claims for compensation for illness associated with smoking. Cases do go to trial, and trials are expensive. By itself, this consideration points to the principle of *caveat emptor* placing liability for harm upon the buyer rather than upon the maker.

Observability

To demonstrate that the market supplies the "correct" percentage of defective stoves, it was necessary to assume that the buyer of a stove knows how careful the stove-maker has chosen to be. With a transaction cost of $200 and an efficient percentage of defective stoves of 5 percent, the buyer pays an expected $230.51 for a working stove. He pays that all at once if the law or a privately arranged contract requires the stove-maker to cover the full cost of defects. He pays that in stages – $209 for the stove itself and the rest as the expected cost of defects – if the law or a privately arranged contract places responsibility for the replacement of defective stoves upon the buyer rather than upon the maker. In either case, the buyer's expected cost is the same.

These two legal regimes cease to be equivalent when the buyer does not know how much the maker has spent to control the percentage of defects. Nothing changes if the maker is held responsible for defects because the full expected cost to the maker is entirely independent of what the buyer does or does not know at the moment of sale. As before, the maker has every incentive to choose the percentage of defects to minimize the expected average cost per working stove. But if the maker bears no responsibility for defective stoves and if the buyer cannot tell at the moment of sale how careful the maker has been, then the maker has no incentive to bear any cost over and above the minimum cost of production. Referring to table 11.1 above, the maker spends $199 to produce a stove with a rate of defects of 9 percent. Competition among stove-makers reduces the price to $199 as well. The buyer is now worse off than he would be if the maker were liable for the full cost of replacing defective stoves *or* if the percentage of defective stoves could be observed at the moment of sale. He pays less for a new stove ($199 rather than $209), but the full cost of a working stove rises from $230.51 to $238.46.

As nobody gains from the buyer's inability to observe the quality of the product, a maker of stoves will do what he can to supply or compensate for the missing information. He may provide a warranty on his product, in effect converting the regime from one where the buyer bears the cost of defects to one where the seller bears the cost of defects. The maker may "brand" his product so that in time buyers will come to know its quality. He may seek to establish a reputation for quality by advertising which may or may not be mendacious or misleading.

Failure of the buyer to observe the percentage of defects would seem to call for a legal regime where responsibility for defects lies with the maker, but it may not matter very much what the law requires because the maker, in his own interest, has an incentive to supply the missing information or to contract around the law, taking upon himself the obligation to compensate the buyer for defects. On the other hand, when differences in quality among products are more subtle and diverse than the mere percentage of defects, the maker's strategies for conveying information may be less successful. Problems of identifying damages, adjudication and observability intersect when there is some question about whether a product conforms to any given standard.

Fault

The word "defective" loads the dice against the maker, conveying the impression that he alone is responsible for defects. That was implicit in the example in table 11.1 where the probability of the stove being defective depended entirely on the maker's expenditure and not at all on how the stove is used by the buyer. Many situations do not conform to that pattern at all. A well-made stove may malfunction if used carelessly. A less-than-perfect stove may or may not cause harm depending on how careful the user turns out to be. Loss of machinery in transit due to the carelessness of the shipper may cause a larger or smaller loss of profit to the manufacturer depending on whether the manufacturer keeps spare parts in inventory. Accidents with ladders typically have more to do with how ladders are used than with how they are made. In general, the risk of harm depends upon how carefully a product is used as well as upon how carefully a product is made. A given accident may not have occurred if either the maker or the buyer had been "appropriately" careful, where appropriate is whatever combination of care by the maker and care by the user would have been agreed upon as part of the sale if such an agreement could be monitored and enforced.

There is a dilemma here. If the maker's care were somehow arranged to be appropriate, then the buyer's care could be rendered appropriate too by requiring the buyer to bear the full cost of accidents or mishaps. Similarly, if the buyer's care were somehow arranged to be appropriate, then the maker's care could be rendered appropriate too by requiring the maker to bear the full cost of accidents or mishaps. (The latter case was, in effect, assumed in the numerical example by making the risk of a defective stove dependent on the maker alone.) As long as only one party's behavior need be influenced, the law can exert that influence by deeming that party to be at fault. When accidents depend on both parties' behavior, the law could, in principle, be designed to minimize the total cost of accidents including the cost of the accidents themselves and of both parties' expenditure to avoid accidents, but it is often difficult to tell what the best law on that criterion would be. Fitting the law to each and every product and to each and every case would constitute a major abandonment of clear and simple rules enabling people to predict the full consequences of their actions. Sometimes one party can be identified as at fault. Sometimes not. The cost of adjudication when fault is disputed can be considerable.

Adjudication becomes especially messy when a defective product increases the probability of an event that might occur regardless. Suppose that the probability of contracting lung cancer rises from 10 percent if one does not smoke to 20 percent if one smokes, and that misinformation by tobacco companies or the spiking of cigarettes to make them more addictive has raised the incidence of smoking to twice what it would otherwise be, so that one-quarter of all smokers' lung cancer can be attributed to the actions of the tobacco companies. A smoker dying of lung cancer has no way of telling whether or not *his* misfortune is the fault of the tobacco company. It seems unreasonable that he should be compensated by the tobacco company for the full cost of his illness, but neither is it reasonable for the tobacco company to bear no responsibility at all. (Consider a more extreme example. Suppose a drug increases the incidence of fatal heart attacks by one per million users. Though a particular user who dies of a heart attack might not have died but for the use of the drug, one would not want to hold the maker responsible for all fatal heart attacks, especially as the drug may actually reduce mortality from other diseases and as substitute drugs may have even greater impacts on the incidence of fatal heart attacks.) The courts could award a fraction of the estimated harm to each possible victim, but courts have not been inclined to act in that way. Typically, smokers who contracted lung cancer have been awarded the full cost of their illness or nothing at all.

Returning to the original problem and pulling these strands together, the case for *caveat emptor* (exempting the maker from responsibility for defective products) rests on the considerable complication and expense in employing the courts to identify fault and to determine the appropriate compensation. Balanced against this is the loss of incentive for care by the maker when the buyer cannot identify the quality of what he buys. The decline in this century of the principle of *caveat emptor* and the considerable willingness of the courts, with the concurrence of the legislature, to arrange compensation for the injured party, may stem from the ever-greater ignorance of the ordinary person about the composition and qualities of the goods he buys. In the nineteenth century, a buyer of a horse or a wagon from the local merchant might be expected to judge quality for himself. In the twenty-first century, the typical buyer of a car, a computer, or a drug produced by a large international corporation has no idea why products work or what dangers lie in their use. Only the automobile manufacturer knows which safety devices are incorporated in the car and which safety devices have been rejected as too expensive.

Murder

All countries punish murder severely. Some countries impose the death penalty. Others impose long imprisonment instead. The choice between these punishments is less susceptible to precise analysis than the choice among rules for product liability, but we need not fall back on the crude supposition that customs are what they are independently of any assessment of the common good. Choice between punishments can, at least in part, be explained with reference to the utility of the citizen.

Long imprisonment was not a serious option until recent times. The Bible sanctioned the death penalty. The Koran sanctioned the death penalty. Every ancient religion sanctioned the death penalty, or accepted it as inevitable. Throughout the world and throughout history until quite recently, every society imposed the death penalty for murder, and, frequently, for many lesser crimes as well. We cannot rule out *a priori* the possibility that the teachings of all religions and the practices of all societies were mistaken or, perhaps, a manifestation of class-based law that could have been jettisoned in a more egalitarian society, but there are reasons for supposing that those teachings and practices were warranted. In ancient times, when the standard of living was very much lower than it is today, imprisonment for murder would have been prohibitively costly and would have constituted a poor deterrent to would-be murderers whose standard of living in prison could not have been much below their standard of living on the outside if they were to survive in prison at all. By comparison with the death penalty, imprisonment would have been so costly and would have deterred so few murders that no reasonable person, however squeamish or kind-hearted, could suppose imprisonment to be the better option.

The balance of considerations is different today. A diversity of practice not noticeably connected to differences among countries in the standard of living suggests a diversity of criteria which may be weighted differently by different people. An important aspect of the problem will for the moment be swept under the rug. Not all murders are equal in the eyes of the law, and sentencing is meted out accordingly. When murder is punished by imprisonment, the term may be long or short depending on the circumstances of the crime. When courts may choose between imprisonment and execution, the latter is typically reserved for the most heinous murders. Ignore such considerations. To focus the analysis, suppose all murders are alike and must be punished identically. Society must choose between punishment by execution and punishment by imprisonment for a fixed number of years. The principal criteria for this choice are as follows.

Deterrence

Deterrence is forward looking. It is the punishment of crime today as a signal to the would-be criminal that he will be punished for similar crimes tomorrow. A law deters when the crime rate is reduced. On this criterion, the best law is whatever serves to minimize the incidence of crime. If the incidence of crime is not reduced, then punishment would not be warranted at all, as, for instance, when the perpetrator of a crime does not know right from wrong. Throughout history, the minimization of the number of murders has been the overriding objective of the law of murder, but the superiority of the death penalty on this criterion is probably less pronounced now than formerly. As mentioned above, imprisonment has become more affordable and more of a deterrent with the widening of the gap between the quality of life in prison and outside. At the same time, the efficacy of the death penalty in containing the number of murders may diminish because the standard for proof of guilt is higher in practice when the punishment is more severe. Judges and juries are expected to convict the accused if they believe him guilty "beyond reasonable doubt." Doubt deemed reasonable when punishment is by imprisonment may, in practice, be deemed unreasonable when punishment is by execution, for imprisonment may be reversed if new evidence eventually reveals the verdict to have been mistaken. In the mind of the would-be murderer, the lower probability of conviction may outweigh the higher penalty, reducing, if not eliminating, the extra deterrence of the death penalty over and above imprisonment. Unlikely to have been of great significance in the distant past, this consideration may be of some importance now. It is said that in the early nineteenth century, the death penalty was abolished for minor crimes because juries simply refused to convict. A similar process may be at work today in the law of murder.

Considering deterrence alone, apart from other aspects of the law of murder to be discussed below, the death penalty is preferable to long imprisonment if

$$M_D < M_I \tag{2}$$

where M_D is the number of murders committed when murder is punished by execution, and M_I is the number of murders committed when murder is punished by long imprisonment.

Punishing the innocent by mistake

Like all human institutions, the legal system works imperfectly. Diligent and honorable scientists cannot guarantee that space probes never fail. Diligent and honorable agents of law enforcement – police, prosecutors, judges, and juries – cannot guarantee that no innocent people are wrongfully convicted of crime. Meticulous care by the police and by the courts reduces the risk of wrongful conviction, but it is beyond the capacity of fallible people to eliminate wrongful conviction altogether. Imprisonment has two advantages over the death penalty: the harm to the innocent is less, and the punishment is reversible if evidence after the trial establishes that a person was convicted by mistake. On the other hand, there may be fewer wrongful convictions with the death penalty than with long imprisonment. The stronger the deterrent, the lower the incidence of crime and the smaller the number of wrongful convictions as well. Considering wrongful convictions alone and abstracting from all other aspects of the law of murder, the death penalty is preferable to long imprisonment if

$$\beta_D W_D < \beta_I W_I \tag{3}$$

where W_D is the number of wrongful convictions when murder is punished by execution, W_I is the number of wrongful convictions when murder is punished by imprisonment, β_D is the "cost" per wrongful conviction when murder is punished by execution, and β_I is the cost per wrongful conviction when murder is punished by imprisonment.

The "cost" of wrongful conviction has a family resemblance to the value of life in cost–benefit analysis. Your cost of wrongful conviction is 1,000 times the amount of money you would be prepared to pay to avoid a 1 in 1,000 chance of being wrongfully convicted. Typically, if not invariably, $\beta_I < \beta_D$, signifying that you would rather be wrongfully imprisoned than wrongfully executed, especially as wrongful imprisonment may be terminated if new evidence comes to light. Ordinarily, $W_D < W_I$, signifying that fewer people would be wrongfully convicted under the death penalty than with imprisonment, for fewer murders would be committed. Thus, it is uncertain whether or not $\beta_D W_D < \beta_I W_I$. The inequality may have held until recently because the death penalty was a sufficiently greater deterrent, but it may be reversed today.

Punishing the guilty

It is this aspect of the law of murder about which people differ most sharply. Two extreme views can be described as *deterrence* and *vengeance*. The discussion of deterrence above took no account of the murderer himself. When the welfare of the murderer is considered, one might define pure deterrence as the minimization of the number of violent deaths, treating murderers and victims equally in the calculation. Ignoring the discomfort of imprisonment as well as the cost of detection and punishment, the sole purpose of the law of murder would be to minimize the number of violent deaths, at the hands of murderers or at the hand of the state. On this criterion, equation (2) above would be transformed into equation (4), indicating that the death penalty is preferable to long imprisonment if and only if

$$M_D + G_D < M_I \tag{4}$$

where G_D is the number of people found guilty of and executed for murder. Pure deterrence recognizes no distinction between the murderer and his victim; the death of the innocent is neither more nor less undesirable than the death of the guilty. Once again, the criterion could justify the death penalty if the death penalty is very much more efficacious than long imprisonment.

Though vengeance and deterrence interact, pure vengeance is unconcerned about the incidence of crime. Pure vengeance looks to the crime that has been committed yesterday rather than to the prevention of crime tomorrow. It is a cry for justice from the relatives of the victims of murder who might extract justice privately if the law will not act on their behalf. On this view, the death penalty is preferable to long imprisonment even if the number of murders deterred is exactly the same. Execution of murderers on this view is a "good" rather than a "bad," and imprisonment would only be preferable to the death penalty if imprisonment were a fate worse than death or if imprisonment were the greater deterrent to crime.

Weighting vengeance and deterrence, and ignoring the risk of wrongful conviction, the death penalty would be warranted if

$$M_D + \gamma_D G_D < M_I + \gamma_I G_I \tag{5}$$

where G_D is the number of people found guilty and executed for murder, G_I is the number of people found guilty and imprisoned for murder, γ_D is one's degree of concern for the executed murderer, and γ_I is one's degree of concern for the imprisoned murderer.

If deterrence were one's only concern in the design of the law, then $\gamma_D > \gamma_I > 0$ on the principle that harm to anybody is deemed unfortunate. If vengeance were one's only concern in the design of the law, then $\gamma_D < \gamma_I < 0$ on the principle that harm inflicted by the state on murderers is *per se* desirable and that execution is a more fitting retribution than imprisonment. Obviously, $G_D < M_D$ and $G_I < M_I$ because the criminal justice system is imperfect.

Some people consider all killing, by the murderer and by the state, as almost equally deplorable. One may see the murderer as an unfortunate by-product of a disturbed childhood in a poorly organized society, or one may have a special abhorrence to killing by the state. Though the hangman does the deed, each citizen is implicated in an execution because he, as voter, commanded the deed to be done. Deterrence would then become the only justification for punishment, and the values of γ_I and γ_D would be positive. Other people believe that everyone must take full responsibility for his actions and see the killing of a murderer by the state as appropriate and right, regardless of the consequence for the incidence of murder. Such people see vengeance as the justification for punishment, and their values of γ_I and γ_D are negative.

The cost of detection, litigation, and punishment

Just as society buys safety in the construction of roads or the provision of medical care, so too does society buy safety through the criminal justice system. Expenditure on the police reduces the incidence of crime, allowing the streets to be patrolled more carefully and more resources to be devoted to each and every investigation. Expenditure on the judiciary reduces the incidence of crime, allowing prosecutions to be conducted more quickly and more thoroughly, and raising the probability that the criminal will be punished in accordance with the law.

A person's trade-off between cost and safety is similar to Robinson Crusoe's trade-off between bread and cheese in chapter 3. Ignoring both the well-being of the criminal and the wrongful conviction of the innocent, a person's taste can be represented by indifference curves over two goods, income and the probability of survival, where income (assumed net of the cost of the criminal justice system) is the value at

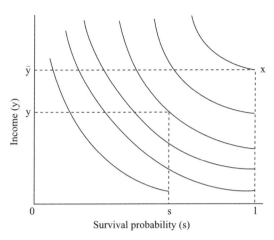

Figure 11.2 A person's indifference curves for income and probability of survival.

current prices of bread, cheese, and all other goods consumed, where the only threat to survival is murder and where all quantities are per year.

The person's indifference curves are shown in figure 11.2 with income, y, on the vertical axis and survival probability, s, on the horizontal axis. The point x, with coordinates $\bar{y}$ and 1, represents the person's situation as it would be if murder vanished spontaneously. His income would be $\bar{y}$ and his survival probability would be 1. Otherwise, his net income is y and his survival probability is s, where

$$y = \bar{y} - c \tag{6}$$

$$s = 1 - m \tag{7}$$

where c is the cost to that person of the criminal justice system, and m is his probability of being murdered in the course of the year.

For depicting the cost of crime, it is helpful to reformulate indifference curves with reference to c and m (the cost per person of the criminal justice system and the murder rate) rather than with reference to y and s. That is easily done. Figure 11.3 is a reconstruction of figure 11.2 with indifference curves looked at not from the origin, 0, but upside-down and back-to-front from the point x. The point x* in figure 11.3 becomes the mirror image of the point 0 in figure 11.2. By construction, the indifference curves are bowed out rather than bowed in and a person's welfare *increases toward the origin* rather than away from it.

The technology of crime prevention can be represented as an extra curve in figure 11.3. This is the dashed curve beginning on the horizontal axis at the point m* (the murder rate as it would be if nothing were spent on the criminal justice system and no punishment were ever inflicted by the state) and rising ever more steeply until the entire national income is devoted to crime prevention and the murder rate is reduced to m**. Note that m** remains greater than 0 because not all murder can be deterred; some murder is inevitably committed no matter how large a share of the nation's resources is devoted to the prevention of crime. Think of figure 11.3 as

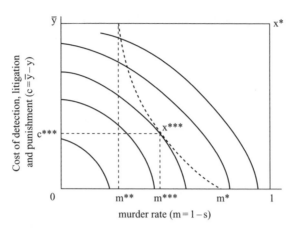

Figure 11.3 Indifference curves for the cost of the criminal justice system and the murder rate.

referring to a typical person so that the cost of deterrence to this person and the cost per head to society as a whole are one and the same.

Optimal deterrence is signified by the point x*** where the "cost of deterrence" curve is just tangent to an indifference curve, the highest (in the sense of making a person as well off as possible) indifference curve attainable with the available technology of crime detection and prosecution. The corresponding expenditure per head on the prevention of murder is c***, and the corresponding murder rate is m***. The common slope of the indifference curve and the "cost of deterrence" curve at the point x*** is the typical person's dollar value of murder prevention, a close relative of the value of life in cost-benefit analysis as discussed in the last chapter. The slope represents the amount of money this person is prepared to pay for a reduction in the murder rate.

When society must choose between the death penalty and imprisonment, each punishment can be represented by a distinct cost of deterrence curve, and each curve is tangent to an indifference curve at a point like x*** in figure 11.3. The punishments can then be evaluated in accordance with the locations of the corresponding x***. The better punishment is whichever brings the person to the "higher" (the closer to the origin) indifference curve. Of course, the locations of the cost of deterrence curves need not remain stationary over time, and, by definition, prosperity increases the average ȳ for society as a whole, so that, as argued above, the better punishment at one time and place need not remain the better punishment everywhere and forever.

Years ago, the cost of execution would have been very much less than the cost of life imprisonment. Today, that is no longer so. The cost of actually putting a person to death may be small by comparison with the cost of keeping a person in prison for the rest of his life, but the full cost of punishment by execution is far greater than the cost of the execution itself. Societies that still impose the death penalty go to enormous effort and expense in litigation to be sure that only the appropriate criminals are executed. Not all murders are alike as we have so far assumed, and the law typically reserves the death penalty for murders that are especially heinous or brutal. Fear of placing a convicted murderer in the wrong category compounds the fear of mistaken conviction. When Canada had the death penalty, the federal cabinet had to approve each execution, and frequently commuted the sentence to life imprisonment. In the United States, a convicted murderer can expect to spend ten to fifteen years in prison while his appeals to higher courts are being considered, at vast expense to cover the cost of lawyers for the defense, lawyers for the prosecution, the court, and imprisonment while waiting for a final determination. Of course, this extra cost per murderer might be offset by a lower murder rate if the death penalty really were a significantly greater deterrent, a question about which there is no firm consensus in the literature of crime and punishment.

Pulling all this together, a citizen would prefer to punish murder by execution rather than by imprisonment if

$$[\alpha M_D + \gamma_D G_D + \beta_D W_D + C_D] < [\alpha M_I + \gamma_I G_I + \beta_I W_I + C_I] \qquad (8)$$

where the subscripts D and I refer to the death penalty and imprisonment, M is the number of murders committed, G is the number of guilty murderers punished, W is the number of innocent people punished for murder by mistake, C is the dollar value of the cost of detection, conviction, and punishment of murderers, and α, β, and γ are a person's weights of the different harms associated with murder, all expressed as dollar values so that the weight attached to C is automatically equal to 1.

Society can be thought of as choosing the punishment for murder and arranging the specifics of the criminal justice system to minimize the weighted sum of all four harms of crime, M, G, W, and C. One favors the death penalty if the weighted sum of the four costs is less when murderers are executed than when murderers are imprisoned. The four harms are weighted in equation (8) by supposedly invariant parameters representing the preferences of the citizen. In reality, the weighting would be more complex. Attainable combinations of M, G, W and C would be represented by a function comparable to the dashed curve showing attainable combinations of M and C in figure 11.3. In a community of identical people, all combinations of M, G, W and C, attainable or not, could be represented by multi-dimensional indifference curves. Society's choice of M, G, W and C would then lie on the highest attainable indifference curve.

Each side of equation (8) is the minimized value of the full social cost of murder when one of the two punishments is in force. The technology of crime detection and punishment varies from place to place and from time to time, but, at any given place and time, society is confronted with a fixed set of choices among the four harms, regardless of anybody's views about their relative importance. By contrast, the weightings of the four harms – α, β, and γ – are a matter of individual taste, and may vary from one person to the next. This is especially evident for the parameter γ which is positive for people who place no weight on vengeance per se and who see punishment as a regrettable necessity, but negative for people who look upon punishment as desirable for its own sake. In fact, our designation of M, G, W, and C as four harms is inaccurate for people in the latter group who see G as a "good" rather than as a "bad." People differ, though less radically, about α and β as well. Some see all violent death, from murder and from wrongful execution, as equally deplorable; for such people, $\alpha = \beta$. Others have a special horror of mistaken execution, holding themselves in some sense responsible or fearing a general corruption of the state from the execution of the innocent; for such people $\beta > \alpha$. Concern for the plight of the guilty may also differ markedly from one person to another.

Is there a natural law of murder that is sufficiently comprehensive and exact to rank execution and imprisonment? Can we speak unambiguously of one punishment or the other as the more conducive to the common good? It has been clear since chapter 1 that the appropriate law must be conditional on the technology of the economy and society. That was evident when patricide was seen as necessary, and therefore just, in some societies, though it is an abomination in others. The law of product safety and the law of murder have both changed radically in many countries over the last one hundred years. All that can reasonably be asked is whether there can be identified a "best" law in the service of the common good at any specific place and time.

As illustrated in the law of product liability, the efficiency criterion (the maximization of expected national income at invariant prices and with adjustments for changes in personal goods normally excluded from the measure of the national income) may, for some torts and crimes, be an adequate indicator of the common good. Behind the veil of ignorance, not knowing one's place in society when the veil is lifted, and as likely to end up as defendant or plaintiff, one might as well opt for the maximization of the national income because whatever maximizes the national income must maximize one's own expected income as well. Efficiency is a reasonable surrogate for the common good not just for the law of product liability, but for most commercial law.

A similar assessment can be made for the choice between imprisonment and execution as punishment for murder as long as the minimization of the number of murders is the overwhelmingly predominant consideration. The assessment changes fundamentally when the choice of punishment requires a balancing of the four harms together, for there is no legal analogue to market-determined prices by which different harms may be compared on a common, universally accepted scale. Just as people differ in the shapes of their indifference curves for amounts of bread and cheese, so too do they differ in their weightings of the four harms. People's weightings may be conditioned to some extent by their circumstances in society, but, even behind the veil, some differences in weightings would normally persist. The veil of ignorance test corrects for people's circumstances in society but not for their tastes. Thus, even behind the veil, there is no universally agreed upon best punishment, no punishment that everybody would choose as in his own interest when he is equally likely to occupy the station of each and every person in society: the law-abiding citizen fearing crime, the wrongfully accused, and the murderer himself. People with different weightings of the four harms are no more likely to agree on the best punishment for murder behind the veil than when the veil is lifted. It is hard to see how differences among people's criteria for the law of murder can be reconciled, except politically when there is a general agreement to accept whatever a majority of voters and legislators decides.

Natural law remains as a goal or ideal. We would all like to think that there is a "best" law out there to be discovered, a law most conducive to the welfare of society as a whole, a law we would all agree to adopt if only we understood the full needs of society and the full technology of social interaction. Sometimes such law can be identified. Sometimes not.

LAW AS A CONSTRAINT UPON THE LEGISLATURE AND THE ADMINISTRATION

The analysis of voting in chapter 9 began with James Madison's gloomy assertion in *The Federal Papers* that "democracies have ever been spectacles of turbulence and contention; have ever been found incompatible with personal security, or the rights of property; and have, in general, been as short in their lives, as they have been violent in their deaths." Madison's concerns were reflected in the exploitation problem in voting about the allocation of a sum of money among the voters themselves. No equilibrium emerged except with the connivance of a coalition of voters, the most likely coalition consisting of a bare majority prepared to take the entire sum for themselves and excluding the minority altogether. Strictly speaking, there is no telling within the formal analysis who the members of the majority coalition will be, but the formation of a majority coalition is facilitated by any pre-existing line of division among voters. Race, religion, ethnicity, location, and language may all serve as badges by which members of a majority coalition are identified. Badges need not be inherently divisive. They become divisive because democracy renders them profitable. The exploitation problem was not just that a majority exploits a minority, but that democracy self-destructs because nobody is prepared to accept the outcome of the vote peacefully. Chapter 9 then identified several defenses of democracy: natural defenses where voting is about matters not reducible to the allocation of a sum of money among voters, procedural defenses in the design of the voting mechanism, and institutional defenses – private property and civil rights – that enable society to avoiding voting about matters equivalent to the allocation of money among voters.

The discussion of civil rights in chapter 9 was brief and formal, almost as though, once enshrined in a constitution, civil rights could enforce themselves. In practice, the protection of civil rights must be assigned to a judiciary with some degree of independence from the legislature and the administration. Defense against exploitation of unpopular individuals or minority groups is the domain of public law, which may be divided into two branches: administrative law placing constraints on the discretion of the bureaucracy, and constitutional law placing constraints upon voters and legislators. A written or unwritten constitution is a defense of civil rights and a specification of the spheres of jurisdiction of the federal and provincial governments in those countries where the powers of lower levels of government are constitutionally entrenched. We consider these matters in turn.

Administrative discretion

A modern society needs a great deal of regulation. Public agencies decide when a person is qualified to become an immigrant, oversee standards of cleanliness in restaurants, check the safety of employment, run schools and hospitals, certify doctors and lawyers, and so on. Public agencies cannot do their job without a certain amount of discretion in their dealings with the public. Parliament can demand certification of doctors, but cannot specify in detail what skill is required, and must trust the certification board to discriminate between good doctors and bad, by examination or by watching candidates at work. Discretion cannot be unlimited, for administrators armed with unlimited discretion could victimize anybody, destroying the independence of the citizen required for the maintenance of democratic government. A few cases will illustrate what may be at stake.

Yick Wo v. *Hopkins* (US Supreme Court, 1886) was about the right to operate a laundry. Ostensibly as a fire regulation, an ordinance of the city of San Francisco required permission of the Board of Supervisors of the city to operate a laundry. Anybody operating a laundry without permission would be imprisoned. Yick Wo, who had been operating a laundry in San Francisco for twenty years in compliance with the earlier fire regulations, was said by the sheriff to be in violation of the new regulations and ordered to close his business. Yick Wo sued the sheriff. The suit eventually reached the Supreme Court. It was noted by the court that "all Chinese applications are, in fact, denied, and those of Caucasians granted," from which it was inferred that the regulations "seem intended to confer, and actually do confer... naked and arbitrary power to give or withhold consent, not only as to places, but as to persons... depriving parties of their property without due process of law." The Supreme Court sided with lower courts in pronouncing the San Francisco regulations to be in violation of the Fourteenth Amendment of the American Constitution, specifically of the clause: "Nor shall any state deprive any person of life, liberty or property without due process of law: nor deny any persons within its jurisdiction the equal protection of the laws."

United States v. *Ju Toy* (US Supreme Court, 1904) illustrates how extensive and how pernicious unconstrained administrative discretion can be. Ju Toy arrived at San Francisco on a ship from China. At that time, Chinese immigration to the United States (and to Canada as well) was prohibited. However, Ju Toy claimed to be an American citizen born in the United States and returning home from a trip to China. The immigration officers refused to believe him. A written appeal to the Secretary of Commerce and Labor was rejected. The case was appealed all the way up to the Supreme Court. The legal question in this case was whether there could be an appeal to ordinary courts of law from a determination by immigration officials with concurrence by the office of the Secretary of Commerce and Labour. A majority of the Supreme Court decreed that there could not, that the decision of the administration would be final and binding, that "due process of law does not require judicial trial" in this type of case. Leave aside the rights and wrongs of the ban on Chinese immigration. That was the law of the land at that time, however unjust it may appear to us today. The matter before the Supreme Court was the limit, if any, upon the authority of immigration officials to determine whether a person was native born. Dissenting from the verdict, a minority of the judges noted that the Act by which Ju Toy was being excluded placed the "burden of proof... upon Chinese persons claiming the right of admission to the United States," giving claimants very little opportunity to verify their claims and creating a state of affairs in which a "citizen of the United States must, by virtue of the ruling of a ministerial officer, be banished from the country of which he is a citizen." A law banning immigration of Chinese could be converted by administrative discretion into a procedure for banishment of some native born Americans unless the courts were prepared to intervene, as they were not in this case. A spirited dissent by the minority judges did succeed in influencing the climate of opinion against excessive administrative discretion.

Flemming v. *Nestor* (US Supreme Court 1960) was about the citizen's right to an old age pension. Ephram Nestor had immigrated to the United States in 1913 and was a member of the Communist Party from 1933 to 1939. From 1935 to 1955, Nestor and his employers contributed to the US government's old age and survivors trust fund to provide him with an old age pension. In 1956, Nestor was deported for having been a communist, his old age pension was terminated and his wife in America was impoverished. The law under which Nestor was deported stipulated that a person not born in the United States, but a legal immigrant, could be banished if he had at any time been a member of the communist party, even at a time when membership itself was not against the law. It is strange that the Supreme Court tolerated a law banishing Nestor for an act which was not a crime when the act was committed, but that is not our concern here. Our concern is with the denial of the old age pension as an administrative decision. The Supreme Court upheld the administration in this case, on the peculiar ground that Nestor's benefits were not an "accrued property right" and "cannot be soundly analogized to that of a holder of an annuity." Once again, victimization of an individual by the administration could have been blocked by the courts, and was not.

Roncarelli v. *Duplessis* (Canadian Supreme Court, 1959) illustrates how an agency of government might destroy a person's livelihood as unofficial punishment for adherence to an unpopular religion. Mr Roncarelli was the owner of a successful restaurant in Montreal and a member of the Witnesses of Jehovah. For some time, Witnesses of Jehovah had been arrested and tried for distributing their magazines, *The Watch Tower* and *Awake*, which were deemed insulting and offensive to the religious feelings of the general population. Mr Roncarelli did not distribute these magazines himself, but he provided bail for his coreligionists. The success of Mr Roncarelli's restaurant depended on his having a permit to sell liquor. Permits were issued by the Liquor Commission which had the authority "to cancel any permit at its discretion." On instructions from Mr Duplessis (who was at once the attorney general and the premier of the province), the administrator of the Liquor Commission cancelled Mr Roncarelli's permit. Mr Roncarelli sued Mr Duplessis, and the case eventually reached the Canadian Supreme Court. The court found for Mr Roncarelli on the grounds that the government's reasons for denying a permit "should unquestionably be such and only such as are incompatible with the purpose envisaged by the statute... There is no such thing as absolute and untrammelled 'discretion,'... for any reason that can be suggested to the mind of the administrator; no legislative act... can be taken to contemplate an unlimited arbitrary power, regardless of the nature or purpose of the statute."

All of these cases may be seen as pertaining to the *rule of law*. We speak of the rule of law as "the absence of arbitrary power on the part of the government" and as a constraint on the society whereby "no man is punishable or can be lawfully made to suffer in body or goods except for a distinct breach of law established in the ordinary legal manner before the ordinary courts of the land."

The protection of civil rights

Though there is no watertight division between administrative law and the protection of civil rights, a rough and ready distinction can be drawn between trespassing on people's rights by the administration in its interpretation of otherwise unobjectionable laws and trespassing on people's rights by the legislature through laws that are inherently discriminatory or in violation of the written or unwritten constitution. The one pits the courts against the bureaucracy. The other pits the courts against the legislature.

The court's willingness to strike down legislation as unconstitutionally discriminatory is dramatically illustrated by the contrast two famous cases, *Plessy* v. *Ferguson* (US Supreme Court, 1896) and *Brown* v. *Board of Education of Topeka* (US Supreme Court, 1954). The first of these cases permitted the United States to segregate people by race; the second overturned the first. *Plessy* v. *Ferguson* was about segregation by race of passengers on railroads. The State of Louisiana assigned white and colored passengers to different coaches. Though seven-eighths white, Plessy was classified as colored and arrested when he insisted on riding in the coach reserved for whites. The Supreme Court denied that "the enforced separation of the two races stamps the colored race with a badge of inferiority" and confirmed the decision of the lower courts to let the Louisiana law stand. Dissenting, a minority of the judges asserted instead that "everyone knows that the statute in question had its origin in the purpose, not so much to exclude white persons from railroad cars occupied by blacks, as to exclude colored people from coaches occupied by or assigned to white persons." Over half a century was to pass before that decision was reversed in *Brown* v. *Board of Education of Topeka*. The case was about segregated schooling rather than travel, but the principle was much the same. The court decreed that "in the field of public education the doctrine of 'separate but equal' has no place. Separate facilities are inherently unequal." It is interesting to speculate whether *Brown* was absolutely necessary, whether the massive change in the climate of opinion after the Second World War could have put an end to legal segregation by legislation without intervention by the judiciary. American federalism might have been an insuperable barrier. Segregation might have been abolished in some states but preserved in others indefinitely.

The constitutional entrenchment of property rights

The protection of private property could be, and to a large extent is, left to the good sense of the legislature. Legislatures can be presumed to understand the benefits of private property – prosperity and democracy itself – and to realize that to undermine private property is to lose almost everything of value in a modern industrial state. Property rights may, nevertheless, be more secure when constitutionally entrenched. A political party in office must resist the temptation to victimize or expropriate its opponents, to enrich its supporters and to preserve itself in office indefinitely. A political party is more likely to restrain itself today, the more certain it can be that the opposition party will be equally restrained tomorrow. A degree of constitutional entrenchment of property may help to provide that certainty. On the other hand, a comprehensive constitutional injunction against expropriation of private property may affect society in unintended and unfortunate ways.

A degree of constitutional protection is provided by the principle of *just compensation*. People can only be said to own property if they are reasonably sure the government will not arbitrarily take it away. The virtues of the institution of private property – the efficiency of the competitive economy and the economic conditions for government by majority rule – require not perfect security of tenure, but more security than there would be if the government of the day had no compunction about canceling one's property rights as it sees fit. A school is to be built in my town. Somebody's property has to be acquired and his house demolished to make way for the new school. Ideally, the municipal government would buy a property from a willing seller. That is not always possible because the owner of the only suitable site may not wish to sell or may try to hold the municipality to ransom. Purchase becomes especially difficult when many adjacent properties have to be acquired to make way for a road. If the municipality were empowered to take the property without compensation, everybody's property would become insecure and the threat of expropriation could be used by the government in office to intimidate its opponents. If every property owner could hold out for a mutually acceptable price, schools and roads might become exorbitantly expensive. The rule within the common law is that the government may take private property but must compensate the owner according to the going market price. The Fifth Amendment to the Constitution of the United States includes the phrase, "nor shall private property be taken for public use without just compensation."

The principle of just compensation can be widely or narrowly interpreted, and there has evolved a large body of law about the boundary between the *taking* of property for which compensation is mandatory and the exercise of the *police power* where people may be affected differently but no compensation is required. Consider the list of public policies with private consequences: My house is expropriated to make way for the construction of a school or a road. My land is flooded when an adjacent river is dammed. My business is ruined when the street on which it is located is converted from two-way to one-way. My distillery becomes valueless when the municipality imposes prohibition. My property loses much of its value because of the noise from a new airport nearby. A municipal ordinance forbids me to drain a swamp on my land for a housing project. An increase in the progressivity of the income tax reduces my net after-tax income if I am rich and increases my net income if I am poor. In all of these cases, public policy transfers income or property from one person or group to another. Some would argue that every one of these transfers is unconstitutional. Others would restrict compensation to the direct taking of tangible property. The courts have no choice but to sort the matter out case by case. *Pennsylvania Central Transportation Co. v. New York City* (US Supreme Court, 1958) was about Grand Central Station in New York. The City designated Grand Central Station a historical site, disallowing the construction of a very profitable skyscraper on the site. The owner of the property sued for compensation, claiming the loss of potential revenue to be a taking and arguing that it ought not to be penalized now for building a beautiful structure a hundred years ago. The court sided with the city that the designation of a building as a historical site, together with restrictions on alterations, is not a taking prohibited by the Fifth Amendment.

Other aspects of the constitutional entrenchment of property rights are illustrated in *Lochner* v. *New York* (US Supreme Court, 1905) about the regulation of the workplace and *Pollock* v. *Farmers' Loan and Trust Co.* (US Supreme Court, 1895) about income tax. In both cases, the Supreme Court interpreted the constitution as imposing a more stringent constraint on public policy than was envisioned by the legislature. *Lochner* was about the constitutionality of a New York law prohibiting bakers from working more than 64 hours a week. A majority of the judges of the US Supreme Court declared the law to be in violation of the US constitution, arguing that the ostensible purpose of the law, to protect public health, was no more than a front for the redistribution of income. In the words of the judgment, "It is impossible for us to shut our eyes to the fact that many of the laws of this character, while passed under what is classed to be the police power for the purpose of protecting the public health or welfare are, in reality, passed from other motives." The precedent in *Lochner* lasted until the 1930s when the court reversed itself on a great deal of social legislation. By then, the prevalent opinion in the United States and Canada was that the benefits to be derived from the institution of private property were not placed in jeopardy by the regulation of hours and wages. Many still believed that the regulation of hours and wages was unwise and that the common good would be best served by leaving that aspect of the market alone, but much of the heat had gone out of the debate because few believed any longer that the regulation of hours and wages was likely to destroy the free market altogether. A consensus seems to have emerged that such social legislation is not forbidden by the constitution and is best left for the legislature to establish or disestablish as it sees fit.

It is hard not to believe that the judges' opinion in *Pollock* on the constitutionality of the federal income tax was conditioned by their opinions about the desirability of the tax. The judgment was ostensibly about whether the income tax is a direct tax. Section 9 of article 1 of the US constitution stipulates that "No capitation or other direct tax shall be laid unless in proportion to the *census* or enumeration herein before directed to be taken." In *Hylton* v. *United States* (1796) the court had decreed that there are only two direct taxes, "capitation or poll taxes . . . and a tax on land." At various times in the nineteenth century, the federal government had successfully levied an income tax. Nevertheless, a bare majority of the court in *Pollock* decided that, as the income tax is imposed on income from land as well as from capital and labor, it must be a direct tax in violation of the constitution. The income tax remained unconstitutional until 1913 when, presumably in anticipation of war, its constitutionality was restored by the sixteenth amendment to the constitution, "The Congress shall have power to lay and collect taxes on incomes, from whatever source derived, without apportionment among the several states, and without regard to any census or enumeration."

A distinction was drawn in the introduction to this book between two sets of rights, property rights – ownership of land, dwellings, factories, and their own skills – that people possess unequally, and civil rights – the right to vote, to free speech, to practice one's own religion, and so on – that people possess equally. Many of the law cases we have been examining can be looked upon as pertaining to disputes over the boundary between these two sets of rights. *Lochner* upheld the right to make contracts against the right to a modicum of leisure. *Pollock* defended what the court saw as a property right in refusing to draw a distinction between *ad hominem* expropriation and a systematic requirement for wealthy people to pay more than a per capita share of the cost of government. The subsequent overturning of these cases was a redrawing of the boundary between rights, enlarging the scope of civil rights and reducing the scope of property rights accordingly.

Jurisdiction of different levels of government

Powers of the different levels of government may or may not be constitutionally entrenched. The United Kingdom and France are "unitary states" with no constitutional sanction for subordinate levels of government. To be sure, the United Kingdom and France have county and municipal governments, but these have no constitutional standing. County and municipal governments may be altered or abolished altogether at the pleasure of the central government. Canada and the United States have "federal governments." The powers of provincial and state governments are set out in the constitution, so that, in Canada for instance, the federal government has no jurisdiction over education or language because these are reserved in the Canadian constitution for the provincial governments. Municipal governments, on the other hand, have no constitutional standing and are entirely under the authority of the provincial governments.

Federalism is a child of taste, fear, and greed. Federal government tends to be established when people in different regions want their governments to do different things, most importantly to protect and foster regionally concentrated language. With nation-wide majority-rule voting, any group constituting a majority within a region but a minority in the country as a whole is placed at the mercy of the majority unless that group's special concerns are protected by the constitutionally guaranteed power of a regional government. This consideration is paramount in Canada where the protection of the French language by a constitutionally sanctioned provincial government was an absolute requirement for Quebec's participation in a united Canada. No constitution can supply absolute protection. A constitution can at best supply a considerable degree of security because it is difficult to amend and cannot be overturned without undermining the legitimacy of the entire government. Federalism may assuage the citizen's fear of predatory government because it may be more difficult to enlarge the powers of government or to replace democracy with dictatorship when there are many governments to contend with, rather than just one. Alternatively, when small countries amalgamate into one large country, federal government may emerge for no better reason than to perpetuate the spheres of authority of the bureaucrats and politicians of the original countries.

Under a federal system of government, where the powers of the different levels of government are entrenched in a constitution, the Supreme Court cannot escape the obligation to resolve disputes over the exact boundaries between domains of authority. There is no other way for such disputes to be resolved. Jurisdiction over unemployment insurance was unassigned in the original Canadian constitution of 1867 because there was at the time no unemployment insurance and none was contemplated. Later on when unemployment insurance was introduced, the Supreme Court was obliged to decide whether it belonged under federal or provincial jurisdiction. The court had no option other than to torture the language of the constitution into a confession on the matter. It had to decide one way or another. Unemployment insurance might have been assigned to the provinces under item 13 of section 92 of the Canadian constitution granting the provinces jurisdiction over "property and civil rights in the province," or it might have been assigned to the federal government under the preamble of section 91 granting the federal government authority to "make Laws for the Peace, Order and Good Government of Canada." For reasons beyond my understanding, it chose to assign jurisdiction over unemployment insurance to the provinces. Subsequently, unemployment insurance was reassigned to the federal government by a constitutional amendment with the concurrence of the federal government and all the provincial governments.

The Canadian constitution is also silent about secession, with no explicit provision for the separation of a province. The closest the Canadian constitution comes to a provision about secession of a province is that any and every clause in the constitution can be amended by the unanimous consent of the federal government and the governments of all of the provinces, with no recourse to a direct vote by citizens. Unanimity of the provinces is widely believed to be at once too stringent a condition for secession and wrong in itself as it places no weight on popular opinion. Nor is there any reference in the constitution to the referendum as a vehicle for constitutional change. The matter became important with the emergence of a strong separatist movement in the province of Quebec. The history of Canada since the 1980s would suggest that most Canadians would be prepared to abide by the outcome of a referendum if the majority for separation were substantial and if the terms of separation were satisfactory.

It is in the interest of all Canadians – in Quebec and in English Canada – that the fate of Quebec be determined within a framework of law. Break-up of a country may be peaceful as in Czechoslovakia or violent as in Yugoslavia. A struggle over secession in Canada is more likely to be peaceful if Canadians can agree in advance upon the rules than if no such agreement is reached. Conflict is less likely to arise if it is known in advance whether and in what circumstances secession would be resisted by force, what the territories of the successor countries would be, how the responsibility for the Canadian national debt would be divided and what percentage of the national vote is required to trigger separation.

In *Reference re Secession of Quebec* (1998), the Canadian Supreme Court accepted a request from the federal government to pronounce on the legitimacy of the separation of Quebec. Specifically, the Supreme Court has been asked these questions: (1) Can Quebec unilaterally separate under the Canadian constitution? (2) Can Quebec unilaterally separate under international law? (3) If there is a conflict between the Canadian constitution and international law, which has precedence? This case placed the Supreme Court in an exceedingly difficult position. A degree of judicial activism was required to establish law where there is none now and where no government is empowered by the constitution to create it. Oddly enough, the Supreme Court refused to provide precise rules about whether, when, and how Quebec may separate from Canada. The Court decreed instead that a vote for separation "with a clear majority on a clear question" in a referendum in Quebec would trigger a "duty to negotiate" upon Quebec and the rest of Canada, with no clear presumption about what the outcome of that negotiation would be.

Judge-made law

Ideally, legislation and adjudication can be kept in two distinct compartments. The legislature makes laws, and the courts apply them. In practice, legislation and adjudication can never be kept entirely apart. There is, first, an unbridgeable gap between the text of the law and the facts of the case at hand. Words denote things imperfectly. Consider, for example, the boundary between patentable inventions and unpatentable scientific principles. How well along to commercial viability must a discovery be before it can be classified as an invention? Who gets the patent when one scientist announces a vague but probably feasible design on day 1 and another scientist announces a similar but better design on day 2? Can a patent on one invention block a second invention which is in some sense dependent on the first? Can a species of animals be patented? It can, but that was uncertain until the courts decreed so. Rightly or wrongly, these matters have been settled by the patent office in the first instance, but ultimately by the courts. A vast doctrine of administrative law has grown up around the question of when it is appropriate for the courts to second-guess or overturn the decisions of administrative tribunals. Lawyers speak in this context of the "open texture of the law," of the room for discretion in the case at hand. Some go so far as to argue that the law is "whatever the judges declare it to be," but the executive and the legislature would make short work of judges whose declarations were too outlandish. Judge-made law is at the root of the expansion of product liability since the 1950s. Over and above the court's responsibility to clarify the law in its application to the case at hand is its responsibility to challenge the legislature when legislation appears to violate the constitution, to victimize particular people or groups of people, or to threaten democratic government?

The dangers of judicial activism

Every branch of government has its vices: the legislature to exploit minorities, the administration to oppress citizens for the benefit of a ruling class, the judiciary to interpret the constitution in accordance with its own preferences or the prejudices of the social class from which the judges are chosen. Pick nine distinguished old folks, dress them in black robes and wigs, tenure them, venerate them, and you can be confident that, sooner or later, they will do something foolish or evil. We have already discussed cases that some readers may see as foolish or evil, though not all readers may agree which cases these are. I would like to close this chapter with three more.

At the head of most people's lists of unfortunate decisions is *Dred Scott* v. *Sandford* (US Supreme Court, 1857). In 1834, the United States was part slave, part free. Slavery was prevalent in the southern states and disallowed in the north. In that year, a slave named Dred Scott accompanied his master from Missouri, a slave state, to Wisconsin, a free state, and then returned with his master to Missouri. On arriving in Missouri, Dred Scott claimed to be a free man because he had become free on entering Wisconsin and because, once free, a person remains so always. The case gradually worked its way up through the lower courts to the US Supreme Court which delivered its verdict in 1857, just three years before the beginning of the US Civil War. A number of possible verdicts were open to the Court. It could have accepted Dred Scott's claim that once free, always free. It could have recognized the de facto situation at the time that migration from a slave state to a free state confers freedom as long as the former slave remains in the free state. Instead, it adopted the extreme pro-slavery position that (1) not being a citizen, a slave is not "entitled to sue as a citizen in a court of the United States," and (2) a slave is property which, like all other property, cannot be seized from its owner in *any* state of the United States. "The right of property in a slave is distinctly and expressly affirmed in the Constitution . . . the Act of Congress which prohibited holding and owning property of this kind in the territory of the United States north of the line therein mentioned, is not warranted by the Constitution and is therefore void."

One can only speculate about the consequences of this decision. Ten years afterwards, slavery was abolished throughout the United States, but the abolition was at the cost of a civil war more bloody and terrible for the people of the United States than any other war in its history. Since that war, it has been asked, over and over again, whether the war was really necessary. Slavery was at that time being abolished throughout the world, in Russia, in the Caribbean, in South America. In many places, abolition was effected peacefully by buying out the slave holders. If slavery is permitted in a country, and if slavery is evil, then everyone in that country, slaveholder and non-slaveholder alike, is guilty of that evil, and it would seem appropriate for everyone to share the burden of its removal. That was the procedure in Russia in 1864 where the holders of serfs were compensated by the state. A million innocent lives could have been spared if that procedure had been adopted in the United States too. Why not? Part of an answer may be that, by entrenching a constitutional right to hold slaves, the Supreme Court hardened opinions and made compromise that much more difficult.

Roe v. *Wade* (US Supreme Court, 1971) struck down state law limiting a woman's right to an abortion. The issue in this case was not primarily whether abortion should or should not be permitted, but who – the state legislatures or the courts – should decide whether abortion is to be permitted. Though abortion had been illegal in certain states since the founding of the United States, the Supreme Court discovered within the constitution a right of privacy that any ban on abortion would violate. In the words of the court, "The right of privacy whether it be founded on the Fourteenth Amendment's concept of personal liberty . . . or the Ninth Amendment's reservation of rights to the people, is broad enough to encompass a woman's decision whether or not to terminate her pregnancy." The Ninth Amendment of the US constitution is, "The enumeration in the constitution of certain rights shall not be construed to deny or disparage others retained by the people." The relevant passage in the Fourteenth Amendment is, "No state shall make or enforce any law which shall abridge the privileges or immunities of the citizens of the United States; nor shall any state deprive any person of life, liberty, or property without due process of law." From that, a woman's right to an abortion was somehow inferred.

Take as a premise that the common good, however defined, is served by a rule permitting a woman to abort her child should she wish to do so. One may hold that view for several reasons. One may believe unwanted children will be badly cared for. One may fear worldwide overpopulation. One may see in many countries a clear choice between abortion today and the slow death by starvation of children tomorrow. One may see abortion as a human right that no state may overturn. The question remains, to whom ought the decision – to allow abortion unconditionally, to ban it altogether, or to allow it on certain conditions – be entrusted? If the constitution were clear on the matter, if it stipulated specifically that abortion is or is not allowed, or if the court's interpretation occurred long enough ago that the constitution would have been amended by now had that interpretation been grossly unpopular, then disallowance of legislation might be reasonable. But judicial innovation on grounds as flimsy as those in *Roe* v. *Wade* serves only to redirect politics from the substantive issue – what to do about abortion – to the composition of the court. If you care, one way or another, about abortion, you must vote for a president who will appoint judges likely to adjudicate as you wish. And, as judges are, more and more, appointed for their anticipated opinions rather than for their learning in the law, the authority of the court as the impartial interpreter of the constitution, and its capacity to challenge the legislatures over central constitutional concerns, are correspondingly diminished.

RJR-McDonald Inc. v. *Canada (Attorney General)* (Canadian Supreme Court, 1995) is about the constitutionality of a ban on tobacco advertising. A federal statute (The Tobacco Products Control Act of 1988) prohibited all advertising and promotion of tobacco products and the sale of tobacco product unless its package includes prescribed health warnings and a list of toxic constituents. The Act was struck down by the Canadian Supreme Court as in violation of section 2(b) of the Canadian Charter of Rights and Freedoms: "Everyone has the following fundamental freedoms:... freedom of thought, belief, opinion and expression, including freedom of the press and other media of communication." A majority of the court decreed that "The prohibition of advertising and promotion of tobacco products violated the right of free expression" and added for good measure that "no direct evidence of a scientific nature showed a causal link between advertising bans and decrease in tobacco consumption." As in the other cases, it is hard to escape the conclusion that judges are simply reading their own preferences into the constitution. Had they chosen to do so, the majority of the court might have concurred with the dissenting minority in drawing a distinction between political and commercial speech, one protected by the Charter of Rights, the other open to regulation by the federal government under the federal government's authority under the constitution "to make Laws for the Peace, Order and good Government of Canada." *RJR-McDonald* has been far less than divisive than *Roe* v. *Wade*, but it remains a manifestation of judicial activism and of the willingness of the courts to encroach unnecessarily on the powers of the legislature.

Adjudication and legislation cannot be entirely distinct. All law is "judge-made" to some extent. Judge-made law fills gaps when the text of the law is incomplete or silent. Laws must inevitably be interpreted in the light of the case at hand, or when new situations conform badly to old prescriptions so that – with little guidance from parliament on how to proceed – the courts must seek rules in commercial custom or in their interpretation of natural justice. Much of the common law, including most of the law of torts and contract, is said to be judge-made in this sense. Over and above that, judges must oppose the legislature when the rule of law itself is in jeopardy. This is explicit in the American constitution which empowers the Supreme Court to strike down legislation causing a person to be "deprived of life, liberty, or property, without due process of law" or "to abridge the privileges and immunities of citizens." There is a written or unwritten equivalent in every democratic country. Though there is no bright line for the legislature between the establishment of general laws and the provision of harm or benefit to particular people or groups of people, some actions by the legislature would be recognized as beyond its constitutional mandate. *Ad hominem* taxation of one's political opponents – a special tax imposed by a liberal government on the ex-cabinet members of the preceding conservative government – is clearly out, and would, one hopes, be effectively blocked by the courts.

Necessary as it is for the preservation of the liberal society, judicial oversight of the legislature is fraught with dangers and difficulties. Constitutions are inevitably vague, and judges are inevitably tempted to fill the interstices of the text with the law as they, personally, would like it to be, encroaching to a greater or lesser extent on the territory of the legislature. Among the dangers in judicial activism are that the judges are wrong in their evaluation of public policy, that politics will be redirected from the election of legislators to the appointment of judges and that courts will lose the moral authority required to uphold the rule of law. Let the courts restrict themselves to the adjudication of civil disputes, to the determination of guilt or innocence of people accused of specific crimes and to an oversight of the legislature extending no farther than is necessary to block victimization or discrimination quite narrowly defined, and the elected officials whose task it is to appoint judges will be content to base their selections on the judges' learning in the law, for we all realize how much is at stake in the maintenance of the rule of law. Let the courts adjudicate cases in accordance with the law as they believe it should be, and the temptation to appoint judges who see matters "correctly" becomes irresistible.

An inescapable dilemma stalks judicial interpretation of the constitution. On the one hand, preservation of government by majority rule voting requires limits beyond which the majority of the day dare not go. Identifiable minorities, unpopular people, politicians out of office and supporters of the opposition party cannot be silenced, oppressed or denied the opportunity to make a living. Good jobs, property, high incomes, and access to the media cannot be reserved for the supporters of the government of the day. Administrators cannot be allowed unlimited scope to interpret the laws as they please. To some extent, society can rely on the good sense of the voters and politicians not to push their advantages too far. Restraint is aided by a written or unwritten constitution interpreted by the judiciary with authority to void unconstitutional legislation. On the other hand, judges empowered to strike down legislation are almost irresistibly drawn to interpret the constitution in accordance with their own preferences, the preferences of the politicians who appointed them, and the preferences of their social class. There appears to be no thoroughgoing resolution to this dilemma. Judicial influence on public policy may be a fair price to pay for the protection of civil rights. Judicial reticence may be required to preserve the respect for the Court without which it cannot effectively challenge the legislature or the administration.

Running through much of this book is a problem that can be encapsulated in the old question, "Who guards the guardians?" Piracy immediately generalizes to all crime. Police immediately generalizes to the entire government with its apparatus of police, courts, army, and civil service. The question is whether and to what extent people empowered to enforce law can be deterred from using their monopoly over the legitimate means of organized violence for their own advantage or to victimize ordinary citizens? Throughout most of history, countries have been ruled by kings, emperors, or dictators who, together with their armies and functionaries, constituted a privileged and self-serving ruling class. But not all governments have been like that, and thoroughgoing predatory government is less prevalent today than in years gone by. The problem is to determine why this is so and what safeguards society can install to direct the government's monopoly of organized violence in the common interest rather than in the interest of some ruling class?

The question was raised in chapter 2, but no answer was provided beyond the general argument that predatory government might be less burdensome to its subjects than the anarchy that all governments must suppress. The question was circumvented in the chapters on markets by the working assumption that property is secure, but a partial answer was nevertheless implied: Where much of the world's work is entrusted to a competitive market, the centralized bureaucracy can be relatively small and, therefore, relatively less able to dominate the rest of society. Voting is obviously crucial as the only non-violent way of replacing an unpopular government with a better alternative. There is, however, no iron-clad guarantee that the right to vote will not be employed to impoverish and disenfranchise unpopular minorities, that a government in office will consent to its displacement in an election, or that an elected government will not be forcibly overturned. As discussed in chapter 10, much depends on what the administration is called upon to do. The more rule-bound the administration, the smaller the perquisites of office and the less the incentive of the government of the day to perpetuate its authority, especially as successor governments would be correspondingly less inclined to perpetuate theirs.

Another consideration is more directly related to the law. There is a sense in which the question "Who guards the guardians?" is fundamentally misleading, for guardians could only be guarded by other guardians who, in turn, would have to be guarded by still other guardians, and so on ad infinitum. To the question, "Who guards the guardians?" there can be only one answer, "Nobody" unless the guardians can somehow be cajoled into guarding themselves.

Discussion of predatory government tends to personify the ruling class. The army, the police, and the civil service are looked upon as moulded, through self-interest or through fear, into a single personality and a single undivided will. Sometimes, in empires and in extreme dictatorships, that is very nearly so. Normally, government is a great collection of people who may not act in unison. Such a government may be held in check by the division of authority among legislature, executive, and judiciary and because obedience within the hierarchy is conditional.

Rules may be self-enforcing. If everybody believes that I am required to act thus-and-so, that the duly-appointed policeman will punish me if I act otherwise and that the policeman himself will be punished by others for failing to punish me appropriately, then I, in my own interest, must act appropriately for fear of what will happen to me if I do not. But I act confidently within the bounds of my rights, knowing that a policeman who interfered with me would not be backed up by others in the police force or in the rest of the community. The forces of society which support the policeman against me when I break the law, would, otherwise, support me against the policeman. The prime minister is obeyed when he acts within the bounds of his constitutionally established authority, but the very people who obey the prime minister when he acts within those bounds withdraw their obedience when he does not or when the rules that established him as prime minister transfer the post to somebody else instead. Government requires cohesion. Laws supply that cohesion through mutually enforcing expectations about how people will behave. As the guardian of the rules and with no separate army to enforce its pronouncements against the rest of the government, the judiciary must be seen as issuing signals indicating when the rules would be broken and when the traditional bonds of obedience might be dissolved.

THE FOUR PILLARS

One cannot state in any absolute or general way whether the greatest danger at the present time is licence or tyranny, anarchy or despotism. Both are equally to be feared.

Alexis de Tocqueville, 1835

The book began in chapters 1 and 2 with an observation and a problem. The observation is that for much – though by no means all – of the population of the world, life is better today than ever before. We have a much higher standard of living. We live longer. We are healthier. We enjoy greater freedom of speech and freedom from predatory government. The ordinary citizen has more influence upon the choice of rulers and the conduct of public policy than ordinary people have had at any time in the past. The problem is to explain why these things have happened. The simple explanation is technical change. The advancement of knowledge has surely made possible the standard of living we now enjoy. While formally correct, this answer is not entirely adequate because it immediately gives rise to other less tractable questions: Why did technical change occur when it did? Why did not the constant scramble for advantage – encapsulated in the story of the fishermen and pirates – destroy the climate for innovation? Or, if piracy is to be controlled, why did the ruling classes fail to employ the advances in technology to suppress ordinary people more effectively than they have ever been suppressed before?

An answer to these questions is suggested by the organization of this book. The four institutions we have studied – property, voting, administration, and law – combine to preserve what most of us see as the good society, enabling us to live our lives as nearly as possible, in this imperfect world, as we would wish. Together, these four pillars of what might be called the *liberal society* are our defense against anarchy on the one hand and despotism on the other. All are essential. Remove one and the entire edifice is sooner or later destroyed.

PROPERTY

The first pillar is property, the private ownership of the means of production. The story in chapter 3 is of how private ownership of the means of production enables the price mechanism to guide the allocation of resources to goods and the allocation of goods to people automatically and without recourse to a comprehensive hierarchy of managers for the entire economy. No central authority decides what to produce or decrees what each person is to earn. Firms must be hierarchical and the civil service must be hierarchical too, but there is no one, all-encompassing hierarchy for the economy as a whole. Establishing order without orders, the price mechanism enlists self-interest in the service of the common good, directing the economy efficiently in the sense that no central authority could rearrange production and distribution to make everybody better off.

The institution of private property may be condemned for its origin in occupation and violence as well as for its unjustifiable disparities of income between the rich and the poor. Neither condemnation can be dismissed out of hand. Nations originate in conquest and plunder. The English landed classes trace their origin to successful Norman bandits. Most of the present inhabitants of North America are descended from European settlers who grabbed the continent from the native tribes occupying territory conquered from other tribes, and so on in an almost infinite regress. Occupants of most of the countries on earth descend from migrant conquerors. Within countries, great fortunes often originate in plunder and chicanery. Apart from the force of custom, the present distribution of wealth is ultimately unjustifiable. By what right is one person born to a rich family, provided the best education money can buy, aided in his search for employment by his family's wealthy and influential friends and supported, if his own earnings prove insufficient, by his family's fortune, while another person is born into poverty, educated in underfunded local schools among other pupils as underprivileged as himself, raised in an atmosphere of violence, mistrusted by potential employers and with no private resources to fall back upon if he becomes unemployed? The existing distribution of property and income is not mandated by some benevolent being in the sky, is not intrinsically just, right or moral, and is, at least in part, the outcome of theft and chicanery made legitimate by the passage of time.

Defense of the institution of private property against these accusations cannot rely on an inherent right to property on a par with civil rights and the right to vote. That argument may appeal to the wealthy but it would not, and in my opinion should not, carry much weight with the poor. A better defense is required to hold the allegiance of the majority of the population with less than the average income per head. A different and stronger argument emerges from the study of economics: The institution of private property is a necessary condition for what most of us, rich or poor, see as a good society. It is a source of general prosperity enabling markets to marshal society's resources efficiently, producing goods people want to consume and providing appropriate incentives for investment and research. It is a requirement for democratic government, upholding majority-rule voting and the rule of law by attending to the allocation of income outside of and independently of the political arena and defending society against the emergence of a predatory ruling class. Regardless of its origin, the existing distribution of property acquires legitimacy in the course of time, becoming an indispensable part of the social capital of the nation.

Yet the institution of private property is not as self-contained as an incautious study of economics might lead one to suppose. The usual exposition of general equilibrium begins with a given allocation among people of all factors of production, and proceeds to identify nice properties of the competitive economy. What needs emphasis here is that the supposedly given allocation of property among people can only be sustained by institutions that are, strictly speaking, external to the market. Private property needs the protection of the state not just from the thief, but from its own inherent limitations. The state must prescribe the boundaries of property rights, resolve disputes among property-holders, and establish a schedule of punishments for crimes. It must specify what I may or may not do with my property, what can be patented and for how long, the terms and conditions for the establishment of corporations, the rights and obligations of shareholders, the governance of the stockmarket, the assignment of wavelengths for radio and TV, the regulation of pollutants and the apportionment among fishermen of the allowable catch when the total catch is restricted to ensure the preservation of the stock of fish. These are among the many and diverse matters that must, one way or another, be resolved politically if the rights of property are to be well defined. Legislature, administration and courts are all essential as technical and social infrastructure without which property rights are meaningless. Only by the intervention of the state can externalities be corrected and the worst excesses of monopoly curtailed. Nor can we be sure that the inequalities of wealth and income in an unconstrained system of private property – in a society where the state protects property rights but lets the distribution of income develop as it may with no attempt to assist the poor or to redistribute property or income at all – will not grow to the point where private ownership of property becomes unacceptable to the great majority of citizens. Some degree of publicly sponsored redistribution is in the interest of the typical citizen and may be required to preserve support in the general population for the private ownership of the means of production.

VOTING

The second pillar of the liberal society is voting for laws and for leaders where the will of the majority prevails. Public decision-making by voting is society's only alternative to autocracy, but decision-making by voting is a fragile instrument, requiring the support of private ownership of property, of an administrative structure and of an independent judiciary. A standard objection to democracy (by which I mean no more than government by majority-rule voting) has for centuries been raised by democracy's enemies and has been recognized as correct, though not, of course, decisive, by democracy's friends. Quite simply, the anti-democratic argument is that, by its very nature, voting is unstable and destined to self-destruct. Inevitably, some majority of voters – usually but not necessarily a majority of the poor – will employ the power of the vote to dispossess the minority mercilessly and completely. Drawn by the powers conferred upon the majority in a democratic society, factions coalesce around any nucleus – income, race, language, location, religion, or social class – to direct the lion's share of the national income to their members. Understanding the danger, the party in office and its supporters are irresistibly tempted to dispense with the elections whenever there is a risk of loss of office at the ballot box. Monarchy, dictatorship of the proletariat, religious oligarchy, or some other form of autocratic government would be established to preserve the authority and the economic privileges of the higher ranks of the people or to defend one's class, ethnic group or religion from exploitation by others.

The force of the anti-democratic argument – as a demonstration of the impossibility of democracy or as a sign of danger that can and must be averted – depends critically on technical, economic, and social conditions. In particular, the viability of public decision-making by voting depends critically on the private ownership of the means of production. Property rights are respected and upheld – even by people with little or no property of their own – as an indispensable requirement for prosperity and for government by majority-rule voting. In a community where all of the means of production is owned and administered by the state, the legislature *must* take upon itself the ultimate responsibility of allocating the entire national income among citizens, for there is no other institution to do so. The whole national income would be up for grabs in the deliberations of the legislature. Each person's prosperity and status would rest entirely on the outcome of the vote. The privileges of majority status and the perquisites of office would be too great to risk at the ballot box, especially as the party now in office would have little ground for trust in the willingness of its successor to step down in its turn. The temptation to rig or abolish elections would indeed be irresistible.

Who is to be the president of the corporation? Who is to be the janitor? Who is to be unemployed when workers are in surplus? Are doctors to be paid more than lawyers, and, if so, by how much? Which towns are to expand and which to contract? Without private property, all of these questions would have to be answered by the legislature, directly or through the intermediary of the civil service. Private property supplies answers and, in doing so, provides the legislature with the option of silence. This is not to deny or to belittle the influence of government on the economy through tariffs, the progressivity of taxation, the old age pension, and in a thousand other ways. It is, rather, to assert that there is a limit to public influence beyond which the powers of office become uncontainable. In a community where the means of production are privately owned and prices are set in the open market, the legislature acquires the option of not concerning itself with the allocation of the national income, or it may be content to influence allocation at the fringes, leaving the core of the market untouched.

With a historically given allocation of property among people, the market automatically generates prices that allocate resources to their most productive use. As a by-product of that allocation of resources, the price mechanism allocates the national income among people in accordance with the earnings of the resources they own. As long as property rights are secure, the assignment of goods to people is arranged without the intervention of the government to determine who gets what. It is this allocative role of property that upholds government by voting, and that compels democratic governments to protect property rights to some extent if democracy is to be maintained at all. The legislature respects existing property rights in the interest of self-preservation.

Property upholds democracy in another respect as well. Democracy requires a viable opposition to the ruling party. It requires that the Liberals are not denied a livelihood while the Conservatives are in office. It requires that the powers of government are not so extensive that opponents of the ruling party can be impoverished. Without private ownership of the means of production, the economy must necessarily be administered by the state. Once the economy is administered by the state, the livelihood of each and every person is at the discretion of the ruling party, for a person denied a job by the government would have no alternative employment. In such an environment, opposition to the party in office can only be maintained at great personal sacrifice. Opposition becomes a desperate if not impossible enterprise, and may be squelched altogether.

There is a natural division of labor between voting and property. Voting cannot allocate the national income without destroying itself, but it can redistribute without too much difficulty. Property, on the other hand, allocates income automatically, but may stand in need of a substantial redistribution of income. Redistribution by voting, while not quite innocuous, is rendered feasible because there is a natural limit beyond which the median voter – the voter halfway along the scale of rich and poor – will not wish to go. The crux of the matter is that the pie shrinks as you share it. A rise in the progressivity of the income tax narrows the gap between the net incomes of the rich and the poor but, at the same time, reduces the national income by weakening the incentive to work and save. In voting on each extra bit of redistribution, a relatively poor person must balance his gain as a recipient of redistribution against his loss from the resulting shrinkage in the national income. The better off one is, the sooner does the loss outweigh the gain. The stopping place for the decisive median voter lies well short of a massive, and costly, transfer to the poor. Contentment of the median voter with the extent of the redistribution of income signifies a degree of acceptance of the existing allocation of the ownership of property which might otherwise be lacking in a system of private property untempered by political intervention. Voting and property reinforce one another, each supporting the other where it is weak and each governing a domain of life from which the other must be excluded if the entire system is to be preserved.

There is nevertheless an unavoidable conflict over the boundary between the domains of property and voting. The ruling principle in the domain of property is that one is entitled to whatever one's income enables one to buy. The ruling principle in the domain of voting is equality among all citizens. The conflict plays out in the determination of public policy in such matters as the provision of education, the provision of medical care and the right to donate money to political parties or candidates for office. Is the education of one's children to be treated as a commodity like bread and cheese that one may purchase in whatever quantity and quality one pleases, or is it a right subsumed under the right to vote available to all citizens equally? Are poor people to be allowed to die because they are unable to afford medical care that would normally be purchased by the rich? Where is the line to be drawn between a right to free speech (which is largely meaningless without a corresponding right of access to the means of communication) and the right to buy votes (which is denied in every democratic country because it would almost certainly lead to the destruction of democratic government)? These questions of policy are beyond the scope of this book. Suffice to say that opinions differ as to the best course of action, that the preferences of the poor would normally be slanted toward equality, that the preferences of the rich would normally be slanted toward property, and that policies differ substantially from one country to the next.

A Rule-bound Public Administration

The third pillar of the liberal society is public administration, the guidance of the bureaucracy by impersonal rules to avoid victimization of people and groups out of favor with the government of the day. It is an unfortunate aspect of the technology of social interaction that many public decisions cannot be made by voting. The legislature can at best conduct a couple of dozen votes a year which must, necessarily, be directed to large political questions, leaving a million details to be sorted out by the civil service, the army, the courts and the police. The day-to-day governance of society – the assessment and collection of tax, the conduct of elections, the maintenance of roads, bridges, and airports, the provision of schooling, the oversight of immigration and foreign travel, relations with other countries, and so on – involves an infinity of small tasks that only a hierarchically organized bureaucracy can perform, though these tasks must ultimately fall within the authority of the legislature. Modern society requires a vast administrative apparatus where each person in the chain of command takes orders from his superior and gives orders to his subordinates.

The bureaucracy has many masters. Elected executives occupy the top ranks of the administrative hierarchy. The legislature supplies laws for the bureaucracy to enforce and programs for it to administer. A written or unwritten constitution subordinates public decision-making to some notion of the common good, which is in part reducible to the principle of equal treatment and to the rules of cost-benefit analysis. Equal treatment requires that any two welfare recipients, children in grade three, cancer patients, or victims of robbery are to be treated alike by the state, at least to the extent that the same resources are devoted to each. Police protection on the block where I live ought not to be significantly better or significantly worse than on the block at the other end of town. One need only state the principle of equal treatment to recognize that it is applied, at best, imperfectly and that there are circumstances where it cannot be applied at all. The principle cannot be applied, for example, in allocating of resources between the education of children in grade three and the alleviation of the suffering of cancer patients when both must be financed from a limited budget, or in deciding whether to locate a new hospital on the east side or the west side of town. For such choices, the administration must have recourse to a more or less precise cost-benefit rule. Values must somehow be placed on the different consequences of public decision-making, so that projects or programs may be undertaken if and only if the balance of costs and benefits is favorable. It is, of course, arguable that a cost-benefit rule is itself a variant of the principle of equal treatment because one cannot predict *ex ante* whether the rule will in time be more beneficial to me or to my neighbor. In practice, the immediate winners and losers from the principle that benefits be weighted equally "to whomsoever they may accrue" know perfectly well who they are, and are actively competing for influence within the legislature.

These two rules for the bureaucracy – "treat everybody equally" and "maximize the gap between benefit and cost" – are not entirely compatible. A benefit-cost rule may bias public policy toward the rich, especially if non-monetary benefits, like time-saving and life-saving, are weighed at the recipient's valuation. An equal treatment rule may benefit the poor who naturally pay less tax per head. Sometimes it is obvious which rule to apply. In a regime of socialized medicine, a benefit-cost test governs the choice of services to provide, while an equal-treatment rule ensures that nobody is favored *ex ante* when it is unknown which services he will require. Sometimes it is unclear which of either of these rules is applicable. It is not accidental that the locating of airports and the closing of military bases is politically contentious, for there is no simple formula in these cases to guide the bureaucracy in deciding what to do.

The greater the tasks of the bureaucracy, the less can it be guided by general rules of conduct. The range of discretion expands together with the authority of the bureaucracy over the economy. Discretion can never be eliminated altogether, and varies from one ministry to the next. It is usually evident how the Ministry of National Revenue ought to behave. The Ministry of Health is probably less rule-bound, and the Ministry of Industry may have even more discretion. The less rule-bound the bureaucracy, the greater the influence of the legislature and the executive over its activity and the more contentious does ordinary politics become.

Administration is never entirely rule-bound or entirely public-spirited. To a greater or lesser degree, all bureaucracies are inefficient, corrupt or predatory. Self-interest, which is normally presumed rampant in the private sector of the economy, cannot be expected to stop short at the door of the public sector. Powers over the economy will inevitably be misused to some extent, and have at times been altogether uncontainable. Hierarchy has throughout history been an instrument of oppression. That an organized few can dominate an unorganized many is reason enough for the absence of any semblance of popular government (except in tribes and city states) throughout most of recorded history. What needs to be explained is not the dominance of the hierarchy in the many times and places where the hierarchy has been dominant, but its subordination to the legislature in many countries today. I have no complete explanation, but something of an explanation may be found in private property and in the law.

Property tempers the administration by reducing the scope of its authority. The smaller the domain of the administration – and the larger the corresponding domain of property, markets and prices – the less does each person's income and status come to depend on the goodwill of the bureaucratic hierarchy and the larger becomes the reward for investment and initiative in producing goods and services and in one's dealings with others in the market. A large organization is likely to be more dangerous than a small one, and an organization encompassing the entire economy – as the bureaucracy must become in the absence of private ownership of the means of production – would be virtually uncontainable, as this century's flirtation with communism has revealed. Size fosters obedience. In a capitalist economy, a civil servant who comes to believe that the actions of his ministry are mistaken or who is asked to do the unconscionable can quit in the knowledge that he can probably find a job in the private sector. Resignation does not lead to ostracism or impoverishment, as it surely would if there were no private sector where one could be employed. The private sector supplies a refuge for people whom the bureaucracy does not employ, and is the matrix of opposition to the bureaucracy as well as to the party in office. Private property constrains the administration by restricting its authority to a domain with fairly well-recognized rules of conduct and by providing an escape from the vengeance of the bureaucracy for those who challenge its authority.

Property tempers the administration in another respect as well. The larger the domain of property, the stronger the signal from the market of what public sector wages ought to be. For example, when almost all medical care is provided in the private sector of the economy, wages of doctors and other medical personnel are determined impersonally like any other market prices, as described in chapter 3. These private sector wages become the standard by which wages of doctors in the public sector – in public health or in the army medical corps – may be set. All that changes when medical care is socialized. Wages of doctors and other medical personnel must then be determined by the legislature or by the administration with little guidance from the market. Doctors' wages become the outcome of a political decision, and the medical profession is automatically transformed into a pressure group seeking alliances with other segments of society in a context of voting not unlike the exploitation problem as described in chapter 9. By itself, this consideration speaks against public provision of medical care, but the argument is by no means decisive. Other considerations – notably a public interest in placing a floor below the very worst consequences of poverty, in removing life itself from the list of things money can buy and in securing the allegiance of the poor to the rules of the liberal society – would seem to push in the opposite direction. To say that full and complete public direction of the economy is destructive of democracy is not to say that public direction is unwarranted in any and every domain of life. The most that can be said is that the larger the scope of the public sector, the higher should be the barrier to the adoption of any new public responsibility. There is a delicate balance to be drawn.

THE LAW

The fourth pillar of the liberal society is the law. Up close, the great institutions of property and voting become an intricate web of rules specifying what one may do, what one must not do and who is entitled to what. Property rules specify people's rights over other people with regard to things. Voting rules specify every detail of the procedure for elections and for the passage of bills in the legislature. Such rules must be interpreted impartially, for neither property nor voting can be sustained if the administration is free and unfettered in its interpretation of the rules in each and every dispute. Interpretation is the task of the judiciary. A "rule of law" protects citizens from the state. Courts must decide when people are guilty of crimes, resolve disputes over the interpretation of the rules of society, including rules about the scope and boundaries of property rights, and block the legislature and the executive when constitutionally guaranteed rights are transgressed. In its classic formulation, the rule of law is juxtaposed with the supremacy of parliament, in a division of labour where parliament has ultimate responsibility for the content of laws and the judiciary ensures that the laws are uniformly and impartially applied.

Though judges are in some broad sense employees of the state, the maintenance of the rule of law requires a splitting off of the judiciary from the rest of the administration and the granting of considerable independence. In no other way can the citizen be protected from an administration that would punish those who displease it on the pretext that the law of the land has been broken. The rule of law is maintained in part by judicial tenure and in part by the withdrawal of obedience by public officials and lay people when government's commands exceed legally established bounds. Once again, the protection of private property by other institutions is reciprocated. An independent judiciary is a defense of property rights, the right to vote and civil rights of all kinds. These rights are at the same time a defense of the independence of the judiciary. Without a large private sector, the scope of the administration would be so wide and its authority over the lives of citizens so extensive that resistance to its authority, legitimate or not, would be futile. A large private sector provides the milieu within which a person may respect judicial pronouncements because he confidently expects others to do so.

There is a technical connection – social technology, but technology all the same – among property, voting, rule-based administration, and law. These four pillars of what we are calling the liberal society stand or fall together.

NOTES

1 HOW DREADFUL LIFE USED TO BE

1 C. Humphreys, *Buddhism*, London, Penguin, 1954, pp. 81–2.

2 Marshall Sahlins, "The original affluent society," chapter 1 of *Stone Age Economics*, London, Tavistock Publications, 1974. Sahlins argued that the transition from hunter-gathering to settled agriculture was a disaster. As hunter-gatherers, people were better fed, healthier, and enjoyed more leisure. Jared Diamond entitled an article on the subject, "The worst mistake in the history of the human race" (*Discover*, pp. 64–6, 1987). The transition from hunter-gathering to agriculture was accompanied by increases in population densities of a hundred fold, but is alleged to have led to a deterioration in the diet and life expectancy of ordinary people that has only been reversed in modern times.

3 Data from M. Livi-Bacci, *A Concise History of World Population*, second edition, Oxford, Blackwell, 1992, chapter 2, section 4, "The tragedy of the American Indios."

4 *Report on the Global HIV/AIDS Epidemic*, UNAIDS, June 2000, www.unaids.org/epidemicupdate/report

5 Wired Health: www.hc.sc.gc.ca/hppb/wired/smoking/htm

6 A. H. Leighton and C. C. Hughes, "Notes on Eskimo patterns of suicide," in A. Giddens, ed., *The Sociology of Suicide*, London Cass, 1971, p. 158.

7 E. Durkheim, *Suicide: A Study in Sociology*, Glencoe, Ill., Free Press, 1951, book two, "Altruistic suicide." For a sympathetic understanding of patricide among very poor or migratory people, see *The Law of Life*, a short story by Jack London about patricide among some North American Indians, and *The Ballad of Narayama*, a beautiful film by Shohei Imamura about tribal people in ancient Japan.

8 Leighton and Hughes, "Notes on Eskimo patterns," p. 195.

9   Marvin Harris, "Murder in Eden," chapter 2 of *Cannibals and Kings*, New York, Vintage Books, 1978. See also, E.A. Hoebel, *The Law of Primitive Man*, chapter 5, Cambridge, Mass., Harvard University Press, 1967.

10 Donald Veall, *The Popular Movement for Law Reform, 1640–1660*, Oxford, Clarendon Press, 1970, chapter 1, "Crime and punishment 1600–1660."

11 Leon Radzinowicz, *A History of English Criminal Law and its Administration from 1750*, vol. 1, London, Stevens, 1948, p. 11, footnote 11.

12 Veall, *The Popular Movement for Law Reform*, chapter 2, p. 6.

13 See Veall, *The Popular Movement for Law Reform*, pp. 27–8.

14 The quotation is from the title page of *Malleus Maleficarum* the great treatise on witchcraft published in 1486, two years after the papal bull of Pope Innocent VIII deploring the spread of witchcraft and instructing inquisitors to extirpate it. See H. R. Trevor-Roper, *The European Witch-Craze of the Sixteenth and Seventeenth Centuries and Other Essays*, New York, Harper & Row, 1969, p. 117.

15 There is considerable variation among historians in their estimates of the number of witches burned at the stake. In *Cows, Pigs, Wars and Witches*, New York, Random House, 1974, p. 207, Marvin Harris asserts that half a million people were executed for witchcraft. In *The Witch-hunt in Early Modern Europe*, New York, Longman, 1995, pp. 24–5, Brian P. Levack estimates that there were about 110,000 prosecutions for witchcraft leading to about 60,000 executions.

16 The Inquisition began in the thirteenth century as persecution of dissident Christian sects. It has been estimated that about 5,000 people were executed for heresy during the Reformation and about 2,000 during the Spanish Inquisition. On the Reformation, see B. Gregory, *Salvation at Stake: Christian Martyrdom in Early Modern Europe*, Cambridge, Mass., Harvard University Press, 1999, p. 6. On the Spanish Inquisition, see J. Contrabras and G. Henningsen, "Forty-four cases of the Spanish Inquisition," in G. Henningsen and J. Tedeschi, eds, *The Inquisition in Early Modern Europe*, Dekalb, Ill., Northern Illinois University Press, 1986. "There is an unjust persecution which the ungodly operate against the Church of Christ; and a just persecution which the Churches of Christ make use of toward the ungodly . . . The Church persecutes out of love, the ungodly out of cruelty," St Augustine, quoted in Henry Kamen, *The Rise of Toleration*, London, Weidenfeld & Nicolson, 1967, p. 14.

17 Kamen, "Economic motives for toleration," *The Rise of Toleration*, pp. 224–7.

18 Quoted by E. M. W. Tillyard in *The Elizabethan World Picture*, London, Chatto & Windus, 1945, p. 9.

19 A. H. M. Jones, *The Later Roman Empire, 284–602: A Social and Administrative Survey*, Oxford, Blackwell, 1964, pp. 17 and 751.

20 J. D. Spence, *The Search for Modern China*, New York, Norton, 1990, p. 125.

21 M. Voslensky, *Nomenklatura: Anatomy of the Soviet Ruling Class*, London, Bodley Head, 1980, p. 179.

22 G. O. Sayles, *The Medieval Foundations of England*, London, Methuen, 1948, pp. 122–5.

23 Veall, *The Popular Movement for Law Reform*, 4. A common test of literacy was to read Psalm 51, known as the "neck verse." By memorizing that verse, a convicted thief might have his punishment commuted from hanging to, perhaps, whipping.

24 A list is contained in Orlando Patterson, *Slavery and Social Death*, Cambridge, Mass., Harvard University Press, 198, appendix C.

25 F. W. Howay, *Voyages of the "Columbia" to the Northwest Coast, 1789–1790*, quoted in Leland Donald, *Aboriginal Slavery on the Northwest Coast of North America*, Berkeley, University of California Press, 1997, p. 172.

26 A. H. M. Jones, *Athenian Democracy*, Oxford, Blackwell, 1969, pp. 78–9.

27 For example, if the pre-war population were 1 million, population had been growing at 2 percent before the war, the duration of the war was 5 years and the post-war population was 900,000, one might infer that, one way or another, 200,000 people died in the war. Two percent of a million is 20,000. Ignoring compounding, we estimate that, but for the war, the population would have grown by 20,000 a year, for a total of 100,000 over the entire five years of the war. We would then estimate that, but for the war, the population would be 1,100,000. As the population is actually 900,000, we would say that 200,000 people perished in the war.

28 R. Hilberg, *The Destruction of the European Jews*, New York, Holmes & Meier, 1985, appendix B. Hilberg's estimate of the Jewish death toll is 5.1 million. In *A Holocaust Reader*, New York, Behrman House, 1976, L. S. Dawidowicz estimated the number at about 6 million.

29 The story is told in Robert Conquest, *Harvest of Sorrow, Soviet Collectivization and the Terror Famine*, Edmonton, Alberta, University of Alberta Press, 1986.

30 Quoted in K. D. Jackson, "The ideology of total revolution," in K. D. Jackson, ed., *Cambodia 1975–1978: Rendezvous with Death*, Princeton, New Jersey, Princeton University Press, 1989, p. 67

31 The story is told in Jasper Becker, *Hungry Ghosts: Mao's Secret Famine*, New York, Henry Holt, 1998. Becker speaks of "millions who have been sacrificed on the alter of Mao's vanity" (p. 299) and he quotes Khrushchev that "Mao thought himself as a man brought by god to do God's bidding" (p. 55). Becker adds that "Mao could not be brought down because he had created a world in which all beliefs and judgments were suspended. No one dared move or act according to what he knew to be true. Instead, even the highest ranking officials moved in a secret society paralysed by an all-pervasive network of informers and spies" (p. 311).

32 See Martin Ravallin, "Famines and economics," *Journal of Economic Literature*, September 1997, pp. 1205–42.

33 Z. Brzezinski, *Out of Control: Global Turmoil on the Eve of the Twenty-first Century*, New York, Scribner, 1993.

34 Napoleon A. Chagnon, *Yanomamo: The Fierce People*, New York, Holt, Rinehart and Winston, 1983, p. 20.

35 *The Economist*, December 21, 1996, p. 60.

2 MAKING AND TAKING

1   The police choose t to maximize $t(1 - t)$ in equation (24). The best tax rate for the police is $\frac{1}{2}$. To see that this is so, suppose instead that $t = \frac{1}{2} + \Delta$ where Δ is any number with an absolute value of less than $\frac{1}{2}$. The value of $t(1 - t)$ becomes $(\frac{1}{2} + \Delta)(\frac{1}{2} - \Delta) = \frac{1}{4} - \Delta^2$ which is as large as possible when $\Delta = 0$ signifying that $t = \frac{1}{2}$.

2   This section draws upon Boaz, M. and Polak, B., "A model of a predatory state," *Journal of Law, Economics and Organization*, 2001, 1–33. The general practice in this book is to cite references for facts but not for ideas. As an introductory text, the book draws upon a literature too vast to be cited in its entirety, with no principle for choosing what to cite and what to leave out. Also, the flow of the argument would be impeded by extensive references to literature the student will encounter in more advanced cources. An exception is made for a couple of articles that are not ordinarily part of the economics curriculum.

3 TASTE, TECHNOLOGY, AND MARKETS

1   Readers with some knowledge of the calculus will recognize that the production possibility frontier and the supply curve are related as integral and derivative.

2   For the student with some knowledge of calculus, the derivation of the demand function in equation (2) from the utility function in equation (1) is obvious. Otherwise, the demand function has to be derived from first principles. To derive equation (2), consider the points α_4 and α_5 in figure 3.4 above. Let the point α_4 represent the combination of bread and cheese $\{b, c\}$, in which case the point α_5 must represent the combination $\{b - \Delta b, c + \Delta c\}$. The main step in establishing the validity of equation (2) is to suppose that the points α_4 and α_5 are very close together so that Δb and Δc are both very small, approaching zero, by comparison with b or c. By construction, the points α_4 and α_5 lie on the same indifference curve and must have the same value of utility. It follows immediately from equation (1) that

$$bc = (b - \Delta b)(c + \Delta c) = bc - c\Delta b + b\Delta c - \Delta b \Delta c$$

from which it follows that

$$\Delta b / \Delta c = b/c + \Delta b/c = b/c$$

as long as the term $\Delta b/c$ is small enough to be ignored. For example, if $b = 10, c = 20, \Delta b = 0.1$ and $\Delta c = 0.2$, then $b/c = 0.5$ but $\Delta b/c = 0.005$. If $b = 10$ and $c = 20$, but $\Delta b = 0.01$ and $\Delta c = 0.02$, then b/c remains at 0.5 but $\Delta b/c$ falls to 0.0005. As Δb and Δc approach zero, the ratio $\Delta b/c$ approaches zero as well, and the ratio $\Delta b/\Delta c$ becomes at once the slope of the indifference curve and the demand price of cheese, as shown in equation (2), at the point $\{b, c\}$.

3   Let x be the share of plot B devoted to cheese. Equating the demand price of cheese from equation (2) with the supply price of cheese along plot B, it follows

that $b/c = 2$ where b and c are Robinson Crusoe's chosen outputs of bread and cheese. Recall that the output of plot B is either 8 loaves of bread or 4 pounds of cheese or some weighted average of the two. When none of plot B is devoted to cheese, the outputs of bread and cheese are 16 pounds and 36 loaves. When a share x of plot B is devoted to cheese, the outputs of bread and cheese are

$$b = 36 - 8x \quad \text{and} \quad c = 16 + 4x$$

When $b = 2c$, as it must be when demand and supply prices are equal, it follows that

$$36 - 8x = 2(16 + 4x)$$

so that $x = 1/4$, $b = 34$ and $c = 17$ as shown in table 3.3.

4   Let $\{c, b\}$ and $\{c + \Delta c, b - \Delta b\}$ be two points on the production possibility frontier. Necessarily,

$$\delta c^2 + \gamma b^2 = D \quad \text{and} \quad \delta(c + \Delta c)^2 + \gamma(b - \Delta b)^2 = D$$

from which it follows at once that

$$\delta[2c\Delta c + (\Delta c)^2] + \gamma[-2b\Delta b + (\Delta b)^2] = 0 \quad \text{or}$$
$$(\Delta b/\Delta c) = (\delta/\gamma)(c/b)\{[1 - \Delta c/2c]/[1 - \Delta b/2b]\}$$

As the two points $\{c, b\}$ and $\{c + \Delta c, b + \Delta b\}$ get closer and closer together, the terms Δc and Δb get smaller and smaller as proportions of c and b respectively. In the limit, the ratios $\Delta c/c$ and $\Delta b/b$ vanish altogether and the expression in squiggly brackets approaches 1. Hence $(\Delta b/\Delta c) = (\delta/\gamma)(c/b)$ which is equation (7).

5   Let s be the share of land devoted to bread, so that $(1 - s)$ is the share devoted to cheese. It follows immediately that $b = 5s$ and $c = 10(1 - s)$. Substituting for s in the equation for c, we see that

$$c = 10(1 - s) = 10(1 - b/5) = 10 - 2b$$

which is equation (13).

6   As shown in the preceding note, $b = 5s$ and $c = 10(1 - s)$ where s is the share of land devoted to cheese. In accordance with equation (1), $u = bc = (5s)(10(1 - s)) = 50s(1 - s)$, so that as explained in note 1 above, u is as large as possible when $s = 1/2$. A person with a uniform plot of land and a utility function represented by equation (1) chooses $s = 1/2$, dividing his land equally between the two goods.

7   Together, equations (2) and (6) $-p^D = b/c$ and $y = b + p^W c$ – imply that $b = p^W c = y/2$ whenever $p^W = p^D$ as is always the case when a person participates in world trade. A table comparable to table 3.5 could be constructed for any utility function whatsoever, but the computation would usually be less straightforward.

8   The general formula is

$$c = 1/2[C + B/p^w]$$

where c is the combined consumption of cheese, C is the combined production of cheese, B is the combined production of bread, p^w is the world price of cheese in terms of bread, and where B and C are amounts produced when each person produces either bread or cheese to maximize the value of his output at world prices.

4 PUTTING DEMAND AND SUPPLY CURVES TO WORK

1   Rewrite equation (4) as $u = u^b + u^c$ where $u^b = (1 - \theta)\sqrt{b}$ and $u^c = \theta\sqrt{c}$. Then let Δu^b and Δu^c be the changes in u^b and u^c resulting from an increase Δc and a decrease Δb that leave u invariant so that the points {b, c} and {b − Δb, c + Δc} lie on the same indifference curve. Necessarily,

$$u^b + \Delta u^b = (1 - \theta)\sqrt{(b - \Delta b)}, \quad u^c + \Delta u^c = \theta\sqrt{(c + \Delta c)} \quad \text{and} \quad \Delta u^b = -\Delta u^c$$

Squaring both sides of the first of these three equations, we see that

$$(1 - \theta)^2(b - \Delta b) = [u^b + \Delta u^b]^2 = [u^b]^2 + 2u^b\Delta u^b + [\Delta u^b]^2$$

As in the derivation of the demand price in the last chapter, we can ignore terms that are the product of two first differences because such terms become very, very small relative to other terms, and, in the limit, vanishing altogether. Also, since $u^b = (1 - \theta)\sqrt{b}$ by definition, the first terms on both sides of the equation cancel out, so that preceding equation reduces to $- (1 - \theta)^2\Delta b = 2u^b\Delta u^b$, or

$$\Delta u^b = -(1 - \theta)\Delta b/2\sqrt{b}$$

A similar line of reasoning establishes that

$$\Delta u^c = \theta\Delta c/2\sqrt{c}$$

Finally, since $\Delta u^b = -\Delta u^c$, it follows that

$$p^D(b, c) = \Delta b/\Delta c = [\theta/(1 - \theta)]\sqrt{(b/c)} \text{ which is equation (5).}$$

2   By definition, $\epsilon^D = (\Delta c/c^*)/(\Delta p^D/p^*)$ and $\epsilon^S = (\Delta c/c^*)/(\Delta p^S/p^*)$ so that $\epsilon^S / \epsilon^D = \Delta p^D/\Delta p^S$ and $\epsilon^S /(\epsilon^D + \epsilon^S) = \Delta p^D/(\Delta p^D + \Delta p^S) = \Delta p^D/t$.

3   The change in production and consumption of cheese can be expressed as a function of the elasticities and the tax rate. From equation (24) and the definitions of the elasticities, it follows that

$$t = \Delta p^D + \Delta p^S = (\Delta c/c^{**})(p^*/\epsilon^D) + (\Delta c/c^{**})(p^*/\epsilon^S)$$

$$= (\Delta c/c^{**})(p^*)[1/\epsilon^D + 1/\epsilon^S]$$

so that

$$\Delta c / c^{**} = (t/p^*)\, \epsilon^D \epsilon^S /(\epsilon^D + \epsilon^S) \quad \text{and}$$

$$L/R = 1/2 \Delta c / c^{**} = 1/2\tau\, \epsilon^D \epsilon^S /(\epsilon^D + \epsilon^S).$$

4   Recall from equation (17) that $(\Delta R + \Delta L)/\Delta R = 1/(1 - B/A)$ where, as illustrated in figure 4.5, B is defined as $t\Delta c$ and A is defined as $c\Delta t$. Thus $B/A = (\Delta c/c)/(\Delta t/t)$ which is the elasticity of tax base to tax rate, called ϵ_{ct} in equation (27). But

$$\epsilon_{ct} = (\Delta c/c)/(\Delta t/t) = (t/p)(\Delta c/c)/(\Delta t/p)$$

where t/p is the tax rate as a proportion of the initial price p, and $(\Delta c/c)/(\Delta t/p)$ is the ordinary elasticity of demand.

5   Multiply both sides by $p/(c\Delta p)$. The equation becomes

$$(p/c)/(\Delta c^p/\Delta p) = (p/c)/(\Delta c^u/\Delta p) + (p/c)/(\Delta c^y/\Delta p)$$

where the expressions on either side of the equality sign are equal to ϵ^M and ϵ^U, the price elasticities for the constant money income demand curve and the constant utility demand curve. The equation can be rewritten as

$$\epsilon^M - \epsilon^U = (p/c)/(\Delta c^y/\Delta p) = [(y/c)/(\Delta c^y/\Delta y)][(p/y)(\Delta y/\Delta p)]$$

$$= \epsilon^Y\,[(p/y)(\Delta y/\Delta p)] = \epsilon^Y\, S$$

as long as $c\Delta p = \Delta y$, so that the expression $[(p/y)(\Delta y/\Delta p)]$ can be rewritten as $[(pc/y)]$ which is s by definition. As long as the change in price is small, the extra income required to keep one as well as before is the extra expenditure required to purchase the original quantity of good in question at the new higher price, the product of the change in price and the quantity of the good consumed. The equality $c\Delta p = \Delta y$ is strictly true for values of c, p, y, Δp, and Δy associated with the point α_4 in figure 4.12. It becomes true for the point α_1 as well when Δp and the corresponding value of Δy are very small because, in that case α_3, α_4 and α_1 are all bunched together. A more direct proof of equation (40) using calculus would be contained in most textbooks of micro economics. The equation itself is a variation of the Slutsky equation. The constant utility demand curve and the constant income demand curve are often referred to as *compensated and uncompensated*. That terminology was avoided here because it tends to obscure the fact that there are many kinds of demand curves, not just two. With numbers in the food and salt example, the estimated values of ϵ^M for food and for salt in accordance with equation (40) are 1.1 [0.5 − (0.3)(2)] and 0.50002 [0.5 − (0.0001)2] as compared with 1.07 and 0.500025 as estimated directly above. The discrepancies are minor and can be accounted for by the fact that the example is about finite changes in prices.

5 TASTE

1 Together equations (40) and (41) imply that $b^{1950*} = c^{1950*} = \sqrt{(b^{1950}c^{1950})} = \sqrt{(15 \times 45)} = 25.98$ so that $y^R(b^{1950}, c^{1950}, p^{2000}) = b^{1950*} + p^{2000}c^{1950*} = b^{1950*} + c^{1950*} = 51.96$ as shown in figure 5.9.

6 TECHNOLOGY

1 Note in passing that the functional form $B = \sqrt{L} + \sqrt{D}$ which served us well for the utility function in chapter 4, is not plausible as an aggregate production function because it implies that neither factor of production is indispensable, that bread can be produced without labor or without land.

2 If $B = AL^\alpha D^{(1-\alpha)}$, then $A(xL)^\alpha(xD)^{(1-\alpha)} = x^\alpha x^{(1-\alpha)} L^\alpha D^{(1-\alpha)} = xB$

3 Though this proposition is true for all α, it will be proved here for $\alpha = 2/3$. From equation (16), it follows immediately that

$$B^3 = AL^2 D \tag{i}$$

Competition for labor ensures that the market-determined wage, w, is $\Delta B/\Delta L$, the increase in B per unit increase in L when D is held constant. Farms hire more and more workers until that is so. From the preceding equation it follows that

$$(B + \Delta B)^3 = A^3(L + \Delta L)^2 D$$

or

$$B^3 + 3\Delta B\, B^2 + 3(\Delta B)^2 B + (\Delta B)^3$$
$$= A^3[L^2 D + 2L\Delta LD + (\Delta L^2 D)] \tag{ii}$$

Subtracting equation (i) from both sides and ignoring all higher powers of ΔB and ΔL (because these are very, very small) we see that

$$3B^2 \Delta B = 2A^3 LD \Delta L \tag{iii}$$

from which it follows that

$$w \equiv \frac{\Delta B}{\Delta L} = \frac{2}{3}\frac{LD}{B^2}$$

or

$$wL = \frac{2}{3}\frac{L^2 D}{B^2} = \frac{2}{3}B \tag{iv}$$

which is equation (17) for the special case where $\alpha = 2/3$.

4 One should remember this formula from high school algebra. Anything growing at a rate of 100n percent is related by this formula to its value in some prior year. The parameter e turns out to be approximately 2.71828.

5 Plugging the assumed values of Y, L and D into the production function, we see that $900 = A15^{2/3} 3^{1/3}$, so that $A = 900/[15^{2/3} 3^{1/3}] = 102.599$.

6 Dividing the expression for $Y(t)$ in equation (20) by the corresponding expression for $Y(0)$, we see at once that

$$Y(t)/Y(0) = [L(t)/L(0)]^{\alpha}$$

or

$$[Y(t)/L(t)]/[Y(0)/L(0)] = [L(t)/L(0)]^{\alpha}[L(0)/L(t)] = [L(t)/L(0)]^{\alpha-1} = 1/2$$

because $Y(t)/L(t)$ is assumed to be exactly half of $Y(0)/L(0)$. Hence, $L(t) = 2^3 L(0) = 120$.

7 In some models, reproducible capital is distinguished from irreproducible land. On the same principle, human capital may be distinguished from pure labor.

8 This is proved in two stages. First, since $k^* = K/Y$, it must be the case that

$$K/k^* = Y = AL^{\alpha}K^{1-\alpha} \qquad \text{(i)}$$

or

$$k^* = K/AL^{\alpha}K^{1-\alpha} = (1/A)(K/L)^{\alpha}$$

or

$$K/L = (Ak^*)^{1/\alpha} = [A\,i/(n+d)]^{1/\alpha} \qquad \text{(ii)}$$

Steady state consumption per head is

$$C/L = (1-i)Y/L = (1-i)A(K/L)^{1-\alpha} = (1-i)A[A\,i/(n+d)]^{(1-\alpha)/\alpha}$$
$$= A^{1/\alpha}[(1-i)i^{(1-\alpha)/\alpha}]/[(n+d)]^{(1-\alpha)/\alpha} \qquad \text{(iii)}$$

9 This is evident from a simple extension of the argument in note 2. If L and D are increased or decreased to xL and xD for some positive value of x, then output in accordance with equation (38) becomes $B^* = A(xL)^{\alpha}(xD)^{\beta} = x^{(\alpha+\beta)}AL^{\alpha}D^{\beta} = x^{(\alpha+\beta)}B$ which is greater or less than xB depending on whether $\alpha + \beta$ is greater or less than 1.

10 Since D is constant, D^{β} must be constant too. The production function in equation (38) can then be rewritten as $B = A^*L^{\alpha}D^{1-\alpha}$ where A^* is a constant term equal to $AD^{\alpha+\beta-1}$. This production function is virtually identical to that in equation (16). It inherits the property that any increase in L leads to a decrease in B/L unless $\alpha > 1$.

7 ASSOCIATIONS

1 The word "surplus" is used with different meanings in different contexts. In chapter 4, it is defined as the value of the opportunity to produce, purchase, sell or consume a good. In chapter 7, it is a sum of money over which people bargain.

2   The allocation of income identified by the maximization of W in equation (3)
     has some degree of independence from the specification of the utility function.
     Consider $u^A(Y_A)$, the utility function of person A. Suppose, in a comparison
     between two possible allocations of a total income of Y between person A and
     person B, the allocation {0.5Y, 0.5Y} yields a higher value of W – and is therefore
     deemed to be more fair and more appropriate – than the allocation {0.6Y, 0.4Y}.
     If so, then the value of W for the allocation {0.5Y, 0.5Y} remains higher than
     the value of W for the allocation {0.6Y, 0.4Y} when the utility function $u^A(Y_A)$
     is replaced by another utility function of the form $v^A(Y_A) = \alpha + \beta u^A(Y_A)$ where
     $\beta > 0$ and α can be anything at all. The reason is simple. Changes in α cancel
     out in the formula, and changes in β increase the values of W for the allocations
     {0.5Y, 0.5Y} and {0.6Y, 0.4Y} by exactly the same percentage, so that whichever
     allocation supplies the larger W for the original utility function supplies the larger
     W for the transformed utility function as well. All that matters for comparisons
     or the fairness of allocations in accordance with equation (3) is the curvature
     of indifference curves which, as explained in chapter 6, can be thought of as
     indicating risk aversion. That is why utilities of different people can be combined
     in equation (3).

9   VOTING

1   As superscripts, G and N refer to "gross" and "net." As ordinary variables, G and
     N refer to guns and population (number of people).
2   This example is based upon Baron, D. and Frerejohn, J., "Bargaining in legisla-
     tures," *American Political Science Review*, 1989, 1181–1206.

10   ADMINISTRATION

1   The derivation of formulae like that in equation (3) would normally be covered
     in high school algebra under the heading of infinite series.
2   The astute reader will have spotted the connection between the derivation of the
     marginal cost of public funds in figure 10.2 and the extended example in chapter
     9 of deadweight loss as a constraint upon the median voter's preferred redis-
     tribution of income. The example abstracted away all public expenditure other
     than for the redistribution of income within a negative income tax, eliminating
     the demand curve in figure 10.2 and providing for a demogrant equal to the
     distance of the supply curve from the vertical axis at a height y_{av}/y_{med} above the
     horizontal axis.
3   What we are calling "rent-seeking" expenditure might be more accurately
     described by the terms "lobbying" or "prize-seeking," but the term "rent-
     seeking" is too well embedded in the literature of economics.

AUTHOR INDEX

SUBJECT INDEX